Office 97 One Step at a Time

Office 97 One Step at a Time

Nancy Stevenson

IDG Books Worldwide, Inc.

An International Data Group Company

FOSTER CITY, CA · CHICAGO, IL · INDIANAPOLIS, IN · SOUTHLAKE, TX

Office 97 One Step at a Time

Published by
IDG Books Worldwide, Inc.
An International Data Group Company
919 E. Hillsdale Blvd., Suite 400
Foster City, CA 94404
http://www.idgbooks.com (IDG Books Worldwide Web site)

Library of Congress Catalog Card No.: 96-79759

ISBN: 0-7645-3150-X

Printed in the United States of America

10 9 8 7 6 5 4 3 2 1

1E/SV/RR/2X/FC

Distributed in the United States by IDG Books Worldwide, Inc.

Distributed by Macmillan Canada for Canada; by Transworld Publishers Limited in the United Kingdom; by IDG Norge Books for Norway; by IDG Sweden Books for Sweden; by Woodslane Pty. Ltd. for Australia; by Woodslane Enterprises Ltd. for New Zealand; by Longman Singapore Publishers Ltd. for Singapore, Malaysia, Thailand, and Indonesia; by Simron Pty. Ltd. for South Africa; by Toppan Company Ltd. for Japan; by Distribuidora Cuspide for Argentina; by Livraria Cultura for Brazil; by Ediciencia S.A. for Ecuador; by Addison-Wesley Publishing Company for Korea; by Ediciones ZETA S.C.R. Ltda. for Peru; by WS Computer Publishing Corporation, Inc., for the Philippines; by Unalis Corporation for Taiwan; by Contemporanea de Ediciones for Venezuela; by Computer Book & Magazine Store for Puerto Rico; by Express Computer Distributors for the Caribbean and West Indies. Authorized Sales Agent: Anthony Rudkin Associates for the Middle East and North Africa.

For general information on IDG Books Worldwide's books in the U.S., please call our Consumer Customer Service department at 800-762-2974. For reseller information, including discounts and premium sales, please call our Reseller Customer Service department at 800-434-3422.

For information on where to purchase IDG Books Worldwide's books outside the U.S., please contact our International Sales department at 415-655-3200 or fax 415-655-3295.

For information on foreign language translations, please contact our Foreign & Subsidiary Rights department at 415-655-3021 or fax 415-655-3281.

For sales inquiries and special prices for bulk quantities, please contact our Sales department at 415-655-3200 or write to the address above.

For information on using IDG Books Worldwide's books in the classroom or for ordering examination copies, please contact our Educational Sales department at 800-434-2086 or fax 817-251-8174.

For press review copies, author interviews, or other publicity information, please contact our Public Relations department at 415-655-3000 or fax 415-655-3299.

For authorization to photocopy items for corporate, personal, or educational use, please contact Copyright Clearance Center, 222 Rosewood Drive, Danvers, MA 01923, or fax 508-750-4470.

ABOUT IDG BOOKS WORLDWIDE

Welcome to the world of IDG Books Worldwide.

IDG Books Worldwide, Inc., is a subsidiary of International Data Group, the world's largest publisher of computer-related information and the leading global provider of information services on information technology. IDG was founded more than 25 years ago and now employs more than 8,500 people worldwide. IDG publishes more than 275 computer publications in over 75 countries (see listing below). More than 60 million people read one or more IDG publications each month.

Launched in 1990, IDG Books Worldwide is today the #1 publisher of best-selling computer books in the United States. We are proud to have received eight awards from the Computer Press Association in recognition of editorial excellence and three from *Computer Currents*' First Annual Readers' Choice Awards. Our best-selling *...For Dummies®* series has more than 30 million copies in print with translations in 30 languages. IDG Books Worldwide, through a joint venture with IDG's Hi-Tech Beijing, became the first U.S. publisher to publish a computer book in the People's Republic of China. In record time, IDG Books Worldwide has become the first choice for millions of readers around the world who want to learn how to better manage their businesses.

Our mission is simple: Every one of our books is designed to bring extra value and skill-building instructions to the reader. Our books are written by experts who understand and care about our readers. The knowledge base of our editorial staff comes from years of experience in publishing, education, and journalism — experience we use to produce books for the '90s. In short, we care about books, so we attract the best people. We devote special attention to details such as audience, interior design, use of icons, and illustrations. And because we use an efficient process of authoring, editing, and desktop publishing our books electronically, we can spend more time ensuring superior content and spend less time on the technicalities of making books.

You can count on our commitment to deliver high-quality books at competitive prices on topics you want to read about. At IDG Books Worldwide, we continue in the IDG tradition of delivering quality for more than 25 years. You'll find no better book on a subject than one from IDG Books Worldwide.

John Kilcullen
CEO
IDG Books Worldwide, Inc.

Steven Berkowitz
President and Publisher
IDG Books Worldwide, Inc.

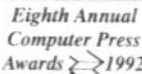
Eighth Annual Computer Press Awards 1992

Ninth Annual Computer Press Awards 1993

Tenth Annual Computer Press Awards 1994

Eleventh Annual Computer Press Awards 1995

IDG Books Worldwide, Inc., is a subsidiary of International Data Group, the world's largest publisher of computer-related information and the leading global provider of information services on information technology. International Data Group publishes over 275 computer publications in over 75 countries. Sixty million people read one or more International Data Group publications each month. International Data Group's publications include: **ARGENTINA:** Buyer's Guide, Computerworld Argentina, PC World Argentina; **AUSTRALIA:** Australian Macworld, Australian PC World, Australian Reseller News, Computerworld, IT Casebook, Network World, Publish, Webmaster; **AUSTRIA:** Computerwelt Osterreich, Networks Austria, PC Tip Austria; **BANGLADESH:** PC World Bangladesh; **BELARUS:** PC World Belarus; **BELGIUM:** Data News; **BRAZIL:** Annuário de Informática, Computerworld Connections, Macworld, PC Player, PC World, Publish, Reseller News, Supergamepower; **BULGARIA:** Computerworld Bulgaria, Network World Bulgaria, PC & MacWorld Bulgaria; **CANADA:** CIO Canada, Client/Server World, ComputerWorld Canada, InfoWorld Canada, NetworkWorld Canada, WebWorld; **CHILE:** Computerworld Chile, PC World Chile; **COLOMBIA:** Computerworld Colombia, PC World Colombia; **COSTA RICA:** PC World Centro America; **THE CZECH AND SLOVAK REPUBLICS:** Computerworld Czechoslovakia, Macworld Czech Republic, PC World Czechoslovakia; **DENMARK:** Communications World Danmark, Computerworld Danmark, Macworld Danmark, PC World Danmark, Techworld Denmark; **DOMINICAN REPUBLIC:** PC World Republica Dominicana; **ECUADOR:** PC World Ecuador; **EGYPT:** Computerworld Middle East, PC World Middle East; **EL SALVADOR:** PC World Centro America; **FINLAND:** MikroPC, Tietoverkko, Tietoviikko; **FRANCE:** Distributique, Hebdo, Info PC, Le Monde Informatique, Macworld, Reseaux & Telecoms, WebMaster France; **GERMANY:** Computer Partner, Computerwoche, Computerwoche Extra, Computerwoche FOCUS, Global Online, Macwelt, PC Welt; **GREECE:** Amiga Computing, GamePro Greece, Multimedia World; **GUATEMALA:** PC World Centro America; **HONDURAS:** PC World Centro America; **HONG KONG:** Computerworld Hong Kong, PC World Hong Kong, Publish in Asia; **HUNGARY:** ABCD CD-ROM, Computerworld Szamitastechnika, Internetto online Magazine, PC World Hungary, PC-X Magazin Hungary; **ICELAND:** Tolvuheimur PC World Island; **INDIA:** Information Communications World, Information Systems Computerworld, PC World India, Publish in Asia; **INDONESIA:** InfoKomputer PC World, Komputek Computerworld, Publish in Asia; **IRELAND:** ComputerScope, PC Live!; **ISRAEL:** Macworld Israel, People & Computers/Computerworld; **ITALY:** Computerworld Italia, Macworld Italia, Networking Italia, PC World Italia; **JAPAN:** DTP World, Macworld Japan, Nikkei Personal Computing, OS/2 World Japan, SunWorld Japan, Windows NT World, Windows World Japan; **KENYA:** PC World East African; **KOREA:** Hi-Tech Information, Macworld Korea, PC World Korea; **MACEDONIA:** PC World Macedonia; **MALAYSIA:** Computerworld Malaysia, PC World Malaysia, Publish in Asia; **MALTA:** PC World Malta; **MEXICO:** Computerworld Mexico, PC World Mexico; **MYANMAR:** PC World Myanmar; **NETHERLANDS:** Computer! Totaal, LAN Internetworking Magazine, LAN World Buyers Guide, Macworld Netherlands, Net, WebWereld; **NEW ZEALAND:** Absolute Beginners Guide and Plain & Simple Series, Computer Buyer, Computer Industry Directory, Computerworld New Zealand, MTB, Network World, PC World New Zealand; **NICARAGUA:** PC World Centro America; **NORWAY:** Computerworld Norge, CW Rapport, Datamagasinet, Financial Rapport, Kursguide Norge, Macworld Norge, Multimediaworld Norge, PC World Ekspress Norge, PC World Nettverk, PC World Norge, PC World ProduktGuide Norge; **PAKISTAN:** Computerworld Pakistan; **PANAMA:** PC World Panama; **PEOPLE'S REPUBLIC OF CHINA:** China Computer Users, China Computerworld, China InfoWorld, China Telecom World Weekly, Computer & Communication, Electronic Design China, Electronics Today, Electronics Weekly, Game Software, PC World China, Popular Computer Week, Software Weekly, Software World, Telecom World; **PERU:** Computerworld Peru, PC World Profesional Peru, PC World SoHo Peru; **PHILIPPINES:** Click!, Computerworld Philippines, PC World Philippines, Publish in Asia; **POLAND:** Computerworld Poland, Computerworld Special Report Poland, Cyber, Macworld Poland, Networld Poland, PC World Komputer; **PORTUGAL:** Cerebro/PC World, Computerworld/Correio Informático, Dealer World Portugal, Mac*In/PC*In Portugal, Multimedia World; **PUERTO RICO:** PC World Puerto Rico; **ROMANIA:** Computerworld Romania, PC World Romania, Telecom Romania; **RUSSIA:** Computerworld Russia, Mir PK, Publish, Seti; **SINGAPORE:** Computerworld Singapore, PC World Singapore, Publish in Asia; **SLOVENIA:** Monitor; **SOUTH AFRICA:** Computing SA, Network World SA, Software World SA; **SPAIN:** Communicaciones World España, Computerworld España, Dealer World España, Macworld España, PC World España; **SRI LANKA:** Infolink PC World; **SWEDEN:** CAP&Design, Computer Sweden, Corporate Computing Sweden, Internetworld Sweden, it branschen, Macworld Sweden, MaxiData Sweden, MikroDatorn, Nätverk & Kommunikation, PC World Sweden, PCaktiv, Windows World Sweden; **SWITZERLAND:** Computerworld Schweiz, Macworld Schweiz, PCtip; **TAIWAN:** Computerworld Taiwan, Macworld Taiwan, NEW ViSiON/Publish, PC World Taiwan, Windows World Taiwan; **THAILAND:** Publish in Asia, Thai Computerworld; **TURKEY:** Computerworld Turkiye, Macworld Turkiye, Network World Turkiye, PC World Turkiye; **UKRAINE:** Computerworld Kiev, Multimedia World Ukraine, PC World Ukraine; **UNITED KINGDOM:** Acorn User UK, Amiga Action UK, Amiga Computing UK, Apple Talk UK, Computing, Macworld, Parents and Computers UK, PC Advisor, PC Home, PSX Pro, The WEB; **UNITED STATES:** Cable in the Classroom, CIO Magazine, Computerworld, DOS World, Federal Computer Week, GamePro Magazine, InfoWorld, I-Way, Macworld, Network World, PC Games, PC World, Publish, Video Event, THE WEB Magazine, and WebMaster; online webzines: JavaWorld, NetscapeWorld, and SunWorld Online; **URUGUAY:** InfoWorld Uruguay; **VENEZUELA:** Computerworld Venezuela, PC World Venezuela; and **VIETNAM:** PC World Vietnam.

3/24/97

CREDITS

Acquisitions Editors
Andy Cummings
Ellen Camm

Development Editors
Michael Koch
Ron Hull

Technical Editor
Forrest Houlette

Copy Editor
Tracy Brown

Production Coordinator
Katy German

Book Designer
Seventeenth Street Studios

Graphics and Production Specialists
Linda J. Marousek
Shannon Miller
Maureen Moore
Andreas F. Schueller

Quality Control Specialist
Mark Schumann

Proofreader
Chris Collins

Indexer
Linda Fetters

ABOUT THE AUTHOR

Nancy Stevenson lives in Indianapolis, IN, and is a freelance writer, editor, and consultant to the publishing industry. In addition to her background as a video scriptwriter and trainer on software products, Nancy has written and contributed to over a dozen books on computer topics. She also has an unpublished murder mystery in her drawer (if any fiction publishers are reading), and enjoys her flute, dog, and travel when she's not writing.

WELCOME TO ONE STEP AT A TIME!

TRY OUT THE
INTERACTIVE TUTORIALS
ON YOUR CD!

The book you are holding is very special. It's just the tool you need for learning software quickly and easily. More than a book, it offers a *unique learning experience*. Along with our text, the dynamic *One Step at a Time On-Demand* software included on the bonus CD-ROM in this book coaches you through the tutorials at *your own pace*. You'll never feel lost!

See examples of how to accomplish specific tasks. Listen to clear explanations of how to solve your problems.

Use the *One Step at a Time On-Demand* software in three ways:

- **Demo mode** shows you how to perform a task in movie-style fashion — in sound and color! Just sit back and watch the *One Step* software demonstrate the correct sequence of steps on-screen. Seeing is understanding!
- **Teacher mode** simulates the software environment so you can practice completing a task without worrying about making a mistake. The *One Step* software guides you every step of the way. Trying is learning!
- **Concurrent mode** allows you to work in the actual software environment while still getting assistance from the friendly *One Step* helper. Doing is succeeding!

Our goal is for you to learn the features of a software application by guiding you painlessly through valuable and helpful tutorials. Our *One Step at a Time On-Demand* software — combined with the step-by-step tutorials in our One Step at a Time series — will make your learning experience fast-paced and fun.

See it. Try it. Do it.

To Meb Boden, my dearest buddy, who manages to stay close no matter what the distance.

And, as always, to G.

PREFACE

Welcome to *Office 97 One Step at a Time,* part of a unique and exciting series from IDG Books Worldwide, Inc. Our goal with this series is to give quick, hands-on training, with help at every step as you're learning the features of Office 97.

Office 97 One Step at a Time has been designed to support your learning in the following ways:

- Lessons are paced to include small, manageable chunks of information so you never feel you're in over your head.
- You learn Office 97 by doing. Each lesson is divided into a number of short exercises, presented in easy-to-follow steps, and with plenty of illustrations to help.
- At the start of each lesson, you learn which files you need to do the lesson, and how much time to set aside to complete it.
- A CD-ROM with sample files accompanies this book. It includes all of the exercises you'll need to complete the lessons, and completed projects that you can compare your results against. This CD-ROM also features our exclusive *One Step at a Time On-Demand* interactive tutorial, which coaches you through the exercises in the book while you work on your computer at your own pace.

Who Should Read This Book

Office 97 One Step at a Time is for people who have only a basic knowledge of computers but who are new to Microsoft Office 97. You will also find this book useful if you have already started using Office 97 but want to learn more about it. This book assumes that you know how to turn on your computer and use the mouse and keyboard to interact with Windows 95. The exercises include completely detailed procedures, so you'll feel comfortable working through these lessons.

How This Book Is Organized

Office 97 One Step at a Time has a very simple structure. The **Jump Start** takes you through a step-by-step tour of essential Microsoft Office techniques and typical features. Don't try to memorize the techniques that you're experimenting with — just follow the steps to get a sense of how Office 97 works. You'll get more information about the techniques and features in the lessons to come.

Part I: Meet Microsoft Office introduces you to the concept of a suite of software products and the Office environment. Lesson 1 teaches you basic Windows skills, Lesson 2 gives you a first look at the Office products and Lesson 3 teaches you some features that all the products have in common, such as ways of getting help and saving files.

After Part I, there is a Part for each software product in the Office suite:

Part II: Word for Windows

Part III: Excel for Windows

Part IV: PowerPoint for Windows

Part V: Microsoft Outlook

Part VI: Access for Windows

Finally, three appendixes cover **Installing Office 97, Answers to Bonus Questions,** and **What's on the CD-ROM.** At the end, you'll also find a **Glossary** of terms and feature names for the various Office products and a **CD-ROM** with sample files (located in the Exercise directory) and templates (located in the Templates directory) for the various Office products.

How to Use This Book

This series is designed for the way people in the real world learn. Every lesson has a consistent structure so you can quickly become comfortable using all the following elements:

- **Stopwatch:** It is best if you can complete each lesson without interruption, so look for the stopwatch symbol at the beginning of each lesson. This stopwatch tells you approximately how much time to set aside to work through the lesson.
- **Goals:** The goals of each lesson are clearly identified, so you can anticipate what skills you will acquire.
- **Get Ready:** Here you find out what files you need to complete the steps in the lessons, and you see an illustration of the worksheet you will create by completing the exercises.
- **Visual Bonus:** This is a one- or two-page illustration with labels to help you more clearly understand a special procedure or element of Microsoft Office.
- **Skills Challenge:** Every lesson ends with a comprehensive Skills Challenge exercise incorporating the skills you've learned in the individual exercises. The steps in the Skills Challenge are less explicit than those in the exercises, so you have a chance to practice and reinforce your Office skills.
- **Bonus Questions:** Sprinkled throughout the Skills Challenge exercise are bonus questions. Check Appendix B for the answers to these questions to see if you got them right.
- **Troubleshooting:** Near the end of each lesson is a series of useful tips and tricks to avoid the traps and pitfalls that many new Office 97 users experience. Look over the troubleshooting tips even if you don't have problems, so you can avoid potential problems in the future.
- **Wrap-up:** Here, you get an overview of the skills you learned, as well as a brief preview of the next lesson.

The One Step at a Time CD-ROM

The CD-ROM that accompanies this book includes the exclusive *One Step at a Time On-Demand* interactive tutorial. This software coaches you through the exercises in the book while you work on your computer at your own pace. You can use the software on its own, or concurrently with the book. In addition, the software includes the entire text of the book so that you can search for information on how to perform a function, learn how to complete a task, or make use of the software itself.

Conventions Used in This Book

Using this book is easy. It follows just a few simple conventions you should know about:

- Instructions to choose a command from a menu are shown this way:

  Select File ➢ Open.

  In this example, *Select* means to click the menu name, File is the name of the menu and Open is the name of the command to select from within the menu.
- In the exercises, information that you should actually type is shown in **boldface**.
- Most exercises and Skills Challenges let you start a project with a file from the CD-ROM that accompanies this book. Before working on these exercises, you should first copy the exercise files to your hard drive (see the CD installation instructions at the end of the book), and open the files from there. If you attempt to work on the files without first copying them from the CD-ROM, you will not be able to save changes to those files.

- You can check your work at any time by opening a file that contains the completed project from the exercise or Skills Challenge. These files are located in the Exercise folder on the CD-ROM along with the rest of the exercise files.

I've tried to make it easy for you to use this book by including several easy-to-understand features. For example, when you see

The text that follows contains a special tip intended to give you some "inside information" that can save you time or frustration.

When you see

The text that follows explains a special note about the subject. Notes tend to be a bit more technically oriented than the rest of the text, but the information they contain is important if you want to know "why" rather than simply "what."

Feedback

Please feel free to let us know what you think about this book and whether you have any suggestions for improvements. You can send your questions and comments to me and the rest of the *Office 97 One Step at a Time* team on the IDG Books Worldwide Web site at `www.idgbooks.com`.

You're now ready to begin. Start with the Jump Start for an interesting look at Office 97, and then learn Office 97 on your own and in your own time, in the lessons that follow.

ACKNOWLEDGMENTS

Many thanks to IDG Books Worldwide for this opportunity to be part of an exciting new *One Step at a Time* series. I owe a debt to Ellen Camm and Andy Cummings for having faith in me and hiring me to write this book, as well as to Michael Koch and Ron Hull, my very user-friendly editors, for working through it with me and providing valuable input. Thanks, too, to Forrest Houlette for his insightful suggestions and tips, to Tracy Brown for her careful copy editing, and to Phyllis Beaty and Katy German and their layout staff for doing such a good job on a tight schedule. My appreciation to you all for making this book a reality.

Special thanks to Tom McCaffrey, Marilyn Russel, and everyone at Real Help Communications, Inc. (`http://www.realhelpcom.com`) for creating the several thousand sound files required for the CD-ROMs in this series, under very aggressive deadlines.

CONTENTS AT A GLANCE

CONTENTS

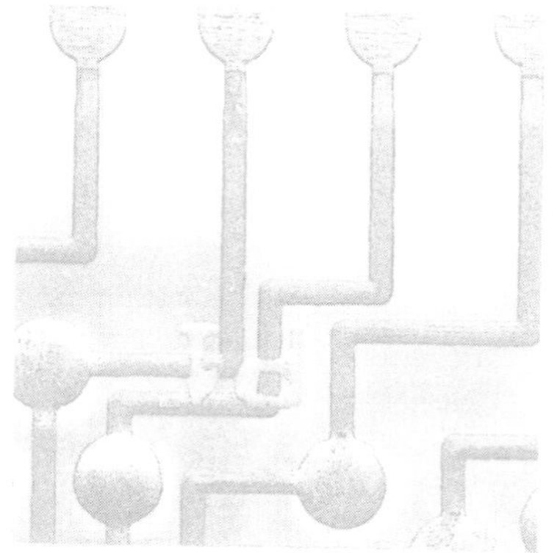

Jump Start

GOALS

In this section, you learn the following:

- Opening programs
- Adding text
- Inserting objects
- Using applets
- Formatting text
- Printing a document
- Saving a document

Get ready

GET READY

You're about to tackle learning of one of the most robust software products on the market today — Microsoft Office 97. This software is actually several software programs bundled together; your challenge is to learn not only the functionality of five distinct programs, but also how they all work together. This warm-up section is included to help you prepare for this challenge. Working through this section will get you used to following the step-by-step structure of this book, and you'll get a glimpse of key functions in several of the Office products.

Don't worry about remembering all the procedures or features you're about to see. You revisit each of them in more detail within the lessons that follow. Just work your way through these steps to get comfortable with the Office environment and the look and feel of its various programs.

For this warm-up, you need to turn on your computer, have the Windows desktop on your screen (this usually appears automatically when you first turn on your computer), and you must have installed Microsoft Office 97 (see Appendix A). Also, be sure that no programs are open and running at the moment.

OPENING PROGRAMS

The first step in working with Office is to take a look at the various programs that comprise it. Therefore, you'll begin by opening some of those programs for a first glimpse.

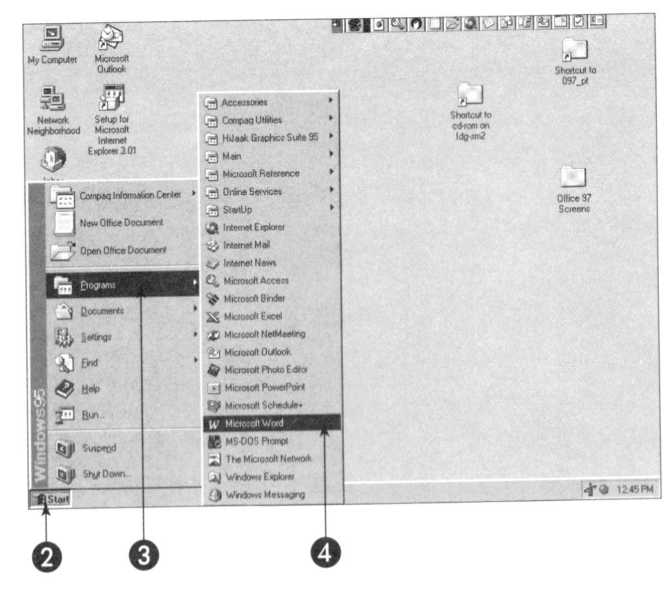

1. Move your mouse pointer toward the lower left corner of your screen.
2. Click the Start button on the Windows taskbar.
3. Move your pointer to the Programs item in the Start menu.
4. Locate the Microsoft Word icon in the submenu that appears, and move your pointer until Microsoft Word is highlighted.
5. Click your left mouse button once (in this book, unless it says otherwise, *click* always means with your left mouse button).
6. Move your pointer back to the lower left corner of the screen.

7. Click the Start button on the Windows taskbar.
8. Move your pointer to the top of the Start menu until it rests on the New Office Document command.
9. Click New Office Document.
10. Move your pointer to the Blank Presentation icon.
11. Click Blank Presentation once to select it.
12. Click OK.

    You now have two Office 97 programs open, Microsoft Word and Microsoft PowerPoint. Although only one may be visible at the moment, you can easily switch between the two programs by pressing the Alt key and the Tab key together (Alt + Tab).

    Try it now.

13. Press Alt + Tab to see the Word screen.
14. Press Alt + Tab again and you see only the PowerPoint screen.

    The illustration to the right shows the Word screen in the foreground and the PowerPoint screen in the background.

ADDING TEXT

In every Office program, you also add text to build a document, whether it's a letter or spreadsheet. That's your next step.

1. Click OK in the PowerPoint New Slide dialog box.
2. Click the box that contains the text *Click to add title.*
3. Type the words **My PowerPoint Presentation**.
4. Click the block that contains the text *Click to add sub-title.*
5. Type your name (for example, I would type **Nancy Stevenson**).
6. Click anywhere outside of the text area.

    Your screen should resemble the illustration to the right. Next, enter some text in a Word for Windows document.

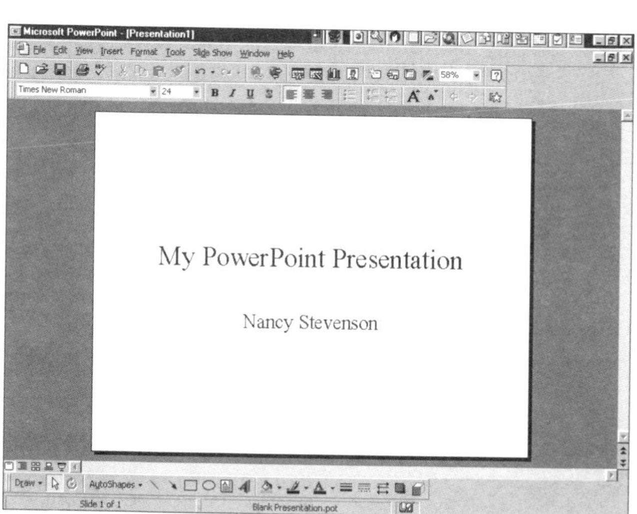

7. Press Alt + Tab.
8. Type **My Word Report**.
9. Press Enter.

If you make a mistake while typing, you can use the backspace or delete key to get rid of the mistake one letter at a time. Another option is to click at one end of a word or phrase and, holding down your mouse button, drag across the text to highlight it. When you press backspace or delete, all the highlighted text is deleted at once. This works the same in any Office program.

INSERTING OBJECTS

In addition to text, you often add other elements such as pictures or charts to documents. Try that now.

1. Click the Insert menu on the Word menu bar.
2. Select Date and Time.
3. Click the second date format (an example of this format is Thursday, September 23, 1999).
4. Click OK.
5. Press Enter twice.
6. Select Insert ➢ Object.
7. From the Object dialog box, click the down arrow in the scroll bar until you see Microsoft Excel Chart.

A scroll bar is a gray bar that can run either along the right side or bottom of a program window, or next to a list. It contains an arrow at either end and a gray rectangle that can move between the two arrows. You move around the page of a document or up and down a list by either

clicking one of the arrows, clicking just above or below the rectangle, or clicking and dragging the rectangle along the scroll bar. You see scroll bars in all Windows-based software programs, including all the Office products.

8. Click the Microsoft Excel Chart option.
9. Click OK.

If the window containing Microsoft Word does not fill the screen, you can enlarge it using the middle of the three control buttons in the upper right-hand corner. These are Windows control buttons (not Office tools). Click the button in the middle — the one with the square symbol on it.

Your screen should now look like the one in the illustration. What you're seeing is actually the tools of Excel within a Word document window. When you insert an object from one Office program into another Office program, you actually open the second program within the first. You get all the functionality of the second program without having to change between the two. When you finish working on the object and close the window of the second program, you are returned to the original program window. By double-clicking the object, you can open the second program again any time you like.

10. Select Chart.
11. Select Chart Type.
12. Click Bar in the Chart type list.
13. Click OK.
14. Click the Data Table tool on the Chart floating toolbar (fifth in from the left) to see the Excel table from which the chart was created.
15. Click the Data Table tool to display the chart format again.

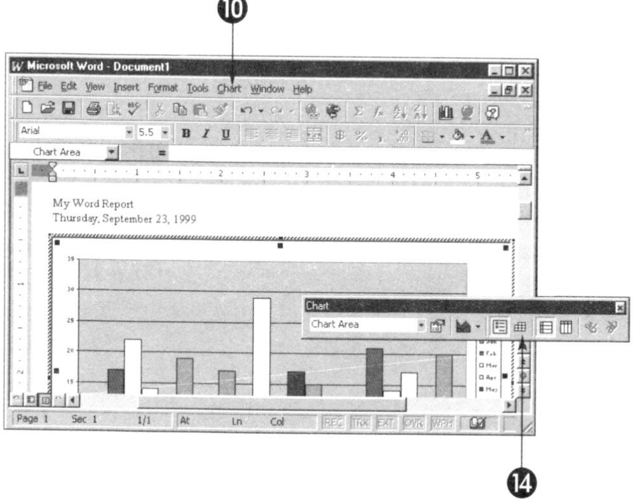

⑯ Click in the Word document anywhere outside of the Excel chart to close Excel and restore your Word toolbars and menus.

USING APPLETS

Applets are small applications included in Office which are available to all the programs. Try using one called WordArt, which offers a gallery of text enhancement effects.

1. Return to PowerPoint, and click the Insert WordArt tool on the Drawing toolbar at the bottom of the screen.

Tools are actually buttons that, when clicked, enable you to perform many of the commands also accessible through menus. Tools are organized in toolbars, and there are usually several toolbars in each Office program for different functions. For example, there might be a Formatting toolbar for formatting text or a Drawing toolbar for drawing objects. You can identify tools by passing your cursor over them and reading the name of the tool from a small callout that appears, called a Tooltip. The Insert WordArt tool has a slightly tilted capital A symbol on it and is near the middle of the Drawing toolbar in PowerPoint.

2. Click the fourth block from the left in the fourth row of the WordArt Gallery.
3. Click OK.
4. Type **Office 97**.
5. Click OK.
6. Move your pointer on the WordArt object until the pointer becomes a four-way pointing arrow.
7. Click and drag the WordArt object until it's centered above the first line of text on your PowerPoint slide.
8. Click anywhere outside of the WordArt object.

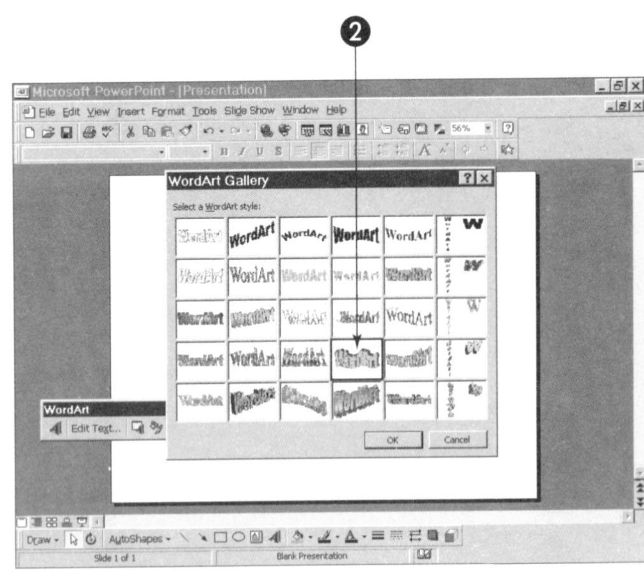

Your PowerPoint slide should look like the illustration to the right. WordArt is just one of several applets that Office provides. Other applets include Microsoft Graph for creating various styles of data charts, and Microsoft Organization Chart for creating organizational and process charts.

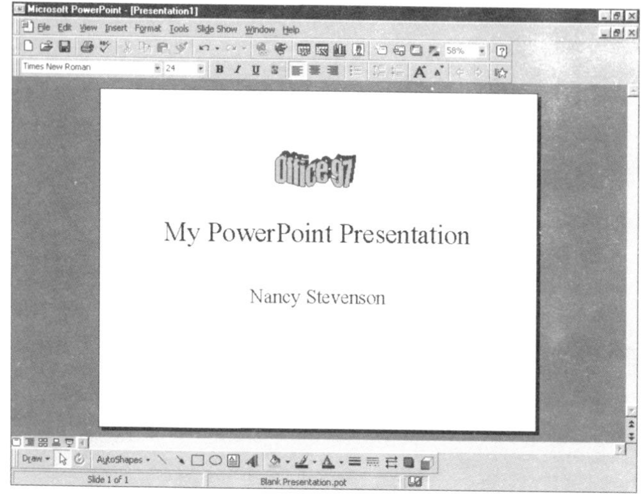

FORMATTING TEXT

Word for Windows and all the Office products offer you many tools for formatting your text; that is, changing the font, font size, or style of the typeface in your document.

1. Return to Word, and click to the left of the text *My Word Report*.
2. Drag your mouse to the right to highlight the entire phrase.
3. Select Format ➢ Font. The Font dialog box in the following illustration appears.
4. In the Font list, use the scroll bar to find the font named Brush Script and click it.
5. In the Font style list, select Bold.
6. In the Size list, use the scroll bar to locate 26 and click it.
7. Under Effects, click in the Shadow check box.

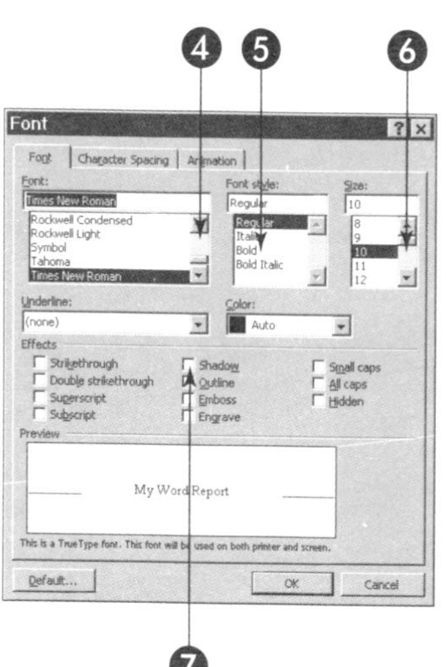

TIP

You frequently see dialog boxes in Office products; they're how you make most choices and settings for your documents. Typically, you see scrollable lists of choices, some lists that drop down when you click the arrow next to them (the Underline and Color choices in this dialog box function that way), and check boxes such as the ones shown in the Effects group box of the Font dialog box. Often, you see a preview that shows you what would happen if you were to apply all the choices you've made. You can usually leave a dialog box without applying your choices by simply clicking Cancel.

Printing a document

8. Click OK.

   Your Word document should now look like the one shown in the illustration to the right.

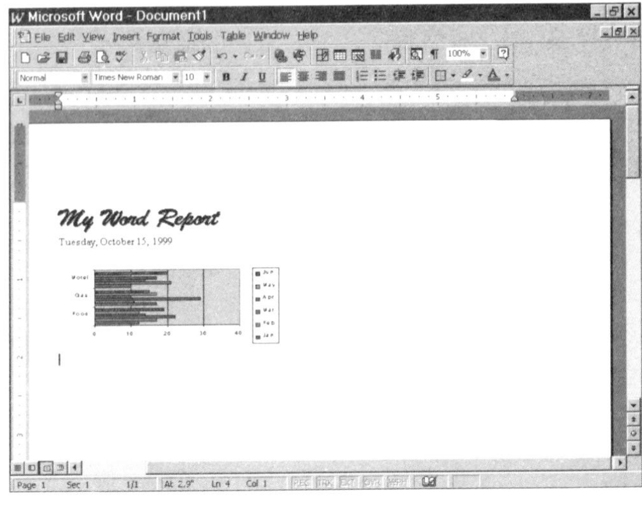

PRINTING A DOCUMENT

Printing an Office document is very easy. Most variations from default settings come when you want to print just a range of pages within your document, multiple copies, or color output. Follow these few steps to print your Word document so you can see how simple printing can be.

1. Select File ➢ Print. The Print dialog box appears.
2. Check the Printer Name to be sure your current printer is selected.

If your printer is not listed in the Printer Name box, click the down arrow to display a list of available printers. If your printer is not listed there, either, you will need to wait until you get to Lesson 8 to print, or get some help from somebody at your office or home in setting up your printer now. Your Windows and printer documentation can also be of help with this process.

3. Click the up arrow in the Number of Copies box to select two copies.
4. Click OK.

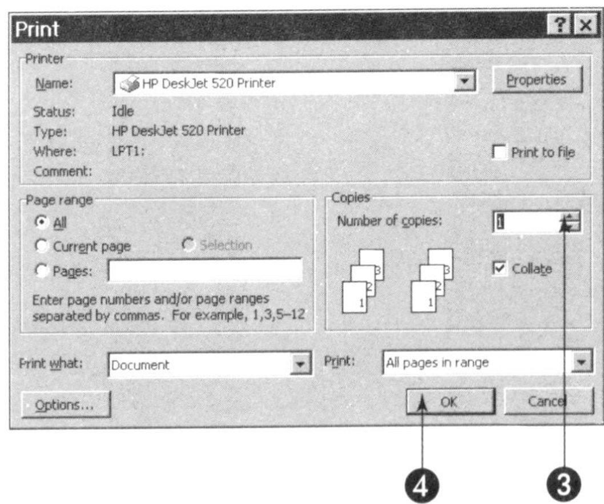

SAVING A DOCUMENT

Well, what's the point of making all these changes to a document if you don't save them for posterity? It's simple, and works the same in just about every Office program.

1. Select File ➢ Save.
2. In the File Name box, type **MyReport**.
3. Open the Save In box by clicking the down arrow.

4. Double-click the (C:) drive.
5. Click the Create New Folder button (it's the third one over from the Save in Field).
6. Type **MyDocs** in the New Folder Name box.
7. Click OK.
8. Click Save.
9. Select File ➢ Exit to close Word for Windows.
10. Select File ➢ Save to save your PowerPoint presentation.
11. Click the down arrow in the Save In box and select (C:).
12. Double-click the MyDocs folder.
13. Type **MyPresentation** in the File Name box.
14. Click Save.

WRAP UP

You've now run through several key functions used in Office programs, including the following:

- Opening and switching between programs
- Adding text and inserting objects
- Using the Office applet called WordArt
- Formatting text in Word and changing chart types in Excel
- Printing and saving files

In the process, you've caught a glimpse of Word and PowerPoint, and some of the tools and menus in Excel. You've seen how getting things done in Office is simply a matter of learning to use the tools, menus, and dialog box choices that the individual programs present you with. You've also seen that many of the features of the Office products work the same, such as making toolbar and menu selections and using scroll bars.

In the lessons that follow, you work with these features and many more until you've mastered Office 97.

PART I

Meet Microsoft Office

This part introduces you to the concept of a suite of software products and the basics of the Office environment. It includes the following lessons:

- Lesson 1: Looking at Office Through Windows
- Lesson 2: Meet Microsoft Office
- Lesson 3: What Do These Programs Have in Common

LESSON 1

Looking at Office Through Windows

GOALS

This lesson will get you comfortable with performing simple tasks in Windows such as the following:

- Moving around the desktop
- Using the Windows taskbar
- Finding files
- Creating folders
- Opening Office programs
- Working with windows
- Setting up your desktop to work with Office 97

Get ready

GET READY

To work your way through this lesson, you need the accompanying CD-ROM where you'll find a folder named Exercise, containing all of the files you need for the lessons in this book.

WHAT IS WINDOWS?

Windows is an interface that enables you to work with your computer through graphical symbols and text rather than text alone. Windows helps you work with the various pieces of information that make your computer run, and Windows makes it easy to run the programs in Office.

All the pieces of the Microsoft Office 97 suite are programs written for the Windows environment. There are certain elements that all Windows programs have in common. They use buttons, called *tools*, as well as menus that contain commands that you select to perform tasks. Each program is viewed within a window (hence the name) and those windows can be manipulated in ways that enable you to easily move from program to program. The illustration at the top right shows a couple of Office programs on the desktop.

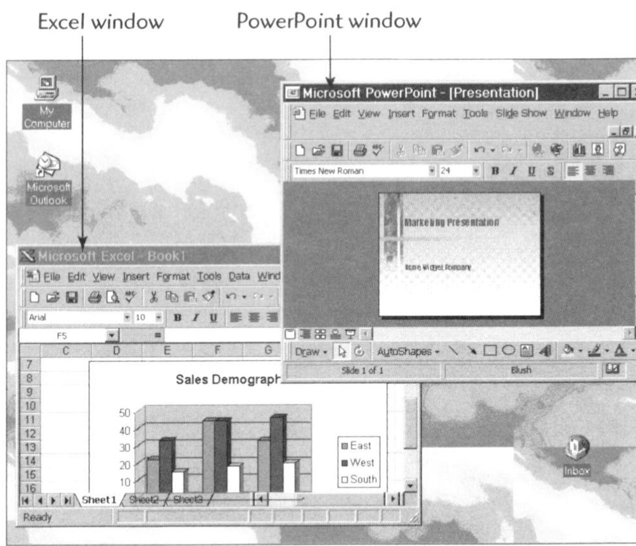

Windows uses a desktop, as shown in the illustration to the right. The desktop is a central place from where all your files and programs can be accessed. Think of this desktop as a metaphor for your desktop at home or in your office. On the surface of your desk are things you use to work, such as files with papers. You have drawers that contain additional tools. The Windows desktop is where you keep folders containing *electronic* files. You open the Start menu as you open a desk drawer to access even more files and software programs. There's even a little icon for old files called a Recycle Bin to throw things in when you don't need them anymore.

You probably have papers on your desk; some of them may be documents someone created in a program such as Word for Windows. In Windows, those documents are saved in computer files and stored in folders. Sometimes you even keep a folder inside another folder, further organizing the information so you can easily find it again. The illustration to the right on the next page shows the My Documents folder and the files it contains.

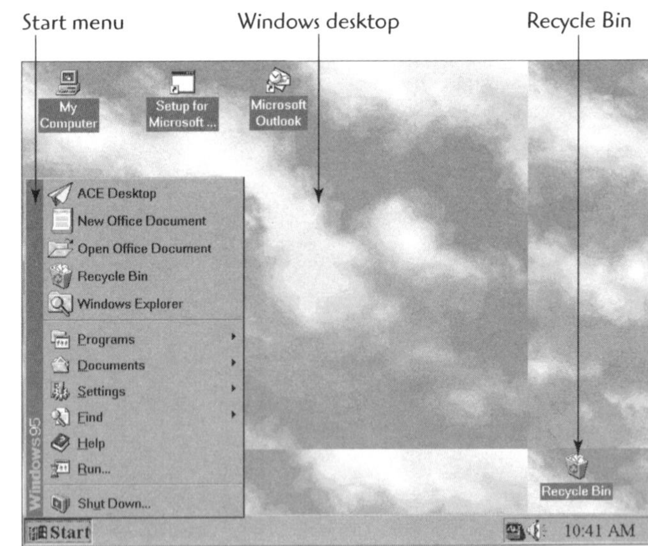

When you open a drawer of your office desk, you probably pull out a pen, calculator, pencil, or ruler to actually do your work. Think of computer programs that way: when you open the Windows Start menu, you can grab Word, which is like a computerized pen, enabling you to write memos and letters; Excel, which is like a sophisticated calculator, creating columns of numbers and tallying them up; and PowerPoint, which can be thought of as a pencil, ruler, and colored markers, all assembled to enable you to draw attractive presentations. Access is like your Rolodex, containing information in an orderly fashion so you can easily look up names and addresses. Outlook is a combination of a few things: your calendar, daily to-do list, address book, and mailbox.

And it's Windows that makes keeping track of all of these documents, tools, and programs simple and efficient.

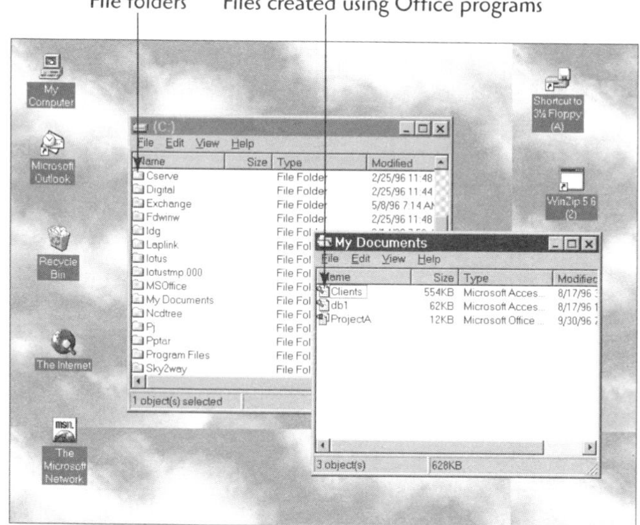

EXPLORING THE WINDOWS DESKTOP

The first step you take in this lesson is to move some items around the Windows desktop. Then, you explore a bit and see how the Windows filing system works.

Moving around icons

Most computers are configured to load Windows when you first turn them on, so start there.

1. Turn on your computer and let Windows load.

What you have on your desktop may not exactly match what I have on mine, or what will appear in the illustrations throughout this book. That's okay; your desk doesn't look like mine either (I hope not, for your sake!). But there are a few things that were created when you loaded Windows 95 that I will assume are still there, such as the My Computer and Recycle Bin icons.

2. Using your left mouse button, click the Recycle Bin icon and drag it to the lower right corner of the screen. (Whenever I say click in these steps, I mean you should use your left mouse button).

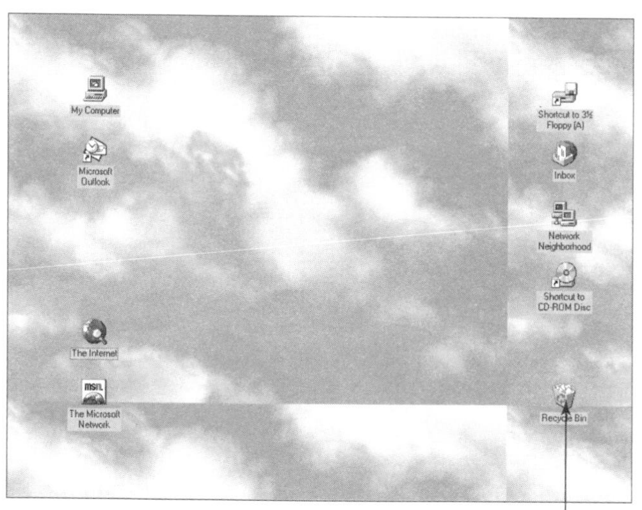

Moving around icons

❸ Click the My Computer icon and place it next to the Recycle Bin.

You can freely move any of these icons around your desktop and organize them in any way you like. You might, for example, put icons that represent shortcuts to your e-mail and Internet connection (which you learn to create later in this lesson) together in one corner of the desktop.

❹ Double-click the Recycle Bin to open the Recycle Bin window.

Your Recycle Bin may have files listed in it. The files in my illustration are files I've recently placed in the trash. However, I haven't actually emptied the trash yet. If I want to, I can move these files back into a folder on my desktop again, thereby retrieving them before they're actually deleted.

The illustration shows some of the elements common to most Windows programs, including the following:

- The *menu bar* containing four menus (File, Edit, View, and Help)
- The *scroll bar* near the bottom with arrows at either end; use this to move around inside the window and see more information
- The *status bar* along the very bottom, summarizing details about what's in the window; in this case, the status bar would show how many files are in the Recycle Bin and the total size of those files
- The *control buttons* in the upper-right corner, which you look at a little later in this lesson

❺ Select File from the menu bar.

The File menu, shown in the illustration, appears. This is called a drop-down menu, because it appears below the filename. Notice that some of the commands on this menu are grayed out and others appear in dark type. The gray ones aren't available, the black ones are. Commands are sometimes only available when you meet some conditions. For example, to activate the Delete command, you would first have to select a file to delete by selecting it in the Recycle Bin list.

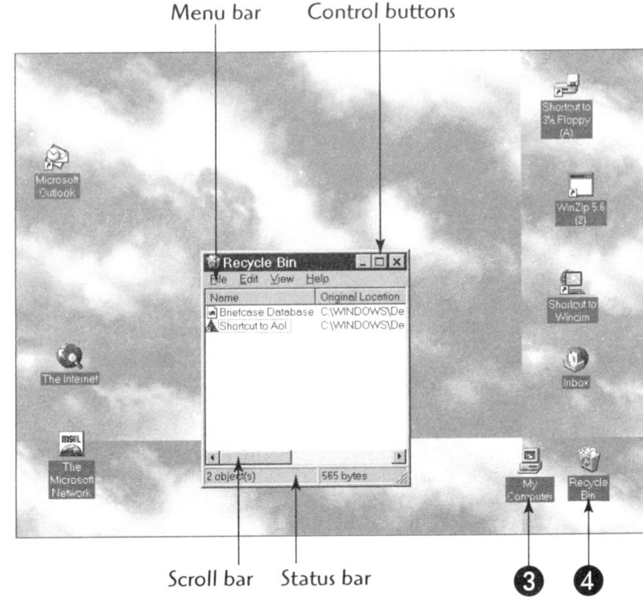

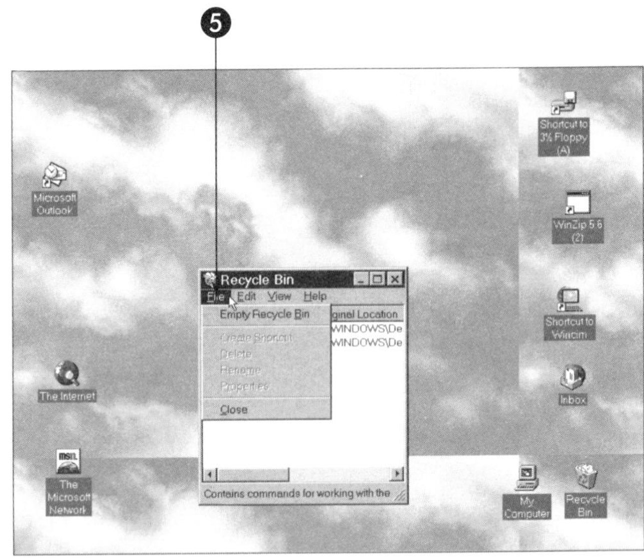

6 Click the Close command at the bottom of the File menu to close the Recycle Bin.

The window disappears, but the Recycle Bin icon is still on your desktop — double-clicking the icon opens that same window again whenever you like. You can see that the icons on the Windows desktop are simply ways to get to the windows that contain the various programs, folders, and files kept on your computer.

TRY OUT THE INTERACTIVE TUTORIALS ON YOUR CD!

Using the Windows taskbar

The Windows desktop also offers a central command feature called the Windows taskbar. Using the taskbar, you can make adjustments to settings that control how Windows works and programs open, and how you search for files, access a help system for Windows, or shut down your computer.

This taskbar isn't always visible, but finding it is simple.

1 Move your mouse pointer to the bottom of the screen. A gray bar appears there with the word Start on a button on the left side.

2 Click the Start button to view the Start menu.

The Start menu is called a *pop-up* menu, because it appears above the button you use to open it.

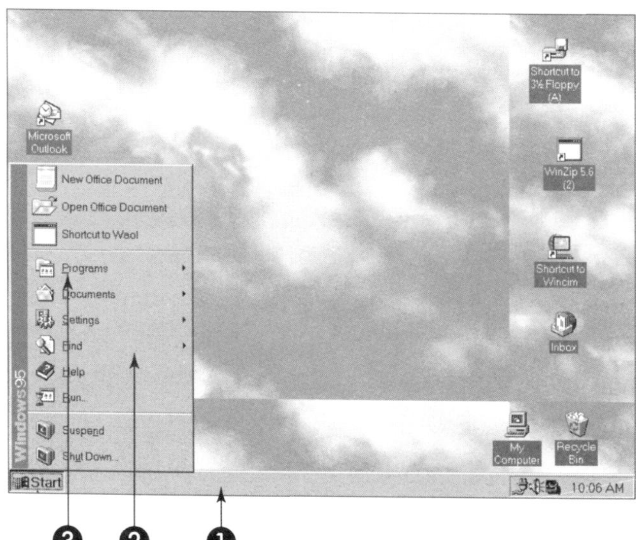

Because this screen happens to be from my laptop computer, a command called Suspend has been added to the Windows Start menu. Some computers have the capability to temporarily shut down using this feature, which is commonly found in portable computers to conserve battery power.

3 Move your pointer up to the Programs item.

Another menu, which is often referred to as a submenu or cascading menu, appears. These are all the programs you have loaded on your computer, and again, are probably different from the ones I have loaded on mine. The submenu is shown in the illustration to the right. Notice that some items on the Start menu and some in the Programs submenu have black arrows next to them. The arrows tell you that another submenu is available.

Notice also that all the Office products — Access, Binder, Excel, Outlook, PowerPoint, and Word — are listed in the Program submenu. You can open any one of them by selecting its name from this list. You see later how opening Office programs works.

4 Move your pointer up to the Accessories item on the Programs submenu.

Using this submenu system takes a little getting used to. If you move up on the Start menu rather than to the right to access the Programs side-menu, you may suddenly find that the Programs side-menu disappears. As you move your pointer over the various program names in the Programs side-menu, other submenus may appear, confusing you as to what selection to make. Don't worry; it takes only a little practice to get comfortable with this. You'll probably be a pro by the time you finish this lesson!

An Accessories submenu appears. This is where Windows programs, such as Calculator and Paint, can be accessed.

5 Move your pointer over the Programs item again.

6 Move your pointer down to the Documents item.

A submenu of documents most recently saved opens. If you have not yet created any Office documents, it is empty.

7 Move your pointer down to the Settings item.

The three options in the Settings submenu (Control Panel, Printers, and Taskbar) enable you to access areas of Windows where you can change settings that control the way your computer, hardware connected to your computer (such as printers and modems), and Windows itself work.

It's time to explore the next item on the Start menu more deeply.

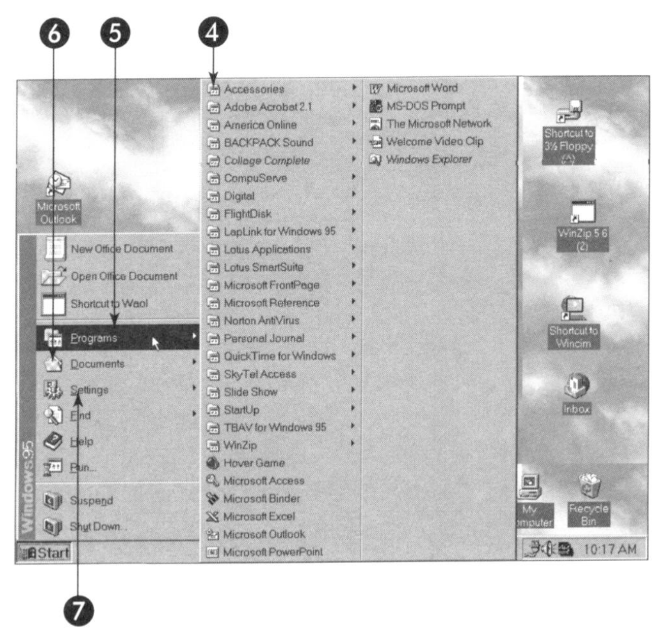

Locating files

Whether you look for a file to open from your desktop or within an application, it's important that you understand how files and folders are organized so you can locate what you need.

You can open files in two ways. First, you can open a document by locating the file and double-clicking it. This opens both the application the file was created in and the file itself. You can also open the application and use the File ➢ Open command to open the file.

There are two methods that help you locate files. If you know where the file is, you can work your way through the various folders and get the file for yourself. The second method uses a Windows feature called Find to locate the folder by an attribute such as its name or a string of text within the document. You can start by locating a file called Contemporary.dot. It's a Word for Windows file, so begin by locating Word.

❶ Open the My Computer window by double-clicking its icon on the desktop.

You probably have at least four items in this window: your floppy drive, usually labeled (A:); Printers; the Windows Control Panel; and the hard drive of your computer, labeled (C:). The hard drive is the permanent storage space inside your computer. All the Office applications, as well as files used to run your computer, are installed to this drive. There may be other items here if your computer is connected to a network or has a CD-ROM drive.

❷ View the folders on your hard drive by double-clicking the icon labeled (C:).

If Office was installed on another drive of your computer or on a network, simply use that drive letter instead of (C:) in the examples.

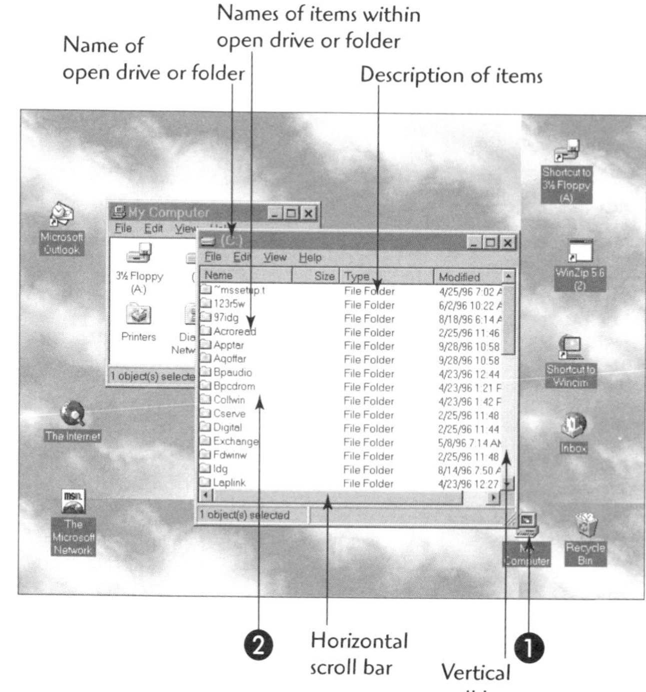

Locating files

Your hard drive contains a different set of files and folders than mine, but you should, nevertheless, be able to get a sense for how files and folders are generally organized. At this level of file management, you're probably looking mainly at *file folders,* rather than individual files. Just as with paper filing systems, you need to work your way to a document by first finding its category and working down to more detailed levels of organization.

These folders are organized alphabetically, so you need to move down the list to locate the Office applications.

3. Click the down arrow on the vertical scroll bar until the folder called Program Files appears and then double-click the folder.
4. Double-click the Microsoft Office folder to view the folders and files within.

   In the window, you see a Microsoft Word icon, which you can double-click to open Word. You're looking for a Word template file, and Office stores all its program templates in a single folder.
5. View the contents of the Templates folder by double-clicking it.
6. Open the Reports folder by double-clicking it.

   There it is, the Contemporary.dot file. You opened the hard drive folder, the Program Files folder, the Microsoft Office folder, the Templates folder, and the Reports folder to get here. Digging down through these various levels of folders gives you several layers of windows cluttering your desktop, as in the illustration to the right.

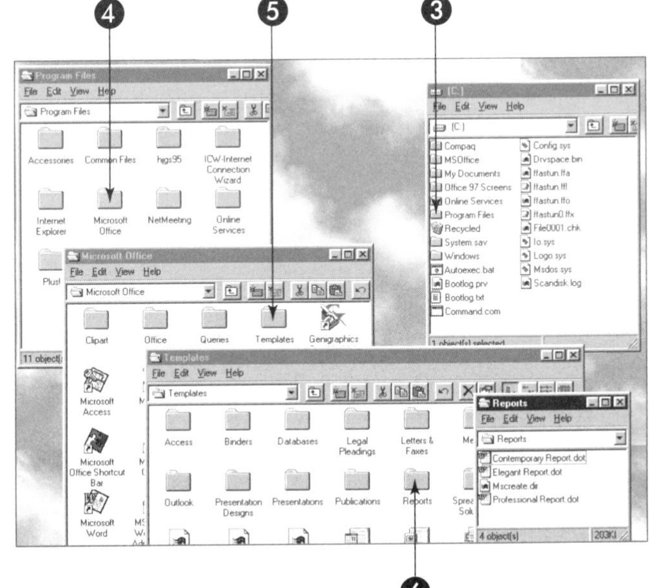

The various files you see as you explore your computer have something in common. All files have three extra letters separated from the filename by a period. This is called an extension. An extension identifies the format in which the file was saved. For example, files saved in Excel have an .xls extension and files saved in Word have a .doc extension. The Contemporary.dot file is a Word template file, a file with certain text formatting settings which you can apply to documents to save you time. Word templates have a .dot extension.

Using File Find

Now that you know the longer method of finding a file, take a shortcut using the Windows Find feature.

TIP

Notice that some windows have icons and some have lists of file or folder names. You can choose to display the files and folders in various windows as either icons or text describing the file. You change this by selecting the View menu in the window and selecting Large Icons, Small Icons, List, or Details.

1. Click the × in the upper right-hand corner of the Reports folder to close that window.
2. Repeat this with all open windows to close them.
3. Click the Start button on the Windows taskbar.
4. Move your pointer to the Find item.
5. From the submenu that appears, move your pointer to Files or Folders.
6. Click the Files or Folders item once to open the Find: All Files dialog box.

   Dialog boxes are opened by menu commands, and you see them often within the various Office products. They enable you to fill in blank spaces called text boxes, use buttons or check boxes, or select from drop-down lists to perform tasks. Sometimes, dialog boxes have tabs that resemble the tabs that divide index cards in a box or sections of a notebook. Tabs help group types of settings together so you can easily find the feature you want to work with.

7. Type the name **Contemporary.dot** in the box labeled *Named.*
8. Click the Find Now button.

   The little magnifying glass icon moves around for a few moments as Windows searches. When it's done, the location of the file

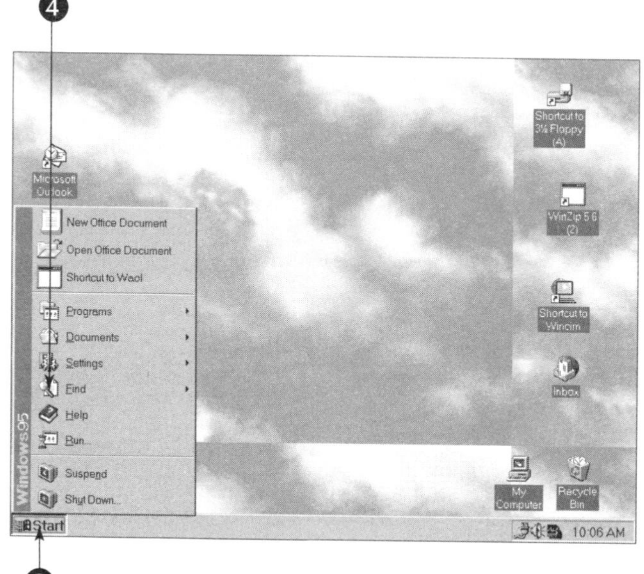

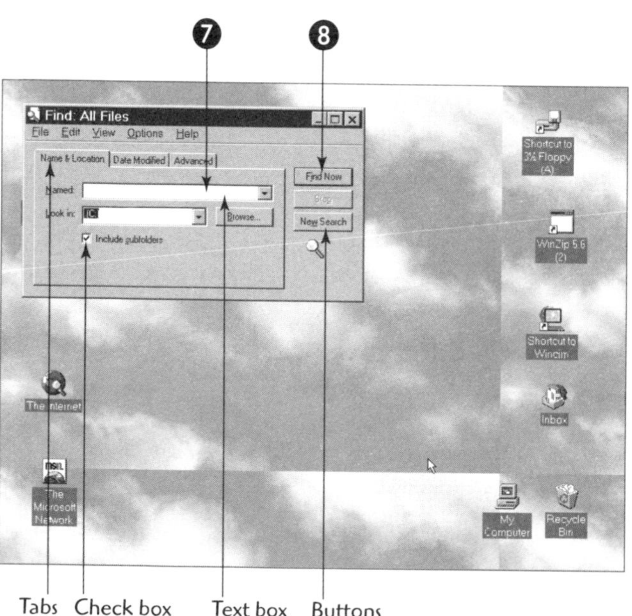

appears in a window at the bottom of this dialog box. When you don't know the location of a file, this can be the fastest way to find it. You can use the File ➢ Open command in the Find dialog box to open the file once it's been located.

9. Click the Close button in the upper right-hand corner to close the Find dialog box.

   The Visual Workout shows you how files are stored in a hierarchy of folders on a typical computer.

ORGANIZING YOUR DESKTOP

Using this system of desktop icons, folders, and files, organize your desktop in the way that best works for you. You can create folders and move files into them. You can even create your own desktop icons as shortcuts to your favorite programs.

Creating folders

Generally, your computer works more efficiently with files located on the hard drive, rather than a floppy disk or CD-ROM. To make your work in this book easier, copy the exercise files into a folder on your hard drive. You can then open and work with the files from that location when instructed to do so.

1. Double-click the My Computer icon on your desktop, if that window isn't open already.
2. Double-click the hard drive (C:).
3. Select File ➢ New, and then choose Folder from the submenu that appears.

   A new folder appears, with the name New Folder.
4. Type **One Step** to name the folder.
5. Place the accompanying CD-ROM into the CD-ROM drive.
6. Back in the My Computer window, double-click the CD-ROM icon, probably labeled (D:), to open the drive where you placed the CD-ROM.

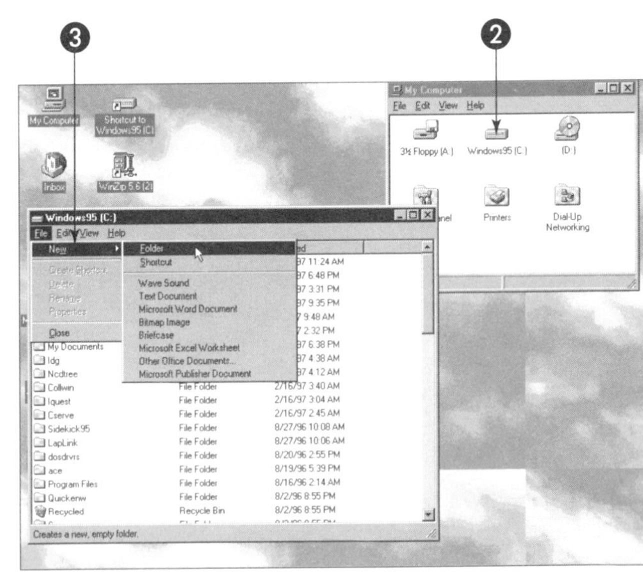

VISUAL BONUS: WINDOWS FILE MANAGEMENT

The figures to the right show the path to get to the Word for Windows application on a typical computer.

The top level of organization is the drive (floppy or hard drive).

There are folders and system files on the (C:) drive. The folders are all listed first, and then the individual files. All folders and files are listed in alphabetical order.

In the Microsoft Office folder, you find shortcuts to the Office applications and subfolders for special Office files.

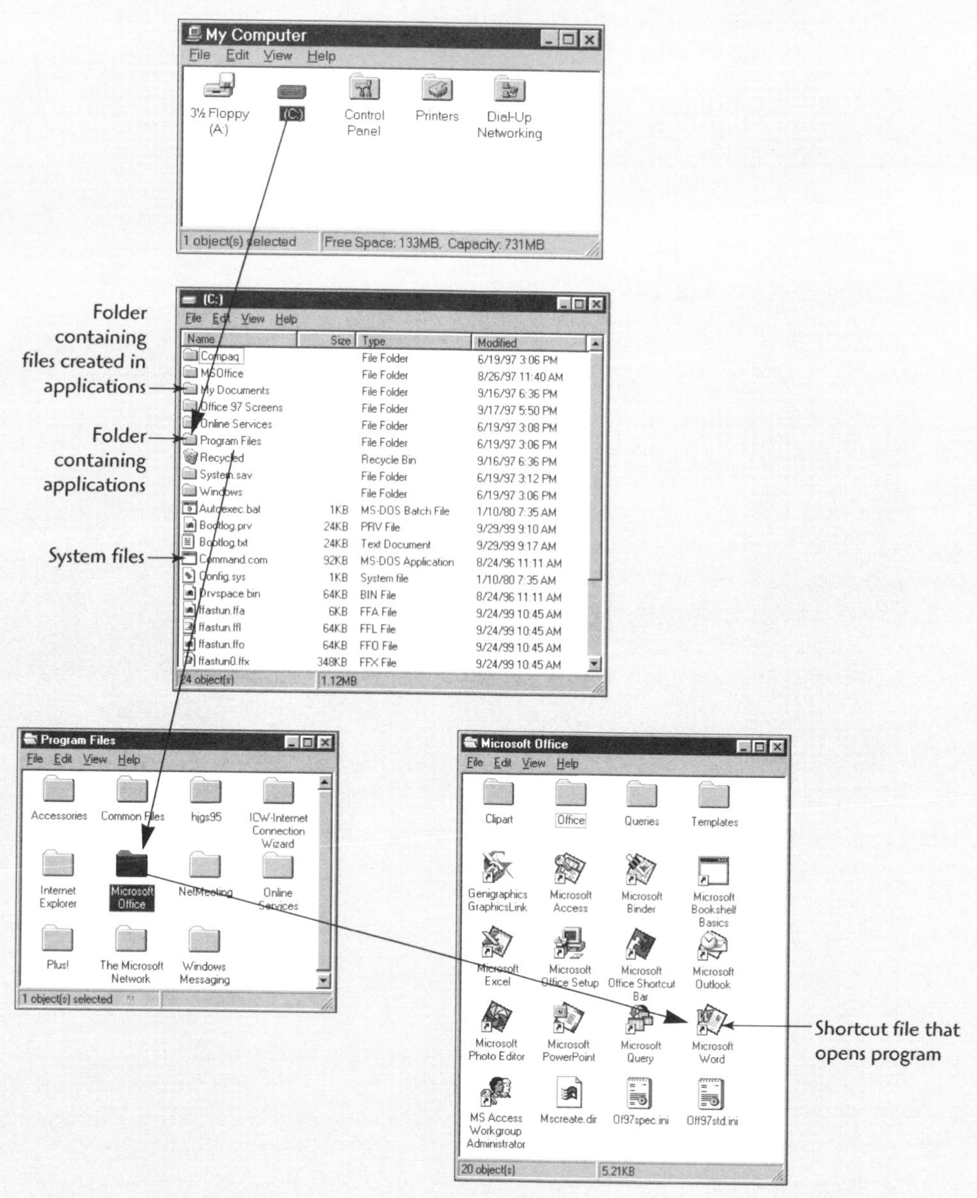

7. Click the folder named Exercise to select it.
8. Keeping the mouse button pressed, drag the mouse (which drags the folder along with it) from the (D:) window to the One Step folder.

   The folder becomes highlighted when you hold the other folder over it, letting you know that if you release your mouse button, the item you're dragging will drop into that folder.
9. Release your mouse button.
10. Double-click the One Step folder.

    All the files for your exercises are now located within this folder, and you can work with them from here.
11. Close all the open windows on your desktop.

Opening Office programs

There are two ways to open your Office programs. You can use the Programs section of the Windows Start menu to go to a particular application and click it. Or, you can use the New Office Document feature that is added to the Start menu when you install Office. In this exercise, you use the latter approach.

1. Open the Start menu from the Windows taskbar and select New Office Document. The New Office Document dialog box appears.

   The icons here enable you to open a new blank document in each of the programs. When you click any of these, a preview of the document type appears in the dialog box. The following is what each opens:

   - *Blank Database* opens the Access for Windows database program.
   - *Blank Document* opens the Word for Windows word processor.
   - *Blank Workbook* opens the Excel for Windows spreadsheet program.
   - *Blank Binder* opens Microsoft Binder.

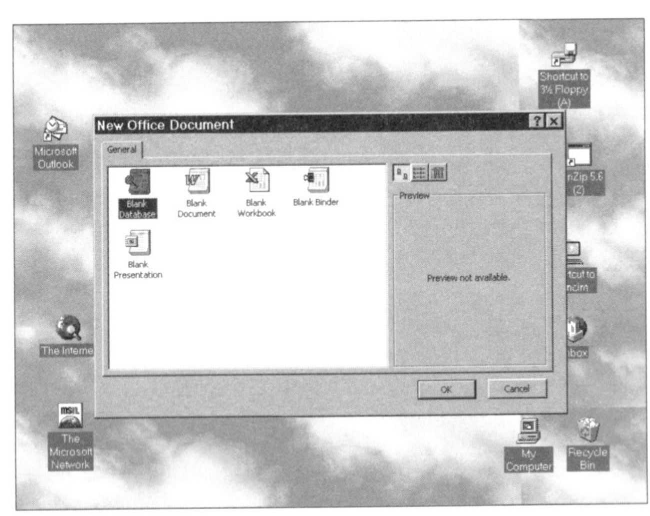

- *Blank Presentation* opens PowerPoint for Windows presentation software.

Microsoft Binder is a feature of Office that enables you to open binders for multiple documents from any of the Office programs. For example, you might want to bind together a spreadsheet, word processing document, and database report into one project binder and give all the documents one title, with the same information in a single header across the documents. This helps you use Office documents in the way that you work; not by software function, but by project or work activity.

2. Double-click the Blank Document icon.

   The Word for Windows application opens in a window on the desktop.

Now try opening Excel, but this time use a different procedure to start the program. (Leave Word open as you follow these steps.)

3. Open the My Computer window.
4. Open the hard drive (C:).
5. Use the scroll bar to move to the Program Files folder and double-click to open it; then double-click the Microsoft Office folder.
6. Using your *right* mouse button, click the file called Microsoft Excel.

   What appears is called a shortcut menu. These floating menus contain some of the most commonly used commands, and appear throughout Office programs when you click with your right mouse button.

7. Select Create Shortcut.

   A new Microsoft Excel icon appears, as in the illustration to the right, with a (2) notation after it. This is basically a copy of the file used to start up the Excel program.

8. Click the new Microsoft Excel file and drag it onto your desktop.

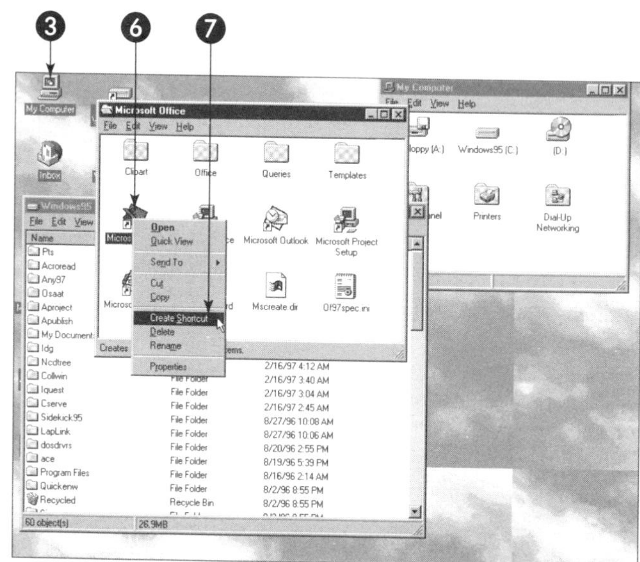

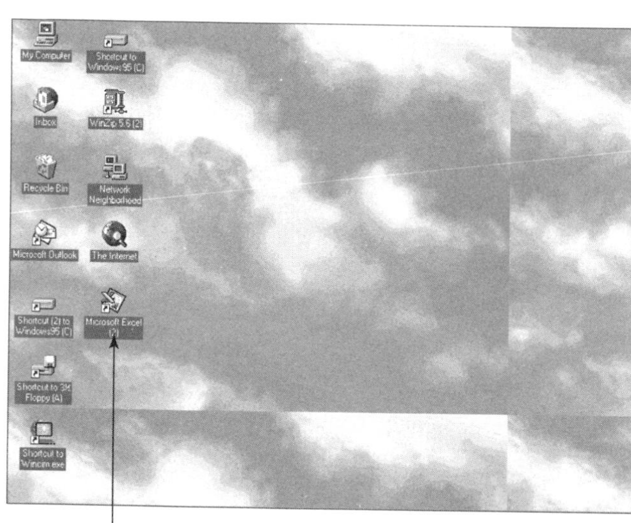

New Excel shortcut

If you inadvertently double-click this icon while trying to select and drag it, Excel will open. That's okay. Just click the Close button in the upper right-hand corner of the Excel window and try again, being careful to click only once on the file.

9. Double-click the shortcut you just created to open Excel.

   You can use this method to create shortcuts to the programs you use most often, so you can open them by double-clicking the shortcut on the Windows desktop.

10. Close all the windows except Excel and Word.

Working with windows

You now have two windows open on your desktop, as shown to the bottom right. You can move open windows around and resize them. You can even drag information from one Office program window to another, which you learn more about in Lesson 2.

1. Click the title bar of the Word window.

   The title bar becomes darkened and the window moves forward. This is now the selected window.

2. Click in the title bar of Word and drag the window to the right side of the screen.

3. Move your mouse pointer to the left side of the Word window until it turns into a two-sided arrow, as shown on the next page at the top.

4. Click and drag the pointer to the right, resizing the Word window to take up about half the width of your screen.

5. Move your mouse pointer to the upper-left corner of the Excel window until the pointer becomes a diagonal two-headed arrow.

6. Click and drag the corner of the Excel window downward about an inch.

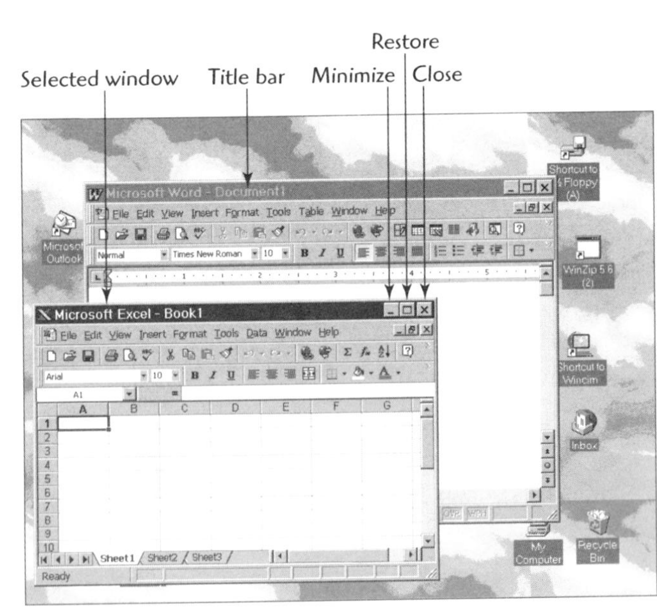

Working with windows

Using the arrow pointer, you can resize windows any way you like. You can drag from a corner to resize but retain the window's proportions, or use the arrow pointer from the top, bottom, or sides of the window to resize and change its shape.

7. In the Word window, click the Minimize button (it's the first of the three buttons to the far right of the title bar).

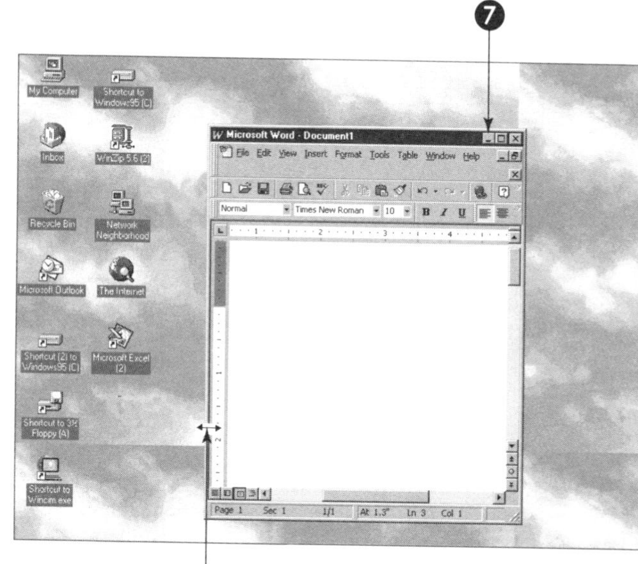

NOTE

If, in moving the Word window around, the Minimize button has moved off the screen, click anywhere on the Word title bar and drag the window back to the middle of the screen.

The Word window disappears, but it's not gone; you can open it again by clicking the Word for Windows button on the Windows taskbar.

8. Move your mouse pointer to the bottom of your screen until the Windows taskbar appears.

The taskbar appears, as in the bottom right illustration, with buttons for both Word and Excel. You can restore the Word window by clicking its button on the taskbar.

9. Click the Word button on the taskbar to open that window again.

Because the taskbar can be accessed no matter where you are in Windows or the Office programs, you can use these buttons to easily move among the programs.

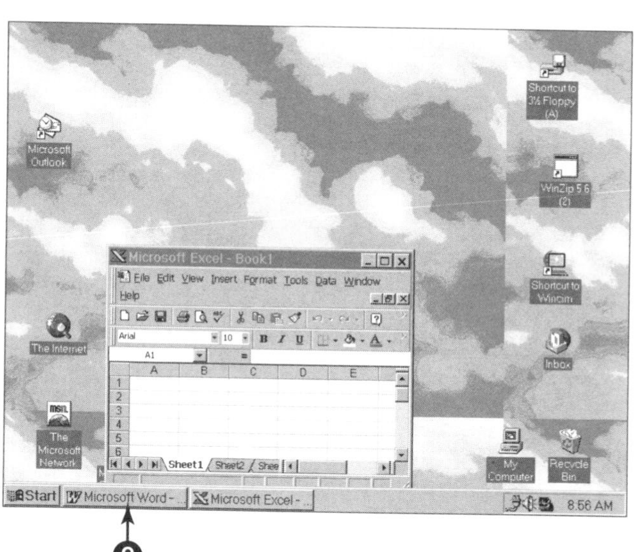

NOTE

You can use the special Windows key on newer keyboards to make the taskbar appear. The key has a little Windows emblem on it. If your taskbar doesn't appear from all windows, select Start ➢ Setting ➢ Taskbar, and click in the check box labeled Always on top *so the taskbar will always be displayed.*

10. Click the Maximize button on the Excel window.

The Excel window expands to take up the entire screen.

Skills challenge

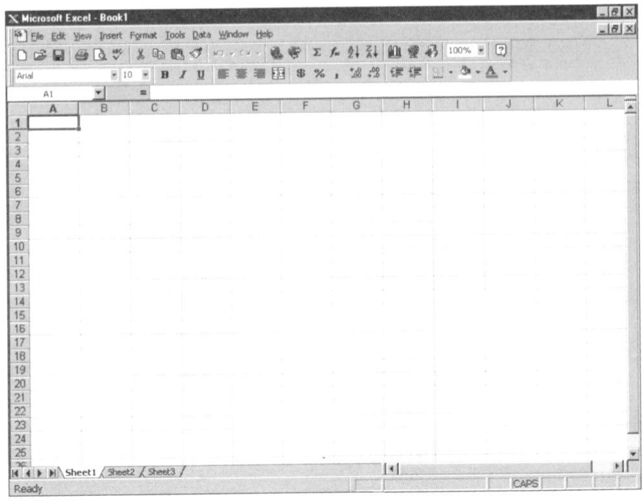

11. Click the Word button on the Windows taskbar.

    The Word window appears. You can also use Alt + Tab to switch back and forth among programs.

12. Close the Word window by clicking the Close button in its upper-right corner.

    Step 12 closes not just the window, but the whole program.

13. Click the Restore button in the Excel window.

14. In the reduced Excel window, select File and then move down the File menu and select Exit.

    You can close a program with its Close button or the Exit command.

SKILLS CHALLENGE: SETTING UP YOUR DESKTOP TO WORK WITH OFFICE

Now that you learned your way around the Windows desktop, here's how to set it up to work with the Office programs.

1. Move the Excel shortcut icon to an empty area of your desktop.
2. Open the My Computer window and locate the MS Office folder.
3. Create a shortcut for another program you think you'll use frequently (Word, PowerPoint, or Access).
4. Drag that shortcut out to your desktop and place it next to the Excel shortcut.
5. Open Excel from the shortcut.
6. Restore the Excel window to fill your entire screen.
7. From the Windows taskbar, open PowerPoint.
8. Minimize Excel.
9. Close PowerPoint.

What are the two ways to close a program?

TRY OUT THE INTERACTIVE TUTORIALS ON YOUR CD!

10 Use the Windows Find feature to locate the file Ex05-1.

Describe how you can get to this file by opening various folders.

11 Create a folder on your hard drive named Workshop on Demand Templates.

12 Move the contents of the Templates folder on the accompanying CD-ROM into that folder.

Besides using the scroll bar, how could you see more of the contents of the (C:) drive window?

13 Close all windows and programs.

TROUBLESHOOTING

You've just begun to explore the Windows environment, and have caught your first glimpse of a couple of Office programs. The following table helps with some common mistakes that a new Windows user might make.

Problem	Solution
I moved a folder into the Recycle Bin and now I need it back.	Double-click the Recycle Bin, and drag the folder back into any open window.
I created a lot of shortcuts and now my desktop is too cluttered.	Click a shortcut with your right mouse button and select Delete from the menu that appears. This won't delete the program, it just gets rid of the shortcut.
I'm trying to create a folder but it tells me I have to rename it.	You can't have more than one subfolder in the same folder with the same name. Choose a different name or move it to another folder.

Wrap up

WRAP UP

You had a quick introduction to some of the basic functions of Windows. These functions will come in handy as you work in and among the various Office programs. You learned the following:

- How to move items around the desktop and find files
- How to create folders and shortcuts to help you set up your desktop the way you please
- The various ways to open, minimize, and close programs

If you want more practice with these skills, set up folders for various projects you might have at work, and move any files that relate to those projects into the folders.

In Lesson 2, you begin to work with the Office products themselves.

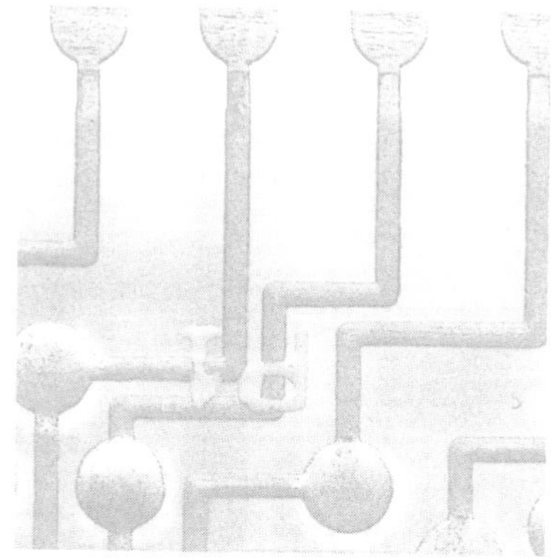

Meet Microsoft Office

GOALS

In this lesson, you get a closer look at the programs that make up Microsoft Office. You learn some of the basics of moving around those programs, including the following:

- Opening Office programs
- Switching between programs
- Opening a Word document
- Opening a PowerPoint presentation
- Exploring an Excel worksheet
- Opening an Access worksheet
- Looking at Outlook

Get ready

GET READY

To complete this lesson, you need the following files: You should have copied these files from the CD-ROM to your hard drive. (See the CD installation instructions for more information.) Ex02-1, Ex02-2, Ex02-3, and Ex02-4.

WHAT IS A SUITE OF SOFTWARE?

A software suite is made up of various individual programs that perform different types of activities, such as word processing or calculating. Microsoft, however, has done much more than just throw several software programs into one box. Office 97 contains features that combine Microsoft's various products and integrate them with each other. This integration involves the following features:

- All the products share a similar look and feel, so learning the products is simpler.
- You can easily take pieces of information from a document created in one program and place them in a document created in a second program. You can even grab an object in one program with your mouse and literally drag it across your screen and place it in another program.
- Office contains several smaller applications called applets which are available to all the programs in the suite. These applets enable you to do things such as build organizational charts and apply fancy text effects.
- You can establish something called a link. With a link, you can copy an object, such as a chart from Excel, into a Word for Windows memo. When you change the data in Excel, it also changes in Word.
- All the products share tools for accessing the Internet, enabling you to go right to Microsoft's home page for product support, upgrade information, and tips for using Office.

What is a suite of software?

VISUAL BONUS: WHAT THE OFFICE PROGRAMS HAVE IN COMMON

This Visual Bonus gives you an idea of how the products share features, and how a similar appearance makes them easy to use.

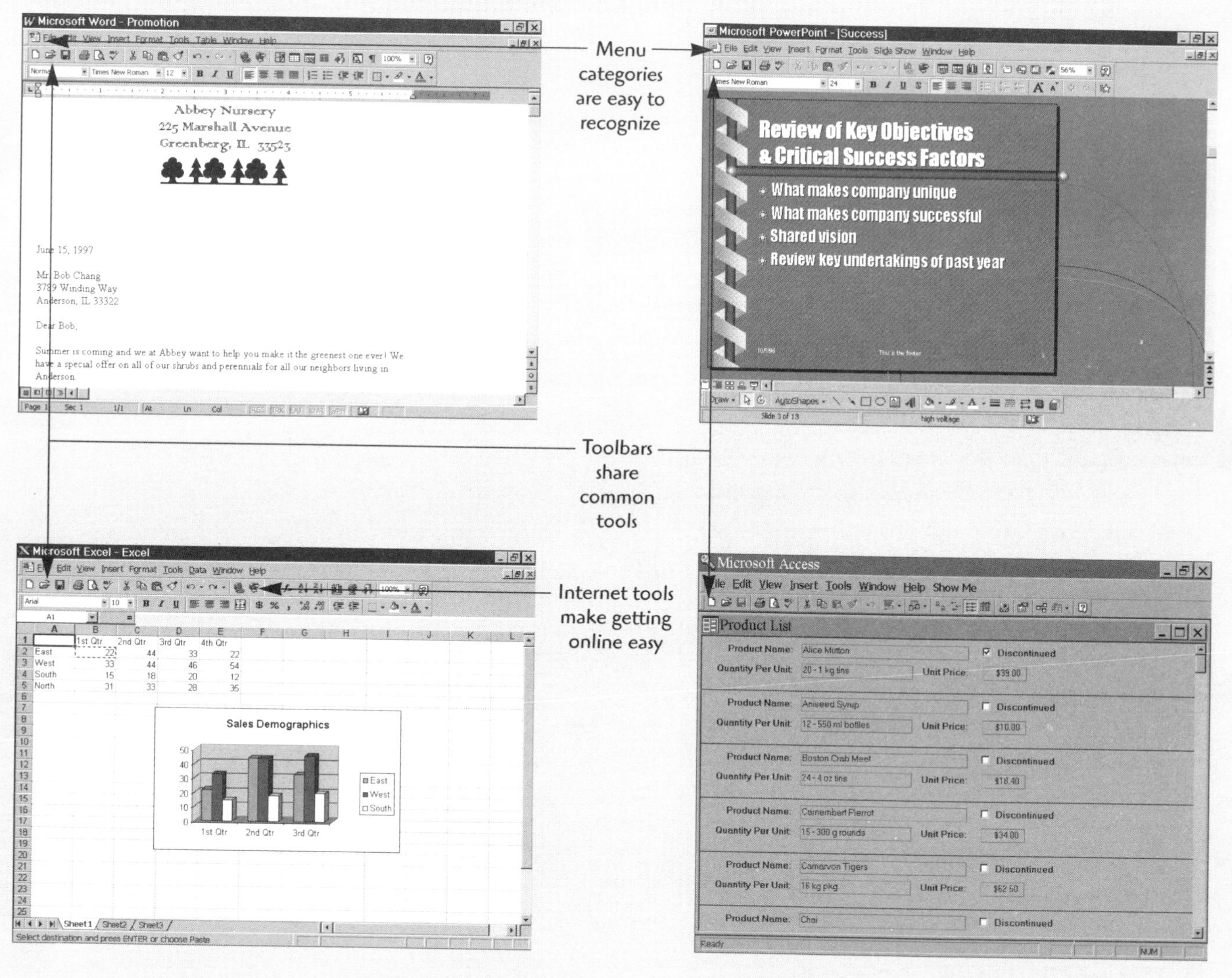

Opening Office programs

Opening Office programs

You'll begin your exploration of Office by practicing a few different ways to open the individual programs.

1. Go to the Windows desktop.
2. Select the Start menu on the Windows taskbar.
3. Choose Programs ➢ Microsoft Word.

   Word for Windows takes a moment to load. When it is finished loading, you see a blank document screen like the one in the illustration to the right. You can begin typing in this blank document, and save it with a specific name after you've entered text.

4. Reduce the Word window by clicking the Restore button in the top right corner (the middle of the three control buttons that has two little square symbols on it).
5. Select the Start menu on the Windows taskbar.
6. Choose Open Office Document to view the dialog box shown in the figure to the bottom right.

   By default, Open Office Document dialog box shows all files created in Office products that have been saved to the My Documents folder. You can use the various fields and buttons here to locate the file you need. Windows will then open the document along with the application it was created in.

7. Place the accompanying CD-ROM in your CD-ROM drive (which I'll assume is D:).
8. Open the *Look in* box.
9. Click (D:).
10. Double-click the Exercise folder.
11. Click the file Ex02-1 and choose Open.

    Excel for Windows opens with the Ex02-1 document displayed, as in the top illustration on the next page.

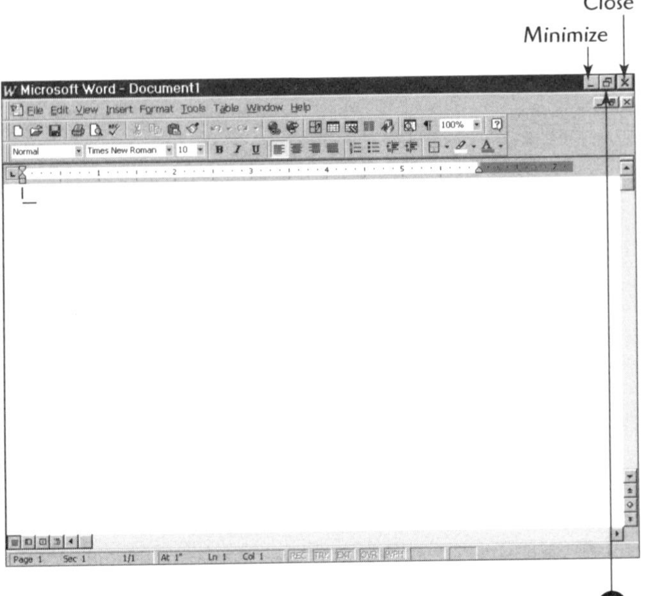

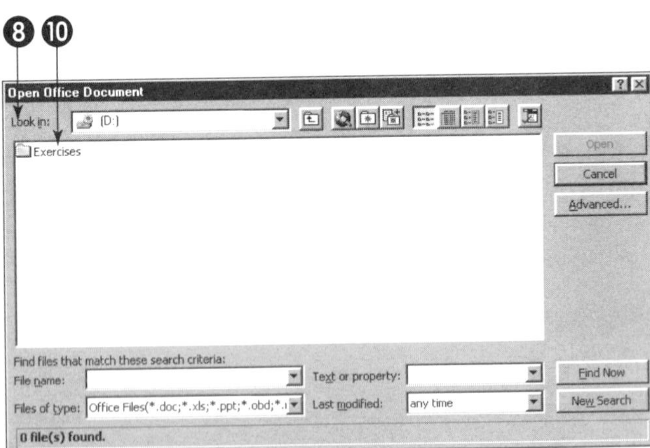

⓬ Click the Restore button to shrink the Excel window.

⓭ Select the Start menu from the Windows taskbar.

⓮ Choose New Office Document.

The dialog box in the illustration to the right appears. From this dialog box, you can choose to select a blank database in Access, a blank document in Word, a blank workbook in Excel, or a blank presentation in PowerPoint.

NOTE

The Blank Binder option opens the Office Binder, which enables you to assemble documents created in several different Office products in one place — for example, to bring an Excel chart, Word table, and Access data form into a project report binder.

⓯ Double-click the Blank Presentation icon.

PowerPoint takes a moment to load. When it does, you see the New Slide dialog box.

⓰ Click OK to open a slide with the Title Slide layout.

A new slide with two text placeholders appears in the PowerPoint Slide View, as in the illustration to the right.

⓱ Click the Restore button to shrink the PowerPoint window.

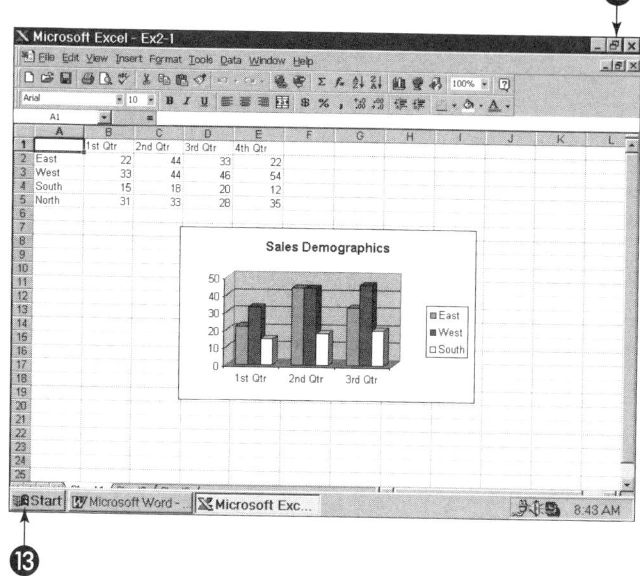

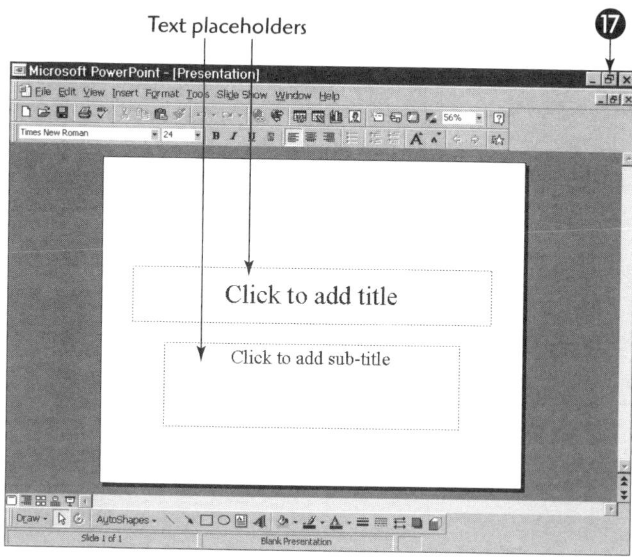

Switching between programs

You now have three Office programs open on your desktop. It's time to practice moving between the programs.

❶ Click the Word window to make it the active window.

❷ Choose the Maximize button in the Word window to enlarge it (oddly enough, it's the same as the Restore button; when a window is reduced in size, the Restore button is called the Maximize button).

Switching between programs

3. Press Alt + Tab.

   The most recent active window, PowerPoint, appears on top of the Word window. PowerPoint is now the active window.

4. Press Alt + Tab again.

   The PowerPoint window disappears, and the Word window becomes the active window. You can use Alt + Tab to switch back and forth among two programs quickly, or click any windows button on the taskbar at the bottom of the screen to make it active.

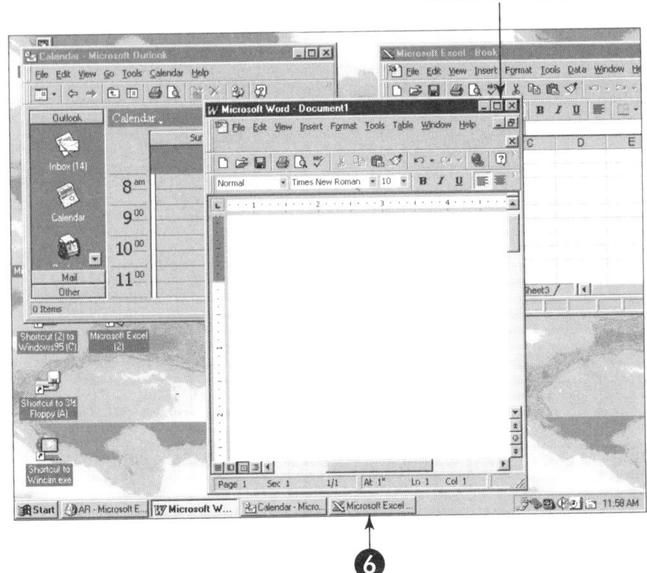

You can also use Shift + Alt + Tab to work your way backward through the previous active windows one by one.

5. Move your pointer to the bottom of the screen until the Windows taskbar appears.

6. Click the button that says Microsoft Excel (some of the letters may be cut off, depending on how many buttons appear on the taskbar at the moment).

   Aside from using Alt + Tab to switch to the last active window, you can make any open window the active window by selecting it from the taskbar.

7. Scroll down in the Excel document until you see the chart.

8. Click the edge of the chart; you should see eight black squares surrounding it.

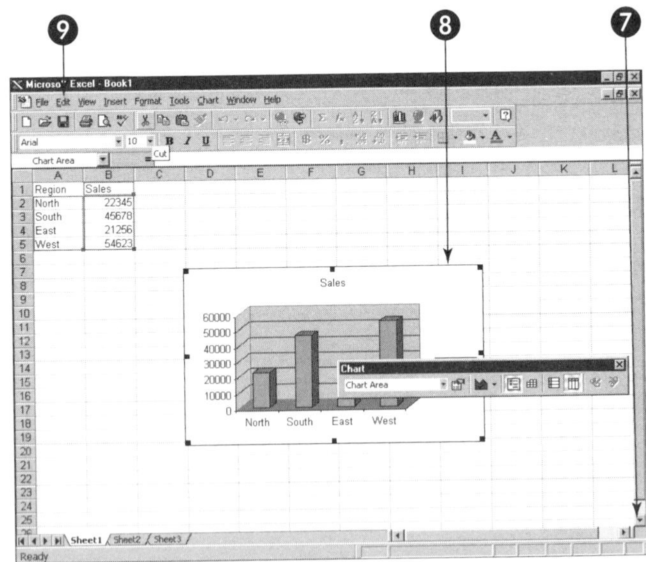

If you need to see more of the Excel window, place your pointer at any corner until it becomes a double arrow and drag to enlarge the Excel window as much as you like.

9. Select Edit ➢ Cut.

10. Click back on the Word document.
11. Select Edit ➢ Paste to paste the chart into the Word document.
12. Move your cursor down to the Windows taskbar and press your right mouse button.
13. Select Minimize All Windows from the shortcut menu that appears.

    All the windows have been minimized and are represented by buttons on the taskbar along the bottom of the Windows desktop.

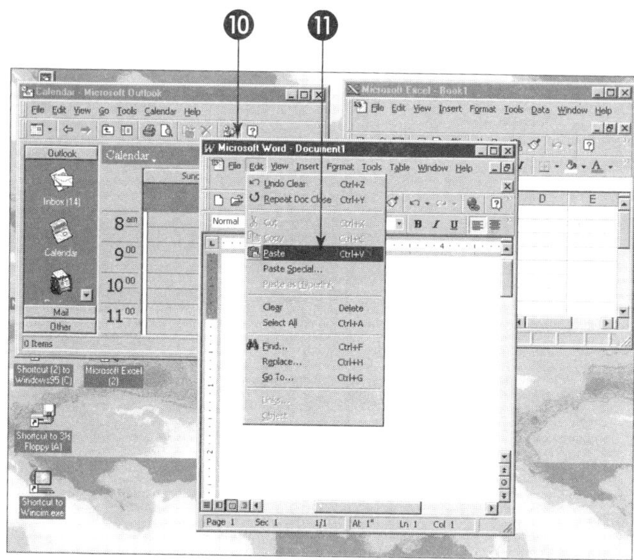

There are also several ways of inserting objects from one program into another using menu commands or tools, which you learn about in other parts of this book. Once inserted, you can open one program within another to edit those objects by clicking the objects.

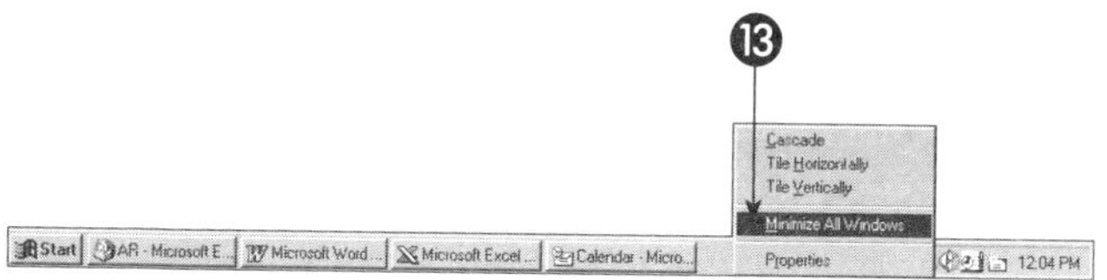

LOOKING AT THE PROGRAMS

Take a closer look at each of the program windows by opening and studying a document in each program. Start with a Word document.

Opening a Word document

As you learned in previous exercises, you can open a program in several ways. If you locate a Word file through your desktop and double-click it, Word will open to that file. If you open Word any other way, it opens to a blank document.

1. Click the Microsoft Word button on the taskbar.
2. If the Word window isn't maximized so that it fills your entire screen, click the Maximize button.
3. Select the File ➢ Open.

   The Open dialog box shown in the illustration to the right appears.

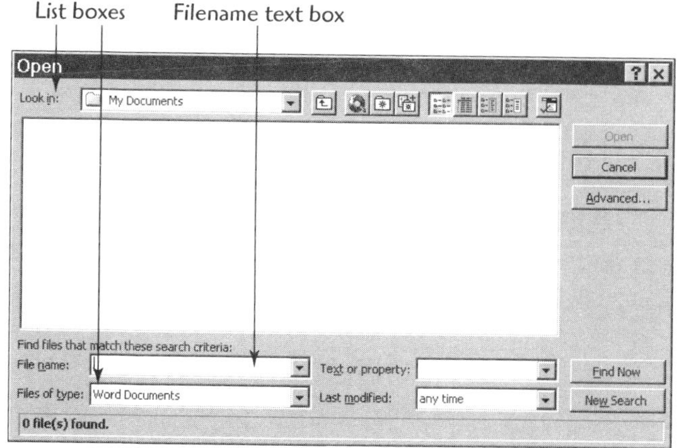

Opening a Word document

Any time you want to open a file in any of the Office programs, you see this dialog box. It may be called something slightly different now and then; for example, when you are inserting a multimedia file, you open it through a dialog box called Insert Sound or Insert Movie. However, the choices in that dialog box are identical to this one.

The following are the settings you can use to locate a file using this dialog box:

- Select the drive where your file is located by opening the *Look in* drop-down list box. This list box includes your hard drive (C:), floppy drive (usually A:), and any network or CD-ROM drives. When you select a drive and directory that contains files, those filenames appear in the large blank area at the middle of this dialog box.
- Designate the kind of file (Word, Excel, graphics, and so on) that you want to open in the *Files of type* drop-down list box. All filenames contain an extension, a three letter designation of the program or type of program in which they were created. For example, Word documents have a .doc extension, while Excel documents have an .xls extension. If you're not sure of the file's extension, select All Files in this drop-down list.
- Type a specific name in the *File name* text box. If you've used the *Look in* drop-down list to open a directory containing files, you can also click the filename when it appears in the window in the middle of this dialog box.

4 Click the arrow on the *Look in* box to open the file.

5 Select (C:).

The major directories on your (C:) drive are displayed, as in the illustration to the left. Your directories will differ from mine, of course, but if you followed the procedures in Lesson 1, you will also have a directory named One Step. During the course of Lesson 1, you copied all the One Step at a Time files into this directory.

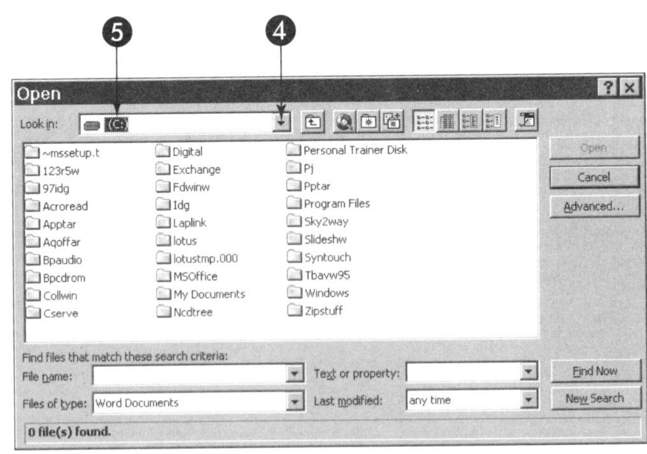

Opening a Word document

NOTE

If you created the One Step directory on your (C:) drive and copied files into it from the CD-ROM that accompanies this book, you should use that directory to open files whenever I direct you to open files from the CD-ROM.

6. Select (D:) from the *Look in* drop-down list to select (D:).
7. Open the Exercise folder by double-clicking it.
8. Click the file named Ex02-2.
9. Click Open to open the file.

   The document in the illustration to the bottom right appears. This is a letter that you'll actually create in a later lesson.

   You can see several elements that you also encounter in the other Office programs: menus and toolbars, which you use to perform tasks; scroll bars to help you move around your document; and the status bar that tells you, for example, what page or line of the document you are currently working in. Other elements, such as the View buttons and rulers, are in some programs but not others. The Windows title bar, which runs across the very top of every program window, gives the name of the program and the name of the currently open file. You'll begin to explore these features in Lesson 3. For now, you'll move on to the next Office program, PowerPoint.

10. Select File ➢ Exit, and don't save any changes if prompted to do so.

NOTE

You can also exit a program by clicking the Close button. If a program is minimized and appears as a button on the Windows taskbar, you can click it with your right mouse button and select Close from the shortcut menu that appears.

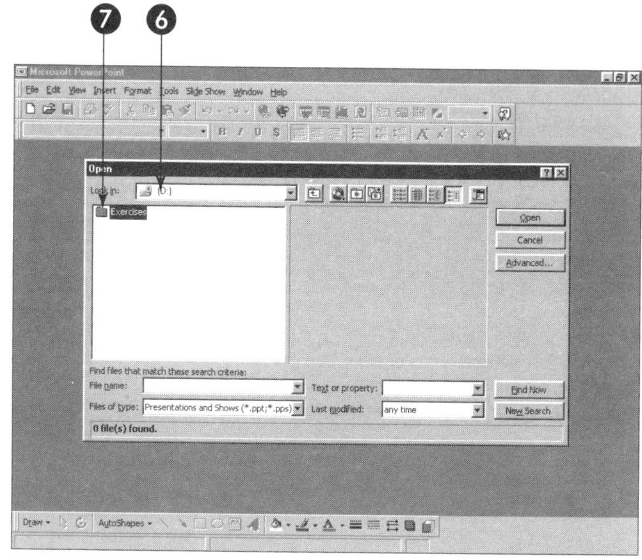

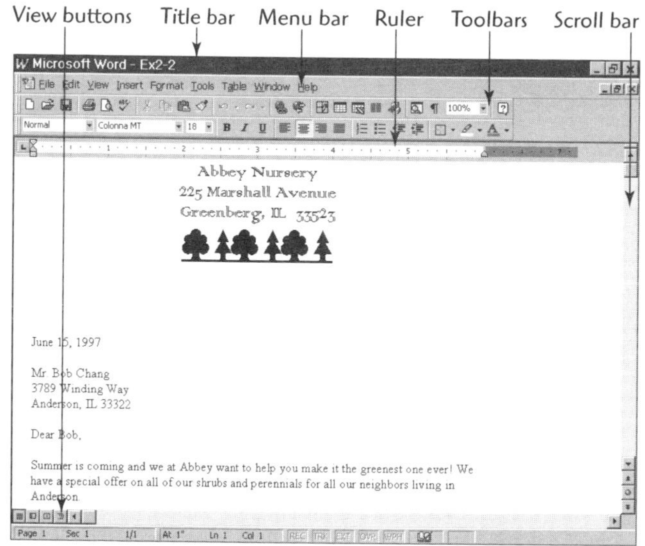

Opening a PowerPoint presentation

Opening a PowerPoint presentation

Next, you'll get your first glimpse of a PowerPoint presentation.

1. Click the PowerPoint button on the Windows taskbar to open the program window.
2. Click the Maximize button to enlarge the PowerPoint window so that it fills the entire screen.
3. Select File ➢ Open.
4. Use the *Look in* drop-down list to locate the Exercise folder in the One Step folder on your hard drive.
5. Select the file Ex02-3 and choose Open.

   The bottom illustration shows the PowerPoint slide image that appears.

   Notice what the Word window and the PowerPoint window have in common. Several of the menus have the same names, such as File, Edit, Window, and Help. Many of the tools on the upper two toolbars are the same. PowerPoint also has view buttons. Right now, you're in Slide View, which is PowerPoint's default view. It shows a single slide from your presentation and the tools you need to add content and apply design elements to the slide. Notice the toolbar across the bottom of this screen; it's a drawing toolbar, useful for creating and modifying the visual elements that are often used in a presentation.
6. Click the down arrow on the scroll bar to take a look at the several individual slides contained in this presentation.
7. Select File ➢ Exit. If prompted to save changes, select No.

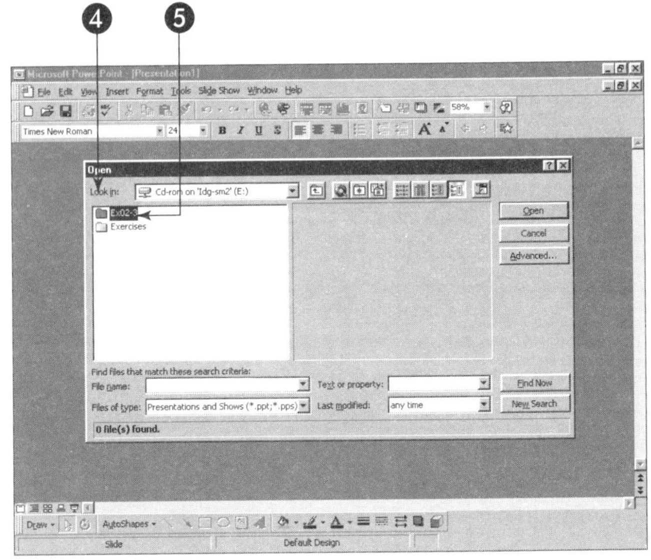

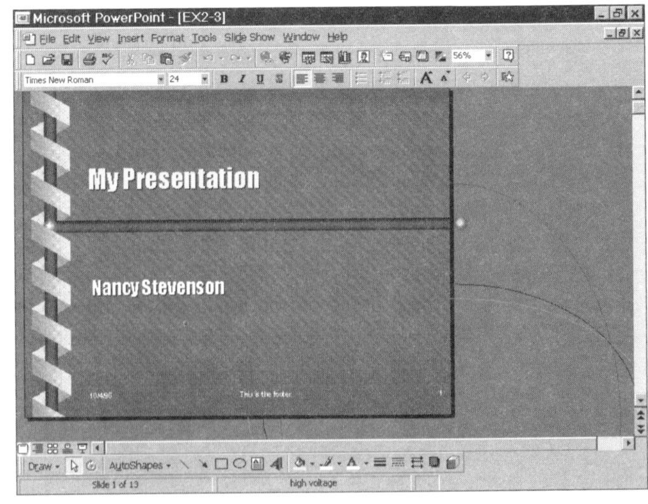

Exploring an Excel worksheet

Excel is the next stop on your exploration of Office. Excel is the calculator extraordinaire of Office.

1. Click the Microsoft Excel button on the Windows taskbar.
2. Click the Maximize button to enlarge this window to fill your entire screen.

The file you opened before is still onscreen, as shown in the illustration to the right.

If you've somehow closed the file, select File ➢ Open and open the Ex02-1 file from the accompanying CD-ROM.

Notice there are some familiar elements here, such as menus and toolbars. However, in place of view buttons found in Word and PowerPoint, there are several tabs at the bottom of the screen labeled Sheet1, Sheet2, and Sheet3. Excel workbooks can be made up of several sheets, each containing different information about the same item, such as a quarterly budget. Each separate box in an Excel worksheet is called a *cell*.

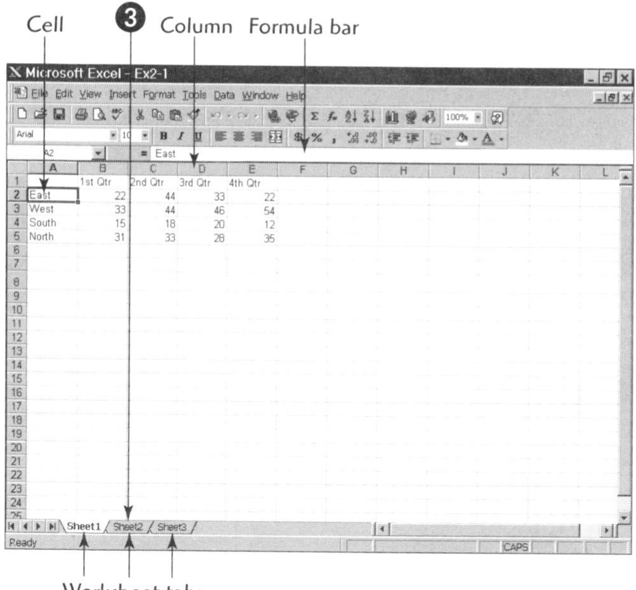

3. Click the Sheet2 tab.

   A different set of data appears, and the Sheet2 tab is now highlighted.

4. Click in the cell with the text *1994*, which places your cursor there ready to enter text.

   Notice that the formula bar now contains the same text. You use the formula bar in Excel to enter information or formulas for calculations.

5. Click the Sheet3 tab and a graph appears.

6. Click anywhere on the graph.

   The floating chart toolbar shown in the illustration to the right appears. You often see floating toolbars appear in Office programs when you are working with specific objects, such as a chart in Excel.

7. Select File ➢ Exit and do not to save changes if prompted.

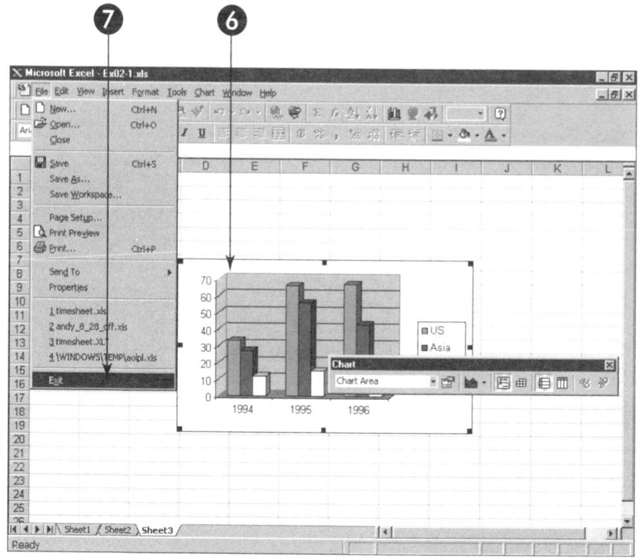

Opening an Access database

Time to move on to Access. Access is a database program used to store and manage data.

Opening an Access database

❶ Select Start ➢ Programs ➢ Microsoft Access.

The Microsoft Access dialog box in the illustration appears. This is actually a sample database provided by Microsoft for the Northwind Trading Company.

When you first open a PowerPoint or Access program, you see an opening dialog box like the one shown in the figure, giving you a few choices of how to open a presentation. In Word and Excel, a blank presentation window simply opens with no choices for you to make.

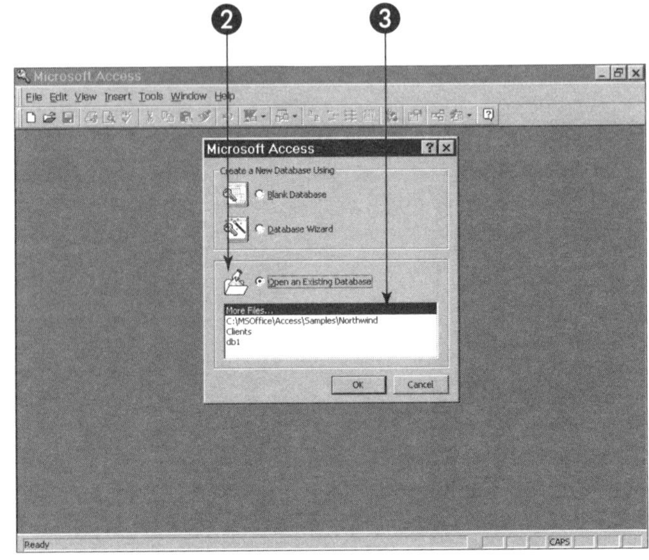

Notice the option of using a Database Wizard. Wizards provide a step-by-step method of creating a new database, presentation, or document by simply responding to questions and filling in blanks. You'll see them used throughout the lessons in this book.

❷ Make sure the Open an Existing Database option button (a.k.a., radio button) is selected.

❸ Double-click the choice More Files....

❹ From the Open dialog box that appears, locate the file Ex02-4 on the accompanying CD-ROM and choose Open.

❺ Click the Forms tab to bring that sheet forward.

The illustration shows the listing of forms that appears. Although you do see a menu bar and toolbar similar to the ones you've seen in other Office programs, things look slightly different. That's because Access databases are typically made up of several pieces, including forms, reports, tables, and queries. A database is simply a set of information, and you can produce a variety of reports and forms based on that information. Think of how your phone book is organized. There's an alphabetical listing by name in the white pages, a listing by business type in the yellow pages, and listings of more specific distinctions, such as restaurants listed by the type of cuisine served. The basic information — a restaurant's name and address — may be the same, but it can be used and viewed in different ways.

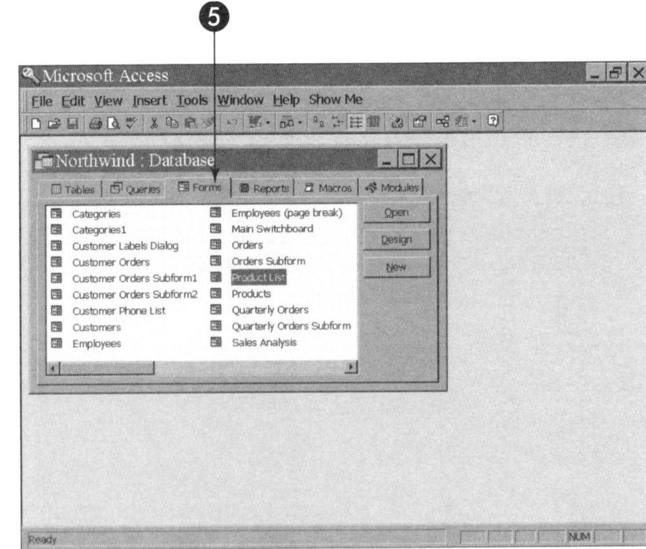

6. Under Form, double-click the Product List.

   The Product form appears. The form shows a listing that is like a product catalog, with Product Name and Quantity Per Unit fields, and which allows you to enter unique information for each product.

7. Click the Close button in the Product form window to close it.

8. Select the Tables tab.

9. Double-click the Products table.

   The table in the illustration appears. This shows some of the same information you saw in the Products form, but this time the information is formatted as a table.

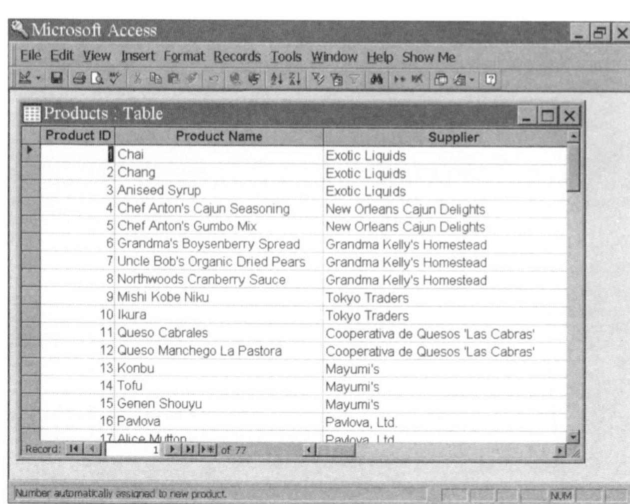

The Access screen in the figure shows a sample database from Microsoft called Northwind. The Show Me menu that appears here doesn't usually appear in Access. It's added to this sample database to provide extra help in learning Access in the form of demos.

10. Select File ➢ Exit and don't save any changes if prompted to do so.

Exploring Outlook

The final element of Office is Outlook. Outlook has multiple uses: it is a program that enables you to send, receive, and manage your e-mail; set schedules; and manage tasks and contacts.

1. Select the Start menu from the Windows taskbar, and then select Programs ➢ Microsoft Outlook.

   The Inbox appears, as in the illustration.

   Outlook has menus and a toolbar that seem similar to those in other Office programs. However, Outlook is different from the other programs in several ways. Think of Outlook as a notebook organizer you carry around with you. It might contain a calendar, an address section, an area for notes, and so on. You carry only one around, but you can certainly make changes and additions as you go through your day. Also, Outlook doesn't create Outlook

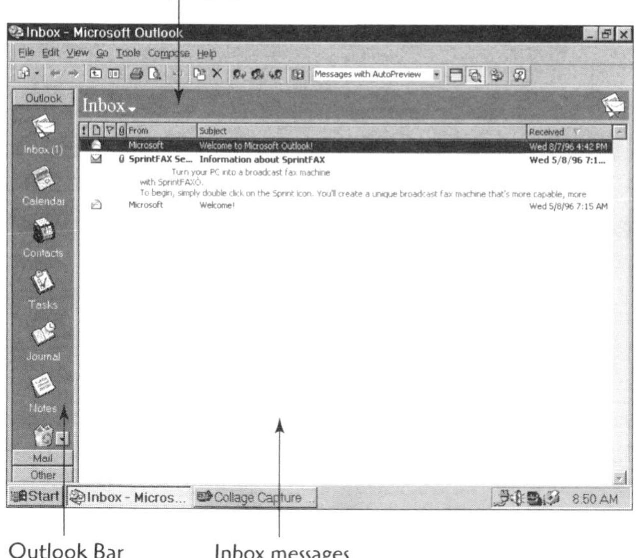

files in the way that Word creates Word documents and Excel creates Excel worksheets. Outlook is a centralized information and mail management program. One other difference from the other Office products is that you don't have to save the information you enter: It's saved automatically as you enter it. This is true of Access, as well.

You can explore the various parts of Outlook using the Outlook bar that runs along the left side of the window.

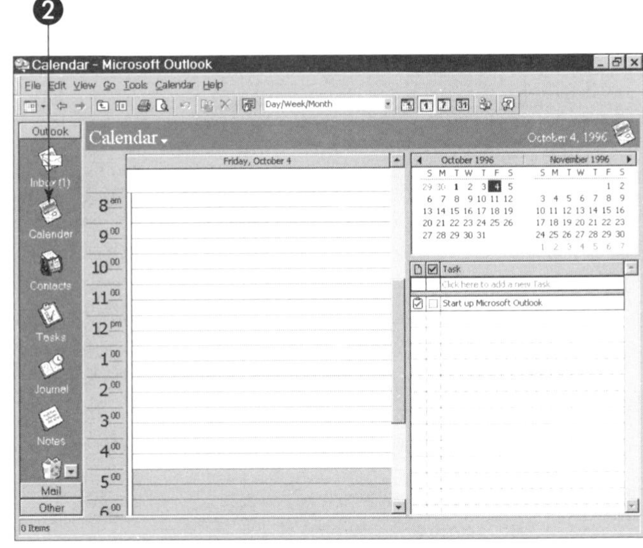

2. Click Calendar to see the Calendar view.

   The illustration shows the Calendar view of Outlook.

   You have three views on this screen: your daily calendar, a monthly calendar, and a task list.

3. Click the Contacts button in the Outlook bar.

   You probably don't have any contacts entered yet, so take a look at the contact list shown in the illustration at the bottom right.

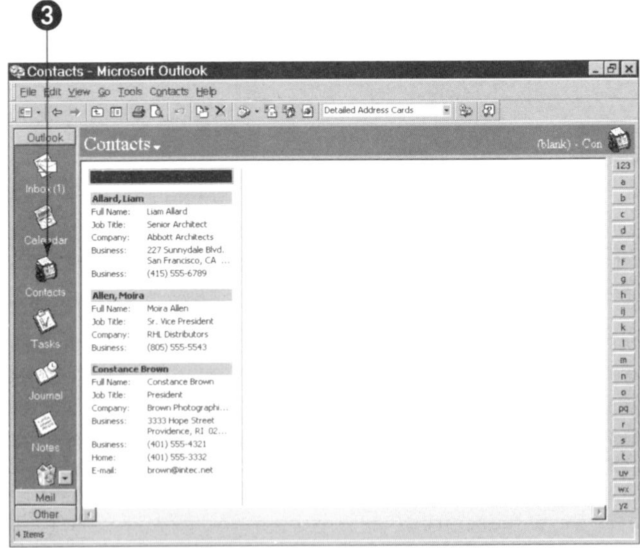

4. Select Contacts ➢ New Contact.

   A new Contact form opens. Here, you enter information about your contacts. By filling out one of these for each contact you have, you can build your own computerized address book over time.

5. Type your contact's name in the Contact Name field.
6. Type the address in the Address field.
7. Click the Close button on the Contact form to close it.

   Now that you've had a chance to see some of the elements of Outlook, you can close the program.

8. Click the Close button.

SKILLS CHALLENGE: USING THE OFFICE PROGRAMS

Now it's time to practice all the skills you've learned in this lesson on your own.

Skills challenge

1. Open Word for Windows.

 *Name four ways to open an Office program.*

2. Maximize the Word window.
3. Open the Start menu, and select Programs ➢ Microsoft Excel.
4. Switch back to the Word Window.

 *Name two ways to switch among open programs.*

5. Reduce both the Word and Excel windows.
6. Make Word the active window.
7. Open the file Ex02-2.
8. Make Excel the active window.
9. Open the file Ex02-1.
10. Move to Sheet2.
11. Click the cell with the text *US* in it.
12. Select Edit ➢ Copy.
13. Make the Word window the active window.
14. Click just below the words *Anderson, IL* in the address block of the letter.
15. Select Edit ➢ Paste.
16. Minimize both the Word and Excel windows.
17. Open the document Ex02-3.
18. Minimize the PowerPoint window.
19. Open Microsoft Outlook.
20. In the Calendar section, click 9:00 in the daily calendar.
21. Type **Learn Microsoft Office**.
22. Close all the programs.

 *Name three ways to close a program.*

TRY OUT THE INTERACTIVE TUTORIALS ON YOUR CD!

Troubleshooting

TROUBLESHOOTING

As you're learning to move among the various Office programs, you may run into some common challenges. I've listed some of them in the following table to help you.

Problem	Solution
I tried to minimize Word; the letter I had open shrunk but Word didn't.	Most Office documents have their own set of Control buttons. Make sure you clicked the Word Minimize button, not the document Minimize button.
I have so many windows open I can't see my desktop; how do I quickly get rid of the clutter?	Click the Windows taskbar with your right mouse button and select Minimize All Windows from the shortcut menu.
I want to keep the windows I have open onscreen, but organize them somehow.	Click the Windows taskbar with your right mouse button and select Tile Horizontally, Tile Vertically, or Cascade to organize the windows.

WRAP UP

You've just begun to explore the different Microsoft Office programs, learning how to move among them with ease. You've learned the following:

- How to open the programs and files within the programs
- How to switch between programs
- Some of the ways that Office programs use a similar interface and features to make learning them easier

In the following lessons, you'll begin to use some of the features you've seen that the programs have in common, such as menus and tools.

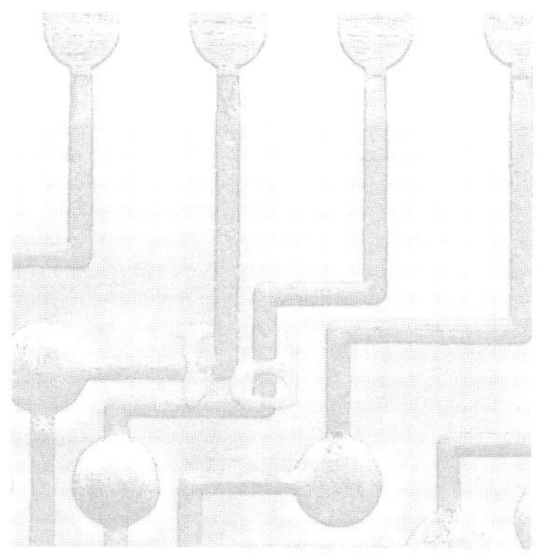

What Do These Programs Have in Common?

GOALS

This lesson explains the following features that all Office programs share:

- Selecting text and objects
- Learning to use tools
- Working with menus
- Moving around your program window
- Cutting, copying, and pasting
- Saving files
- Using Help features

Selecting objects

GET READY

To complete this lesson, you need the files Ex03-1, Ex03-2, and Ex03-3 from the Exercise folder in the One Step folder on your hard drive.

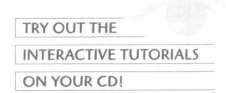

TRY OUT THE
INTERACTIVE TUTORIALS
ON YOUR CD!

SELECTING IN OFFICE PROGRAMS

In order to perform many of the tasks you want to accomplish in Office programs, you first have to learn about selecting things. You can select anything from a single character to an entire multiple page document. You can select objects such as drawings or charts. You can select the cells of an Excel worksheet or a record in an Access database.

Once you've selected something in an Office program, whatever action you perform next (such as deleting or formatting or resizing) will affect the selected item. There are a few different ways to select items, depending on the type of object you're selecting and the program you're using at the moment.

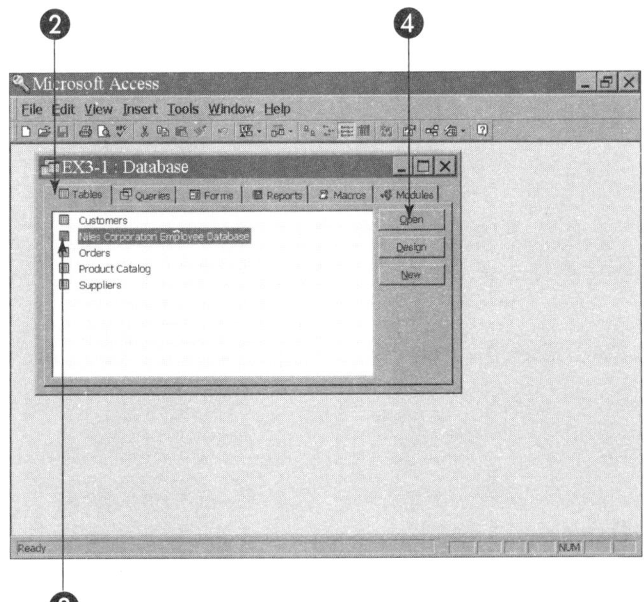

Selecting objects from lists, tables, and worksheets

Try a few of these methods to select items in Access and Excel.

1. Open the file Ex03-1.
2. Click the tab named Tables.

   The illustration to the right shows the Tables panel of an Access database. Notice the two tables listed on this panel.
   You can select any item in a list such as this by clicking it. When you do, the item is highlighted to indicate that the object is selected. The action you take, such as choosing to open or design the table, will affect the selected database.

3. Select the Niles Corporation Employee Database.
4. Click Open.

   An Access table, shown in the illustration on the next page, looks much like an Excel worksheet. It is made up of cells, and each cell can contain data. The cells are organized in rows and columns. You can select single cells, groups of cells, whole rows, or whole columns. You can even select the entire table.

5. Move your cursor between the first and second cells in the top row until it turns into a white cross.
6. Click once to select the cell to the right of the cursor.
7. Move your cursor to the cell containing the text *Arturo* and click to place your cursor between the letters *t* and *u*.
8. Drag your cursor to the right to highlight the letters *uro*.
9. Type **her**.

   Notice that once you have selected text, you can replace it by typing the new text.

10. Move your cursor to the top of the column with the title Last Name until the cursor becomes a downward pointing black arrow (the selection pointer shown in the illustration to the right).
11. Click once to select the entire column.
12. Move your cursor to the gray block on the left of the third row down.
13. Click once to select the entire row.
14. Move your cursor to the cell with the number 4 in it until your cursor becomes a white cross.
15. Click and drag down to select the two cells below this one. Use this method to select a set of cells.
16. Select Edit ➢ Select All Records to select the entire table.

    These methods of click and drag, or using special cursors to select cells, rows, or columns, also work in Excel and in Word tables.

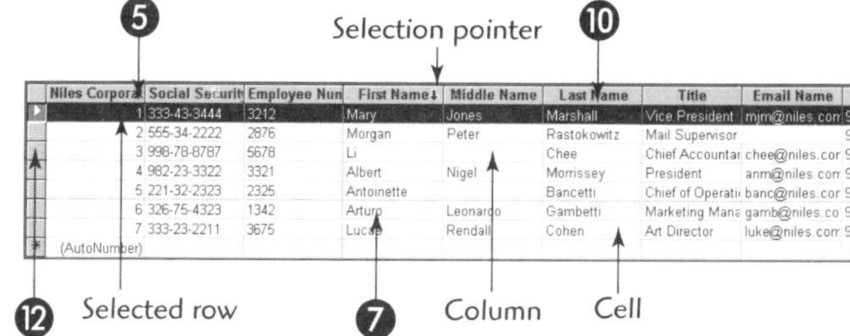

Selecting text and objects

Now take a quick look at selecting text and objects in Word.

1. Select File ➢ Exit.
2. Open the file Ex03-2.

3. Move your cursor to the left of the line *Sun Announces Newest Product Line.*

   Your cursor should change to an arrow pointing upward and to the right, as shown in the illustration. This change occurs when you place your cursor in the selection bar. The selection bar is the area on the left of a Word document that enables you to select an entire line, or set of lines, of text at one time.

4. Click once to select the line of text to the right of the cursor.
5. Click again and drag your cursor down to the end of the first paragraph.
6. Click anywhere within the text to deselect these lines.
7. Press Ctrl and click to the left of any line to select all the text in the document.
8. Place your cursor to the right of the word *Announces* in the heading.
9. Double-click to select the entire word to the left of the cursor.
10. Move your pointer to the left of the first line of the second paragraph until the cursor becomes an arrow pointing upward and to the right.
11. Double-click to select the entire paragraph.

    You can use the selection bar and methods such as Ctrl and double-clicking to select a single word, line of text, paragraph of text, or all the text in a document. You can also move your cursor to any point in the text and simply drag to select it.

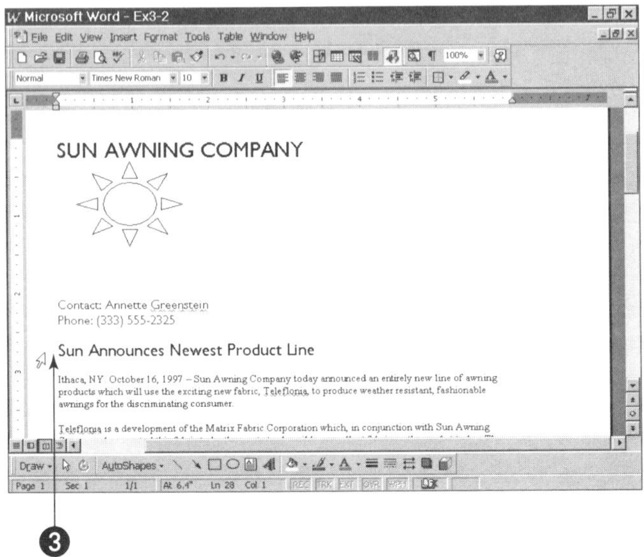

Note that when you select a cell in Excel, the formula bar across the top of the worksheet is where you select and edit the text contained in the cell.

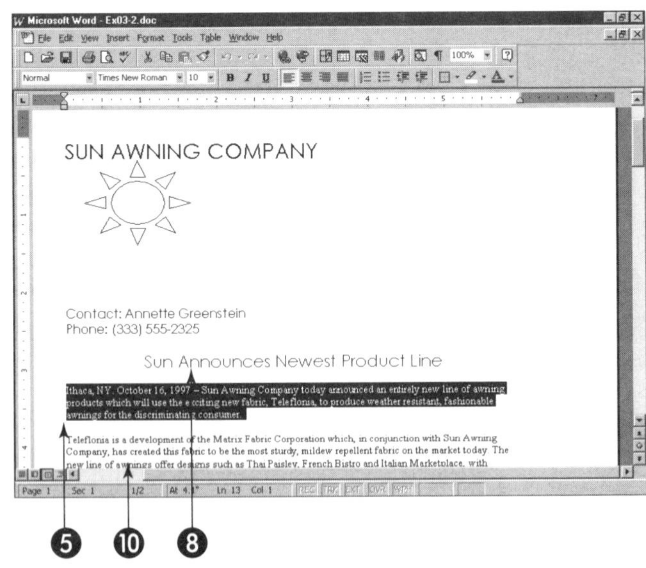

Now try selecting a drawing object.

12. Press the Page Up key on your keyboard to move to the top of the document.

⓭ Click in the middle of the sun object.

When you select a drawing object by clicking it, eight square boxes called handles appear to define the parameters of the object. You can now resize the objects by dragging these handles, or move it using a four-way pointing arrow cursor that appears when you move your cursor over the object. This is true of drawings, clip art, tables, multimedia objects, and charts that you use in any Office program.

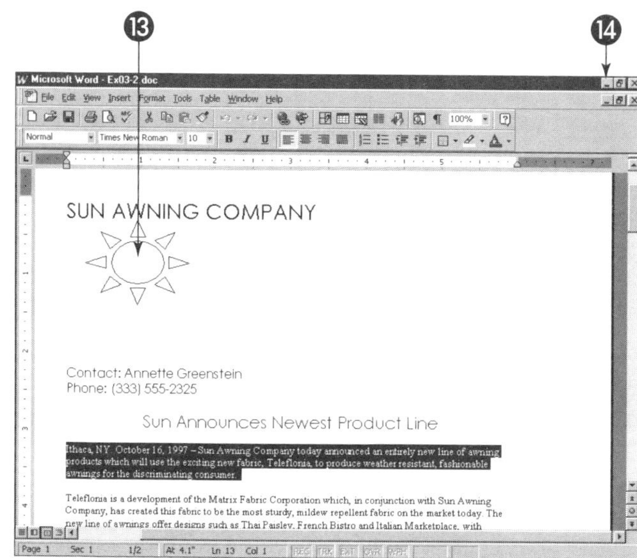

You learn more about this in Lesson 17, which discusses manipulating objects in PowerPoint presentations.

⓮ Click the Minimize button to minimize the Word window.

USING TOOLS AND MENUS

Tools and menus are common to every Office program, and in fact, to most Windows software. You use tools and menus to request functions such as saving a file or formatting selected text in boldface. Actually, just about every tool function is also accessible through a menu command, but the tool is a bit of a shortcut. Rather than open a menu and select a command, which can involve two or three selections, a tool only requires you to click it once to achieve the same results.

These tool shortcuts are typically available for the most commonly used functions in a program. Because of this, the toolbars that appear when you open Office programs won't include every command you can find through menus.

You can customize Office toolbars to include the tools you want, rather than just the ones that appear by default. This is done by selecting View ➢ Toolbars and choosing the Customize option in the dialog box that appears. It would be better, however, to leave such customization until you've reached the end of this book so that the directions and illustrations match your own screen.

Learning to use tools

It's time to get some practice using both tools and menu commands to perform common tasks in Excel.

Learning to use tools

Tools are those cute little icons you see across the top and sometimes the bottom of the screen. One has a picture of scissors, one a little book, another a little brush, and so on. Tools functions are invoked by clicking a tool button on a toolbar. Doing so results in a variety of actions. The figure to the right shows the different tools.

Get acquainted with the tools by following these steps:

1. Open the file Ex03-3, shown in the illustration.
2. Click cell A1 (the cell that contains the word *Population*).
3. Click the Bold tool.
4. Click cell B1 and drag your mouse to cell G1 to select all the dates in the top row.
5. Click the Italic tool.
6. Click the Center tool.

Your Excel worksheet should now look like the one shown in the illustration to the right. Now see how making the same types of changes works using menu commands.

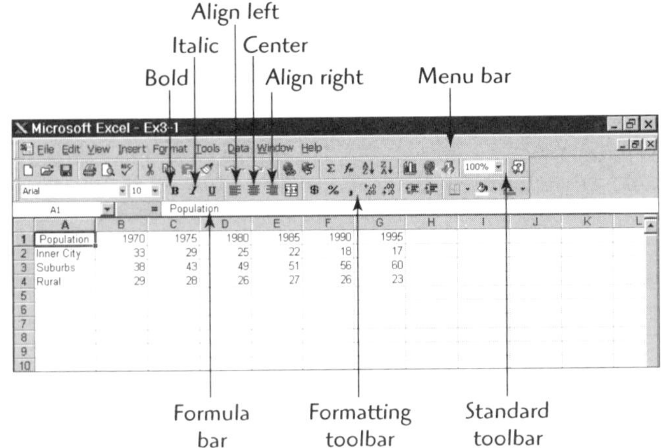

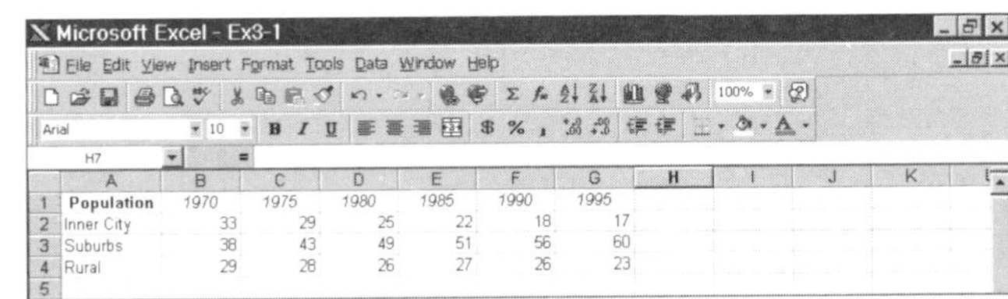

Using menus

Menus are another way to do many of the things you do with tools. Menu functions are invoked by opening a menu and selecting a command from it.

Follow these steps to center text using menu options:

1. Select all the cells with data values in them (B2 through G4).
2. Select Format ➢ Cells.
3. Select the Alignment tab.
4. Open the drop-down list titled *Horizontal.*

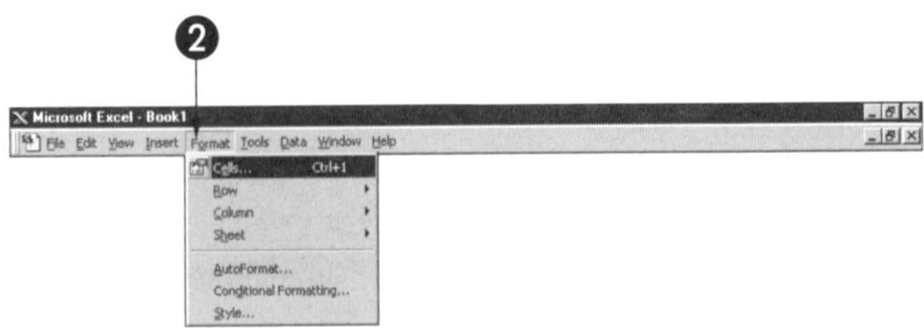

5. Click Center to select Center alignment.
6. Click OK.

   Notice it took you five steps to perform alignment action on the selected text in the preceding steps, and it took only one step when you used the Center alignment tool. However, if you wanted to change several elements for these cells, such as alignment, number format, and font, making all the changes at once from the Format Cells dialog box might be easier. Dialog boxes reached through menu commands can offer you more control than tools. For example, a tool used to enlarge text may do so only by a preset increment, whereas in a dialog box you can type in the precise measurement for the text size that you want. Also, the Format Cells dialog box offers vertical as well as horizontal alignment controls that can be set separately.

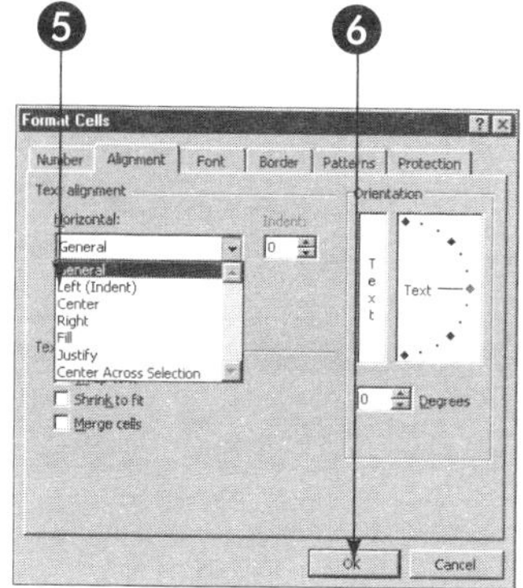

7. Open the View menu.
8. Select Header and Footer.
9. In the *Header* drop-down list, select Page 1.

   There is no tool for adding a header on any of the default toolbars, so you have to perform this task using menus.

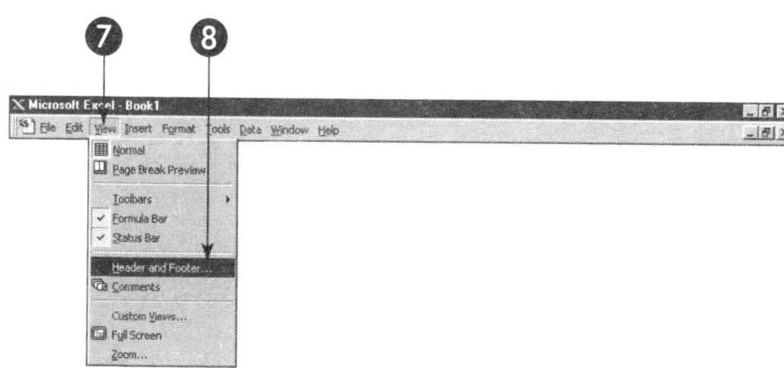

10. Open the File menu.
11. Select Save (or click the Save tool).

    Whether you perform this task using the menu command or Save tool, the Save dialog box appears. You take a closer look at the process of saving files later in this lesson.

12. Click Cancel to close the Save dialog box.
13. Click the Minimize button to minimize the Excel window.

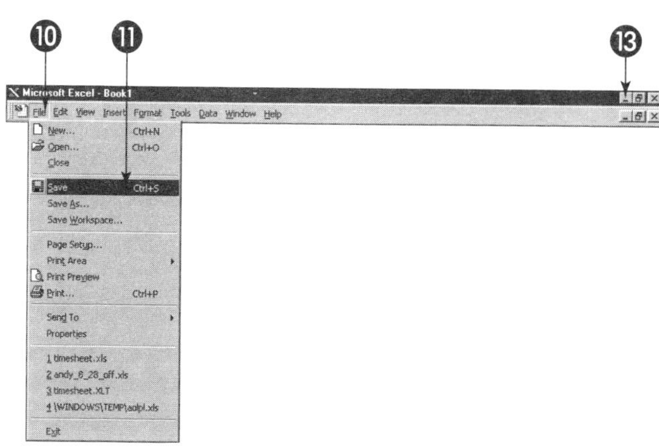

WORKING IN DOCUMENTS

The tasks of moving around your document window, deleting or copying objects, and saving files are all performed in pretty much the same way in all the Office programs. You get some practice now with these procedures. As you work through these exercises, you also get more practice in using both tools and menu commands.

Moving around your program

Moving around your program window

Within each of the Office programs there are tools to navigate around the program screen itself, as well as its individual pages, slides, sheets, or records. Many of these navigation tools work in exactly the same way from program to program.

1. From the Windows taskbar, restore Word for Windows; the file Ex03-2 should still be open.
2. Press Page Down on your keyboard to move down the page; this feature typically moves you about a third of a page at a time.
3. Press Page Up to return to the top.
4. Press the down arrow key on your keyboard to move down line by line until you reach the end of the page.
5. Press the Ctrl + Home keys to return to the beginning of the document.
6. Press Ctrl + End keys to move back to the end of the document.

Using Page Up, Page Down, Home, End, and the up and down keys on your keyboard, you can quickly move by one line, a portion of a page, or to the beginning or end of your document. However, the scroll bars provide an alternative method of moving quickly through a document using your mouse.

Scroll bars come in two varieties: horizontal and vertical. A horizontal scroll bar runs along the bottom of a document and is used to move from side to side. A vertical scroll bar runs along the right side of a document and is used to move up and down from the first to last page of a document. In the case of a PowerPoint presentation, the vertical scroll bar moves you from one slide to the next when you're in Slide View.

Both types of scroll bar are made up of a few basic elements, as shown in the illustration to the right. Use the vertical scroll bar to move around this document.

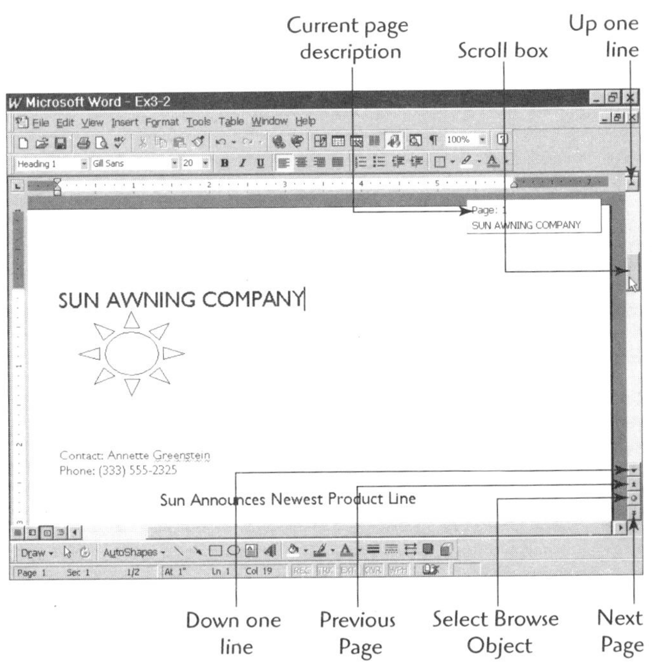

The Select Browse Object button is unique to Word for Windows; however, the other programs in Office have Find and Go To commands in their Edit menus to perform many of the same functions.

7. Click the bar above the scroll box to move up one screen.

8. Click the Previous Page button to move to the beginning of the previous page.

9. Click the Select Browse Object button.

   A pop-up list of choices appears, as shown in the illustration to the right. As you place your cursor on each one of these squares, its function is described in the bottom of the pop-up box. You can use these choices to find and go to a particular item in your Word documents.

10. Click the choice in the lower left-hand corner called Go To.

11. In the Find and Replace dialog box that appears, type **2** to go to Page 2.

12. Click Go To.

   The Find and Go To features, whether reached through the Select Browse Object button in Word or the Edit menu in the other Office products, can be invaluable for getting around, especially in longer documents. The Select Browse Object feature in Word can also be used for other things, such as locating a specific table or picture in a document or locating a specific heading.

   There is another quick way to go to a specific page using the scroll box in the scroll bar.

13. Click the scroll box and drag it up.

   As you drag the scroll box, a callout with the page number and first line of the page appears. Using this, you can quickly drag down a multiple page document and release the scroll box at exactly the page you want.

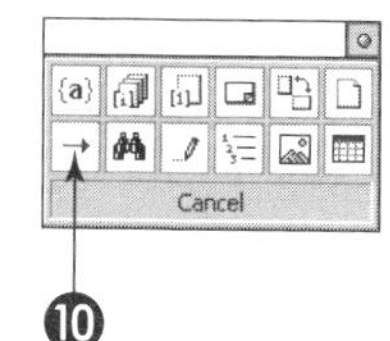

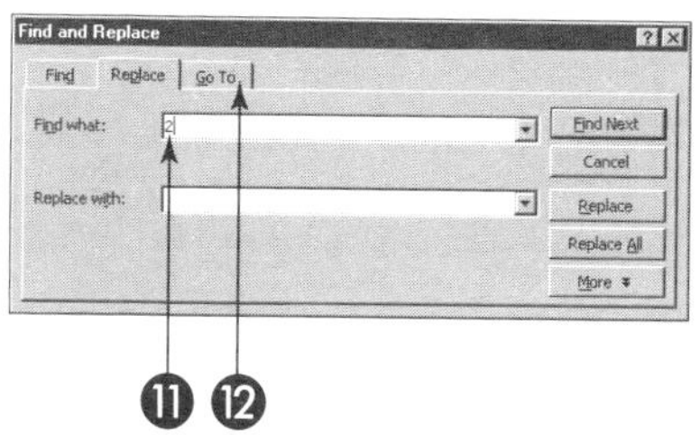

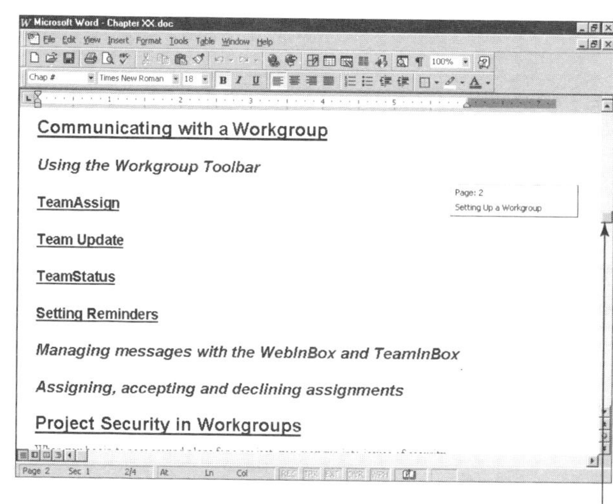

Cutting, copying, and pasting

Using the selecting skills you learned in this lesson, you can begin to take advantage of the Cut, Copy, and Paste functions that are found in all Office programs. Cut removes an item from a document, while Copy duplicates it and leaves the original in place. These features make use of something called the Windows Clipboard. This is a temporary holding place where any object or text that you have cut or copied is placed, ready to be pasted to another location in the same document or even to another file. You can cut and paste just about anything from one Office program document to any other Office program document. One important warning: The Clipboard only holds one thing at a time — if you place something else there, it overwrites the first item.

1. Select the first line of the document, *Sun Awning Company.*
2. Open the Edit menu.
3. Select Copy.
4. Press the Next page button on the vertical scroll bar.
5. Open the Edit menu.
6. Select paste to place the copy of the text at the beginning of page two.
7. Select *Florida Splash.*
8. Choose the Cut tool.
9. Place your cursor at the beginning of *French Bistro.*
10. Choose the Paste tool to place the original text in a new location.

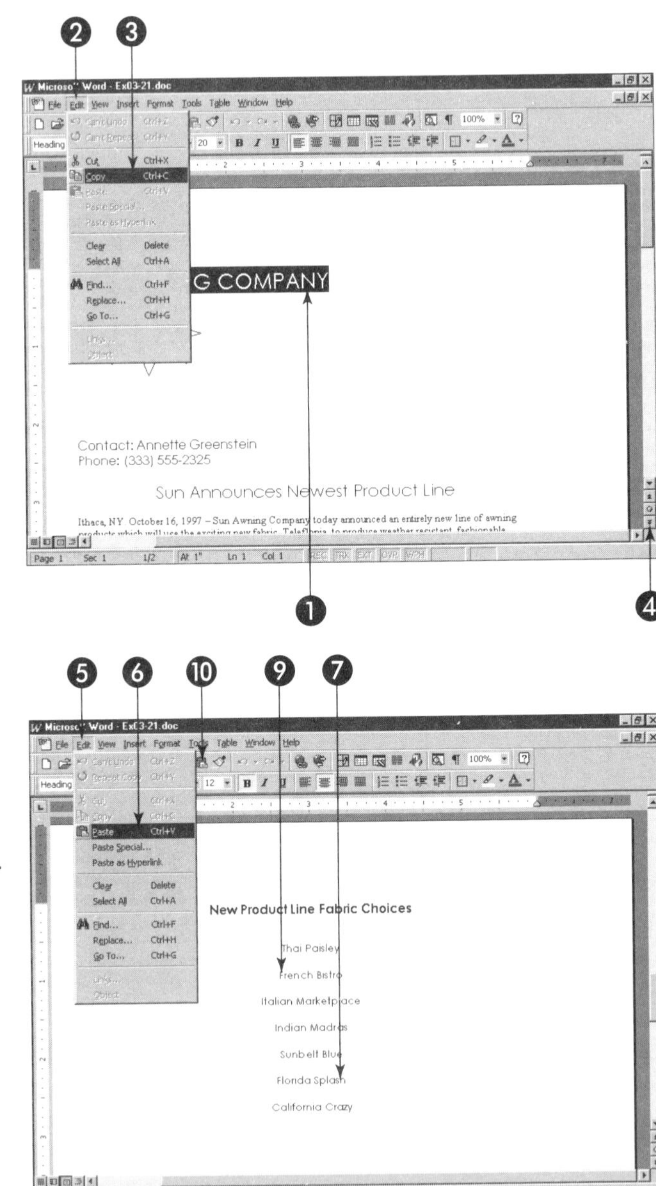

SAVING A DOCUMENT

Now it's time to save the changes you made. Saving a file for the first time is slightly different than saving a file all subsequent times.

Saving files

A very important piece of advice in the world of computing is: Save your files! Use these steps to do so often with your Office documents.

1. Open the File Menu.

2. Select Save to see the Save As dialog box shown in the illustration to the right.
3. In the *File name* box type **Sun**.
4. Open the *Save in* list by clicking the arrow next to it.
5. Double-click on the (C:) drive.
6. Double-click the MyDocs folder (or the My Documents folder) to open it.

You should have created the MyDocs folder in the Jump Start section at the beginning of this book. If you don't have the folder anymore, or you didn't create it then save the file in the My documents folder.

7. Click Save to save the Sun file to the folder.

If you have saved a file once, selecting Save or clicking the Save tool will simply save the document and not open the Save dialog box. If you want to save a document with a different name, select File ➢ Save As and the same dialog box will open to enable you to enter a new name. The original file will still be available, as well as this version of the file with another name.

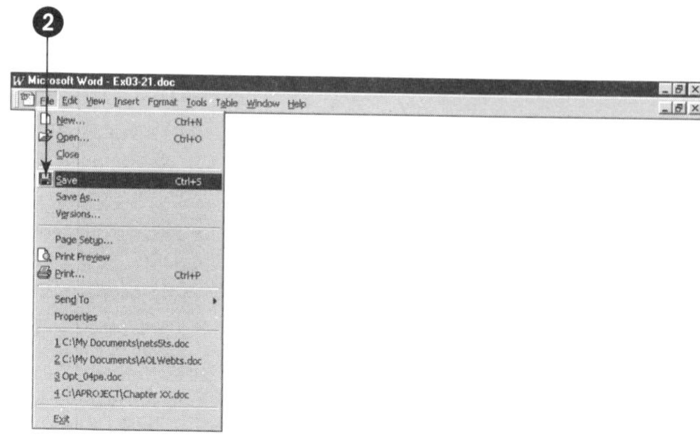

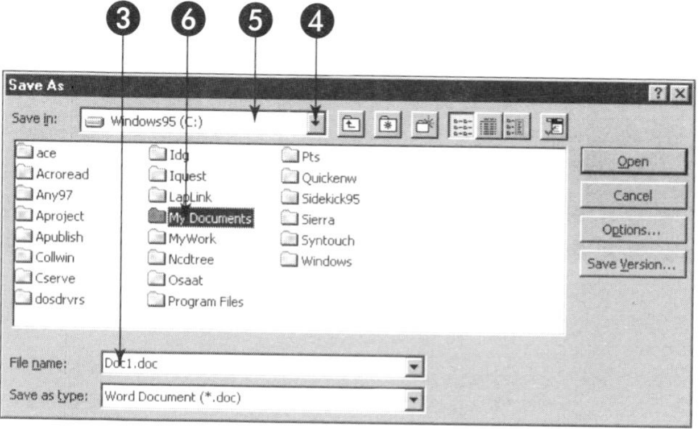

GETTING HELP

There are several ways to get help while using Microsoft Office, and each way functions the same way in each program. This makes the help features easy to learn and use. The following list briefly describes the help features:

- *Office Assistant* is a handy feature that enables you to type in a question and select from several possible types of help. Office Assistant sometimes offers to show you how a procedure is performed.
- *Help Contents and Index* is a database of information about topics which you can search by typing in a term or choosing from broader categories of information.

Using help features

- *What's This?* is a feature that turns your mouse pointer into a help tool. When you've selected What's This?, you can click any one screen element and a brief description of its function appears.
- *Microsoft on the Web* offers several ways to get online help from Microsoft's Web page.

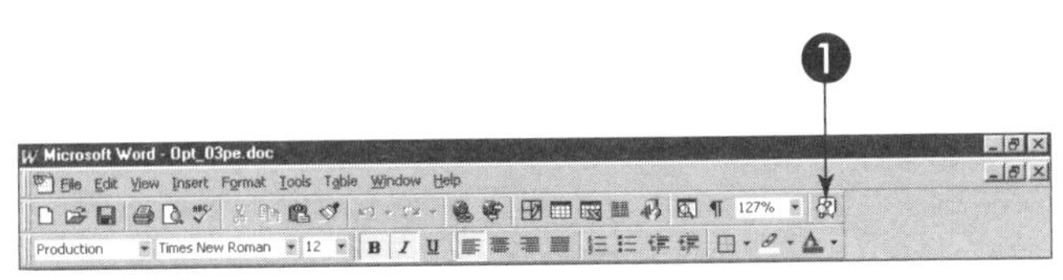

Using help features

Look at how the first three features work with the same problem. Say you want to know how to copy a block of text. Start by seeing what the Office Assistant, a new feature in Office 97, has to offer.

1. Choose the Office Assistant tool. (It's the one with a question mark on it at the far right of the top toolbar.)

   The illustration to the right shows the Office Assistant, an animated paper clip, with its menu of choices displayed. The choices relate to saving a document, the last action you took in the program. Office Assistant figures that your problem is related to the last thing you tried to do. However, if you want help with a different task, you can type a question and the Assistant will respond with new options.

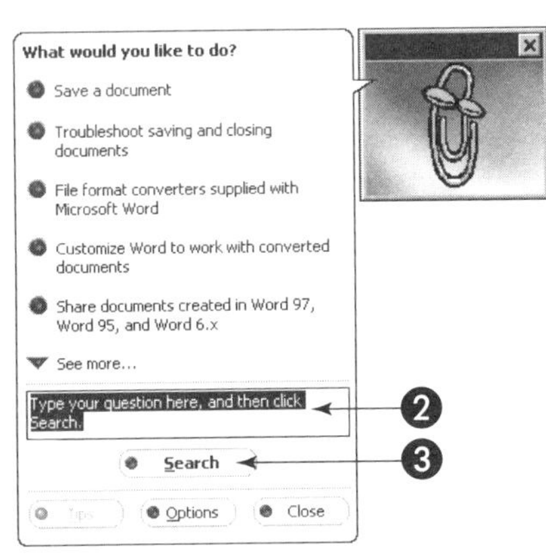

2. Type **How do I copy text?**
3. Click the Search button.

   The Office Assistant "thinks" about that for a moment, and then displays several possible relevant areas of information.

4. Click the blue button next to the choice Move or Copy Text and Graphics. Information on that topic appears, as shown in the illustration.
5. Close the help information box by clicking the close button in its upper right-hand corner.

   This offers some basic information and additional buttons to help you narrow down the specific type of information you'd

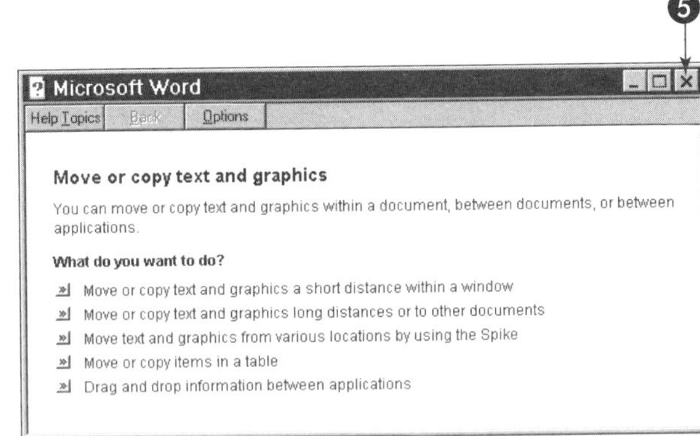

like on the topic. Look at how the other help features address this same question.

1. Open the Help menu.
2. Select *What's This*. The pointer changes to an arrow and question mark together.
3. Click the Copy tool to see a description of how the tool works.
4. Click anywhere on the document to remove the description.
5. Open the Help menu again.
6. Select Contents and Index.
7. Select the Index tab.
8. Type the word **copy** in the first field to quickly move to that topic in the index list.

You can also use the scroll bar in this dialog box to scroll down the list of index topics until you find the one you need.

12. Scan the list of topics concerning copying (use the scroll bar if you need to) and select the one that reads copying text and graphics.
13. Click Display.

    A list of topics, such as the one in the illustration to the right, appears. If you select the second option, you get exactly the same information that the Office Assistant provided, but you get there with a key term rather than typing a question. Often the information you get to is identical, but you might be more comfortable with one method over another. Try the method that seems most logical to you based on what you know about the feature you're looking for help on; whether you know its exact name, what it does, or where it's located, for example.

14. Close the help box.
15. Select File ➢ Exit and choose not to save changes if prompted.

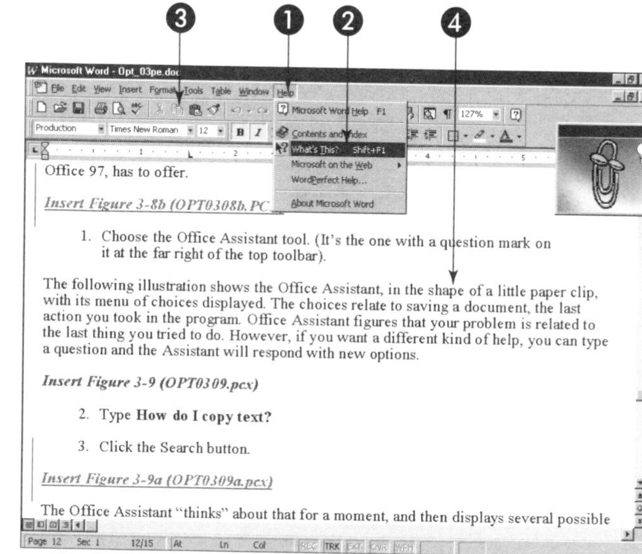

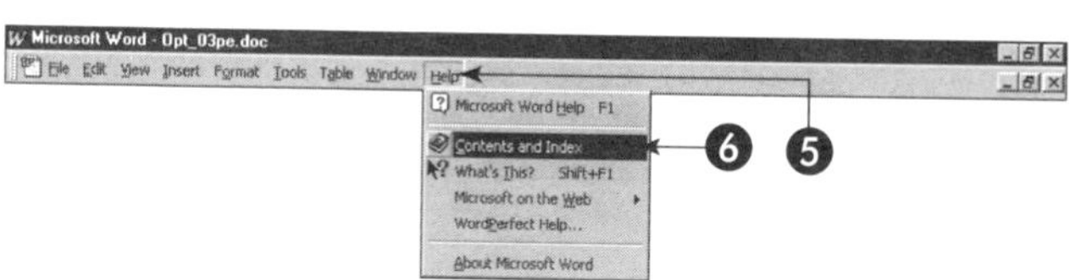

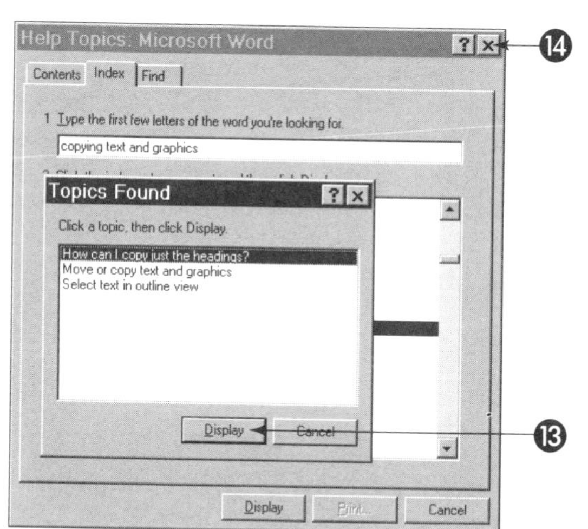

Skills challenge

SKILLS CHALLENGE: EXPLORING WHAT OFFICE PROGRAMS HAVE IN COMMON

Practice makes perfect! Work through this exercise to get that little extra bit of practice with Office.

TRY OUT THE INTERACTIVE TUTORIALS ON YOUR CD!

1. Restore the Excel window with the file Ex03-3 opened.

If, for some reason, you closed Excel and didn't save the changes already made to the file in this lesson, you can open the file Ex03-4 in the Exercise folder in the One Step folder on your hard drive.

2. Select the entire contents of Sheet1.
3. Using a tool, change the text size to 12 point.

How would you perform the same procedure using a menu command?

4. Copy the selected text.
5. Move down the worksheet until Row 30 is visible onscreen.

There are six different ways to move down in a document. Can you name them all?

6. Paste the text you copied into Row 30.
7. Ask the Office Assistant, **How do I delete a worksheet from Excel?**

What keyword or words could you use to search the Contents and Index feature of Help to get the same information?

8. Close all Help windows.
9. Select Row 33.
10. Delete the entire row using a menu command.
11. Use the What's This? help feature to get a description of the function of the Cut tool in Excel.

12. Move to the right in your document until Column Y is displayed onscreen. (Hint: Use the horizontal scroll bar.)
13. Using the home key, display cell A1 on your screen.
14. Replace the word *Population* in Cell A1 with the words **Census Data**.
15. Select the word **Data** in the formula bar.
16. Delete the selected text.

Name three ways to delete something.

17. Save this file with the name **Census**.
18. Close all Office programs.

TROUBLESHOOTING

Because the functions described in this lesson work similarly in all Office programs, learning them now will give you a head start. This table offers some solutions to problems you might encounter with these features.

Problem	Solution
I just cut a block of text from my report and now want it back.	Use the Undo feature in the Edit menu or the Undo tool, or simply paste the cut text back where it was.
The Office Assistant keeps appearing asking if it can help and I find it annoying.	Select Options on the Assistant screen, and deselect *Display alerts* from the Office Assistant dialog box.
I want a copy of the same document with the same name, but in a different folder.	You can select File ➢ Save As and keep the same filename, but change the directory in the Save As dialog box.
There is no scroll bar in Access when I display a form; how do I get to the next form?	Access provides its own navigation arrows on forms to move from one record to another; look for a set of right- and left-facing arrows on the bottom of the form itself.

Wrap up

WRAP UP

In this lesson, you picked up a lot of muscle in the area of functions common to all Office programs. You exercised the following skills:

- Selecting text and objects and using both tools and menu commands to perform procedures on selected elements
- Moving around your document windows using both your keyboard and mouse
- Cutting, copying, and pasting text using the Windows clipboard
- Saving files and closing Office programs

In Lesson 4, you begin to explore the world of Word for Windows in more detail, making further use of all of the skills you learned here.

PART II

Word for Windows

This part introduces you to the world of Word for Windows, Office 97's word processor. It includes the following lessons:

- Lesson 4: Creating and Saving Documents
- Lesson 5: Getting Your Document in Shape
- Lesson 6: Punching Up Your Documents
- Lesson 7: Putting Information in Its Place with Tables and Charts
- Lesson 8: Printing Your Word Document
- Lesson 9: Merging Your Mail

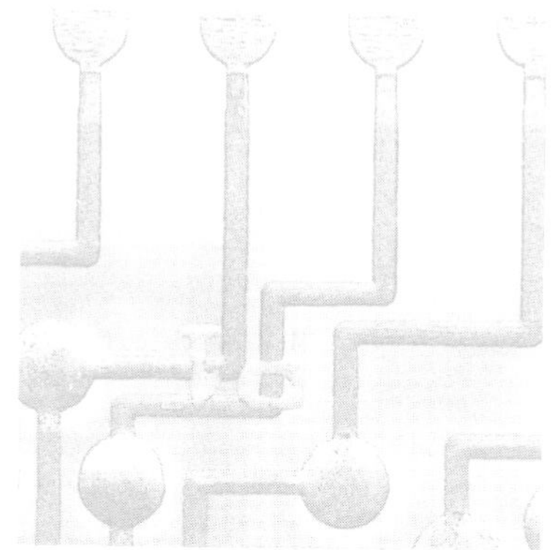

Creating and Saving Documents

GOALS

In this first lesson on Word for Windows, you master fundamental skills such as the following:

- Understanding templates
- Running the Letter Wizard
- Entering text
- Saving a Word document
- Closing a Word document
- Navigating around your document
- Changing Word views

Get ready

GET READY

To complete the exercises in this lesson, you need to have installed Word for Windows as part of the Office suite of software.

You also need the file Ex04-1 from the Exercise folder in the One Step folder on your hard drive.

When you're done with these exercises, you will have created a document that looks like the letter on the facing page (although the name of the letter author, company, and return address will be your own).

TRY OUT THE INTERACTIVE TUTORIALS ON YOUR CD!

CREATING YOUR FIRST DOCUMENT

A document created in Word for Windows can run the gamut from a simple letter to a multiple page newsletter with pictures and fancy text effects. That novel you're going to write someday is a document. A recipe for your Aunt Tilly is a document. A report on the average rainfall in the Arizona desert is a document.

So, what do all documents have in common? Typically, documents use text. That text has a certain design, called a font. That font can have effects applied to it, such as bold or italic. The text has size, which is measured in something called points. Text is aligned somehow on a page: that is, the text has a point of origin, which is typically on either the left side, right side, or center of a page.

Every document in Word is based on something called a *template*. Templates are like the foundation of a house: They provide the basic outline and structure for the house; you fill in the contents and details. A template contains, at a minimum, a designated font and the alignment and size for text that you enter. In addition, templates can contain different text fonts and sizes for different levels of text, placeholders that indicate what text you should enter to complete a document, and graphic elements such as a border or lines. However, the template is only a beginning; you can change anything you like about the template settings and add to your document after you open a new document.

Templates in Word are categorized and named by their function. There are report, memo, letter, and fax templates. There are résumé and Web page templates. There is a blank document template, which is the most basic and flexible template — it contains only font, font size, and alignment settings.

Stevenson Leisure Products
5566 Pendleton Road
Marblehead, IN 44456

September 6, 1999

RE: Pool Clean Order

CONFIDENTIAL

Mr. Al Smith
Enchanted Pool Products
2222 Maple Drive
Fairfield, MI 05555

Attention: Ordering Department

Dear Al,

Subject, Order No. 334-J

This will confirm our phone conversation today, when I placed an order for 32 gallons of Pool Clean. As agreed, the discount price for this product is $37.95 per gallon.

I will expect delivery no later than October 22.

Sincerely yours,

Nancy Stevenson
President

cc: Mary Jo Minton
Chloro Chemicals

Understanding templates

In addition to templates, Word for Windows has something called *wizards*. A wizard is more than a design framework for your document; a wizard actually walks you through the creation of a document step by step, giving you the chance to answer questions and make choices about how you intend to use the document. The wizard then creates the skeleton of a document based on your input.

In the exercises that follow, you'll use both templates and wizards to create your first Word documents.

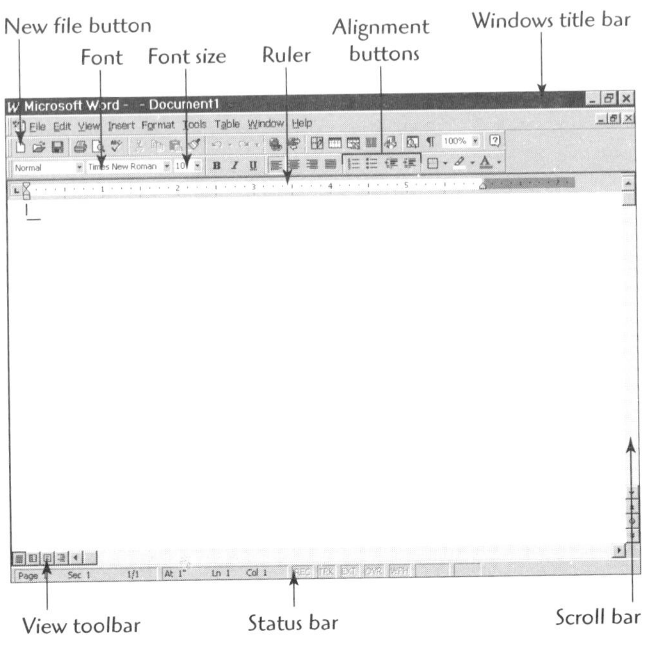

Understanding templates

The best way to understand how a template impacts your document is to see one in action.

1. Click the Start button on the Windows taskbar.
2. Choose Microsoft Word from the Programs selection.

   After a brief introductory screen, Word's main screen appears, as shown in the illustration to the right.

   When you first enter Word, a new document is already open for you. This document is temporarily named Document 1, until you save it with a new name. This document is based on the blank document template. Take a moment to look at the Word screen. It contains many of the common elements that have been described in the first few lessons of this book, such as toolbars and menus. Notice the items that have been predetermined by the blank document template: On the second toolbar from the top, there are settings for font (Times New Roman), font size (10 points), and text alignment (align left).

   If you wanted to, you could begin to type in this document at this point. On the other hand, if you want to choose a different template on which to base your document, you would need to open a new document. Do that now.

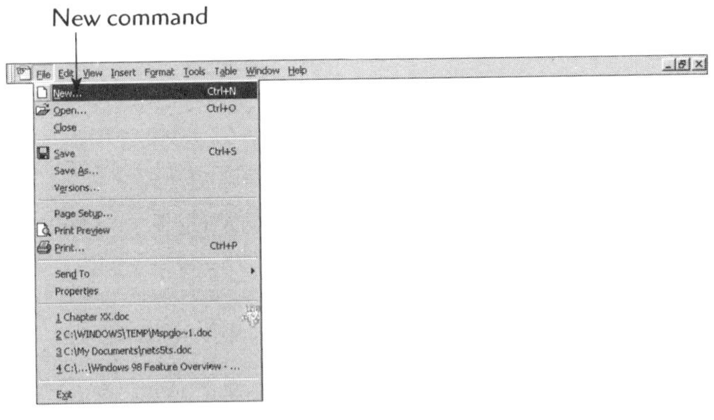

There are two ways to open a new file; you can select the New command from the File menu, which gives you the option of opening a document based on a template, or you can use the New file button on the

far left of the top toolbar, shown at the top of the preceding page, to open a blank document based on the Normal template.

At this point you will see the New dialog box, shown in the illustration to the right. This dialog box first appears with the General tab selected. The General panel contains the Blank Document template.

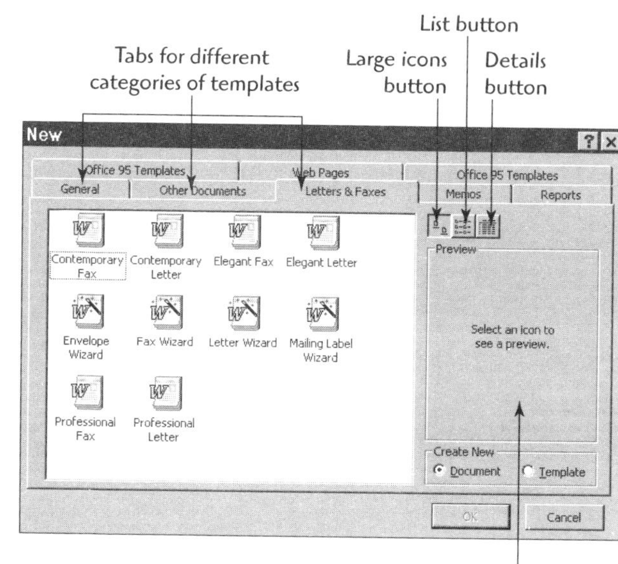

3. Select the Letters & Faxes tab (shown in the illustration) to see more templates.
4. Select the Elegant Letter template.

   A preview of this template appears on the right side of the dialog box. Notice that both templates and wizards are available to you.
5. Select the Letter Wizard to see a preview of how this document would appear if you used the Wizard to create it.

   You can move around the tabs of this dialog box and preview different templates and wizards to get an idea of what's available to you. There are three buttons above the Preview box that enable you to change how you view the available template files: Large icons, Lists, and Details. The first is the default and enables you to view files as large icons.
6. Click the second button and you see a list of files by name.
7. Click the third button and you get the details about each file, such as the type of file and the date it was last modified.

Notice that at the bottom right-hand corner of the New dialog box is a section labeled Create New. In this section are two option buttons called Document and Template. This feature enables you to create a new file as a template. Then, if you make changes to it — for example, add a company logo to a fax cover sheet template — and save it, it will be available as a brand new template. By default, this is set to create a document, rather than a template, and in most cases you would just leave that setting alone when you create a new document.

VISUAL BONUS: THE WORD TOOLBARS

This visual bonus gives you the rundown on Word's Standard and Formatting toolbars.

The Standard Toolbar

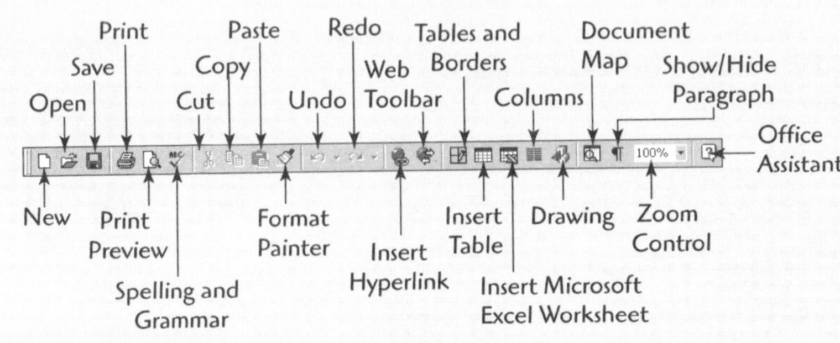

The Formatting Toolbar

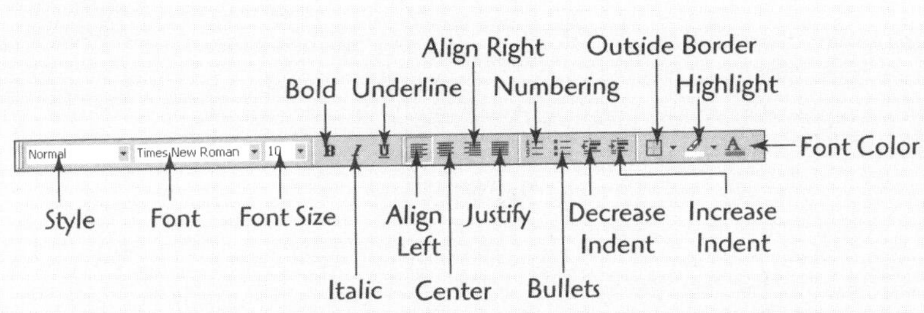

Running the Letter Wizard

The Letter Wizard, like all the wizards in Office, is designed to save you time and enable you to take advantage of professional document design expertise.

1. If the New dialog box is no longer open, click to open the File menu and then select New.
2. Select the Letters and Faxes tab of the New dialog box.
3. Select the Letter Wizard.

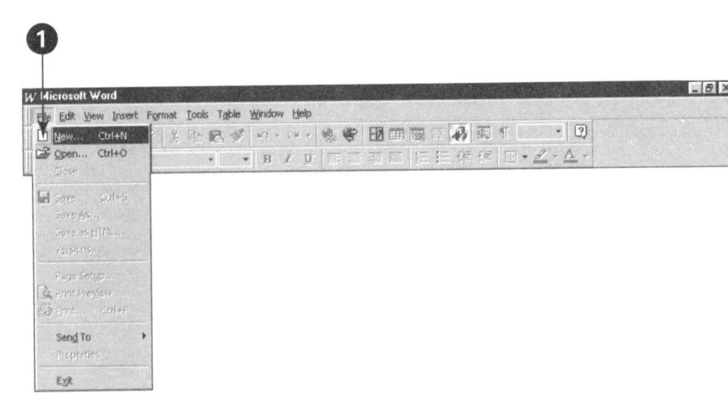

Running the Letter Wizard

4 Choose OK to begin to run the Letter Wizard (or simply double-click the filename Letter Wizard to run it).

The Office Assistant appears. The Office Assistant is a help feature that looks like a little box with a character resembling a paper clip in it. It's part of the Help system for all the Office products that you were introduced to in Lesson 1. The Assistant starts you off on the Wizard by asking you to choose whether you are going to generate a single letter or a larger mailing.

5 Select the *Send one letter* option.

The first Letter Wizard screen appears. The Assistant displays a brief explanation of the choices offered in this dialog box.

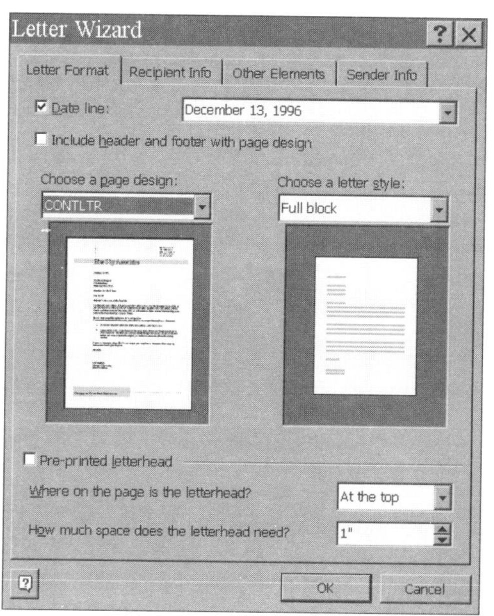

A Wizard displays its various steps as sequential tabs in a dialog box. These tabs are in the suggested order for moving through the choices offered by the Wizard. However, if as you proceed with the Wizard you decide you'd like to go back to change an earlier setting, you can just click that tab to return to that step.

You can make the following settings for your document in the first tab of the Letter Wizard:

- *Select the* Date line *check box to display a date in your letter. When you do, a drop-down list becomes available with various formats for dates. The default format is the standard for business letters.*
- *Select the second check box to include a header or footer on your page. For this exercise, leave this check box unmarked.*
- *Choose a page design. Clicking the arrow in this drop-down box reveals a list of four page styles: Contemporary, Elegant, Normal, and Professional. When you select a style, a preview of it appears beneath the drop-down list.*
- *Choose a letter style. This drop-down list offers variations of what elements in your letter are indented on the page. For example, the Modified Block style has an indented signature line.*

Running the Letter Wizard

If you want to print this letter on stationary or letterhead, check the Pre-printed letterhead *check box. When you do, the last two options become available, enabling you to make adjustments to the position of the letter in relation to the elements on the letterhead. For this exercise, leave this check box unchecked.*

6. Select the Date Line option and leave the default date style.
7. Select the Contltr (Contemporary Letter) style.
8. Select the Full Block style.
9. Select the OK button.

   This moves you to the next tab in the Wizard sequence, Recipient Info. Here you can enter information about the person to whom your letter will be addressed. This tab is shown in the accompanying illustration:

   You can do the following on this tab:

   - You can use information you have previously stored in your Office Address Book to automatically fill in the name and address information of your letter. (You can learn more about using Address Book in Lesson 9.)
   - You can simply type in a recipient's name.
   - Fill in a delivery address, pressing Enter at the end of each separate line of the address.
   - Finally, you can choose a style of salutation. This is the form of the recipient's name that will be used in the greeting. Informal will use the first name of the person as you entered it in the *Recipient's name* box; Formal or Business will use the name with its title (such as Mr. Smith or Dr. Jones) followed by a colon or comma, respectively; Other provides different options such as Dear Mom and Dad or To Whom It May Concern.

10. Type **Al Smith**.
11. Type **Enchanted Pool Products** [Enter] **2222 Maple Drive** [Enter] **Fairfield, MI 05555**.

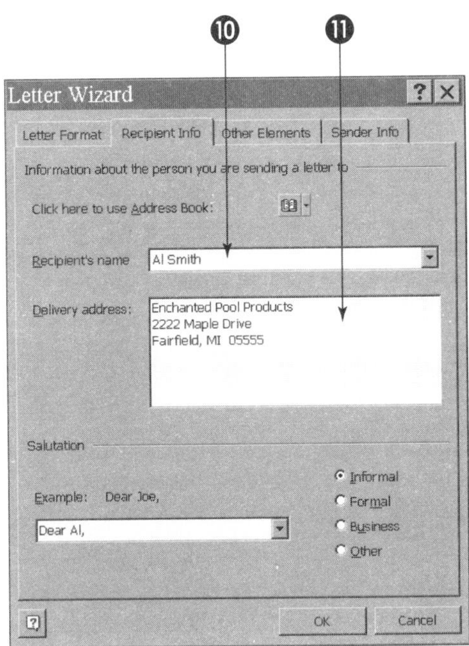

⑫ Select Informal.

⑬ Choose the OK button to proceed to the next Wizard tab.

This is the Other Elements tab of the Letter Wizard.

Here you can choose to include a reference line to refer to an earlier correspondence, for example. You can put mailing instructions such as Personal or Confidential on your letter. If you want to direct your letter to a particular person's attention, add a subject line, or note that a copy of your letter is going to someone else, you make those settings here.

⑭ Select the *Reference line* check box and choose RE: from the corresponding drop-down list.

⑮ Place your cursor after RE: and type **Pool Clean Order**.

⑯ Select *Mailing instructions*.

⑰ Use the corresponding drop-down list to choose CONFIDENTIAL.

⑱ Select the *Attention* check box.

⑲ Place your cursor after the word *Attention* and type **Ordering Department.**

⑳ Select the *Subject* check box.

㉑ Place your cursor after the word *Subject* and type **Order No. 334-J**.

㉒ In the *Cc:* text box, type **Mary Jo Minton** [Enter] **Chloro Chemicals**.

㉓ Choose the OK button to proceed.

The final tab of the Letter Wizard, Sender Info, appears as shown in the illustration.

This tab is used to input your name and return address information if desired, as well as the closing of the letter.

㉔ Type your name in the *Sender's name* box.

㉕ Type your company name and address in the *Return address* box.

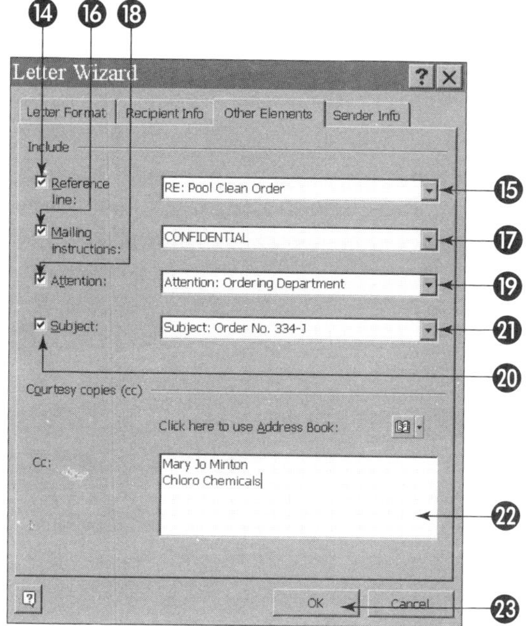

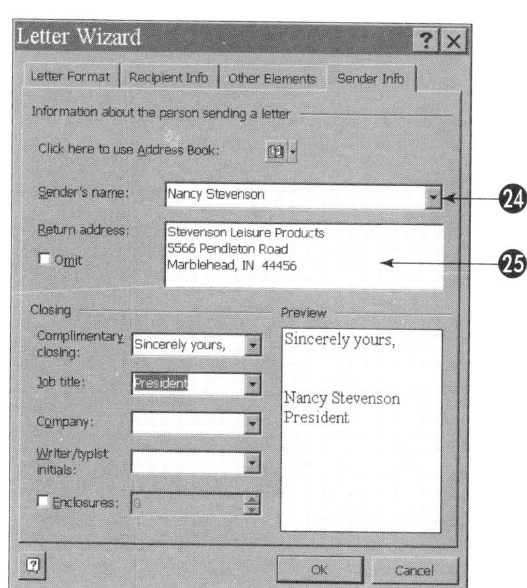

Entering text

26. Open the *Complimentary closing* drop-down list and select Sincerely yours.

27. Type your job title in the *Job title* box.

    You can indicate a number of items you want to enclose with your letter by selecting the *Enclosures* check box and using the corresponding arrow keys to select a number of enclosures. Notice that as you have typed information into this dialog box, a preview of the closing of your letter appears.

28. Select OK to complete the Letter Wizard.

When you end the Letter Wizard, the Office Assistant appears on your screen, offering you some different options such as making an envelope or rerunning the Wizard. You learn about creating envelopes with Word in a later lesson. For now, if you wish to send the Office Assistant away, just click the close button in the upper right-hand corner of the Assistant window.

Entering text

When you finish the Letter Wizard there is a placeholder for the actual letter text, which you can see highlighted in the illustration to the right. To enter text, follow these steps:

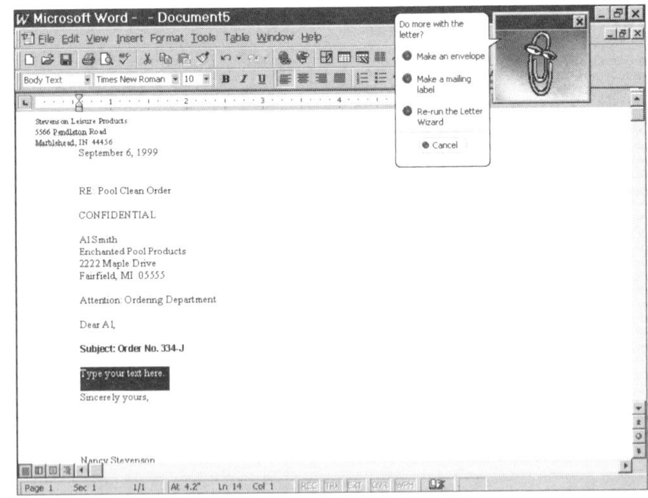

1. Type: **This will confirm our phone conversation today, when I placed an order for 32 gallons of Pool Clean. As agreed, the discount price for this product is $37.95 per gallon.**

   Notice that you don't have to press Enter at the end of a line. Word has a feature called text wrapping, which automatically breaks a line at the most appropriate place and sends your cursor to the beginning of the next line. The only time you need to press Enter is when you want to begin a new paragraph.

2. Press Enter.

❸ Type: **I will expect delivery no later than October 22.**

You now have a complete letter with proper return address, date, sender's address, closing, and complimentary copy notation. To see how the actual letter will appear, use the Print Preview feature.

❹ Click the File menu to open it.

❺ Select Print Preview.

A view of the entire letter appears, as shown to the right. Notice that the return address appears in the upper right-hand corner. This is a result of the full block letter style you selected while running the Letter Wizard.

Notice that, according to the Print Preview, the letter is a bit high on the page. There is too much blank space at the bottom of the page. You can fix that by adding some blank lines higher up in the letter. You can place two of these after the return address and three after the date.

❻ Choose the Close button on the Print Preview toolbar to return to your document.

❼ Move your mouse cursor just before the month in the date line.

❽ Press Enter two times.

❾ Move your mouse cursor to the beginning of the reference line (before the letters *RE*).

❿ Press Enter three times.

⓫ Take a look at what that did to make your letter look more balanced on the printed page by once again looking at Print Preview. Select File ➢ Print Preview.

Notice the letter is much more pleasing to the eye.

⓬ Choose the Close button on the Print Preview toolbar.

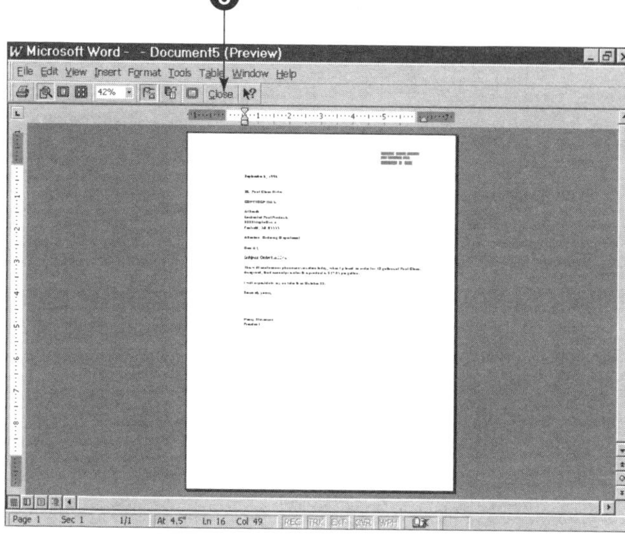

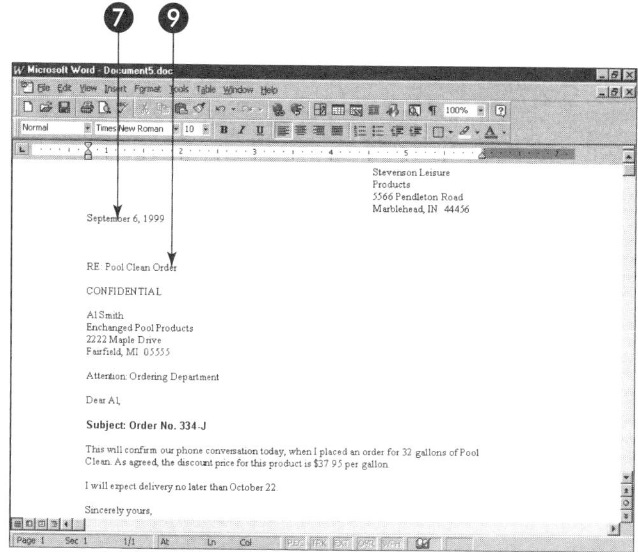

Saving a Word document

SAVING AND CLOSING YOUR WORD DOCUMENT

When you have created a document and added a little text to it, it's a good idea to save the file. That way you don't run the risk of losing your work in the event of a computer crash or power outage, which happens more often than you'd think. After you save the file initially, it's also a good idea to save it periodically as you work on it so you don't lose any changes you may make.

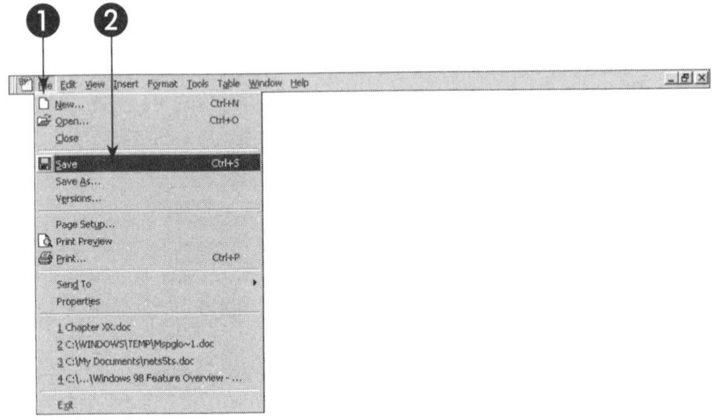

Saving a Word document

Until you save a file, it has a temporary designation of *Document #* (where # represents the number of new, unsaved documents you have created since you opened Word).

1. Click the File menu to open it.

2. Select Save.

   The Save As dialog box appears, as shown in the accompanying illustration. The suggested filename is the name of the Wizard file you ran to create this document, Letter Wizard.

   You can use the drop-down list in the *Save in* box and the three buttons to the right of it to browse around your hard drive, floppy drives, or any network drives your computer may be connected to. You can create a new folder in Word for your work and save this file there.

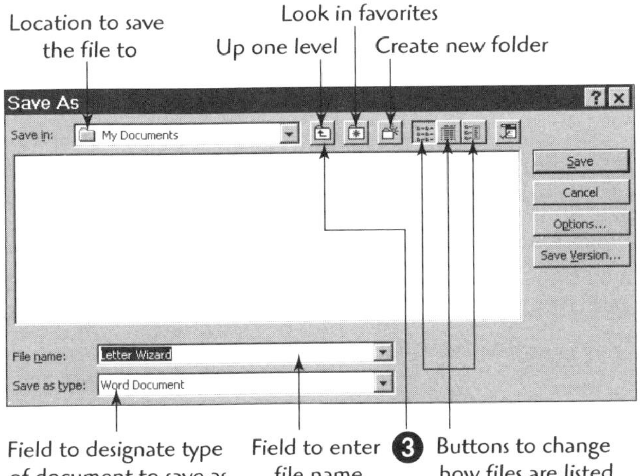

3. Click the *Up one level* button.

   You now see all the programs loaded on your computer's hard drive. Word for Windows is within the folder called Microsoft Office, which is in the folder called Program Files.

4. Double-click the folder named Program Files and then the one called Microsoft Office.

   The folders within the Microsoft Office folder are displayed.

5. Double-click Winword, which is the folder containing Word for Windows files, so the Winword folder appears in the *Save in* field.

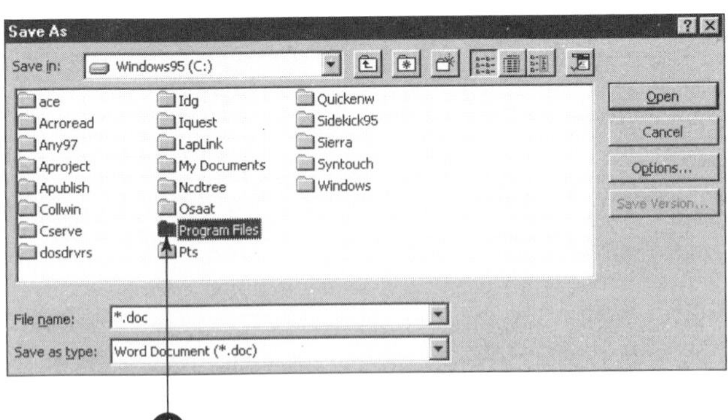

6. Click the Create New Folder button.

   The dialog box in the following illustration appears, enabling you to designate a name for the new folder.

7. Type the folder name **My Work**.

8. Click OK to return to the Save As dialog box.

   Your new folder name is now listed along with the other folders in the Winword folder.

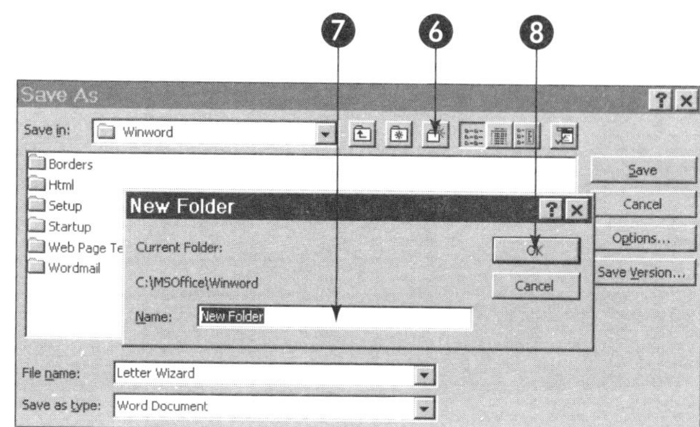

9. Double-click the My Work folder to open it.

10. Place your cursor in the *File name* box.

11. Click and drag your mouse to highlight the name of the Letter Wizard.

12. Release the mouse button and type **Pool Clean**.

    The new name replaces the suggested filename. The default type of file is Word Document, which is typically the file type you want. If, however, you are saving the file for someone who uses a different word processor, such as WordPerfect, or as a new Word template that you could base future documents on, you can use the drop-down list in the *Save as type* box to change the file type.

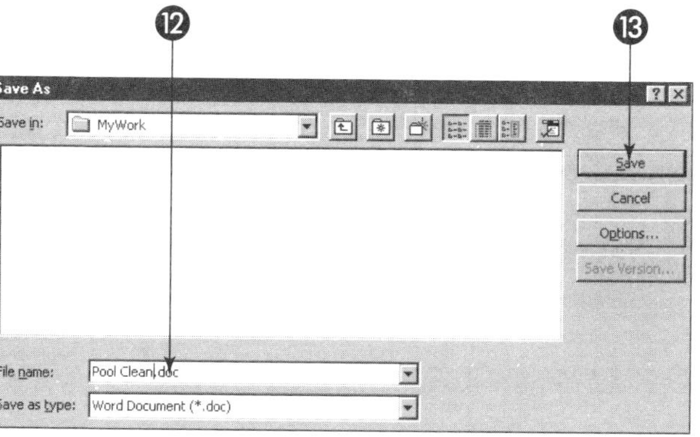

13. Choose the Save button to save the file in the location and with the name you've designated.

    The title bar of the file now lists the name Pool Clean. In the future, you have two options for saving this document.

    - You can simply save again to save changes with the same filename. To do this, you can either choose the Save button on the toolbar or Select File ➢ Save.
    - You can save the file with a different name. This actually creates a second file. The first file exists as the last saved version, and the new file is where your current changes will be saved. This can be useful to create a copy of a document or save various drafts of a document for future reference or comparison. To save a file with a new name, select File ➢ Save As. The same Save As dialog box appears, and you can use the same settings to save the file with a new filename.

Closing a Word document

Closing a Word document

If you've just saved a file and you're ready to close it, do the following:

1. Click the File.
2. Select Close.

   The document closes, but Word remains open.

   If you haven't saved the file since you last modified it, things work a little differently. First, open the document again and make a few changes.

3. Select File.
4. Select Pool Clean from the list of recently opened files at the bottom of the File menu.
5. Place your cursor before the text *Al Smith* in the sender address.
6. Type **Mr.** and one space.
7. Select File.
8. Select Close.

   The message in the illustration to the right appears, asking whether you want to save changes to the file.

9. Click Yes to save changes.

   If you decide not to save the changes, select No. The file would then close and no changes made since the last time you saved the file would be kept. If you selected Cancel, your attempt to close the file would be aborted, and you'd be returned to the document window.

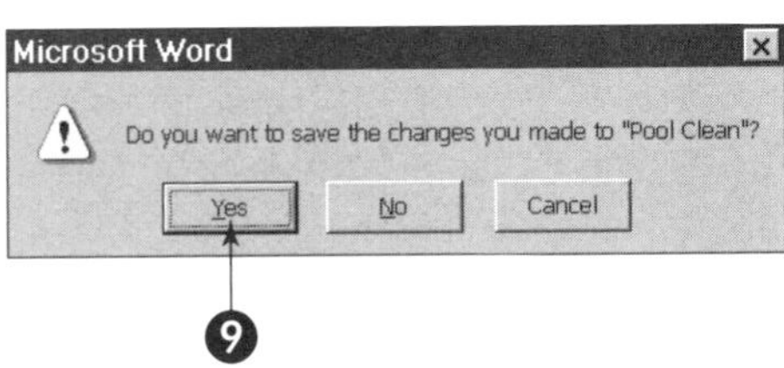

MOVING AROUND WORD

Once you have entered text in a Word document, perhaps even several pages of text, you may need to move around the document to revise or add text. In the following exercises, you practice moving around a Word document. In Lesson 5 you begin to use the editing tools that Word provides to make changes to your text and format text elements on your page.

Navigating around your document

For this exercise, open the file Ex04-1 in the Exercise folder you copied from the CD-ROM. This is a marketing plan for a film company, based on the Contemporary Report template. It consists of a title page, and two pages with text and a table. You use this report to practice moving around a document.

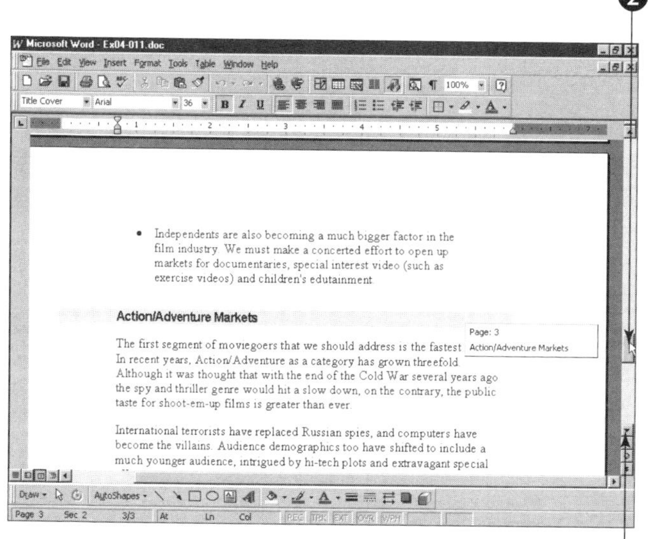

1. Click the down-pointing arrow at the base of the scroll bar to move down line by line until you reach the second page.
2. Click the scroll box and drag it down until you reach Page 3.

   Dragging the scroll box moves you more quickly through a document. As you move the scroll box, a small box appears containing the number of the page that is displayed if you release the mouse button. This feature makes it easy to know where you have moved in the document.

If you only want to move a page at a time, click above the scroll box to move up one page and click below the scroll box to move down a page.

For much larger documents, however, it might be easier to go directly to a specific location. The Go To feature of Word enables you to go directly to a particular spot in your document.

3. Select Edit.
4. Choose Go To.

   The Find and Replace dialog box shown in the accompanying illustration appears. This dialog box contains tabs for Find, Replace, and Go To. On the Go To tab you can choose to go to various elements in your document, such as a table, object, or line. The default choice is page number, which you will probably use most often, to take you to a specific page in the document.

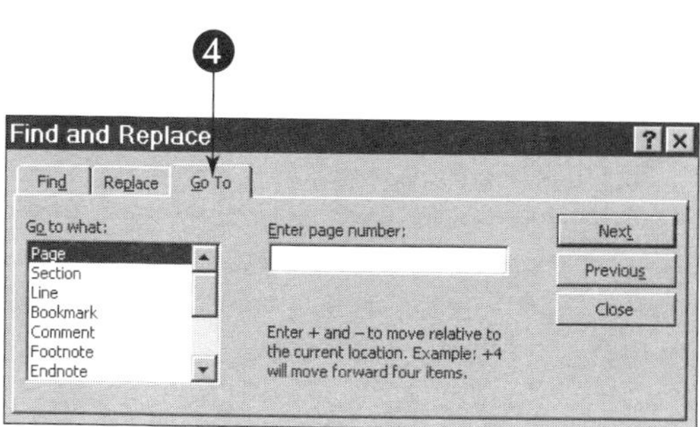

5. Type the number **1** in the *Enter page number* box.
6. Choose the Next button.

   Page 1 appears on your screen. To make it easy to continue searching, the Find and Replace dialog box remains onscreen. If you want to find another page to review, you can simply type a new page number.
7. Choose the Close button to remove the Find and Replace dialog box from your screen.

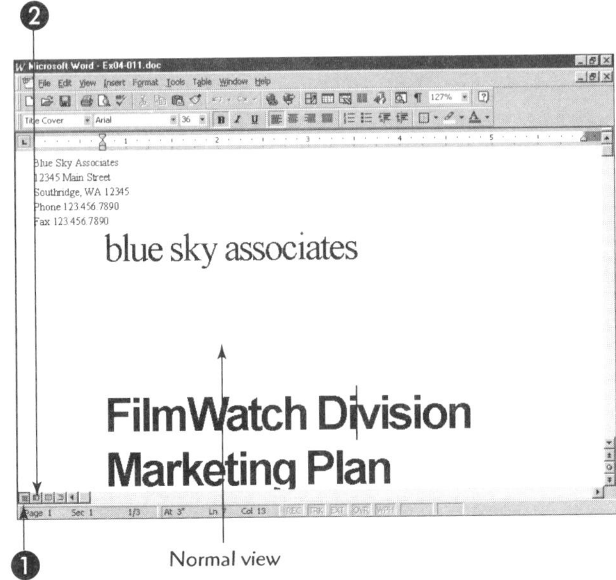

Changing Word views

Word for Windows provides different views of your document to help you work on it. You can change views using the view buttons near the bottom left-hand corner of the screen.

1. Choose the Normal view button.

   The Normal view appears for the title page in the Ex04-1 file. The Normal view fills your document window with the white space of the document, providing the cleanest view for entering the contents of your document. There is no real attempt to indicate the actual page edges in this view; breaks between pages are indicated with a faint dotted line.
2. Choose the Online Layout view button.

   Online Layout view takes advantage of the fact that you can publish a Word document in HTML format, which is the format used for documents published on the World Wide Web (WWW). This view approximates how someone viewing your document on a Web site would see it. There is a section on the left that provides an outline of topics in your document that you can open and close to show greater or lesser detail, and the document itself on the right. Only one page can show in the document window at a time. When you're in Online Layout view, the view buttons don't appear at the bottom of the screen. To move to another view, you must use menu commands.
3. Click the View menu to open it.

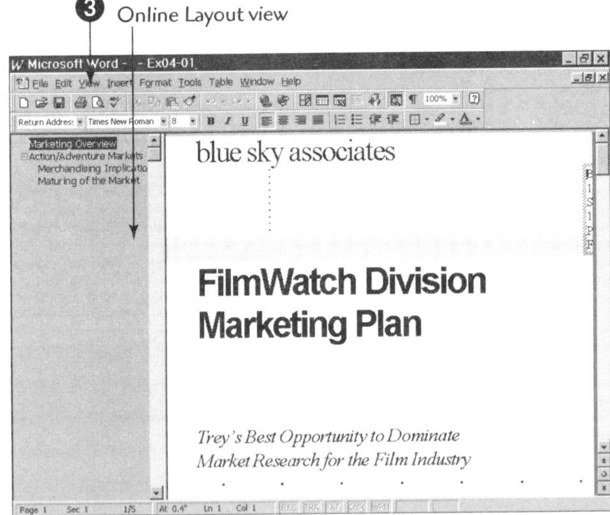

4 Select Page Layout.

Page Layout view appears. This view is similar to Normal view, except that the top, right, and bottom edges of a printed page are represented by gray space around the white area of your document, as seen in the accompanying illustration. Notice that there is a gray space between pages. This view is useful when you want to see how your document flows from one page to the next, or work with the layout of elements on your page relative to the page dimensions, such as charts, tables, pictures, and text.

5 Choose the Outline view button.

Outline view displays the contents of your document in a traditional outline format, with text indented beneath headings in a hierarchy structure. In this view, you can display just headings, or any level of detail beneath the headings that you wish. The accompanying figure shows a document in Outline view. Notice that when you are in this view there is an additional toolbar that enables you to open and close headings to reveal more or less detail, and to promote or demote headings to change their position in the outline hierarchy.

6 Move your mouse pointer to the plus symbol to the left of the heading Marketing Overview. The pointer changes to a four-way arrow.

7 Click the arrow symbol to select this heading and all of its subheadings.

8 Choose the Collapse button from the Outline toolbar.

All the subheadings disappear. They have temporarily been collapsed or hidden from view. The wavy line under the heading indicates there are collapsed headings underneath it.

9 Choose the Expand button.

The subheadings appear again.

10 Click the small box symbol to the left of the heading that reads Changes in the Industry.

11 Choose the Promote button.

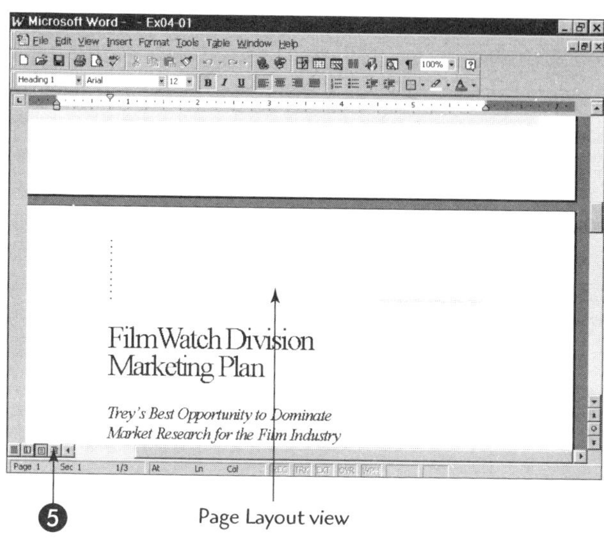

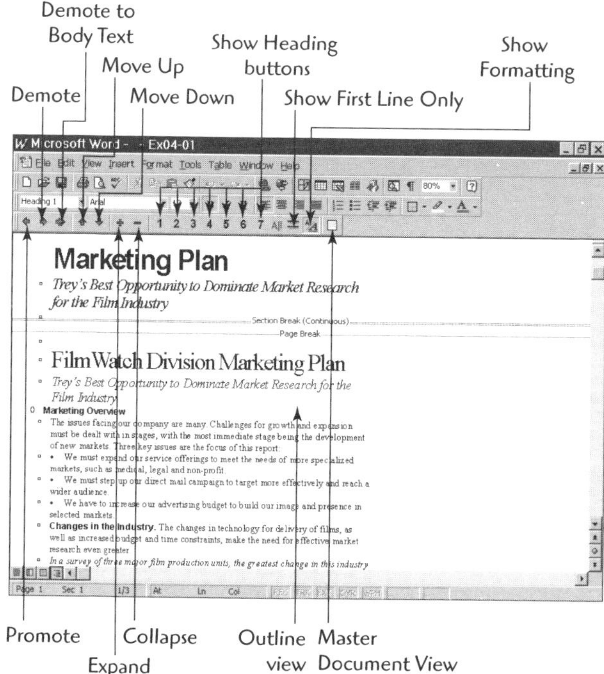

The heading has moved up to a higher level heading, and the plus symbol to its left indicates that the headings that follow are now subordinate to this heading in the outline structure. The Outline view is a great place to look at the structure of the contents of your document, to see if you have organized your thoughts and topics logically.

12. Select File ➢ Close and choose No when asked if you'd like to save your document.

TRY OUT THE INTERACTIVE TUTORIALS ON YOUR CD!

SKILLS CHALLENGE: CREATING A WORD DOCUMENT

In this exercise, you open a document based on a Word template, enter text in that document, save it, preview it, and move around the document. This exercise brings together all the skills you learned in this lesson.

1. Open Word for Windows.
2. Select File ➢ New.
3. Select the Office 97 Templates tab of the New dialog box.
4. Open the Elegant Report template.

Do you remember how to see templates listed by file details rather than large icons in the New dialog box?

5. Click the first line of the document and type **Blue Sky**.

Can you identify in which view this document appeared?

6. Using the scroll box, move to the second page of the document.
7. Change to the Outline view.
8. Collapse all the headings under the heading How to Customize This Report.
9. Demote the heading More Template Tips.
10. Move to Normal view.
11. Save the file in the WinWord folder, within a new folder you create now called **Reports;** name the file **Blue Sky**.
12. Move to the first page of the document.
13. Place an extra line before the words *Blue Sky* at the beginning of the document.

How can you see how your printed document will look without actually printing it?

14. Select File ➢ Close.
15. Make the right selection from the resulting dialog box to close the document and save changes to it.
16. Open the Blue Sky file you just closed.
17. Save the file to the My Work folder with a different name: **Proposal**.

If you wanted to save this as a WordPerfect file, what change would you make in the Save As dialog box?

18. Close the file and exit Word for Windows.

Troubleshooting

TROUBLESHOOTING

You learned a lot of the basics of creating, moving around in, and saving a document in Word for Windows. The following table might answer some questions that have come up during this lesson.

Problem	Solution
While running a wizard, I need to go back and make a change.	Select the tab in the Wizard dialog box where the entry is to return and change it.
I want to save this document as a template.	Select File ➢ Save As and select Document Template in the *Save as type* drop-down list.
I'm in Online Layout view and the view buttons are gone.	To move to a different view, select the View menu and choose a view from the list of commands.
In a 56-page report, I want to get to Page 43.	Select Edit ➢ Go To and type **43** in the *Enter page number* box.
My cursor jumps down two spaces at the end of a line.	Remember not to press ENTER at the end of lines unless it's a new paragraph; Word wraps text for you automatically.

Although you may run into some of these challenges as you learn Word, most are not fatal, and finding solutions to them is all part of the learning process.

WRAP UP

Before you hit the showers, go over the following things you learned in this lesson:

- You learned how to create a new Word document using a template or a wazard.
- You began to get familiar with the elements of the Word screen, such as toolbars, menus, and view buttons.
- You entered some text and saved the document you created.
- You practiced moving among Word's various views, and learned to use some of the features of the Outline toolbar.

For more practice, open a document based on the Professional Resume template and enter the text for your own résumé.

In Lesson 5, you begin to see how Word features enable you to easily set up your page, and format and edit text in your document.

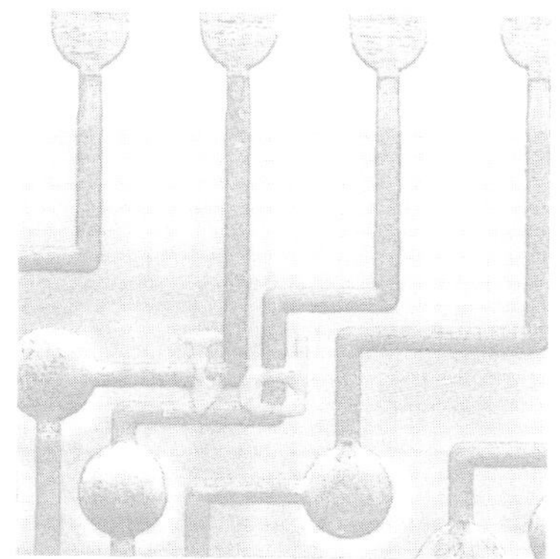

Getting Your Document in Shape

GOALS

This lesson introduces ways you can use Word features to format and edit the contents of your documents, including the following:

- Setting margins and tabs
- Using indents
- Modifying paragraph spacing
- Selecting, cutting, copying, pasting, and deleting text
- Using the Undo/Redo command
- Moving text with drag and drop
- Realigning text
- Changing fonts and font size
- Applying effects to text
- Assigning styles
- Copying formats

Setting margins

GET READY

To work through this lesson, you need the files Ex05-1 and Ex05-2 you copied to your hard drive from the accompanying CD-ROM.

When you complete the Skills Challenge at the end of the lesson, you will have produced a document that looks like the illustration to the right.

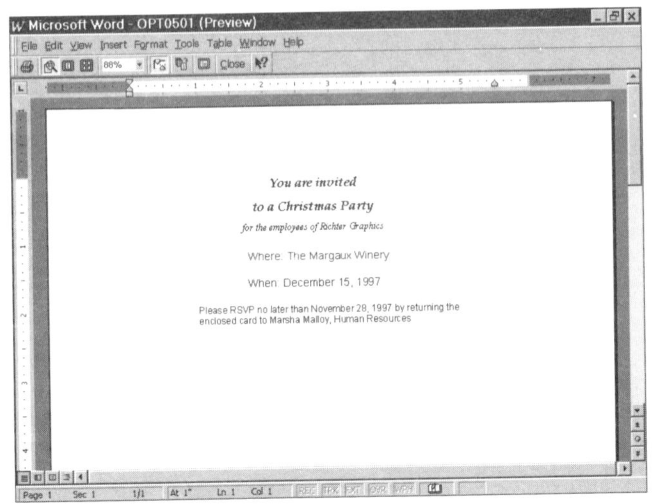

SETTING UP YOUR PAGE

When you use a word processing program such as Word for Windows, the goal is to create a document that looks good on a printed page. Although that page doesn't exist until you print it, you still need to plan the printed page and arrange the page area as you work on your computer screen. The Word features that work with the arrangement of text on your page include the following:

- *Margins*, which comprise the blank border on the outer edges of your page where text won't print
- *Tabs*, which are stopping points that can bet set, enabling you to place text at various points across your page
- *Indents*, which enable you to set the position of whole lines or blocks of text relative to the left margin of your document

Setting margins

Because margins determine the overall parameters for where text appears on an entire page, it is a good idea to set your margins first.

1. Open the Ex05-1 file.
2. If you are not in Page Layout view, click the Page Layout view button.

   You'll see the document shown in the accompanying illustration. This is a memo regarding the construction of a new home.

   The margins are indicated by the dark gray areas of the rulers. Changing the margin settings is easy. You can practice this by changing the left margin.

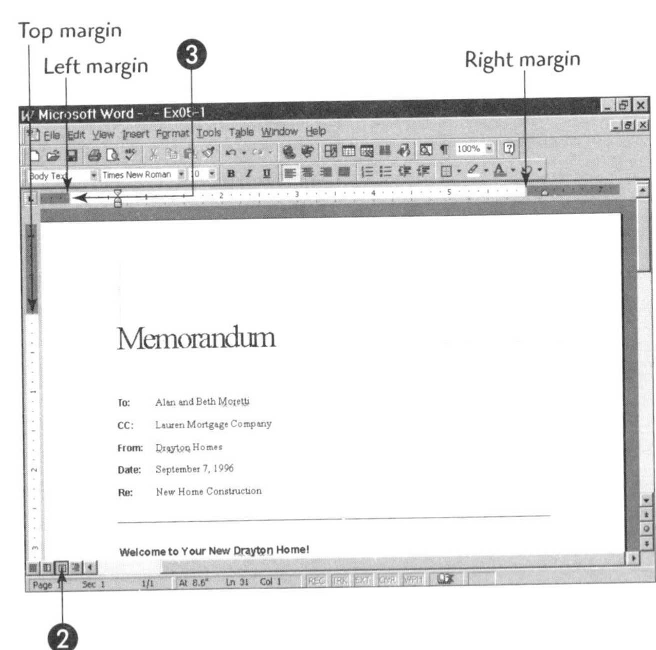

3. Place your mouse pointer on the thin gray line between the darker gray margin and the white area of the ruler.

   Your mouse pointer changes to a two-sided arrow and the label Left Margin is displayed.

4. Click your left mouse button and drag the margin half an inch to the right.

5. Release the mouse button and your memo text has shifted to the right to match the new margin setting.

Indents are set relative to margins. When you change a margin, any indents are maintained relative to the margin. So, for example, when you perform the preceding steps to move the left margin of this memo, notice the indented information about the Option Package moves over, maintaining the same relative position to the right of the new margin setting.

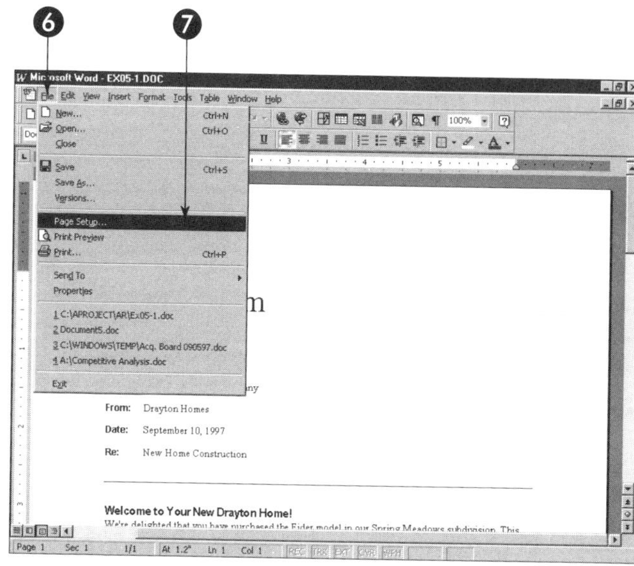

There is another way to change margins, using the Page Setup dialog box. This method enables you to be a bit more precise in your settings. Move the right margin using this method.

6. Click the File menu to open it.

7. Select Page Setup.

   The Page Setup dialog box appears, as shown in the accompanying illustration.

8. Click the upward-pointing arrow on the Right margin setting until it reads 1.5.

   The preview area of the Page Setup dialog box shows your new margin setting.

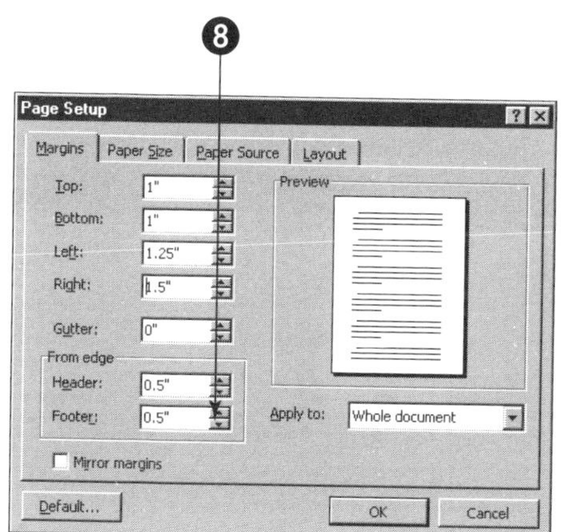

Notice the arrow controls you use to set margin settings have predetermined settings, and won't enable you to set margins more finely than a tenth of an inch. To enter a margin setting of 1.25, for

example, you have to enter the number yourself, or use the arrows on the margin settings to reach 1.2, and then place your cursor after the 2 and type ***5***.

9. Choose OK.

   The text in the memo shifts to the new right margin setting.

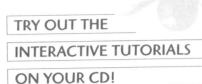

TRY OUT THE INTERACTIVE TUTORIALS ON YOUR CD!

Setting tabs

Whereas margins determine the overall parameters for where text appears on an entire page, a *tab* enables you to set one specific point across the width of the page. For example, you might set a tab at 4.5 inches from the left margin to align numbers in a short column (for longer columns, you would use the column or table features of Word). Outlines also use tabs to move from one indented level in the outline structure to the next.

Tab stops can be set in four varieties:

- *Left tabs.* When you set this tab, typed text inserts itself to the right of the tab stop, as with the following numbers, which line up on their left side:

  1,234.56
  3.786

- *Right tabs.* When you set a right tab, typed text inserts itself to the left of the tab stop. The same numbers line up on their right side:

  1,234.56
  3.786

- *Center tabs.* Center tabs cause typed text to fan out on either side of a center point, as in the following example:

  1,234.56
  3.786

- *Decimal tabs.* These tabs are useful when typing numbers. Text typed at a decimal tab lines up at the decimal point:

  1,234.56
  3.786

Setting tabs

When you first open a Word document, there are left tab stops preset every quarter inch along the page, indicated by pale gray marks appearing just below the horizontal ruler measurements. You can delete these tabs, or add new ones anywhere you like on the ruler.

It's time to get some practice setting tabs. There are two ways to do this. The first method uses the ruler and Tab tool. You can see the Tab tool in the illustration to the right.

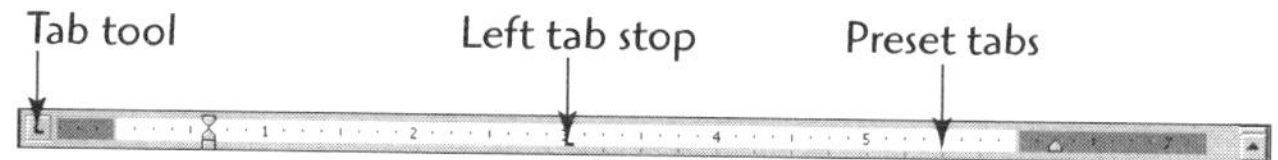

1. Use the scroll bar to move to the bottom of the page.
2. Place your cursor before the text *Mark Anderson, Drayton Homes.*

   The Tab tool currently displays an L shape, which is the symbol for a left tab. Click the tab tool to see the different tab styles.
3. Click the Tab tool.

   The L changes to a horizontal line with a vertical line extending upward from its center. This is a center tab.
4. Click the Tab tool again.

   A reversed L symbol appears. If you set a tab when this symbol is on the tab tool, you are setting a right tab.
5. Click the Tab tool one more time.

   A symbol similar to the center tab appears, but there is a small decimal point next to it. This is the decimal tab.
6. Click the Tab tool to return to the left tab setting.
7. Place your mouse pointer on the horizontal ruler at the three-inch mark and click.

   An L symbol appears at the three-inch mark on the ruler, and all preset tabs before the three-inch mark disappear.
8. Press the Tab key on your keyboard.

   The signature line has been indented, as shown in the illustration to the right. Without this new tab setting, if you wanted to tab this text to the three-inch mark, you'd have to move it through every preset tab setting until you reached three inches. This would involve 12 keystrokes — a very cumbersome operation if you did this with several lines of text. With the new tab setting,

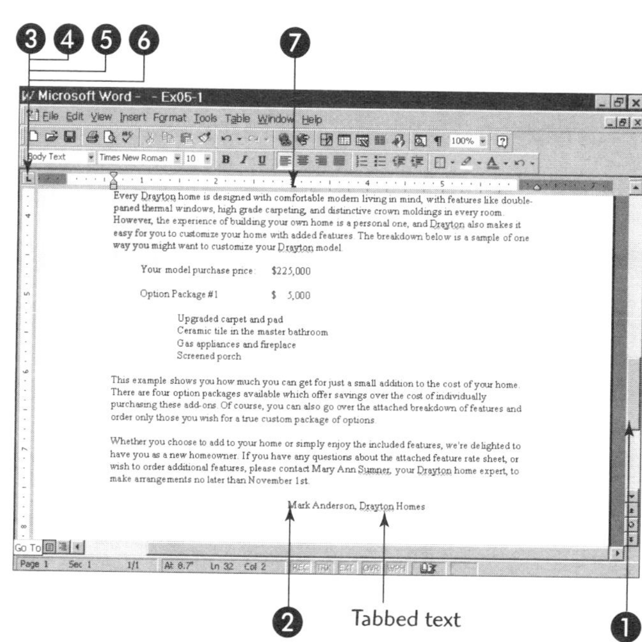

you can move the text to the three-inch position with one keystroke.

Removing a tab is also simple. You can remove this tab and set it again using the second method.

9 Click the tab stop you placed with your cursor and drag it off the ruler.

The text moves back to its original position, and all the preset tab stops have returned.

10 Make sure that your cursor is before the text *Mark Anderson* and click the Format menu.

11 Click Tabs.

The Tabs dialog box appears, as shown in the illustration.

12 Type **3.0** in the Tab stop position field.

13 Leave the Alignment of the tab set on Left and choose Set.

14 Click OK to return to your document.

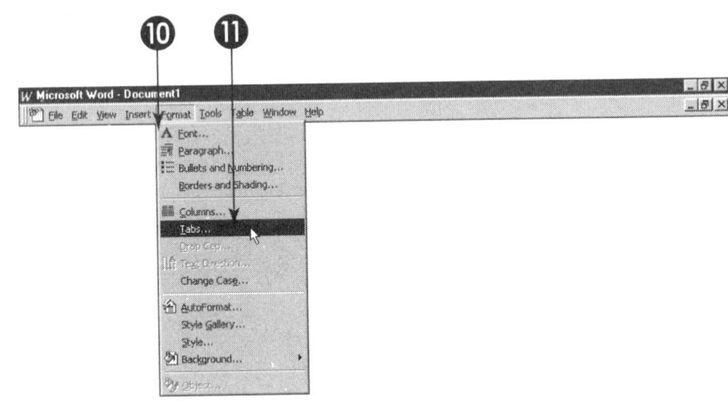

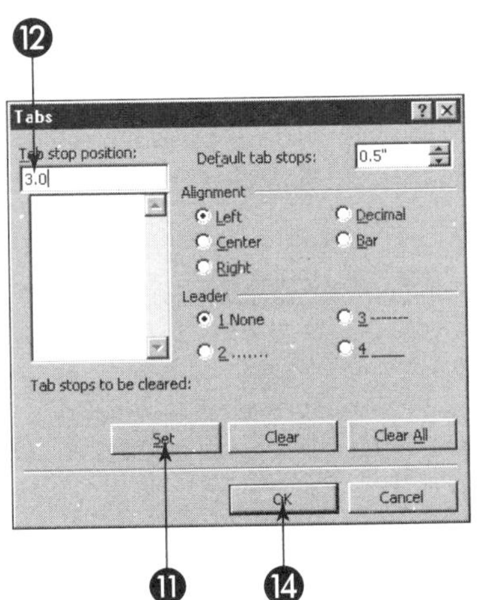

TIP

If you want to clear tab settings, you can use the Clear or Clear All buttons in the Tabs dialog box.

Using indents

Notice the text that discusses the option package immediately after the second paragraph of this document. It's indented away from the left margin. In fact, the first two lines are indented to one point and the details of the option package are indented even further. Could you get this indented effect by setting tabs? Yes. But using an indent is not only faster, it makes changing the contents of your document simpler.

You typically use indent settings on a block of text, so the whole block shifts to originate from a distance relative to the margin. If you decide to move the indented text, you can just select the block and move the indent. If you move the margin, the indented text stays indented relative to the new margin setting. If you tab to indent each line of the text and you add or delete text, you have to manually adjust all the tabs you've inserted to make the text line up again.

Here's how indents work:

1. Select the first two paragraphs of the memo.

   Take a look at the horizontal ruler. Notice a little hourglass-like symbol appears on the ruler at the left margin's edge. This symbol is made up of the following three parts:

   - The top triangle is the first-line indent. If, for example, you select a paragraph and move the first-line indent symbol in five spaces on the ruler, the first line of the paragraph moves in that far, but the rest of the lines stay the same.
   - The bottom triangle is a hanging indent. A hanging indent is the reverse of a first-line indent. If you select a paragraph and move the hanging indent marker half an inch to the right, the first line begins at the same spot but all the following lines move five spaces in from it.
   - The small box beneath the hanging indent is the left indent symbol. If you select a paragraph and move the left indent half an inch to the right, the whole paragraph moves five spaces. Any hanging or first line indent settings would be maintained, relative to the new left indent position.

2. Move your mouse pointer to the ruler and rest it over the indent markers until the words First Line Indent appear.
3. Click your mouse and drag the first line indent marker to the one-inch mark on the ruler.

   The first line of the paragraph moves in, but all the other lines retain their origination point at the left margin, as shown in the following illustration.

4. Select the third paragraph.
5. Click the hanging indent marker and drag it half an inch to the right.

Left indent

First-line indent

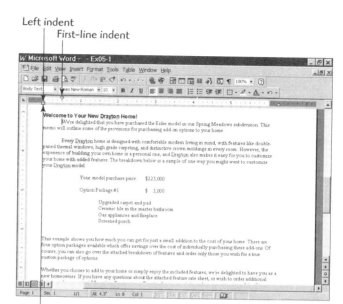

Hanging indent

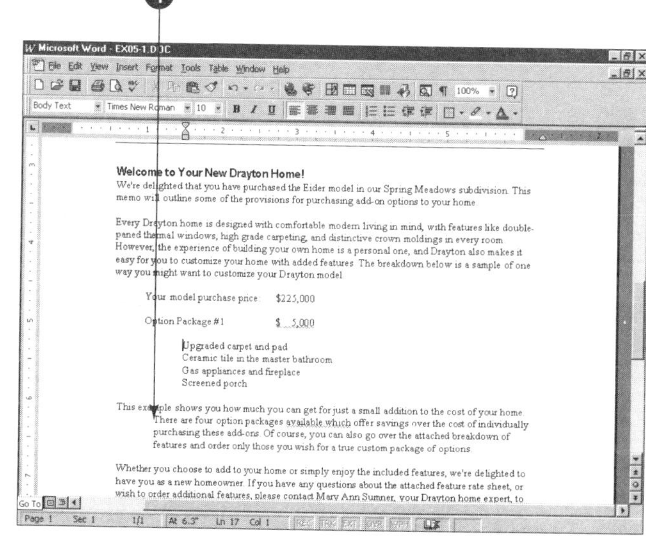

5 Getting Your Document in Shape

The first line of the paragraph stays on the left margin, but the lines that follow it are indented.

6. Place your cursor at the beginning of the line that says *Upgraded carpet and pad.*

   Notice that the whole hourglass configuration consisting of the Left indent, First Line indent, and Hanging indent markers is at the one-and-a-half inch point on the ruler. By moving this entire symbol, you move all lines in a block of text to line up along a single indent setting.

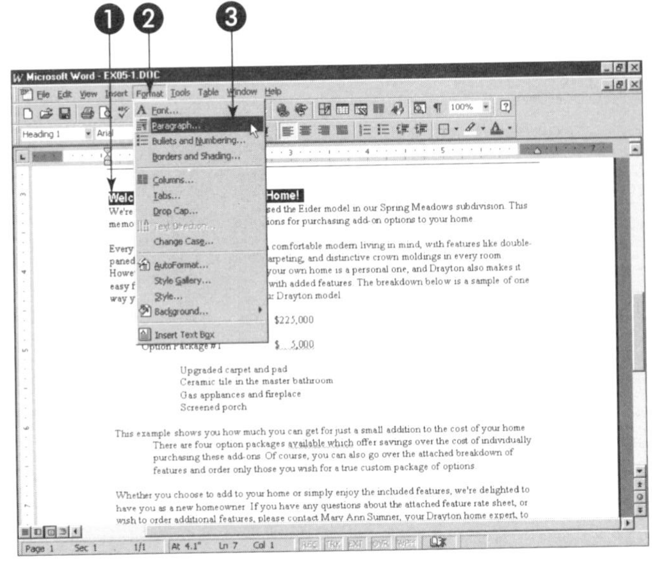

Modifying paragraph spacing

Another skill you should develop for arranging text on your page is modifying the spacing between lines of text. Notice that the heading at the opening of the document in the file Ex05-1 is right up against the first line of text. The heading might look better with some space between the two lines. To change the spacing, follow these steps:

1. Select the heading *Welcome to Your New Drayton Home!*
2. Select Format.
3. Select Paragraph.

   The Paragraph dialog box, shown in the accompanying illustration, is displayed. These settings are applied to selected text; or, if you have no text selected, they change the line spacing for all text you enter from this point on.

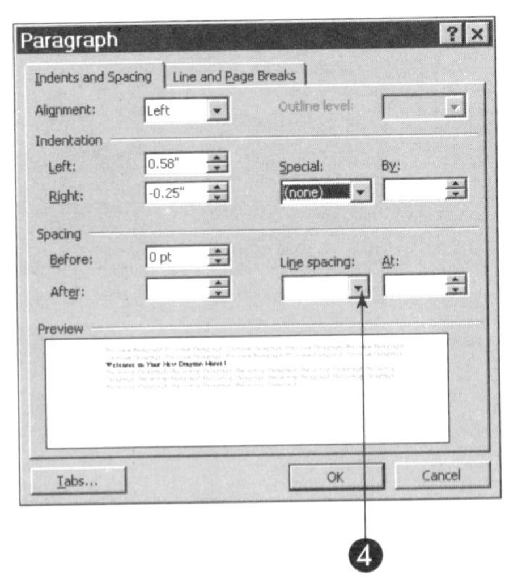

Notice that the Paragraph dialog box also offers an option to the method described in the previous section for setting indentations. Here you indent selected text by setting the Indentation measurements and choosing any special effects, such as a hanging or first line indent.

4. Click the arrow to display the drop-down menu for Line spacing.
5. Select Double to apply double-spacing to this line.

The Preview shows how the first line of selected text will be spaced from the second line using this setting. If you want to use a setting other than single, one and a half, or double, you could set the number of points to use in the Before and After fields, and choose either At Least or Exactly in the *Line spacing* drop-down list. At Least ensures that automatic spacing provides at least the number of points you enter (but could include more than that); Exactly constrains the line spacing to precisely the setting you enter in the *Before* and *After* boxes.

6. Choose OK.

   The spacing in the document is shown in the illustration to the right.

   If you want an entire document to be spaced differently from the default single spacing, change this setting before you begin typing any text. If you want to change spacing after having entered text, you will have to select the text and then use the Paragraph dialog box to make changes to it. A shortcut is to use Edit ➢ Select All if you want to select all the text in your document to change its spacing.

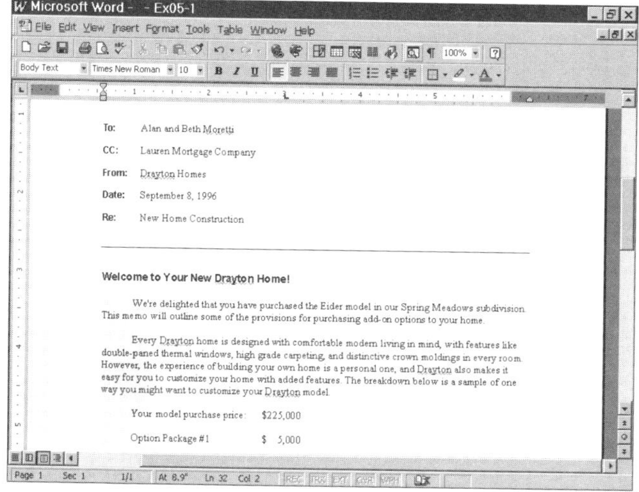

WORKING WITH TEXT

Writing a document is an iterative process. You may write one draft, and decide to make changes: You might add more text, delete some other text, or move text around to organize the flow of your thoughts differently. You may do this several times before you create a finished document.

Word for Windows enables you to easily move, delete, or copy anything from a single letter to whole pages of text. These features not only work within a single document, but they also enable you to take elements of one document and place them in another.

Cutting, copying, pasting, and deleting text

For this exercise, you need the file Ex05-2. So, you first need to close the file Ex05-1 (if you haven't done so already), and then open the file Ex05-2.

Working with text

1. Close the file Ex05-1 without saving the changes.
2. Open the file Ex05-2.

   This annual meeting notice was based on the Normal template (the template used for any blank document you create). There are several elements that need attention in this first draft.

   The address of the company should be moved down to the bottom of the form to indicate where the form should be returned. It is probably a good idea to have the company name both at the top to identify whose annual meeting it is, and again at the bottom as part of the address block. One line is duplicated and should be cut from the notice. These changes require the use of the Cut, Copy, Paste, and Delete functions of Word.
3. Select the two lines of the address at the top of the document.
4. Choose the Cut button on the toolbar.

   The text disappears. It has actually been cut from this document and placed on the Windows Clipboard. The important thing to remember about this Clipboard is that it can only contain one item. If you were to cut something else, it would erase this text from the Clipboard and place the new item there. Cut is used when you want to take something from one place and paste it into another place right away.
5. Move your mouse pointer to the bottom of the page.
6. Choose the Paste button on the toolbar.

   The address appears at the bottom of the page. Now you will copy the name of the company and place it at the bottom of the page to complete the address block. When you copy, Word will place a copy of the selection on the Clipboard, and the same caution about losing the text given for cutting still applies.
7. Select the company name, *Worldwide Wood Products Corporation.*
8. Choose the Copy button.
9. Place your cursor before the number *23* in the address line.
10. Choose the Paste button.

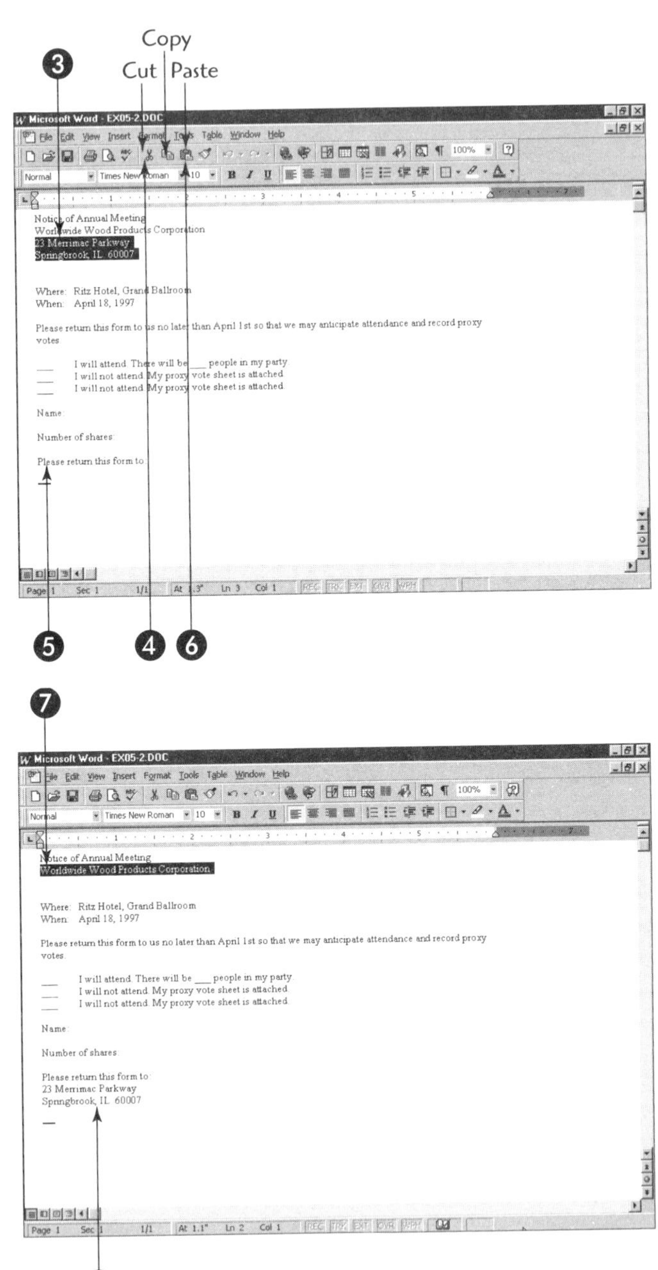

The text has been duplicated near the bottom of the page, as shown in the illustration to the right.

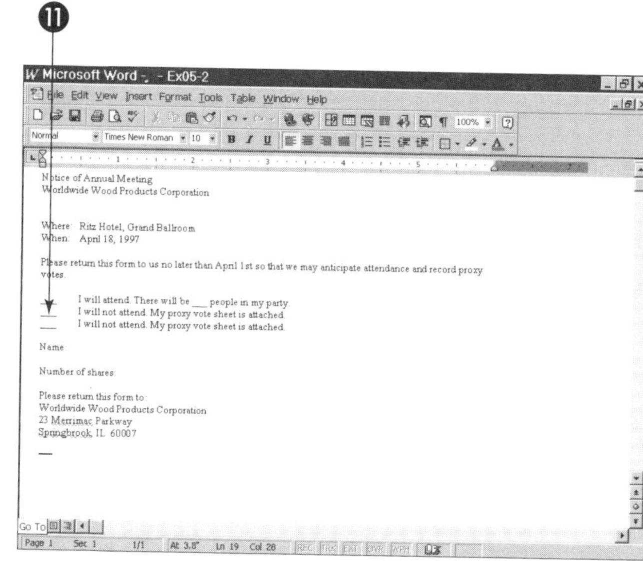

You can also perform the Cut, Copy, and Paste functions by selecting the various commands from the Edit menu.

Now take care of that duplicated line in the middle of this form.

11. Select one of the lines that reads *I will not attend. My proxy vote sheet is attached.*

    There are several methods you can use for cutting text. Try any of the options offered in Step 10.

12. Press Backspace on your keyboard, press Delete on your keyboard, or select Edit ➢ Clear.

Using the Undo/Redo command

What do you do if you delete something and then realize you shouldn't have? One of the most wonderful features in Word is the Undo/Redo feature. It enables you to undo a wide variety of actions. You should use the Undo feature soon after the action you wish to undo. Once you save the document, undoing an action becomes impossible. If you perform several subsequent actions, undoing an action becomes too cumbersome.

Say, for example, you realized that the line you just cut should stay in your document, but it needs to be slightly modified so it isn't an exact duplicate of the line preceding it.

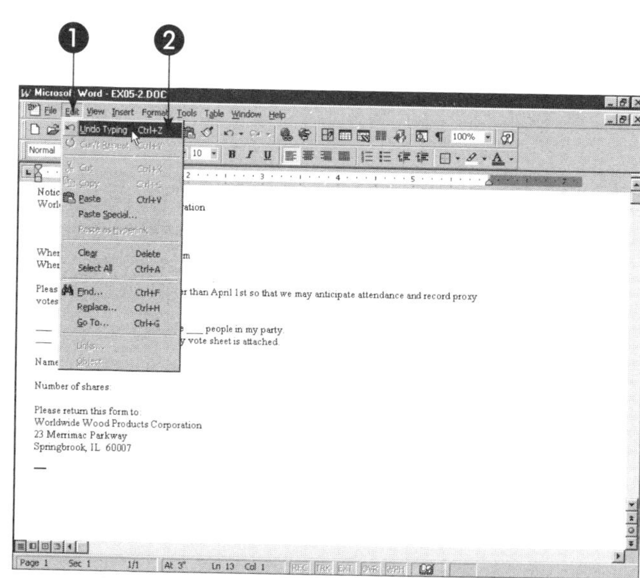

1. Select Edit.
2. Select Undo Typing. The deleted line returns.
3. Place your cursor within the line, before the word *attached.*
4. Type **not** and a space.
5. Place your cursor at the end of the line (after the word *attached*).

6. Insert a space (by hitting the spacebar), and type **I waive my right to proxy vote.**

   The capability to undo your delete action saved you having to retype that sentence. With a whole paragraph or even pages of text, the undo function is invaluable. You can undo almost any action. For example, you can use Undo if you apply formatting to text, indent text, or paste a block of text into your document and then change your mind. You can perform a single Undo or Redo function with these commands in the Edit menu, or by clicking the Undo or Redo buttons on the toolbar.

   You can undo and redo more than just your last action using the Undo or Redo buttons on the toolbar. However, you undo and redo multiple actions in the order they were performed; if you delete text then perform several other tasks, you can use the Undo function and sequentially undo all the actions you've performed, back to your deleting action. However, you'll have to gauge whether losing all the other actions you performed in between is more trouble than undoing your delete. Practice using the Undo function with multiple actions.

7. Click the arrow next to the Undo button.

   The accompanying illustration shows the list of tasks you've performed, with the most recent one at the top. By dragging down the list, you can select however many of these tasks you wish to undo.

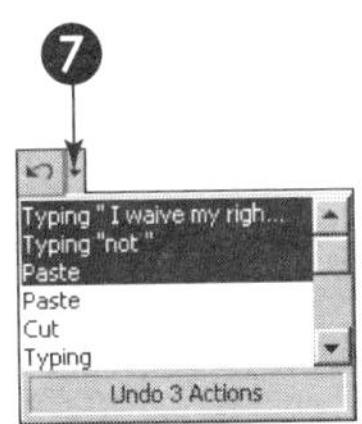

8. Drag your mouse pointer to select the first two items on this list.
9. Click your mouse, and the list disappears.

   You have undone the change of adding two text items to this line of your document.

10. Click the arrow next to the Redo button.
11. Select the first two items and click.

    The text reappears.

Moving text with drag and drop

Cut and Paste is one way to move a block of text or object, such as a drawing, from one place in a document to another. However, there's another method that's often faster and easier. You can use your mouse to simply drag a selection to a new location in a document.

1. Drag your mouse pointer across the text to select the sentence that begins *Please return this form to us. . . .*
2. Release your mouse button.
3. Place your mouse pointer anywhere in the area of the highlighted text.
4. Press your left mouse button, and drag the text (without letting go of the mouse button).

   Your mouse pointer changes to a small, dotted, vertical line. As you drag the text, this pointer indicates the location it will move to if you release the mouse button.
5. Place the dotted line pointer just before the first word of the phrase *Please return this form to:* and release the mouse button.

   The sentence has been moved to the new location in one action, instead of using the cut and paste function.

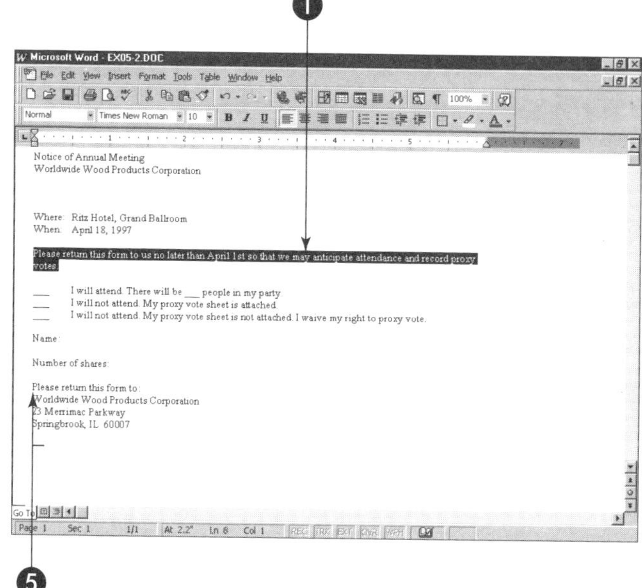

Aligning text

By default, text you type in a Word document is aligned at the left margin. When you're positioning text on a page, you sometimes want to realign it. That is, you may want the text to be aligned in the center of your page, or aligned to the right margin. This can be done either with buttons on the Formatting toolbar or with menu commands. You use a combination of these in this exercise.

The Justify alignment choice adjusts the spacing between the letters in your text to spread a line evenly across your page. This can cause rather odd spacing between letters in words, and some people don't like

Aligning text

the Justify alignment for that reason. However, because all lines begin and end at exactly the same point on either side of the page, the text forms a uniform block without the ragged edge of left or right alignment. Try them all and see which you prefer.

1. Select the first two lines of text.
2. Choose the Center button on the toolbar.

   The text appears centered between the right and left margins.

3. Select the last four lines of the document.
4. Select Format.
5. Select Paragraph.

   The Paragraph dialog box, shown in the following illustration, appears.

6. Click the arrow to display the drop-down list for the Alignment setting.
7. Choose Right.
8. Click OK.

   This last alignment change should make your document look like the illustration at the bottom right.

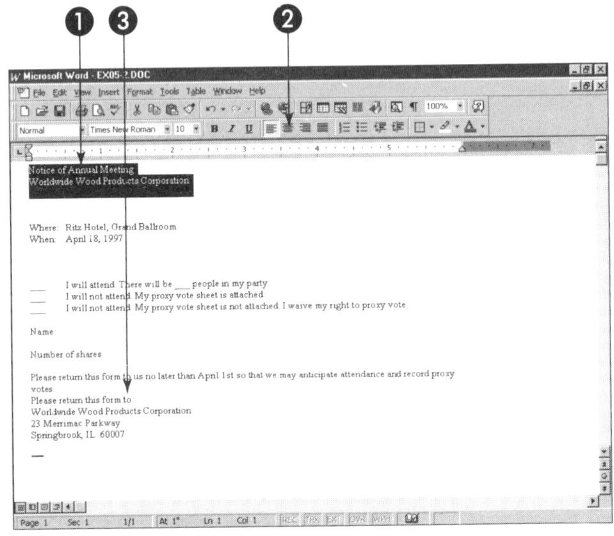

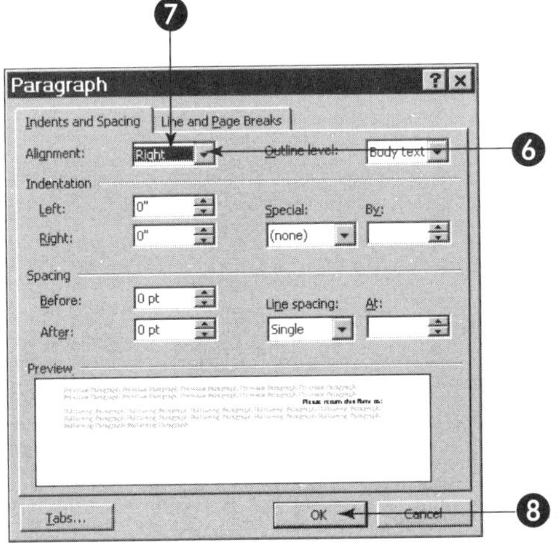

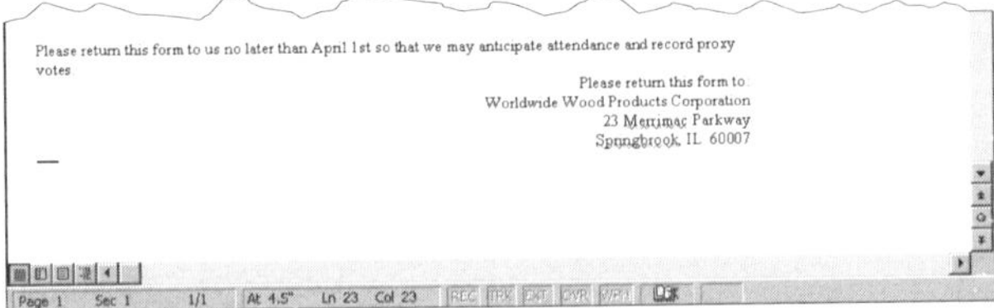

EDITING TEXT

Aside from positioning text on your page, there are several things you can do to make the text itself more attractive and readable. In the Normal template, which is the one applied when you open any blank document, your text is 10 point in size and uses the Times New Roman typeface (or *font*) by default.

A point is a standard measurement of type size, which is $^{1}/_{72}$ of an inch. 10 points make your letters $^{10}/_{72}$ of an inch tall. Typically, business letters use either a 10 or 12 point setting for text.

A font or typeface is a design set for letters, numbers, and characters. One font might be used for headings in a document, and another for the body text. However, a good rule of thumb is to not use more than two fonts on a single page. Otherwise, your document becomes busy and difficult to read.

You can change the font, adjust its size, and apply effects, such as boldface and italic. You can even save sets of these formatting attributes as something called styles, and apply them to selected text again and again.

Changing fonts

Often the heading or title of a document looks better if it is emphasized by formatting. In this exercise, you change the font of the first two lines of the Annual Meeting notice.

1. Select the first two lines of text.
2. Click the arrow next to the Font button on the toolbar (this button contains the name of the current font, Times New Roman).
3. Drag the scroll bar to the top of the list.
4. Choose the font named Arial.

The result is shown in the figure at bottom right. Arial is a typeface often used for headings. It offers a clean, easy-to-read look.

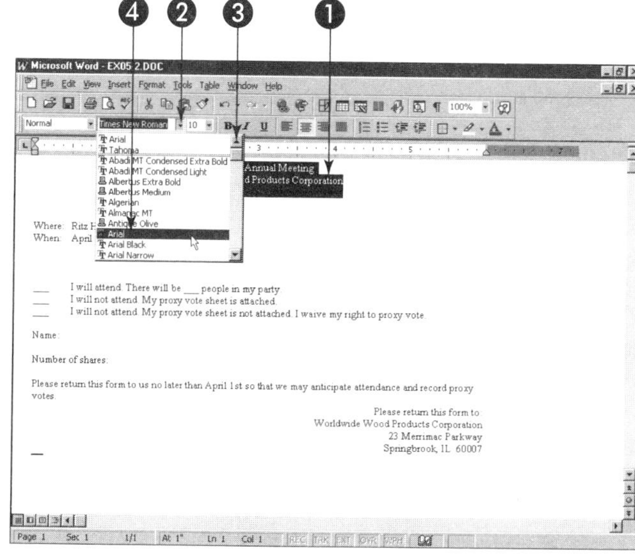

NOTE

When you have made font selections for a document, the most recently used fonts will be listed at the top of the Font drop-down list, with a line between those fonts and the alphabetical listing of all fonts. Word assumes if you use a font once in a document, you may want to use it again — this saves you from having to scroll through a long list. Because it's a good idea to limit yourself to a few fonts and use them consistently in a document, it's a good idea to have these handy.

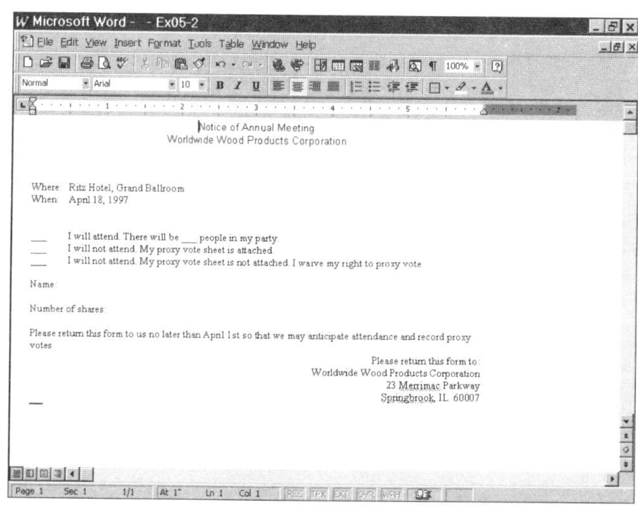

You can also change the typeface of the address to Arial. This time, you'll use the Font dialog box to make the change. This will enable you to preview the appearance of the font before you apply it.

5. Select the last three lines of the document.
6. Select Format.
7. Choose Font.

   The Font dialog box shown in the following illustration appears.

   This dialog box offers you a central place to make changes to text. If you want, for example, to change the font, font size, and color of your text, you can open this dialog box and make several changes at once. You can do that now, starting with changing the font of this text, and continuing over the next few exercises to make all changes to this text at once.
8. Drag the scroll bar in the Font list to the top.
9. Choose Arial from the list.

   A preview of how this font would look applied to the text appears at the bottom of the dialog box.

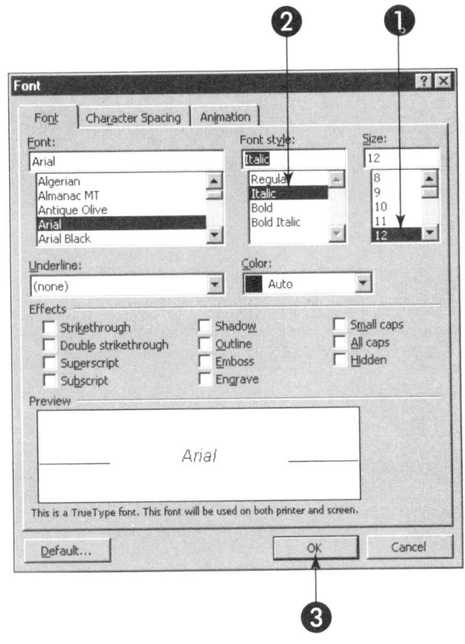

Working with font size and effects

Now change the font size of this text.

1. Choose 12 from the Size list in the Font dialog box.
2. Choose Italic from the Font style list.
3. Choose OK to accept both changes you made to the text.
4. Select the first two lines of the document.
5. Click the arrow of the Font Size button, and select 16 point.
6. Choose the Bold button on the toolbar.
7. Place your cursor just before the address block at the end of the document (before the word *Worldwide*) and press enter.

   You can begin to see how these easy text formatting changes make this a more attractive and balanced document.

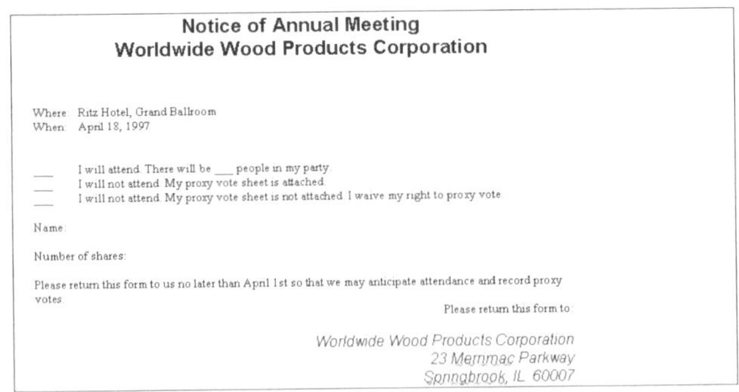

Notice of Annual Meeting
Worldwide Wood Products Corporation

Where: Ritz Hotel, Grand Ballroom
When: April 18, 1997

___ I will attend. There will be ___ people in my party.
___ I will not attend. My proxy vote sheet is attached.
___ I will not attend. My proxy vote sheet is not attached. I waive my right to proxy vote.

Name:

Number of shares:

Please return this form to us no later than April 1st so that we may anticipate attendance and record proxy votes.

Please return this form to:

Worldwide Wood Products Corporation
23 Merrimac Parkway
Springbrook, IL 60007

FORMATTING SHORTCUTS

If you find that you frequently use certain combinations of formatting, there are some easy ways to apply them all at once. One way is to use styles, and the other is with the Format Painter tool.

Assigning styles

A style is a saved combination of formatting settings. Styles are built into templates on which you base your document. You can select text and apply a style to it. You can try that with the location and date of the meeting in our annual meeting document.

1. Select the two lines that begin with the words *Where* and *When*.
2. Select the Style button on the toolbar (it currently says Normal for normal body text).
3. Choose Heading 2.

   The style has applied font (Arial), font size (12 point) and an italic effect to the text.

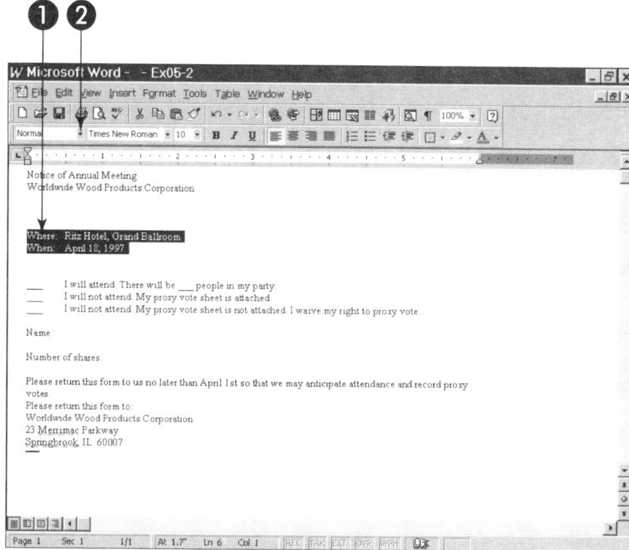

If you want a style applied only to a single paragraph, you don't have to select text to apply it. Place your cursor anywhere in a paragraph and select the style. The whole paragraph (that is, from the beginning of the paragraph to the point where you press Enter*) changes to the new style.*

You can create a new style yourself and use it in future documents.

4. Select Format.
5. Select Style.
6. From the dialog box that appears, choose the New button.

   The New Style dialog box appears.

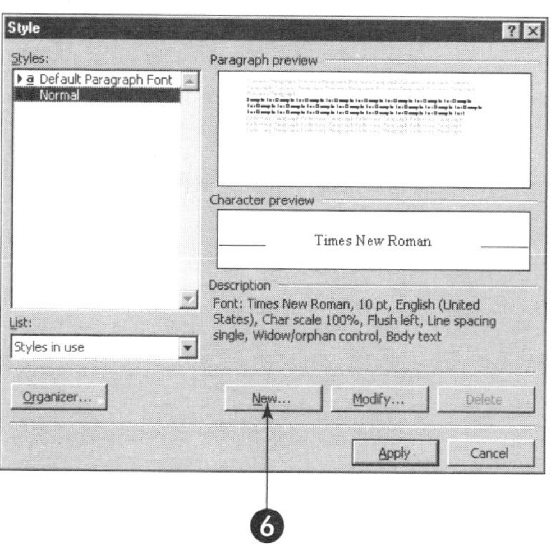

Copying formats

If there is a style that has some of the elements you'd like in the new style, you can save time by selecting it from the *Based on* drop-down list in the New Style dialog box. If you don't have a style with some of the components you want in mind, leave the *Based on* setting at Normal. This style has only font, font size, and alignment settings so you can customize it easily.

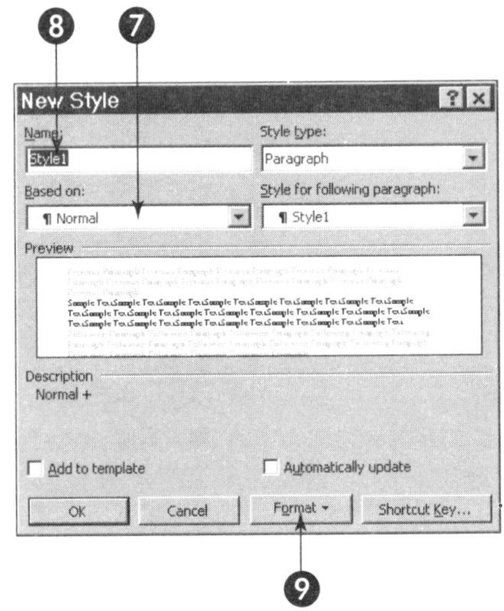

7 Select Normal in the drop-down list.

8 Type the name **MyStyle** for the style in the Name box.

Notice there is a description area at the bottom of this dialog box. Currently, it says Normal. You can now proceed to add whatever formatting settings you want to the Normal style.

9 Choose the Format button. A list of different formatting settings appears.

10 Choose Font. The Font dialog box appears.

11 Select the Bold Italic effect and change the font to 12 point.

12 Choose OK to return to the New Style dialog box.

The description in the New Style dialog box now says "Normal + Font: 12 pt, Bold, Italic." You can repeat this procedure to make changes to other types of formats using the Format button.

13 Choose Close to save the new style and close the Style dialog box.

14 Select the two lines of text, *Name:* and *Number of Shares.*

15 Open the Style drop-down list on the toolbar. Your new style is now on the list.

16 Click the style MyStyle and the selected text becomes bold, italic, and 12 point.

Copying formats

It's also easy to copy the format of one piece of text to another using the Format Painter tool.

1. Select the word *Where.*
2. Choose the Format Painter tool (it looks like a little paintbrush).

   The mouse pointer turns into a small paintbrush symbol that you use to copy the format of the selected text to any text you drag your mouse pointer over.
3. Drag your mouse pointer across the line *Please return this form to.*

   Your document should now look like the illustration to the right.
4. Close without saving changes.

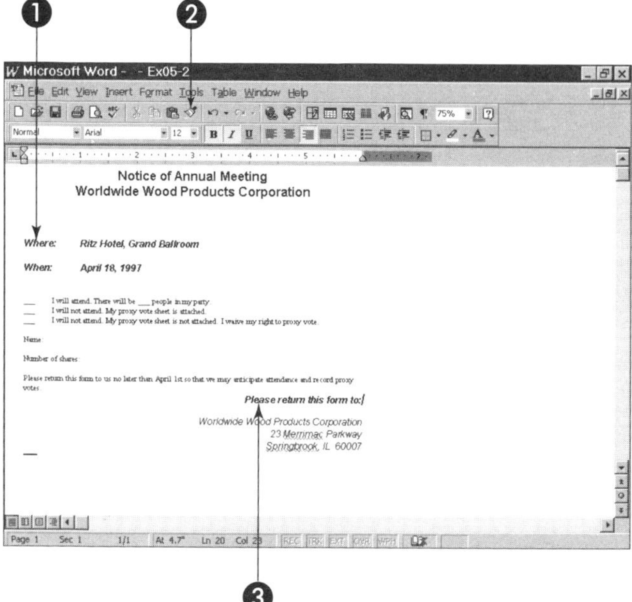

SKILLS CHALLENGE: CREATING AN INVITATION

In this exercise, you practice all the skills you've learned in this lesson to create an invitation to a company party.

1. Open a document based on the blank document template.
2. Type the following text, pressing Enter as needed to create new lines:

   You are invited [Enter]

   to a Christmas Party [Enter]

   Where: The Margaux Winery [Enter]

   When: December 15, 1997 [Enter]

   Please RSVP no later than November 28, 1997 by returning the enclosed card to Marsha Malloy, Human Resources [Enter]

   for the employees and valued customers of Richter Graphics
3. Select the first two lines.

TRY OUT THE

INTERACTIVE TUTORIALS

ON YOUR CD!

Skills challenge

4. Center the text on the page.

Aside from using the Center button on the toolbar, what is the other way to change text alignment?

5. With the text still highlighted, select Format ➢ Font.
6. Change the text to Book Antiqua font, Bold Italic font style, and 16 point.
7. Choose OK to apply the font changes.
8. Select all the text in the document.

How do you quickly select all text in a document without using your mouse?

9. Select Format ➢ Paragraph.
10. Change Line spacing to 1.5.
11. Choose OK to apply the paragraph formatting.

    At this point, your document should look like the illustration to the left.

12. Select the last line, beginning with the text *for the employees....*
13. Drag this text up to move it just below the second line of text (after *to a Christmas Party*).
14. Center this text and italicize it using the buttons on the toolbar.
15. Select the last four lines of text.
16. Using the Style drop-down list on the toolbar, change the style of this text to Heading 3.
17. Select the last two lines of text beginning with *Please RSVP....*

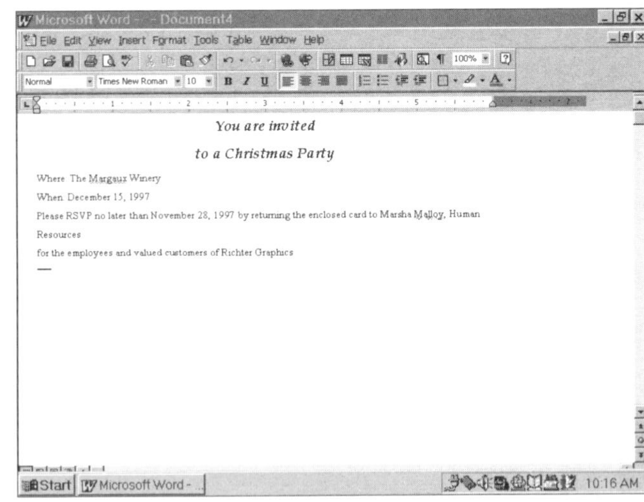

18 Indent the text to the one-inch mark on the ruler.

The boss just came in and said it's going to be an employees-only party!

19 Delete the text *and valued customers* from the third line.

If you Cut text, is it deleted?

20 With the last two lines of text still selected, change its font size to 10 point.

21 Select the two lines that begin *Where*: and *When*:.

22 With the Tab tool displaying a left indent marker, click the 1.75-inch point on the horizontal ruler to place a tab stop.

23 Place your cursor in front of *Where:* and press Tab on your keyboard to tab this text to the 1.75-inch point on your page.

24 Repeat this procedure to tab the line beginning with *When:* to the 1.75-inch point.

Identify the three fonts used in this document. How was each applied?

25 Select all the text in the document.

26 Move the right margin to 5.5 inches.

Your document should now look like the illustration to the right.

27 Close and save as **Party**.

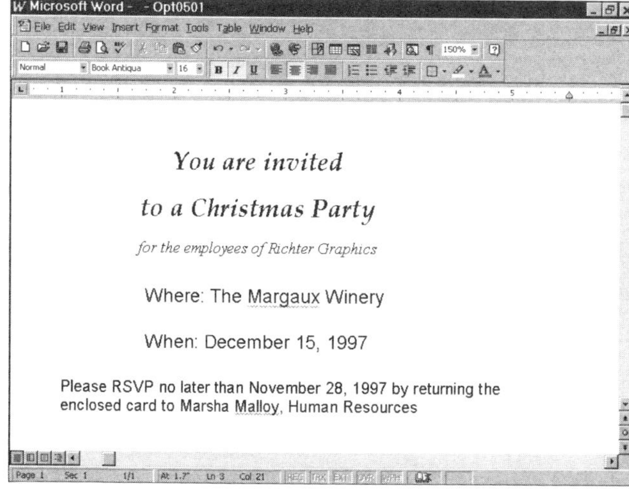

Troubleshooting

TROUBLESHOOTING

Completing this lesson means you've mastered many of the skills needed to produce attractive documents. In addition, many of the tools and procedures you learned here will be useful in all the other Office programs. This table offers solutions to some questions or challenges you might have encountered in practicing these skills.

Problem	Solution
I changed the size of the type, now the lines run together.	Select Format ➢ Paragraph and adjust the line spacing to be greater.
I set several tabs and now want to get rid of them all.	Select Format ➢ Tabs and choose Clear All.
I saved a style and now I can't find it.	Styles that aren't part of a document's template have to be loaded into the document. Select Format ➢ Style Gallery and choose your style from the list there.
I applied a font to text and it's all little pictures.	Some fonts, such as Wingdings, are symbol fonts, made up not of letters and numbers but of images, such as scientific symbols.

WRAP UP

You've practiced quite a few skills in this lesson, including the following:

- Setting tabs and margins and indenting text using both toolbar and menu commands
- Changing the spacing between lines of text using the Paragraph dialog box
- Cutting, copying, pasting, and deleting text, and changing your mind with the Undo/Redo function
- Moving and realigning text on your page

- Formatting text with fonts, font sizes, and effects such as Bold and Italic and even shortcuts such as styles and Format Painter to copy styles from one piece of text to another

If you'd like more practice with these skills, try creating a flyer promoting a yard sale at your house next week.

In the following lesson, you start working with objects other than text that can help add flair to any document.

Punching Up Your Documents

GOALS

In this lesson, you discover ways to add visual style to Word documents, learning skills such as the following:

- Inserting clip art
- Using WordArt
- Moving and rotating objects
- Drawing shapes and lines
- Resizing objects
- Grouping and ungrouping objects
- Formatting line styles
- Working with color and patterns
- Applying borders
- Creating columns
- Changing the order of objects

Inserting clip art

GET READY

To complete this lesson's exercises, you need the files Ex06-1, Ex06-2, and Ex06-3, which you copied to your hard drive from the accompanying CD-ROM.

When you're done with this lesson's exercises, you'll have created the document shown on the facing page.

ADDING OBJECTS

Word processors such as Word for Windows enable you to go far beyond simple text. You can easily add ready-made pictures, create drawings, and add columns to your page. You can even design enhanced text effects such as curved text using a small application called WordArt, which is built right into Word. In this section, you practice adding ready-made art and drawing your own objects.

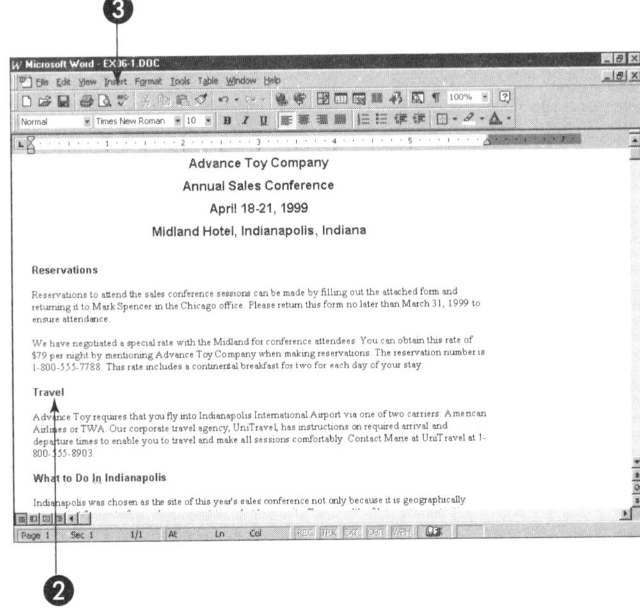

Inserting clip art

Word contains a built-in collection of multimedia files called Clip Gallery. One part of Clip Gallery contains ready-made line drawings called clip art. Placing one of these pictures into a document involves opening the Gallery, selecting a picture, and opening it.

1. Open the file named Ex06-1.

   The document shown in the following illustration appears. This is an announcement of an annual sales conference for the Advance Toy Company. To make it more visually interesting, add some clip art.

2. Place your cursor on the blank line following the heading Travel.
3. Click the Insert menu.
4. Select Picture.
5. Choose Clip Art from the side menu that appears.

   The Clip Gallery dialog box appears, as shown in the illustration to the right.

   The Clip Gallery includes tabs for Clip Art, Pictures, Sounds, and Videos.

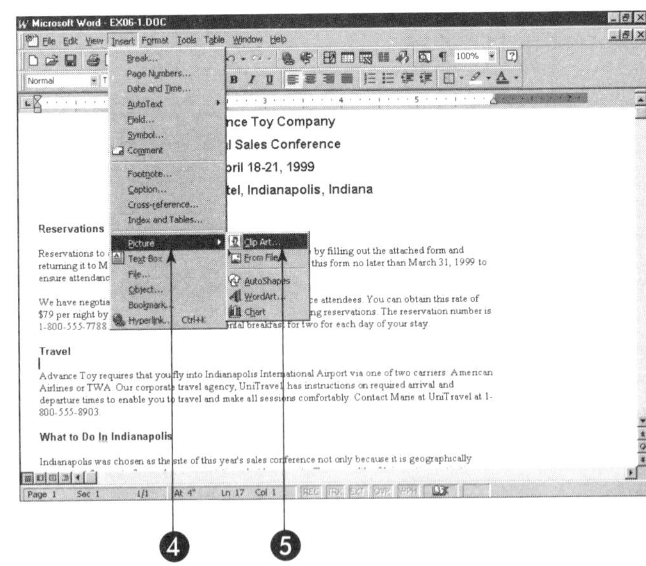

Advance Toy Company

Annual Sales Conference

April 18-21, 1999

Midland Hotel, Indianapolis, Indiana

Reservations

Reservations to attend the sales conference sessions can be made by filling out the attached form and returning it to Mark Spencer in the Chicago office. Please return this form no later than March 31, 1999 to ensure attendance.

We have negotiated a special rate with the Midland for conference attendees. You can obtain this rate of $79 per night by mentioning Advance Toy Company when making reservations. The reservation number is 1-800-555-7788. This rate includes a continental breakfast for two for each day of your stay.

Travel

Advance Toy requires that you fly into Indianapolis International Airport via one of two carriers: American Airlines or TWA. Our corporate travel agency, UniTravel, has instructions on required arrival and departure times to enable you to travel and make all sessions comfortably. Contact Marie at UniTravel at 1-800-555-8903.

What to Do In Indianapolis

Indianapolis was chosen as the site of this year's sales conference not only because it is geographically convenient for most of our sales representatives, but because it offers a wealth of leisure-time activities. Besides the world-famous Indianapolis 500 racecourse, there are professional theatre, opera, ballet and a wide variety of musical performances available to the out of town visitor. Our hotel is one block away from the historic Union Station, a renovated 1800's train station with shops and restaurants. We are directly across the street from a museum of American Indian arts, and a short drive away is the world's largest children's museum.

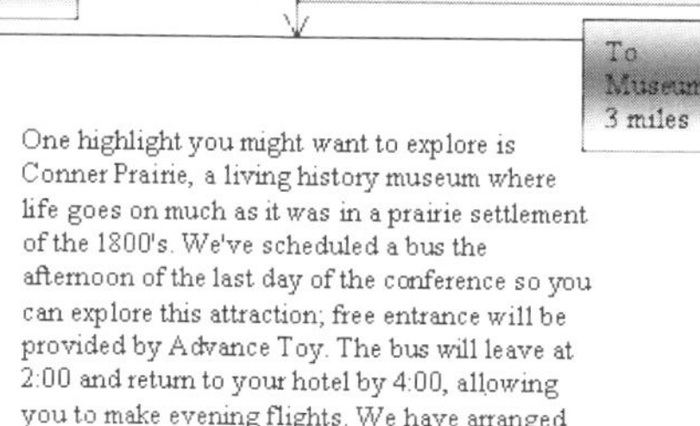

One highlight you might want to explore is Conner Prairie, a living history museum where life goes on much as it was in a prairie settlement of the 1800's. We've scheduled a bus the afternoon of the last day of the conference so you can explore this attraction; free entrance will be provided by Advance Toy. The bus will leave at 2:00 and return to your hotel by 4:00, allowing you to make evening flights. We have arranged for late checkout for all attendees to accommodate this excursion. If you're interested in taking advantage of this trip, please notify your manager no later than March 31, 1999.

See You There
We're looking forward to a great conference with seminars and panel discussions on topics that will help you do your job better. Any suggestions for additional topics should be forwarded to the office of the President, Amy Scott, as soon as possible.

Inserting clip art

❻ If you are not on the Clip Art tab, click it now.

The categories of clip art are listed on the left side of the tab. A preview of the various clip art files within the selected category appears in the middle.

❼ Select the Travel category by clicking it at the end of the category list.

❽ Use the scroll bar in the preview area to locate the image of the airplane that looks like the one in the bottom-right illustration.

❾ Click the airplane, and then choose Insert.

The airplane clip art image appears in your file with eight square handles around it. These are *resizing handles,* and you use them to change the dimensions of objects. They appear when you click an object, indicating it is currently selected. The clip art has appeared at the left margin of your document, as shown in the illustration to the right.

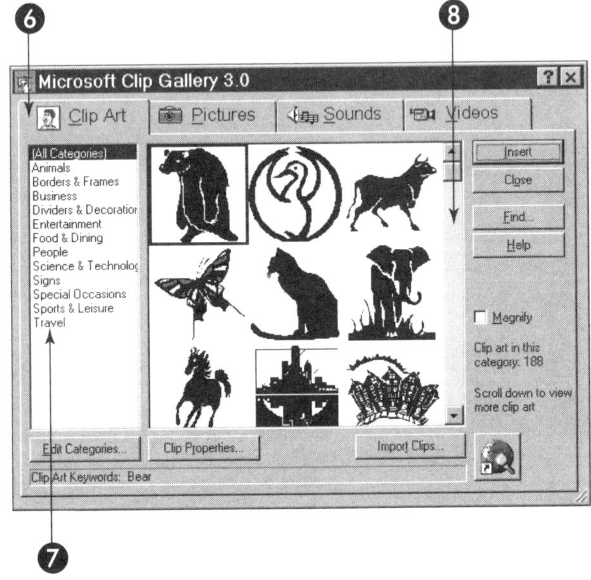

You aren't confined to using the images in the Clip Gallery. You can also bring in graphics files from any location you like, such as files located on your hard drive, a CD-ROM, floppy disk drive, or network. When you're in the Clip Gallery, simply choose Import Clips. An Add Clip Art to Clip Gallery dialog box appears, which you can use to browse for a file. When you locate a file and choose Open, that file is added to the Clip Gallery.

❿ Click the File menu.

⓫ Select Save.

⓬ Name the file **Art** and choose Save.

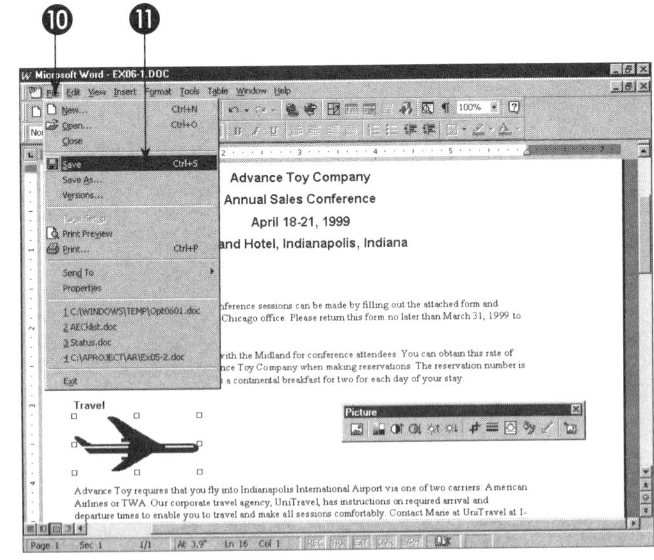

Note that when you insert any object such as clip art or WordArt, (discussed next), you sometimes need to adjust the way text wraps around that object on a page. Text can continue right through such an object, or avoid it entirely if you choose a feature called text wrapping. *You*

can control text wrapping by selecting the object and then selecting Format ➢ Object and choosing a style on the Wrapping tab.

Using WordArt

WordArt is one of several small applications, called *applets*, that are built into Word for Windows. This applet has features for creating interesting text effects and is very simple to use. You'll replace the typed company name at the top of the current document with a WordArt version.

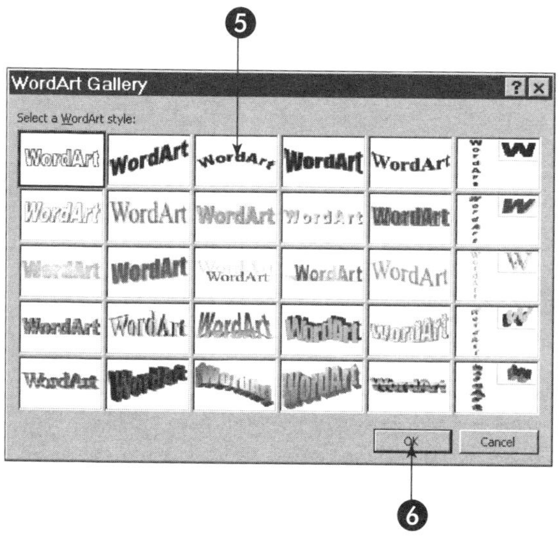

1. Place your cursor at the top of the Word document, and select the *Advance Toy Company* line of text.
2. Delete the text by using Backspace or Delete on your keyboard, and then press Enter.
3. Place your cursor on the first blank line of the document.
4. Select Insert ➢ Picture ➢ WordArt.

   The WordArt Gallery opens, as shown in the illustration at the top right. These built-in styles provide ways to enhance text for emphasis, create a company logo, or arrange text vertically on your page.

5. Click the curved selection in the top row, third from the left.
6. Choose OK.

   The Edit WordArt Text dialog box appears, as shown in the accompanying illustration.

   This dialog box has only a few simple elements. Drop-down lists enable you to make changes to the font and font size of the text, and two buttons enable you to make text bold or italic. Finally, a large window in the center highlights the words *Your Text Here*.

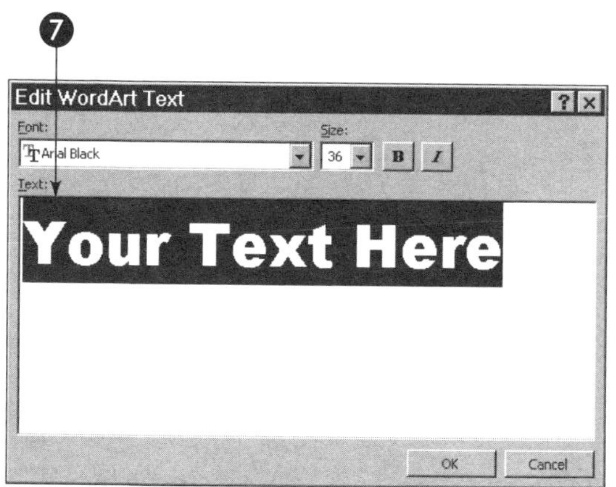

7. Type the words **Advance Toy Company**, which will replace the placeholder text automatically.

   The text appears in a preset font, but you can change the font if you like.

8. Select the words you just typed.
9. Click the arrow on the *Font* drop-down list and use the scroll bar to locate and select Century Schoolbook.
10. Click OK.

   The WordArt object appears on your page.

TRY OUT THE
INTERACTIVE TUTORIALS
ON YOUR CD!

Moving objects

You may need to move the WordArt object to the top of the document. Moving objects is simply a matter of clicking and dragging them to a new position.

1. Move your mouse pointer over the WordArt object until your pointer appears as four arrows.
2. Drag the WordArt object to the top of your page.

You can also move things more precisely: Select the object, and then choose Format ➢ Object. In the dialog box that appears, select the Position tab and enter horizontal and vertical measurements on the page where you'd like the object placed.

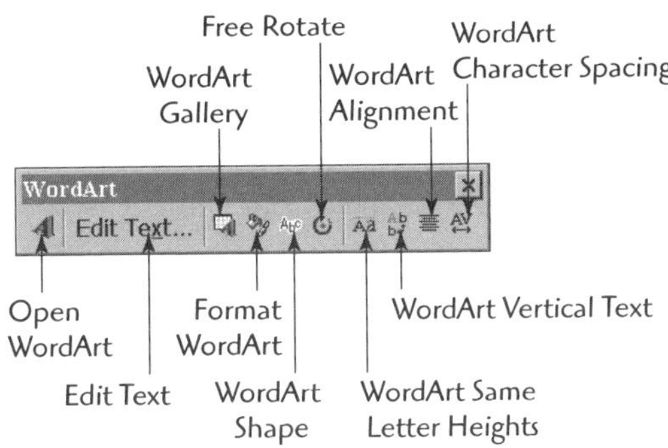

Notice the WordArt toolbar in the accompanying illustration. This toolbar appears when you select a WordArt object. Using this toolbar, you can make formatting changes to your WordArt object or reenter the applet at any time. Try one of these tools now.

3. With the WordArt object selected, choose the WordArt Same Letter Heights button on the WordArt toolbar.

   All the letters stretch to be the same height on the page.

Drawing shapes and lines

Word for Windows has its own drawing feature built right in. This feature enables you to draw simple figures such as squares and lines in your document, or you can get more sophisticated and actually build your own drawings.

1. Choose the Drawing button on the Standard toolbar.

   The Drawing toolbar appears along the bottom of your screen. The tools you'll use in this exercise are called out for you on this illustration, and more details about the other tools are provided in the next Visual Bonus. You're going to draw a map of the hotel in the sales conference document.

2. Locate the section of the document with the heading *What to Do In Indianapolis.* Place your cursor at the end of the first paragraph in this section.
3. Press Enter 15 times.
4. Choose the Rectangle button on the Drawing toolbar.
5. Place your mouse pointer, which has changed to a crosshair shape, at the top of the blank area between the two paragraphs.
6. Click and, without letting it go, drag to the right and down to create a rectangle approximately two inches tall and six inches wide.

   As you draw an object, a faint image of it appears, indicating the shape and size of the object if you were to release your mouse button at that point.

TIP

Use the horizontal and vertical rulers to help you judge the length and width of the object as you draw it.

7. Choose the Rectangle tool again.
8. Draw a rectangle in the upper left-hand corner of the larger rectangle.

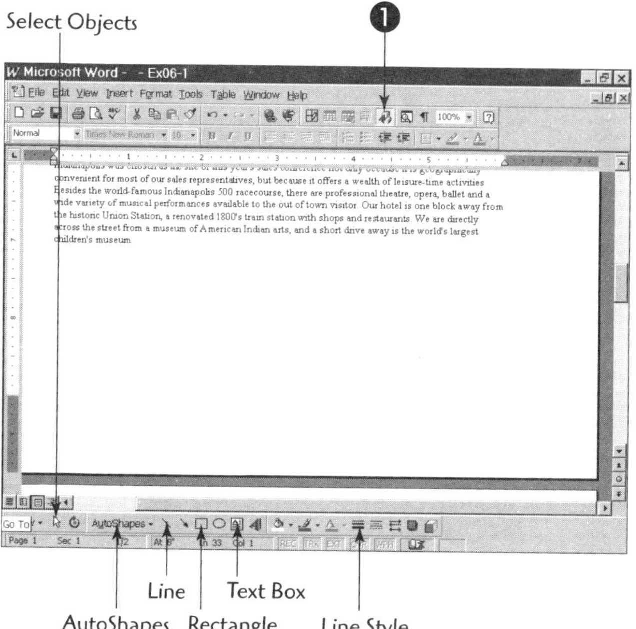

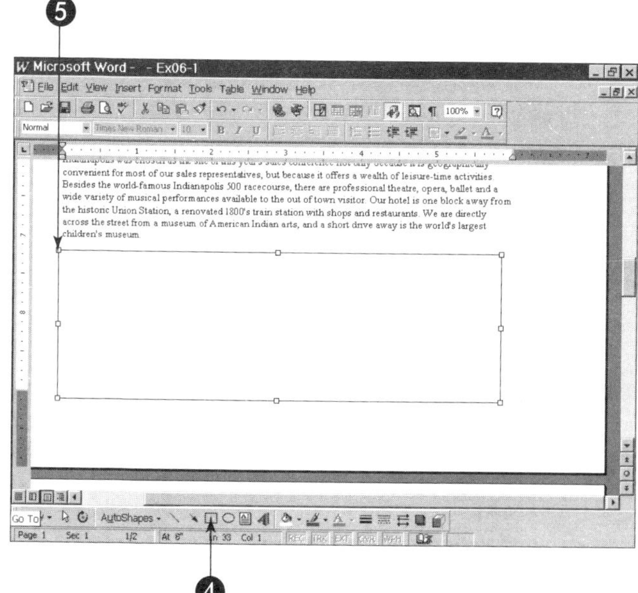

9. Repeat the preceding two steps, creating four rectangles placed approximately as shown.
10. Choose the Text Box button on the drawing toolbar.
11. Place your cursor in the rectangle in the middle of the drawing.
12. Type **Midland Hotel**.
13. Use the Text Box tool again to enter labels in each of the rectangles as shown at the bottom right.

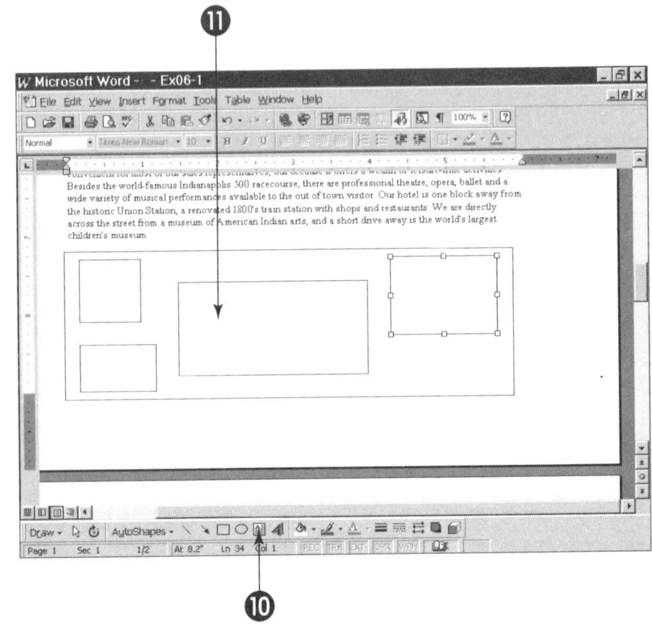

Text Boxes replace a feature called Frames from previous versions of Word for Windows. Basically, if you wanted to create text that you'd like to move around your page or position on a drawing, you used to have to place a frame around that text. In this latest version of Word, you should create any text you want to move around your page in a text box. However, if you ever open a Word document that uses frames from a previous version, Word 97 will support those frames, so you won't lose that formatting.

To indicate something that is just off the area of the map, you can place an arrow on the page. You can use the Arrow tool to do this, or draw a line and add arrows to it with the Arrow Style button.

14. Choose the Line button on the drawing toolbar.
15. Place your cursor at the bottom edge of the rectangle with the words *Midland Hotel* in it.
16. Drag down until the line reaches the bottom of the surrounding rectangle and release your mouse button.
17. With the line selected, choose the Arrow Style button on the drawing toolbar and select the second style from the top.

You have created an arrow like the one shown in the illustration. Now add a callout explaining what the arrow indicates. (A callout is simply a text element combined with a pointer that explains something in a drawing, such as a map or diagram.)

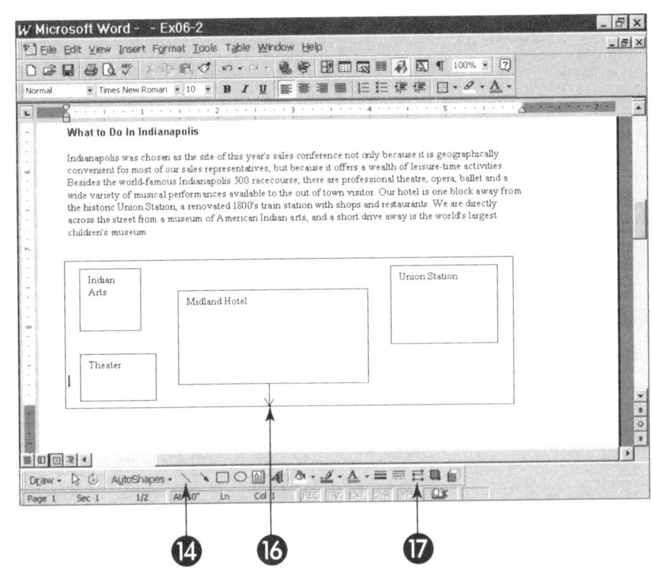

18. Choose the AutoShapes button on the drawing toolbar.
19. Select Callouts from the menu.
20. From the side menu that appears, select the callout style that is the second down on the left.
21. Place your mouse pointer in the middle of the line you've just drawn.
22. Press your left mouse button and drag to the right and down to draw a callout box.
23. Release your mouse button and the callout box is open, ready for you to enter text.
24. Select the Text Box tool.
25. Click in the callout box and type **To Museum, 3 miles**.
26. Click anywhere outside the drawing objects.

The map you've drawn should resemble the one in the illustration to the right.

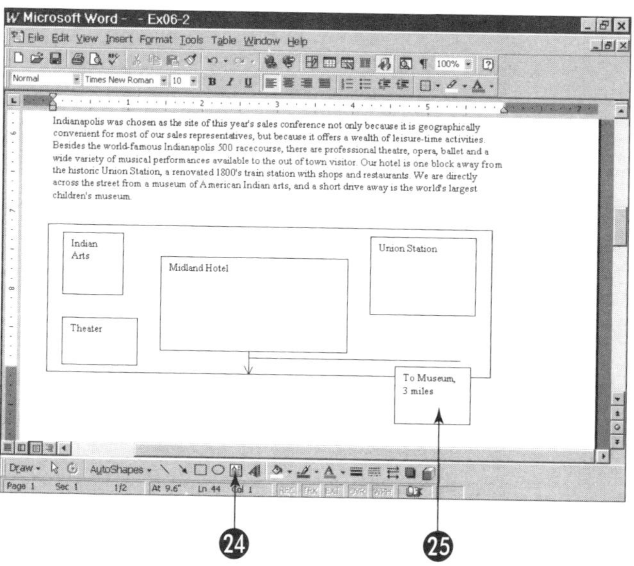

WORKING WITH OBJECTS

Once you've drawn or inserted objects (such as the map you've just created) or clip art pictures, you can make them fit your document by resizing them. You can also group objects together to make one large object; once you do, you can more easily apply formatting to it and move it around your page.

Resizing objects

There are several methods you can use to change the dimensions of objects in Word. This exercise starts by using the resizing handles that appear when an object is selected.

1. Scroll up your page until the clip art airplane you inserted earlier is visible.
2. Select the clip art object.

Resizing objects

VISUAL BONUS: THE DRAWING TOOLBAR

This Visual Bonus shows you the various tools available in Word for creating and editing drawings.

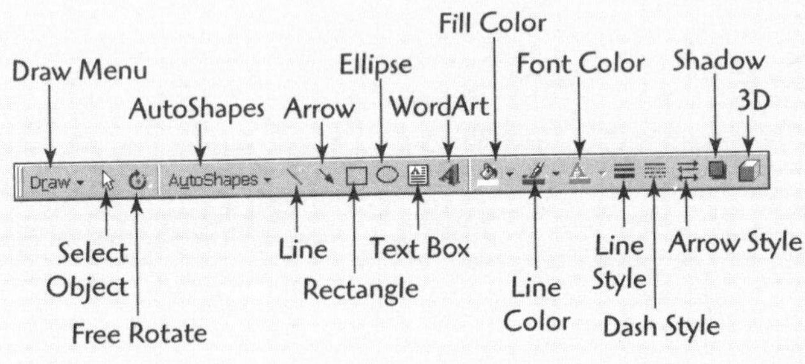

The Draw and AutoShapes menus are pop-up menus that contain multiple submenus.

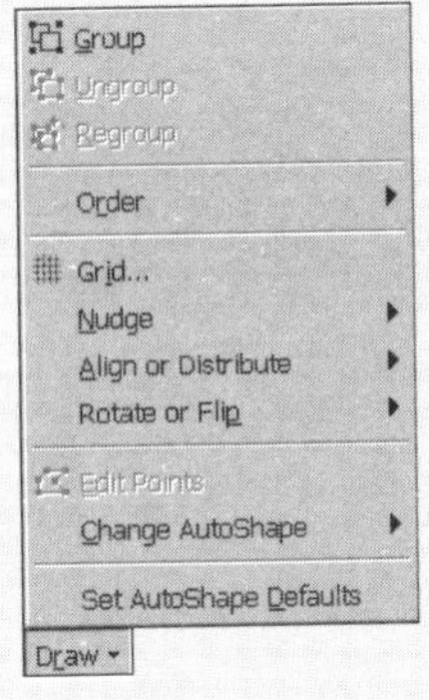

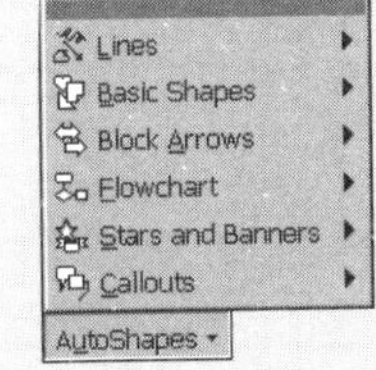

You can drag on the resizing handles (which appear when you select an object) to change the object's size.

❸ Click the top right-hand corner handle.

❹ Drag about half way to the left margin and release your mouse.

The object has become smaller, and may also have moved down within the lines of text that previously followed it.

❺ If necessary, move the clip art object up under the heading Travel.

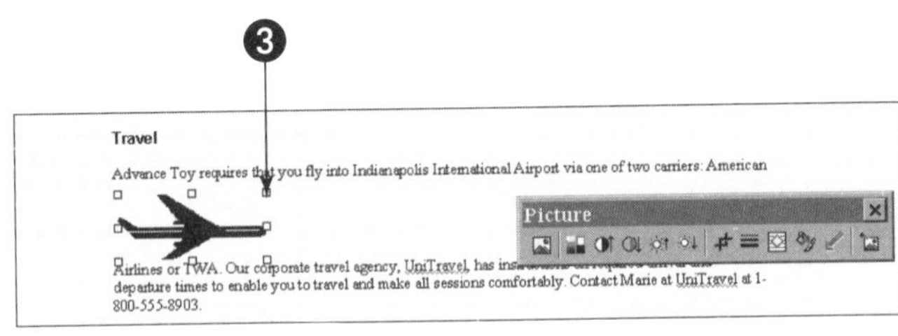

You can use resizing handles in three different ways:

- The *corner handles* enable you to resize objects in the direction in which you drag the handle, while maintaining the original proportions of the object.
- The *side and bottom handles* enable you to resize objects in the direction in which you drag the handle, but the original shape of the object will change proportion. If you use this method to resize a square, for example, you will probably end up with a rectangle. To retain the perfect square, you should use the first method.
- To resize the object in the direction of the center of the object while maintaining its original proportions hold down the Ctrl key while dragging.

Line resizing handles work similarly, but only two exist: one at each end of the line. You can select the line and when your mouse pointer appears as a two-headed arrow, drag the line toward or away from its center to shorten or lengthen it.

6. Move your mouse pointer over the side resizing handle on the right of the object until your pointer becomes a double arrow.
7. Hold your mouse button down and drag the side of the object to the right about half an inch.

   The object has become elongated beyond its original proportions. Although the left side stayed where it was, the right side (the side on which you dragged the resizing handle) moved out further to the right.
8. Save the file.

It's a good idea to save your files frequently while working on them. Drawings and clip art pictures sometimes take more memory than text files and can cause computers to crash or shut down. If that

happens you may lose your document or any changes you've made to it since you last saved it. Save often!

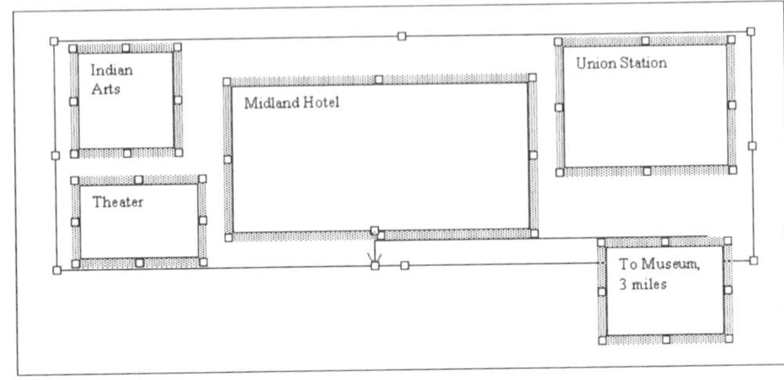

Grouping and ungrouping objects

If you've drawn several objects, or inserted several clip art objects, you may want to group them together. You group objects so you can move them as a single unit, making it quicker than moving several smaller ones, and also enabling you to retain the objects position relative to each other. For example, if you wanted to move the map you created earlier somewhere else in your document, it would be easiest to move the map as one object.

1. Scroll down in your document until you see the map you drew earlier.

Just in case you've lost your file or your place, you can open Ex06-2 which you copied from the accompanying CD-ROM; it contains all the changes you've made to Ex06-1 up to this point.

2. Click the large outside rectangle to select it.
3. Hold down Shift and click each of the other rectangles, the line, the callout object, and the text boxes in turn.
4. Release Shift. All the objects should be selected, with handles around each.
5. Select the Draw menu.
6. Choose Group.

   The multiple sets of handles have been replaced by a single set of handles as in the illustration to the right. The object can now be moved, resized, and even formatted as a single object.

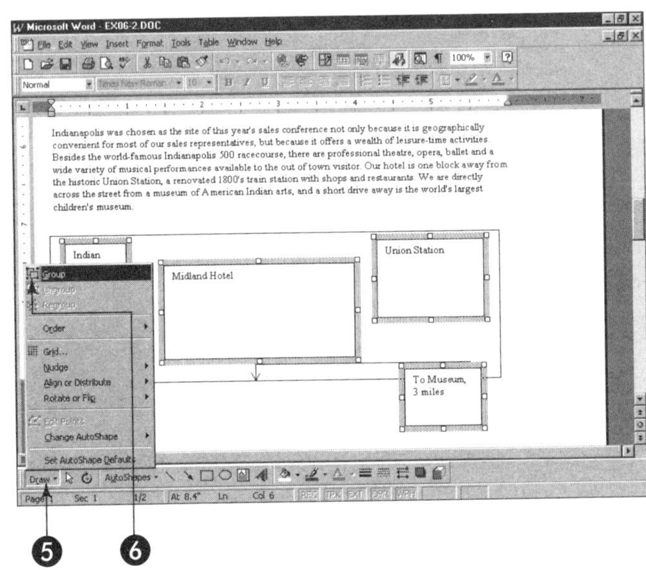

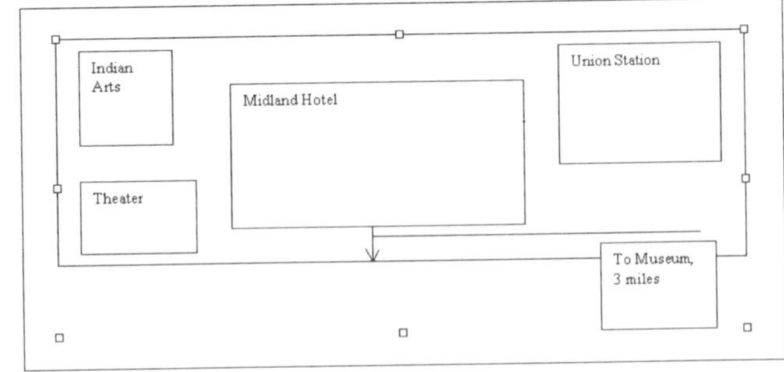

FORMATTING OBJECTS

The simple objects you draw in Word can be given even greater visual interest by using formatting tools to add color or patterns. In addition, you can use a variety of line style settings.

Of course, any color formatting you apply to a Word document will only be worthwhile if you have a color printer. However, even a black-and-white printer can take advantage of some patterns or colors to produce grayscale shading that give some interest and depth to your objects.

Formatting line styles

You already applied one line style when you added an arrow to the line you drew in the map. Try using some other formatting tools for lines.

1. Scroll to the top of the document.
2. Choose the Line tool.
3. Place your mouse pointer at the left margin between the *Advance Toy Company* WordArt object and the first line of text, *Annual Sales Conference.*
4. Click and drag horizontally, straight across your page to the right margin of the document.

   You have drawn a line that should look something like the one in the illustration at the top right.
5. With the line selected, choose the Line Style button. The pop-up menu appears.
6. Select the first of two $4\,^1/_2$ point double-line styles near the bottom of this menu.
7. Choose the Arrow Style button.
8. From the pop-up menu that appears, select the style with a diamond shape at both ends of the line.

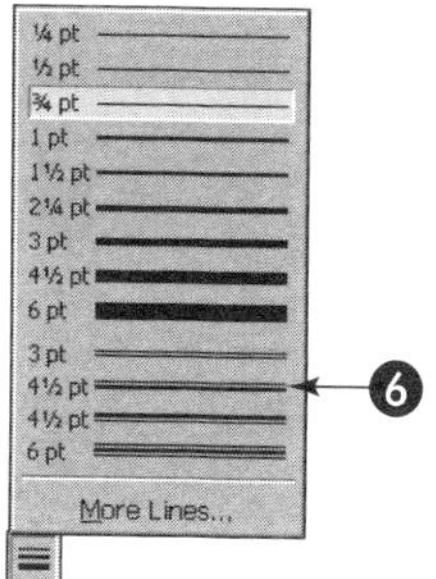

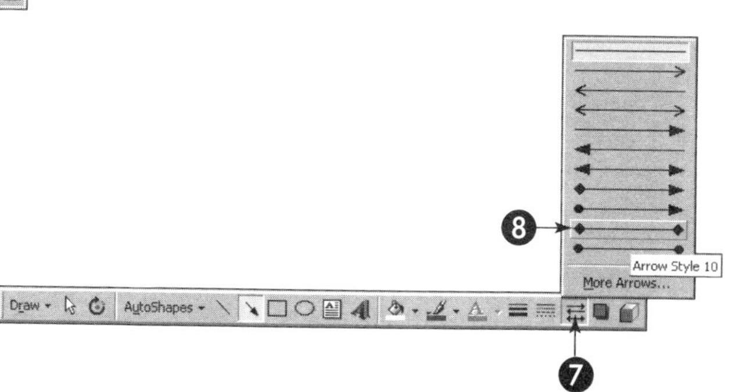

The line should now have a double-line style and the two-sided arrow style applied.

Advance Toy Company

Annual Sales Conference

April 18-21, 1999

Midland Hotel, Indianapolis, Indiana

Working with color and patterns

Objects can be filled with color and various patterns that are built right into Word.

1. Scroll down in your document until you see the map.
2. Select the map, which is a grouped object.
3. Click the arrow on the right side of the Fill Color button. A pop-up palette appears.
4. Click a light blue square.

   The entire object is filled with a blue color.
5. Click the Fill Color arrow again to display the same pop-up palette.
6. Select Fill Effects from the bottom of the palette.

   The Fill Effects dialog box appears. Here you can select from four tabs:

   - *Gradient* is used to apply a graduated lighting effect to your fill color.
   - *Texture* gives you access to textures such as marble or wood.
   - *Pattern* offers a palette of various patterns, such as stripes, brick, and thatch.
   - *Picture* enables you to select a picture file. With this tab you could use a picture of yourself that you have scanned into a computer file and make it the background fill for an object in your Word document.
7. Click the Gradient tab.
8. Choose the lower left choice in the preview squares labeled Variants.
9. Choose OK to apply the gradient to your map.

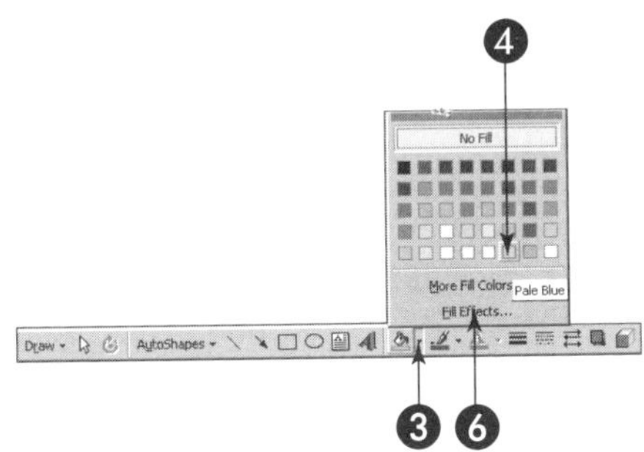

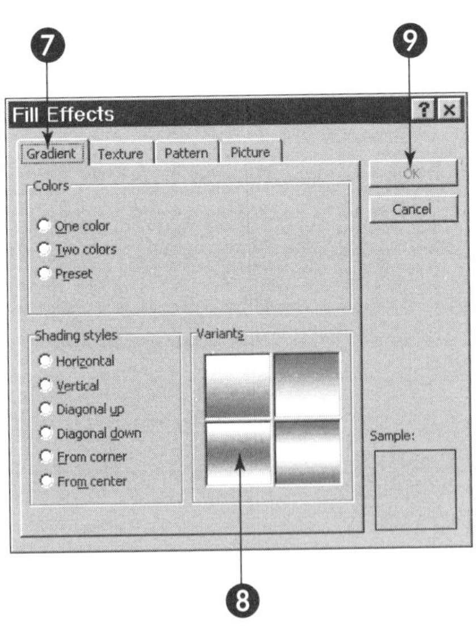

If you want to apply the same fill color to a series of objects quickly, Word makes it easy. Instead of choosing a color from the pop-up palette, click the part of the Fill Color tool with the small paint bucket icon on it, rather than the arrow next to it. This automatically applies the last selected color to any selected object.

USING BORDERS AND COLUMNS

To help set off text in your document and arrange text on your page, Word offers two features: Borders and Columns. The Borders feature places a visible edge or edges around selected text, setting that text off from other elements of the document. The Column feature enables you to flow the text of your document in two or more columns across the page, in a format similar to a newspaper or magazine.

Applying borders

Borders are very simple to apply, and can help organize and emphasize information in your document.

1. Select the words *Midland Hotel, Indianapolis, Indiana*, near the top of the document.

   You can use the Border tool in two ways: You can click the part of the tool that has an image of a border style on it to apply the last selected style, or you can use the arrow key on the right of the tool to choose among several variations on border styles.

2. Click the arrow on the right side of the border button.

   A drop-down list of border choices appears, as shown in the accompanying illustration. Using the choices on this list, you can surround the selected text with a full border, or place a border on any side of it.

3. Select the bottom-border style, which is the middle choice in the top row of the drop-down list.

Applying borders

The bottom border line appears, providing a neat divider between the heading text and the body text of the document. Now apply another border and format it.

4 Scroll to the bottom of the document.

5 Select the last heading, *See You There*, and the paragraph below that heading.

6 Click the arrow on the Border button.

7 Select the first option, the full border.

8 Click the Format menu.

9 Select Borders and Shading.

The Borders and Shading dialog box appears, as shown in the illustration at the bottom right. Here you can choose a setting for the border and format the line that forms the border for style, color, and width. You can also use the Shading tab to add a shade of gray to fill the inside of the border.

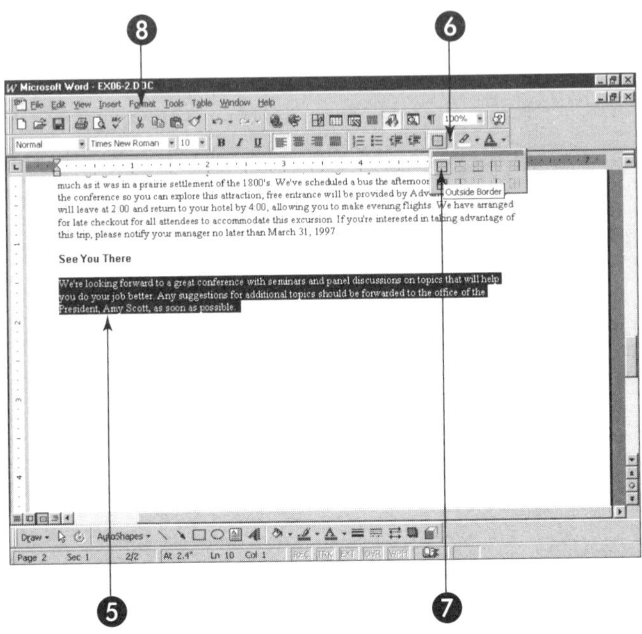

TIP

For an interesting text effect, you can apply a border to text, shade that border in black, then format the text to be white. This creates a reversed text effect — bright white against a black background.

10 Select the seventh style down in the Style list (the first double line style).

11 Select the Shadow option under Setting.

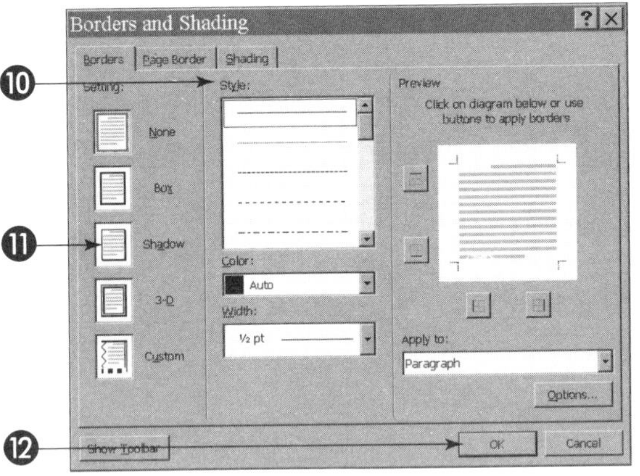

TIP

You can also use the Page Border tab of this dialog box to apply a border to the entire page.

12 Choose OK to see how your formatting looks.

Your full border should now look like the one in the illustration to the right.

See You There

We're looking forward to a great conference with seminars and panel discussions on topics that will help you do your job better. Any suggestions for additional topics should be forwarded to the office of the President, Amy Scott, as soon as possible.

Creating columns

You can use columns to create documents such as newsletters or book pages. The Column option controls the width and number of columns. Narrower column widths make your text easier to read. Often, creating columns enables you to fit more text on a single page. Columns work particularly well where you have several shorter topics making up a larger document, as with a newspaper.

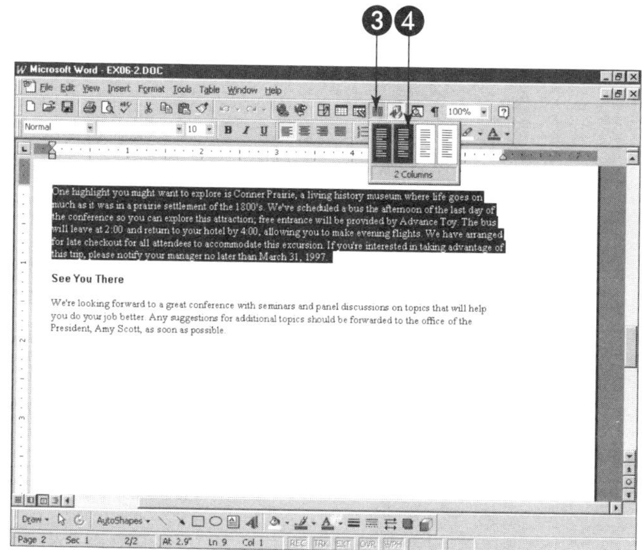

1. Scroll to the top of the document.
2. Select all the text from the first heading (*Reservations*) to the end of the paragraph ending in the text, *no later than March 31, 1997*.
3. Choose the Column button on the toolbar.

   A drop-down list appears with four columns across it. You can actually choose up to six columns by simply continuing to drag beyond the four-column display.
4. Click the first column in the drop-down list and drag across to highlight the first two column symbols; then release your mouse button.
5. Scroll to the top of your document, which should now look like the illustration to the right.

   If you move around your document to see how the columns look, you'll notice that the map, which is too wide to fit in a single column, is now off the printable area of the page. This problem is easily fixed by resizing the map object.
6. Select the map (remember, it's now one large object so you can resize all these drawings all at once).
7. Press the Ctrl key, and then click the top left corner and drag toward the center of the map to resize it to about half of its original size.
8. Select the newly sized map and drag it back into place within the text area.

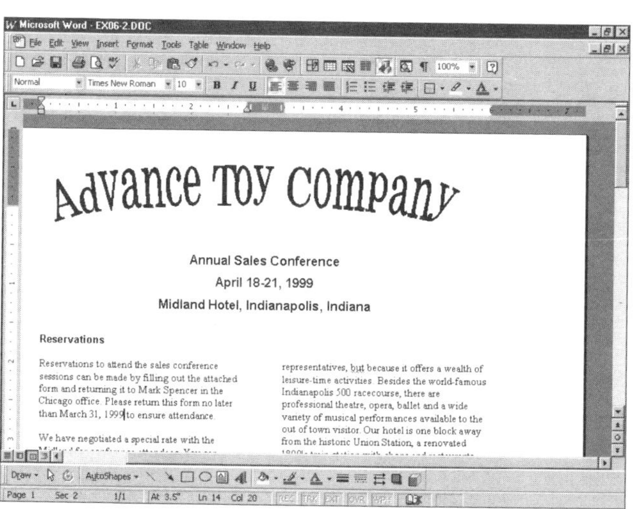

Rotating objects

In resizing objects with text boxes in them, you may find that some of the text in the text boxes is no longer visible. In this example, you could remedy that by ungrouping the objects (Drawing ➢ Ungroup), and then individually resizing each text box until all the text shows.

The illustration to the right gives you a view of your entire document. Here, you can see how your columns, borders, and added artwork have helped to enhance the look of the piece.

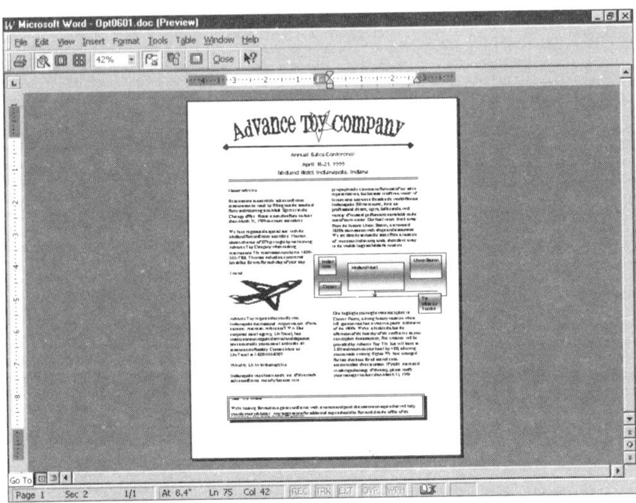

MANIPULATING OBJECTS

Once you create or insert objects into a Word document, you may want to manipulate those objects so they are placed at an angle on the page. You may even have more than one object; in that case, you may want to stack these objects on your page, making it appear that one is on top of another. Learning about rotating and prioritizing objects can help you do these tricks.

Rotating objects

Sometimes it's helpful to be able to rotate objects on a page, either to fit them into a proscribed space or to position them relative to other objects. You'll try that with a new object that you'll draw and then rotate. The object you'll work with is a star that is part of the Advance Toy Company's logo.

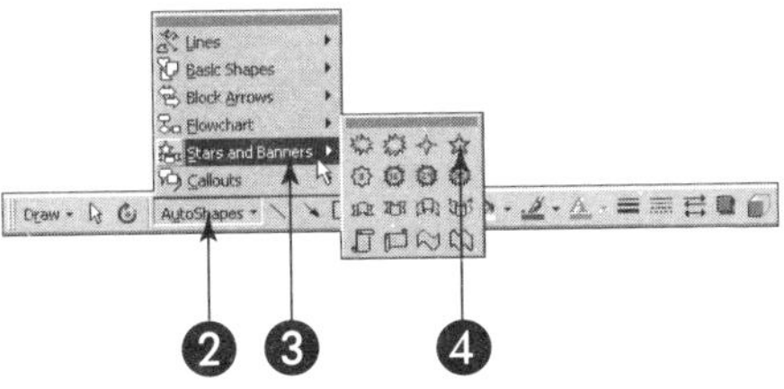

1. Move to the top of the document.
2. Select the AutoShapes button.
3. Choose Stars and Banners from the pop-up list.
4. In the side menu that appears, select the five-pointed star (top row, far right).
5. Draw this shape so it's about the same size and position as shown in the accompanying illustration.

Advance Toy Company
Annual Sales Conference
April 18-21, 1999
Midland Hotel, Indianapolis, Indiana

The star you've drawn is blocking one of the letters. You can rotate it slightly to avoid this overlap.

6. Select the star object.
7. Choose the Free Rotate button.

   Four round green handles appear around the shape. When you move your mouse pointer over one of these handles, your pointer changes to a curved arrow.

8. Drag on one of the handles to reposition the shape as shown in the illustration to the right.

   As you drag, a faint outline of the star appears, indicating its new position should you choose to release your mouse button at that point.

9. When the image of the rotated object is in the right position, release your mouse button.

Changing object priorities

One other skill you'll find useful when working with drawings is the ability to place objects in a certain order relative to each other. Just as you can have a stack of pages on your desk, with the top one covering those beneath it, you can order drawing objects to give the appearance that one is on top of another.

1. Select the star shape you've just rotated.
2. Drag on the top handle to resize as large as the letters of the company name.

   Notice that the star now covers up the text. To bring the text in front of the star, you need to change the order of the objects.

3. Select the star.
4. Click the Draw menu.
5. Select Order.
6. From the side menu that appears, select Send to Back.
7. Close the file without saving changes.

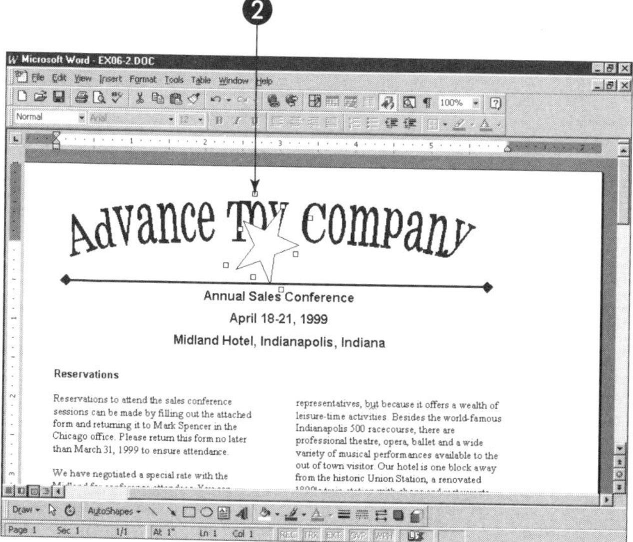

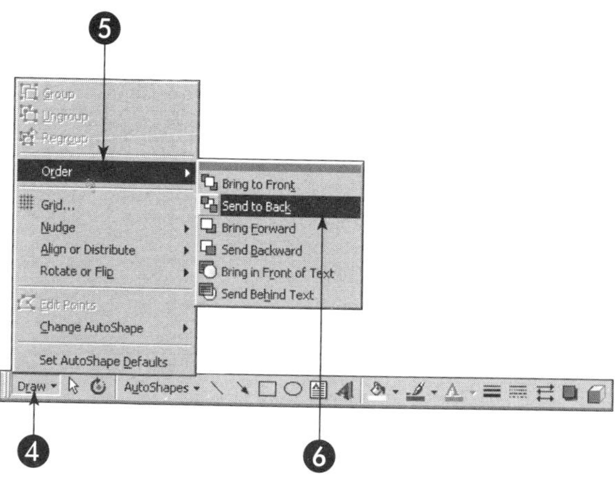

Skills challenge

Notice the third and fourth commands here, Bring Forward and Send Backward — not to be confused with the Send to Front and Send to Back commands. If you have several objects on top of each other, say four or five, the Bring Forward and Send Backward commands move the selected object forward or backward only one place in the stack. The Send to Front and Send to Back commands, on the other hand, move these objects all the way to the front or all the way to the back of the stack, respectively.

The star now appears behind the text.

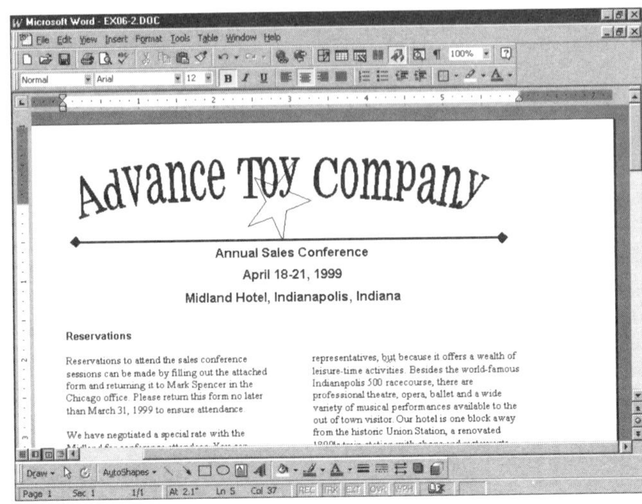

SKILLS CHALLENGE: CREATING A SIMPLE NEWSLETTER

In this Challenge Skills, you'll use the skills you've learned in this lesson for creating and editing objects to design a simple newsletter.

1. Open the file Ex06-3.
2. Delete the first heading, *Online Art.*
3. Select Insert ➢ Picture ➢ WordArt.

What is another way to open WordArt?

4. Choose the WordArt style in the fifth row from the left, fourth down.
5. Choose OK.
6. In the Edit WordArt Text dialog box, type **Online Art**.
7. Change the font to Brush Script MT (or any typeface you prefer if this one is not available).
8. Choose OK.
9. Move the WordArt object to the top left corner of the page.

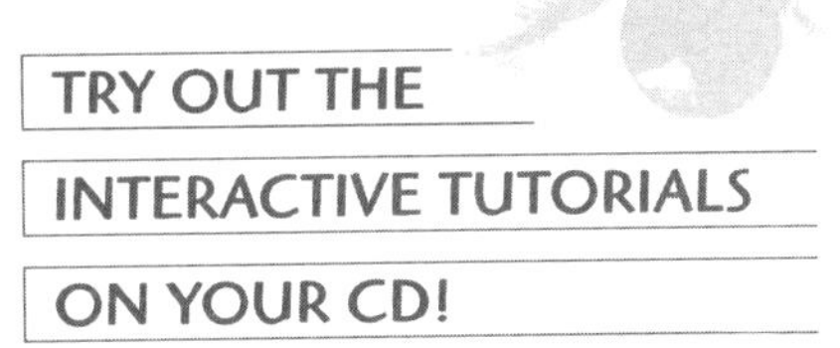

10. Adjust the text wrapping so the rest of the heading doesn't overlap the WordArt. (Hint: Select Format ➢ WordArt and use the top and bottom style from the Wrapping tab.)

    At this point, your newsletter should resemble the one in the accompanying illustration.

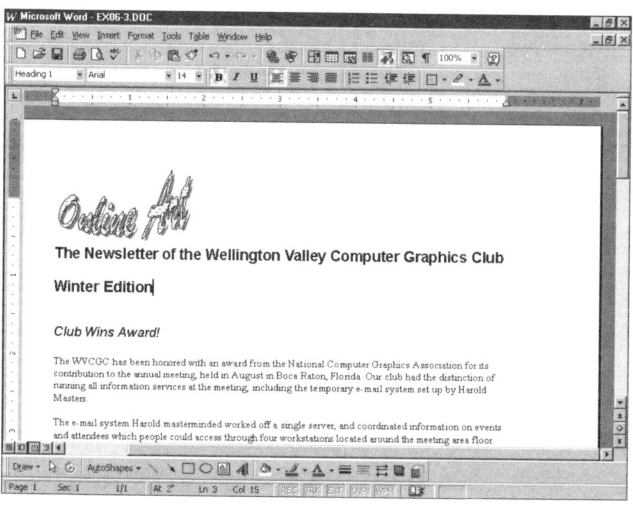

11. Put the text from the heading *Club Wins Award!* to the end of the document in two-column format.
12. Draw a line just under the words *Winter, 1997-98* from the left margin to the right margin.
13. Format the line with the 3pt double line style.
14. Place your cursor just at the end of the story about the Christmas party, on the first blank line after the sentence ending with the words *please return it promptly!*
15. Insert the clip art object in the Special Occasions category that contains party hats and streamers.

How can you add new clip art to the Clip Gallery?

16. Apply a full border to the heading and paragraph of text beginning *Meeting Announcement.*
17. Draw a rectangle about one inch wide and half an inch high centered beneath the *Meeting Announcement* paragraph.
18. Draw a larger AutoShape (about two-inch square) on top of the first one using the Basic Shape that looks like a rectangle with rounded corners (first row, second down).
19. Change the order of the two objects so the rectangle is in front.

    This drawing should look like the one in the illustration to the right and resemble a computer disk.

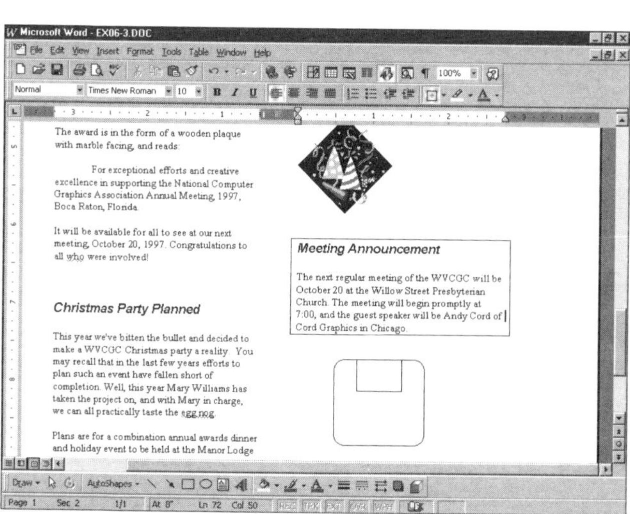

20. Create a text box within the rectangle portion of the drawing you've just created and type **WVCGC**.
21. Resize the text box (if necessary) to fit all this text on one line.
22. Select the AutoShape of the rectangle with rounded corners and add a pale gray fill color to it.

What other fill effects can be added to objects?

23 Group the various parts of your drawing so they become a single object.

24 Switch to Print Preview to see the newsletter you've created, which should resemble the one shown in the illustration to the right.

25 Close the file without saving changes.

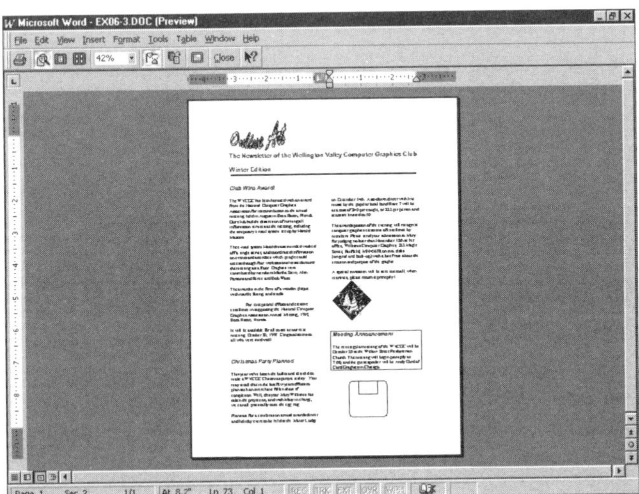

TROUBLESHOOTING

Using objects such as clip art and WordArt can really spice up a document. Using them takes a little practice, however. While you're practicing, you may run into some of the common challenges listed in the following table.

Problem	Solution
I put clip art in text and it covers the text.	Select the object, and then select Format ➢ Object and choose a text wrapping style that bypasses text.
How do I edit a WordArt object?	Select the object and use the tools on the floating toolbar that appears.
I drew three circles and want to move them all to the next page.	Use the Shift key to select all three, and then select Draw ➢ Group and move them as a single object.
I applied a border, but it just underlined the text.	You used a bottom border; click the arrow on the Border tool and choose another border style.

WRAP UP

You've picked up quite a bit of information in this lesson about adding elements to give your document visual punch:

- You learned how to insert clip art and WordArt and draw objects using Word's drawing toolbar.
- You formatted objects with styles and fill colors.
- You applied borders and created columns.
- Finally, you learned to manipulate objects in your document using the rotating, order, and group features of Word.

If you want more practice in these skills, try creating a newsletter for your own group or company. Have fun creating drawings and using elements such as clip art and WordArt to spice up your page.

In the next lesson, you'll learn how easy it is to create tables and charts in Word to help you convey a lot of data clearly and concisely.

Organizing Information with Tables and Charts

GOALS

In this lesson, you'll learn about features of Word such as the following:

- Inserting a table
- Adding text to a cell
- Selecting and aligning text
- Inserting rows and columns
- Adjusting the size of rows and columns
- Using Table AutoFormat
- Modifying borders, lines, and text
- Inserting a chart

Inserting a table

GET READY

To complete this lesson, you'll need the files Ex07-1 and Ex07-2 which you copied to your hard drive from the accompanying CD-ROM.

When you finish the exercises you'll have created the document shown on the facing page.

TRY OUT THE
INTERACTIVE TUTORIALS
ON YOUR CD!

CREATING A TABLE

Tables are a great way to show a lot of information in a concise, easy-to-read way. Tables are useful for statistics or lists of items you want to compare side by side. They provide a way for people to look up the intersection of two pieces of information: For example, every year you look up your net income in a row of a table and your tax due in a corresponding row (married, single, and so on). The IRS tax table is a perfect example of how a lot of information can be placed in a convenient format using a table (and those tables are much easier to read than the instructions themselves, right?).

Inserting a table

Creating a table is one of the easiest processes in Word.

1. Open the file Ex07-1.

   This is a memo giving the results of a survey of wine consumption in the United States. The results of a product testing for three products has to be summarized in this memo. A table is the perfect way to present this information.

2. Place your cursor on the blank line beneath the heading Product Testing Results.

3. Choose the Insert Table button on the Standard toolbar.

   A drop-down palette of squares appears.

4. Click the first square and drag your mouse to highlight four rows of squares down and four columns over.

   The squares in the Insert Table palette represent cells. A *cell* is a single unit of a table, representing the intersection of a column and row. When you have selected a certain number of cells and

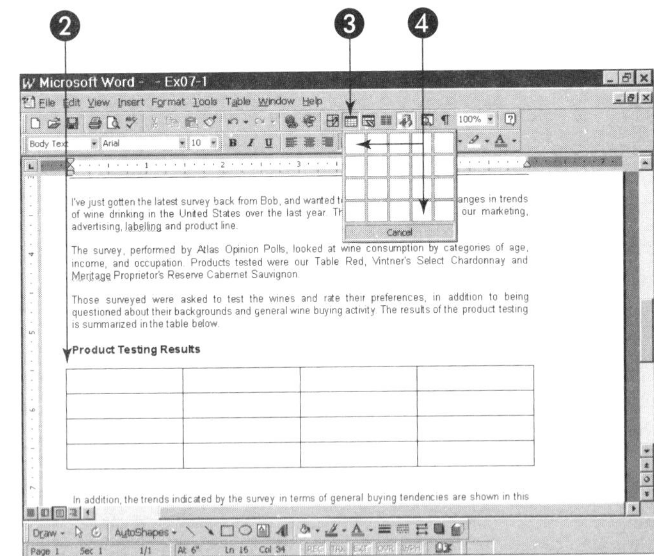

Meritage Vintners

Memo

To: Mary Lou Pachino
From: Roger Marx
Date: October 17, 1999
Re: Trends in Wine Consumption

I've just gotten the latest survey back from Bob, and wanted to share with you some changes in trends of wine drinking in the United States over the last year. These trends could impact our marketing, advertising, labeling and product line.

The results of the product testing is summarized in the table below. The table shows the average score on a scale of 1-100 for each product.

Product Testing Results

MERITAGE VINTNERS PRODUCT TESTING AUGUST, 1999				
Product Name	Acidity	Flavor	Nose	Body
Table Red	45	67	55	48
Vintner's Chardonnay	58	77	80	79
Meritage Reserve	88	89	89	92

In addition, the trends indicated by the survey are shown in this chart.

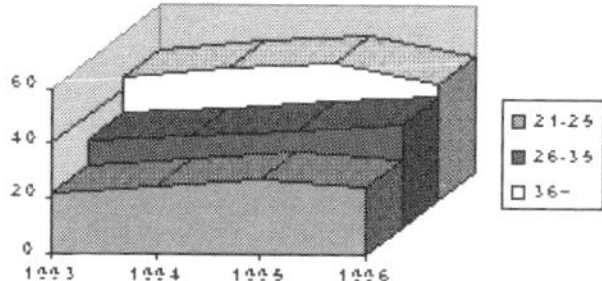

Page 1

released your mouse button, a blank table consisting of four rows and four columns appears at the cursor.

You can also create a table by selecting Table ➢ Draw Table and using the tools on the Tables and Borders toolbar to draw a table and each of the rows and columns in it. You'll see this toolbar later; however, the Insert Table button is the simplest way to actually create a new table.

5. Save your file with the new name **Wine** (File ➢ Save As).

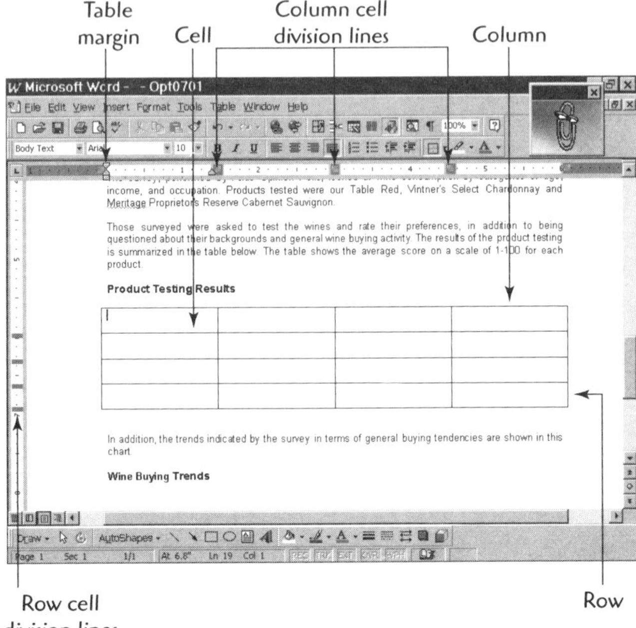

Adding text to a cell

Although easy to create, what good is an empty table? What you need now is some text in the individual cells.

1. Place your cursor in the top left cell (if it's not already there).
2. Type **Product Name**.
3. Press TAB to move to the next cell to the right.
4. Type **Acidity**.

   Notice that text typed in cells of a table aligns to the left by default; although you can change that, as you will see shortly.

5. Press Tab again to move to the next cell to the right.

You can also move back one cell at a time using Shift + Tab.

6. Type **Flavor**.
7. Press your right arrow, which is another way to move to the next cell to the right.
8. Type **Body**.
9. Click in the second cell down on the far left of the table.

⑩ Type **Table Red**.

⑪ Press the down arrow on your keyboard to move down one cell.

⑫ Type **Vintner's Chardonnay**.

⑬ Using the text shown in the illustration to the right, use your Tab key and arrow keys to move to the remaining blank cells and enter the rest of the text.

Product Testing Results

Product Name	Acidity	Flavor	Body
Table Red	45	67	48
Vintner's Chardonnay	58	77	79
Meritage Reserve	88	89	92

TIP *If you make a mistake while typing in a table cell, simply use the Backspace or Delete key to correct it.*

Selecting and aligning text

Text in tables can be formatted in all the ways that regular Word text can be formatted. Aligning text in a table is only slightly different, in that alignment isn't relative to the sides of the page, but to the sides of the cell in which the text is located. Practice selecting text in a table, and then aligning the headings of our table to be centered. You can select single cells, whole rows, or whole columns in a table.

❶ Place your pointer to the left of the row that begins *Table Red.*

Your pointer should change to a left-facing arrow when it is over the selection bar that runs along the left margin.

❷ Click in the selection bar; the entire row is highlighted.

❸ Click outside of the table to deselect the row.

❹ Move your mouse pointer over the column with the word *Acidity* in the first cell.

Your mouse pointer becomes a small, black, downward-facing arrow, as in the illustration.

❺ Click to select the column.

❻ Move your pointer to the cell that contains the number 48 until the pointer becomes a white, left-facing arrow.

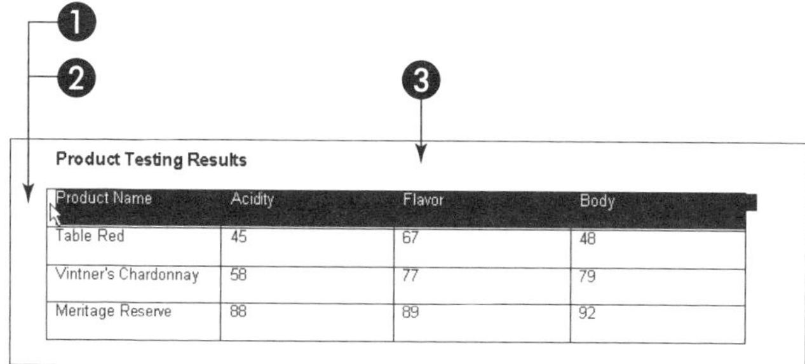

Product Testing Results

Product Name	Acidity	Flavor	Body
Table Red	45	67	48
Vintner's Chardonnay	58	77	79
Meritage Reserve	88	89	92

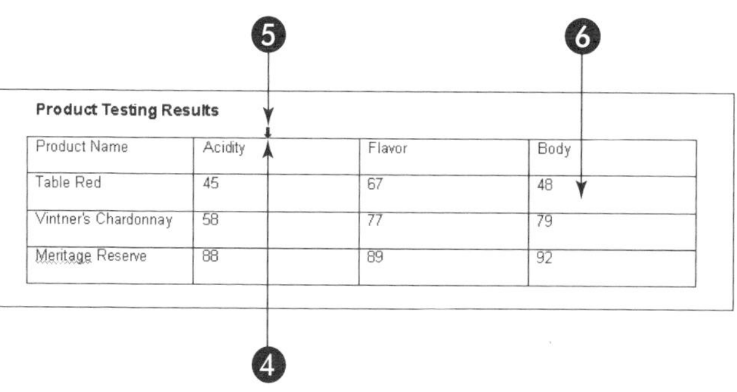

Product Testing Results

Product Name	Acidity	Flavor	Body
Table Red	45	67	48
Vintner's Chardonnay	58	77	79
Meritage Reserve	88	89	92

7. Click to select the single cell.

   Okay, now that you've got the hang of selecting the various pieces of a table, you can work on aligning the headings.

8. Select the top row starting with the cell containing the words *Product Name.* (Hint: Use the selection bar on the left edge of your page.)

9. Choose the Center button on the Formatting toolbar.

   The text is centered within each cell.

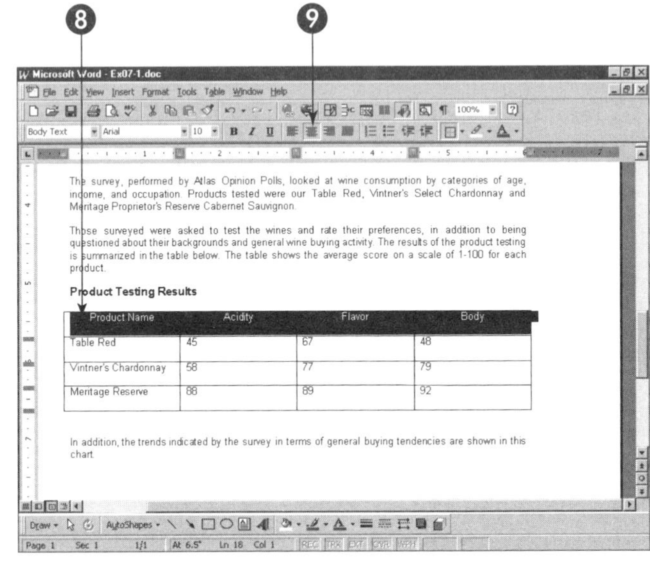

Inserting rows and columns

You are not limited to creating tables with four rows and four columns. You can add or delete as many rows and columns as you like.

1. Select the column that is headed by the cell containing the word *Body.*

2. Click the Table menu.

3. Select Insert Columns.

   A new blank column appears to the left of the column you selected when you chose the Insert Column command. If you select a column in your table, the command available in the Table menu is Insert Column; likewise, if you select a row, the command changes to Insert Row. Try using the Table and Borders toolbar to add a row to the table.

4. Select Table.

5. Choose Draw Table.

   The Tables and Borders toolbar appears. You can use the tools in this toolbar to draw a single cell to a whole table. You can also format elements of your table with these tools.

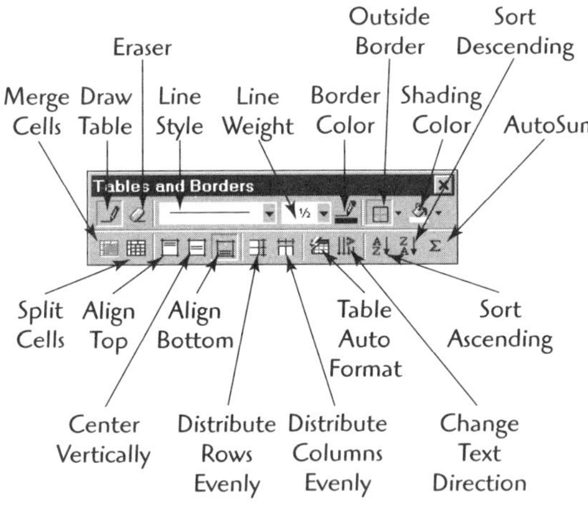

6. Select the Draw Table tool.

7. Place your pointer above the table, near the upper-left corner of it.

8. Click and drag to draw a new row at the top of the table that runs the length of the current rows.

   The row that appears is empty, with no column dividers in it. You can create dividers within a row or column that you draw in this way by simply drawing in the lines. You use this row for a table title, so no dividers are necessary.

9. Type **Meritage Vintners Product Testing**.

10. Press Enter.

    Notice that the row expands to accommodate the second line of text you've entered.

11. Type **August, 1996**.

12. Move your poiner to the first blank cell of the column you inserted earlier.

13. Type **Nose**.

14. Enter the numbers shown in the following illustration.

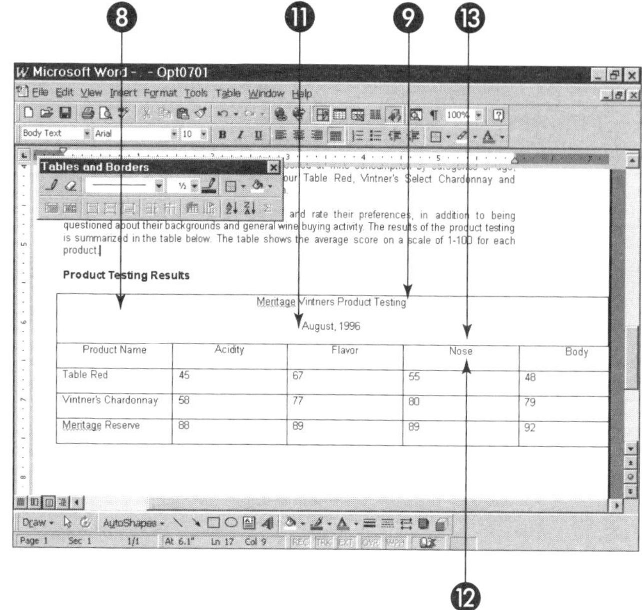

Adjusting row and column size

Notice that the table is now too wide to fit within the margins of the memo. To make it fit, you can adjust the width of the columns so they don't take up so much space. There are two ways to do this: Use your mouse to move column dividers, or use the Table menu. Try both.

1. Select the two columns with the headings *Product Name* and *Acidity*.

2. Move your pointer to the dividing line between these two columns.

   Your pointer should appear as two lines with arrows pointing off to each side, as in the following illustration.

3. Drag your mouse slightly to the left.

   As you drag, you will see a dotted line indicating the new location of the line if you release the mouse button at that point. Make sure to move this dotted line no further to the left than the last letter of the longest line of text in the first column.

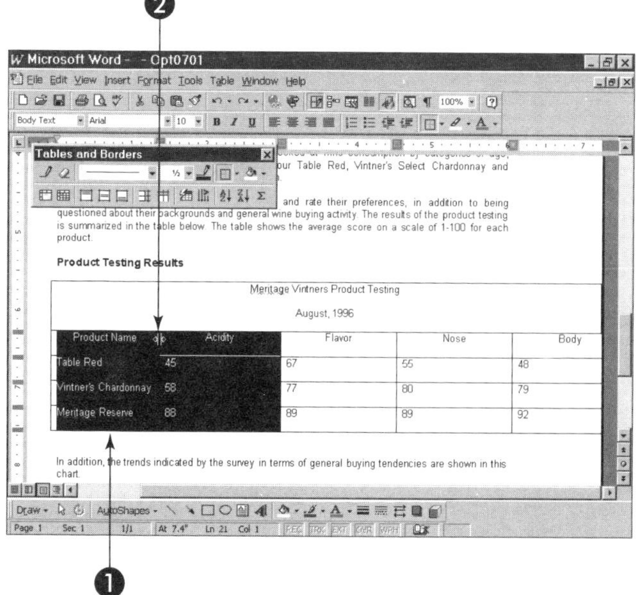

Adjusting row and column size

4. Release your mouse button.

   The first column has been made slightly narrower than the other columns in the table. Use the menu command to change the width of the remaining columns.

5. Select the three remaining columns.
6. Click the Table menu.
7. Select Cell Height and Width.

   The Cell Height and Width dialog box appears. Here you can set exact measurements for rows and columns.

8. Choose the Column tab.

   The Column tab is shown in the following illustration.

9. Use the arrows in the *Width of columns* field to change the measurement to 1 inch.
10. Choose OK.

    The four columns have now adjusted, but what about that top row? It's still too wide. Use the mouse to adjust it.

11. Move your mouse pointer to the far right side of the top row, until your pointer becomes two lines with two arrows.
12. Click and drag the right edge of the top row until the dotted line lines up with the right edge of all the other rows.
13. Release your mouse button and your table should look like the illustration to the right.

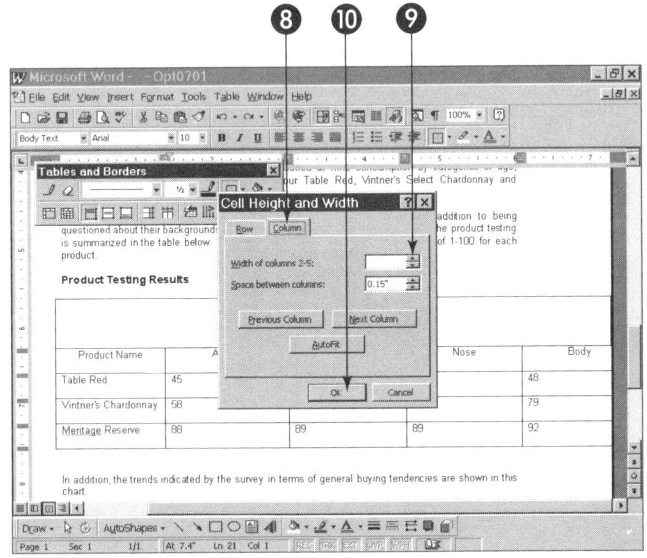

Meritage Vintners Product Testing August, 1996				
Product Name	Acidity	Flavor	Nose	Body
Table Red	45	67	55	48
Vintner's Chardonnay	58	77	80	79
Meritage Reserve	88	89	89	92

FORMATTING A TABLE

You can format each cell of your table just as you would any text in a Word document — using different fonts, font sizes, and effects such as bold or italic. However there is a built-in feature called Table AutoFormat that makes formatting tables much simpler.

Using Table AutoFormat

You could use various formatting tools to change the style of the text in your table, to add or change the thickness of borders, and apply a background color to cells. Or you can let Word do all that for you with its AutoFormat feature.

1. Place your cursor anywhere within the table.
2. Click the Table menu.
3. Select Table AutoFormat.

   The Table AutoFormat dialog box appears.

4. Select the Colorful 2 Format.

   Notice in the preview of the format that the top row is shaded and there are no dividing lines between rows and columns.

5. Scroll down the *Format* list.
6. Select Grid 3.

   This time the preview shows a format with a shaded top column, and lines between columns, but not rows. You can move around the list of AutoFormats in this way and use its preview feature to see the variety of styles built into AutoFormat. For now, try out one more style and apply it.

7. Select the Classic 2 format.
8. Choose OK to apply the format.

If there are any formatting elements you'd like to change, you can use the check boxes under the section labeled Formats to apply them. For example, if you'd rather keep the font you have now, deselect the Font *check box and the font associated with the AutoFormat won't affect your text.*

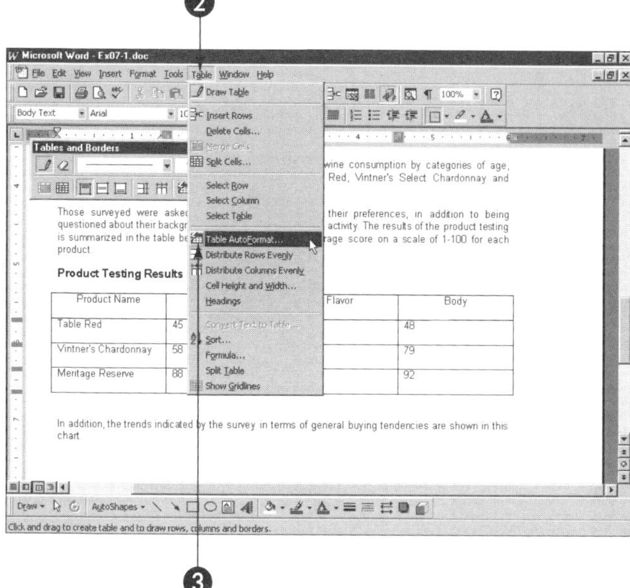

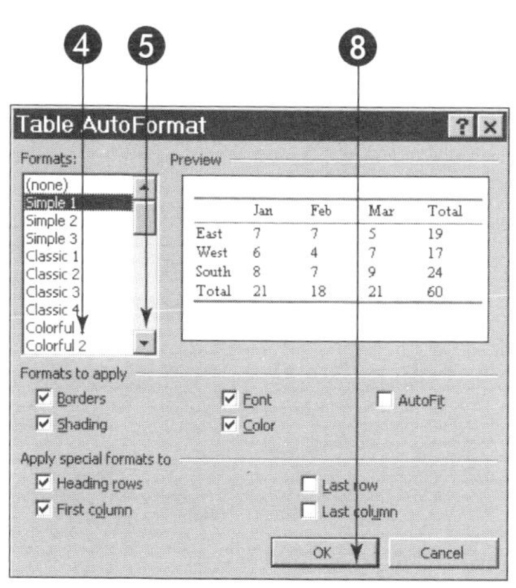

Modifying borders, lines, and text

Of course, you can modify this format in any way you like. In the steps that follow, you apply a full border using the tools on the Tables and Borders toolbar and add a dividing line between two columns in the table.

1. Select the entire table.
2. Select the Border tool.

   A drop-down list appears with a choice of border styles.

3. Click the first border style (the full border).

   Now add a dividing line between the product names and the rankings.

4. Select the Draw Table tool.
5. Place your cursor between the words *Product Name* and *Acidity.*
6. Draw a line between the first column and second column. Be careful not to touch any of the text in the columns.

   Finally, to make the title of the table stand out, format that text differently.

7. Click and drag to select the text in the title (the top row).
8. Select Format.
9. Select Font.
10. Using the settings in the Font dialog box that appears, change the text to be Small caps, Times New Roman font, and 12 point.
11. Choose OK to save these settings.
12. Select Format.
13. Select Paragraph.
14. Change the Spacing After to 6 point.

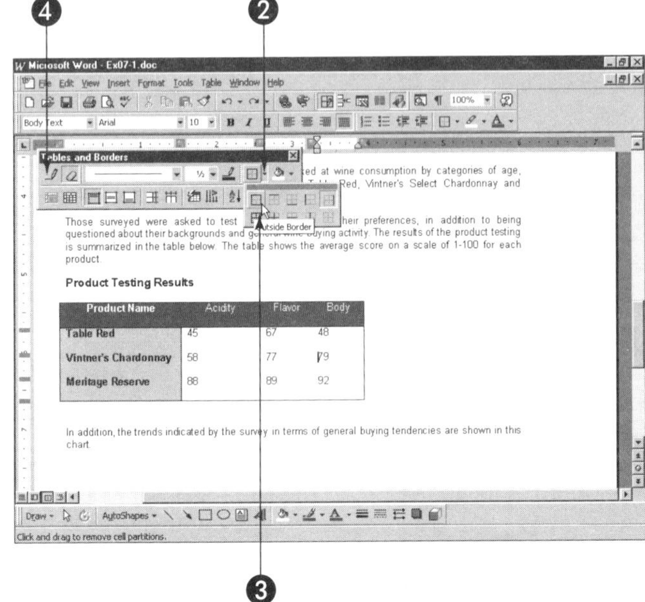

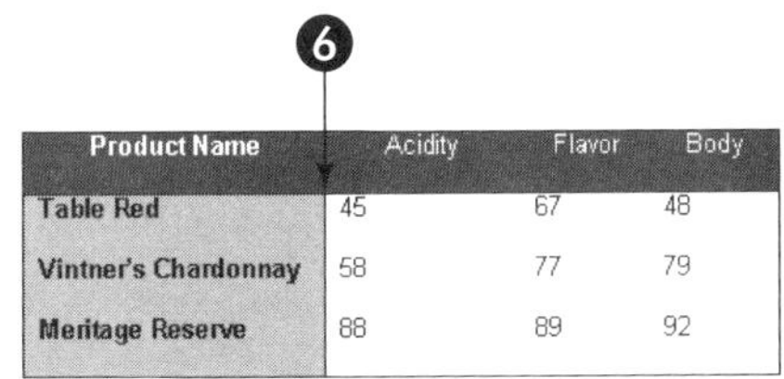

Product Name	Acidity	Flavor	Body
Table Red	45	67	48
Vintner's Chardonnay	58	77	79
Meritage Reserve	88	89	92

⓯ Choose OK.

You should now have a table like the one in the illustration to the right.

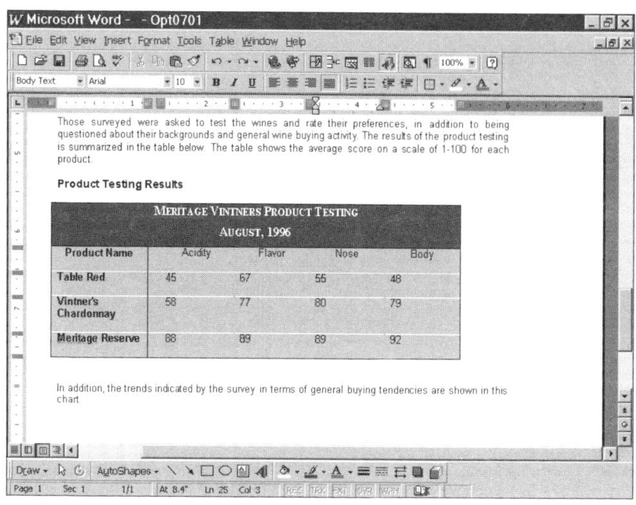

CREATING A CHART

A chart is a visual representation of numerical data. Charts come in many forms: bar charts, pie charts, line charts, and so on. Whatever style you select, the actual chart elements (bars, pie wedges, lines, for example) correspond to values in a spreadsheet of rows and columns. Charts are a great way to help your reader understand complex information quickly; with a chart, it's easy to spot overall trends and relationships among sets of data which might not be readily apparent from rows and columns of numbers.

There are actually two ways to create a chart in Word. One is inserting an Excel chart, and you can learn more about creating and formatting Excel charts in Lesson 13. The other method uses an applet called Microsoft Graph 97. This charting program enables you to type in information in a simple spreadsheet-like interface, and then insert a chart based on that data into your Word document. You use this method in this lesson.

Inserting a chart

In this exercise, you'll use the applet Microsoft Graph 97 to create a simple chart.

❶ Place your cursor at the end of the memo, after the last sentence.

❷ Press Enter twice.

❸ Select Insert.

❹ Select Object.

❺ Select Microsoft Graph 97 Chart in the Object Type list.

❻ Click OK.

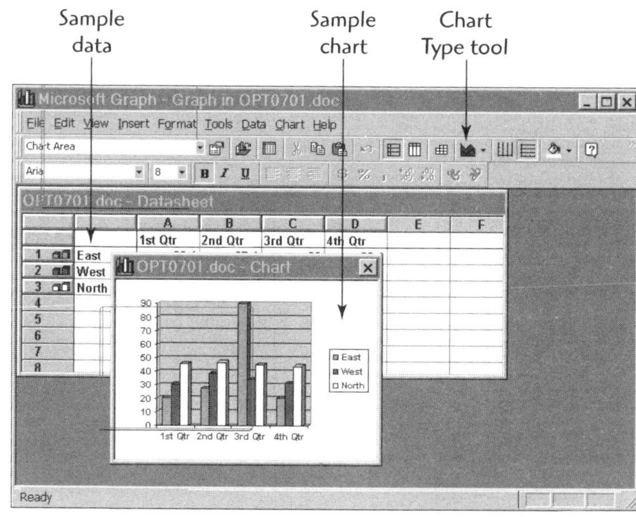

Inserting a chart

❼ Enter the information in Table 7-1 on the spreadsheet replacing the sample data.

TABLE 7-1 CHART DATA TO ENTER

	1993	1994	1995	1996
21-25	22	25	27.3	25
26-35	31	33	35	38
36+	44	47	49	42

TIP

Changing a table you create to a chart is easy to do. Select the portion of your table you want to turn into a chart, and then select Insert ➢ Object and format the chart.

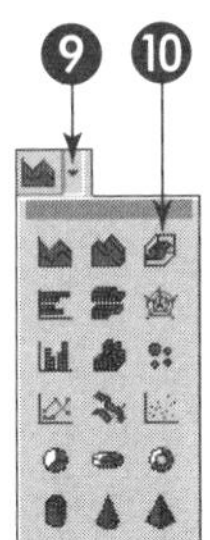

❽ Select the window containing the preview of the chart.

❾ Click the arrow on the right side of the Chart Type tool on the toolbar.

The choices of chart types appear.

You can try selecting different chart styles here and see how they appear in the chart preview window. Bar charts, line charts, cylinder, pyramid, and area charts are useful for showing overall trends. Pie charts are good for comparing parts of a whole, such as the mix of occupations in an overall population. Scatter and radar charts compare several sets of data.

❿ Select the 3D Area chart style.

The chart preview in the following illustration appears. The *y* axis labels (the age range labels) make it rather cluttered. Just get rid of those.

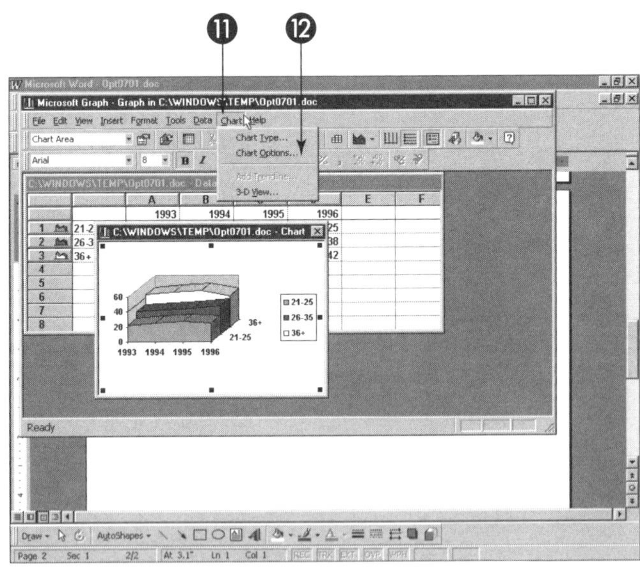

⓫ Select Chart.

⓬ Select Chart Options.

⓭ Select the Axes tab of the Chart Options dialog box.

⓮ Click the check box labeled *Series (y) axis* to deselect it.

⑮ Choose OK.

TIP

If you want to make any changes to your chart you can simply double-click it to bring up the Microsoft Graph 97 window. For more detailed information about formatting charts, see Lesson 13.

⑯ Use the scroll bar to view both pages of the document.

⑰ Click back in the Word document screen to place the chart in your memo.

⑱ Choose the Print Preview button.

The preview shown in the figure to the right appears, displaying the chart and table elements you've just created.

⑲ Choose the Close button to close Print Preview.

⑳ Select File ➢ Close and save the file when prompted by Word.

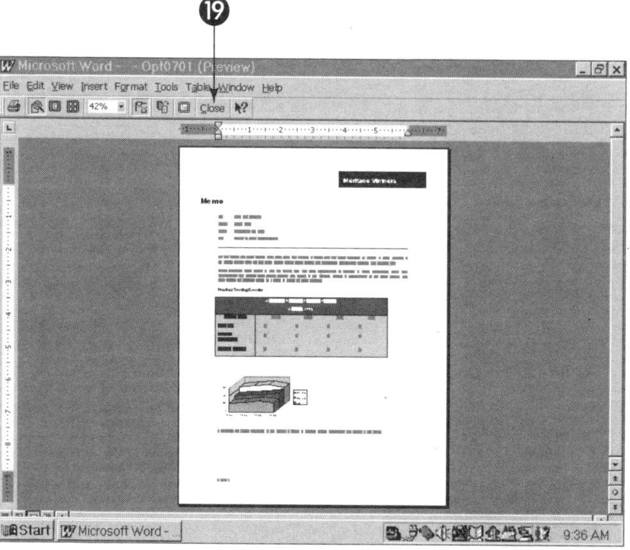

VISUAL BONUS: CHART TYPES

Chart types work best with different kinds of data. Here are some ideas for how to use them.

Bar charts show trends over time, such as sales per region over the course of a year.

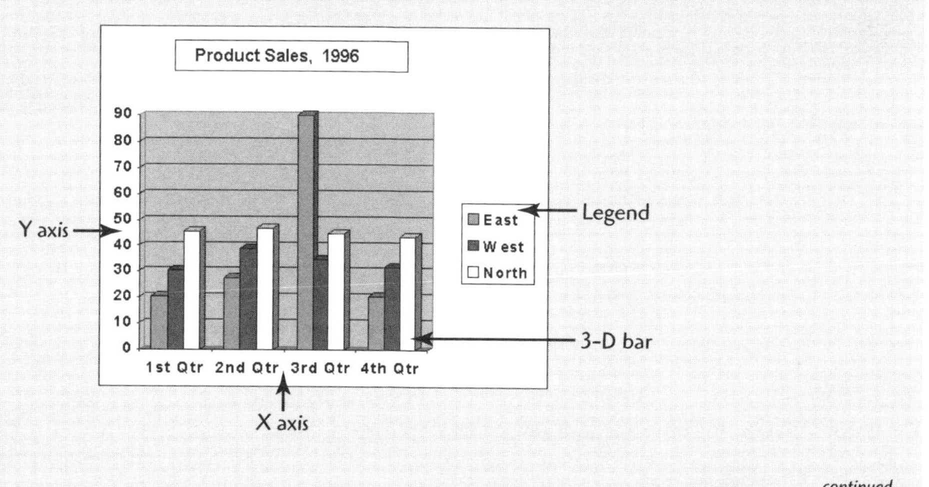

continued

Skills challenge

VISUAL BONUS: CHART TYPES *(continued)*

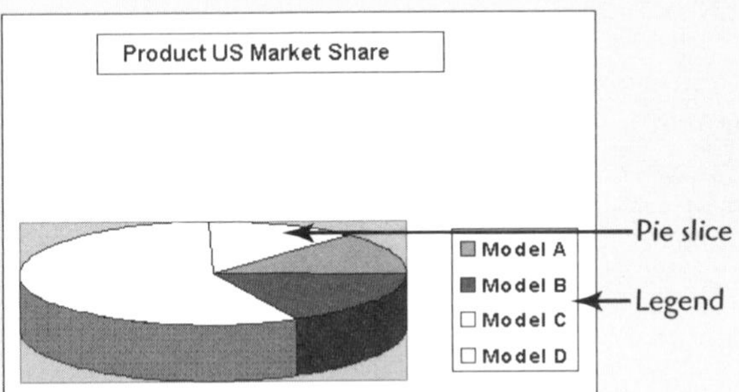

Pie charts display parts of a whole, such as percentages of market share.

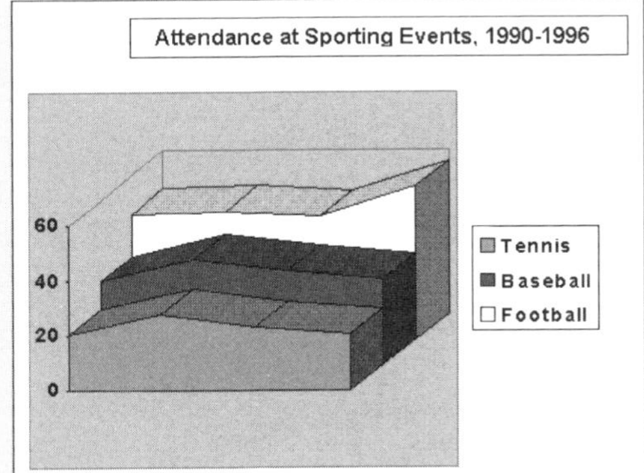

Area charts, whether in the shape of a block, pyramid, or cylinder, compare trends in different data sets.

SKILLS CHALLENGE: BUILDING A TABLE AND CHART

TRY OUT THE INTERACTIVE TUTORIALS ON YOUR CD!

Now that you know about putting information in its place with tables and charts, it's time for that last bit of practice.

1. Open the file Ex07-2.
2. Place your cursor on the first blank line at the end of the memo.

Skills challenge

3. Create a table with three columns and three rows.

   1 *Name two ways to create a table.*

4. Add one row to the table.
5. Enter this text in the first cell: **Genre**.
6. Move to the next cell in the top row.
7. Type **1985**.
8. Move to the far right cell in the top row.
9. Type **1995**.
10. In the column headed Genre, enter these three items: **Mystery**, **Romance**, **and Biography**.
11. Complete the rest of the information shown in the illustration.

Genre	1985	1995
Mystery	35%	45%
Romance	40%	37%
Biography	22%	18%

12. Change the width of the columns to 1 inch.

   2 *Name two ways to change column or row size.*

13. Format the table with the Columns 5 format.
14. Insert a column to the left of the column headed *1985*.
15. Type a heading of **1980**, and then below it, three entries of **39**, **21**, and **40**.

How would you move the entire table to the right so it lines up with the left edge of the text in the memo?

16. Place your cursor beneath the table and press ENTER.
17. Insert a Microsoft Graph object.

Troubleshooting

18. Enter the information for 1995 from the table in the data sheet, as shown in the illustration, and format it as a 3D pie chart. (Hint: To delete the rows you don't need from the sample data, select them, and then select Edit ➢ Clear ➢ Contents.)

19. Click back on the Word document to display the final document.

20. Click the chart once and move it to the center of your memo.

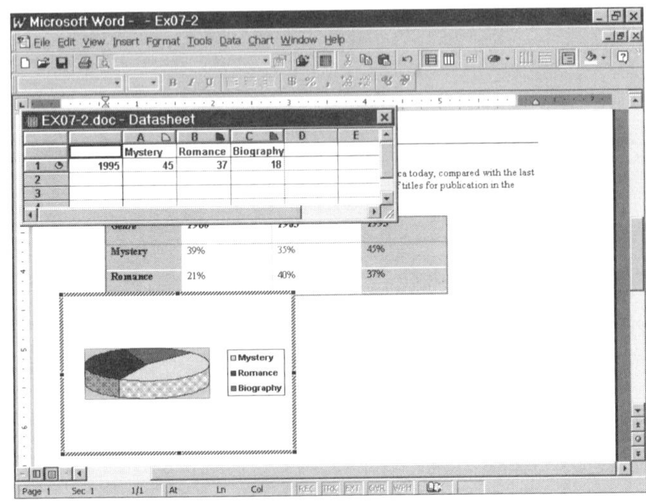

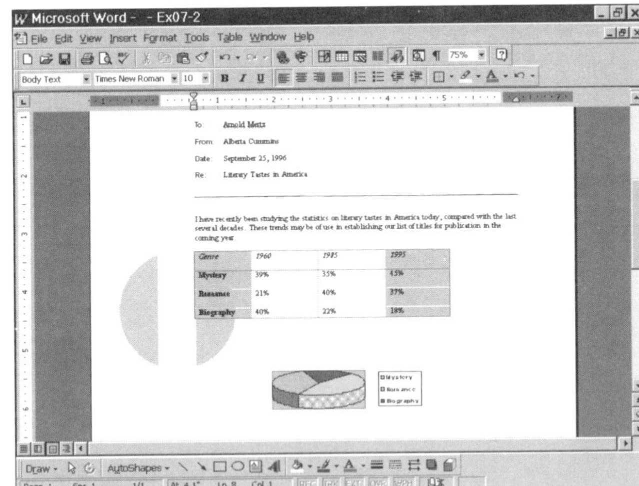

TROUBLESHOOTING

Table your frustrations — you're doing a great job! However, some challenges you might encounter using tables and charts are addressed here to keep you going.

Problem	Solution
I try to make a column narrow by dragging the cursor, but only one row changes size.	Be sure to select the whole column before dragging the dividing line, or drag the Column Division Line on the ruler instead.
I did some resizing of my columns but now they're all different sizes.	Use the Distribute Columns Evenly tool on the Tables and Borders toolbar. (There's also a Distribute Rows Evenly tool.)
I entered the data for my bar chart, but I want the information on the x-axis to go on the y-axis and vice versa.	If your chart data doesn't read quite right, try selecting Data, and switching from Series in Columns to Series in Rows.

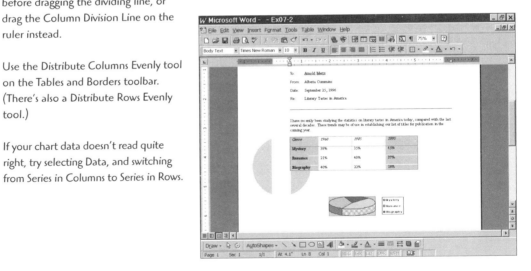

WRAP UP

In this lesson, you've picked up a lot about creating tables and charts, including the following:

- Inserting a table or chart into your document
- Entering data in cells
- Formatting elements of your table and chart

If you'd like a practice project for revisiting these features, try creating a table about your family: List each person's name, and fill in columns listing each person's hobby, age, and favorite type of music. You could also create a chart showing who spends the most time on your home telephone in a single day. (Hint: Try a pie chart.)

In the next lesson, you'll find out how to print documents so you can see what they look like on paper.

Printing Your Word Document

GOALS

In this lesson, you'll learn the skills needed to print documents, including:

- Selecting page orientation
- Adding headers and footers
- Using Print Preview
- Selecting a printer
- Selecting a portion of your document to print and making multiple copies

Get ready

GET READY

To work through this lesson, you need the files Ex08-1 and Ex08-2, which you copied to your hard drive from the accompanying CD-ROM, and a printer installed and connected to your computer.

SETTING UP YOUR PAGE AND PRINTER

When you installed Office 97, the software searched for your printer and set up all the programs to send documents to that printer. You won't usually have to make any changes to that setting. But suppose you get a new printer? Or what if you like to print to the laser printer down the hall for letters on stationery, but prefer your desktop printer for drafts of reports? Because of these typical scenarios, you have to know how to tell Word where to send printed documents and how to setup documents so that what you see on screen is what you get on paper.

If you are on a network — that is, if your computer is tied into a company-wide system of computers — setting up a printer can be a bit more complicated. You may not have access to certain printers or permissions to print to them. These things would need to be changed by your MIS or computer support person. But don't worry, he or she will probably only need to make changes once, and you'll be all set to print as you please.

Selecting paper size and orientation

Several of the settings that relate to how your document prints are located in the Page Setup dialog box. Page Setup is where you choose the paper size, set margins, choose the page orientation, and designate from which tray in your printer your pages will print.

If you want choices other than the default choices in Page Setup, it's a good idea to make changes before you enter your document's contents. If you change

things such as margins and page orientation after you've entered and formatted your document, the shift in layout on your page may ruin many of the settings you've made.

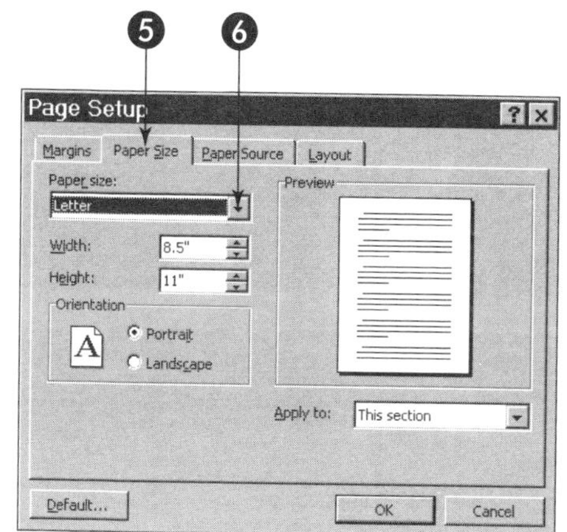

1. Open Word for Windows.
2. Open the file Ex08-1.
3. Select File.
4. Select Page Setup.

   The Page Setup dialog box appears, as shown in the illustration to the right. Default settings here are to print on letter-sized paper in a portrait orientation, which is usually fine for the majority of documents you print.
5. If the *Paper size* tab is not displayed, select it.
6. Open the Paper size drop-down list.

   You have the following seven choices in the *Paper size* drop-down list:

   - *Letter* is the standard U.S. business letter size of 8.5 × 11 inches.
   - *Legal* formats your document to an 8.5 × 14-inch size.
   - *Executive* is a standard letter stationery size of 7.25 × 10.5 inches.
   - *A4* is the standard European size for letters (210 × 297 mm).
   - *No. 10* is the U.S. letter envelope size of 4.125 × 9.5 inches.
   - *DL* is the European letter envelope size (4.33 × 8.66 inches).
   - *Custom* is for output sizes you set yourself.
7. Make sure Letter is selected in the Paper size drop-down list.

   The width and height of the selected paper size is given just beneath the *Paper size* box. To create a custom page size, select Custom from the *Paper size* list, and make measurement settings in the *Width* and *Height* boxes.

Now take a look at the next area of the Paper Size tab: Orientation. *Orientation* relates to whether your document will print vertically or horizontally. Portrait orientation is used in typical business letters, with the 8.5-inch side of the paper across the top and the 11-inch side down the side. Landscape is printed with a horizontal orientation: The longer side of the paper runs across the top. A table of information with many columns across might require landscape orientation.

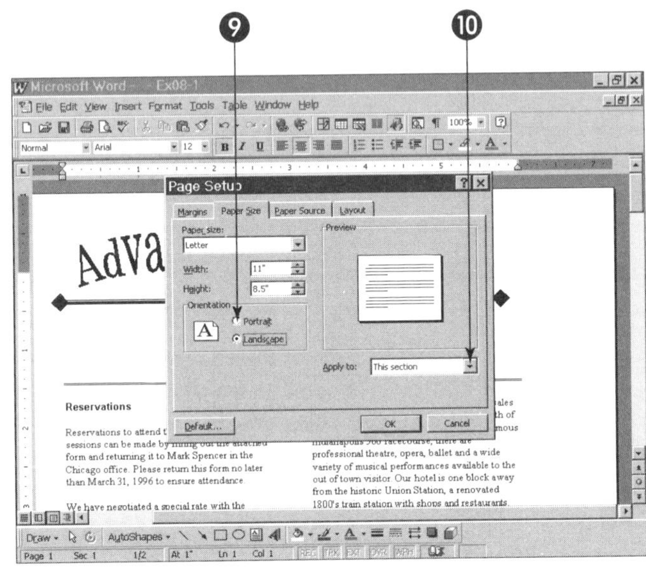

8. Click the Landscape orientation. A preview of Landscape output appears as in the *Preview* box in the following illustration.
9. Click the Portrait orientation.
10. In the *Apply to* drop-down list, select Whole Document.

If you want just one section of the document to be changed to specific settings, insert section breaks in your document (Insert ➢ Break ➢ Section) and then select This Section from the Apply to *drop-down list in this dialog box.*

11. Select the Paper Source tab.

    Here you can change to different paper trays for printing. For example, many office printers are set up with plain paper in one tray and company letterhead in a second tray.

12. Choose OK to save the Page Setup settings.

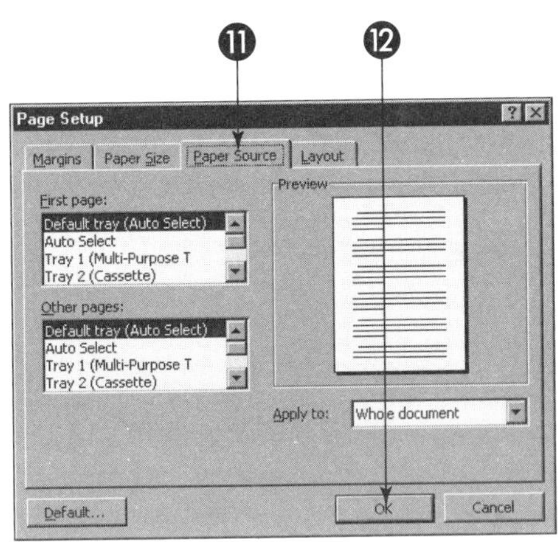

Adding headers and footers

Headers and footers are elements that appear on every page of your document. They typically contain information such as page numbers, the date the document was printed, the author of the document, and so on. Although you can add headers and footers before you even begin typing your document, many people leave this to the end of the process, just before printing their first draft. Adding headers and footers is easy to do. Just follow these steps:

Adding headers and footers

1. Select View.
2. Choose Header and Footer.

   A view of your document appears, showing the text of your document grayed out, a header section defined by a dotted line border, and the Header and Footer toolbar.

3. Choose the *Switch Between Header and Footer* button on the Header and Footer toolbar.

   The Header section disappears and the Footer section appears.

4. Click the Insert AutoText button on the toolbar.

   A list of options drops down, including Page, Created by, Filename, Last Printed, and so on. These are automatic text entries that Word can place in your header or footer based on information stored with your document.

5. Select Filename. The filename appears on the left side of the footer box.

It's a good idea to place the filenames of documents in their draft versions. When you go back to make revisions, if you've forgotten what you named the file, the name is right there on your draft.

6. Press Tab.
7. Click the Insert Date button.

   The current date is placed in the center of the footer.

8. Place your cursor after the date and press Tab again.
9. Choose the Insert Page Number button.

   The page number is inserted right justified in the footer box because tabs are set for left, center, and right in the header and footer sections. Notice that the text styles of these entries differ slightly; the filename is 12 point type size and the header and footer are 10 point. Typically, it is better to have consistent and slightly smaller text in your header and footer.

10. Select all the text in the footer.

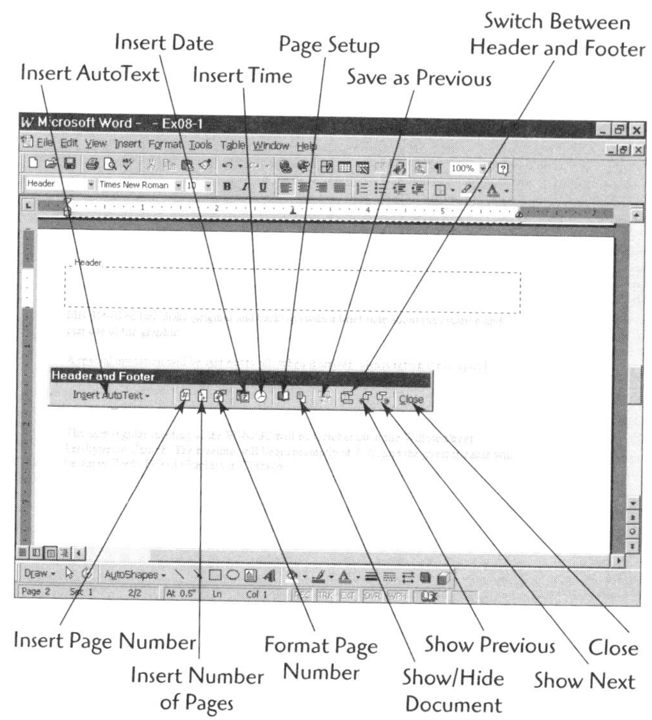

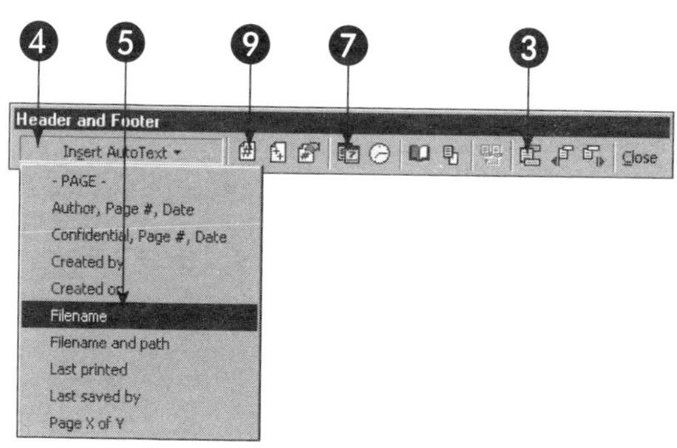

8 Printing Your Word Document

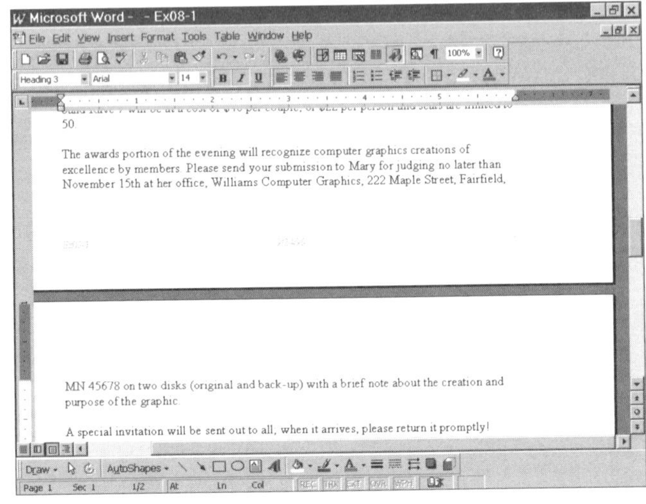

11. Select the 9 point setting in the Font Size drop-down list on the Standard toolbar.
12. Choose the Close button on the Header and Footer toolbar.

    Make sure you are in Page Layout view (View ➢ Page Layout).
13. Scroll to the bottom of your document page.

    The footer text appears in gray, as in the illustration to the right.

Using Print Preview

To save paper (and time), it's a good idea to see how your document will print before you actually print it . You can do this with a feature called *Print Preview*. Print Preview uses a feature called WYSIWYG (pronounced *wizzy-wig*). This stands for What You See Is What You Get. It's a technology that represents your printed document based on your printer and the page setup settings. Print Preview can show you if the elements on your page are balanced in a well-designed way, and if elements of your document are falling outside of the printable area of the document.

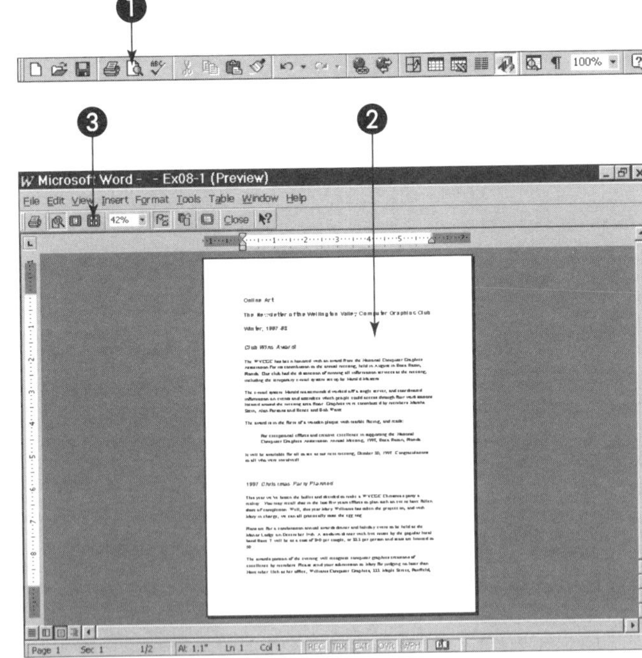

1. Click the Print Preview button (or select File ➢ Print Preview).

   The illustration to the right shows the print preview of the first page of a document. Notice that the mouse pointer is in the shape of a small magnifying glass.
2. Click your mouse pointer anywhere on the document preview.

   The preview zooms in to show more detail of the area you clicked. You can use this Magnifier mouse pointer, which is the default pointer in Print Preview, to zoom in to your document, or you can make zoom settings with the Zoom Control button. If you want to see more than one page, you can use the Multiple Pages button to see as many pages as you like at a time.
3. Choose the Multiple Pages button and drag your mouse pointer to select two pages.

Your preview now shows the two pages of your document on one screen, as in the illustration to the right.

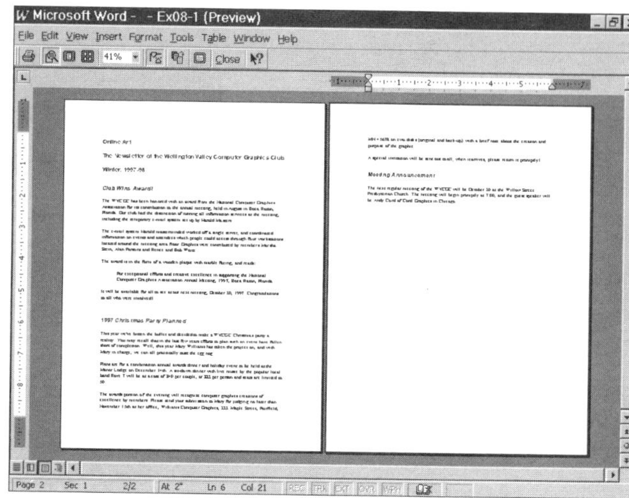

4 Choose the Full Screen button to see more page area.

The Full Screen View gets rid of the Windows title and status bars.

5 To close the Full Screen, click the Close Full Screen command on the floating Full Screen menu.

Notice that the gray areas on either side of the two rulers in Print Preview indicate the margins of the document. You can adjust the margins right in Print Preview by simply dragging the margin icons on the rulers.

At this point you have the following two options:

- If you are happy with the Print Preview and all your default printer settings are fine, you can print right from here by clicking the Print button.
- If you see something in your document you'd like to change before printing, or if you want to modify your printer settings, click Close to close Print Preview and return to your document. For the purpose of this lesson, close the document first and then look at printer settings.

6 Choose Close to close the Print Preview and return to your document view.

Selecting a printer

You install printers and set a default printer in Windows. This has probably already been done either by Windows itself when you installed it or by your computer support person. If not, you can designate the default printer by selecting the Windows taskbar, and then Settings and Printers. Double-click the Add Printer icon to start the Add Printer Wizard, which will walk you through the printer installation process.

Selecting a printer

Once you have installed and set up a default printer, you can easily print to that printer from Word. You can also determine settings in Word to print a document to a printer other than the default (as long as that printer is also installed in your Printer directory). The printer you select can affect what size pages you can print and what color you can print in.

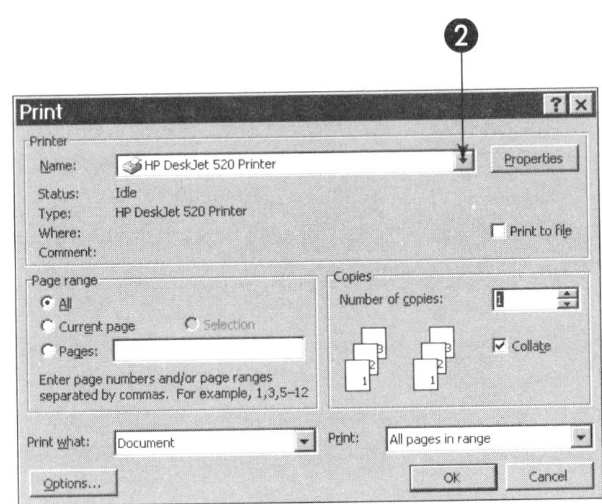

1. Select File ➢ Print.

   The Print dialog box appears, as shown in the illustration to the right. The top section of this dialog box, labeled Printer, is where you designate a printer for this print job. The default printer set in Windows should be listed here.

2. Open the drop-down list in the *Name* box.

   All installed printers are listed here. This may also include faxing software; to fax a document from Word you simply print to the faxing software. Details about the selected printer are also listed, including the type of printer and its status — *status* meaning whether the printer is busy.

To print the document not to a printer but to a file, select a printer and click the Print to file *check box in this section of the Print dialog box. You print to a file (rather than just save the file) if you want to save a file with a particular printer language included. If you do this, you can print the file at a later time from a computer that doesn't even have Word installed on it.*

   If you choose a printer other than the Windows default printer, this changes the default printer designation for Word documents, but not the default printer for your computer. For example, if you were to change the printer for Word and then open PowerPoint, PowerPoint's default printer would still be matched to the Windows default printer. To change Word back to the Windows default printer, select that printer again in the Name field in the Print dialog box.

3. Be sure the default printer is selected.

❹ With your default printer displayed in the *Name* box, choose the Properties button.

A dialog box like the one shown in the illustration appears. These settings offer the paper size, black-and-white or color, and orientation options available to the selected printer itself. For example, the printer shown in the illustration has no option for color printing because it is a black-and-white printer.

You have three options for dealing with the shading and colors in your printed documents, controlled from the Printer dialog box:

- If you have a document that consists of text only and you want to print in black-and-white, select *Black Text*. Everything on your printed page appears in black.
- If you have graphics such as clip art or drawings in your document, or you've used any patterns in your borders or drawings, use the *Grayscale* option. This enables your printer to print shades of gray to help delineate the various areas of graphics.
- If you have selected a color printer, use the *Color* option to print in color. Of course, if you have a color printer but don't want to print this particular document in color, you can choose the Black Text or Grayscale option.

❺ Choose OK to return to the Print dialog box.

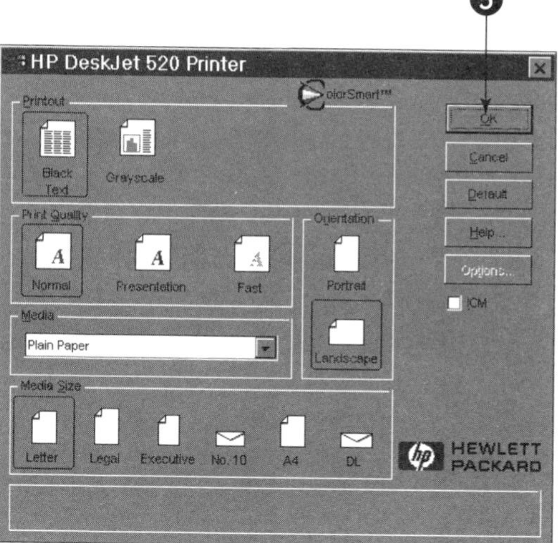

MAKING PRINT SETTINGS

There are two simple settings to make before finally printing your document: what part of your document you want to print, and how many copies you'd like to have printed. Both of these are set in the Print dialog box.

Using the Print dialog box settings

Using the Print dialog box settings

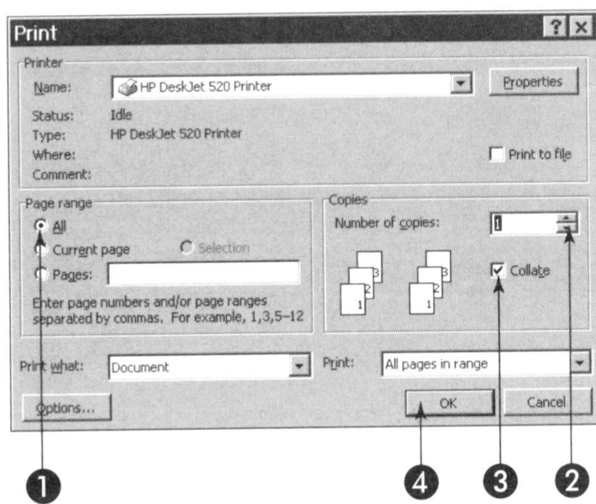

Look at the Page range section of the Print dialog box. You have the following four options:

- *Select All* if you want to print your entire document.
- *Select Current* page if you want to print the page where your cursor currently appears.
- *Pages* can be used to enter a range of pages to print. You can enter a range such as 5–10 to get pages 5–10 inclusive. You can also enter a series of page numbers, such as 10, 15, 21. Or you can use a combination of these — indicate ranges and single pages this way: 1–3, 4–6, 21.
- If you select text before you open the Print dialog box, the choice *Selection* is available to you. This will print only currently selected text.

❶ Click the All option button.

You can print as many copies of your document as you like. To designate the number of copies to print, do the following:

❷ Set the *Number of copies* field for 2 copies using the up or down arrow, or by typing **2** in the field.

If you are printing multiple copies of a document and you haven't selected the *Collate* check box, all the copies of Page 1 will print out first, and then all the copies of Page 2, and so on. You can collate the pages so that each complete set of copies prints out together.

❸ Click the *Collate* check box.

❹ Choose OK in the Print dialog box to print the document.

❺ Select File ➢ Close to close this document and select No when asked if you want to save changes.

SKILLS CHALLENGE: PRINTING AN INVITATION

In this exercise, you apply all the skills you just learned to print an invitation.

TRY OUT THE INTERACTIVE TUTORIALS ON YOUR CD!

1. Open the file Ex08-2.
2. Look at the document in Print Preview.

Where are the margins indicated in Print Preview?

3. Close the Print Preview.
4. Change the orientation of the document to Landscape.

   Notice how the change in orientation shifted the drawing away from the center of the document.
5. Look at the invitation in Print Preview again.
6. Look at the page in Full Screen view.

If you want to see several pages of a document in Print Preview, how do you display them?

7. Close the Full Screen view.
8. Close Print Preview.
9. Open the Header view.
10. Type the following header: **Merry Christmas, Season's Greetings, Happy Hanukkah, Merry Christmas, Season's Greetings**.

If you want to put your name in the header, what's the quickest way to do that?

11. Change the font in the header text to 10 point Brush Script MT (or another script font if this one is not available to you).
12. Center the header text.
13. Close the header view.
14. Open the Print dialog box.

15. Set the printer up to print in Grayscale.
16. Adjust settings to print three copies.

If you want multiple copies to print in complete sets, what setting do you choose?

17. Print the document.
18. Close the file without saving changes.

TROUBLESHOOTING

You're doing a great job! The following table suggests a few things to watch out for as you print Word documents.

Problem	Solution
A piece of clip art gets cut in half when I print.	It's placed outside the printable area of the page; check your page in Print Preview and move anything that appears cut off to a location within the document area before printing.
I entered a footer, but it didn't print.	It may be off the printable area of the page; change the location where your footer prints in the Page Setup dialog box (File ➢ Page Setup).
The graphic I put in my newsletter doesn't print.	If you select Fast Print Quality in the Printer dialog box, a draft prints without graphics. Select File ➢ Print ➢ Properties, and choose Normal Print Quality.

WRAP UP

You've learned a lot about getting your Word documents to print properly, including the following:

- Setting up orientation in Page Setup
- Creating headers and footers
- Using Print Preview to make sure your document will print correctly
- Choosing a printer to print to and making settings in the Print dialog for the number of copies and section of your document to print

If you'd like more practice with these skills, try printing a much longer document, such as a 10-page report, and making selections to print only pages 3 through 7, collate copies, and place a graphic object, such as clip art, in a footer (see Lesson 6 if you need help with the clip art).

In Lesson 9, you learn Mail Merge, a very handy procedure for generating mass mailings.

Merging Your Mail

GOALS

In this lesson, you discover one of the most time-saving features of word processing — mail merge. You'll master the following skills:

- Creating the main document
- Building the data source
- Placing merge fields in your document
- Using Word fields and queries
- Viewing and checking a mail merge
- Printing to a printer or document

Get ready

GET READY

To work through this lesson, you need the files Ex09-1 and Ex09-2, which you copied to your hard drive from the accompanying CD-ROM. You should also have a printer connected to your computer, and both paper and #10 envelopes available.

When you complete this lesson, you'll have created the personalized letter like the one on the facing page.

TRY OUT THE
INTERACTIVE TUTORIALS
ON YOUR CD!

WHAT IS A MAIL MERGE?

Mail merge is a pretty simple concept: You take a document (such as a form letter) and a set of information (such as the names and addresses of all your clients) and you merge them. When you merge the form letter and the list of names, you can generate a mass mailing. Each copy of the document you print will be personalized with a different name and address. A mailing to hundreds of clients can therefore be accomplished by typing the letter once, combining it with your client list, and printing it.

Want an easy way to visualize a mail merge? Think of that junk mail you get every month that tells you that you may have already won 10 million dollars. The form letters in this type of mailing usually call you by your first name repeatedly; they may even tell you that the loot will be delivered to your specific address, accompanied by TV cameras and a dozen roses. Each personalized piece of information is inserted in those letters, on a grand scale, with a mail merge process.

Although names and addresses are common uses of mail merge, you can take it even further. For example, you can create a mail merge for your monthly billing. You can create a billing letter, personalize the name and address, and place the current month's outstanding balance in the third sentence. All you need is a data set including name, address, and account balance. A data source can be a Word table, Excel worksheet, or Access database.

Abbey Nursery
225 Marshall Avenue
Greenberg, IL 33523

June 15, 1999

Mr. Bob Chang
3789 Winding Way
Anderson, IL 33322

Dear Bob,

Summer is coming and we at Abbey want to help you make it the greenest one ever! We have a special offer on all of our shrubs and perennials for all our neighbors living in Anderson.

For the remainder of June all shrubs and perennials will be priced at 20% off. Just bring in this letter and our friendly staff will be glad to help you choose the perfect complement for your yard. We'll even give you all the advice and support you need to plant your purchases so they'll thrive for years to come.

Bob, we at Abbey look forward to seeing you in the next few weeks. Happy Summer!

Sincerely,

The Abbey Nursery Staff

What is a mail merge?

You do all this with a *field*. A field is like a code that tells Word where to get information, and to place that information where the code is in a document. A Name field, for example, is a placeholder for all the names of your clients in your client list. Word reads the field called Name, and goes looking for all the entries in the corresponding field in the client list.

VISUAL BONUS: HOW MAIL MERGE WORKS

A mail merge typically involves a data source, a form letter, and output, as seen in this Visual Bonus.

June 15, 1999

«Title» «FirstName» «LastName»
«Company»
«Address1»
«City», «State» «PostalCode»

Dear «FirstName»,

Summer is coming and we at Abbey want to help you make it the greenest one ever! We have a special offer on all of our shrubs and perennials for all our neighbors living in «City».

For the remainder of June all shrubs and perennials will be priced at 20% off. Just bring in this letter and our friendly staff will be glad to help you choose the perfect complement for your yard. We'll even give you all the advice and support you need to plant your purchases so they'll thrive for years to come.

«FirstName», we at Abbey look forward to seeing you in the next few weeks. Happy Summer!

Mail merge fields

A form letter with mail merge fields.

Title	FirstName	LastName	Company	Address1	City	State	PostalCode
Mr. & Mrs.	James	Simms		223 Elm Street	Anderson	IL	33322
Ms.	Margaret	Cushing		299 Main Street	Medville	IL	33222
Mr.	Bob	Chang		3789 Winding Way	Anderson	IL	33322
Dr.	Mary Lou	Pike	Medical Arts, Inc.	325 Medical Way	Johnson	IL	33332
Mr. & Mrs.	John & Dierdre	Mantagni		69808 Fisher Parkway	Medville	IL	33222
Rev.	Harriet	Lennon		P.O. Box 3434	Anderson	IL	33322

Field names

A data source; in this case, a listing of customers with names and addresses.

continued

VISUAL BONUS: HOW MAIL MERGE WORKS *(continued)*

Abbey Nursery
225 Marshall Avenue
Greenberg, IL 33523

June 15, 1999

Mr. Bob Chang
3789 Winding Way
Anderson, IL 33322

Dear Bob,

Summer is coming and we at Abbey want to help you make it the greenest one ever! We have a special offer on all of our shrubs and perennials for all our neighbors living in Anderson.

For the remainder of June all shrubs and perennials will be priced at 20% off. Just bring in this letter and our friendly staff will be glad to help you choose the perfect complement for your yard. We'll even give you all the advice and support you need to plant your purchases so they'll thrive for years to come.

Bob, we at Abbey look forward to seeing you in the next few weeks. Happy Summer!

Sincerely,

The Abbey Nursery Staff

A personalized letter resulting from the mail merge.

SETTING UP THE MAIL MERGE

The first step to performing a mail merge is creating the document and the data source. In this exercise, an example is used of a small company sending a mailing to customers in the area, notifying them of a sale.

Creating the main document

Creating the main document

The main document can be a form letter, an invoice, an invitation — any type of document. The idea here is that the document will go to many recipients, and some unique information must be included to personalize it.

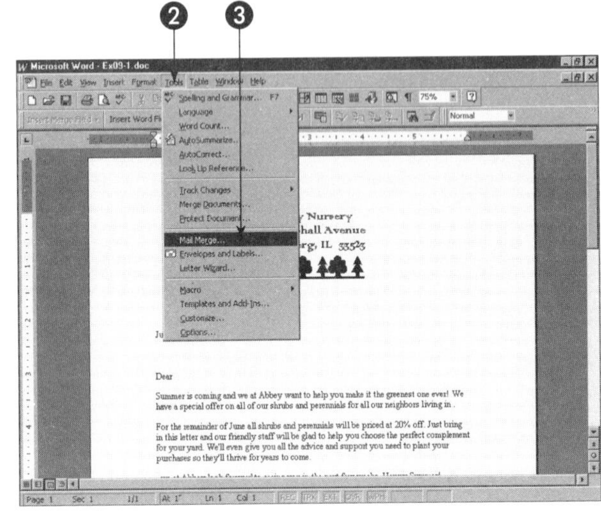

1. Open Word for Windows. (If it's already open, close all documents and open a new document.)
2. Select Tools.
3. Choose Mail Merge.

   The Mail Merge Helper dialog box appears. The three steps of a mail merge are outlined here: creating a main document, getting the data to merge with the document, and performing the merge. First, you create a form letter.

4. Click the Create button.
5. Select Form Letters from the drop-down list.

Other choices in the drop-down list include Envelopes, Labels, and Catalog. Don't let this confuse you, you can always come back and create the envelopes for your letter; once you've created the data source and saved it, you can use it again and again with different types of documents.

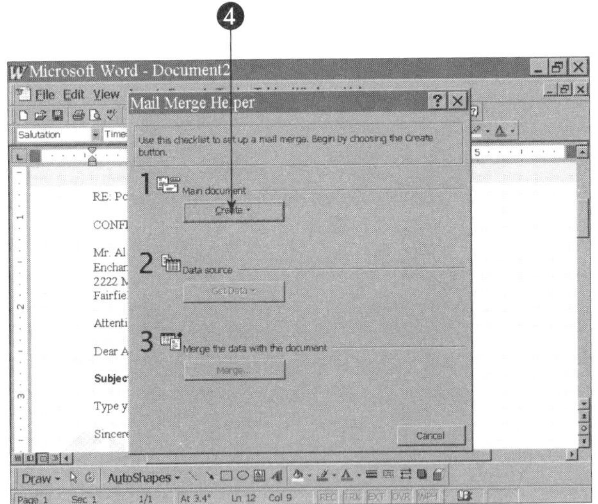

A dialog box appears giving you two choices: to create a form letter within the active window (which would currently be Document1, assuming you've just opened Word for Windows), or open a new window (Document2). In these steps, you'll use the blank document that's currently open.

6. Select Active Window.

   You are returned to the Mail Merge Helper, but there is now a second button available under the first step called Edit. You use that button to go to a document, enter the text of your letter, and place merge fields within it.

Creating the main document

If you prefer, you can type your document before initiating the mail merge. When you reach this step, choose Edit and insert the merge fields in your document.

❼ Click Edit.

❽ Select Form Letter: Document1 to go to the document where you can create your letter.

Now you are in the regular Word window, with Document1 (at this point, a blank document) displayed. Notice there is a new toolbar showing beneath the Formatting toolbar, which is shown in the illustration to the right. You'll see how several of these tools function as you use them in exercises throughout this lesson.

To save time typing a letter, you can insert a file from the accompanying CD-ROM containing a letter already created in Word. However, keep in mind that you could also type a letter or other document.

❾ Click the Insert menu.

❿ Select File.

⓫ In the Insert dialog box that appears, locate the file Ex09-1 in the Exercise folder on your hard drive.

⓬ Click OK to insert the file.

This is a letter from a nursery to customers about a plant sale. Notice there is no return address, and no name in the greeting. In addition, at the end of the first paragraph there is a space between the last work and period, where the name of the recipient's town should go. Finally, at the beginning of the third paragraph, the writer intends that the customer's first name should be inserted before the comma that begins the paragraph.

When you create a document for a mail merge, you should plan out these elements in advance. You can use merge fields to add little personal touches throughout a letter to make it more friendly and persuasive.

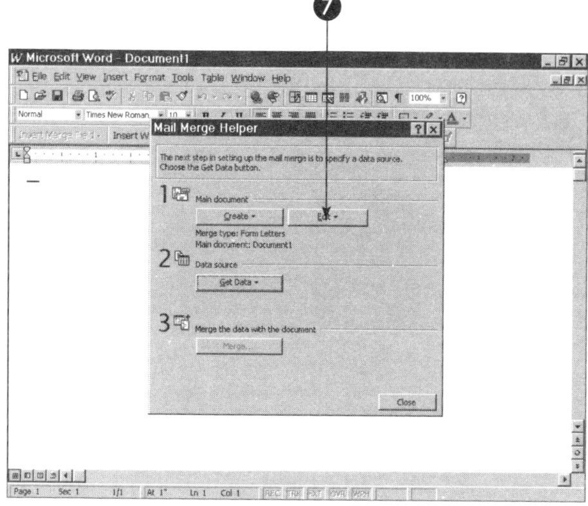

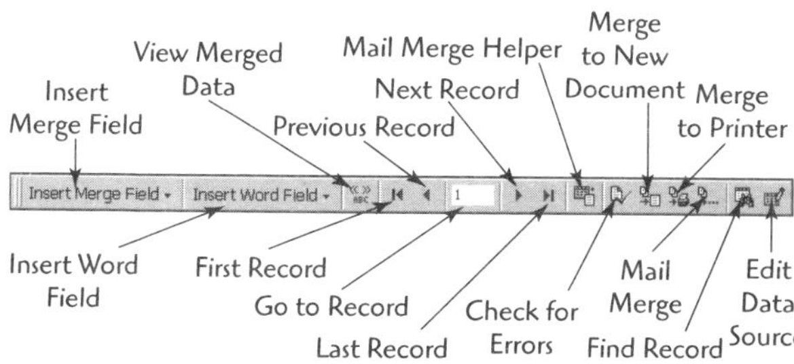

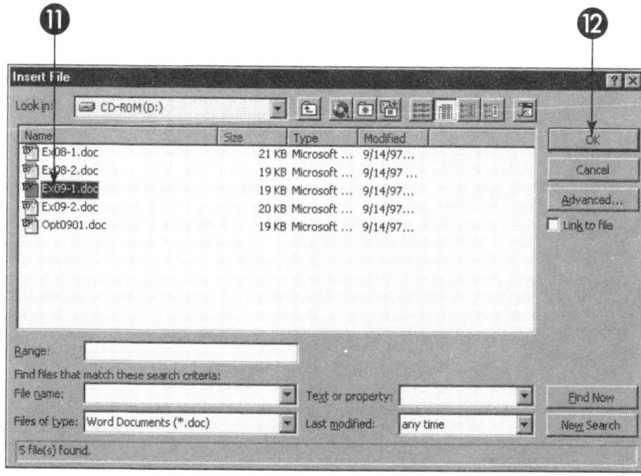

Building the data source

Now it's time to create the source of data for the mass mailing.

1. On the Mail Merge toolbar, select Mail Merge Helper to return to that dialog box.
2. Click Get Data.

   There are four choices in the drop-down list that appears:

   - *Create Data Source* enables you to design a simple database and enter records into it.
   - *Open Data Source* would be your selection if you have a database of records you've already created, either in Word or an application such as Access.
   - *Use Address Book* gives you access to the Outlook or Personal address books (see more about this in Lesson 16).
   - *Header Options* enables you to specify one file for the document header and another for merging with the rest of the document.

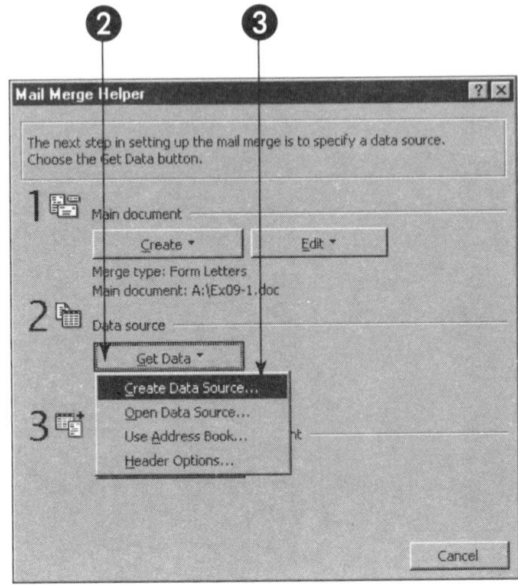

3. Select Create Data Source.

   The Create Data Source dialog box appears.

   This dialog box already contains many common field names, such as FirstName, LastName, Company, and Title, as well as several fields for addresses. You can remove fields that you don't need for your document; add fields that don't appear here but that you'd like to use, such as SpouseName; or move the fields around using the Move up and down arrows.

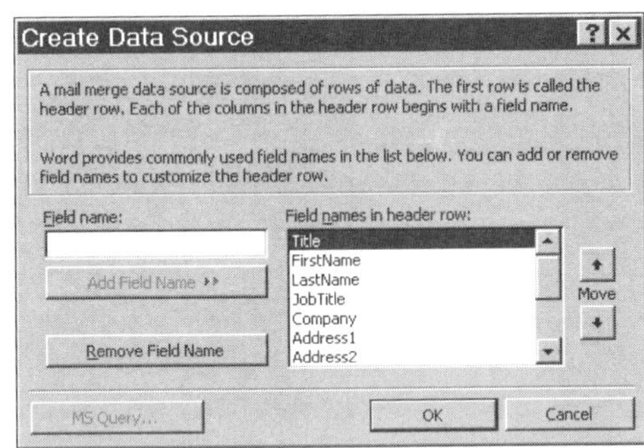

The fields you end up with in this list are the fields that appear on all of your database records. You can always ignore superfluous fields: They won't affect your merge document unless you place a merge field for them in it. However, if there are, say, three or four fields you don't need, removing them from this list makes it faster to enter and edit information in your database records.

4. Click the field name JobTitle.
5. Click Remove Field Name.

   The field disappears from the List, and appears in the *Field name* box. When anything is entered in the *Field name* box, either as a result of a removed field name or something you've typed, the Add Field Name button becomes available. Clicking this will add whatever field name is entered here to your list.

6. Repeat Steps 4 and 5 to remove the following four fields: Address2, Country, HomePhone, WorkPhone.
7. Click OK to proceed.
8. Type the file name **Clients** in the *File name* box of the Save As dialog box to save the data source file.
9. Choose Save to save the file.

   The dialog box shown in the illustration at bottom right appears, telling you that your data source has no records. You have the option of editing the data source to add records, or going to the merge document and adding merge fields. Either way, you proceed with building the data source.

10. Choose Edit Data Source.

    The Data Form appears as shown on the next page. To build a database for your mail merge, you need to create several records by entering information in these forms.

11. Enter the following information in this form:

Title:	**Mr. & Mrs.**
FirstName:	**James & Martha**
LastName:	**Simms**
Address1:	**223 Elm Street**
City:	**Anderson**
State:	**IL**
PostalCode:	**33322**

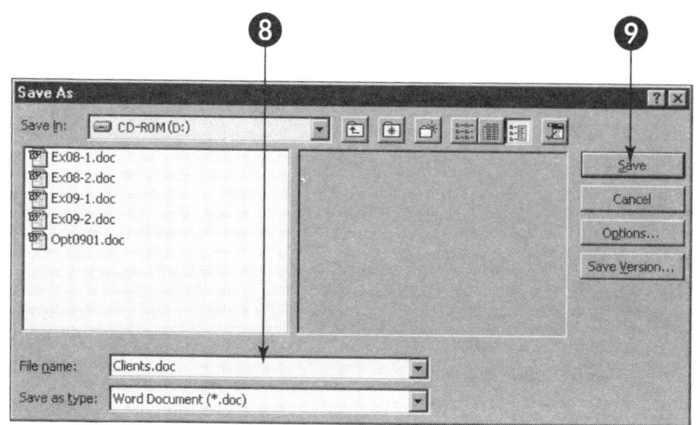

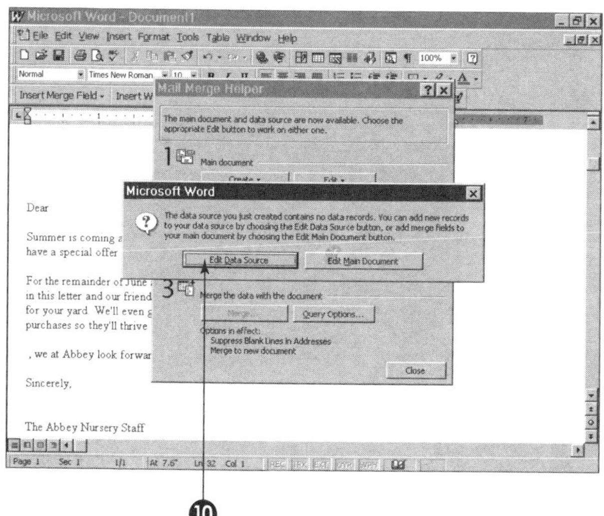

12. Choose Add New to add the next record.
13. Using the information in Table 9-1, add another five records to this database.

TABLE 9-1 DATA SOURCE RECORDS FOR MAIL MERGE

Record #	Title	FirstName	LastName	Address	City	State	Zip
2	Ms.	Margaret	Cushing	299 Main Street	Medville	IL	33222
3	Mr.	Bob	Chang	3789 Winding Way	Anderson	IL	33322
4	Dr.	Mary Lou	Pike	325 Medical Way	Johnson	IL	33332
5	Mr. & Mrs.	John & Dierdre	Mantagni	69808 Fisher Parkway	Medville	IL	33222
6	Rev.	Harriet	Lennon	P.O. Box 3434	Anderson	IL	33322

14. After you enter the above records, use the Record navigation buttons at the bottom of the Data Form to move back to record 4.

    Dr. Mary Lou Pike gets her mail sent to her office. You need to add company information for her.

15. Type **Medical Arts, Inc.** in the Company field.
16. Choose OK to save the database and return to your main document.

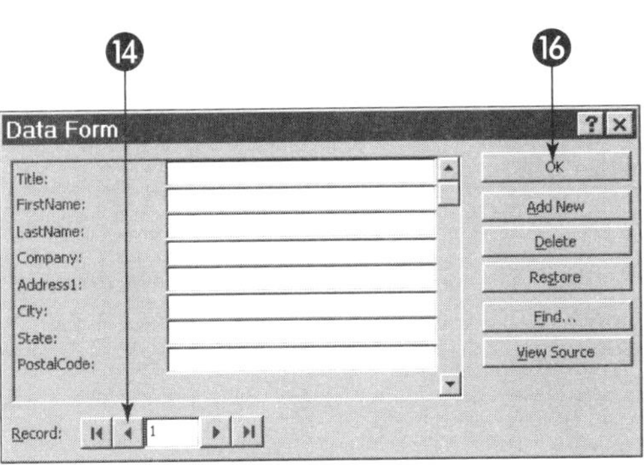

Placing the merge fields

It's time to enter merge fields in the form letter you typed. The merge fields in the letter will correspond to the fields in your database.

1. Scroll to the top of the document.
2. Place your cursor halfway between the date and salutation.
3. Choose the Insert Merge Field button on the Mail Merge toolbar.

   The drop-down list with the field names in your data forms appears. If you choose a different data source, they change to reflect that database's field names.

4. Select Title.

   A merge field appears in your document. This is the code Word needs to tell it where to go in the database to place information at this spot in each letter.

5. Press the spacebar once to put a space between the Title (Mr., Ms., and so on) and the FirstName.
6. Choose the Insert Merge Field button again and this time select FirstName.
7. Press the spacebar once.
8. Choose Insert Merge Field ➢ LastName.
9. Press Enter.
10. Choose Insert Merge Field ➢ Company.

    Because one record has an entry in the Company field, you must include the merge field here. Records with no information in that field will not include an extra line for it, but the one record with an entry will have this extra line in the address.

11. Press Enter.
12. Choose Insert Merge Field ➢ Address1.
13. Press Enter.
14. Choose Insert Merge Field ➢ City.
15. Type a comma, and then a space.
16. Choose Insert Merge Field ➢ State.
17. Press the spacebar once.
18. Choose Insert Merge Field ➢ PostalCode.
19. Move your cursor to the salutation, after the word *Dear.*
20. Press the spacebar once.
21. Choose Insert Merge Field ➢ FirstName, and then type a comma.
22. Place your cursor at the end of the last line of the first paragraph, just before the period.

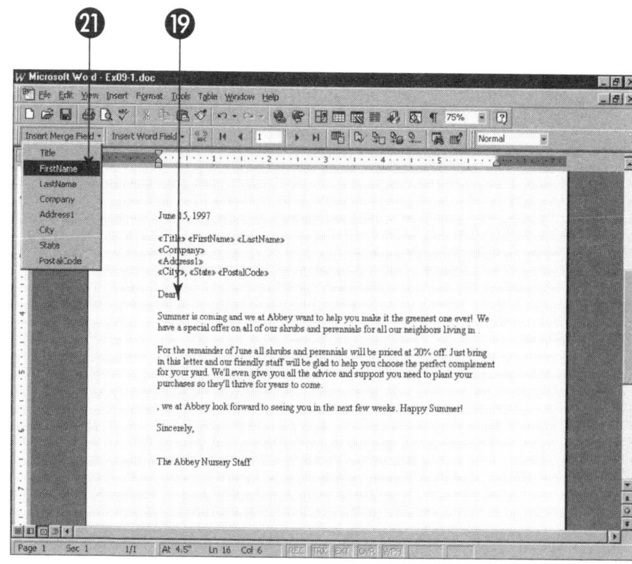

23. Choose Insert Merge Field ➢ City.
24. Finally, place your cursor at the start of the last paragraph, just before the comma.
25. Choose Insert Merge Field ➢ FirstName.

    You have now entered all the merge fields for your letter, and your document should look like the one in the illustration to the right.

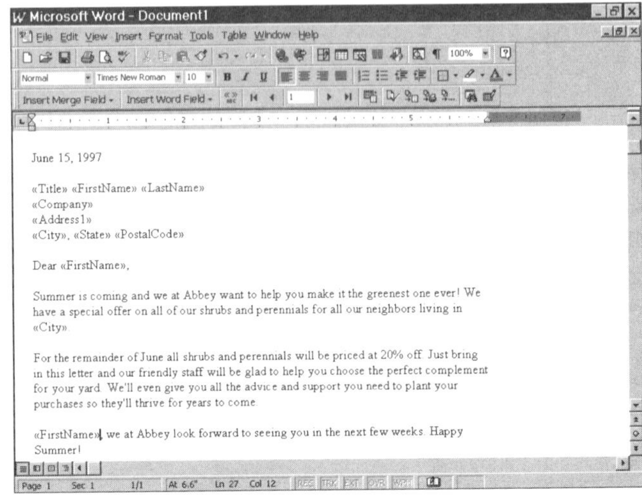

Using Word fields and queries

You can define which records you want included with your mail merge, and you can customize the information to be included in each document. To do so, you can insert *Word fields* in a document or use a *query* to filter and sort your records. You look at both of these procedures in this exercise.

Notice the button on the Mail Merge toolbar called Insert Word Field. These fields are basically formulas that help you control what information is included in your documents.

There are six types of Word fields available to you:

- *Ask and Fill-in* fields pause during printing your documents, and give you a chance to enter additional information for each letter. Use this if you'd like to add a personal note to each letter, or a unique password for a new customer account, for example.
- *If... Then... Else* enables you to enter a condition that must be met and the resulting action or actions. For example, If State = *IL*, then *We're nearby, so come on over.* And If State = *IN*, then *When you're next in Illinois, please visit us* might make a logical addition to your sample mailing.
- *Merge Record #* and *Merge Sequence #* will add the number of the merged data record in your document and the sequence of merged data records, respectively. In the case of a mail merge where you print only selected records from the data source, merge record would differ from merge sequence.
- *Next Record* and *Next Record If* enable you to print more than one set of data within a single document.

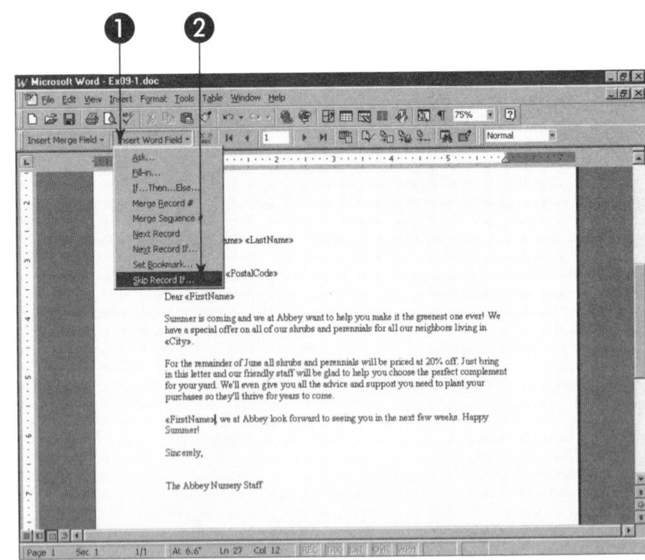

- *Set Bookmark Field* enables you to associate some information in your document with a bookmark, which can be placed in your document as many times as you like. Then, if the original information changes, all the bookmarks will be updated automatically.
- *Skip Record If* enables you to enter a condition that, if met, will result in that record not being merged.

Try one of these fields in your current mailing. If the creator of this letter decided he didn't want to send it to customers located in the city of Johnson, he could use a Word Field.

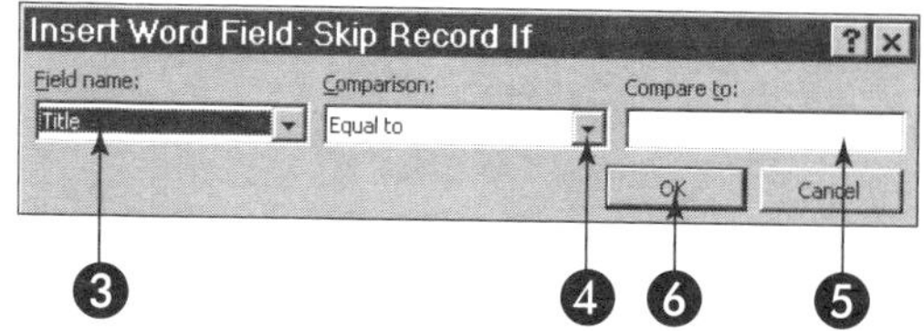

1. Choose Insert Word Field.
2. Select Skip Record If from the drop-down list.
   - A dialog box appears, as shown to the right.
3. In the *Field name* drop-down list, select City.
4. In the *Comparison* box, select Equal to.
5. In the *Compare to* box, type **Johnson**.
6. Choose OK.

Another way to affect which records will print, or in what order they will print, is to use Query Options. You perform a query through the Mail Merge Helper.

7. Choose the Mail Merge Helper button on the Mail Merge toolbar.

Once you've created a document and data source and inserted merge fields in your document, the third option in the Mail Merge Helper dialog box becomes available. There are now two buttons: Merge and Query Options.

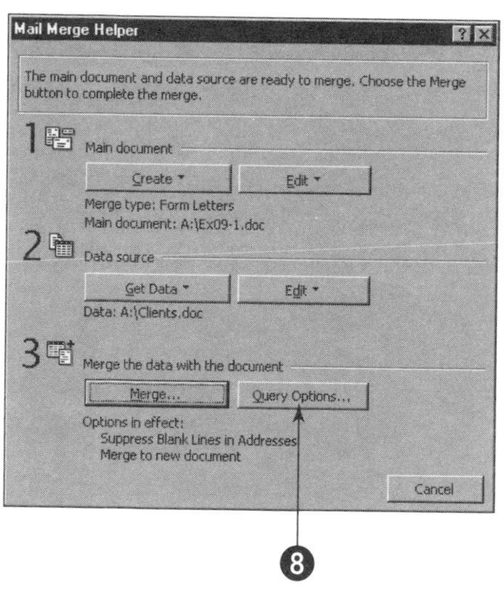

8. Choose Query Options.

The Query Options dialog box appears, as shown in the illustration on the next page.

9. In the *Field name* drop-down list, select State. (See figure on next page.)
10. In the *Comparison* drop-down list, select Equal to. (See figure on next page.)

9 Merging Your Mail

Merging document and data

⓫ In the Compare To field type **IL**.

Now any records that contain addresses outside of the state of Illinois will be filtered out of the mail merge.

⓬ Select the Sort Records tab of the Query Options dialog box.

The Sort Records panel appears.

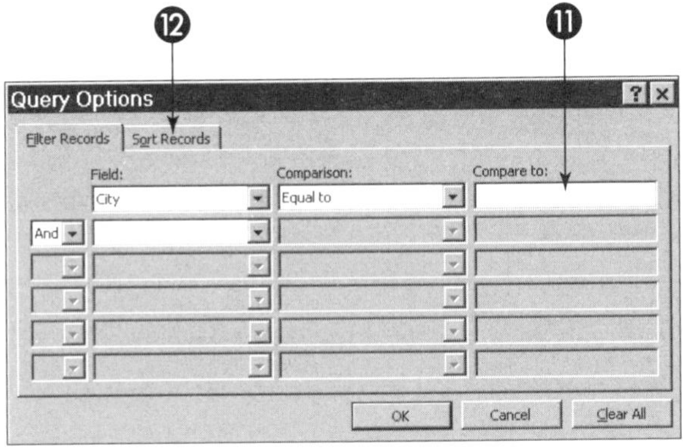

If you're doing a bulk mailing, sorting by PostalCode is a good idea. Because you need to sort and bundle the mail by ZIP code, printing out letters and envelopes in that order can save you time.

⓭ Select the Sort By field and choose LastName.

You can also choose a second and third sort criteria. For example, if you sort by City you might also want to sort by LastName, so all those living in the same city would print in one group, alphabetically by last name.

⓮ Choose OK.

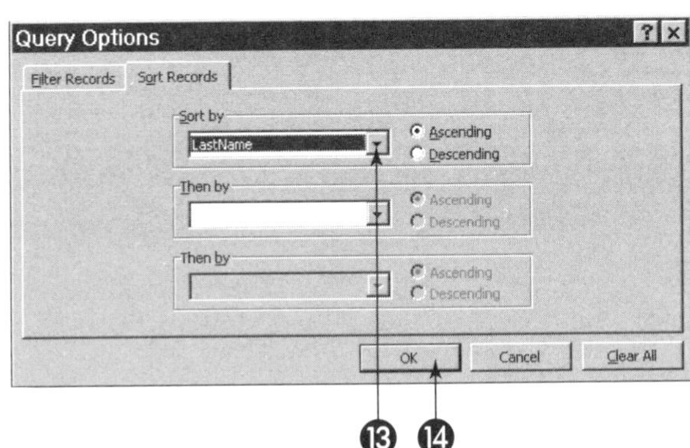

MERGING DOCUMENT AND DATA

At this point, you have the following options:

- You can view the letters that would result from performing a mail merge.
- You can run a check for errors in the merge before performing any of the above actions. This check looks for things such as fields that don't match the fields in your data source.
- You can merge your letters to a new document, creating one large file containing all the letters, one after the other, that would result from combining your data and document.
- You can merge to your printer, proceeding to print out these letters without previewing or saving them to a document.
- You can print the documents to e-mail.

It's always a good idea to view your merged document before printing. Look for extra spaces or lines and fields that don't make sense in context. For example, you might have used the salutation Dear *with a* LastName *field code, only to realize that you need a* Title *field (Mr., Ms., and so on) in front of it.*

Checking the merge

Now it's time to see how your settings created customized form letters.

1. Choose Close to close the Mail Merge Helper.
2. Choose the Check for Errors button on the Mail Merge toolbar.

   The Checking and Reporting Errors dialog box appears.

   You have three options here. If you want to check for errors without actually performing the merge, select the Simulate the Merge and Report Errors in a New Document option. If you want errors reported as the merge occurs, select Complete the merge, pausing to report each error as it occurs. If you want to go ahead with the merge, but have errors reported at the end, select the last option.
3. Select the Simulate option.
4. Choose OK.

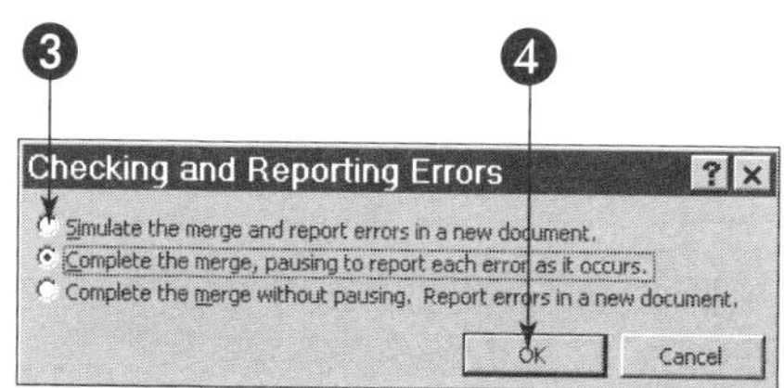

In this case, everything checks out okay. But suppose that after placing all your merge fields in the document you decide to use a different data source to generate the mailing. What would happen if that data source didn't include one of the merge fields already placed in your document? In that case you'd see an Invalid Merge Field message similar to the one in the illustration to the right, indicating that there is a merge field in the document that doesn't correspond to the merge fields in the data source.

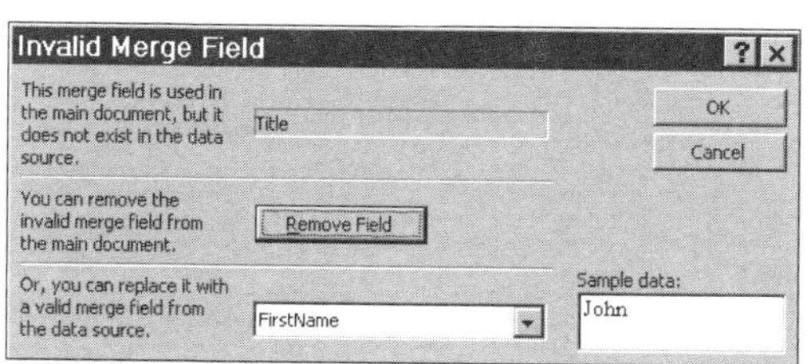

5. Choose OK to close the Check for Errors notification box.

   Now it's time to see what this mailing is going to look like.

6. Choose the View Merged Data button to see the letters that would result from the merge.

   This doesn't actually perform the mail merge: It simply enables you to preview the merge.

7. Scroll through the letters that now appear.

   Notice a few things: The letters have been sorted alphabetically, and no letter was generated for Dr. Mary Lou Pike, because she lives in Johnson and you told Word to skip any records for that city.

   At this point you should look for any problems with spacing or extra blank lines you might have missed. You can then click the View Merged Data button again to return to the main document window and make changes, if necessary.

8. Choose the View Merged Data button to toggle back to the main document.

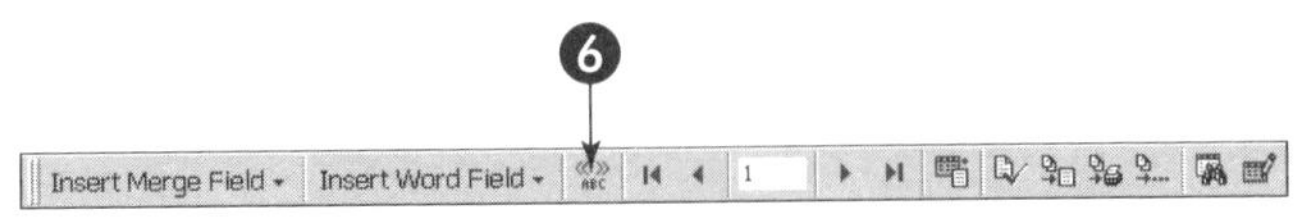

Merging to a printer or document

At last it's time for all this hard work to pay off.

1. Choose the Mail Merge Helper button.

   The Mail Merge Helper dialog box now looks like the illustration to the right, with a list of Options at the bottom of the window. Take a look at some of those options.

2. Choose Merge.

   The Merge dialog box appears.

   This is where you can designate to print or not print blank lines if a field is empty. Remember only one of your records had a company name? Selecting a blank line when data fields are empty in this dialog box would cause everybody but that person to have a blank second line in their address.

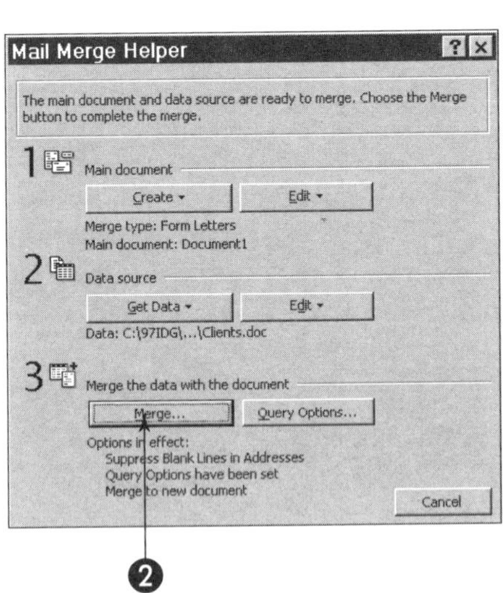

Merging to a printer or document

You can also designate that only a certain range of records should merge by entering the record number in the From and To fields.

3. Open the *Merge to* drop-down list.
4. Select Printer.
5. Choose Merge.

   The Print dialog box appears. Make sure all settings for your printer are accurate.

6. Choose OK to print.

   Your letters will now print out in the sorted order.

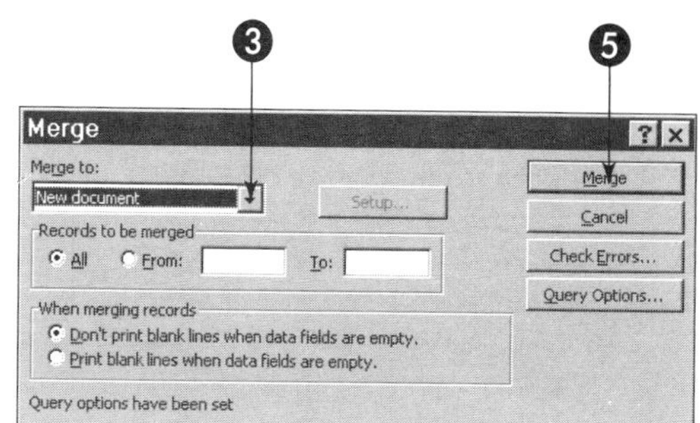

If you want to print your mail merge to stationery, be sure to load the stationery in your printer prior to printing the mail merge. You might want to merge to a document, and then print just the first page of that document to see how the letter lines up on the stationery printout.

If you had selected Print to a New Document, that document would have appeared on your screen and you could save that file of letters and print them now or later.

If you want to print to either an e-mail or fax, you have to use the Setup button in the Merge dialog box to designate a field in your data source that contains e-mail or fax addresses. You can also type in a subject line at that time.

SKILLS CHALLENGE: CREATING AN ENVELOPE MAIL MERGE

In this exercise, you practice your skills by generating envelopes for the mailing you just printed.

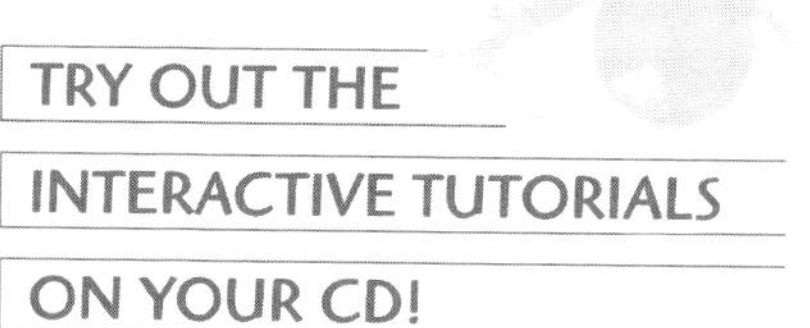

Skills challenge

If, for some reason, you don't still have the Clients database displayed, the same data is available in the file Ex09-2 which you copied to your hard drive from the accompanying CD-ROM. Simply choose to open this data source in the Mail Merge Helper.

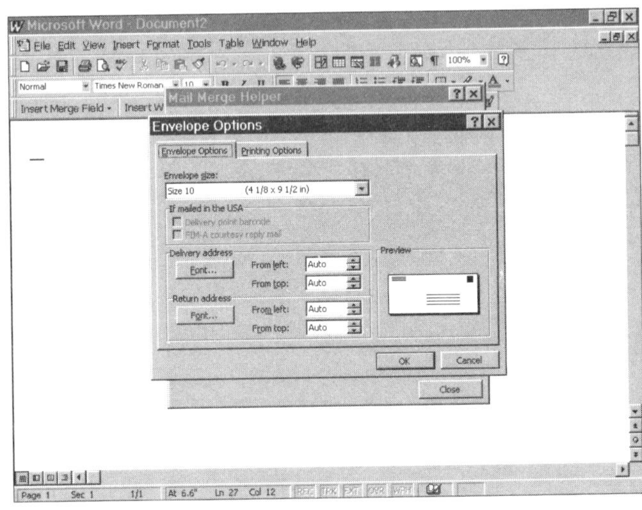

4. Open the Mail Merge Helper.
5. Create a Main Document using Envelopes as the type.
6. When prompted, choose to create a new document.
7. Open the Clients data file.
8. Choose to set up the Main Document.

   The Envelope Options dialog box appears, as shown in the illustration to the right.

9. Choose OK to accept the default settings.

   The Envelope Address dialog box shown in the following illustration is displayed.

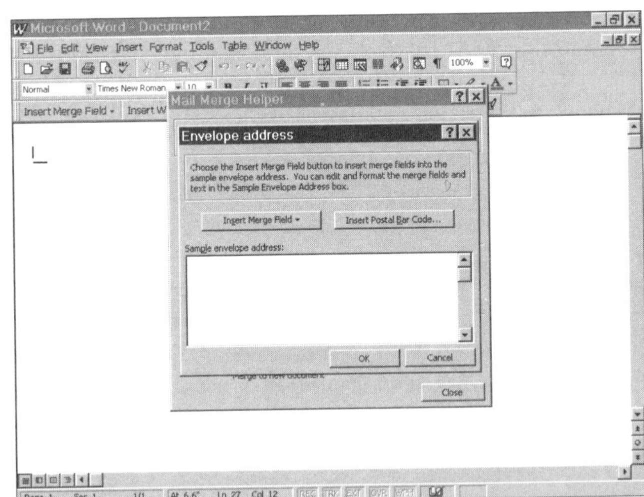

10. Insert Merge fields for Title, FirstName, LastName, Company, Address1, City, State, and PostalCode, with appropriate spaces and line breaks to form an address block.

If you want a blank line to appear for any records with no data in the Company field, where do you check that setting?

11. Choose OK to return to the Mail Merge Helper dialog box.
12. Choose Close to close the Mail Merge Helper and see your Main Document.
13. Insert a Word Field to place the Merge Record # in the upper left-hand corner of the envelope and press ENTER.
14. Enter the following return address: **The Abbey Nursery, 225 Marshall Avenue, Greenberg, IL 33523**.
15. View the merged document.

16 Use the Next Record and Previous Record arrows to look at the different merge documents.

2 *How do you quickly move to the last record?*

17 Return to the Mail Merge Helper.

18 Select the Query Options dialog box and sort the records by first name.

To sort records so that all the records from a particular PostalCode appear in a group, and the higher ZIP codes print first, what settings would you make in the Query Options dialog box?

19 Return to the Main Document and view the results of the sort.

The illustration to the right shows how a preview of an envelope should look.

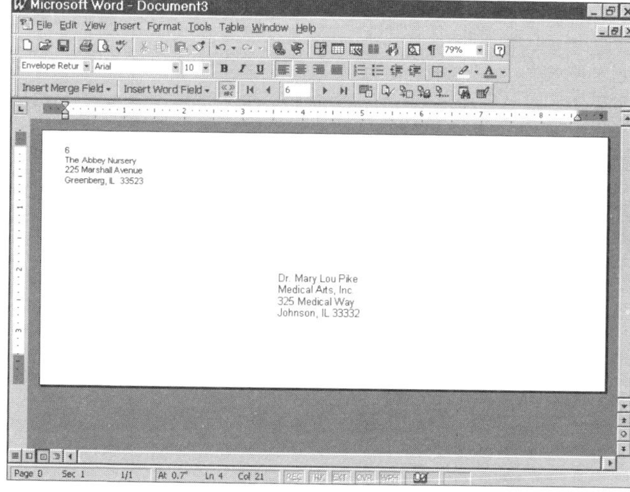

20 Print the merge using the Merge to Printer button on the Mail Merge toolbar.

Before you print, be sure your envelopes are loaded in your printer and that everything is set up to feed the envelopes properly. If you're in doubt, you can change the settings by selecting Tool, Envelopes, and Labels, and adjusting the options in the Envelope Options dialog box that appears.

21 Select File ➢ Close.

22 When prompted, don't save the changes to the documents.

Troubleshooting

TROUBLESHOOTING

You've had the help of Mail Merge Helper in getting through the steps of a mail merge. However, like any other procedure, you'll sometimes come across challenges you can't solve alone. Table 9-1 provides some answers to some of those questions that might come up.

Problem	Solution
I want to make a small change to only one of my letters.	You can either use the Ask or Fill-in Word fields to be prompted for a change as you merge, or merge to a document and then edit that one page of the document.
I have 355 records in my mail merge. How can I find the preview of just one of them?	Use the Find Record button on the Mail Merge toolbar, and then enter information about the record by field to locate it.
I want to use an Access database for my data source; how do I do that?	Using the Get Data button in the Mail Merge Helper ➢ Open Data Source; in the Open Data Source dialog box that follows, change the file type to Microsoft Access Database, locate your file, and open it.

WRAP UP

You've mastered the simple skills you need to make your mailings much easier. You've covered the following:

- Creating both a main document and data source for your mailings
- Making the choices involved in performing a mail merge
- Printing a mail merge letter, and generating mailing envelopes easily

Wrap up

If you want more practice with these skills, try preparing a mass mailing of letters and envelopes for your business or personal Christmas card list.

In Lesson 10, you start to explore the world of numbers with the Office suite accountant, Excel for Windows.

PART III

Excel for Windows

This part introduces you to Excel for Windows, Microsoft's spreadsheet application. It includes the following lessons:

- Lesson 10: Looking at the Anatomy of a Workbook
- Lesson 11: Editing Workbook Sheets
- Lesson 12: Adding Formulas for Success
- Lesson 13: Building Charts
- Lesson 14: Printing from Excel

LESSON 10

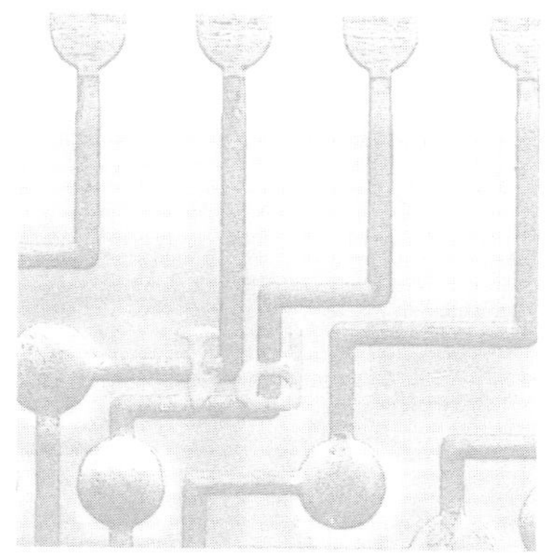

Looking at the Anatomy of a Workbook

GOALS

In this lesson, you'll be introduced to Excel, Office 97's spreadsheet program. You'll learn how to do the following tasks:

- Opening an Excel workbook
- Moving around an Excel workbook
- Naming worksheets
- Moving and copying worksheets
- Adding new worksheets
- Saving a workbook

Opening an Excel file

GET READY

To complete this lesson, you will need to have successfully installed Excel for Windows. You will also need the file Ex10-1 which you copied to your hard drive from the accompanying CD-ROM.

When you complete the exercises in this lesson, you'll have a document that matches the illustration at bottom right.

TRY OUT THE INTERACTIVE TUTORIALS ON YOUR CD!

UNDERSTANDING WORKBOOKS

Excel is a spreadsheet program. A spreadsheet program is used to create tables of data on which calculations can be performed. People use Excel to create budgets and documents to track performance or results.

Microsoft has organized each Excel file into what is called a workbook. A *workbook* is like a notebook that contains worksheets. You can have a workbook with only one worksheet filled out, or you can use several worksheets, each containing different data about the same project or topic. You could, for example, create a single workbook for a particular client, and use a different worksheet for that client's transactions during each month of the year. In fact, every workbook can contain over 200 worksheets.

Worksheets themselves consist of columns and rows of data. You can apply formulas to this data to add it, subtract it, multiply it, divide it — in other words, use any mathematical operation on data. You can also easily turn the data into impressive looking charts to show trends or percentages visually. Over the next few lessons, you'll learn how to do these things. But now, it's time to get your first glimpse of an Excel workbook.

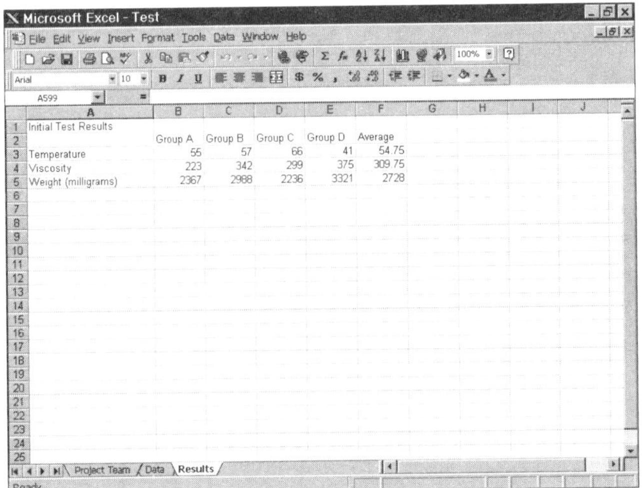

Opening an Excel file

The first thing to learn is what's involved in opening an Excel file.

1. Click the Start button on the Windows taskbar.
2. Select Programs.
3. Select Microsoft Excel.

Moving around a workbook

A blank workbook like the one in the illustration to the right appears. The workbook is temporarily titled Book1. Notice that there are already three worksheets in this workbook, with their name tabs near the bottom of your screen. The rows and columns of the active sheet (Sheet1) are visible. The rows have numbers running along their left side. The columns are designated with letters. Each point of intersection of a row and column is a box called a cell. Cells are named for that intersection. The cell at the intersection of Column B, Row 3, for example, is named B3.

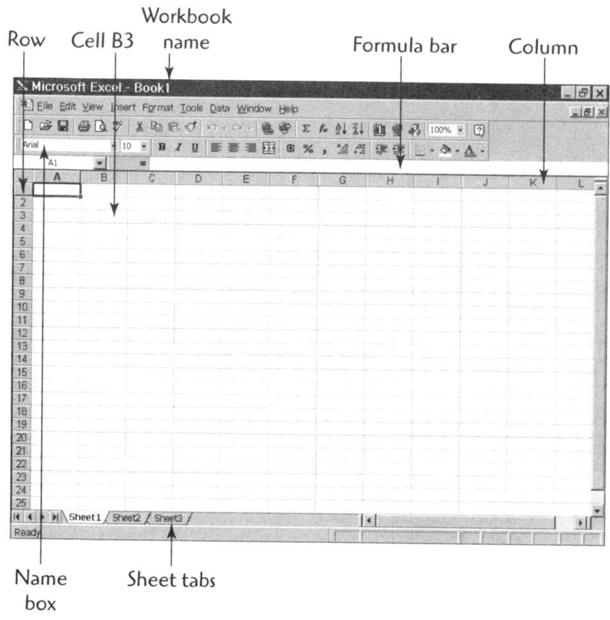

3. Click the cell at the intersection of Column G, Row 8. The name of the cell appears in the Name box.
4. Click the box containing the letter for Column C. This selects the entire column.
5. Click the box that contains the number for Row 2. This selects the entire row.
6. Click cell A1.
7. Type **Budget**.

Notice that as you type the letters not only appear in the cell, but also in the formula bar along the top of the worksheet. If you enter a formula to perform calculations on data in a cell, the result of the calculation will appear in the cell, but the formula is displayed in the formula bar.

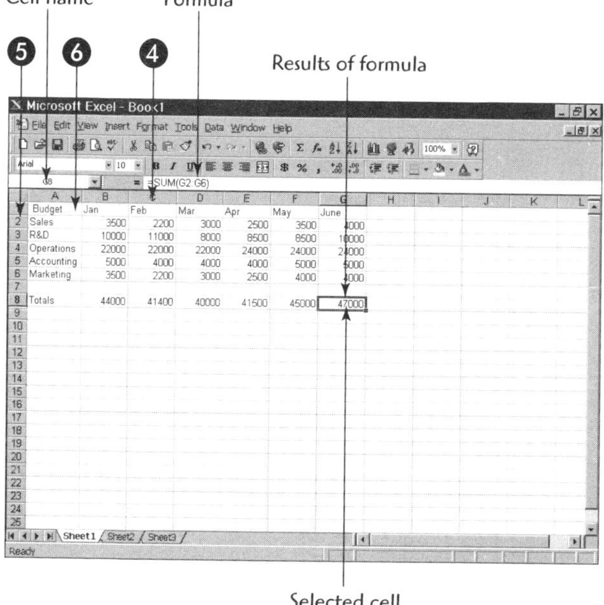

Moving around a workbook

Workbooks have three worksheets in them by default, and you can create many, many more. Each worksheet has thousands of empty rows and dozens of columns, so learning to get around them is the first skill to practice.

1. Close the current workbook and open the file Ex10-1.
2. Click the tab for Sheet2. Sheet2 is now the active sheet.

Moving around a workbook

VISUAL BONUS: AN EXCEL WORKBOOK

This Visual Bonus gives you an idea of how the pieces of an Excel workbook relate to each other.

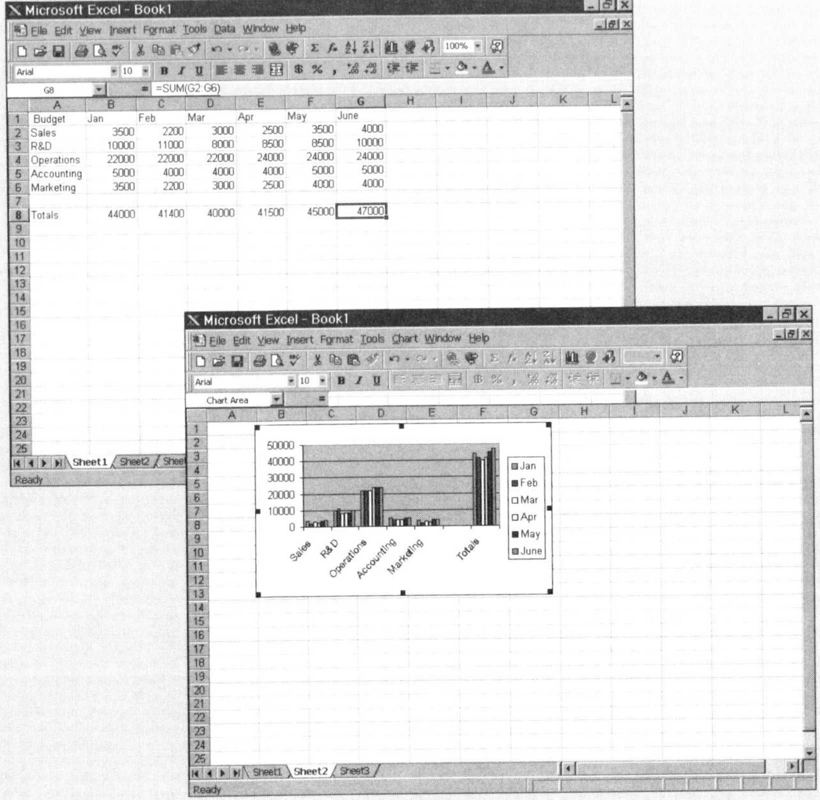

Each sheet is held in the workbook like pages in a binder. Make a sheet active by clicking its tab. Sheet2 contains a chart based on the numbers on Sheet1.

3. Click the right arrow key on the horizontal scroll bar repeatedly to move across the worksheet. Stop when you reach the column titled G8.

   By default, there are over 200 columns in a single spreadsheet, however you can add columns as you need them. Now you can see how many rows are available.

4. Click the down-pointing arrow on the vertical scroll bar continuously. Stop when you reach row 500.

There are fifty thousand rows in each Excel worksheet. You can also add rows — but let's hope you never have to! With all those rows and columns, it's helpful to be able to go to a particular row quickly. You can do that using the Name box.

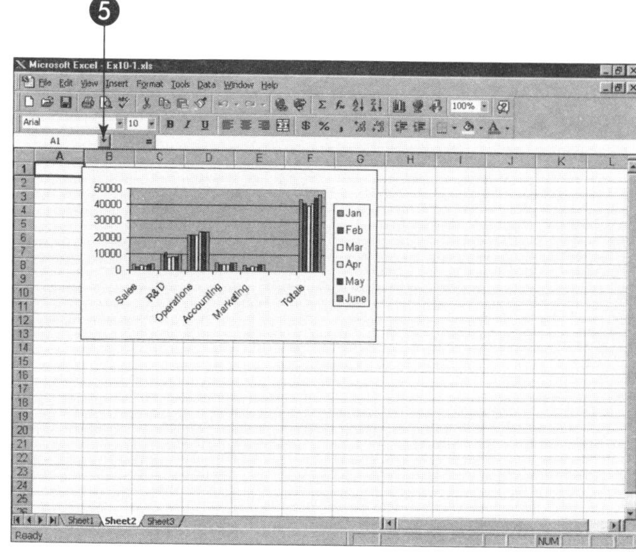

5. Click the arrow on the Name box (at the left end of the formula bar).
6. Type **A10000** and press Enter.
7. Click on the scroll box in the vertical scroll bar and drag it to the top of the bar to return to the first row.
8. Click the tab for Sheet3; a blank worksheet appears.

WORKING WITH WORKSHEETS

To organize your workbook, it's helpful to understand how to manipulate the worksheets that it contains. In the following exercises, you'll practice naming, moving, and adding new worksheets to a workbook.

Naming worksheets

Although worksheets are named Sheet1, Sheet2, and so on when you first create them, you can name them something a little more specific to your contents.

1. Right-click the tab for Sheet3.
2. Select Rename from the shortcut menu.
3. Type **Sales**.
4. Select the tab for Sheet2.
5. Double-click on the tab.
6. Type **Chart**.
7. Select the tab for Sheet1.
8. Double-click the tab.
9. Type **Budget**.

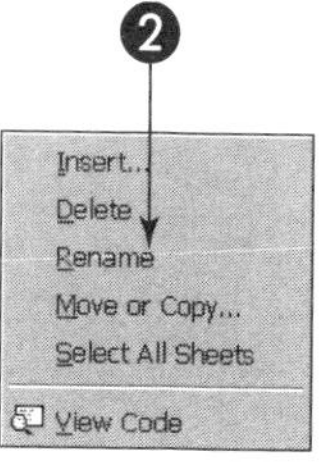

Moving worksheets

You can use these two methods — selecting the Rename command from the shortcut menu or double-clicking the tab itself — to rename each tab. It can be very helpful in navigating around your workbook if each worksheet is named to reflect its contents.

Moving worksheets

Just because you build a worksheet in the Sheet 3 position, for example, you aren't stuck with that. You can easily change which worksheet goes where.

1. Right-click the Budget tab.
2. From the shortcut menu, select Move or Copy. The dialog box shown in the illustration to the right appears.

   You can choose to move or copy a sheet to a different workbook by clicking the arrow on the *To book* box and selecting (new book). This opens a new workbook with a single sheet. You can also move or copy a worksheet to another location in the current workbook.

3. Click Sales in the *Before sheet* list.
4. Click OK. The sheet moves to the right in the order of sheets.

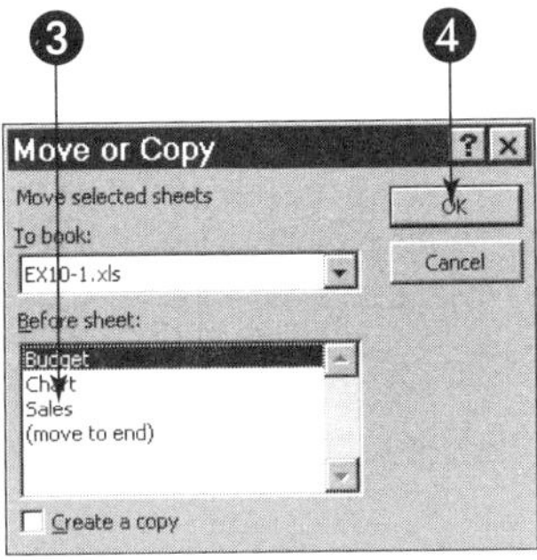

Copying and adding new worksheets

In addition to moving existing worksheets, you can make copies of sheets or add additional blank worksheets to your workbook.

1. Select Edit ➢ Move or Copy Sheet.
2. Click the *Create a copy* check box.
3. Select *(move to end)* in the *Before sheet* list.
4. Click OK.

   A fourth sheet tab appears at the far right, titled Chart(2). You can now rename the new sheet and modify its contents as you wish.

   Next, add a new worksheet. This is a simple one-step procedure.

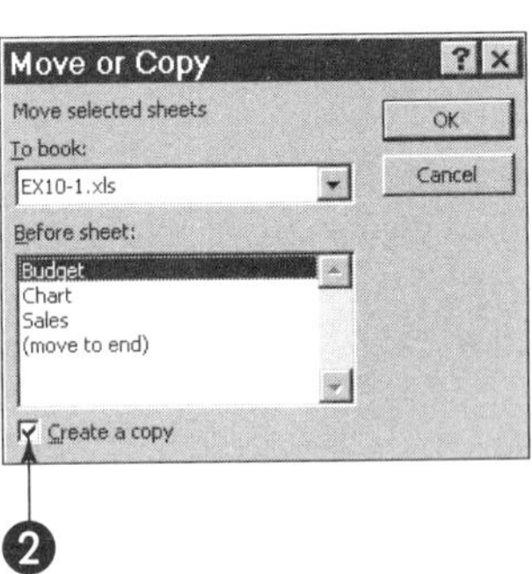

5 Select Insert.

6 Select Worksheet. The new sheet appears.

By default, all new workbooks have three worksheets. You can change that default to more or less sheets. Select Tools ➢ Options. On the General tab of the Options dialog box, use the arrows in the Sheets in New workbook *box to set a new default.*

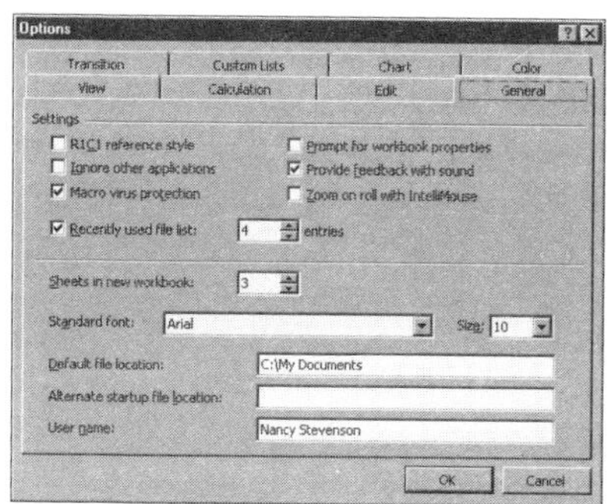

Saving a workbook

As with any other software application, it's wise to save files often so you don't lose your valuable work. Here's how you save in Excel:

1 Select File ➢ Save. The Save As dialog box in the illustration to the right appears.

2 Select the MyDocs directory you created in earlier lessons. If you don't have this directory, create it now using the Create New Folder button in the Save dialog box.

3 Enter the name **MyWorkbook** in the *File name* box.

Notice that Excel files are saved in the Microsoft Excel Workbook format. An extension of .xls appears at the end of all Excel filenames. Once you've saved a file, if you want to save a workbook with a different name, you can select File ➢ Save As and enter a new workbook name in the *File name* box.

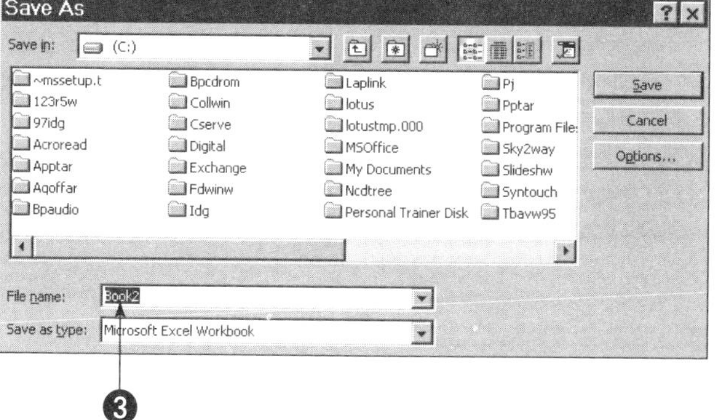

SKILLS CHALLENGE: CREATING A WORKBOOK

It's time to practice all you've learned by working with another workbook and making changes and settings.

1 Close any open files.

2 Open the file Ex10-2.

3. Select cell F3.

What is the formula displayed in the formula bar calculating?

4. Using the Name box, go to cell F600.
5. Return to cell A1.
6. Rename Sheet1 with the name **Results**.

What are the two ways to rename a worksheet?

7. Make a copy of the Results worksheet and place it at the end of the workbook.
8. Rename the copy of the Results worksheet **Final**.
9. Make a copy of the Results worksheet and place it in a new workbook.
10. Add two new worksheets to the new workbook.

How can you set up Excel to provide five worksheets in each new workbook by default?

11. Name Worksheet 1 **Project Team**.
12. Name Worksheet 2 **Data**.
13. Save the new workbook with the name **Test**.
14. Close Excel.

TRY OUT THE INTERACTIVE TUTORIALS ON YOUR CD!

TROUBLESHOOTING

This lesson got you on the road to learning the features that make Excel the best-selling spreadsheet program today. However, you might encounter some challenges as you explore Excel. The following table offers some troubleshooting advice to help you out.

Problem	Solution
I want to copy a worksheet to another existing workbook.	Open the other workbook; when you select the Move or Copy command from the Edit menu, the workbook will be listed in the *To book* box.
I moved all the way over to Column DD; how do I get back to A1 quickly?	You can use the Name box and enter A1, or press Ctrl + Home.
I have 20 worksheets in my workbook; how can I see the names of tabs farther to the right?	When you have more tabs than can show in the space provided, use the set of four arrows to the left of the sheet names to display additional tabs.

WRAP UP

In this lesson, you've caught a glimpse of how Excel files are organized. You learned the following:

- Excel workbooks are collections of worksheets containing cells, rows, and columns
- How to use worksheets, including renaming, moving, and creating them
- How to save Excel files

In Lesson 11, you'll begin to add data to your workbook and format that data.

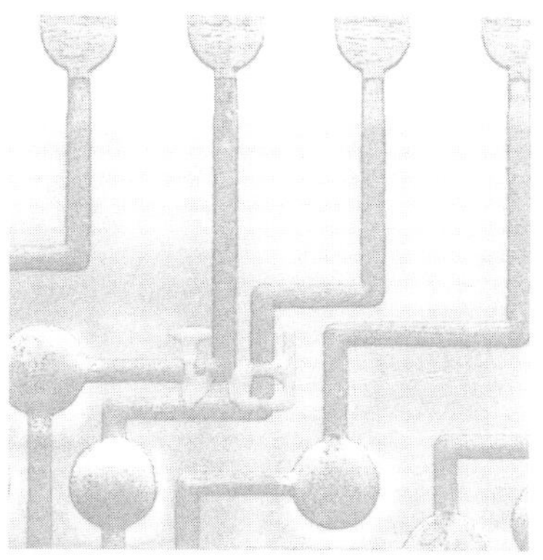

Building Worksheets

GOALS

It's time to build your first Excel worksheet! As you do, you'll pick up the following skills:

- Entering information in cells
- Filling in data by example
- Adding a title
- Changing font type and size
- Applying shading and borders to cells
- Aligning text
- Formatting numbers
- Adding and rearranging columns and rows
- Resizing columns and rows

Entering information in cells

GET READY

To complete this lesson, you need the files Ex11-1 and Ex11-2, which you copied to your hard drive from the accompanying CD-ROM.

At the end of these exercises, you'll have built an Excel worksheet like the one in the illustration to the right.

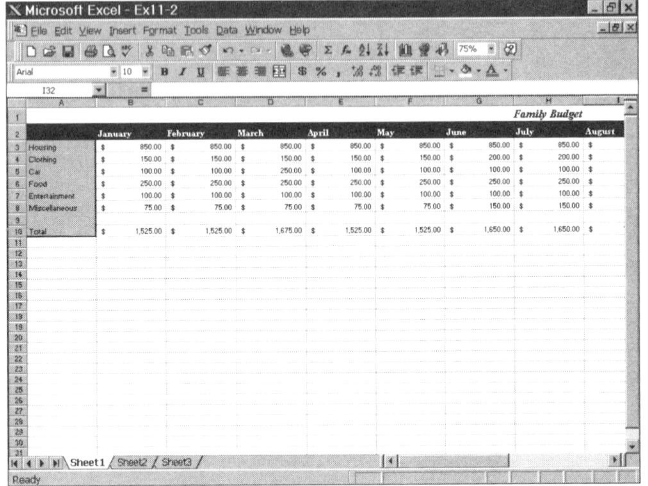

ENTERING DATA

Building a worksheet in Excel involves three basic steps: entering the data, formatting the data, and applying formulas to the data. An example of this process is entering a column of numbers representing income for the month of August, formatting the numbers as currency, and applying a formula to add them together to reflect the total income for the month. This lesson will take you through the first two steps: entering and formatting data.

Data is entered into individual cells of the worksheet, and, except for a few shortcuts, is simply a matter of typing what you want in each cell.

Entering information in cells

You begin by entering the numbers that represent a family budget.

1. Open Excel.
2. Select cell A2.
3. Type **Housing**.
4. Press Enter.
5. In cell B2, type **850**.
6. Continue entering the information listed in Table 11-1.

   Notice that some text entered into column A is too wide for the column. The end of the words appear cut off. Don't worry; you fix that later in this lesson. For now, add the column headings to your worksheet.

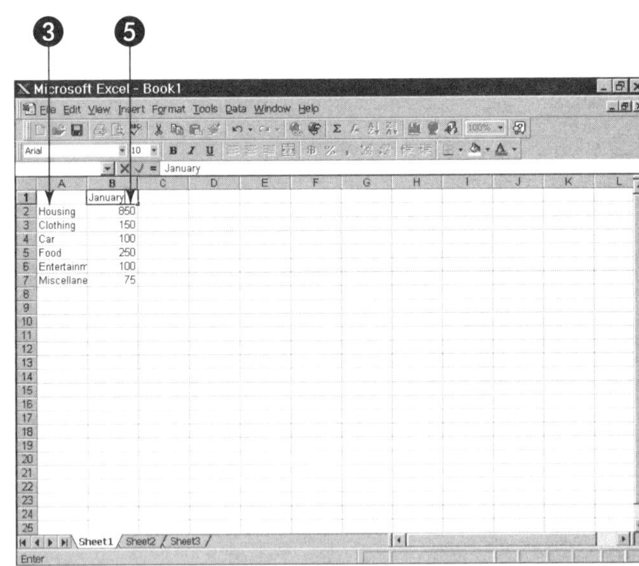

TABLE 11-1 DATA FOR WORKSHEET EXAMPLE

Cell Reference	Data
A3	Clothing
B3	150
A4	Car
B4	100
A5	Food
B5	250
A6	Entertainment
B6	100
A7	Miscellaneous
B7	75

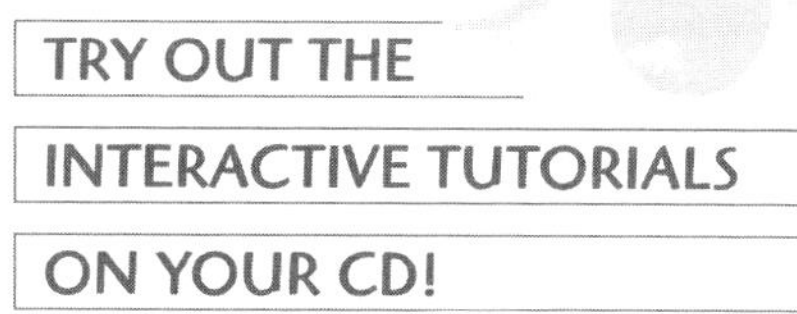

Filling in data by example

You don't have to enter all the data in a worksheet yourself. Excel is capable of filling an entire series of cells with the same number. Excel can even project a trend and enter the logical data to complete a series for you. For example, if you enter January as a column heading, Excel can complete the series by entering the other months of the year in subsequent column headings.

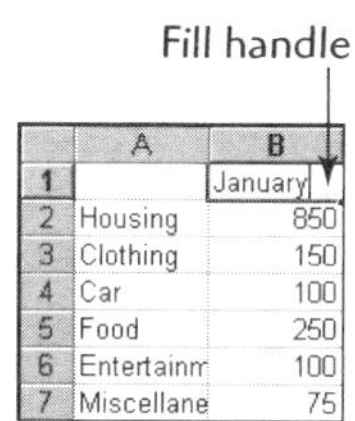

❶ Select cell B1.

❷ Type **January**.

With cell B1 still selected, as in the illustration, there is a small handle in the bottom-right corner of the cell border. This is called the fill handle. You can use this to complete a logical series of text or numbers.

❸ Click the fill handle for cell B1; your cursor changes to a crosshair.

❹ Drag to the right to highlight cells C1 to G1.

❺ Release your mouse button and Excel fills in the rest of the months in the series for the cells you've selected.

❻ Select cell B2.

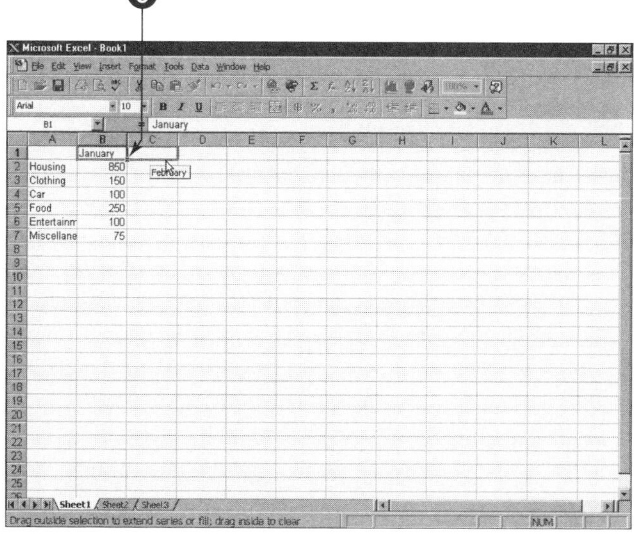

7. Click the fill handle and drag to highlight C2 through G2.

When you release your mouse button this time, Excel has copied the original number into each of the other cells you selected. This fill feature is especially handy in budgets, where one item, such as the housing cost in this example, stays constant over a period of several months or years.

To automatically enter a series of numbers, enter the first two values (to indicate a trend) and then use the fill handle to complete the series. For example, if you entered 2 in cell A1 and 4 in cell B1, and then selected those two cells and dragged the fill handle from B1 over cells C1 through F1, the numbers 6, 8, 10, and 12 would be entered automatically.

Adding a title

Quite often it's helpful to have a title for your worksheet. A title should be placed in the first row of a worksheet. However, you don't want the text of a title to stop and start at the wall of each cell. That's where the capability to merge cells of a single row come in handy.

1. Select row 1 by clicking the number 1 on the far left of the row.
2. Select Insert ➢ Rows.
3. Select cells A1 through G1.
4. Click the Merge and Center tool.
5. Type **Family Budget**.

   The title is automatically centered in the merged cells. However, it would be better if you could format the title to stand out from all the other text in the worksheet. Give that a try.

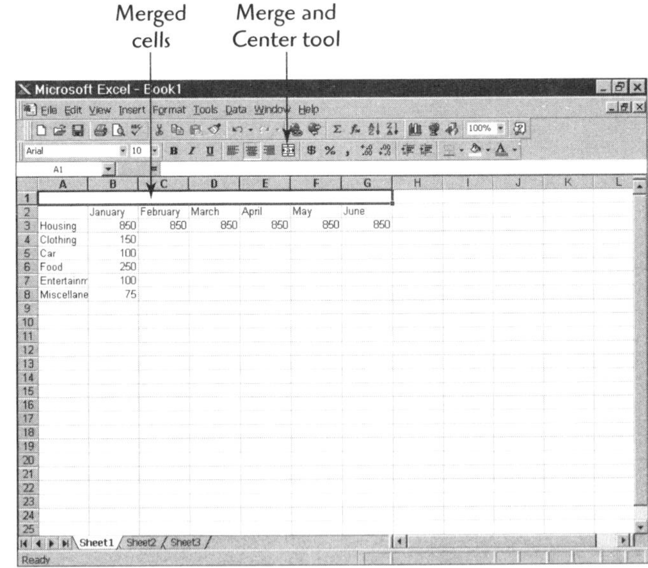

FORMATTING DATA

You can format text and numbers in Excel with all the tools you've already used in Word. You can change the font and font size, add styles such as bold, italic, or underline, and adjust alignment. You can even modify the color of shading in each cell or apply borders to cells.

When formatting in Excel, you often want to format numbers to be a specific type of number, for example, currency, date format, or percentages.

Formatting text

Start by formatting text — something practiced in Word.

1. Select Row 2.
2. Select Format ➢ Cells. The Format Cells dialog box appears.
3. If it's not already displayed, select the Font tab.
4. Select Times New Roman from the *Font* list.
5. Select Bold in the *Font style* drop-down list.
6. Select 11 in the *Font size* drop-down list.
7. Choose OK.
8. Select the cell containing the title *Family Budget.*
9. Choose OK to save the cell formatting.
10. Open the *Font* drop-down list on the toolbar and select Times New Roman.
11. Select 14 points in the *Size* drop-down list on the toolbar.
12. Using the Bold and Italic buttons on the toolbar, make the title bold and italicized.

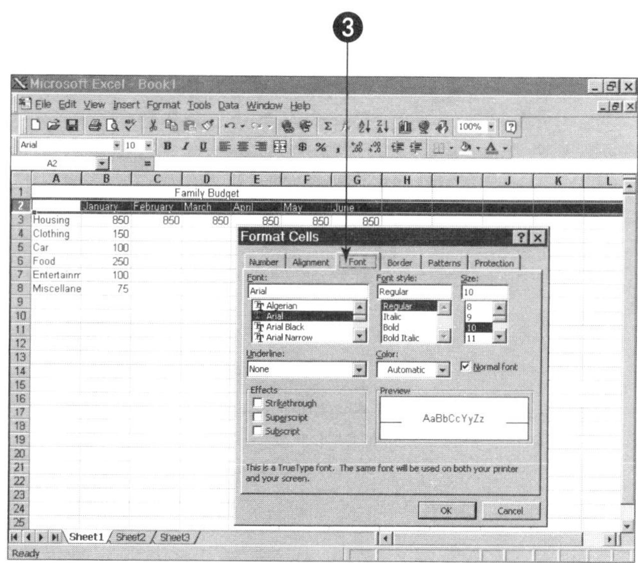

Formatting cells

Note that you don't have to select text within a cell to format it; just select the cell itself and any formatting changes you select will be applied to all text in the cell. However, if you want to format only a portion of text in a cell, select that portion in the Formula bar before applying formatting.

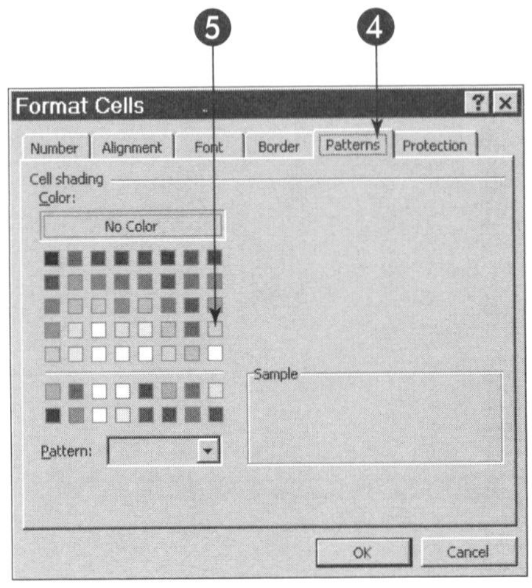

Formatting cells

You can also format the background and border effects used on individual cells in your worksheet. Using these formatting features, you can differentiate certain blocks of cells from others in your worksheet.

1. Select cells A3 through A8.
2. Select Format.
3. Choose Cells.
4. Select the Patterns tab.
5. Select a light gray cell shading (the color sample block four down in the far right-hand column of samples).

If you want to fill a cell or cells with a pattern, such as stripes, rather than a color, use the Pattern pop-up menu in the Format Cells dialog box.

6. Select the Border tab.
7. Click the Outline Preset.
8. In the *Line style* list, select the fifth style down on the right side (a thick solid line).
9. In the Border styles, select the option with a border on the right side of the cells.

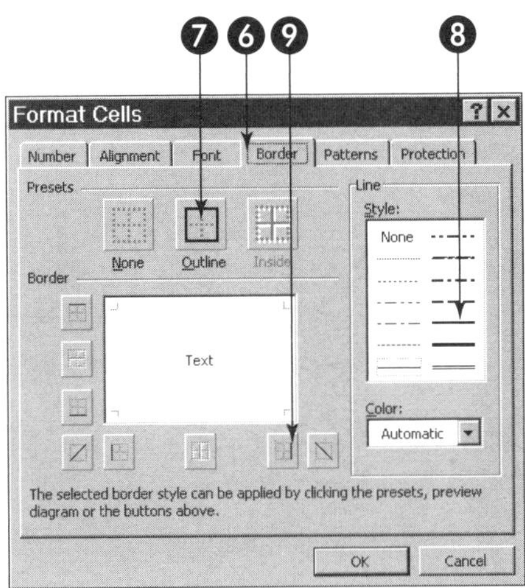

10. Select cells B2 through G2.
11. Open the Border drop-down menu on the toolbar.
12. Select the bottom border style. Your spreadsheet should now look like the one in the illustration to the right.

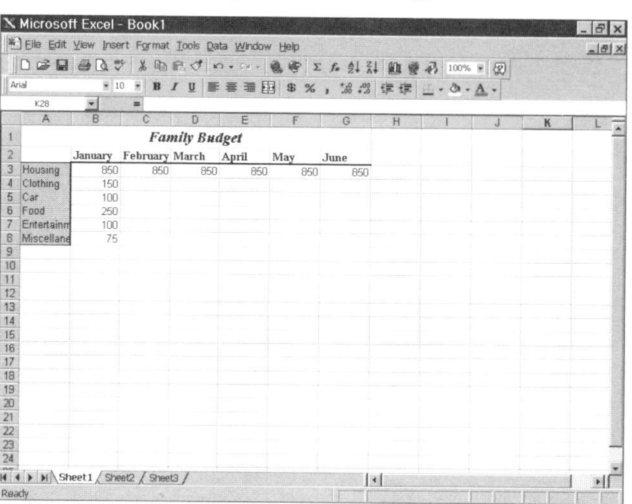

Aligning text

Sometimes you will prefer to center text, such as column headings, in cells; other times you will prefer to have things left- or right-aligned.

Note that there is a relationship between how you format numbers and alignment. For example, currency will be right aligned so the dollars line up down the column.

Practice aligning text.

1. Select Row 2.
2. Click the Center button on the Formatting toolbar.

   Aligning text is simple, using either the toolbar or the alignment tab of the Format Cells dialog box. However, you should notice something interesting about applying this and other formatting. If you select an entire row or column and apply formatting, such as center alignment, any text you add to any cell in that row or column will be formatted automatically. If you select only a set of cells in a row or column and apply formatting, text entered in other cells in the same row or column will have to be formatted manually.

   You should also notice that Excel applies certain default alignment depending on what you enter. The text you entered for Column A and Row 2 was automatically aligned to the left; however, the numbers you entered in Row 3 and Column B were aligned to the right. Numbers are typically aligned to the right so that their final numerals line up.

3. Select cells B3 to B8.

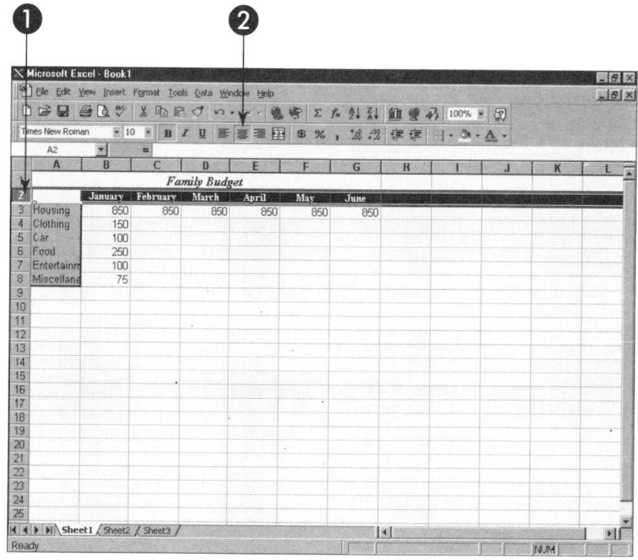

Formatting numbers

4. Click on the Align Left tool on the toolbar.

   Notice how odd the numbers look lined up this way. When numbers include decimal points, this alignment looks even stranger. Although you might want to change alignment for column, row, or worksheet headings, Excel's default alignment for numbers is usually best.

5. Click the Undo tool to undo your formatting change.

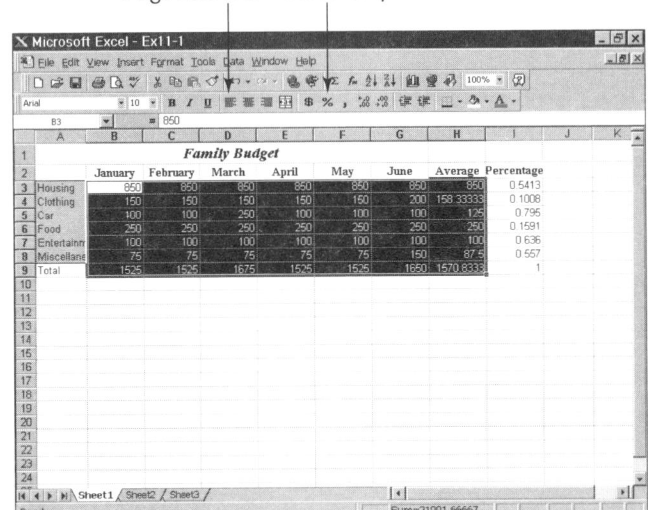

Formatting numbers

Being able to easily assign the appropriate format to numbers is a great time-saver. Rather than type dollar signs and decimal points for all the currency in a budget, for example, you need only type numbers and apply currency formatting. In order to try this out with a few different types of numbers, work with a different version of the family budget you've been working with.

1. Close the current file and save it with the name **Budget**.
2. Open the file named Ex11-1.
3. Select the block of cells ranging from B3 to H9, as in the illustration to the right.
4. Select Format ➢ Cells.
5. Select the Number tab.
6. In the *Category* list, select Currency. Notice there are several currency formats to choose from; for U.S. dollars, the default choice is correct.
7. Choose OK.

   All the numbers you had selected are now formatted as currency, with dollar signs and appropriate decimal points. Turn your attention to that last column, which reflects what percentage each average cost is of the total average cost.

8. Select cell I3 through I9.
9. Click the Percent Style button on the toolbar.

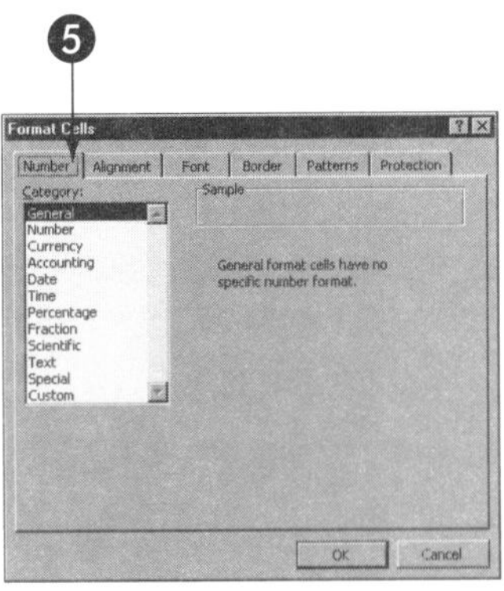

Adding columns and rows

Your worksheet should now look like the one in the illustration to the right.

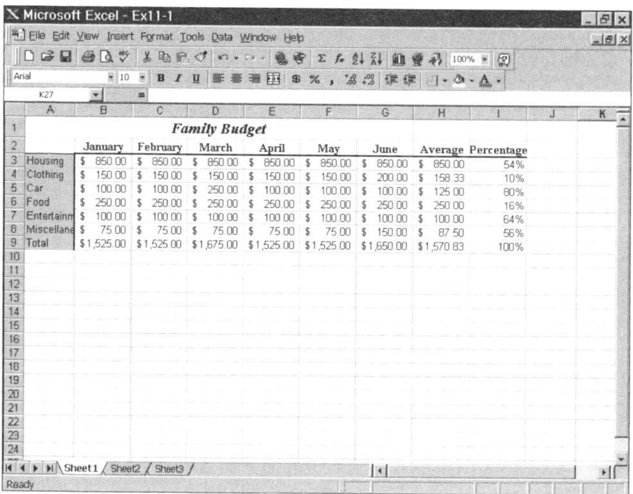

WORKING WITH COLUMNS AND ROWS

Columns and rows are also important in achieving a polished look for your worksheet. Sometimes you'll need to add or rearrange columns or rows, and often you'll need to resize them to accommodate text comfortably. Try this now with the family budget.

Adding columns and rows

Excel offers great flexibility in adding new columns and rows, or rearranging those you've already created.

1. Select column H.
2. Click the Insert menu.
3. Select Column. Notice that the new column appears to the left of the selected column.

TIP

If you insert a new row using the same procedure, it is inserted above the selected row.

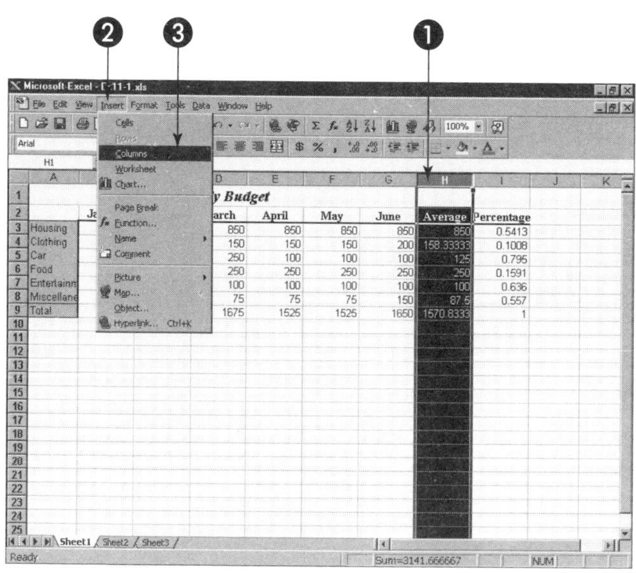

4. Click the column H heading with your right mouse button.
5. Select Insert from the shortcut menu. A new column is automatically inserted.
6. Repeat the above step until you've inserted four more columns, one for each remaining month of the year.
7. Use the fill handle from cell G2 (June) to fill in the months in the new columns, using the dragging method discussed earlier.
8. Select column N.
9. Select Insert ➢ Column.
10. Select column O.

⓫ Select Edit ➢ Cut.

⓬ Select column N.

⓭ Click the Paste button on the toolbar. All the data from column O is pasted into the selected column.

You can move entire sections of data around in your worksheet by inserting blank rows or columns and using the cut, paste, and copy features. However, keep in mind that any formulas you've applied (you learn more about formulas in Lesson 12) work relative to named cells; rearranging whole rows and columns might change the cell references in those formulas, so it's best to arrange them before you create any formulas.

Resizing columns and rows

Several words in Column A are cut off because of the column width. It's time to fix that.

❶ Place your mouse pointer between the column headings for Columns A and B. Your pointer changes to a two-way pointing arrow.

❷ Click and drag the pointer until the measurement readout shown in the accompanying illustration reads 14.00.

You can also adjust the height of rows in your worksheet. You might want to do that to provide more space between numbers in a large spreadsheet, for instance. Rows can be resized in the same way you've just resized a column. However, if you want to resize a whole range of rows or columns to a new, uniform size, it's better to use menu commands.

❸ Select Rows 3 through 9.

❹ Select Format ➢ Row ➢ Height. The Row Height dialog box appears.

❺ Type **15** for the new row height.

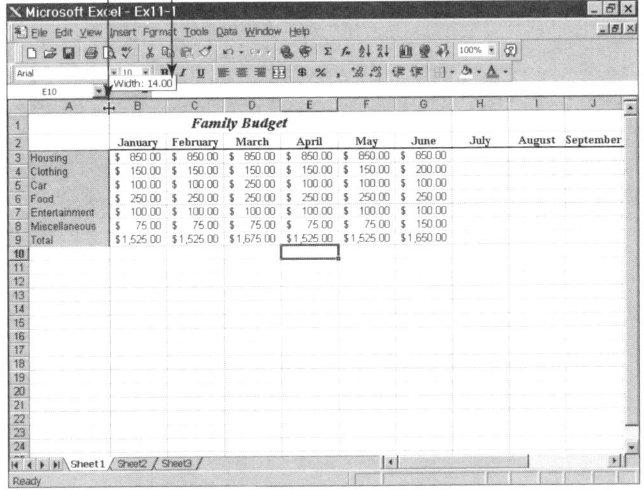

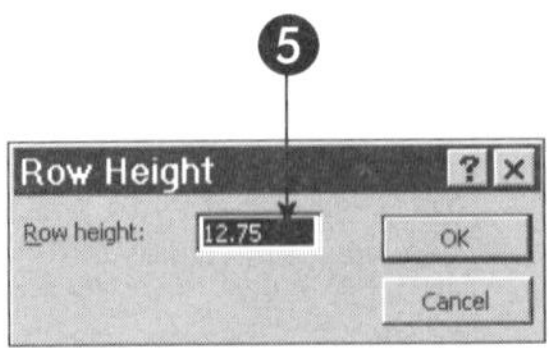

6. Choose OK. The rows are now uniformly higher, making the text within them easier to read.

TRY OUT THE
INTERACTIVE TUTORIALS
ON YOUR CD!

SKILLS CHALLENGE: BUILDING A BUDGET

This Skills Challenge continues with the Family Budget you've been building throughout this lesson. If you haven't saved that file or you no longer have it onscreen, you can open the file Ex11-2 to complete the following steps.

1. Using the fill handle, carry each of the budget figures for June across to December.
2. Change the Clothing expense for September to $250 (school's open!).
3. Format all the numbers in your worksheet to the Times New Roman font.
4. Format Row 2 to be shaded black.
5. Format all text in Row 2 to be white.

What tool could you use to quickly change font color?

6. Merge cells in the top row so that your worksheet title is centered above the entire range of columns.
7. Increase the height of Row 2 to be 20.25.

Name two methods of changing column or row size.

8. Apply a thick bottom border line to the range of cells A3 through A9.
9. Insert a row above the current Row 9 (between Miscellaneous and the Total).

If you select a column and insert a new column, does the new column appear to the left or right of the selected column?

⑩ Widen all columns from B through O to 16 points.

⑪ Center the text in Row 2.

⑫ Format the text in cells A3 through A10 to be bold.

TROUBLESHOOTING

You've picked up quite a bit about entering and formatting data in your worksheet. As you use the various features and practice building your own worksheets, you might encounter a few of the challenges listed in the table below.

Problem	Solution
I entered a value and then applied percentage format and my 10 percent became *1000.00%*.	You must type percentages in as decimal values; for example, 10 percent is .10. Percentage format will then return *10%*.
I have 20 rows of numbers. How can I quickly fill three more columns to repeat these numbers without filling row by row?	Select the entire range of cells in the rows, and then use the fill handle on the bottom right cell in the range of cells and drag.
I formatted my column headings to be bold, but new column headings don't appear bold.	Don't select a range of cells in a row before formatting, select the entire row so any new text in the row also takes on this applied formatting.

WRAP UP

You mastered two of the three major tasks you can perform with an Excel worksheet in this lesson, entering text and formatting the worksheet. You learned the following:

- How to format text with font, alignment, and number type formatting
- How to format cells with shading and borders

- How to merge cells to create a worksheet title
- How to insert, resize, and move columns and rows of data around your worksheet

In Lesson 12, you tackle the third major set of features used to build a worksheet: the formulas and functions that enable you to apply calculations to your data.

LESSON 12

Adding Formulas for Success

GOALS

In this lesson, you learn how to manipulate the numbers in your Excel worksheet. You'll practice the following:

- Entering formulas
- Using functions within formulas
- Using formulas in combination
- Copying formulas
- Finding and resolving errors in formulas

Get ready

GET READY

To complete the exercises in this lesson, you need the files Ex12-1, Ex12-2, and Ex12-3, which you copied to your hard drive from the accompanying CD-ROM.

When you're done with the exercises, you'll have created several documents, including the one in the illustration to the right.

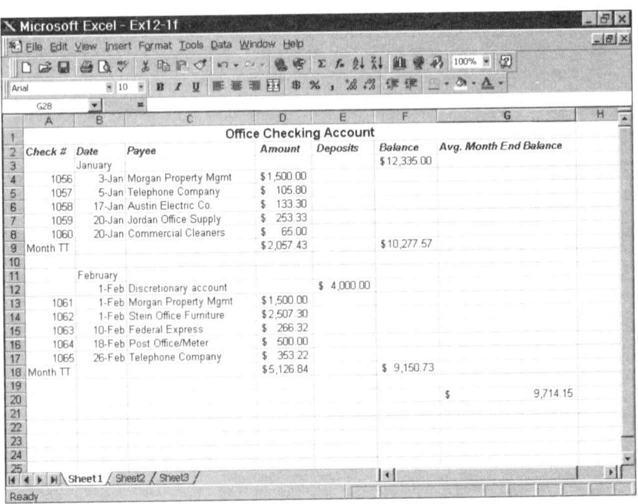

HOW DOES EXCEL CALCULATE?

Excel can take the data you enter in your worksheet and perform any calculation that you can with a calculator or a slide rule. You can add simple columns of figures, or multiply the value in one cell by the value in another and have the result entered in a third cell. You can even place the average of a column of figures in one cell, and then perform a calculation on that cell to figure what percentage that number is of a number in yet another cell.

The clue to calculations in Excel is understanding that you create formulas to designate a function to be performed to a particular range of cells. You already learned how to refer to Excel cells, such as A1 or G7, reflecting the intersection of a particular row and column. In this lesson, you learn how to enter cell references into formulas to get the results you want.

Entering formulas

You will work with an Excel file that has checking account activity recorded. In this exercise, you apply formulas to keep a running total of checks written in a given month and subtract checks from a running balance.

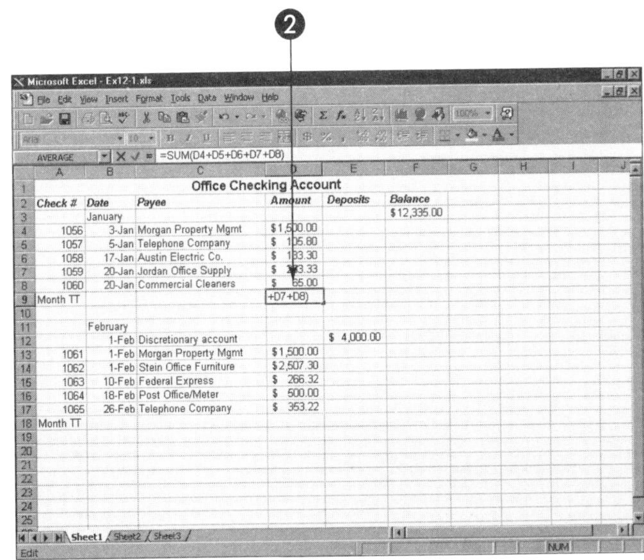

1. Open the file Ex12-1.
2. Select cell D9.
3. Type = (the equal sign indicates the beginning of a formula).
4. Type (.

   Note: Every formula argument begins and ends with a parenthesis.

VISUAL BONUS: HOW FORMULAS RELATE TO WORKSHEET CELLS

This Visual Bonus gives you an idea of how a simple formula in Excel works.

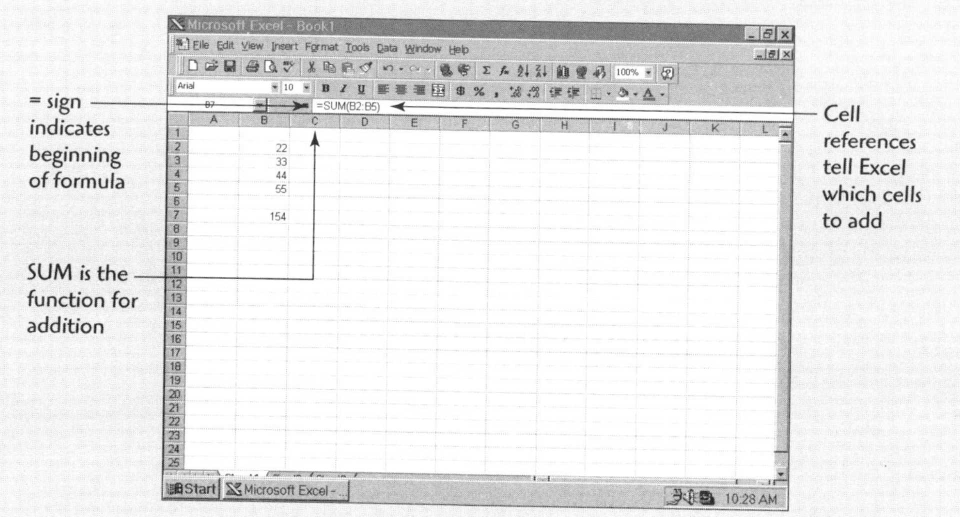

Here's a simple addition formula entered in the formula bar. The cell you've selected, which the results of this formula will be placed in, is in the Cell name field to the left of the formula.

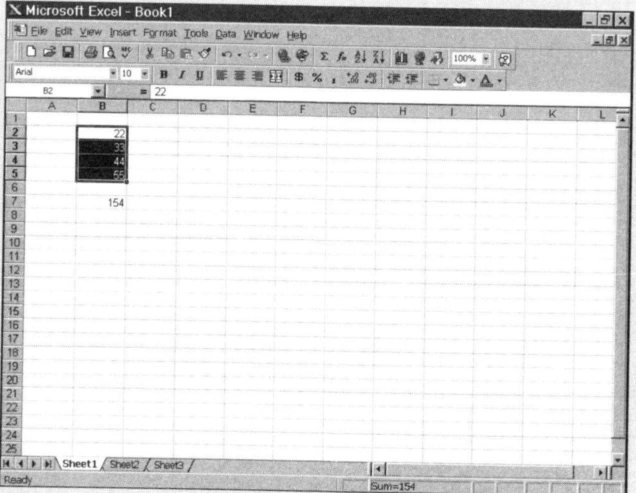

Here are the cells included in the formula's reference.

continued

VISUAL BONUS: HOW FORMULAS RELATE TO WORKSHEET CELLS *(continued)*

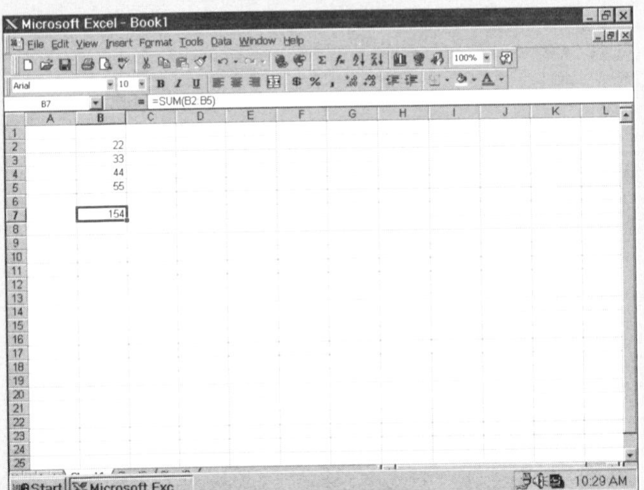

When the formula is entered in the Formula bar it returns a value in the selected cell.

Then type **D4+D5+D6+D7+D8)**. This formula has five cell references, and the plus sign tells Excel to add the values in those cells.

5. Press Enter.

That's it! The total of the amounts in cells D4 through D8 ($2,057.43) is entered in cell D9. One of the nicest things about using formulas to perform your calculations is that if you change a value in the named range, the formula automatically recalculates the total. For example, if you discover that you incorrectly entered one of the check amounts when you get your bank statement, you can simply change the check amount, and the total for the month would adjust automatically.

TRY OUT THE INTERACTIVE TUTORIALS ON YOUR CD!

Using functions within formulas

Functions are commonly used operations that Excel can perform, such as SUM to add a range of numbers, or COUNT to count the number of cells that meet certain criteria. *Arguments* are the values on which those operations are performed. (The argument in an Excel formula must appear in parentheses.)

Using functions, you can quickly add columns of numbers to a sheet. Try that with the checks written in February; this time use your mouse to indicate a range of cells.

1. Select cell D18.
2. Type **=SUM(**. *SUM* is the name of a function that adds all the values between the parentheses.
3. Using your mouse, click and drag over the range of cells from D13 through D17.
4. Type **)** and press Enter.

The total for the range of cells from D13 to D17 ($5,126.84) appears. Notice that while you were selecting the cell references with your mouse, a dotted line border appeared around the selected range and a small callout like the one in the illustration to the right told you the number of rows and columns currently selected so you would make no mistake about exactly which cells were included.

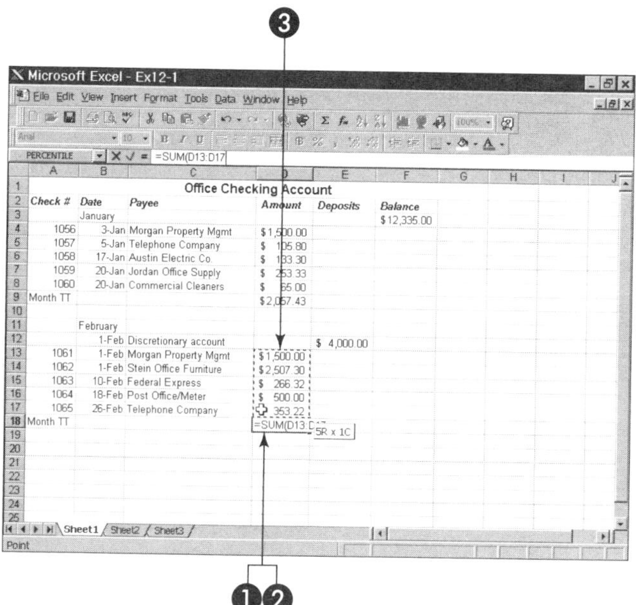

If you want to enter a range of cells into a formula without using the mouse, use a colon. In this example, the formula would read =SUM(D13:D17). This saves you having to type the name of each cell with a + symbol between them. In a larger range of cells references, this can be a big time-saver.

One time-saver you should be aware of is the AutoSum button on the toolbar. If you select an empty cell and click AutoSum, a formula is automatically entered to sum up all values in that column directly above the selected cell.

Using formulas in combination

Now use subtraction in a calculation of the month-end balance for both January and February.

1. Select Cell F9.
2. Type **=(F3-D9)**. The minus sign in this argument is all you need to subtract one cell from another.
3. Press Enter.
4. Select cell F18.
5. Type **=(F9-D18+E12)**.
6. Press Enter.

   In this formula, you told Excel to take the month-end balance for January in Column F (cell F9), deduct the total number of checks written in February (cell D18), and add in the deposit made in February (cell E12). So not only can you perform several types of calculations in the same formula, but you can perform calculations involving cells that contain formulas.

Microsoft Excel - Ex12-1.xls

F18 =(F9-D18+E12)

	A	B	C	D	E	F
1			Office Checking Account			
2	Check #	Date	Payee	Amount	Deposits	Balance
3		January				$12,335.00
4	1056	3-Jan	Morgan Property Mgmt	$1,500.00		
5	1057	5-Jan	Telephone Company	$ 105.80		
6	1058	17-Jan	Austin Electric Co.	$ 133.30		
7	1059	20-Jan	Jordan Office Supply	$ 253.33		
8	1060	20-Jan	Commercial Cleaners	$ 65.00		
9	Month TT			$2,057.43		$10,277.57
10						
11		February				
12		1-Feb	Discretionary account		$ 4,000.00	
13	1061	1-Feb	Morgan Property Mgmt	$1,500.00		
14	1062	1-Feb	Stein Office Furniture	$2,507.30		
15	1063	10-Feb	Federal Express	$ 266.32		
16	1064	18-Feb	Post Office/Meter	$ 500.00		
17	1065	26-Feb	Telephone Company	$ 353.22		
18	Month TT			$5,126.84		$ 9,150.73

TIP

One serious word of caution is warranted here. Because Excel calculates based on cell references, if you change your worksheet around, you run the risk of getting the wrong value returned by the formula. For example, if you added an additional check or deposit for February after creating the formula in cell F18, the cells in which the check or deposit were entered wouldn't be included in the results of the formula. If you do make changes after creating formulas, be sure to check the formulas to be certain they include all rows and columns that you want included.

Now, use the AVERAGE function and try to figure out what the average month-end account balance is for this checking account. This example applies a formula containing a function on two cells that contain formulas.

Using formulas in combination

7. Select cell G20.
8. Type =.
9. Select Insert.
10. Select Function.

    The Paste Function dialog box shown in the next illustration appears. Excel functions are divided by category, such as financial and statistical. If you're not sure which category a function should fall into, you can select the All category here to see all the functions available. Notice that a description of the function you select appears at the bottom of this dialog box.

11. Select Statistical in the *Function category* list.
12. Select AVERAGE in the *Function name* list.
13. Choose OK. The Average dialog box appears so you can enter the argument for this formula.
14. Type **F9,F18**. This indicates the cells whose values Excel should average. A comma is used to separate the two values in an average formula.
15. Choose OK. The average of the two named cells is returned in cell G20.

    Functions can get quite complex: You can use functions for obscure things, such as the "cumulative beta probability density function" in a statistical calculation, or something a little closer to home; the calculation of payments for a loan, such as a mortgage, based on a set interest rate. However, the basic operators you use with these functions are constant. Table 12-1 shows you the use of various symbols in creating formulas with or without functions.

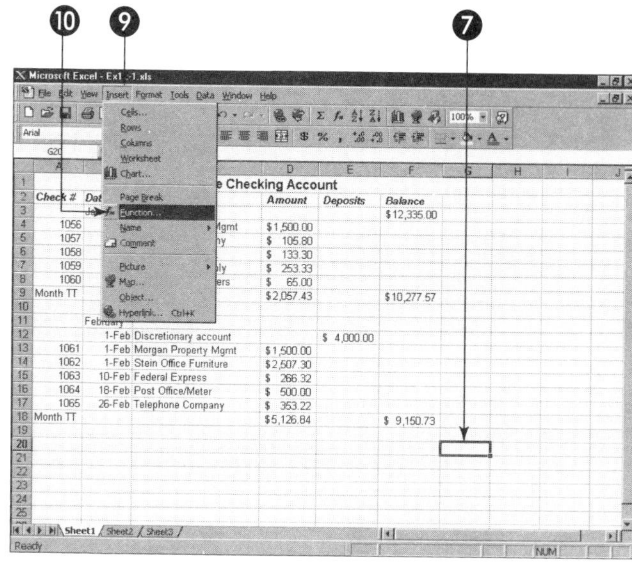

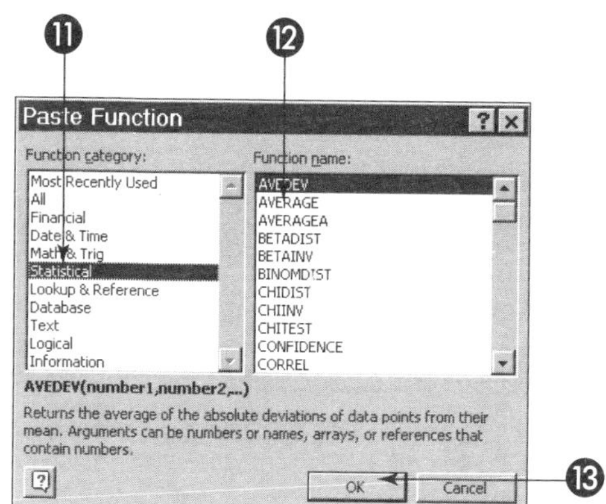

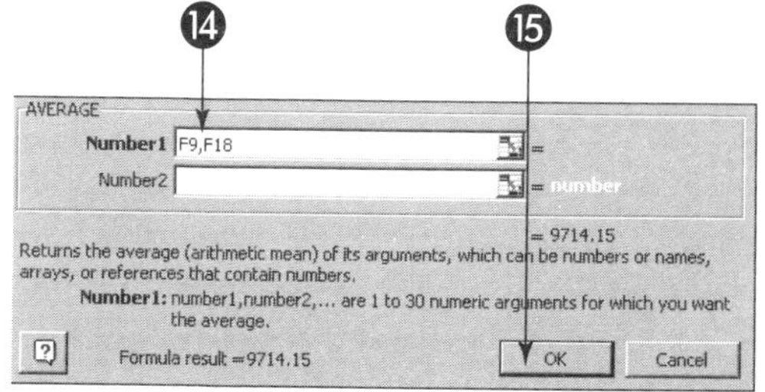

You can use cell references or actual numeric or text values in formulas. For example, if you want a particular cell to contain the sum of 3+5, enter this formula: ***=SUM(3+5)***.

TABLE 12-1 OPERATORS FOR CALCULATING EXCEL FORMULAS

Operator	Use	Example
+	Add	D5+D7
-	Subtract	D5-D7
*	Multiply	D5*D7
/	Divide	D5/D7
%	Percent	20%
=	Equals	D1=B1
>	Greater than	D1>B1
<	Less than	D1<B1
>=	Greater than or equal to	D1>=B1
<=	Less than or equal to	D1<=B1
<>	Not equal to	D1<>B1
:	Indicates a range	D5:D7
,	Combines multiple references	D5,D7,D8

You can use the Logical categories of functions, such as IF and TRUE along with operators such as >= to create formulas like this: IF the value in cell D7 is greater than or equal to the value in cell D5, enter TRUE. With this formula, if the value in cell D7 is not greater than or equal to the value in cell D5, the word FALSE would be entered in the cell where you placed this formula.

WORKING WITH FORMULAS

As you can see from the preceding section, formulas can be as straightforward or complex as you care to make them. They can utilize functions, such as SUM or AVERAGE, or simple operators like the minus or plus symbols. However, all formulas, simple or complex, have several things in common. You copy and move formulas to new cells in the same way, and there are several ways to find errors within your formulas.

Copying formulas

Sometimes you want to use the same calculation on different sets of numbers in a worksheet. To save time, you can copy one formula to another cell. You do that because Excel uses what are called *relative references* in formulas. Rather than cell references indicating a specific numbered cell, they indicate a cell located in the worksheet relative to the cell where you're entering the formula.

For example, if you create a formula in cell C10 to add all the values in cells B3 to B9, Excel actually adds all the values in the seven cells one column to the left of C10, rows 3 to 9. If you copy this formula to cell E10, the formula will now be adding cells D3 to D9: the same row numbers one column to the left of E10.

1. Close the file Ex12-1 without saving changes.
2. Open the file Ex12-2.

   The illustration to the right shows the file Ex12-2, a spreadsheet listing typical weather activity around the country in a given year. Notice that cell C11 holds the total of the numbers in column B. Click cell C11 and you see the corresponding formula in the Formula bar. Notice that column E represents the same kind of total column for all the values in column D, however, no formula has been entered. Now copy the formula from C11 to D11.

3. Select cell C11.
4. Click the Copy button on the toolbar.
5. Select cell E11.
6. Click the Paste button on the toolbar.

   The formula has been copied; the relative reference to cells one column over have changed the formula to reference column D. Note that when you *move* a formula, rather than copy it, the cell references do not change.

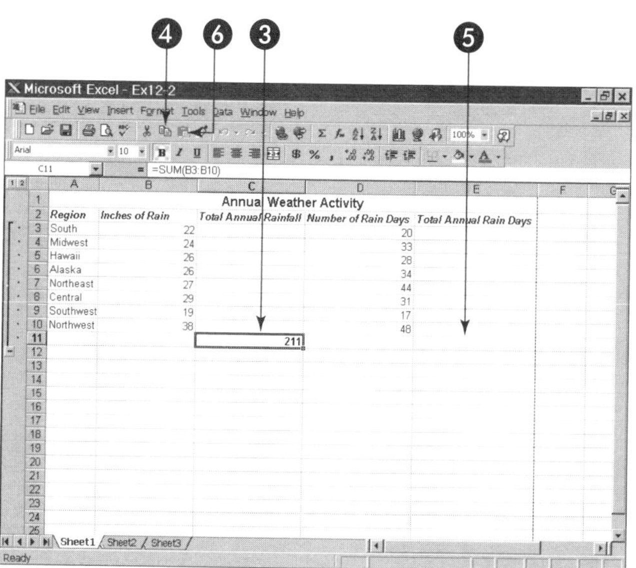

12

Adding Formulas for Success

TIP

If you want a formula to contain absolute references (references to specific cells rather than the relative location of cells), you can precede the parts of the cell name in the formula with a dollar sign. For example, the formula in C11 could have been entered as =SUM($B$3:$B$10). Then, if you copy the formula into another cell, it will return the same result.

Finding errors in formulas

As you're learning to use formulas and functions in Excel, you'll probably make your share of errors in formula syntax. It's not hard to make a mistake with the proper order of symbols in a formula, or to choose the wrong function or cell references to create a proper argument. Errors in formulas occur when you type text where Excel expects a numerical value, or when a cell referenced in the formula no longer exists, or if you have left out a symbol, such as a parenthesis at the front of your argument. Excel assists you with finding these errors.

1. Select cell B11.
2. Enter this formula: **=AVERAGEB3:B10**.
3. Press Enter.

   The cell returns the error value #NAME?. This is an error code that indicates a problem with the syntax in the argument. Can you spot the problem? You neglected to enclose your argument in parentheses. Table 12-2 lists some of the common error values and their meanings.

   One way to ensure your fomulas have the proper syntax is to use the Paste Function feature (as opposed to entering the formulas yourself). The Paste Function feature enters your parameters with the correct syntax automatically. Try that now.

4. Press Backspace to delete the current formula.
5. Select Insert ➢ Function.

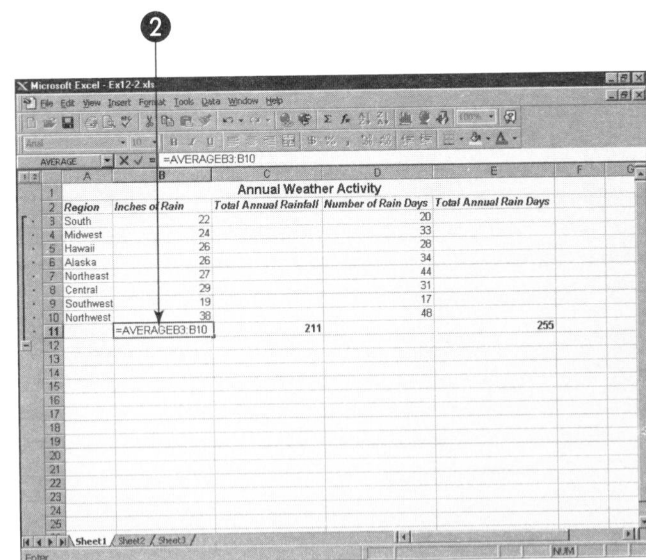

TABLE 12-2 COMMON FORMULA ERRORS

Error Value	Meaning
#####	The column isn't wide enough to display the results of the formula.
#VALUE!	The wrong type of argument or operator is used; for example, using text where a number is called for.
#NAME?	Excel doesn't recognize an entry in the formula; for example, if you misspell a function.
#NUM!	The function can't find a result or the result is too large or small to be represented.
#REF!	A cell reference is invalid; the cell may be missing.

6. From the Paste Function dialog box, select AVERAGE.
7. Choose OK. The range you just entered manually appears in the next dialog box.
8. Choose OK to accept the cell references. The formula has been successfully entered in the cell.
9. Close the file Ex12-2 without savings changes.

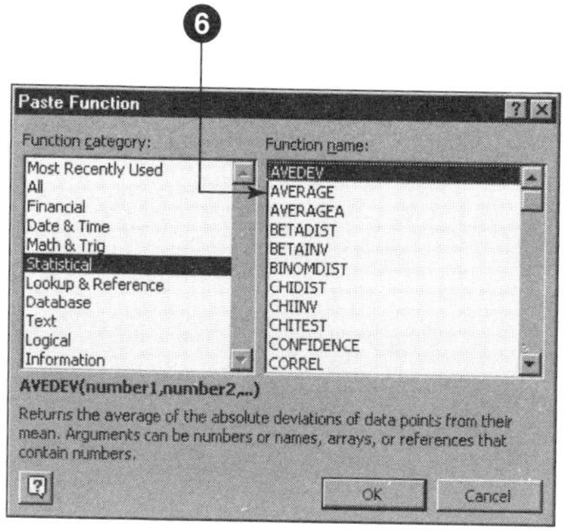

SKILLS CHALLENGE: ADD FORMULAS TO A DEPARTMENT BUDGET

Although logical in their structure, Excel formulas take some getting used to because of all the variables you could include. Use this Skills Challenge to practice using formulas.

1. Open the file Ex12-3 from the accompanying CD-ROM.
2. Enter a formula in cell B8 to total all the values in Column B.

How do you use your mouse to complete a formula?

TRY OUT THE
INTERACTIVE TUTORIALS
ON YOUR CD!

Skills challenge

3. Use the AutoSum button in cell C8 to total the values in that column.
4. Use a function to create a formula in cell D8 to total the numbers in that column.

What operator do you use to designate a range of cells?

5. Insert a function in cell B10 to count the number of values entered in Column B. (Hint: Use the Count function in the Statistical Function category.)
6. Copy the resulting formula in cell B10 to cells C10 and D10.
7. Use cells B12, C12, and D12 to enter average costs in each of those three categories. (Hint: use the AVERAGE function on rows 3 through 7 in each of those columns.)

What would be the fastest way to place this formula in all three cells?

8. Use formulas to create totals for Rows 3 through 8 in Column E.

4 *What is the total of costs for this budget?*

9. Check your totals against those in the file Ex12-3 on the accompanying CD-ROM.
10. Close the file and save it with the name **Formulas**.

TROUBLESHOOTING

Using formulas to calculate is one of the major features that sets Excel apart from a simple table or database. Although you've picked the basic methods of creating and copying formulas, you may run into some of the problems listed in the table below as you use formulas.

Problem	Solution
After pasting a copy of a formula in a cell, a moving border remains on the original cell.	That border will remain so you can paste as many copies as you like of the formula. Just begin typing any value or formula in another cell and it will disappear.
I got a message that I created a circular reference.	When you make a reference in a formula to the cell where you're entering the formula, Excel repeats the calculation endlessly. Click OK on this message and Excel will display a Circular Reference toolbar to help you find the circular reference.
I copied a formula and the cell references didn't change.	Be careful not to enter formatting for numbers in your cells; using a dollar sign before values in formulas, for example, can cause them to become absolute values that won't change when you copy the formula.
I have numbers in the cell but they aren't being calculated as numbers in my formula.	If you have General formatting applied to numbers Excel treats them as text. Apply a numeric format such as currency or percent to the cell.

WRAP UP

In this lesson, you learned all the basics of Excel formulas and functions, including the following:

- Entering formulas in cells using your keyboard, your mouse, or the paste function feature

Wrap up

- Copying formulas to other cells
- Identifying errors in formulas and solving them

In Lesson 13, you learn how to turn the data in your Excel worksheet into attractive and informative charts.

Building Charts

GOALS

In this lesson, you learn just how easy it is to take worksheet data and turn it into an impressive Excel chart. You learn the following:

- Using Chart Wizard
- Changing the chart type
- Adding titles and labels
- Working with the legend
- Adding gridlines
- Using 3-D effects
- Applying formatting to chart elements

Get ready

GET READY

To complete this lesson, you need the files Ex13-1 and Ex13-2, which you have copied to your hard drive from the accompanying CD-ROM.

In this lesson, you generate a chart like the one in the illustration to the right.

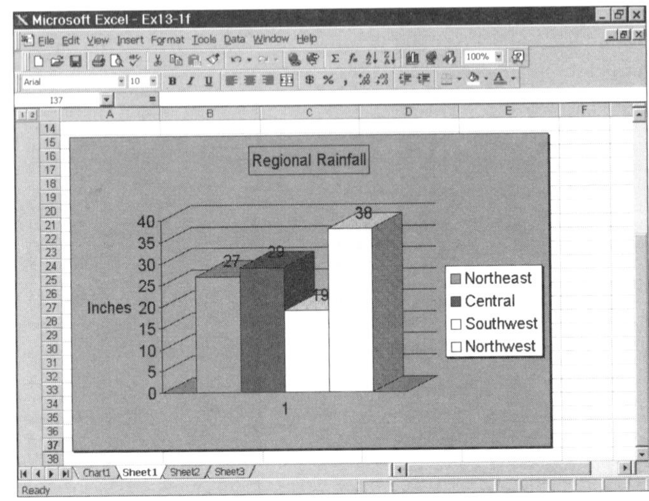

HOW EXCEL GENERATES CHARTS

The good news is, in Excel, you don't really have to create charts; they are automatically generated from the data entered in your worksheet. What you do have to do with Excel charts is make choices about how to represent the selected data: whether to display a pie chart or bar chart, whether there should be color in the background, if a legend should appear at the side of the chart, and so on.

Using Chart Wizard

One of the easiest ways to generate a chart from data you enter in a worksheet is by using Chart Wizard. Chart Wizard is a simple four-step process of making selections to produce a finished chart.

1. Open the file Ex13-1. This is a worksheet you used in Lesson 12.
2. Select Insert ➢ Chart. Step 1 of the Chart Wizard dialog box, Chart Type, appears, as in the illustration to the right.
3. With the Column chart type selected, choose the *Stacked column with 3-D visual effect* subtype (the middle subtype in the second row of choices).

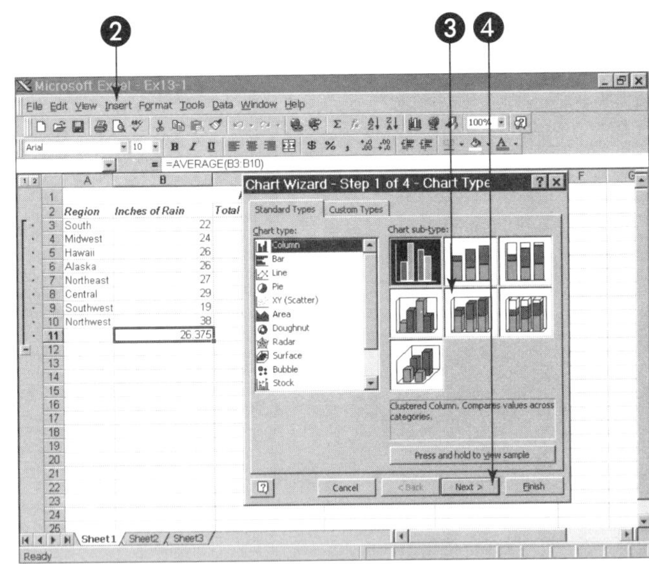

To see how this chart type looks with the current worksheet's data, click the bar under the subtype chart samples for a preview.

4. Choose Next to move to the next step in the Chart Wizard. The Chart Source dialog box appears.

VISUAL BONUS: HOW WORKSHEET DATA BECOMES A CHART

This Visual Bonus shows you how the data in your worksheet relates to the pieces of a chart.

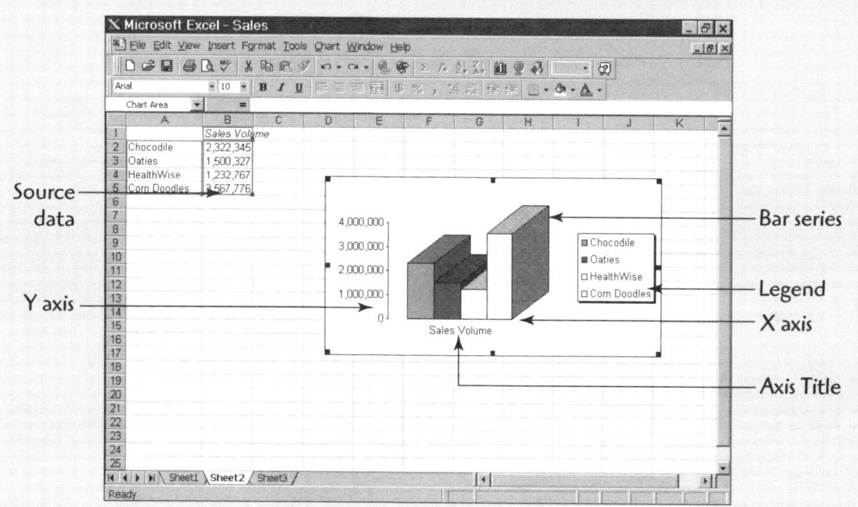

A standard bar chart shows overall trends in performance.

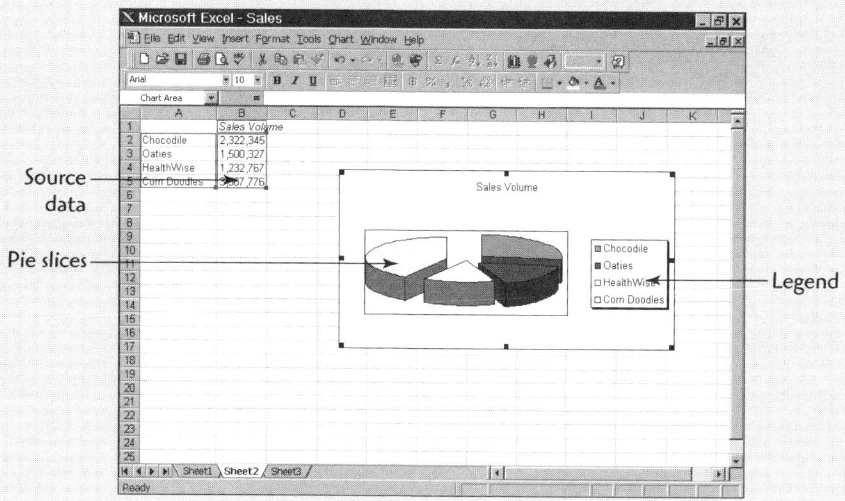

A pie chart shows the pieces that make up the whole.

Using Chart Wizard

This is where you tell Excel on which data to base the chart. The preview appearing here indicates how the chart looks using all the data in the current worksheet. This is a pretty busy chart, showing information for eight different regions of the country with two sets of data: rainfall and rain days. It's never a good idea to show too much information in a single chart; it can be very difficult for others to decipher, so you should choose a smaller range to display.

5. Click in cell A3 on the worksheet.
6. Drag your cursor until the range from A3 to B6 is surrounded by a blinking, dashed gray line.

   The range you've just selected with your mouse appears in the *Data range* box in the Chart Source dialog box of the Chart Wizard.

   You can also type in this data range. However, it's important that you enter each piece of information with dollar signs preceding it. Because the chart has an active link to this data, any change to data in these cells updates in the chart. Usually, you don't want the chart changing if you add a column or row or move the data, and these dollar signs guarantee your chart is based on this absolute data, rather than its relative position on the worksheet.

7. Choose Next to proceed to Step 3 of the Chart Wizard, the Chart Options dialog box shown in the illustration to the right.
8. On the Titles tab, enter the following label in the *Chart title* text box: **Annual Rainfall in Inches**.
9. In the *Category (X) axis* text box, type **Region**.
10. In the *Value (Z) axis* type **Inches**.

    Notice that a preview of all your changes shows in this dialog box. This is very helpful when you are first building charts and are unsure of which axis is which and where labels and titles will appear on the chart. Because only one series of data is represented here, rainfall in inches, the legend to the right of the chart doesn't serve much purpose. Get rid of that now.

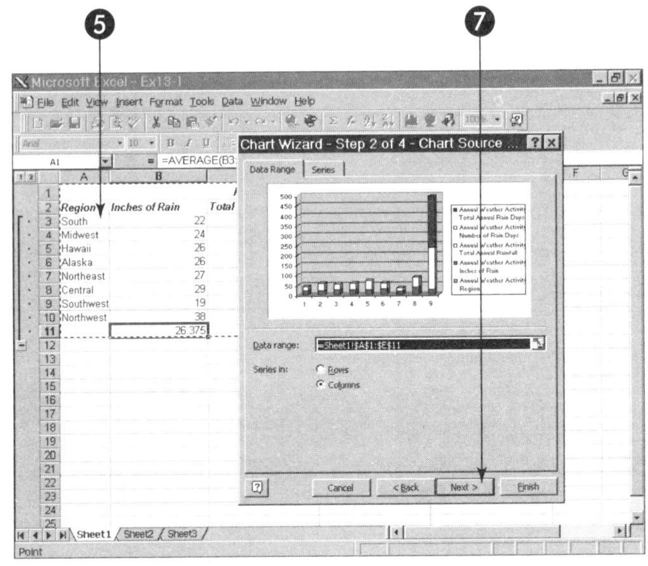

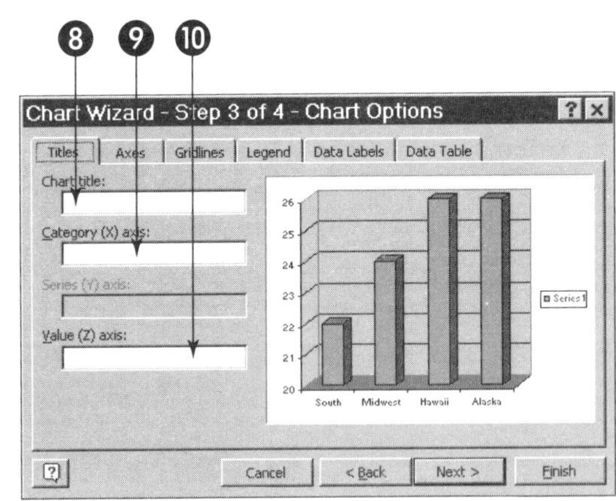

⓫ Select the Legend tab.

⓬ Click the *Show legend* check box to deselect this choice. It disappears from the preview.

⓭ Select the Data Labels tab.

⓮ To show the values right on the bars, click the *Show value* radio button. The exact number of inches for each bar appears in the preview.

⓯ Choose Next to move to the fourth and final Chart Wizard dialog box, Chart Location, shown in the bottom right illustration.

In this dialog box, you determine where the chart will appear. Your choices are on a new sheet in this workbook, or as an object on one of the existing sheets.

⓰ Click the *As new sheet* radio button.

⓱ Choose Finish to complete the Chart Wizard.

The new sheet displays with the finished chart on it. Notice that the new sheet created during this process is named Chart1.

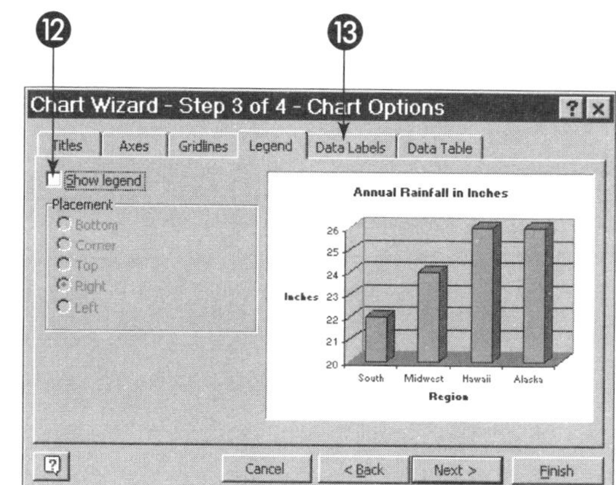

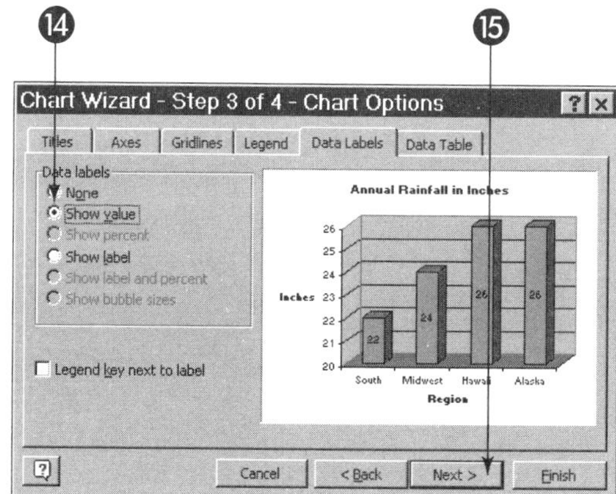

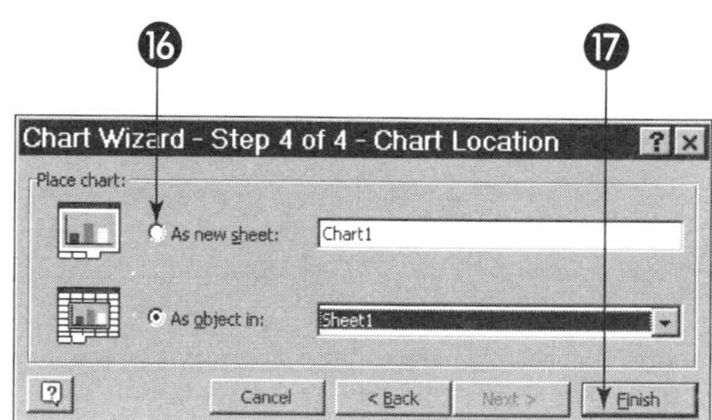

Changing the chart type

Different types of charts work well with different types of information. A bar or column chart helps you compare data for different items side by side. A pie chart, on the other hand, shows how the pieces of a whole are apportioned. A line chart is useful for showing trends over time, such as a growth in population or progress toward a goal.

You may create one kind of chart, and then decide that the information would be better represented by another. Or you may want to try different chart types to see which works best. Trying on different chart types is easy:

❶ Make Sheet1 the active worksheet.

❷ Click the Chart Wizard button on the toolbar.

Changing the chart type

3. In the first Chart Wizard dialog box, choose Line for the chart type.
4. Choose Next.
5. In the next dialog box, designate a data range of A7:B10. You can do this by dragging over these cells with your mouse or typing in the range.
6. Choose Finish. The chart in the center right illustration appears.

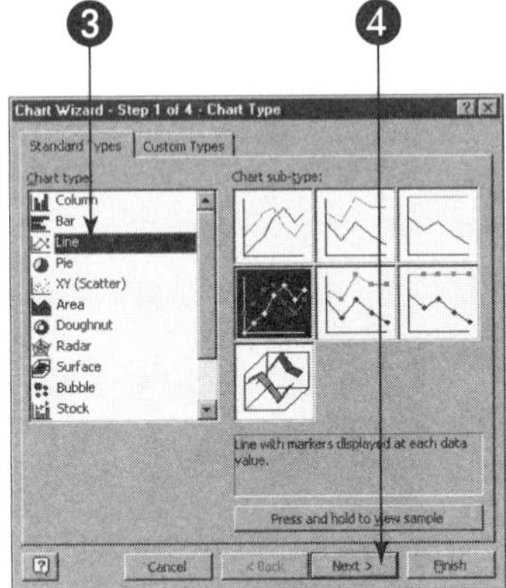

Because you didn't get to the part of the Chart Wizard that enables you to choose where to place the chart, it appears on whatever sheet was active when you started Chart Wizard. You can always create a new sheet and cut and paste the chart onto it.

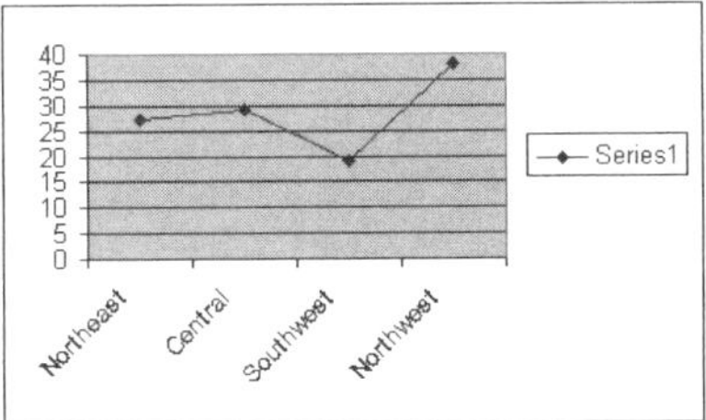

7. Click the Chart menu.
8. Select Chart Type. The Chart Type dialog box appears.
9. Select the Pie chart type.
10. Click the *Press and Hold to View Sample* button. Using this preview capability you can try out different chart types easily.
11. Select the Custom Types tab in the Chart Type dialog box. Try a few of these on for size.
12. Select the Columns with Depth chart type.
13. Choose OK to apply the new chart type.

Notice the custom chart types offer somewhat more creative designs for charts. Using the standard chart types, or these custom chart types, you can find one that conveys your information most clearly, and has the visual appeal you want. Because you didn't use the Chart Wizard to add on titles, labels, and legends, you need to add those to this chart yourself.

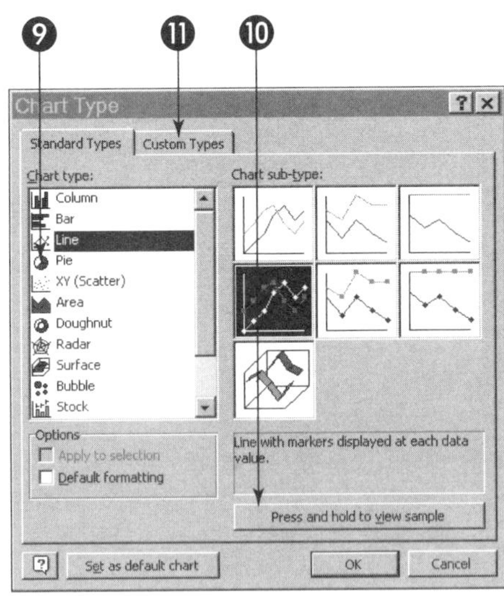

Adding titles

Once you've found the basic chart type you prefer, you can modify its elements almost any way you like. For one thing, you can include titles for the chart and each chart axis. as you need them.

1. Select the chart.
2. Select Chart ➢ Chart Options.
3. Select the Titles tab to see the Chart Options dialog box shown in the illustration to the right.
4. Enter the following chart title: **Regional Rainfall**.
5. Click OK. The title appears above the chart.
6. Right-click the title.
7. Select Format Chart Title from the shortcut menu that appears. The Format Chart Title dialog box shown in the bottom right illustration appears.

   Using the three tabs in this dialog box, you can modify the font and alignment for the title, as well as fill the area of the title box with a color or pattern and apply a border around it.
8. Select the Patterns tab if it's not already selected.
9. Click on the Automatic radio button in the Border section to apply a border to the chart title.
10. Select the Font tab.
11. Select the Times New Roman font for the title.
12. Choose OK to apply the formatting choices to the title.
13. Click anywhere outside of the title to see the new border surround it.
14. Select Chart ➢ Chart Options.
15. Select the Titles tab.
16. In the *Category (Y) axis* box, type **Inches**.
17. Choose OK to apply the axis title.

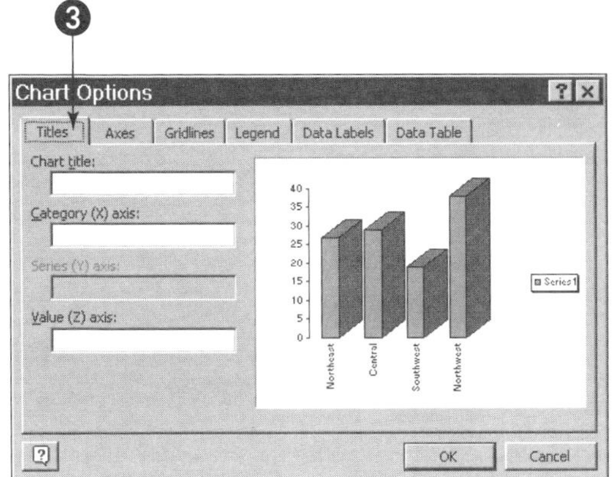

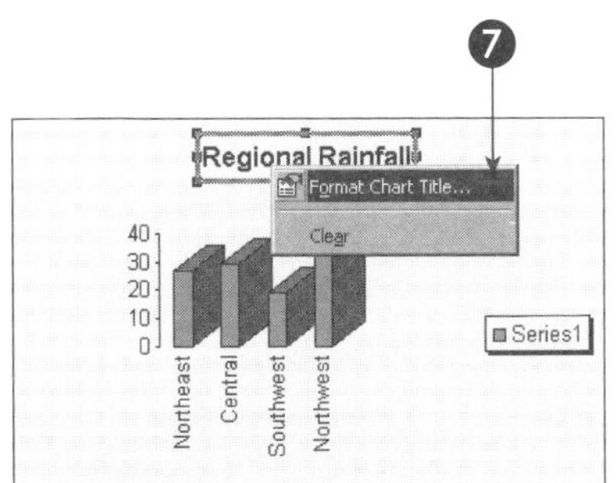

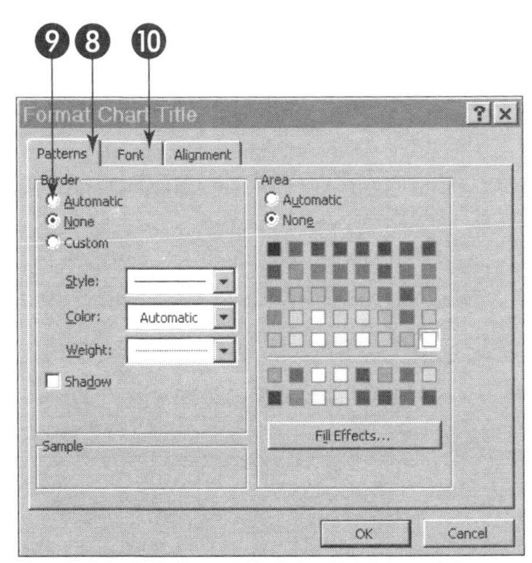

13 Building Charts

You can right-click either of the axis titles to format them in the same way you formatted the chart title.

Working with legends and labels

In addition to adding chart and axis titles, you can include labels on your bars and a legend to explain the chart features. In this chart, labels and a series legend will be included. First, you'll arrange the data a little differently to see how helpful a legend can be. You'll also make some modifications to the labels on the bars.

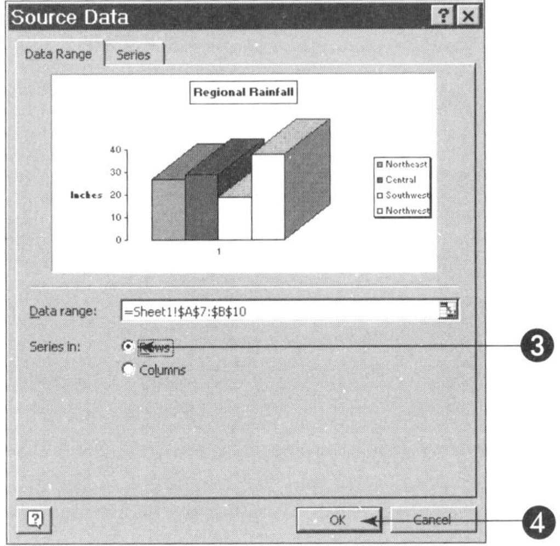

1. Select the chart.
2. Select Chart ➢ Source Data.
3. In the Source Data dialog box that appears, choose to display the series in rows instead of columns. A preview appears, as shown to the right.

   In your source data, the regions of the country are the rows, so it makes sense to arrange the series of data by rows. Notice the difference it makes to the legend in this preview. With the series in columns, there was only one series, and therefore the legend had only one key in it, which was hardly useful. With series for the regions, a legend is useful to label the y axis.
4. Choose OK.
5. Select Chart ➢ Chart Options.
6. Select the Legend tab.
7. Click the *Left* radio button to place the legend to the left of the chart.
8. Click the Data Labels tab.
9. Click the Show Value option button. The numerical value for each bar, as opposed to the name of the bar, is displayed.

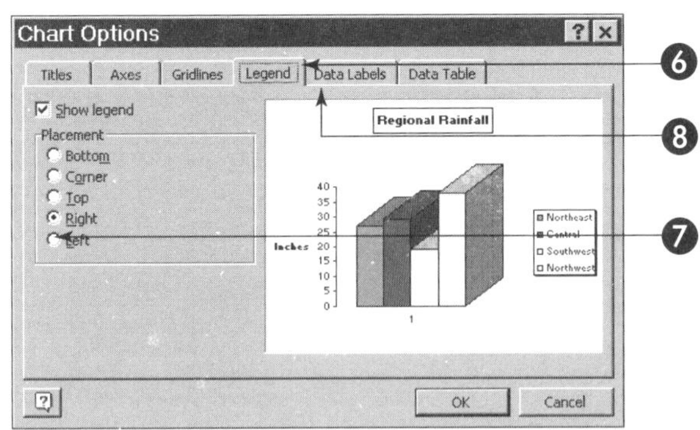

Depending on the information in your chart, you can choose to show other information such as the percent value, or both a text label and percent value. However, you can only select one of these data label options for your chart.

FORMATTING A CHART

In addition to the formatting you can apply to titles, there are several formatting changes you can apply to the elements of the chart itself. You can add gridlines to your chart, apply 3-D effects, and modify the fonts and background patterns used.

Adding gridlines

Gridlines help the reader of your chart understand the data. Gridlines are set at regular intervals against which the elements of the chart are measured. You can add horizontal or vertical gridlines to a chart, separately or in combination. Once again, the preview capability helps you try out different combinations to see how they work with your chart.

You should still be in the Chart Options dialog box.

1. Select the Gridlines tab. Some of the choices here may vary depending on the chart type you're working with.
2. Click in the *2-D walls and gridlines* check box to deselect it. With 3-D bars, this 2-D effect can make gridlines difficult to read.
3. Place a check mark in all of the four available check boxes on this panel and take a look at the preview.

   You can see that using too many gridlines can make a chart busy and difficult to read. Try just the major gridlines.

4. Click in the *Minor gridlines* check box under Category (X) axis and Value (Z) axis, respectively, to deselect them.

   This effect works much better. The major function of gridlines is to make the numerical values of chart elements easy to read. Looking closely, you realize that only the horizontal gridlines

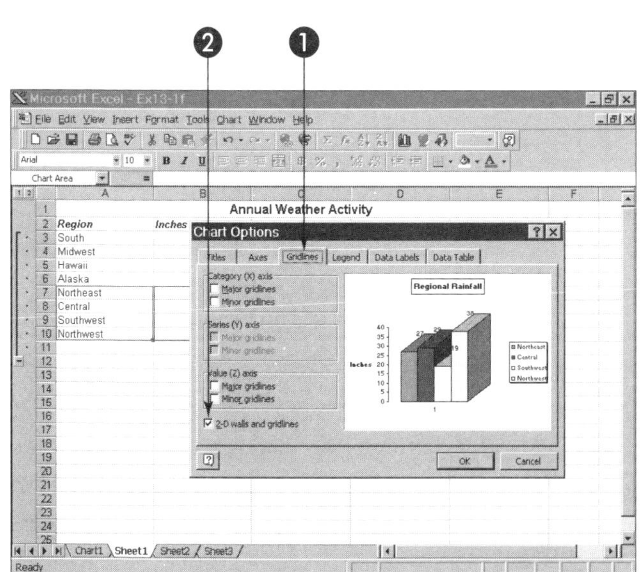

help you line up the bars with numerical data. Get rid of the horizontal gridlines and see what happens.

5. Click in the Category (X) axis *Major gridlines* check box.
6. Choose OK.

   This is the right combination of gridlines for this particular chart, which you determine here in this dialog by previewing the different combinations. Now that you can clearly see the values of each bar against the gridlines, you might reconsider showing value labels on the bars themselves. Although Excel offers you a lot of flexibility in modifying the various elements of a chart, everything you do should be done with the readability of the chart for the reader in mind.

Using 3-D effects

3-D effects can make charts more visually appealing. They can also make charts more difficult to read if they're not formatted correctly. For example, the slant to the 3-D columns in your chart makes it difficult to read where values lie on the *y* axis. You apply a 3-D chart type when you first create the chart. Excel then enables you to modify default 3-D settings to make the effect either more or less apparent.

1. Right-click the chart and select 3-D View from the shortcut menu. The 3-D View dialog box appears.
2. Click the large down arrow two times, until the *Elevation* box reads 5. The Elevation angle is slightly decreased.
3. Click the curved right-facing arrow next to the *Rotation* box until that box reads 10. The rotation angle is slightly decreased.
4. Choose Apply to see these effects on your own chart.
5. Choose OK. The top two illustrations on the next page show the original chart, and the chart with 3-D changes.

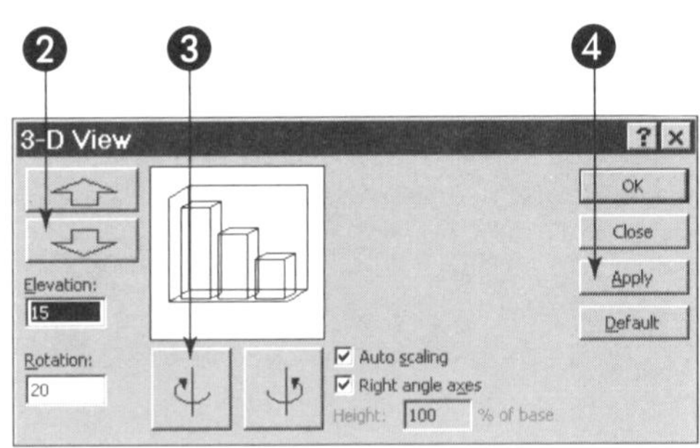

Formatting chart elements

You can format any element of a chart by clicking it with your right mouse button and selecting the Format command from the shortcut menu; you can also double-click an element to format it. You saw an example of this in formatting the chart title. Now try formatting the entire chart.

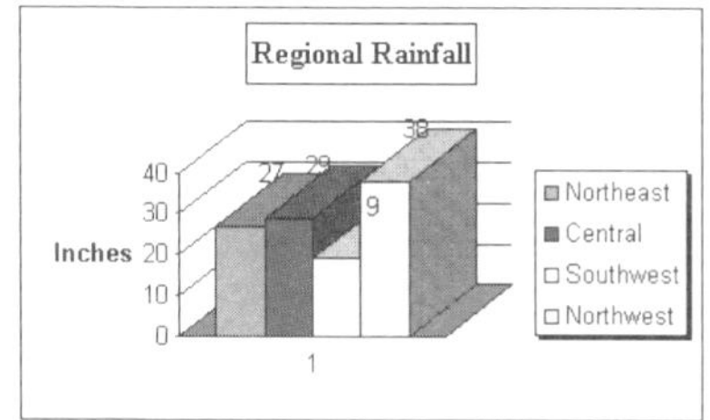

Before

❶ Right-click the chart.

When you move your pointer around a chart, a small callout appears telling you the name of each element. When you see that callout, double-click to access formatting for that element. To format the background for the whole chart, the callout should read Chart Area.

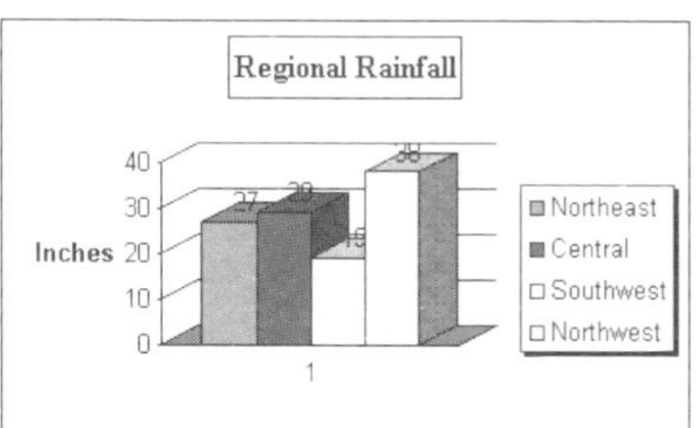

After

❷ Select Format Chart Area on the shortcut menu.

❸ Select the Patterns tab.

❹ Click a light blue color in the Area color palette.

❺ Click in the *Shadow* check box to add a shadow to the border surrounding the chart.

❻ Select the Font tab.

❼ Change the font size to 9 points.

❽ Choose OK.

The chart now appears as in the bottom right illustration. Using these various formatting settings, you can change such elements as the legend, the bars in a bar chart or pie wedges in a pie chart, and the data labels.

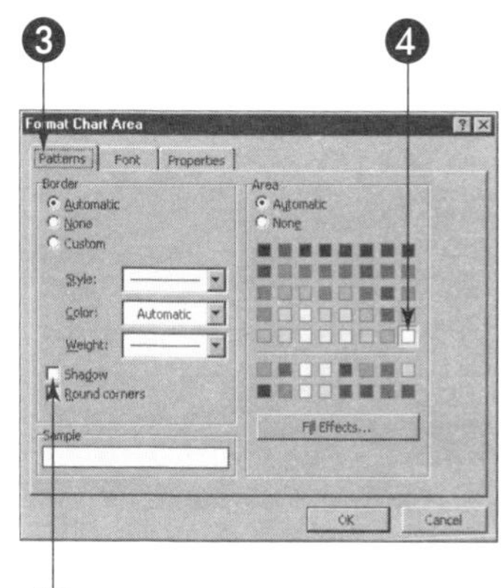

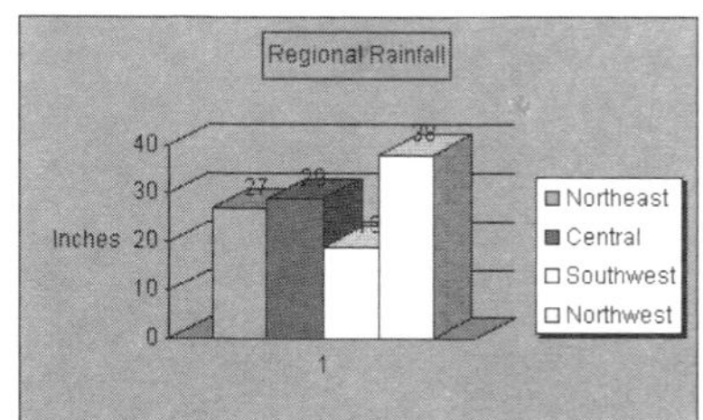

SKILLS CHALLENGE: CREATING A PIE CHART

To further practice your charting skills, create a pie chart.

❶ Open the file Ex13-2, which you copied from the CD-ROM.

❷ Select Insert ➢ Chart.

Skills challenge

3. Select the Explored pie with a 3-D visual effect chart type.
4. Choose the cell range A2:B6 for your source data.

1 *What are two ways of designating source data?*

5. Place the chart on a new sheet in the workbook and complete the steps in the Chart Wizard.
6. Add the following title to the chart: **Breakdown of High School Curriculum**.
7. Show percent labels on the individual pie wedges.
8. Change the font of the chart title to 14 point.
9. Change the data labels to 12 point, bold.
10. Change the 3-D view to 10 Elevation.

How do you determine that a chart will have a 3-D effect applied?

11. Change the background of the Chart Area to a pale green shade.
12. Apply a border to the chart title.
13. Move the legend to the bottom of the chart.
14. Change the chart type to an Exploded Doughnut (Honest, that's what it's called!).

How do you preview how a chart type will look with your chart?

15. Close the file without saving changes.

TROUBLESHOOTING

Charts in Excel can be simple or highly complex. You learned the basics of creating charts here, but as you continue to experiment, the troubleshooting tips in Table 13-1 may help you out of a tight spot.

Problem	Solution
I created a pie chart but there's only one single slice in it.	Check the Source Data dialog box to see if you chose to show data by row or column. Changing this should give you multiple pie slices.
There's a big space between two of the bars in my chart.	You probably included a blank row or column in the source data. Delete the row or column in the data source range.
I want to make the legend larger so it can be read more clearly.	Select the legend, and then place your cursor at its corner till it becomes a two-way facing arrow. Click and drag the corner until the legend is the size you wish.

WRAP UP

You've done a great job of getting through all that's involved in creating and formatting an Excel chart. You learned the following:

- Using the Chart Wizard to create a chart
- Modifying a chart to add labels, titles, and legends
- Formatting chart elements with font, background pattern, and 3-D effects

In Lesson 14, you learn how to print what you've created in Excel.

Printing from Excel

GOALS

Now that you know all about creating worksheets, building formulas, and generating charts, you probably want to print what you've created. In this lesson, you learn the following:

- Choosing the page orientation for your worksheet
- Setting margins
- Scaling output
- Adding headers and footers
- Printing row and column headings
- Hiding columns or rows
- Setting the Print Area
- How to print selected text, pages, or sheets

Changing page orientation

GET READY

To complete this lesson, use the files Ex14-1 and Ex14-2, which you copied to you hard drive from the accompanying CD-ROM.

SETTING THE SIZE OF PRINTED OUTPUT

Excel worksheets aren't like Word documents: each one is a slightly different size depending on how many columns and rows you create and how you resize them. Because worksheets are difficult to read if all the columns across don't print on a single page, getting the size of your worksheet output right can be the most important step you take before printing.

So, before you print what you create, you have to choose a few settings. For one thing, you have to designate in which direction you want your file to print on the page. Worksheets that contain several columns across, for example, often work better with landscape rather than portrait orientation. You should look at the way page margins affect how much of your worksheet area can print on each page. In many cases, you may need to scale the output so all your columns and rows fit.

Changing page orientation

A worksheet with 3 columns across and 50 rows down might do best printed like a typical business letter, with portrait orientation; but when you need to print 12 columns across, it's time to switch that orientation around. Here's how you do it:

1. Open the file Ex14-1. Be sure that Sheet1 is the active worksheet.
2. Select File ➢ Print Preview.
3. Press Pg Dn (page down).

Notice that the default page orientation setting, portrait, is currently in effect. Because the columns running across the worksheet are too wide for this orientation, Excel places the last four columns on a second page. This would make this worksheet more difficult to read. Let's change the orientation.

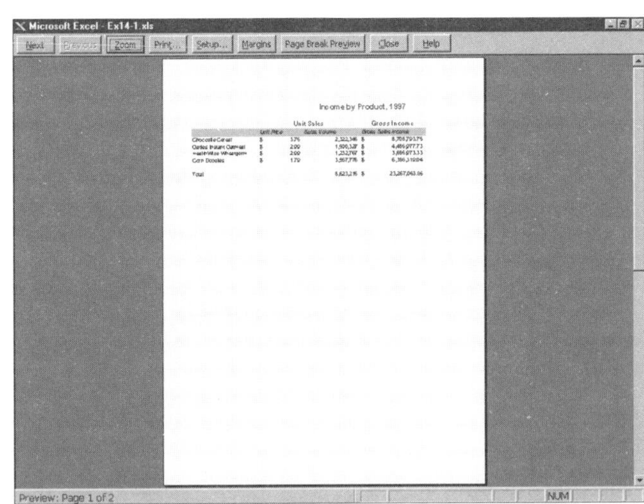

4. Choose the Setup button from the Print Preview toolbar. The Page Setup dialog box appears.

5. Click the radio button labeled Landscape.

6. Choose Print Preview.

   You return to Print Preview, but you still have one column that doesn't fit across a single page. You have to look at some other options for this page setup.

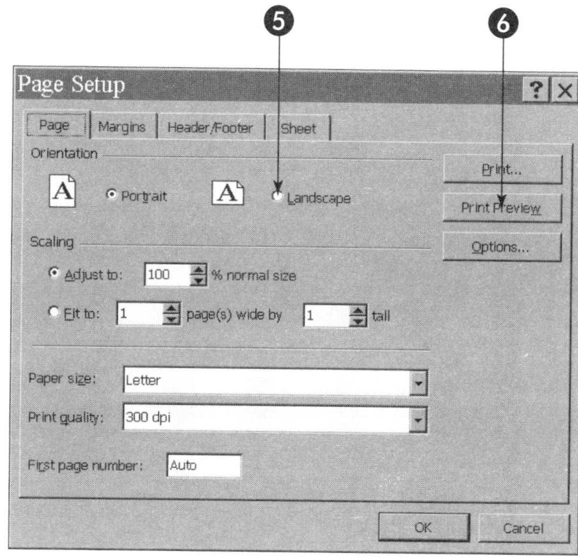

Setting margins

Margins, which comprise that blank area around the edge of your document, can be adjusted to help you fit just a bit more on the printed page.

1. Click the Setup button again.
2. In the Page Setup dialog box, select the Margins tab.
3. Using the setting arrows, change the Left margin to 0.75.
4. Using the setting arrows, change the Right margin to 0.75.
5. Choose Print Preview.
6. Click the Margins button to see your margin settings more clearly.
7. Press Pg Dn (page down).

   Adjusting margins before printing can sometimes help you fit your worksheet across or down a page, but in this case, it's not enough. You still have columns falling onto the next page, but there are a couple of other things you can do about that.

You can also change margins by dragging the margin lines displayed after you click the Margin tool in Print Preview.

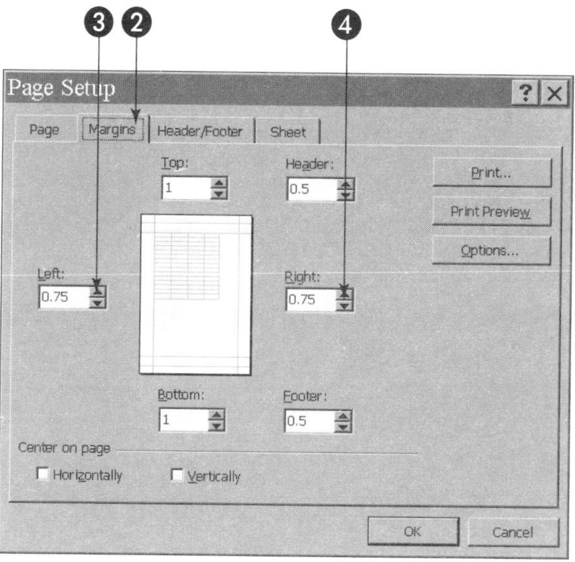

Scaling output

With Excel, you have the ability to scale your printed output to fit more on each page. You control this in the Page Setup dialog box.

1. Click the Setup button in Print Preview. The Page Setup dialog box appears.
2. Select the Page tab. The accompanying illustration shows the default Scaling settings on this tab.

   The Scaling section of this tab enables you to control your output size in two ways. You can adjust the output to a percentage of normal size, or you can make settings to limit exactly how many pages will print. Try both.
3. In the Adjust To setting, use the arrow keys to make the output 95 percent of normal size.
4. Choose OK to see the results in Print Preview.
5. Press Pg Dn (page down). You still have a column falling on a second page.
6. Click the Setup button to display the Page Setup dialog box again.
7. This time, click the option button for *Fit to* and leave the setting at 1 page wide.
8. Choose Print Preview. The worksheet fits across your page in Print Preview.

   If you were to click the Setup button again and look at the Scaling section, you would notice that the *Adjust to* box has changed to 90 percent of normal size, automatically calculating the percentage required to fit this worksheet across one page. You can use any combination of these methods — changing the orientation, adjusting margins, scaling to a percentage of normal size, or fitting to a single page across — to get your output right before you print.
9. Click the Close button in Print Preview to return to your document view.

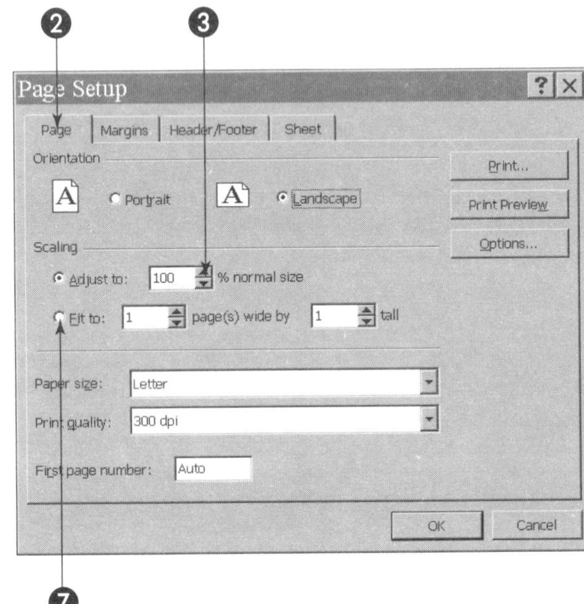

CHOOSING WHAT TO PRINT

Before you print, you can determine what should appear on your worksheet and what portion of the entire workbook you want to print. With Excel you have a lot of flexibility: You can choose not to print certain rows or columns in a worksheet, print just selected text or a whole workbook, or repeat row and column headings on each and every page.

Adding headers and footers

Because a worksheet printout can run across several pages, it's sometimes useful to place information such as the name of the worksheet, its author, or date last updated across the top or bottom of each page. To do that, use the Header and Footer feature.

1. Select View ➢ Header and Footer. The Page Setup dialog box appears with the Header/Footer tab already selected.
2. Click the arrow on the *Footer* drop-down list.
3. Select Page 1.

   This places a page number at the bottom of each page. By default, that number appears centered. If you want to change that, use the Custom settings.
4. Click Custom Footer. The Footer dialog box appears.
5. Click in the Right section box.
6. Click the Page Number button in the middle of the dialog box (it's the second button from the left with the image of a little page with a number sign on it) to place the page number on the right of the printed page.
7. Highlight the &[Page] text in the *Center section* box and press delete.
8. Click in the Left section box.
9. Click the *Date* button. The current date will be printed here.
10. Choose OK.
11. Choose Print Preview to see your footer in place.

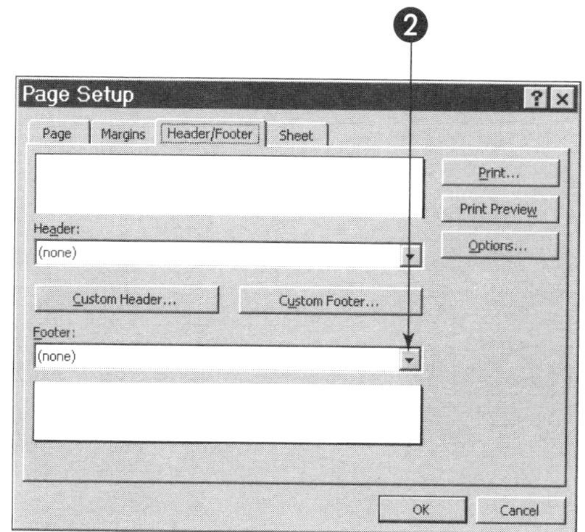

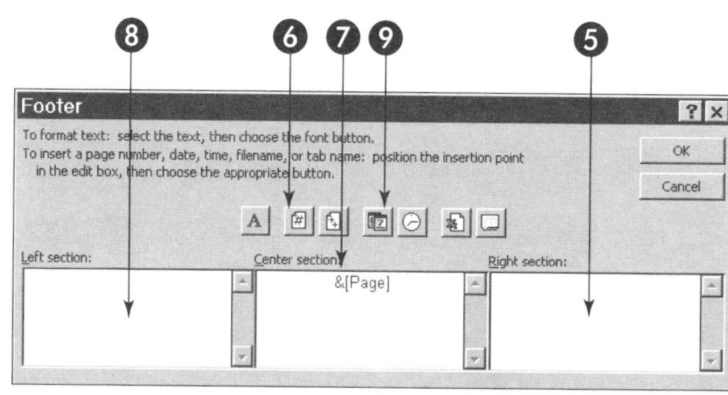

If you want to begin numbering pages at a number other than 1, you can change the First page number *box on the Page tab of the Page Setup dialog box.*

Printing row and column headings

If your worksheet spreads over several pages, it can be helpful to your readers to repeat column and row headings on each page of output. Here's how that's done now.

1. Click the Setup button on the Print Preview toolbar.
2. Select the Sheet tab.
3. Click the check box for *Row and column headings.*

   You may also want to repeat certain rows or columns at the top or side of each page. For example, this worksheet has a row containing column headings with a row of subheadings beneath it; you might want to repeat that row at the top of each page.

4. Click the box at the end of the *Rows to repeat at top* box. The small window shown in the illustration to the right appears.
5. Click the number 3 at the beginning of row 3 on your worksheet. The designation for row 3 appears in the Rows to repeat at top window.
6. Press Enter. You are returned to the Page Setup dialog box with the code for row 3 entered in the *Rows to repeat at top* box.
7. Choose OK to close the Page Setup dialog box and Close to close Print Preview.

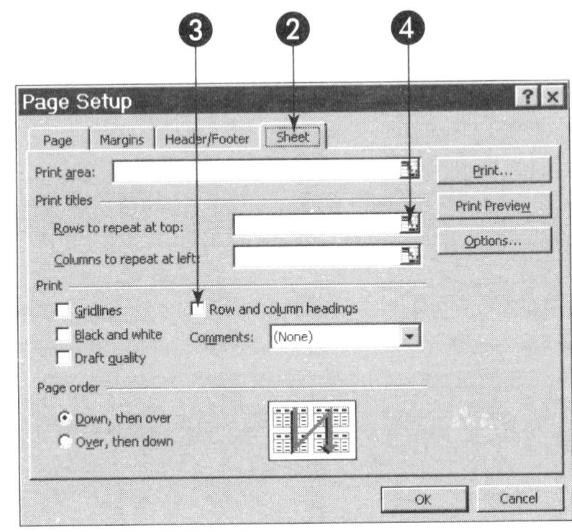

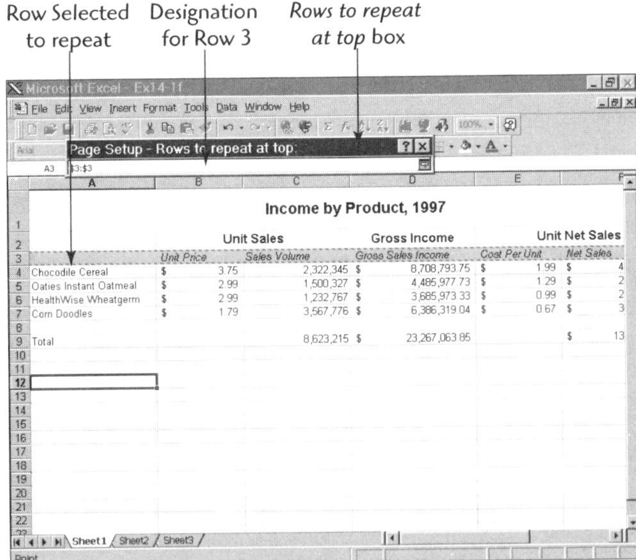

Hiding columns or rows

While there are some rows and columns you want to repeat on each page, there are others you don't want to print at all. For example, you might want to print out a worksheet of employee performance ratings, but hide the column that shows each employee's performance bonus amount.

Hiding columns or rows

1. Select column G.
2. Select Format.
3. Choose Column.
4. Select Hide from the side menu that appears.

   The selected column disappears from your onscreen display of the worksheet.

5. Select File ➢ Print Preview.

   Column G has also disappeared from the preview of the printed output of this worksheet. If you want to unhide this column, select Format ➢ Column ➢ Unhide. Any hidden columns reappear.

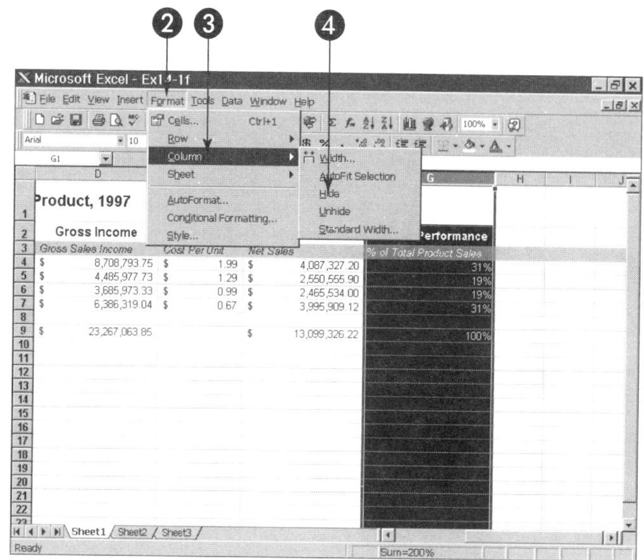

Specifying what to print

The Print Area border marks the portion of a worksheet that will appear on printed pages.

You can use the Print Area command on the File menu to set a default print area. For example, if you usually print only the first three columns of your worksheet for your weekly staff meeting, you could set your print area for those first three columns. That way when you print, those three columns will print by default.

1. Close the Print Preview.
2. Select the first seven rows in the worksheet.
3. Select File.
4. Choose Print Area.
5. Select Set Print Area from the side menu that appears.
6. Click the Print Preview button on the toolbar.

   Only the first seven rows of the worksheet are selected to be printed. You can clear this setting by selecting File ➢ Print Area ➢ Clear Print Area.

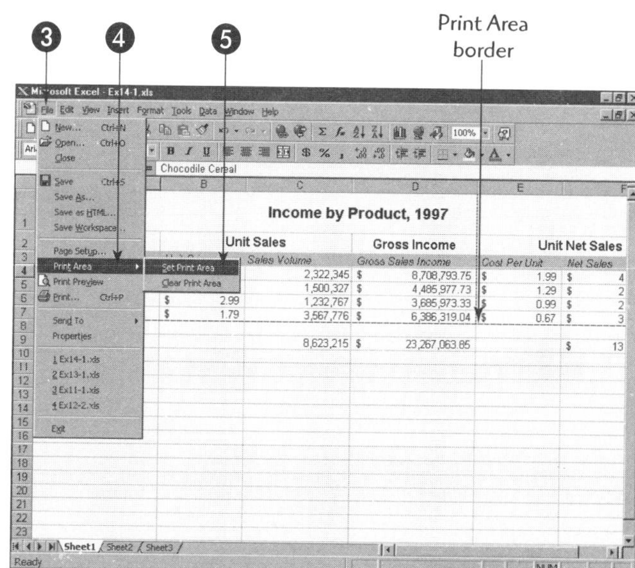

Specifying what to print

There are more ways to designate exactly what part of your workbook you want to print. These methods are handled through the Print dialog box.

7. Click the Print button on the toolbar in Print Preview. The Print dialog box appears.
8. Make sure the Print range is set for All. If you wish to print only certain pages, use the Pages From/To settings.
9. In the Print what section, make sure *Active sheet(s)* is selected. If you wanted to print all sheets in the workbook, or only cells you have selected, you could use those settings here to do so.
10. Leave the Number of copies set at 1.
11. Click OK to print.

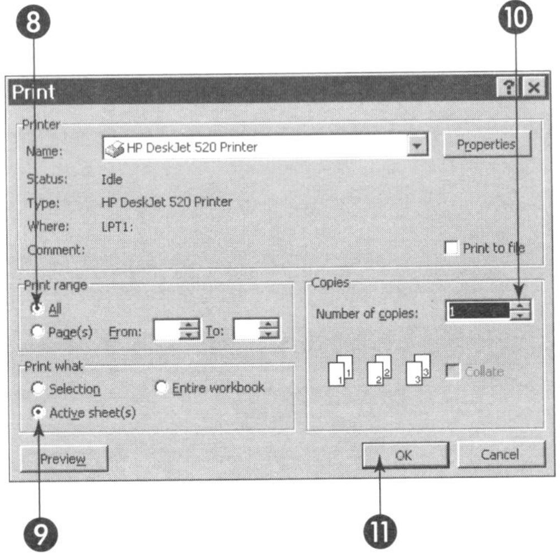

SKILLS CHALLENGE: PRINTING A WORKSHEET

Okay, I hope you were paying attention, because now you get to practice all the details of printing your Excel worksheet on your own.

1. Open the file Ex14-2 in the Exercise folder on your hard drive.
2. Set the orientation for the worksheet to Landscape.
3. Preview the worksheet to see if all columns will fit on the sheet.

Name four ways you can adjust sizing of output.

4. Add a footer to the worksheet.
5. Change the margins of the worksheet so all the rows fit on one sheet.

Name two methods of changing margins.

6. Add a footer to the worksheet with the date on the left and the page number in the center.
7. Make changes to scaling to print the worksheet at 90 percent of normal size.

TRY OUT THE
INTERACTIVE TUTORIALS
ON YOUR CD!

8. Make settings to print two copies of the worksheet.
9. Print the two copies of the active sheet.
10. Change the orientation of the page to Portrait.
11. Preview this output.
12. Make settings to print the worksheet to one page wide.

What percentage of normal size should be used to print this worksheet on a single page?

13. Change the page numbering to begin at Page 20.
14. Hide Rows 20 and 21.

Why could hiding these rows confuse the readers of your spreadsheet?

15. Set the Print Area to include all the rows and columns except Row 23, the Total Sales row.
16. Select the first five rows.
17. Print one copy of the selected rows.
18. Close the file without saving any changes.

TROUBLESHOOTING

You've mastered the essentials of printing your Excel worksheet just the way you want it. However, as you've seen, there are many variables to control your output, and you may run into a few challenges. the table on the next page may help you deal with them if they occur.

Wrap up

Problem	Solution
I added a footer but none printed.	If your top and bottom margins are too wide to accommodate a header or footer, they just won't print. Make your top and bottom margin settings smaller and your footer should print.
I want to print two nonconsecutive sets of pages.	Click the Pages button in the Print dialog box type your two page ranges like this example: 3-5, 10-15.
There are two printers in my office and my worksheet printed to the wrong one.	You have to change the default printer in your Print dialog box.

WRAP UP

You've done a great job learning the basics of generating output from Excel. In this lesson you've covered the following:

- Adjusting the size of your output using margins, scaling, and orientation
- Adding headers and footers, hiding columns or rows, and selecting the Print Area
- Determining the number of copies and page to print

If you'd like more practice with printing from Excel, try creating a longer Excel worksheet and print it with both Portrait and Landscape orientation; try printing an entire workbook that contains multiple worksheets.

In Lesson 15, you move on to learning about the presentation portion of Office 97, PowerPoint.

PART IV

PowerPoint for Windows

This part introduces you to PowerPoint for Windows, a program that enables you to build effective presentations. It includes the following lessons:

- Lesson 15: Creating Presentations
- Lesson 16: Building Your First Presentation
- Lesson 17: Going Public with Your Presentation

LESSON 15

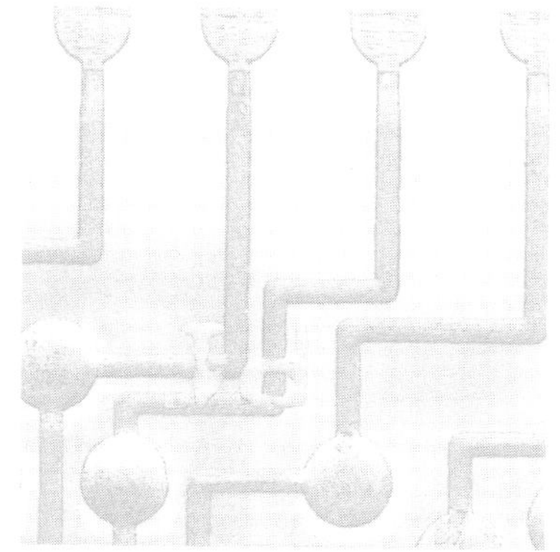

Creating Presentations

GOALS

In this lesson, you learn the following PowerPoint skills:

- Preparing for your presentation
- Viewing a slide show
- Starting PowerPoint
- Selecting a template
- Selecting an AutoLayout
- Working with placeholders
- Using tools
- Changing the presentation template
- Using PowerPoint views

Get ready

GET READY

To complete the exercises in this lesson, you need the files Ex15-1, Ex15-2, and Ex15-3 in the exercise folder you copied from the CD-ROM.

TRY OUT THE INTERACTIVE TUTORIALS ON YOUR CD!

PRINCIPLES OF GOOD DESIGN

The ability to present information well may be the most valuable skill you develop in your job, but nobody teaches you how to do it. You learned grammar and writing in school, so you can immediately put word processing skills to work. You took math courses and accounting theory; therefore Excel has immediate application to procedures you understand. But with PowerPoint, just knowing the names of the tools and menus doesn't mean you know how to build an effective presentation.

Presentations are the combination of words and visuals used to inform or persuade people in a way that is easy to understand. That means you have to consider your audience's knowledge of the topic. You have to know what they expect to get out of listening to you or viewing your presentation before you even begin working with PowerPoint.

What makes a presentation different from a simple talk to a group is the addition of visual elements. These elements can be printed words alone, which help the reader remember the key ideas of a presentation, or they can be drawings, animations, or photographs, which help the audience visualize a process or concept. Studies have shown that the addition of visuals to a learning experience dramatically increases retention. So if you want your audience to remember what you're saying, the addition of visuals can be your greatest ally.

However, when you build a PowerPoint presentation, it's easy to get carried away with the tools it provides to add art, fancy text effects, and color. It's not unusual to get so carried away with using these features that your presentation becomes unreadable. Never forget that the materials you're preparing with PowerPoint are, in most cases, going to be viewed in a darkened room with audience members sitting 20 or 30 feet away. Even when viewed one-on-one in a well-lit room on a single computer screen, a presentation must be kept simple and clear to be understood. Also remember that neither the speaker nor the visual materials should be the focus of your audience's attention. You want them focused on the ideas you are presenting. Just as you shouldn't wear bright, distracting colors when making a presentation, you shouldn't overdo your visuals.

How can you ensure effective visuals? Here are a few points to remember:

- Keep your text concise; six to seven words maximum per line is a good rule of thumb.
- Keep the overall content of each page manageable; five or six lines of text is the most you should place on any one slide.
- Use color consistently. This gives a feeling of cohesiveness to your presentation, and gets the audience comfortable with the general look of things. A PowerPoint feature called design templates, which you learn about later, goes a long way toward assuring a consistent look and color scheme.
- Use dramatic effects, such as WordArt, enhanced text, or sound bites sparingly; they can be distracting and even annoying with repetition.
- Avoid using elements that work slowly because of hardware limitations. For example, if you give an onscreen presentation on a computer with low memory, playing animation sequences is painfully slow.
- Try to arrange for good presentation equipment, whether a slide projector, overhead projector, or computer workstation. The last thing you need to worry about when standing in front of 100 people is faulty equipment.
- Finally, prepare. No amount of animation, clever sound bites, or bright colors can make a badly organized, insubstantial presentation succeed.

Looking at sample presentations

In this exercise, you take a look at two PowerPoint presentations. The first is a badly organized, badly designed presentation. The second is a much more effective use of PowerPoint's features to get a message across.

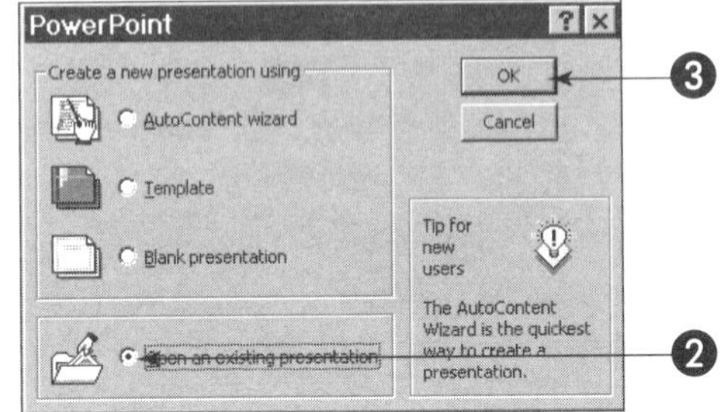

1. From the Windows taskbar, select Microsoft PowerPoint to open the program.
2. On the initial PowerPoint screen select *Open an existing presentation*.
3. Click OK.
4. In the dialog box that follows, locate the folder where the exercise files are stored.
5. Select the file Ex15-1 and choose Open.

   The presentation opens to the Slide view, which is a view of a single slide. There are other views in PowerPoint, which you learn about later in this lesson. For now, you are going to move to a view called Slide Sorter, which enables you to see all the slides in a presentation in miniature.

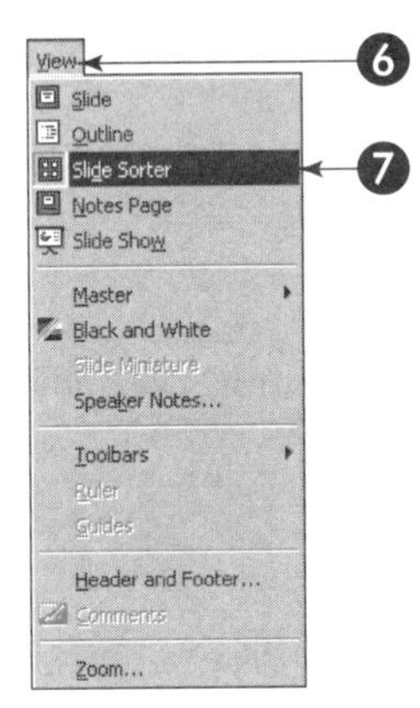

6. Click the View menu.
7. Select Slide Sorter.

   The view in the illustration to the right appears.

   Take a moment to look over these slides. Notice that some are overcrowded with text, making them difficult to read. Others have too many graphics and charts on one slide. If you study the contents of each slide, you find there is lack of organization to the ideas and even misspellings and poor grammar. Any of these problems can make a good presentation fail.

   Now, look at the other presentation.

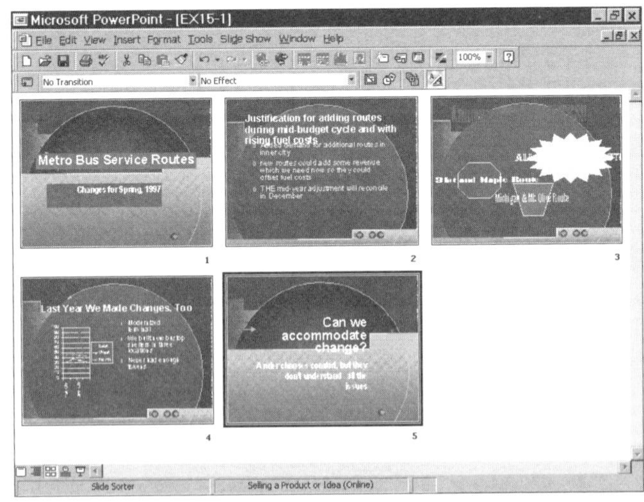

8. Select File ➢ Open.
9. From the dialog box that appears, locate the file Ex15-2 on your hard drive, select it, and choose Open.

⑩ When the presentation opens, select View ➢ Slide Sorter, if you haven't done so already.

The Slide Sorter view displays the presentation as shown in the illustration to the right.

Notice the difference between this and the first presentation. Slides aren't overcrowded with text, and there is no more than one chart or drawing per page. This presentation is much less distracting to a viewer, and offers a much more pleasant audience experience.

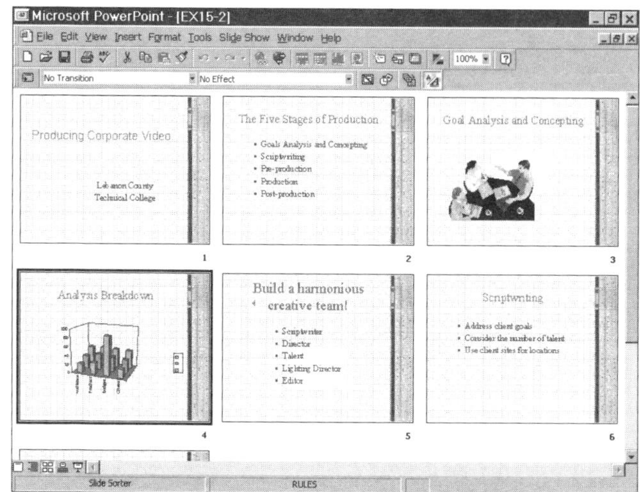

PREPARING FOR YOUR PRESENTATION

There are several things you can do to prepare for a presentation before using PowerPoint. In the second presentation, it's obvious the creator answered some basic questions, such as the following:

- *What is my message?* The focus of your presentation should be appropriate to the occasion. You should try to provide enough information to cover the topic, but not so much that you overwhelm your audience.
- *What do I want my presentation to achieve?* Are you trying to sell something, present information, or persuade people to adopt your point of view? If you were presenting three plans for the reorganization of the company and wanted your audience to choose the second one over the others, how could you make the presentation of the second plan more appealing?
- *Who is my audience?* Are you talking to experts who know the definition of the jargon you're using, or to people who aren't familiar with the topic? Can everyone in your audience read English equally well, or would you get your message across better with more visuals and less text? If you're making a presentation to a group of accountants, charts and graphs of hard data may be better received than clever cartoons and animations.

Preparing for your presentation

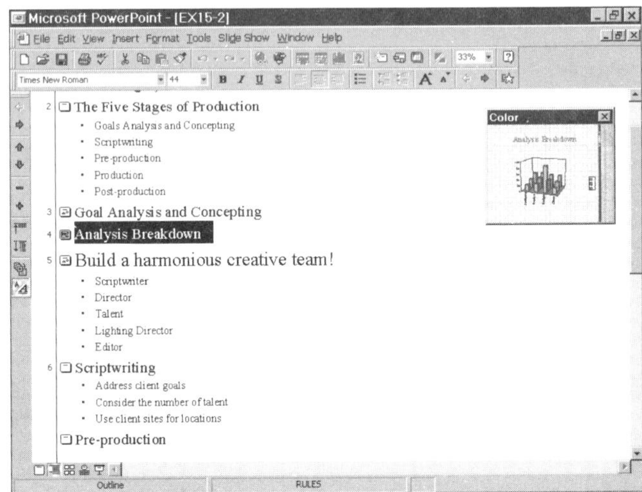

After you answer these questions, you can begin to design your presentation. Consider how to best organize the information. PowerPoint's Outline view, shown in the illustration to the right, can help you do that. You learn more about using Outline view in Lesson 16.

Consider any time constraints. PowerPoint has a feature that enables you to rehearse your presentation and record the time you take to display each slide. However, before you start building slides, you should have a general idea of timing: Do you have five minutes or an hour? There's no point in building 25 slides in PowerPoint if you don't have enough time to present them. Your PowerPoint slides should reinforce the key ideas of your presentation, not repeat the text verbatim. A PowerPoint presentation is meant to, in most cases, work in conjunction with a speaker, or at least a recorded narration.

If you plan to deliver your presentation on a computer screen with recorded narration, so that no live speaker is present to answer questions or interact with the viewer, you need to build more of your content into the slides. An example of this kind of presentation is a single computer workstation with a product presentation at a trade show booth where someone may or may not be present to talk to all the people who view the slides. Deciding what part of your message to show on slides and what to have the speaker to say is basic to planning and designing your presentation.

Offering your audience printed handouts, which are simple to generate from a PowerPoint presentation, is strictly optional. Some people find it helps their audience follow along and refer back to earlier points so they don't get lost. Others feel their audience spends more time reading and noisily turning pages than paying attention to the speaker. This may also vary from audience to audience. It is, however, one item to consider in planning how you will best convey information to your viewers. The good news is, besides actually printing the handouts, there are no additional steps to creating them, once you've created your presentation.

CREATING A PRESENTATION

Creating a basic presentation is pretty easy because PowerPoint offers several design shortcuts that make even the most simple presentation look professional. PowerPoint includes a wide variety of pre-existing "layouts." *Layouts* are arrangements of common slide elements, such as titles and bulleted lists. All the layouts (except the blank layout) provide you with placeholders. *Placeholders* are like little "Your Message Here" blocks, indicating where you should place certain elements in your presentation. Placeholders also automate the entry and formatting of your content.

PowerPoint also comes with dozens of built-in templates. *Templates* are like those plywood figures at amusement parks, with brightly painted bodies, and a hole where the head should be; you stand behind the figure and place your own head there to give life to the cutout. In a similar way, templates are files that provide the design framework for a presentation: the colors, patterns, and pictures creating a backdrop for the words and other elements you place in your slides to bring your presentation to life.

You can even create your own templates and save them for future use. When you save a file, just select the option button for Template instead of Document in the Save As dialog box.

Starting PowerPoint

Time to get some practice with the options presented to you when you first start PowerPoint.

1. On the Windows Taskbar, click Start ➢ Programs.
2. Choose PowerPoint from the list of available programs.

   The first screen you see contains the following four options:

   - *AutoContent wizard* walks you through the process of creating a new file, in this case a presentation, step by step. (You run through this wizard at the end of this lesson.)

Selecting a template

- *Template* enables you to base your presentation on predetermined designs and formatting elements. Select this if you don't want to be walked through the whole process of creating a presentation.
- *Blank presentation* enables you to start with a blank page; the only design element you are asked to apply is a layout for the first slide. Select Blank presentation if you don't want PowerPoint to provide any design elements or advice.
- *Open an existing presentation* enables you to open a previously saved presentation (including any presentations copied from the accompanying CD-ROM).

3. Select Template.
4. Choose OK to proceed.

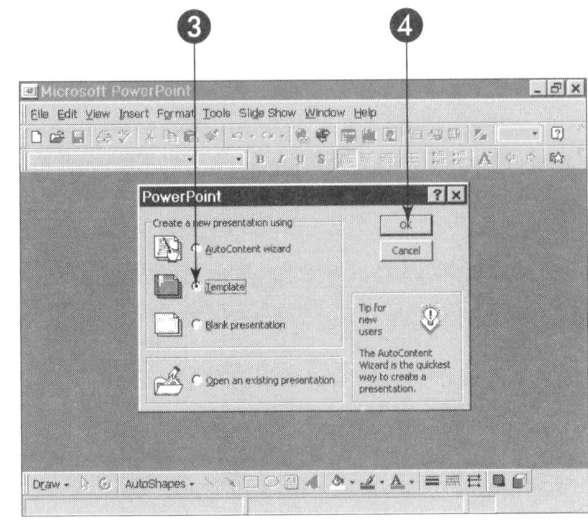

Selecting a template

At this point, you see the New Presentation dialog box shown in the following illustration, which has three tabs: General, Presentation Designs, and Presentations.

1. Select the General tab (if it's not already selected).

   The only template contained here is Blank presentation. This template has some text styles and formatting applied, but no graphic or design elements present.

2. Select the Presentations tab.

   The templates contained here are named by the type of presentation they are suited for, such as a Business Plan or Training presentation. Presentation templates not only contain all the style, formatting, and design elements of the presentation design templates, but also several slides are created by these templates with placeholders for the type of content you might include. For example, the Company Meeting template includes

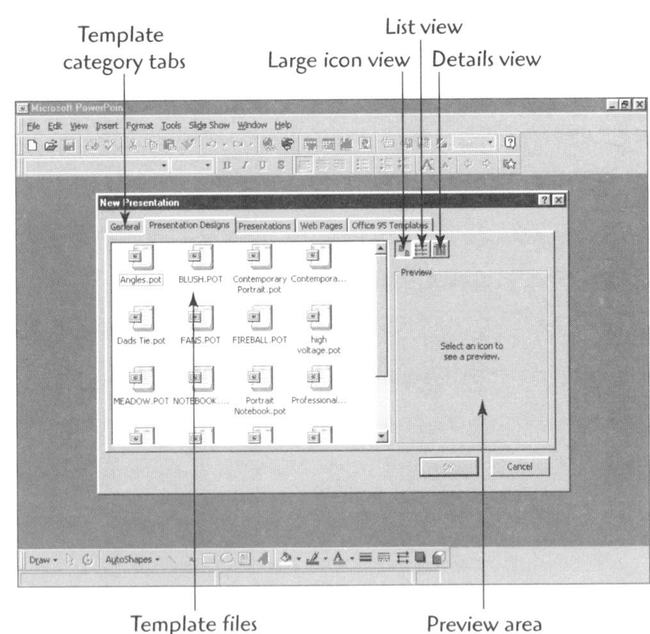

slides titled Organizational Overview and Top Issues Facing Company, with bullets suggesting the content you might enter on each slide.

3 Select the Presentation Designs tab.

This tab contains templates named by the look of the presentation, such as Blue Diagonal or Professional. If you only want design elements including text styles, text formatting, background colors, patterns, and graphic elements such as borders or clip art, you can use one of these templates.

4 Select the Blush template file from the Presentation Designs tab.

Notice that a preview appears in the box to the right of the template icons. You can change how you view the list of available templates by using the three buttons above the Preview. The first icon is currently selected: It displays file icons.

5 Select the List button to see the templates listed by name.

6 Select the Detail button to see the templates listed by name, size, type, and the date the file was last modified.

7 Choose OK to proceed with creating a presentation based on the Blush template.

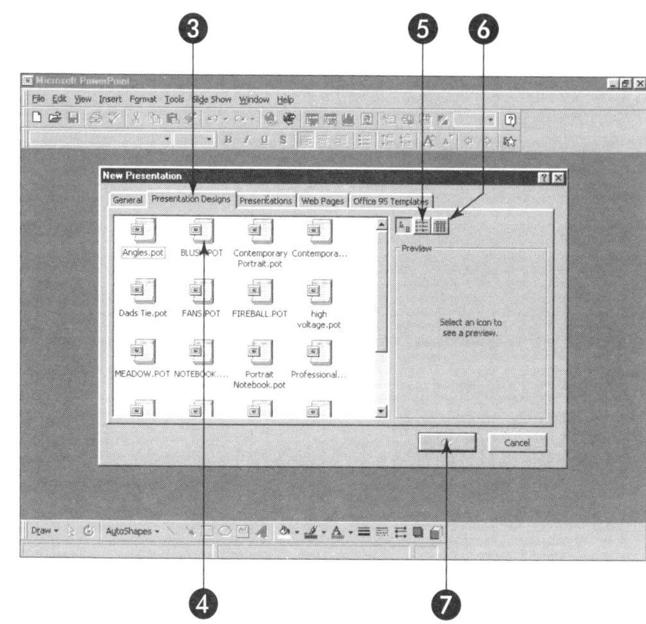

WORKING WITH LAYOUTS

The New Slide dialog box appears, as shown in the illustration to the right. You choose a layout for your slide here.

Remember, a layout provides placeholders for certain common presentation elements, such as a title, bulleted list, chart, or piece of clip art. Layouts are also referred to as AutoLayouts in PowerPoint.

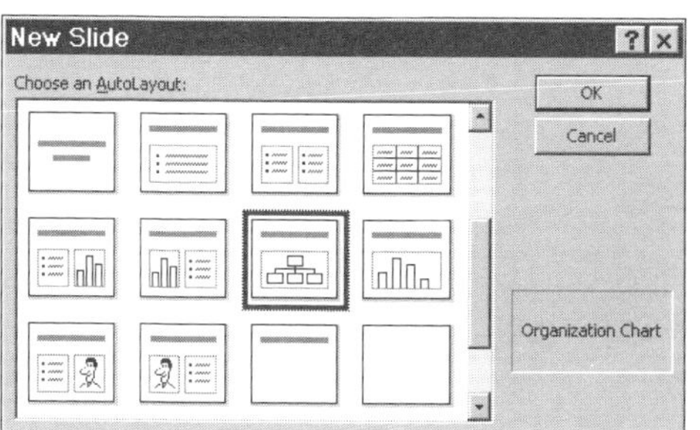

Selecting an AutoLayout

While a template places design elements on all your slides, AutoLayout places content placeholders. Each slide can have a different layout (whereas a presentation can have only one template applied). Here's how to select and apply a layout to your slide.

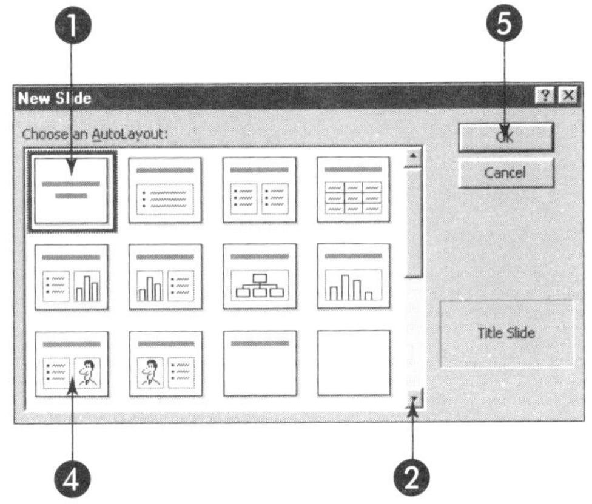

1. Select the first AutoLayout displayed in the New Slide dialog box.

   The name of the layout is shown in the box at the bottom right-hand corner. This one's called *Title*.

2. Click the down arrow at the bottom of the scroll bar to see additional layouts.

   Notice the various symbols used in the layout thumbnails, as described in the following table.

TABLE 15-1 SYMBOLS FOR PLACEHOLDERS IN AUTOLAYOUTS

Symbol	Placeholder
Thick gray line	Title or subtitle
Bullets with wavy lines	Text (formatted as bulleted lists)
Bar chart	Chart object
Boxes connected with lines	Organizational chart object
Picture	Clip art object
Movie slate	Movie object
Empty box	Object (usually from another Office application or applet)
Nine cells with text	Table

3. Scroll to the top of the layout list.
4. Select the Text & Clip Art layout (the third down on the left with title, bulleted list, and clip art symbols).
5. Choose OK to see your first slide.

Working with placeholders

Welcome to your new PowerPoint presentation! You're now looking at the first (and, for now, only) slide in your presentation. You see how this slide should look in the following illustration.

Take a look at all the menus and toolbars that appear around the PowerPoint screen in just a moment. First, identify the placeholders provided by your layout choice.

Notice that each of the three placeholders of the layout you selected appears on your slide, along with a patterned background supplied by the Professional template. Placeholders appear in the location determined by the layout, but you can move them around the slide if you like.

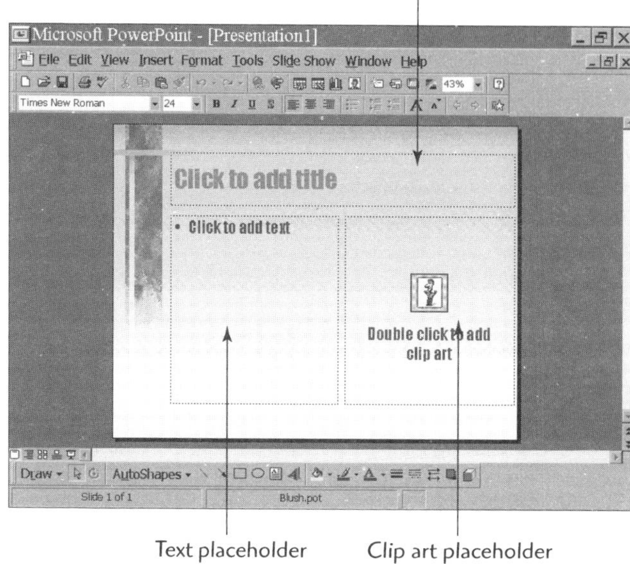

1. Click once anywhere on the clip art placeholder.

   A thick, shaded gray line appears around the placeholder and your cursor changes to a crosshair with arrows on all four ends. This cursor symbol means you can move the placeholder if you like. Try it.

2. Move the clip art placeholder by dragging it around your screen.
3. Select Edit.
4. Select Undo Move Object to move the clip art placeholder back to its original position.

Don't worry if you move a placeholder around and can't get it back where it belongs, you can always reapply a layout to snap things back where they started. You do this by selecting Format ➢ Slide Layout. From the Slide Layout dialog box that appears, select the layout and then click the Reapply button.

5. Click the title placeholder.

   A thick, shaded gray line appears around it, and the middle turns white, with a blinking, line-shaped cursor. This cursor indicates where text will begin if you start typing.

6. Type this title: **My First Presentation**.

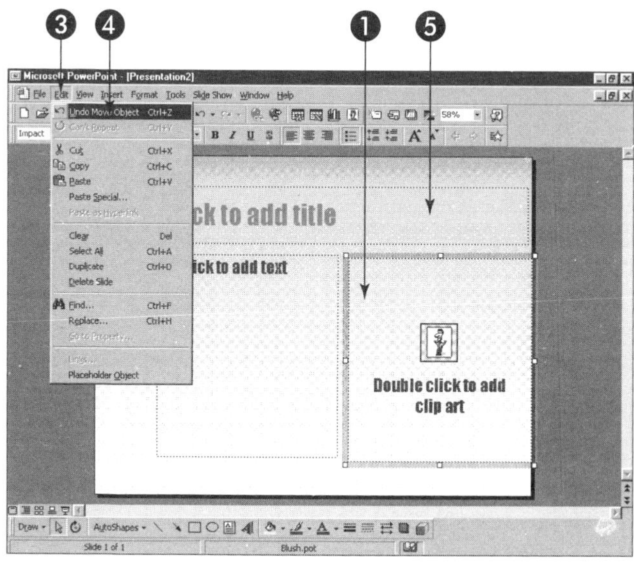

7. Click anywhere outside of the title placeholder to see your text in place on the slide, as shown in the illustration to the right.

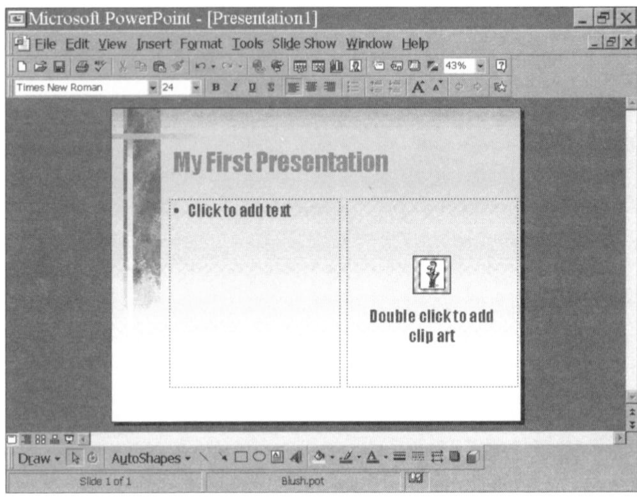

Text placeholders provide a place for you to enter text easily. Bulleted list placeholders, for example, automatically format each new line with a bullet when you hit Enter. *Other types of placeholders, such as clip art or chart placeholders, enable you to reach dialog boxes or other applications where you can create that type of object. You do this by double-clicking on this kind of placeholder. You see how this works in Lesson 17.*

LEARNING TO USE POWERPOINT TOOLS

Take a moment to examine the PowerPoint screen and all those little buttons and other elements surrounding your slide. In this section, you focus on the tools, which are shortcuts to getting things done in PowerPoint. In the next section, you take a closer look at menus, which offer another way to get things done.

The hardest part of learning any Windows-based program these days is memorizing the functions of each tool. Here are some exercises and tips to help you.

■ Looking at toolbars

When you select View ➢ Toolbar, a submenu appears, listing all of the toolbars available to you in PowerPoint.

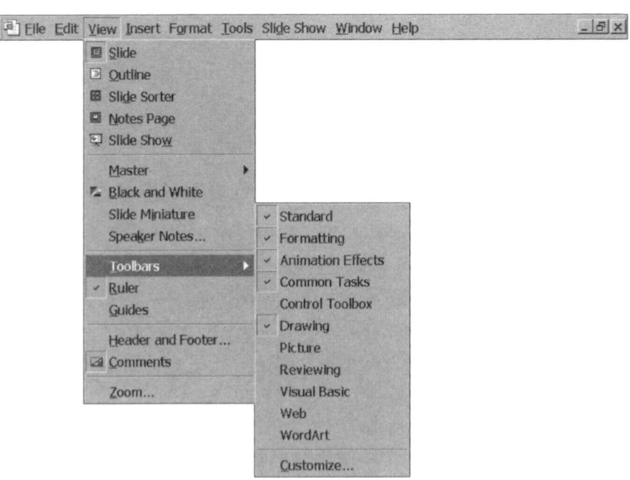

The toolbars that are checked appear on your screen by default. To display any toolbar, click next to it and a check mark appears. To stop displaying a toolbar, click next to it again and the check mark disappears.

Examine the toolbars on the top of the PowerPoint screen. The top row of buttons make up the Standard toolbar; the one just under that is the Formatting toolbar.

Learning to use PowerPoint tools

Take a look at the bottom of the screen shown at the top of the preceding page; here are two more sets of tools. The set of five tools in the left corner of the bottom of the screen is used to navigate among PowerPoint's different views. This isn't a toolbar you can choose to display or hide; it's a permanent set of tools that is always right where you see it now. The bottom row of buttons is the Drawing toolbar, which is used for drawing and formatting objects.

VISUAL BONUS: LEARNING POWERPOINT TOOLS

When you first open a PowerPoint presentation, you're surrounded by tools! This Visual Bonus provides a quick introduction to each toolbar and its buttons.

The Standard toolbar offers tools used to manage files, cut and paste text, insert objects, and apply certain design elements to slides.

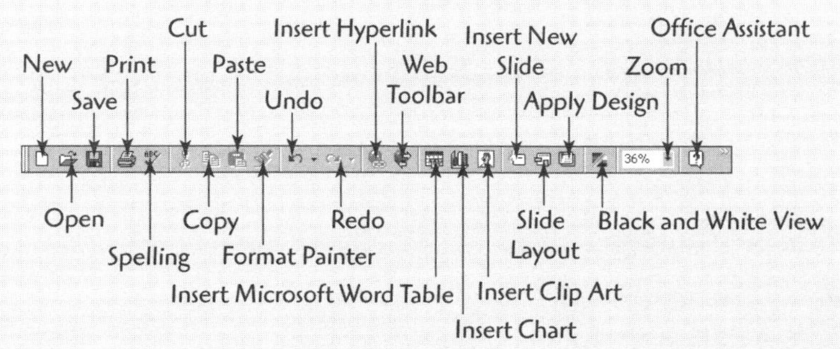

The Formatting toolbar contains tools for setting the font type and size, text special effects, spacing, alignment, and animation effects of objects in a presentation.

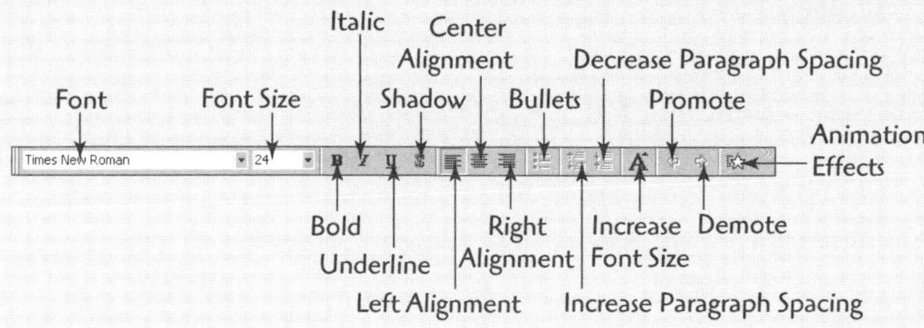

15 *Creating Presentations*

Using tools

Use these tools to switch among PowerPoint's five views.

Outline View
Notes Page View
Slide View
Slide Show View
Slide Sorter View

The first button on the left of this toolbar opens the Drawing menu; all the other tools are used for drawing or formatting shapes on your slides.

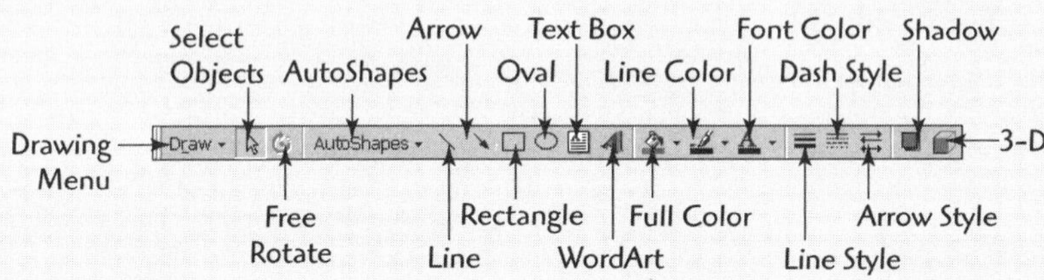

Using tools

It's time to practice using a few of these tools.

1. Place your mouse pointer over any tool on the Standard toolbar without clicking your mouse button.

   After a moment, a tool tip appears showing you the name of the tool in a little box just below your pointer. This is a handy way to learn the name of tools, or to remember those you've forgotten. First you'll use the Formatting toolbar.

2. Select the title object of your slide. The text opens, ready for editing.

3. Select the text *My First Presentation* by clicking at the front of the text and dragging your mouse cursor to the end of the line to highlight it.

4. Click the Bold button (in the Formatting toolbar, with a letter B on it).

5 Click the Bold tool again to remove the bold formatting.

6 Click the Font tool.

When you click this arrow, the drop-down list shown in the following illustration appears. With this type of tool, you make a selection from a drop-down menu by either clicking your choice, or using the scroll bar to locate it, and then pressing Enter.

7 Select the Arial font by clicking it in this list.

8 Click anywhere outside of your slide to deselect the title and see your changes in place.

Next, familiarize yourself with a couple more tools. First, create a new slide and save your presentation.

9 Click the New Slide tool on the Standard toolbar.

The New Slide dialog box appears, enabling you to select a layout for your new slide. Many tools in PowerPoint will open dialog boxes so you can make selections to perform procedures, such as creating a new slide.

10 Select the Title Slide layout (the first one).

11 Choose OK.

You now have a presentation consisting of two slides, so you should save your presentation.

12 Click the Save tool.

13 Complete the choices in the Save As dialog box to save this file with the name **My Presentation**.

Here are the three basic types of tools you encounter: toggle functions, tools that offer a selection through a drop-down list (or sometimes a pop-up palette of choices), and tools that take you to a dialog box to begin a procedure. You'll have plenty of practice with all these tools as you go through the tasks involved in building a PowerPoint presentation. For now, take a look at how you can do many of the same things you just practiced, and more, with PowerPoint menus.

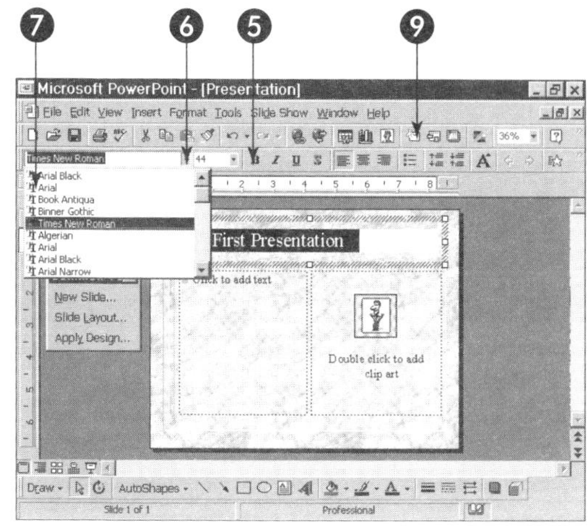

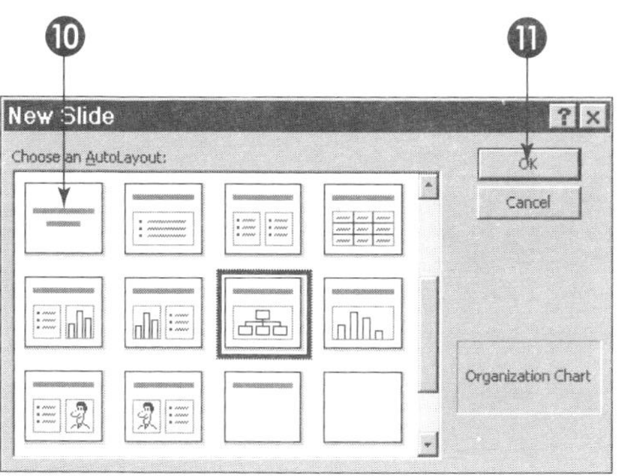

Using menus

USING MENUS

Buttons that you find on toolbars are actually shortcuts to performing functions that can also be accessed through menu commands. However, some functions have no toolbar shortcuts, and must be accessed through menus.

Many of the menus you see in PowerPoint are common to several of the Office programs and contain similar commands, so if you completed previous lessons in this book and are familiar with menus in any other program in Office, you have a head start.

■ Exploring menus

The following table provides an overview of the commands you find in the various menus of PowerPoint. The best way to learn these commands is to actually use them to perform tasks. I refer to both toolbar and menu commands in various exercises in the rest of this section so you can begin to get used to them.

TABLE 15-2 POWERPOINT MENU COMMANDS

File	Types of Commands
File menu	Open, close, save, print, or send files to another application or e-mail.
Edit menu	Select, cut, copy, paste, clear, and duplicate text or objects. In addition, it contains commands that enable you to Undo and Redo your last action, and Find and Replace specific text.
Insert menu	Create new slides, duplicate slides, insert items like slide numbers and the date on your slides, or insert slides from other locations into your current presentation. In addition, there are several types of objects, such as pictures and charts, that you can place in your presentation using the Insert menu.

File	Types of Commands
Format menu	Apply common text formatting, including modifying bullet list styles, changing text alignment, adjusting line spacing, and changing the case of text. Change your choice of layout, template, or color scheme from this menu, and get to property dialog boxes for colors and lines and drawing objects.
Tools menu	Access all the options for common functionality in the program through the Options dialog box. Check for correct spelling and style, and choose the language used for these checks. Manage presentations and customize PowerPoint.
Slide Show menu	Make settings for how your presentation will run if you display it on a computer screen, including the addition of sounds, animation, special effects for the transition between slides, and even recorded narration.

In addition, the Window and Help menus you saw earlier in this book, and in every other Office application, appear on the PowerPoint menu bar.

Changing the template

Try one exercise to practice using menus. Here, you apply a new presentation template to your slides to see how easy it is to try on new looks for your presentation.

1. Select Format.
2. Click Apply Design.

   In the Apply Design dialog box, you can select another design template on which to base your presentation. This dialog box can also be reached using the Apply Design tool on the Standard Toolbar.

3. Click the template named Meadow. A preview of the template appears.

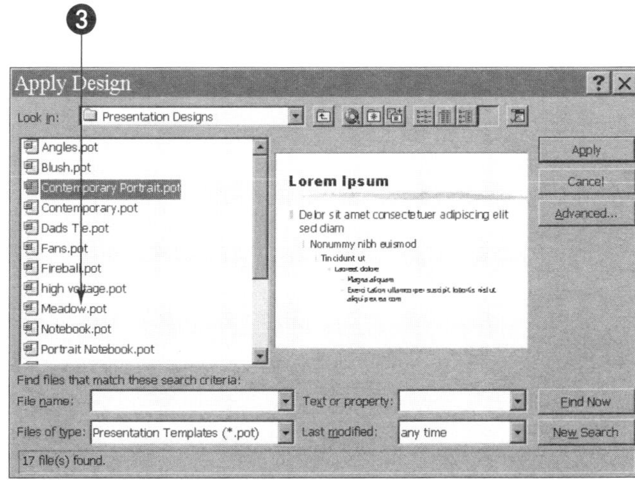

15
Creating Presentations

4. Choose Apply.

   Take a moment to study the changes the new template has applied to your presentation. Try to identify the settings and elements that were applied by the template, such as graphics, font, and font size.

5. Select File ➢ Close.

6. Choose No when asked if you wish to save your changes.

UNDERSTANDING POWERPOINT'S VIEWS

There are several elements involved in creating a presentation. There's the text you use to get your ideas across. There are the graphic elements you use to visually reinforce your ideas. You might want to make notes for either yourself or your audience to help you present information and them to retain it. To help with these various aspects of building a presentation, PowerPoint has provided five different views. To practice using these views, open the file Ex15-3, which you copied to your hard drive from the accompanying CD-ROM.

■ Using Slide view

The view you've been looking at so far is Slide view, shown in the illustration to the right. Slide view enables you to work on the design of your slides and insert elements. Slide view displays a single slide and the tools you need to adjust a slide's content, including rulers and a variety of toolbars.

In this view you can do the following:

- Enter text
- Edit text
- Add objects to your slides, such as charts and clip art
- Format and manipulate objects
- Draw and format shapes

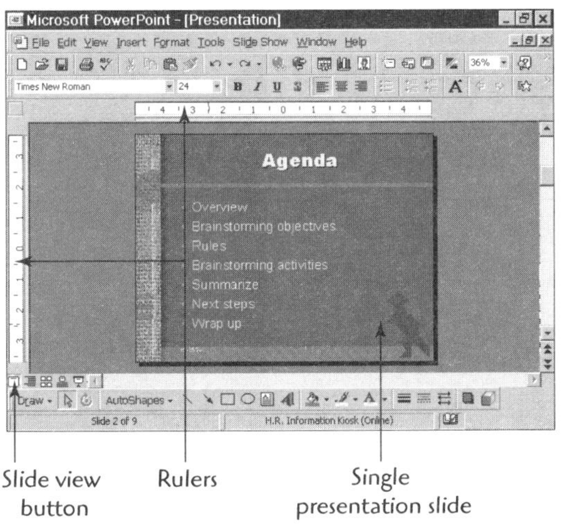

This view is best used for the actual slide design, creating arrangements of text and objects in your presentation.

Using Outline view

The Outline view helps you organize your ideas and concepts. Any text you enter here appears on your individual slides in Slide view, and any text you type in Slide view appears in the Outline view. So how do you decide where to enter text? Although you can easily enter text in the Slide view, typing text into the Outline view can be quicker (just like typing in a word processor), and enables you to see the organization of information in your presentation as you build it.

The illustration to the right shows a presentation in Outline view. There is a special toolbar that appears in this view; it runs down the left side of the screen. These tools enable you to display the varying levels of detail in your outline, or to rearrange the items in the outline. There is also a floating preview box. This preview corresponds to whatever outline item you have selected (or wherever your cursor is resting). Each slide is numbered along its left side.

The special outline toolbar provides the functions you need to view and reorganize your outline. The bottom right illustration shows the Outline toolbar in detail.

Practice using the Outline view to see different levels of outline detail, move a slide in the presentation, and enter and change the level of an outline item. Choose the Outline view button to move to the Outline view first.

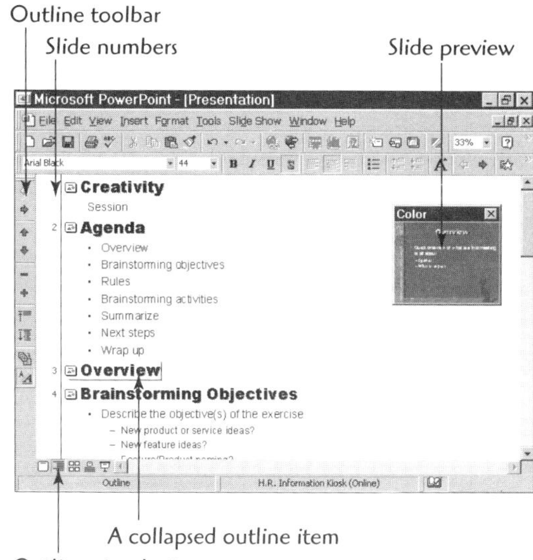

1. Place your cursor before the word *Agenda* in Slide 2.

If you don't see the Agenda heading, use the scroll bar to move up or down in the outline until it appears.

2. Choose the Collapse tool on the Outline toolbar.

   The bulleted items underneath the title *Agenda* disappear, and you see a wavy, gray line under the title. This line indicates that there is more detail to this heading that isn't currently visible.

3. With your cursor still before the heading *Agenda,* choose the Move Up tool.

   Agenda and all its bullet points move up in the sequence of slides to become Slide 1.

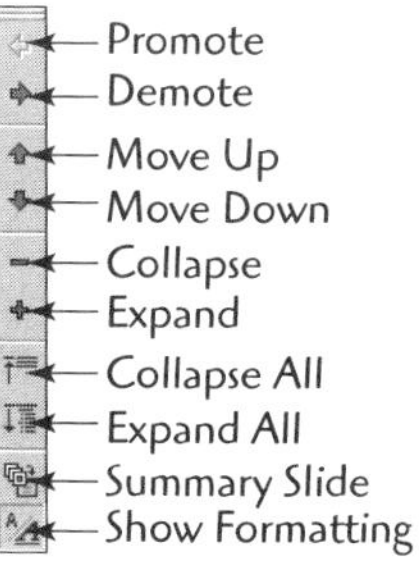

15 Creating Presentations

4. Choose the Collapse All button to see just the headings for each of the slides in this presentation.

   Your outline now looks like the one in the illustration to the right.

   Notice the blank slide at the end of this presentation. Add some text to it.

5. Place your cursor next to the icon for Slide 9 and type **Assignments**.

6. Press Enter.

   When you press Enter, a new slide appears. If you want to create another slide, type another title. But, if you want to create details for Slide 9, you have to demote this new item to become a bullet point under *Assignments*.

7. With your cursor still on the Slide 10 item in the outline, choose the Demote button.

   This will indent the item in the outline, making it subordinate to the heading and part of Slide 9.

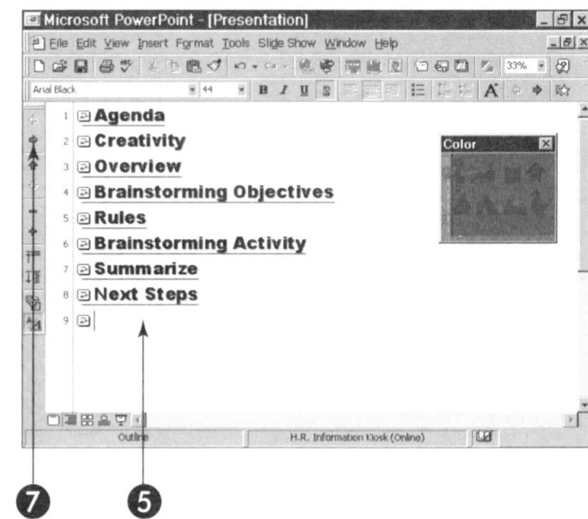

Using Slide Sorter view

Although, as you saw in the previous exercise, you can move slides around your presentation in Outline view, it's sometimes easier to reorganize your presentation in Slide Sorter view.

1. Choose the Slide Sorter button to move to the Slide Sorter view. Slide Sorter view also has its own toolbar, displayed at the top of the screen, beneath the Formatting toolbar.

   Slide Sorter view gives you a thumbnail view of the overall flow and look of your slides. Use Slide Sorter view to see the flow of slides in your presentation and get a feel for the consistency of graphics and other design elements. You can rearrange slides, delete slides, duplicate slides, and preview transition effects between slides in this view. Practice some of these functions now.

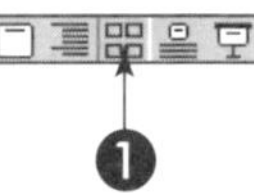

2. Click Slide 4 (Brainstorming Objectives) to select it. A black border appears around it.

❸ Click and drag this slide up between Slide 2 and Slide 3.

A long vertical line should appear between Slides 2 and 3. This line indicates where your slide will be placed if you release your mouse button.

❹ Release the mouse button and Slide 4 should have been moved to become Slide 3.

If you put the slide in the wrong spot, practice dragging it until it appears in the correct place.

❺ Select Slide 1 (Agenda).

❻ Select Edit ➢ Duplicate.

The selected slide is duplicated. This can be useful if, for example, you want to use a title slide at both the opening and closing of your presentation. At this point, you can move this slide duplicate to the end of the presentation using the drag-and-drop method just described.

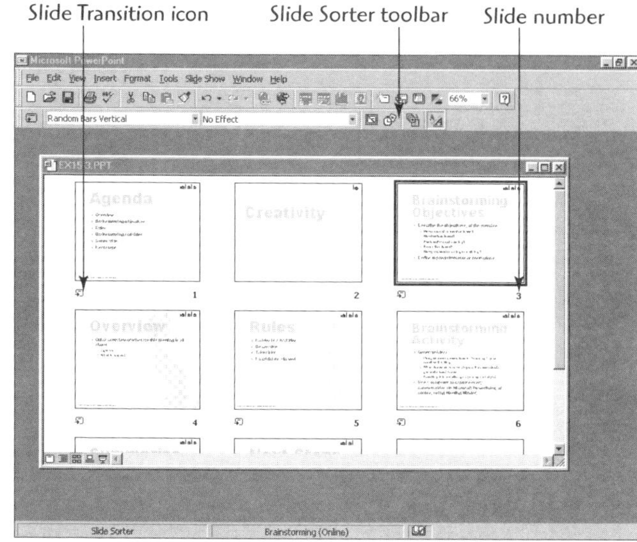

Using Notes Page view

You use the Notes Page view to add and view notes for your presentation. This view enables you to create speaker notes to remind you of important background information as you present your slides. You can then print out these notes, which contain an image of a slide and the notes that accompany it, something like the page shown on the screen in the following illustration.

Entering a note is a simple process.

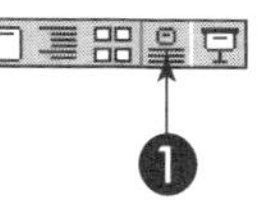

❶ Click the Notes View button to move to the Notes View.

❷ Click the notes area. A gray dashed border surrounds it.

❸ Choose the Zoom button and select 50 percent to view your text more easily as you type.

❹ Type the following text: **Don't forget to provide background on how we got where we are today**.

❺ Click anywhere outside of the notes area to move out of editing mode.

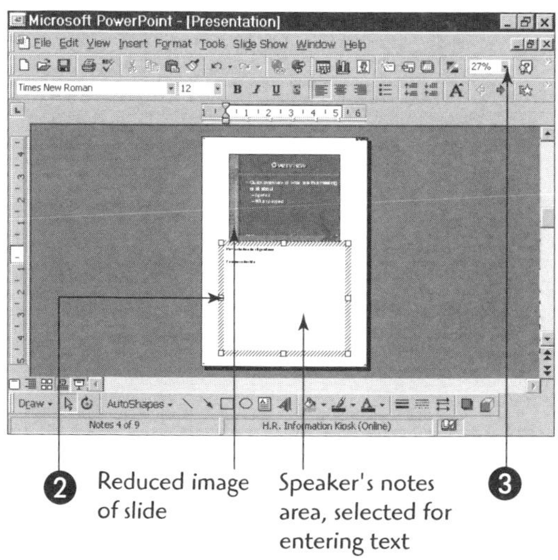

6. Choose Zoom from the toolbar, and select Fit from the bottom of the *Zoom* list.

   Your notes page returns to full view, with your new note in place. You learn more about printing notes in Lesson 17.

Using Slide Show view

The last view in PowerPoint is really the simplest. Slide Show view enables you to see your presentation as your audience will see it, as shown in the following illustration.

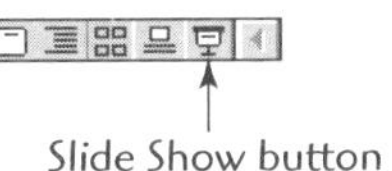

Slide Show button

1. Choose the Slide Show view button.

   You now begin previewing your slides full screen, just as you would see them in an onscreen presentation. The presentation begins at the slide you had selected in the Notes Page view.

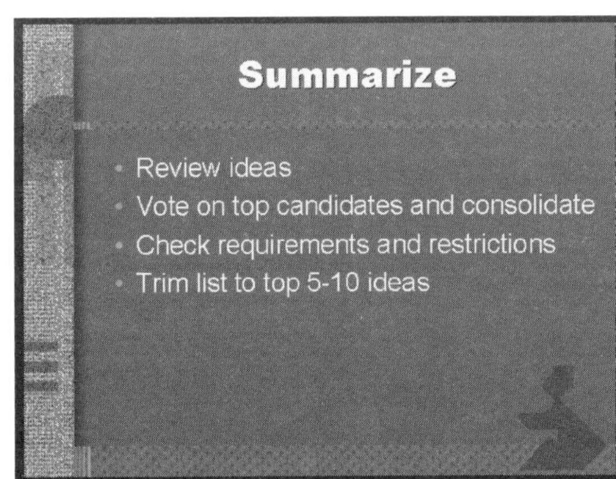

2. Press the right arrow key on your keyboard to move forward to the next slide.

   Notice the transition effect between slides. A transition effect is the way in which the new slide replaces the current one on the screen, such as flying in from the side or raining down from the top. You can also use other methods to move in your presentation.

3. Click your mouse once to move to the next slide.
4. Press Enter, which is another method to move forward to the next slide.
5. To go back a slide, use the left arrow key.
6. To leave the Slide Show, press Esc.
7. Select File ➢ Close and do not save changes to the file when asked.

SKILLS CHALLENGE: USING THE AUTOCONTENT WIZARD

One of the easiest ways to begin a new presentation with PowerPoint is using AutoContent Wizard. This selection takes you through choices that help determine some of the design and content choices for your presentation. The following steps walk you through this process.

1. Select File ➢ New. The New Presentation dialog box appears.

When you first open PowerPoint, how do you start the AutoContent Wizard?

2. Select the Presentations tab.
3. Click AutoContent Wizard (it's at the top of the list; use the scroll bar to locate it if you need to). Click OK to proceed.
4. The first wizard screen is shown in the illustration. This screen shows you the various choices you are asked to make during the wizard procedure.
5. Choose Next to proceed. The next dialog box offers you options for the type of presentation you want to create. These are basically the various Presentation templates, divided by categories such as Corporate and Personal to make your selection simpler.
6. Click Corporate to see the templates related to business.

Name three elements or settings for your PowerPoint slides that can be contained in a template.

7. Click the Company Meeting choice in the list of presentation templates.
8. Choose Next to proceed.

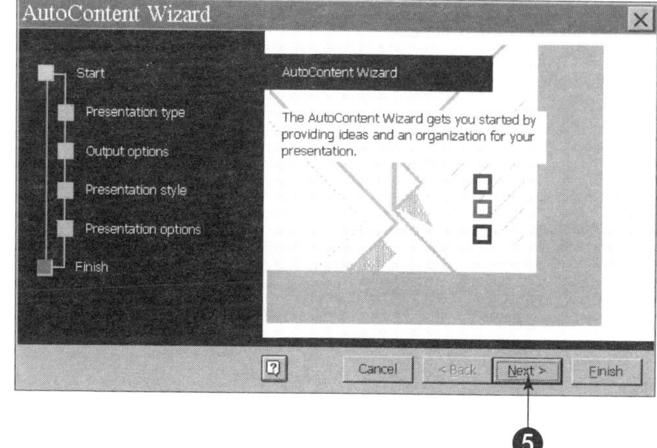

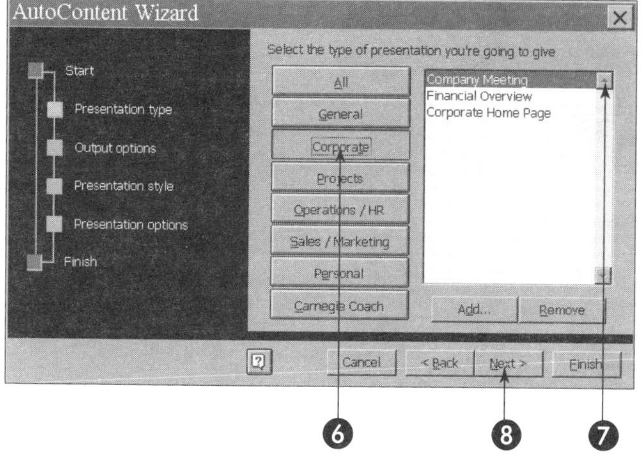

Skills challenge

9. The next dialog box asks whether you'll be presenting these slides for formal/information presentation, handouts, or on the Internet. This selection influences choice of backgrounds (some background templates don't work as well on Web pages). Choose Next to accept the default choice and proceed.

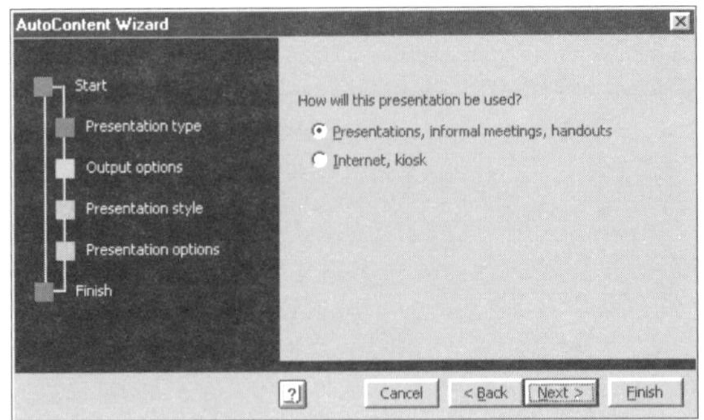

10. The next AutoContent Wizard dialog box asks you to specify the way you'll output your presentation (such as overheads, slides, or onscreen). You don't have to decide now, but it is helpful if you can make this determination before you begin building slides. If you change output choices after creating slides, some of the elements on the slides themselves may have to be rearranged to accommodate the new output choice. Choose Next to accept the *On-screen presentation* option and proceed with the last step in the wizard.

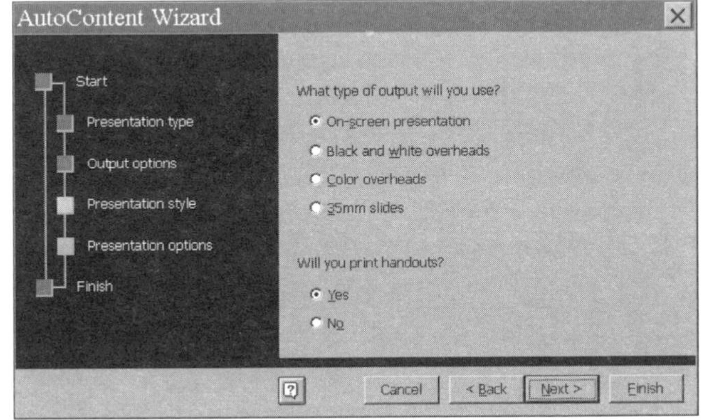

11. The final AutoContent Wizard dialog box asks you to enter a title for the presentation, your name, and any additional information (for example, the date of the presentation) in three text fields. Type **My Project** in the *Title* box, and type your name in the *Name* box.

12. Choose Next to go to the final wizard dialog box. At this point, you can click the gray box next to any of the wizard choices you've completed to return and make changes. To complete the wizard, choose Finish.

13. The presentation appears on your screen in Outline view.

    Now use some of the skills you learned in this lesson to see what the wizard provided.

14. Make sure your cursor is on Slide 1, My Project. Choose the Slide view button to move to slide view.

15. Click the title object to open it for editing. Replace the title *My Project* with the words **Project Presentation**.

16. Click anywhere outside of the title object to deselect it.

17. Move to the Slide Sorter view using the View menu. Select View ➢ Slide Sorter.

What is the other method of displaying the Slide Sorter view?

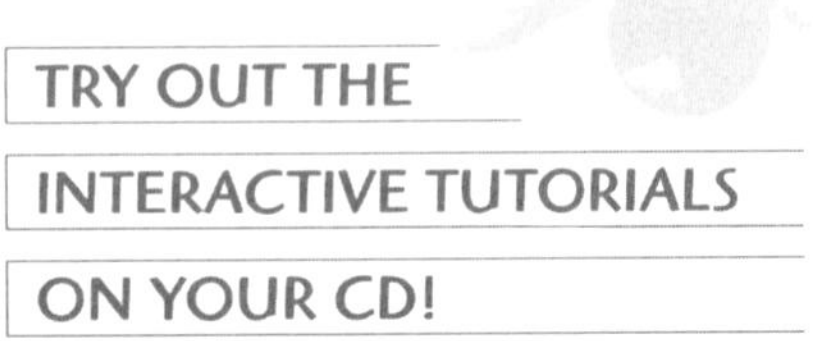

18. Click Slide 3 to select it, and then drag it to the left so that it becomes Slide 2.
19. Choose the Notes Page view button.
20. Click the notes area, and type **Provide statistics here**.
21. Select the text you just typed using your mouse. Make the text bold and apply a shadow to it.

In the previous step, there are two ways to achieve these text formatting changes. What are they?

22. Select File ➢ Save, and save this file with the name **Project Presentation**.

TROUBLESHOOTING

There are some questions that often come up in designing effective presentations. Some are listed in the following table, along with suggested solutions.

These are all common mistakes that most of us make in learning our way around a new program. Above all, don't stop when you encounter a few problems. You soon overcome them!

Problem	Solution
I always run overtime on my presentations.	Use visuals, such as charts or drawings, to make some of your points and save time.
I chose the wrong template.	Select Format ➢ Apply Design and select another template.
I chose the wrong layout.	Select Format ➢ Slide layout and choose another layout.
I moved a placeholder and want to put it back.	If you just did this, select Edit ➢ Undo. If you did it a few actions ago, select Format ➢ Slide layout and reapply the layout.

continued

Wrap up

Problem	Solution
I deleted a placeholder.	Select Format ➢ Slide layout to reinsert the placeholder on your slide.
I entered Slide Show view by mistake and can't get out.	Press Esc.

WRAP UP

In this lesson, you've been introduced to several key concepts concerning successful presentations, and you've practiced the following skills:

- Planning your presentation to convey your message the best way
- Creating a new PowerPoint presentation using a template or the AutoContent wizard
- Exploring the various toolbars and menus and learning to create a new slide and change your presentation design template using these commands
- Exploring PowerPoint's five views, and seeing how each helps you to work with various aspects of your presentation

If you want to practice these skills further, try running through the AutoContent wizard again, but this time, make choices that would be more appropriate for a personal presentation about your last vacation.

In Lesson 16, you tackle the process of building your first complete PowerPoint presentation, adding text, clip art, and a chart.

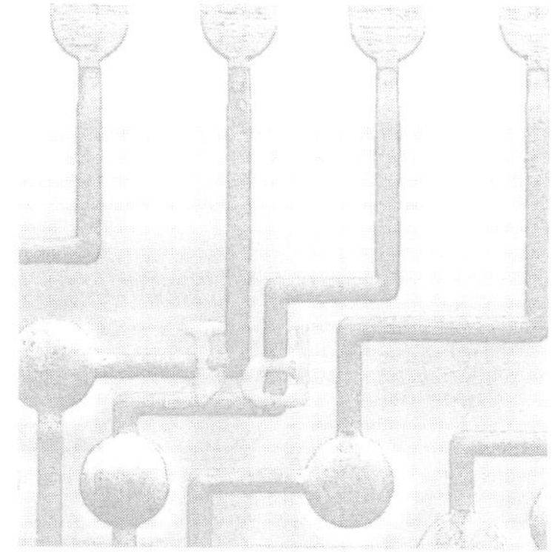

Building Your First Presentation

GOALS

In this lesson you learn the basics of building a presentation, including the following:

- Adding text to your slides and formatting the text
- Adding a new slide
- Adding a clip art object and working with objects
- Using Handout Master
- Creating a presentation from a presentation design
- Using AutoShapes and drawing freehand
- Resizing drawings

Get ready

GET READY

In this lesson, you build your own presentation. The final version of the presentation has been copied to your hard drive from the accompanying CD-ROM, named Ex16-1, should you need to refer to it or use it in the Skills Challenge at the end of the lesson. You'll also need the file Ex16-2 from the accompanying CD-ROM.

In the exercises in this lesson, you create a presentation containing slides like the one shown on the facing page.

TRY OUT THE INTERACTIVE TUTORIALS ON YOUR CD!

STARTING WITH AN OUTLINE

There are basically two ways to enter the text for your presentation: You can enter an outline, much like an outline in Word for Windows or any other word processor, and that outline is automatically turned into individual slides by PowerPoint. Or, you can enter text on each individual slide, in which case PowerPoint creates the corresponding outline. You can even use a combination of the two methods within the same presentation.

You'll begin building your first presentation in the Outline view of PowerPoint, and then move to the Slide view to format text and insert other types of objects on your slides.

Entering outline text

The Outline view was made for entering text: It uses tools and a structure you might recognize from the Word for Windows outlining feature.

1. Open PowerPoint.
2. From the opening screen, select Template.
3. Choose OK. The New Presentation dialog box appears.
4. Select the Presentation Designs tab.
5. Click the Blush template.
6. Choose OK. The New Slide dialog box appears.
7. Choose OK to accept the default Title Slide AutoLayout.

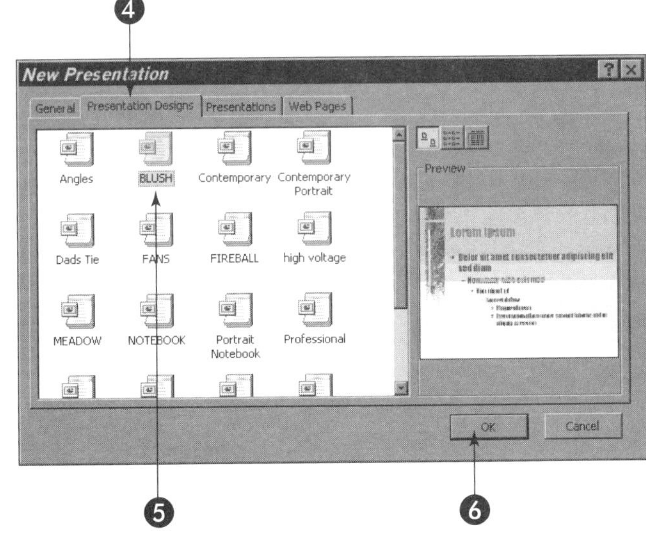

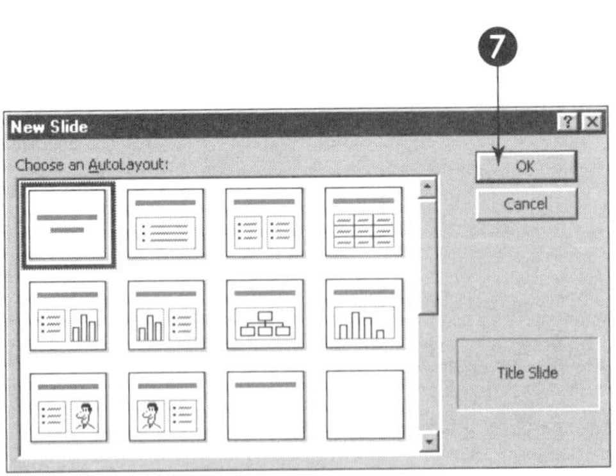

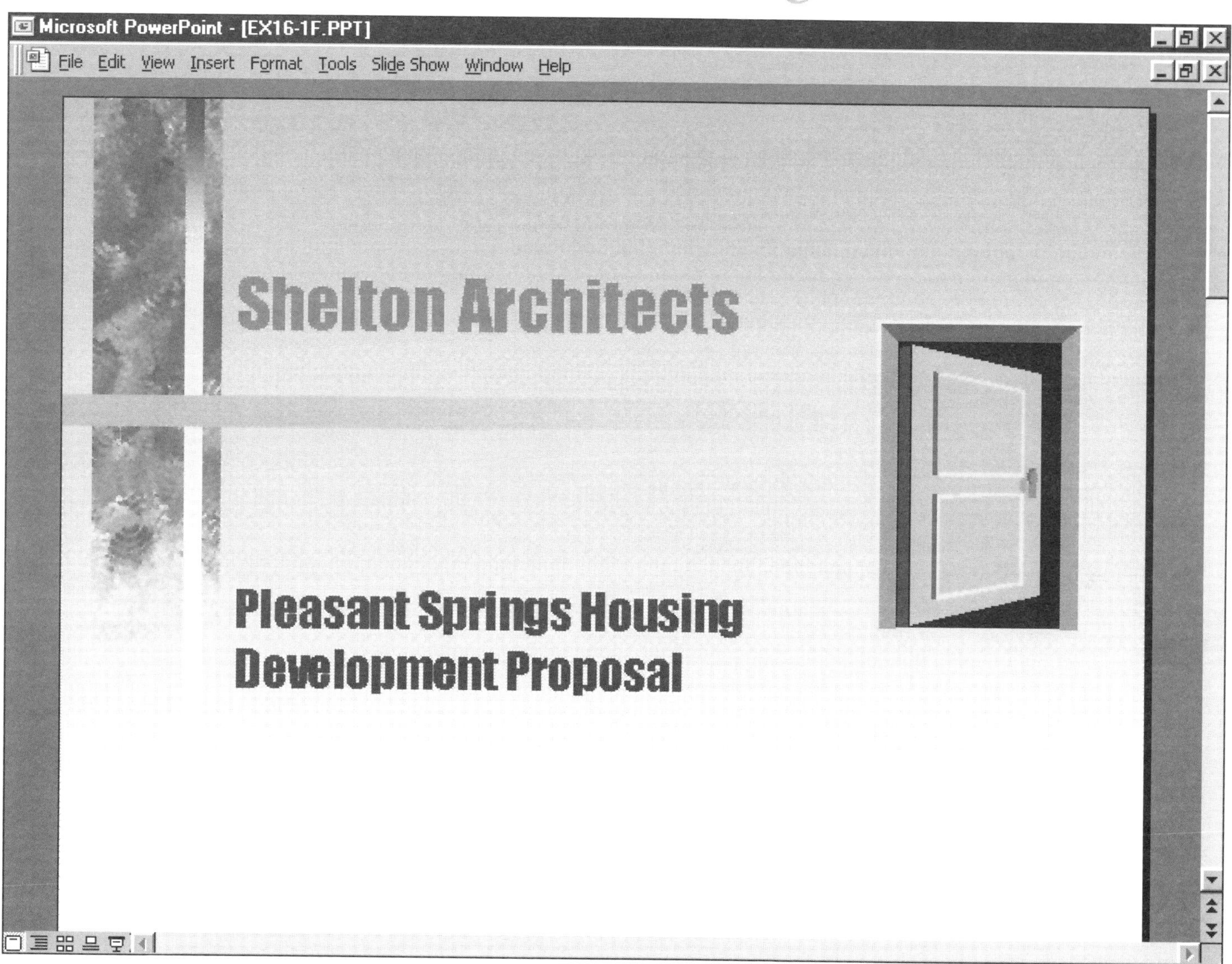
Microsoft PowerPoint - [EX16-1F.PPT]
File Edit View Insert Format Tools Slide Show Window Help
Shelton Architects
Pleasant Springs Housing
Development Proposal

Entering outline text

The template appears on your screen in Slide view. The colors, design, and font formatting have been brought in by the template; the two text placeholders, one for the title and one for a subtitle, belong to the Title Slide AutoLayout.

8. Click the Outline view button. The Outline view appears.
9. Type **Shelton Architects**.
10. Press Enter.
11. Type **Pleasant Springs Housing Development Proposal**.
12. Press Enter. Notice that you now have three numbers and slide icons running along the left of the text. This indicates three separate slides in your presentation.
13. Switch to Slide view.

    Notice that the note in the status bar at the bottom of the screen says Slide 3 of 3. By default, PowerPoint has applied the AutoLayout containing a title and bulleted list of text to the second and third slides, because that is typically what follows a title slide. Notice that the third slide is blank, because you haven't added any text to it yet in Outline view.

14. Switch back to the Outline view.
15. Select the second line of text by clicking the slide icon to the left of it.
16. Press the Demote button on the Outline toolbar.

    By demoting the second line of text, you made it part of the first slide, subservient to the title text. You now have two slides instead of three. You can use the demote and promote tools to move lines of text in or out in an outline, to greater or lesser levels of detail.

17. Switch to Slide view. The first slide now contains a title and subtitle corresponding to the outline structure, as in the illustration to the right.

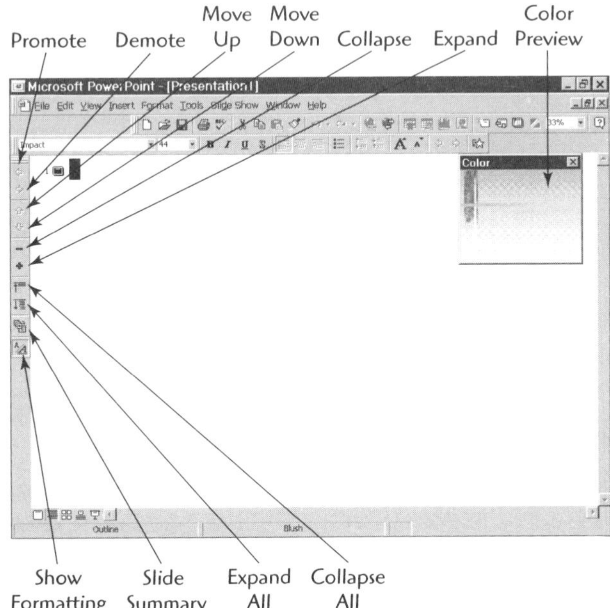

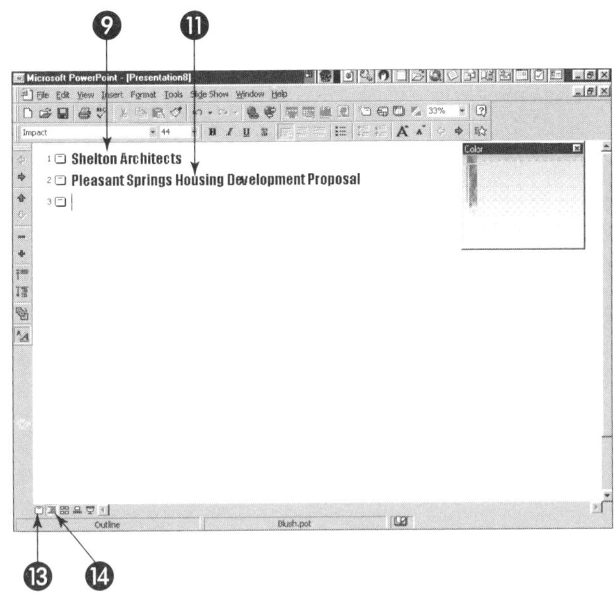

18. Switch back to Outline view.
19. Click next to the icon for Slide 2 to place your cursor there.
20. Type **Background** and press Enter.
21. Press Tab. This is another way to demote a line of text. Notice this line of text has a bullet before it, because this layout has a bulleted list for the second placeholder.

NOTE

Although you can create several levels of text on a single slide, a title and subheading or bulleted list of text is usually the most you want to create. More than two levels of text in a slide can make it too busy and difficult to read. If you have several subpoints to make, consider creating separate slides for each.

22. Type **Incorporated 1968** and press Enter. The next line of text appears at the same level as the line before it.
23. Type **Member National Architects Association** and press Enter. Notice the slide color preview build as you continue to enter text.
24. Type **Winner of 1995 NAAC Award** and press Enter.
25. Click the Promote tool to move the next line of text up in the outline hierarchy, thereby making it the title of a new slide.
26. Type **Design Process** and press Enter.
27. Type **Qualifications**. Your outline should look like the one in the illustration to the right.

    Before you go any further, it's a good idea to save your presentation.

28. Select File ➢ Save. Save the presentation with the name **JobBid**.

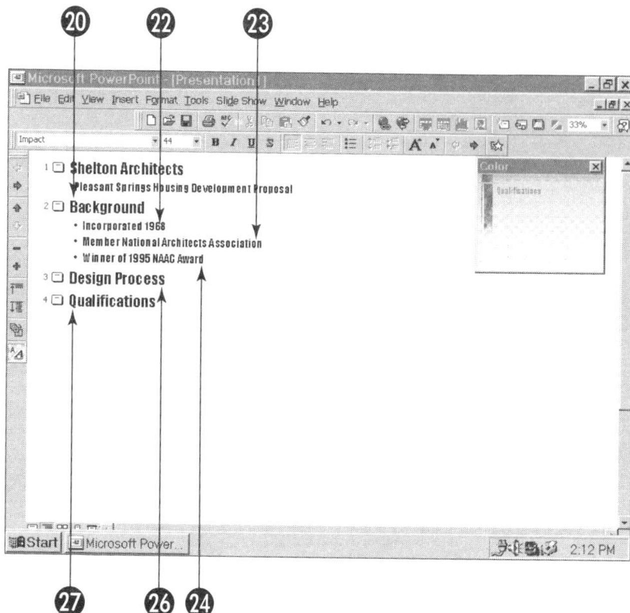

Reorganizing the outline

Reorganizing the outline

Once you've entered some text in your outline, it's a simple matter to reorganize that text and even manipulate it so you can view different levels of detail in your presentation. For example, you can look at just the titles of each slide to see how the major topics of your presentation flow one to another.

1. Select Slide 4 by clicking the slide icon to the left of the text *Qualifications.*
2. Click the Move Up button on the Outline toolbar. *Qualifications* becomes Slide 3 in the presentation.
3. Select Slide 2, titled *Background.*
4. Keeping your mouse button pressed, drag the slide icon down. A black line indicates where the slide will be placed should you release the mouse, as in the illustration to the right. Release the mouse button when the line is between the third and fourth slide.
5. Click the Collapse All button on the Outline toolbar.

   The detail text under the first and third slide is hidden, but a wavy, gray line indicates there's more detail here. Notice that the Color preview of the slide itself still displays the detail text: expanding and collapsing only impacts the text in your outline. This helps you to focus on as much or as little detail as you need to organize your presentation contents.
6. Select the Slide 1.
7. Click the Expand button on the Outline toolbar. Only Slide 1 expands to show all its detail.

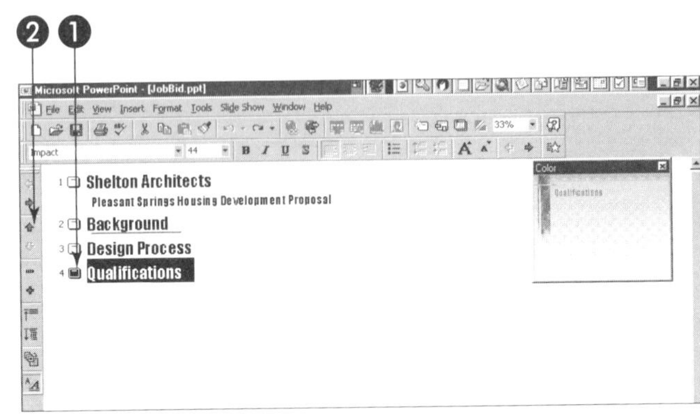

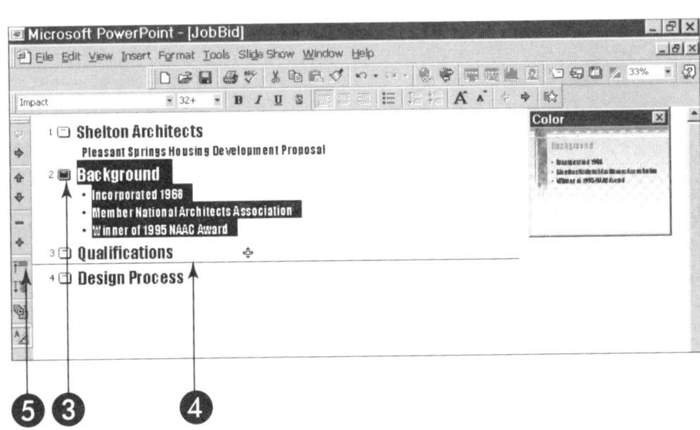

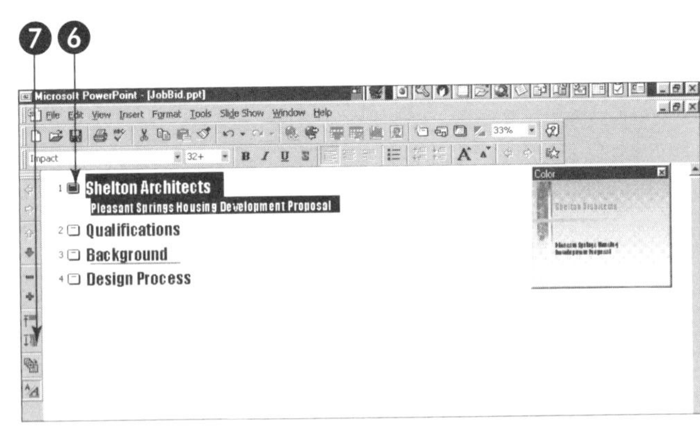

ADDING ELEMENTS IN SLIDE VIEW

Using Outline view can be the fastest way to add text, but when you're ready to focus on the design of the individual slides, it's useful to move to the Slide view. Here you can continue to add or edit text, as well as insert design objects such as clip art or drawings.

Adding text to slides

While text you've entered in Outline view will appear in your slides, text you add to layout placeholders in your Slide view will also be reflected in your Outline view.

1. Switch to Slide view.
2. Using the scroll bar, move to Slide 2, titled *Qualifications*.
3. Click the bulleted text placeholder (where it says Click to add text). The placeholder opens with your cursor at the first bullet point.
4. Type **20 major housing developments completed** and press Enter. This begins a second bullet point.
5. Type **Experience with passive solar design**.
6. Click anywhere outside of the text placeholder.
7. Switch to Outline view. The text entered in the Slide view appears in the outline, as shown in the illustration to the right.
8. Select Slide 4.
9. Switch to the Slide view.
10. Click the Slide Layout button on the toolbar.
11. Select the Title Only layout and choose Apply. The bulleted text placeholder disappears.
12. Click the Text Box button on the Drawing toolbar.
13. Click the slide and drag to draw a small rectangle.

   This rectangle is a text box. It's a way of placing a text object on the page outside of a text placeholder. A text box is kind of like a text drawing object. You might use a text box to place a label on a piece of clip art, for example, or to place the word *Stop* in the middle of a drawing of a stop sign. Although the text in placeholders will meet most of your needs, occasionally you'll want to create your own text objects, and the text box is how to do it.

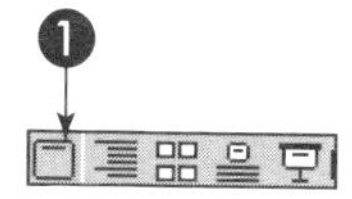

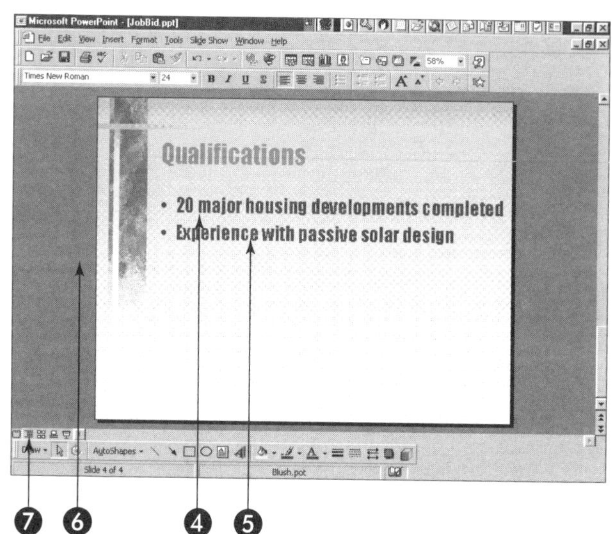

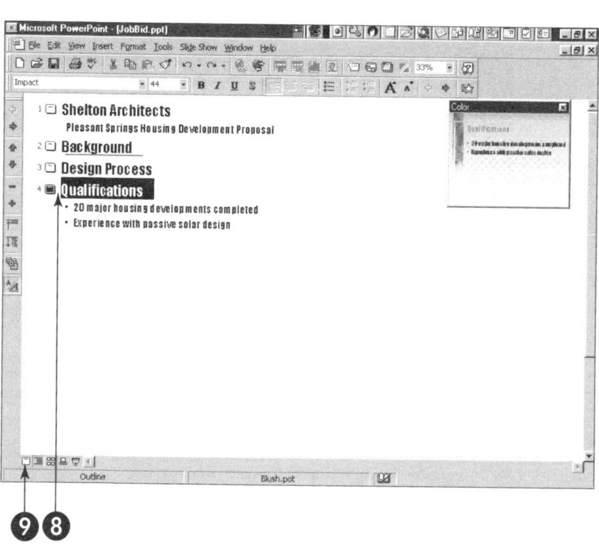

14. Type **Award Winning!**
15. Switch to Outline view.

    Notice that while the text box shows on the color preview, it does not become part of the outline. Nothing you enter in a text box is included in the outline for a presentation. Also, the slide icon for the fourth slide now looks slightly different; the image of a little drawing on it indicates that a drawing object has been placed on this slide.

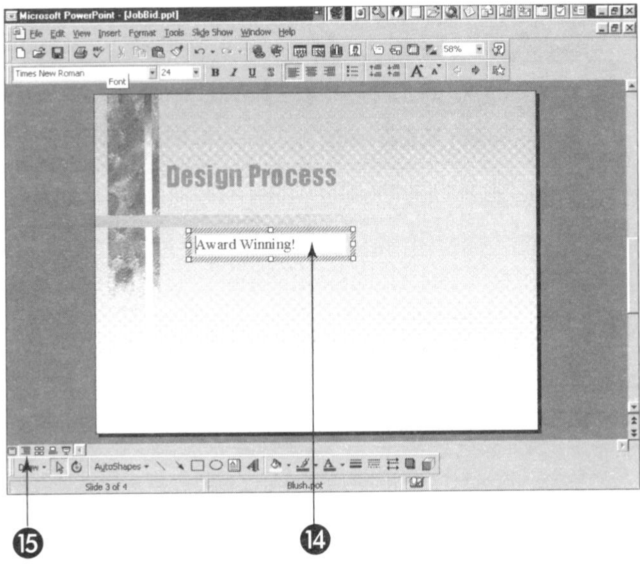

Formatting text

The ways you choose to format text in a PowerPoint presentation can be as important — or more important — than the formatting of text in a Word for Windows letter. After all, the text in your PowerPoint presentation might end up a foot tall on a presentation screen, so it should look its best!

1. Switch back to Slide view, displaying Slide 4.
2. Select the text, *Award Winning!*
3. Click the Shadow button on the toolbar.
4. Use the *Font size* drop-down list on the toolbar to change the font to 48 points.
5. Select the title text.
6. Click the Format menu.
7. Select Font. The Font dialog box appears.

   If you are working through this book in sequence, this Font dialog box should look very familiar. It's identical to the dialog box used for formatting text in Word for Windows. Although the font and formatting for text in placeholders is preassigned by the template you've chosen, you can change that formatting using the tools on the formatting toolbar or in this dialog box.
8. Change the font to Baskerville.

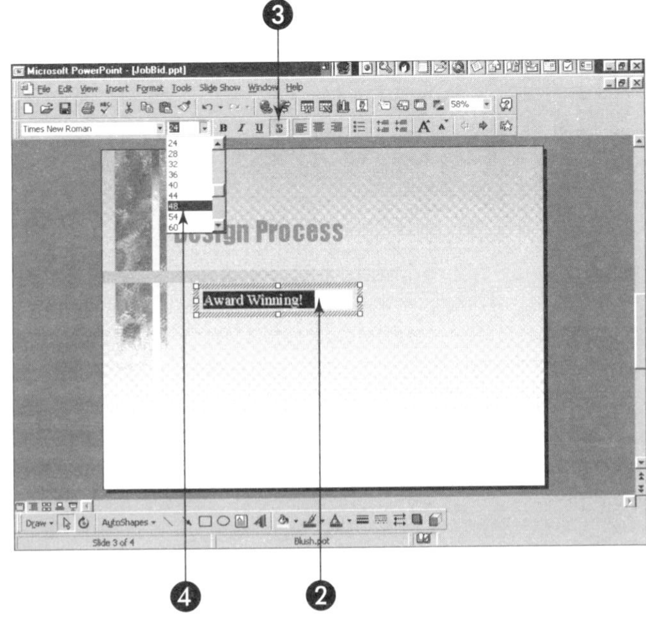

9 Select Bold, Italic style, and choose OK to apply the new formatting.

10 Choose OK to apply the new formatting.

Adding a new slide

In the Outline view, you can add a new slide by pressing Enter at the end of an upper-level line of text, or by promoting a line of text to the first level. In Slide view, it works a little differently.

1 Click the New Slide button on the toolbar.

2 Select the Text & Clip Art AutoLayout from the New Slide dialog box.

3 Choose OK to create the new slide.

The new slide is inserted after the slide you have displayed onscreen when you create it. However, you can easily use the Outline view or Slide Sorter view to easily move slides around your presentation.

4 Switch to Slide Sorter view.

5 Select Slide 2.

6 Click the New Slide button.

7 Select the Bulleted List AutoLayout in the New Slide dialog box and choose OK.

The new slide appears after the second slide. Notice that new slides automatically take on the formatting of the template the presentation is based on. You can also use the Slide Sorter view and Outline view to delete slides from a presentation.

8 With the third slide selected (the new, blank one) press the Delete key.

9 Switch to Outline view.

10 Select Slide 4 (the other blank slide).

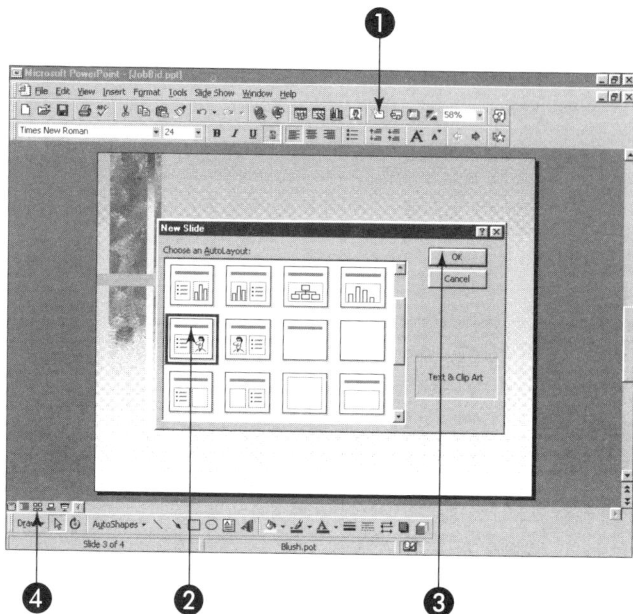

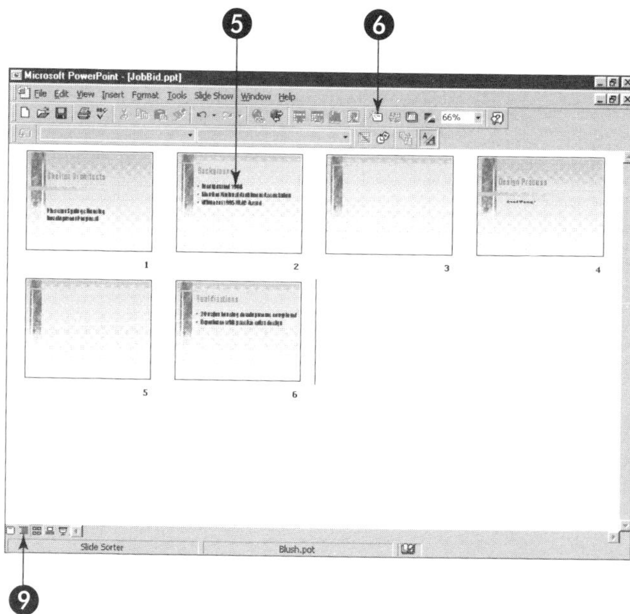

⓫ Press Backspace.

Backspace, Delete, and Cut all work to get rid of a selected slide in Outline view or Slide Sorter view.

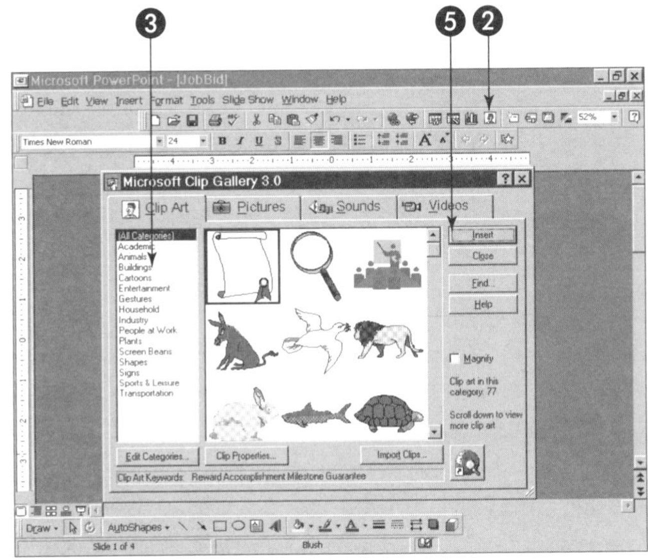

WORKING WITH OBJECTS

Although text-only presentations can be perfectly acceptable, sometimes you want to add objects such as pictures, charts, or drawings to help you make a point or add visual interest. In this section, you add a simple clip art object and learn some simple ways you can manipulate it. Later in this lesson, you work with drawings, charts, and tables.

Adding a clip art object

Clip art is a ready-made line drawing, sometimes with color added, that you can place on your slides. A collection of clip art comes with PowerPoint, and is contained in an area called the Clip Gallery. This gallery also contains multimedia clips, such as sound and animation clips. Placing clip art in your presentation is simple. You simply select the picture you want from the Clip Gallery and insert it on your slide.

1. Display Slide 1 in Slide view.
2. Click the Insert Clip Art button on the toolbar. The Clip Gallery appears.
3. Select the Buildings category in the list on the left side of the Gallery. If you don't know which category to search, choose All Categories in this list to display all clip art.
4. Click the picture of a door.
5. Choose Insert to place the picture in your presentation.

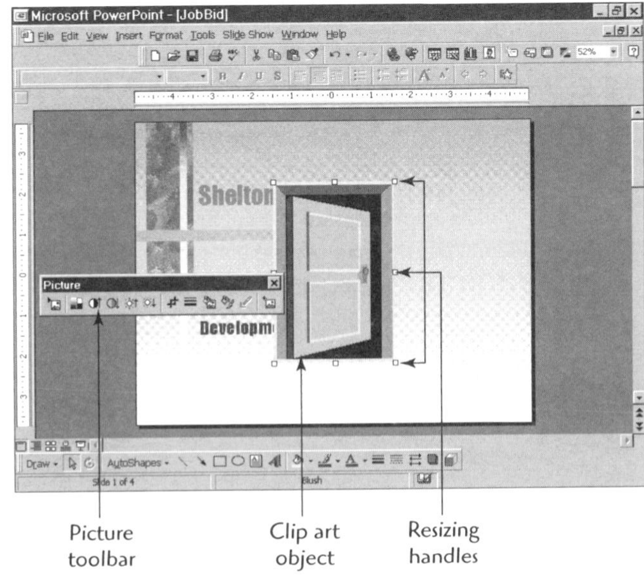

There are many collections of clip art available, and you can use the Clip Gallery to insert a clip from a disk or CD-ROM, giving you much more variety of the visuals you can add to your slides.

Manipulating objects

Typically, clip art objects don't insert where you want them on your slide, or are even the size you'd like them to be. As with the picture of the door in the previous illustration, placed smack in the middle of the slide, inserted objects sometimes overlap text or are out of proportion with the rest of the elements on the slide. Luckily, it's easy to move and resize these objects.

The eight squares around the outside of the object are called resizing handles. You've seen these on objects in Word and Excel. Practice using them again here.

1. Place your mouse pointer on the bottom right corner handle of the clip art object until it turns into a two-way pointing arrow.
2. Click and drag the arrow; as you do a dotted, white outline appears (shown in the illustration), showing you the new size of the object should you release the mouse button.
3. Drag until the outline appears to be about half the size of the original object and release your mouse button.

   Dragging on the corner resizing handles changes the size of an object while keeping its original proportions. If you drag on any of the side, top, or bottom handles, the picture will resize, but lose its original proportions and become narrower, wider, squat, or elongated, depending on the handle you drag.
4. Move your pointer over the picture until it becomes a four-way pointing arrow.
5. Click and drag the object to the middle of the right side of the slide.
6. Release your mouse button. The object has been moved, as shown in the illustration to the right.

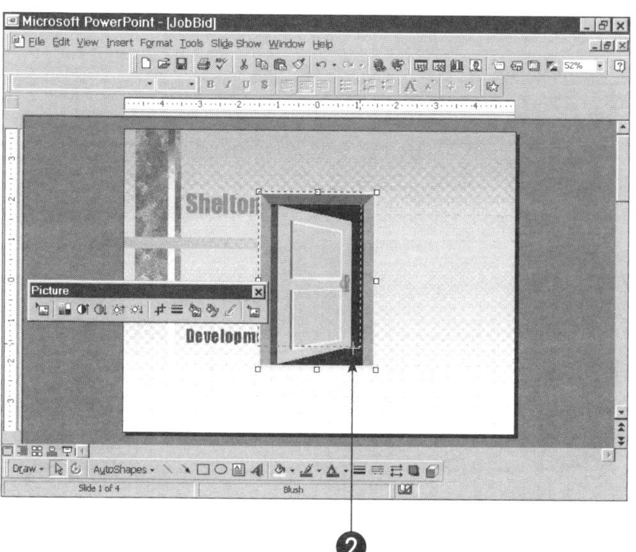

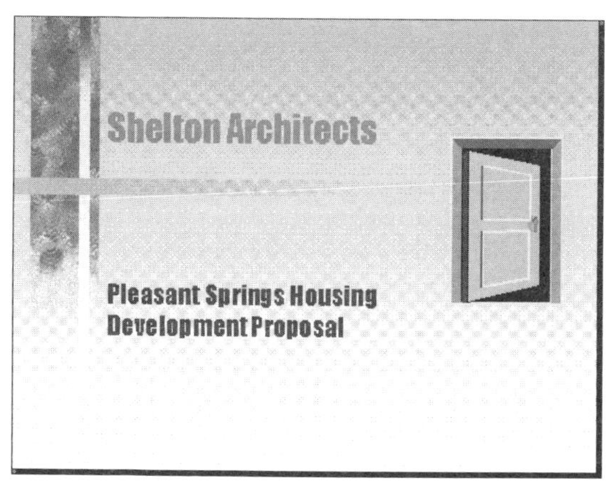

USING POWERPOINT MASTERS

It takes time to add text or objects slide by slide, no matter which view you use to do so, especially with a longer presentation.

Adding a logo

However, PowerPoint offers a handy shortcut that can save you time with elements you want to have appear on every slide. Called a *master,* this feature enables you to enter text or an object, such as a company name, presentation date, or logo, only once. Anything you enter on a master appears on every slide. There are four masters: Slide Master, Title Master, Handout Master, and Notes Master.

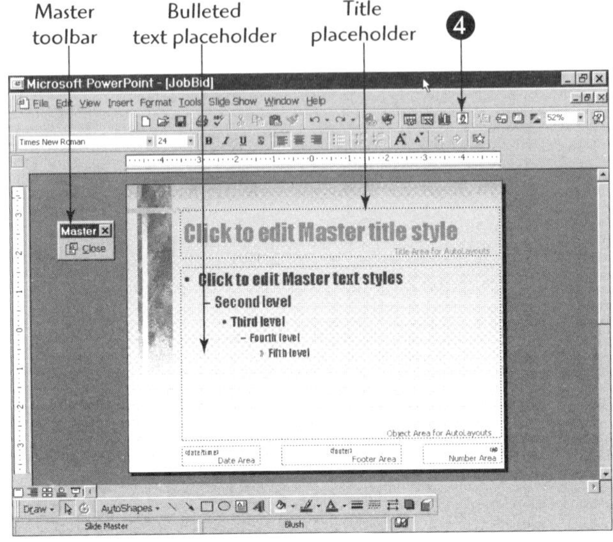

Adding a logo

A master is commonly used to add a company name or logo to every slide. Here's how it's done.

1. Select View.
2. Choose Master.
3. Choose Slide Master. The Master view appears.
4. Click the Insert Clip Art button on the toolbar.
5. Select the Skyscraper clip and choose Insert.
6. Click a corner resizing handle of the clip art object and resize it to be about half of its original size.
7. Move the clip art object to the lower-right side of the Master slide.
8. On the Master floating toolbar, click the Slide Miniature button. A small black-and-white slide appears, showing you the placement of the new object.
9. Click Close on the Master toolbar to close the Master view.

The Slide Sorter view now shows the new clip art object appearing on every slide except the title slide (title slides have their own master). You cannot move, delete, or format this object in any view but Slide Master. However, you can choose not to display any background elements from the master on an individual slide or all slides; this will remove all design elements from the template as well as items you've placed in the Master view. You do this by selecting Format ➢ Background, and clicking in the *Omit background graphics from master* check box, and then choosing to Apply this to the selected slide or Apply To All.

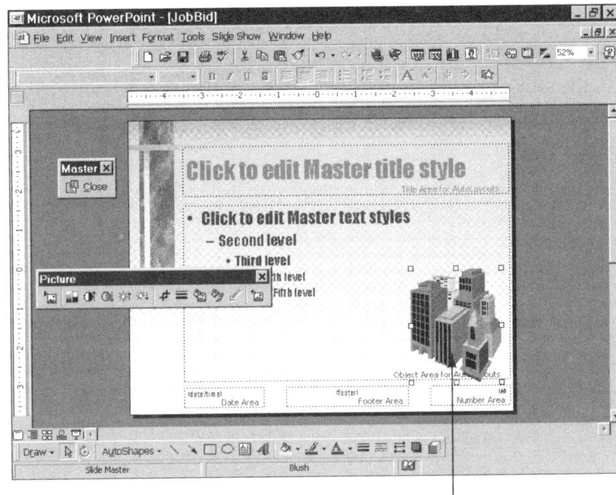

Creating handouts

Slides aren't the only products of PowerPoint for which you can use master views. You can also add elements to audience handouts and speaker's notes using their own master views.

1. Select View ➢ Master ➢ Handout Master.
2. On the Handout Master toolbar, click the Show Positioning of 3-per-Page Handouts button. The illustration to the right shows the resulting Handout Master view.
3. Click the Text Box button on the Drawing toolbar.
4. Click next to the middle slide on the Handout Master. A small text block opens up, ready for editing.
5. Type **Shelton Architects**.
6. Select File ➢ Print.
7. In the lower portion of the Print dialog box, click the arrow for the *Print what* drop-down list and select *Handouts (3 slides per page)*.
8. Click OK to print. Your presentation handouts will print with the master text on each page.
9. Close the file, saving any changes that you've made. The final saved version of this file is on the accompanying CD-ROM with the name Ex16-1F.
10. Close PowerPoint.

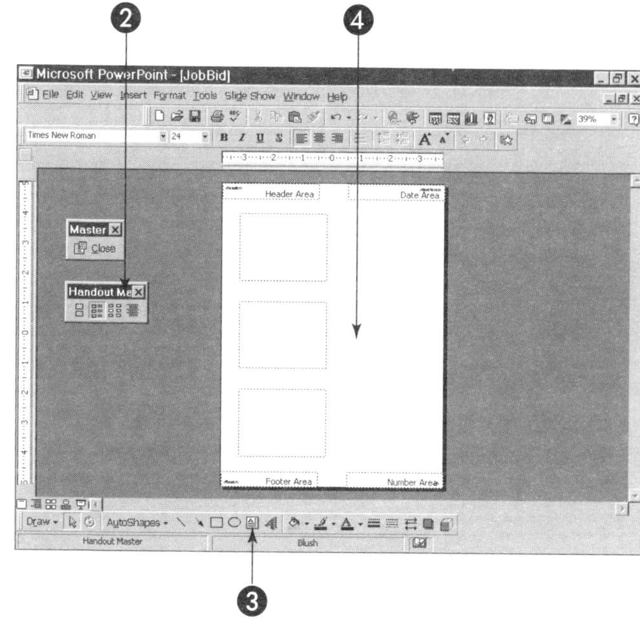

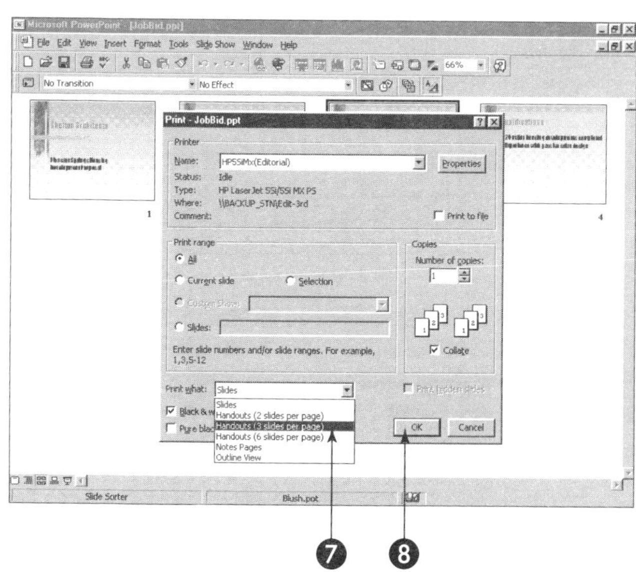

EXPLORING PRESENTATION DESIGNS

In the preceding exercises, you used a template to build a presentation. That template, selected from the Presentation Design templates, included graphic elements as well as color and font formatting. Using the template, you were able to quickly provide an attractive and professional look for your slides.

PowerPoint also has Presentation templates, which provide more than color and design elements. Presentation templates actually offer content and structure for typical business presentations.

Using a design template

When you base a presentation on one of these templates, several slides are created with suggested text already in place.

Some templates even help you become a better presenter. Microsoft has added Dale Carnegie methodology to some templates, such as the Facilitating a Meeting template. These templates offer tips and suggestions for effective presenting.

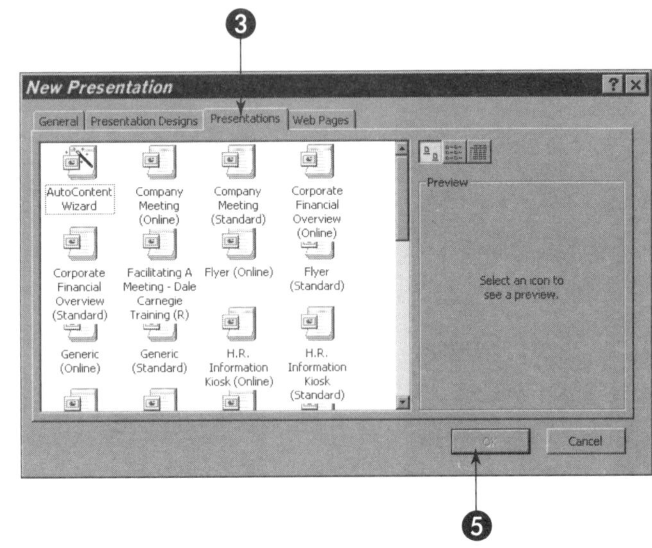

Using a design template

In this exercise, you begin to build a presentation based on a template.

1. Open PowerPoint.
2. From the opening dialog box, select Template, and then choose OK.
3. In the New Presentation dialog box, select the Presentations tab.
4. Select the Marketing Plan (Standard) template.
5. Choose OK to apply it.
6. Switch to the Slide Sorter view.

   Notice a few things about this presentation. First, it has 17 slides with sample content entered on them. Some headings are simply placeholders for your actual text entry, such as [Product Name] in the title of the first slide. Other headings, such as Product Packaging, you may want to keep as you fill in your own marketing strategy. Bullet points have suggested text and, in many cases, subheadings that make suggestions as to what might be discussed at a particular point in the presentation.

   Presentation templates are suggested structures that can be modified in any way you like. For example, you can delete whole slides, add slides, replace text, or add to it. However, if you select a presentation template that relates to your topic area, it can be a great head start in building a well organized presentation.

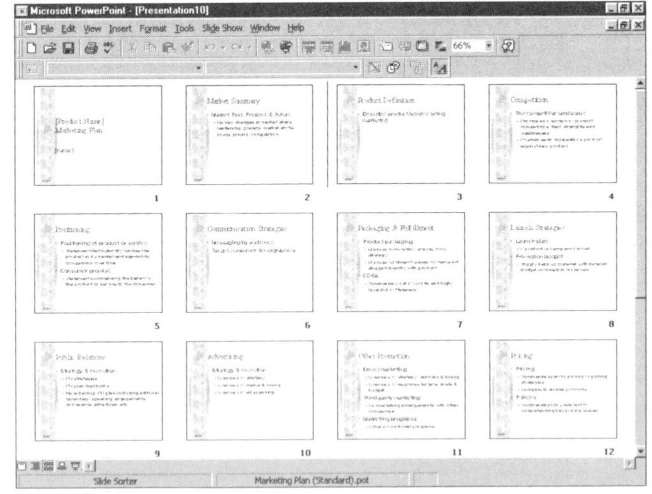

7. Select Slide 1.
8. Switch to Slide view.
9. Click the title placeholder.
10. Select the text *[Product Name]*.
11. Type **PlanAhead Calendars** and press Enter.
12. Select the subtitle placeholder.
13. Select the text *[name]* and replace it with your own name.
14. Move to Slide 2.
15. Select the text in the bulleted list placeholder.
16. Type **Where we've been** [Enter] **Where we're going**.

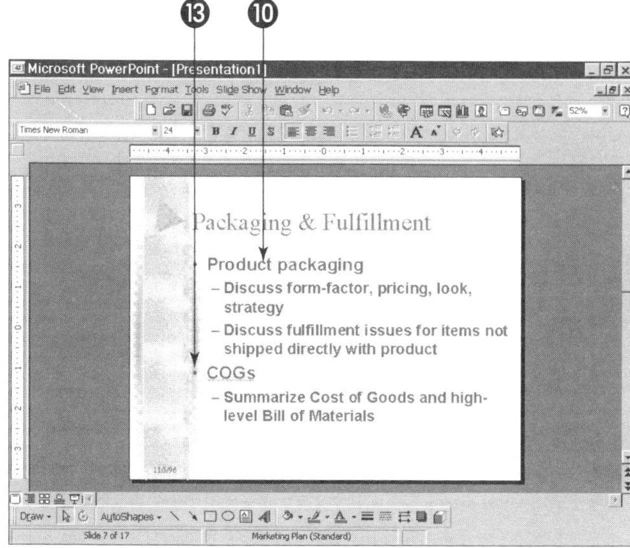

Applying a different design

Whichever template you choose for your presentation, you can always change to a different one. When you change the template, the contents don't change; only the background graphics and color scheme, as well as any text formatting.

1. Click the Apply Design button on the toolbar. The Apply Design dialog box opens.
2. Click the Up One Level button.
3. Double-click the Presentation Designs folder. The presentation design templates are now listed.
4. Select Meadow.
5. Choose Apply.

   The same 17 slides are there, but a new background, color scheme, and text treatment are applied.

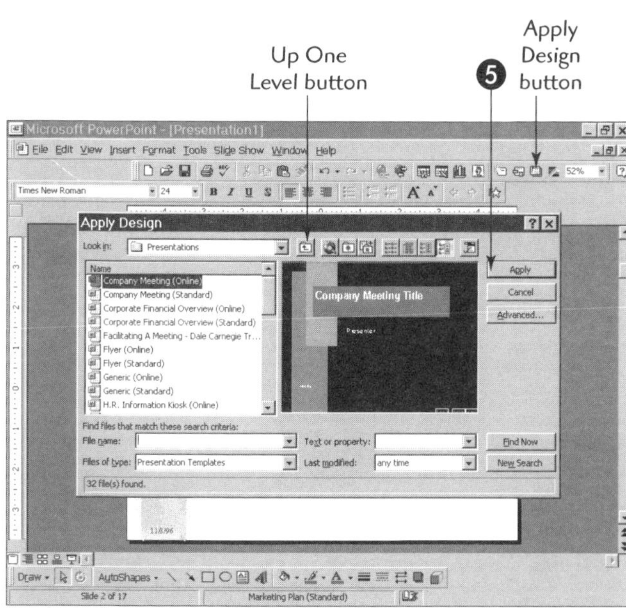

USING DRAWING TOOLS

Earlier in this lesson, you added clip art objects to a presentation. Often, such ready-made drawings are a quick, easy way to add visual interest to a presentation. However, there are times when you want to create your own drawings, and this is easy with the tools PowerPoint provides.

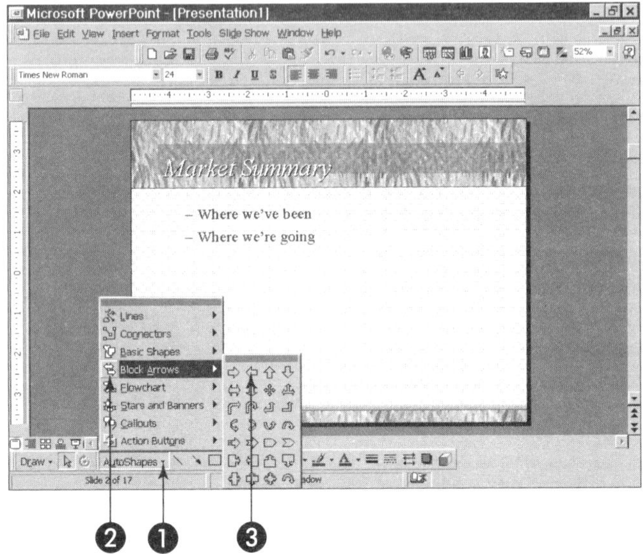

Using AutoShapes

AutoShapes is a set of drawing tools that enables you to create predefined shapes by simply clicking your slide. This tool includes shapes such as stars, smiley faces, arrows, and triangles. Display the second slide (titled "Market Summary") on your screen for this exercise.

1. Click the AutoShapes menu on the Drawing toolbar to open it.
2. Move your pointer to the Block Arrows selection; the submenu appears.
3. Click the left-pointing arrow in the top row of choices.
4. On the slide, click below the bulleted list, flush left.
5. Select AutoShapes ➢ Block Arrows, and then the right-pointing arrow (the first choice in the top row).
6. Click to the right of the first arrow on your screen. Your slide now looks like the on in the illustration to the right.
7. Move to Slide 3.

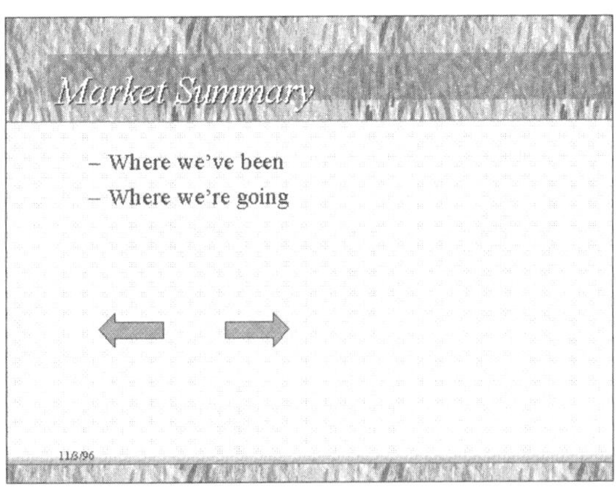

TIP

If your arrows are not positioned in the same place as the arrows in the preceding illustration, you can easily move them around your slide. Place your mouse pointer over an arrow until it becomes a four-way pointing arrow. Click and drag the arrow to wherever you'd like it on your slide.

8. Select AutoShapes.
9. Select Flowchart.
10. Click the *Flowchart: Multidocument* shape (the fourth from the left in the second row from the top).
11. Click the slide and drag your cursor about two inches down and to the right.

   You have the choice of clicking the slide to place the default sized AutoShape there, or clicking and dragging to draw a shape in the size you want. You can also resize a drawing object using the eight resizing handles that surround it when it's selected; you see how to do that later in this lesson.

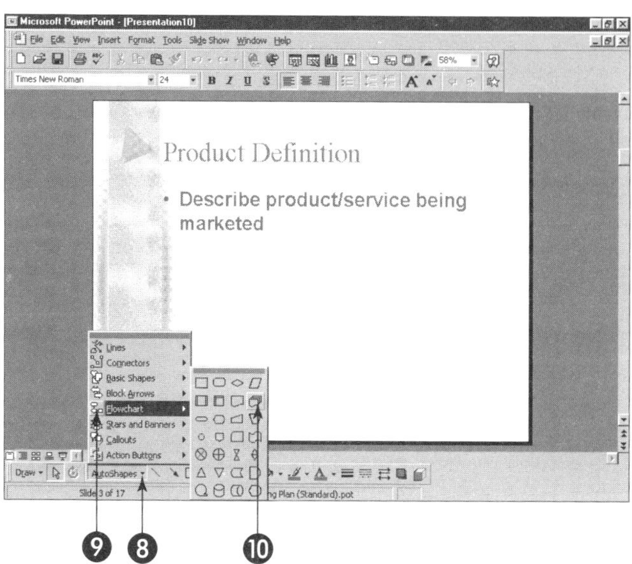

Some common shapes — a line, rectangle, and oval — have their own tools on the Drawing toolbar for quicker access. Each is also available in the appropriate category in the AutoShapes menu.

Drawing freehand

Drawing predefined shapes isn't the only way to draw in PowerPoint. AutoShape also has tools that enable you to draw freehand, just as you would with a pencil or crayon. This kind of drawing is a little trickier, but sometimes it's the best way to make your point.

1. Move to Slide 4.
2. Select AutoShapes ➢ Lines.
3. Click the Freeform tool (in middle of the second row).
4. Draw a landscape. First, draw the top of the mountains across the slide, and then bring your cursor back along the bottom of the slide to meet with your starting point.
5. Double-click when you reach the original start point of the line so your final landscape looks something like the one in the illustration.

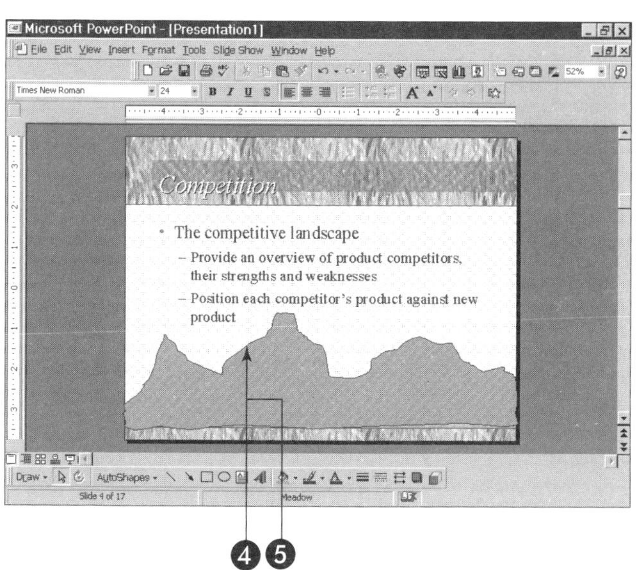

When you draw your freeform line so your end point matches your start point, you create a shape that fills with the default color associated with this template. If you don't connect the start and end points, you end up with just a freeform line. Freeform drawing is difficult to master, and you may need to practice it several times to get the hang of it. If you need to, select what you've drawn by clicking it, press Delete, and draw it again until you're happy with it.

Grouping drawings

It is sometimes practical to treat several drawing objects as a single object. This enables you to move, resize, and format all the objects at once, rather than separately. In PowerPoint, this is called grouping.

1. Switch to Slide 2.
2. Select the first arrow.
3. Hold down the Shift key and select the second arrow.
4. Select Draw ➢ Group.

   The two arrows now have one set of handles. You can see the difference in the illustration, which shows two sets of arrows, one grouped and the others separate objects.
5. Select the arrows object.
6. Select Drawing ➢ Align or Distribute. If no commands are available, click Relative to Slide, and then reopen the Align and Distribute menu.
7. Select Align Center from the submenu.

   The two grouped objects can be treated as one so that you can, for example, move it with your mouse cursor or align it relative to the edges of your slide. To ungroup a grouped object, select it, and then select Drawing ➢ Ungroup.

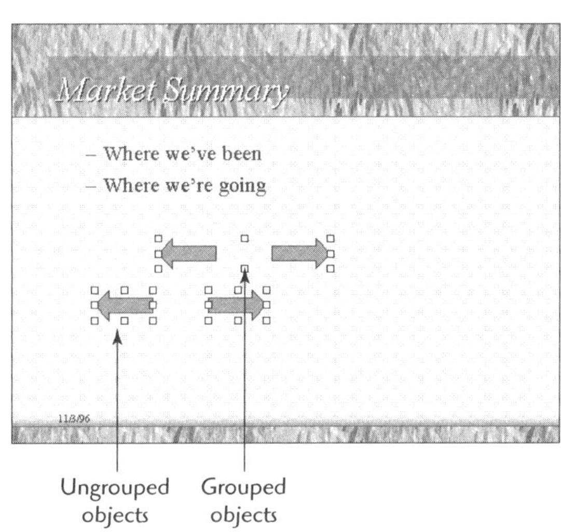

Rotating drawings

Grouped or not, all objects can be moved to different angles on your slides.

1. Move to Slide 3.
2. Select the drawing object.
3. Click the Free Rotate button on the Drawing toolbar. The object's handles become four round handles.
4. Move your pointer to the top left handle. Your pointer is now shaped like a little circle with an arrow.
5. Click the handle and pull the object around about 30 degrees to the right.

   The pointer becomes a circle with four arrows, and a dotted-line image of the object appears, as in the illustration. This line indicates the object's new position should you release the mouse button.
6. Release the mouse button and click anywhere outside the slide area.

   To help you align and rotate objects more precisely, you can display guides. Guides consist of two intersecting lines; that point of intersection can be moved anywhere on your slide by moving each of the lines separately. You can then use either the intersection, or the relationship of those lines to a point on either ruler, to position objects.
7. Select View ➢ Guides.

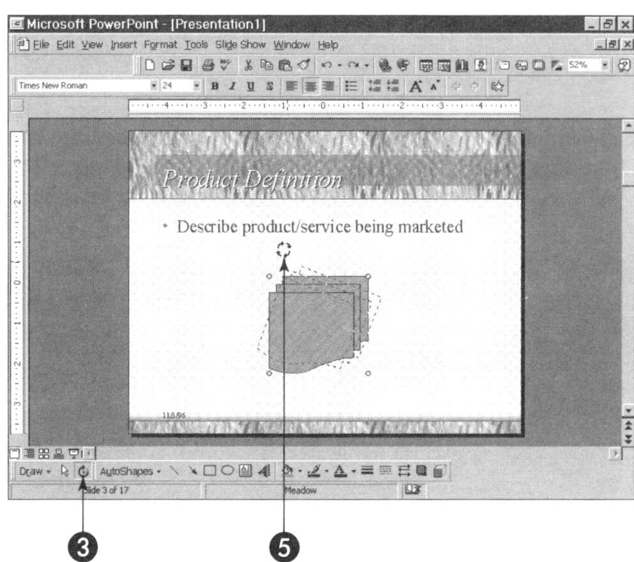

FORMATTING DRAWINGS

When you complete your drawing, you can use a variety of formatting tools to add color and depth to it. You can also modify its size and shape once it's been drawn.

Adding color and patterns

Drawing objects appear filled in with a color that is determined by the template. You can change that color, and even use fill effects such as patterns and gradients to customize each object.

Adding color and patterns

1. Select the drawing object on Slide 3.
2. Click the arrow on the side of the Fill Color tool. The illustration to the right shows the pop-up palette that appears.
3. Select the pink block. The object is now filled with pink.
4. Select the drawing object again.
5. Click the arrow on the side of the Fill Color tool.
6. Select Fill Effects. The Fill Effects dialog box in the bottom illustration appears.
7. With the Gradient tab selected, click the top left block in the Variants section of the dialog box. A sample of this effect appears in the lower right-hand corner.
8. Choose OK. The object now has a gradient effect that makes light seem to shine on it from above.
9. Click the arrow on the right of the Fill Color tool and select Fill Effects.
10. Select the Pattern tab.
11. From the *Background* drop-down list, select the pink block.
12. From the *Foreground* drop-down list select the black block.
13. Click the Light Horizontal pattern (fourth block from the left, second row down).
14. Choose OK.

The drawing of pieces of paper now has a pattern reminiscent of the lines on a pad of paper. You can use any number of gradients and fill patterns. If you want a wider choice of colors, you can also select More Colors from the Fill Colors pop-up palette. This offers you an expanded palette of colors, and a tab for creating your own custom colors.

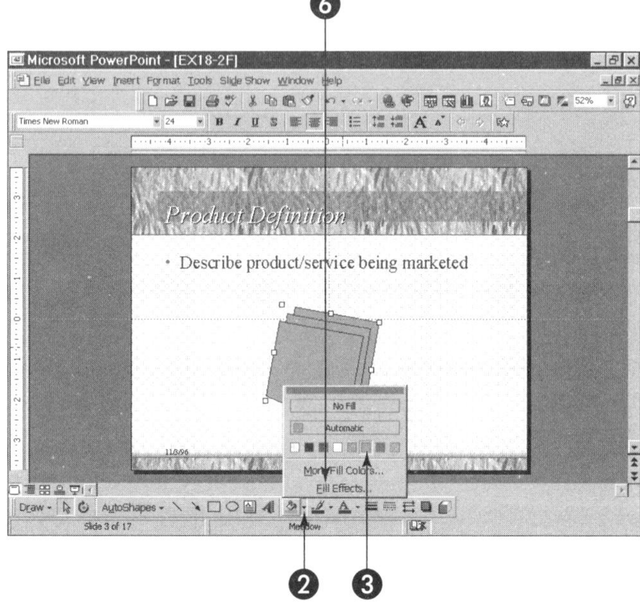

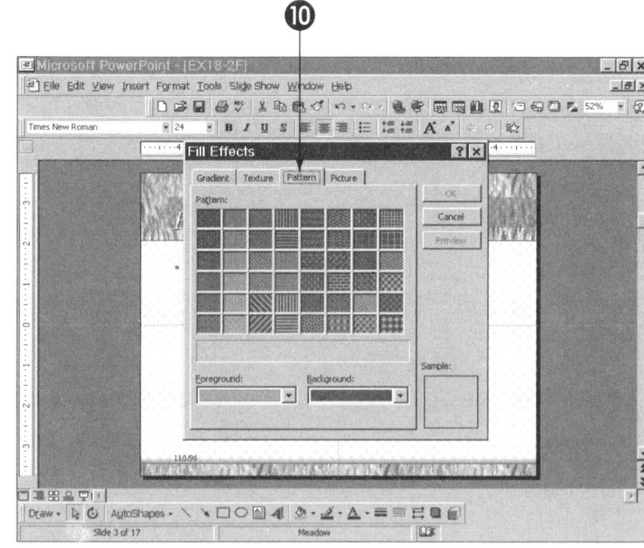

Formatting drawing objects

The width of lines that define the outer edges of a drawing object and the shadow effects you can apply to a drawing help you add depth and perspective to objects.

1. Move to Slide 2.
2. Select the grouped arrow object.
3. Click the Line Style button on the Drawing toolbar.
4. From the pop-up palette of line styles that appears, select $2\,^1/_4$ pt.
5. Click the Shadow button on the Drawing toolbar.
6. Select Shadow Style No. 9 (the first choice in the third row down). Your arrows are now defined by a bolder, outside line and have added depth from the shadow effect, as in the illustration to the right.
7. Move to Slide 4.
8. Select the freeform drawing object.
9. Click the 3-D button on the Drawing toolbar.
10. Click the 3-D Style 11 from the pop-up 3-D palette (the third from the left, third row down from the top).

    Your landscape drawing now has some perspective to it. You can use any combination of line style, shadow, and 3-D effect to give simple line drawings more impact.

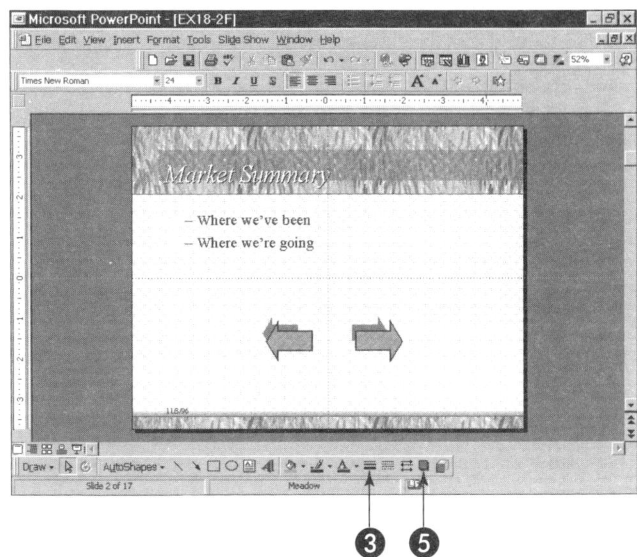

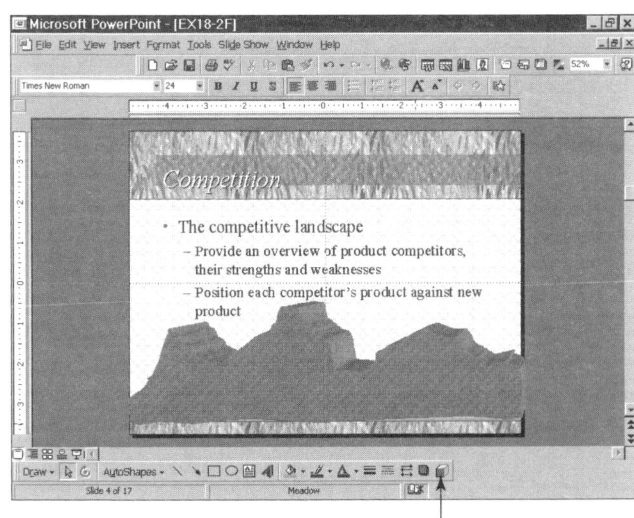

Resizing drawings

Drawings don't always appear exactly the size you want when you place them on a slide. For that reason, easy-to-use resizing features are available in PowerPoint.

1. Move to Slide 2.
2. Select the drawing object. Eight resizing handles appear.

Resizing drawings

3. Place your mouse pointer over the right top corner handle until your pointer turns into a line with an arrow at either end.
4. Click and drag up about a half an inch.
5. Release your mouse. The arrows have been resized, but kept their original proportions.
6. Move your pointer to the top middle handle until it becomes a two-way pointing arrow.
7. Click and drag upward about a half an inch. When you use the top, bottom, or side handles to resize, the object doesn't retain its original proportions.
8. Select Format ➢ Object. The Format Object dialog box appears.
9. Select the Size tab.
10. Highlight the measurement in the *Height* box and type **3**.
11. Highlight the measurement in the *Width* box and type **5**.
12. Choose OK. The arrows appear with their new measurement, as in the bottom illustration.

   To change the size of an object, you can either use the resizing handles or the exact settings in the Format Object dialog box. You can also use settings on the Position tab of the Format Object dialog box to place objects at precise locations on a slide.

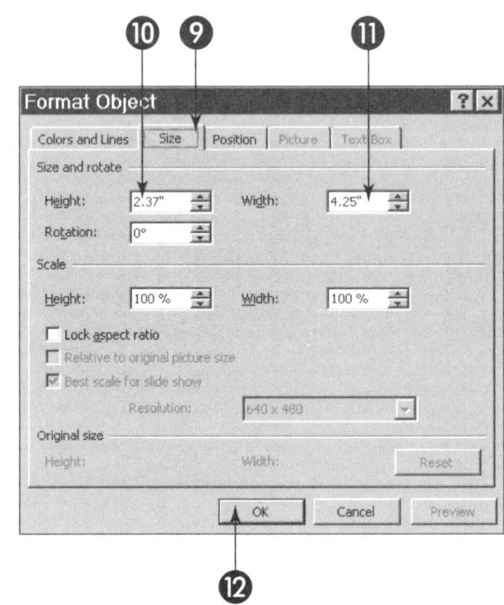

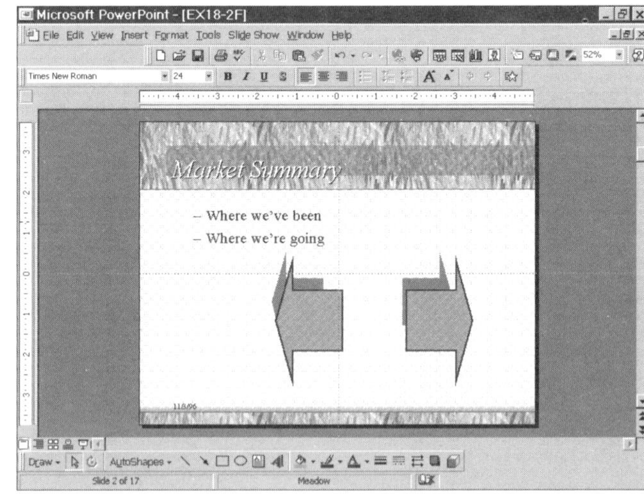

SKILLS CHALLENGE: ADDING VISUAL EXCITEMENT TO A PRESENTATION

Features such as drawing can be the most creative and fun part of building a PowerPoint presentation. First, you'll practice moving around the various views of a presentation, then flex those creative muscles a little more by working through the second part of this exercise.

1. Open a new PowerPoint file and use the Professional template.
2. Apply the Title Slide AutoLayout to Slide 1.

3. Enter the following text, with the indentation for different levels as indicated, in the Outline view:

Bosworth Auto Sales
    Fleet Sales Program
Bosworth Experience
- **26 years in business**
- **Second generation management**

Fleet Sales Savings
- **Discounts for 5 or more vehicles**
- **Free logo and company name detailed on all vehicles**

4. Move the Slide 3 to become the Slide 2.

What are the different ways you can change the order of slides in a presentation?

5. Collapse all the detail in the Outline view.
6. Expand the detail for Slide 3 only.
7. From Slide view, add a new slide using the Title Only layout.

If you use a layout with two placeholders but you only enter text in one, what appears in the empty placeholder when you print the slide?

8. Type this title: **Guaranteed Satisfaction**.
9. Format the new title as Arial typeface, 48 point, bold.
10. Insert the clip art image of a sports car on the slide.

How do you control where on your slide a clip art image appears?

11. Resize the image, keeping it in proportion, to be half its original size.
12. Move the clip art image to the bottom of the slide, beneath the title.
13. Add the text **Bosworth Auto Sales** in the lower left-hand corner of the Slide Master.

TRY OUT THE
INTERACTIVE TUTORIALS
ON YOUR CD!

Skills challenge

14. Change the background of Slide 3 so the master elements don't appear on it.
15. Close the file and save the changes with the file name **Bosworth**.
16. Open the file named EX16-1 in the Exercise folder on your hard drive. This is a file you began to build earlier in this lesson.
17. Move to the second slide.
18. Draw a simple house using a combination of AutoShapes and the Freeform tool. Include the frame, a window, a door, a chimney, and a squiggle of smoke coming out of the chimney.
19. Group all the objects you created to make the house.

How do you ungroup grouped objects?

20. Use the Fill Effects to add a brick pattern to the house frame.
21. Use the Gradient effect to make light seem to shine from the top of the roof of the house.
22. On Slide 3, draw an AutoShape banner and with that object selected, type the text **1st Place**.
23. Change the fill color of the banner object to dark pink.

What two PowerPoint features can you choose to display to help you position objects on screen?

24. Close the file without saving it. The saved version of the file, which you copied from the accompanying CD-ROM, is named Ex16-2.

TROUBLESHOOTING

This lesson hopefully brought out the artist in you, but you may still have an occasional creative difference with PowerPoint. Table 16-1 offers some troubleshooting tips to help you out of those tight spots.

Problem	Solution
I want to put our company logo at the top of every slide, but the title for each slide is in the way.	You can move placeholders in Master view, too. Select View ➢ Master ➢ Slide Master, and drag the title placeholder to a new location. Repeat this with Title Master.
I have a whole outline in Word which would be the perfect basis for my presentation.	Don't retype it all! Select Insert ➢ Slides from Outline. Select your Word file from the Insert Outline dialog box. If it has tabs for indentations or was created using Word's outlining feature, it should come in perfectly.
I want to rotate an object exactly 180 degrees; any shortcuts?	Select the object, and then Draw ➢ Rotate or Flip ➢ Flip Horizontal. You get an exact mirror image of the original.
I drew something freehand and want to move one corner slightly.	Select the object, and then select Draw ➢ Edit Points. Multiple editing handles appear; click and drag on them to reshape the object.
I want to move a whole drawing object, but very slightly.	Select the object and then select Draw ➢ Nudge, and select a direction to nudge it from the submenu that appears.

WRAP UP

In this lesson, you picked up some great skills for adding visual interest to a presentation, including the following:

- Creating a new file based on a PowerPoint template
- Entering and reorganizing text in Outline view
- Entering and formatting text in Slide view

Wrap up

- Inserting clip art objects and moving and resizing them on a slide
- Using PowerPoint's Master views to save time entering text or objects that should appear on every slide
- Using drawing tools to create and format objects
- Adding color, patterns, and line styles to drawings

If you'd like some further practice with these skills, try creating a presentation describing your last vacation. Use drawing tools to draw scenes and objects you mention, and tables and WordArt to help get information across.

In Lesson 17, you take the final step in preparing your slide show for its final presentation.

Going Public with Your Presentation

GOALS

After you create your presentation, you still have several choices to make about how to print or present it. The good news is that all of the options are very easy to use. In this lesson, you learn the following:

- Printing slides
- Printing speaker notes and audience handouts
- Generating slides
- Adding transitions
- Adding animation effects
- Adding narration and sounds
- Running a slide show

Get ready

Get Ready

To complete this lesson, you need the files Ex17-1 and Ex17-2, which you copied to your hard drive from the CD-ROM. You also need a sound card installed and configured properly on your computer to use the PowerPoint features that place sound or music on your slides.

TRY OUT THE INTERACTIVE TUTORIALS ON YOUR CD!

POWERPOINT'S PRESENTATION CHOICES

Once you build the slides in your presentation, you have to decide how you want to make that presentation. You can do any of the following:

- Print paper copies of each slide and copy them onto overhead sheets to generate overhead transparencies
- Print paper copies of speaker's notes or audience handouts
- Save to a file formatted for 35mm slides and send that file to a slide bureau to produce the slides
- Add transitions between slides, set timing, and include animated elements to produce an onscreen slide show
- Print the outline of your presentation

Any one of these output choices is easy to produce once you have created your presentation. The following Visual Bonus gives you an idea of how your presentation corresponds to the different types of output.

CREATING OUTPUT

If you're not showing your PowerPoint presentation onscreen, your choices are determined by the settings you make in the Print dialog box. You saw this dialog box in other Office products. However, PowerPoint offers many more options for creating output for a presentation. You can save to a 35mm slide file format, or you can print individual slides, speaker notes, audience handouts, and an outline of your presentation.

■ Printing slides

Most people don't create their own slides; they create a PowerPoint file and send it to a slide bureau. In general, any slide bureau can create slides from PowerPoint presentations without you converting anything or saving the file in any special format. You can either send a disk with your presentation on it to the bureau, or send it online. Many slide bureaus can turn around 35mm slides in a couple of days, or even overnight (with accompanying rush charges).

PowerPoint has built in a wizard to prepare your file for a slide bureau called Genigraphics. The installation of this wizard isn't typical. To install it, you need to run Office setup again. Once installed, select File ➢ Send to, and then select Genigraphics from the side menu that appears.

If you are intending to generate your final presentation to slides, keep in mind the following:

- Printing slides can be expensive; double-check spelling and grammar, and check to make sure nothing is falling outside the printable area of your slide before sending your file to a bureau.
- Slides work well with darker background designs, because the light that shines through them makes the designs crisper, while paler designs can appear washed-out.
- It's a good idea to get two sets of slides for a presentation, especially if you're going to use them several times or take them on the road. If you lose one slide or want to create a second version of the presentation, you'll already have your backup set available.
- When presenting a slide show, always check the equipment you'll be using and make sure it's working properly. There's nothing more embarrassing than a presentation halted because of a snagged slide.

Creating output

VISUAL BONUS: HOW POWERPOINT GENERATES OUTPUT

PowerPoint is able to generate several different types of output: print, slides, overhead transparencies, and even support materials, such as audience handouts. This Visual Bonus shows you how each of these relates to the file you created.

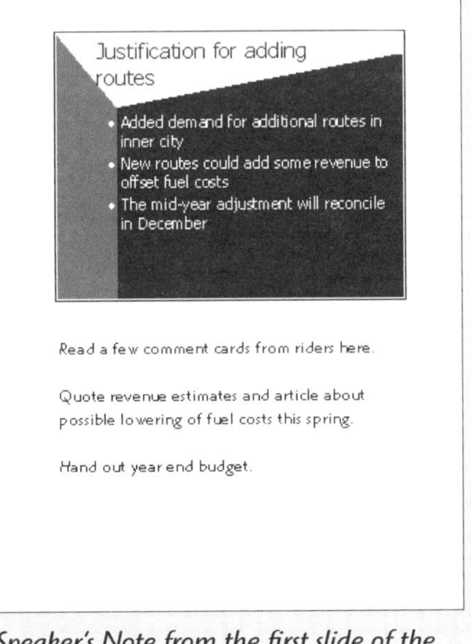

Speaker's Note from the first slide of the presentation.

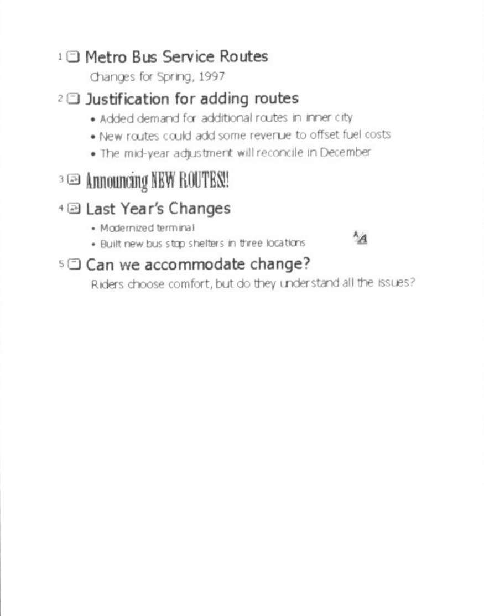

An outline of the entire presentation can easily be printed.

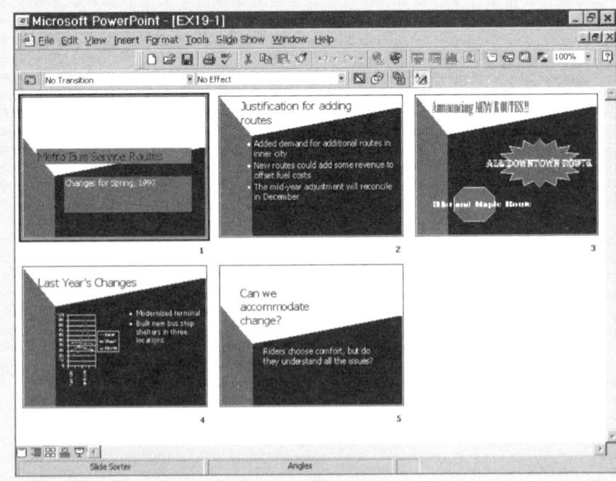

Slide Sorter view of a presentation.

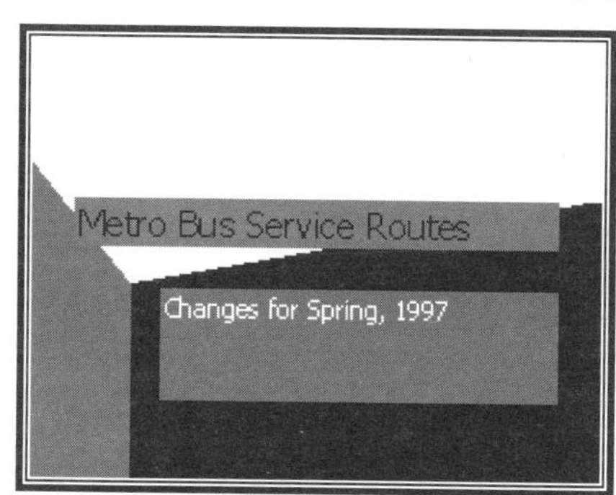

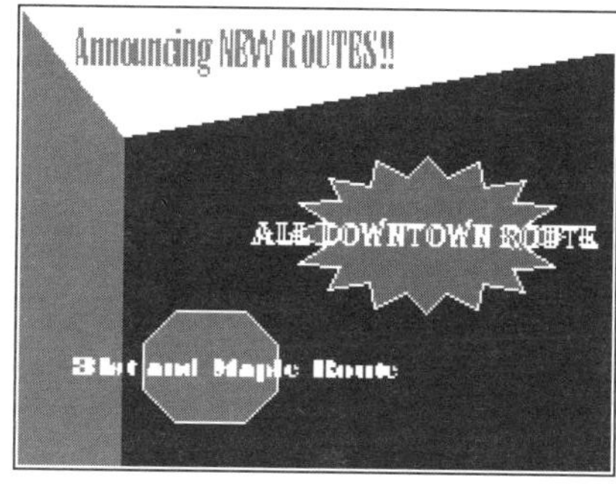

Audience handout from the first two slides of the presentation.

35mm slides are generated from a file saved in the proper format.

Printing to paper or transparencies

Printing to paper or transparencies

You may want to print a paper copy of your presentation or create overhead transparencies. Both are simple to do.

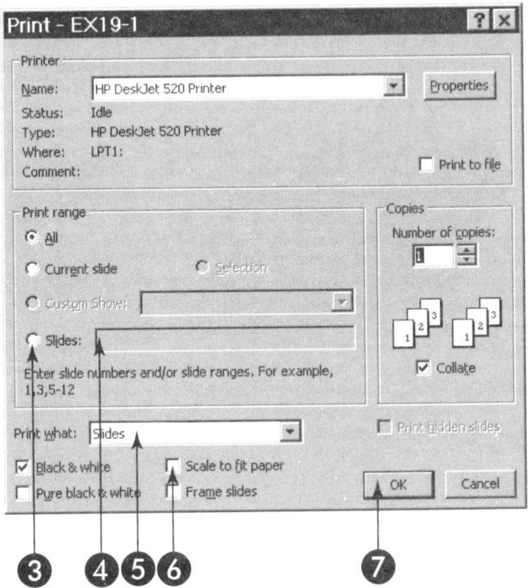

1. Open the file Ex17-1 from the accompanying CD-ROM.
2. Select File ➢ Print. The Print dialog box, shown in the illustration to the right, appears.
3. In the Print range, click in the Slides radio button.
4. Type **2-4** to print only slides 2, 3, and 4.
5. In the bottom of this dialog box, check the Print what box to make sure that Slides is selected.

   You can choose four settings here by clicking any of the check boxes at the bottom of the dialog box.

   - *Black & white* enhances the appearance of color slides when printed in black-and-white.
   - *Pure black & white* uses only black to print; shadings and colors are treated as either black or white, with no gray.
   - *Scale to fit paper* adjusts the size of your slide to fill the paper when you print.
   - *Frame slides* places a border around the edge of all the slides.
6. Select *Scale to fit paper* and *Frame slides*.
7. Choose OK to print.

   The three slides should print to your designated printer.

If you want to print out hidden slides in your presentation, click the Print hidden slides *check box in the lower right-hand corner of the Print dialog box before printing.*

To print overhead transparencies from your slides, you follow the same basic procedure outlined above, with one additional step.

Printing to paper or transparencies

8. From the Print dialog box, choose Properties. The printer's Properties dialog box appears, as in the illustration to the right.
9. In the *Media* drop-down list, select Transparency.
10. Choose OK, proceed with any other print settings, and choose OK again to print.

    Selecting Transparency instructs your printer to wait a few minutes after printing each page on a transparency film sheet, so each sheet can dry properly. However, if you have a laser printer, this option is not necessary.

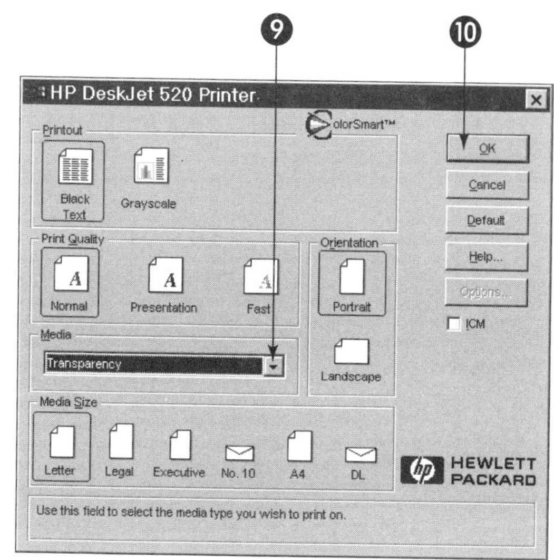

■ Printing speaker notes, audience handouts, or an outline

Whether you print speaker notes, audience handouts, or an outline, your presentation is determined by a single setting in the Print dialog box. In the Print What drop-down list, you have a choice of three kinds of Handouts, Notes Pages, or Outline View. Choose your preference and print.

Here's what you'll get:

- *Handouts* are miniature images of your slides, and can be printed two, three, or six to a page. With a shorter presentation, two or three slides per page is a nice choice because it leaves space on the page for your audience members to take notes. However, with a long presentation, having six slides to a page saves your audience from carting home a lengthy printout.
- *Notes pages* gives you a single page for each slide, with the slide image on the top of the page and any speaker's notes you add printed beneath.
- *Outline View* gives you a printout of your presentation's text as it appears in the Outline View. You can make changes in your Outline View before printing to affect the appearance of the printout, including collapsing or expanding the details displayed and zooming to decrease the type size and fit more on a page.

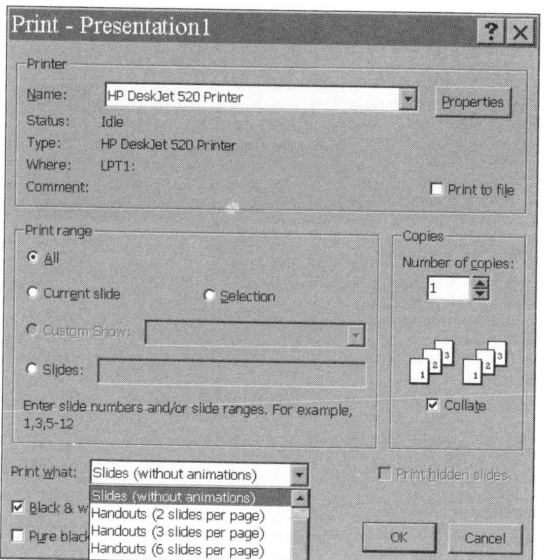

RUNNING A SLIDE SHOW

If you intend to run your presentation onscreen, you can do several exciting things to add punch to your show. PowerPoint has built-in transition effects you can use between slides, easy to use animation for text and objects, and the capability to record narration and add sounds to your presentation. These features become even more important if your presentation has to stand on its own, say at a kiosk or trade show booth, with only the viewer present.

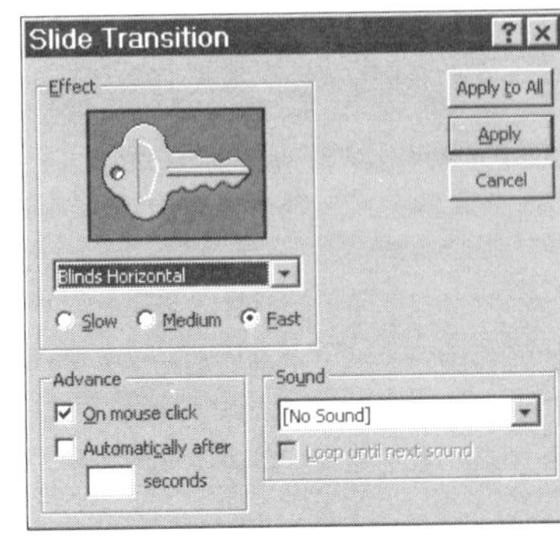

Adding transitions

You can introduce each new slide in several ways. As a new slide appears onscreen, it can replace the previous slide, or appear using a variety of animated transition effects. Your next slide can seem to fly in from the left side of the screen, rain down from the top of the screen, or fade in from a solid black screen.

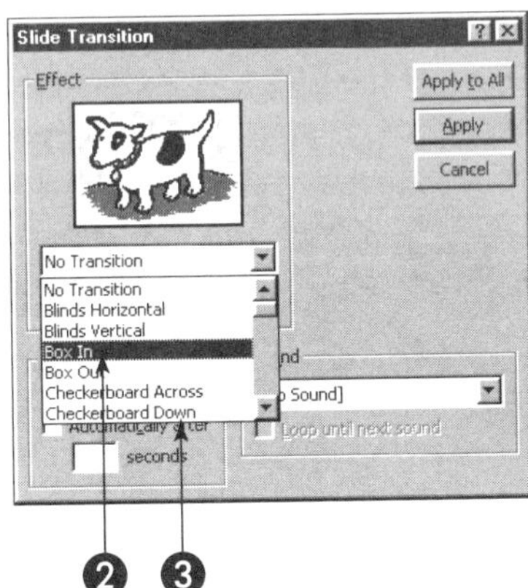

1. Select Slide Show ➢ Slide Transition. The Slide Transition dialog box appears.
2. Select *Box In* from the Effect drop-down list. Notice the preview of how the image will appear in the box above the drop-down list.
3. Select *Checkerboard Down* from the drop-down list. Again, notice the preview of the effect.
4. Click the Medium radio button to adjust the speed of the effect.
5. In the Advance section of the dialog box, select the *Automatically after* check box.
6. Type **5** for the number of seconds to wait before advancing.

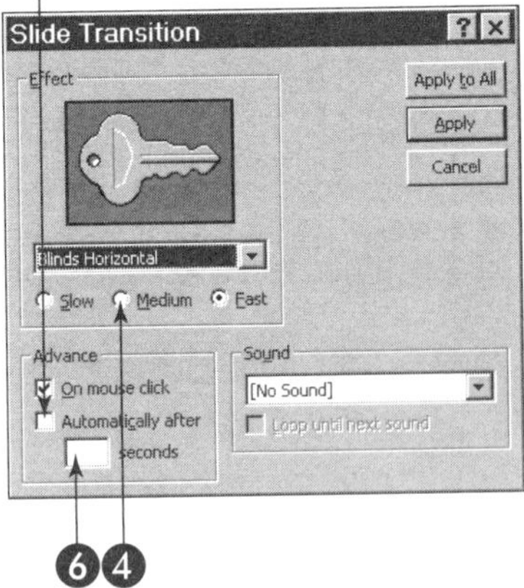

You can also use a mouse click to advance to the next slide, rather than have the presentation timed to move forward automatically. The automatic advance setting is useful for stand-alone presentations.

7. To associate a sound with the transition, select Laser from the *Sound* drop-down list.
8. Choose Apply to All.
9. Select the Slide Show view button in the lower-left corner of your PowerPoint window.

   The slide show plays, using the transition effect and sound you selected. You can use different transitions between each slide by choosing Apply instead of Apply to All in the Slide Transition dialog box. This applies the transition to the current slide only; you have to individually select and apply transition effects to each of the other slides in your presentation.

Adding animation effects

In addition to animated effects between slides, elements on each slide can be made to appear with an associated effect.

1. Display Slide 1 in Slide View.
2. Select the title text object.
3. Click the Animation Effects button on the toolbar (it looks like a star in a hurry). The Animation Effects floating toolbar appears.

You can also select Slide Show ➢ Preset Animation to apply these effects.

4. Click the Camera Effect button (third from the left in the second row down).
5. Select the Slide Show view button to begin running the show from the current slide.

   First, the slide checkerboard transition effect displays the slide, minus the title. The title then appears, as if with a camera click. You can sequentially cause text to appear onscreen by applying an effect first to the title, and then the text.

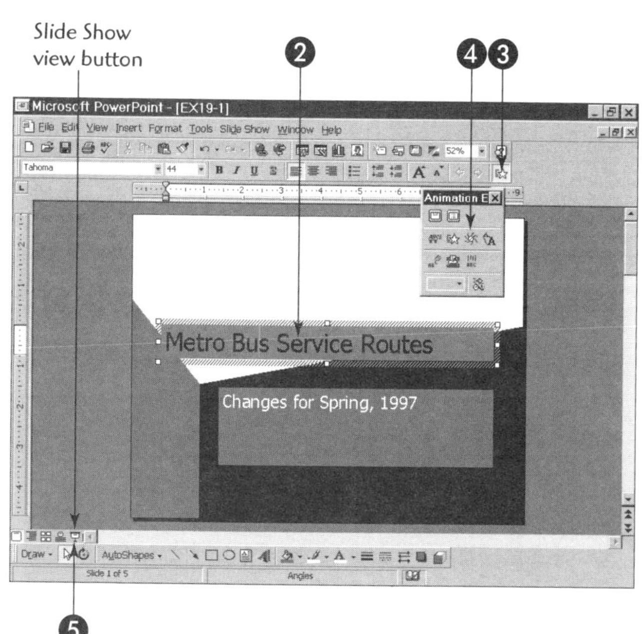

6. Press Esc to stop running the slide show.
7. Move to Slide 2.
8. Select the bulleted list of text. The choices in the Animation Effects floating toolbar change slightly.
9. Select the Typewriter animation effect (second from the left, third row down).
10. Select the Slide Show button to run the show.

   Each letter of the bulleted list appears as if being typed on your screen. You can also apply any of these animation effects to objects, such as clip art, charts, or drawings. Be careful how you use these effects; too many sounds and animations can be distracting to your viewers. Consistency is also helpful to your viewers: They begin to anticipate that a certain effect signals the introduction of a new topic, while another occurs when you pause for audience questions.

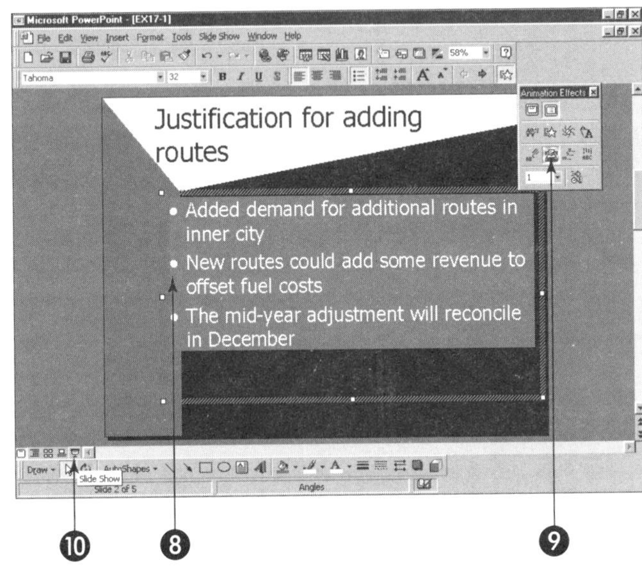

Adding narration

To add narration to your slide show, you need a sound card and microphone attached to your computer.

1. Click the Slide Show menu.
2. Select Record Narration. The Record Narration dialog appears.

   To save the narration in a separate but associated file, click the *Link narrations in* check box. This saves space in your presentation file. The Settings button takes you to another dialog box where you can set the quality of the recording. The lower the quality — for example, telephone quality versus radio quality — the less memory you use. The Current recording quality settings are listed at the top of the Record Narration dialog box. This tells you how much time you can record before you run out of space on your hard drive.

3. Choose OK to proceed. Your slide show plays.

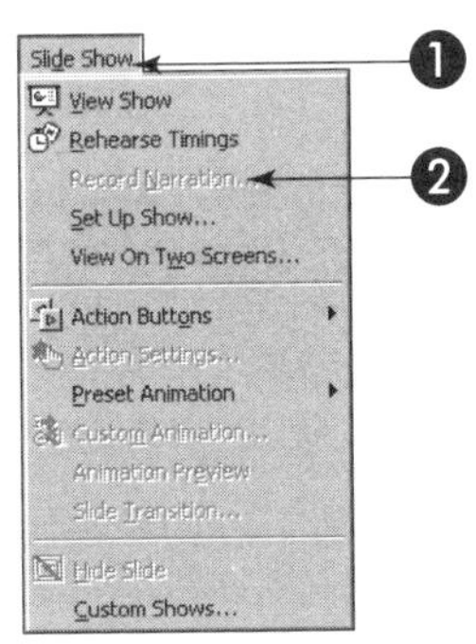

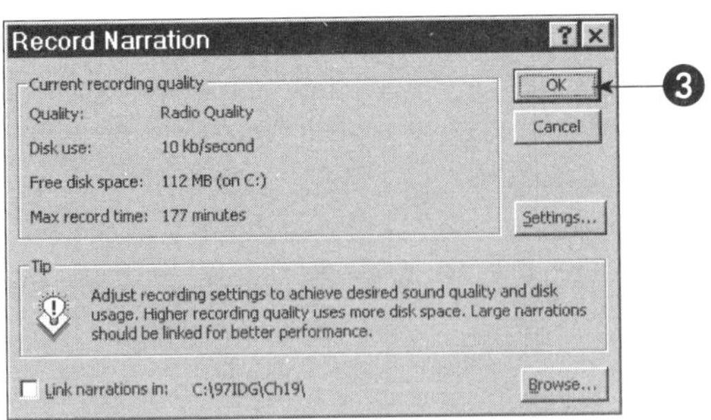

4. Record your narration timed to your slides. For this exercise, read the slide contents as they appear. Use mouse clicks to move through the presentation.

   At the end of the show, a dialog box asks if you want to save the timing of the presentation, or the narration. It's possible to set timings separate from the narration by selecting Slide Show ➢ Rehearse Timings. If you've done this and don't want to override the settings, select No here.

5. Select Yes to save timings.
6. When asked, say Yes to reviewing timings in Slide Sorter view. Notice the slide times beneath each slide.
7. Select the Slide Show view to run the show. Your narration plays along with your slides.

   You can go back and rerecord your narration as many times as you like to get the timing and pace just right.

Running a slide show

You've run slide shows by selecting the Slide Show view button on your PowerPoint screen, or selecting Slide Show ➢ View Show. This runs the show from the currently displayed slide in Slide View, or from the currently selected slide in Outline or Slide Sorter view. You can make certain settings control how your slide show will run.

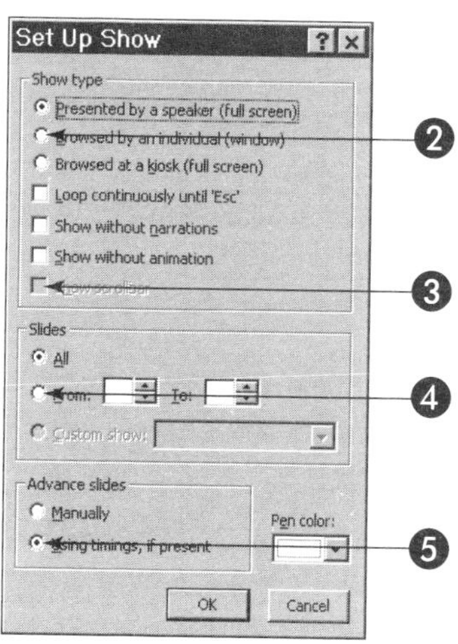

1. Select Slide Show ➢ Set Up Show. The dialog box in the illustration to the right appears.
2. Select the *Browsed by an individual* radio button.
3. Make sure the *Show scrollbar* check box is checked. This provides scrollbars for the viewer to navigate from slide to slide.
4. Change settings in the From and To fields in the Slides section to include only Slides 1 through 3. This is useful for creating different versions of the same presentation.
5. Under *Advance slides*, choose the *Using timings, if present* radio button and click OK.

If you want to present the slide show manually, the Pen color option becomes available. This relates to the capability to make notes right onscreen as you make a presentation. You do this by right-clicking during the presentation and selecting Pen from the shortcut menu that appears.

If you make all your animation settings and then decide, for example, to make your presentation on a computer with less memory, you can also select to Show without narration or animation to make the show proceed more quickly.

6. Run the slide show.

   Because you chose to have an individual view the show in a window, the show now runs with scroll bars and some Web navigation tools showing onscreen. These tools enable the viewer to access the Web during the presentation, assuming the computer is set up for this.

   You can stop a screen show at any time by hitting ESC. Unless you have chosen to loop the show continuously in the Set Up Show dialog box, it will also stop automatically when it reaches the end and return you to whatever view you were in when you began the show.

7. At the end of the slide show, close the file without saving changes. The saved version of this file was copied from the accompanying CD-ROM, and is named Ex17-1.

SKILLS CHALLENGE: SETTING UP A SLIDE SHOW

There are hundreds of variations on how you can set up the pieces of a slide show to run on your computer. Practice a few more ways in the following exercise.

TRY OUT THE INTERACTIVE TUTORIALS ON YOUR CD!

1. Open the file Ex17-2.
2. Select Slide Show ➢ Slide Transition.

3. Apply the Cover Down transition to all slides to occur automatically after three seconds.
4. On the title slide, animate the title with the Drive In effect.
5. Apply the Camera animation effect to the bullet list on the second slide.

How do you apply an animation effect using a menu command?

6. Record Narration using telephone quality. Read the contents of the slides as they appear, and use mouse clicks to advance through your presentation.
7. On Slide 4 only, set the Blinds Horizontal slide transition to occur with the sound file named ~PP932.wav.
8. Set up the slide show to run continuously, using all slides.
9. Set up the show to run using timings.

What are two ways to apply timing to your show?

10. On Slide 3, add the Flying animation effect to the clip art object.
11. Run the slide show.
12. Run the show again, without the narration, and play only Slides 2 through 5.
13. Close the file without saving changes. The saved version of this file was copied from the CD-ROM with the name Ex17-2.

TROUBLESHOOTING

This lesson was the payoff for learning to build PowerPoint presentations: the moment you actually see them printed out or run onscreen. Table 17-1 provides a few answers for questions that might come up as you generate output for your presentation.

Wrap up

Problem	Solution
My 35mm slides came back with an odd looking font.	If you use an unusual font in your presentation, you may have to let your slide bureau know the name of the font or even supply it for them to use in producing the slides.
I created a presentation with color but the slides printed in black-and-white.	Did you select the check box for *Black & white* in the Print Dialog box? Deselect it and try again.
My presentation runs very, very slowly.	A few options: Run it on a faster computer, free up some memory, run the presentation without animations, or delete some graphics from slides.
Not all my slides appear when I run my slide show.	Make sure you haven't selected to hide any slides, or chosen in the Set Up Show dialog box to show only a range of slides.

WRAP UP

You've learned the essentials of generating presentation output in this lesson, including the following:

- Printing paper slides, transparencies, notes, handouts, and outlines
- Generating 35mm slides
- Making settings to add simple transitions, animations, and narration to your presentation

For more practice, create a presentation with a slide describing each member of your family. Add sounds, animations, and narration that are appropriate to each person's personality.

In Lesson 18, you begin taking a look at Microsoft Outlook, and seeing the many ways it can help organize you and your Office documents.

PART V

Microsoft Outlook

This part introduces you to Microsoft Outlook, which offers you functionality in three areas: scheduling, contact management, and e-mail. It includes the following lessons:

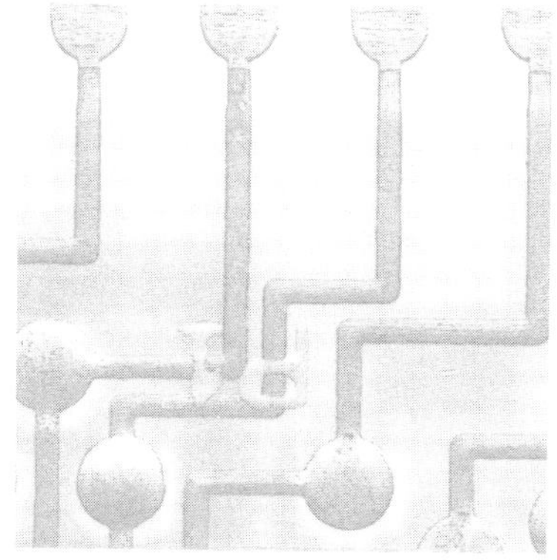

Managing Your Schedule

GOALS

Outlook is a marvelous feature of Office 97, bringing together scheduling, contact management, and e-mail to make your life simpler. In this lesson, you'll be introduced to Outlook, and learn the following:

- Using the Outlook Bar
- Adding appointments
- Adding events
- Requesting a meeting
- Changing views
- Using the Task Pad
- Changing Task Pad views

Get ready

GET READY

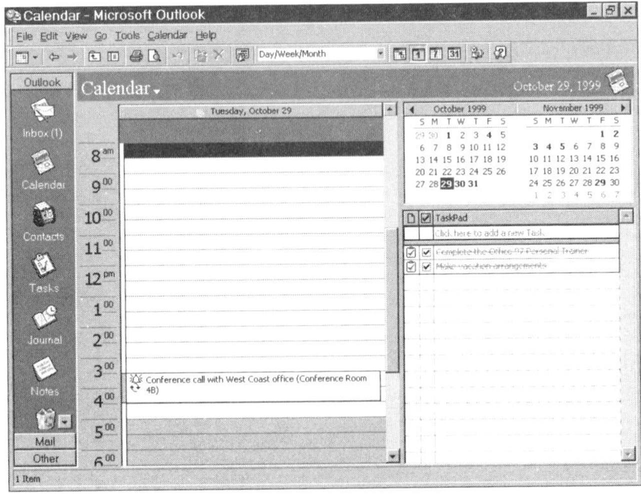

In this lesson, you begin building your own Outlook schedule from scratch. I'll assume you have not added any tasks, contacts, or messages to Outlook, and are using it for the first time.

In the exercises that follow, you create a calendar like the one in the illustration.

FIRST LOOK AT OUTLOOK

Outlook is the happy combination of two programs named Schedule+ and Exchange in the previous version of Microsoft Office. Outlook offers you functionality in three areas: scheduling, contact management, and e-mail. In addition, Outlook can help you organize the work you need to perform with the other Office programs by creating task lists, keeping records of documents you've worked on in a journal, and attaching documents to Outlook elements such as e-mail or appointments.

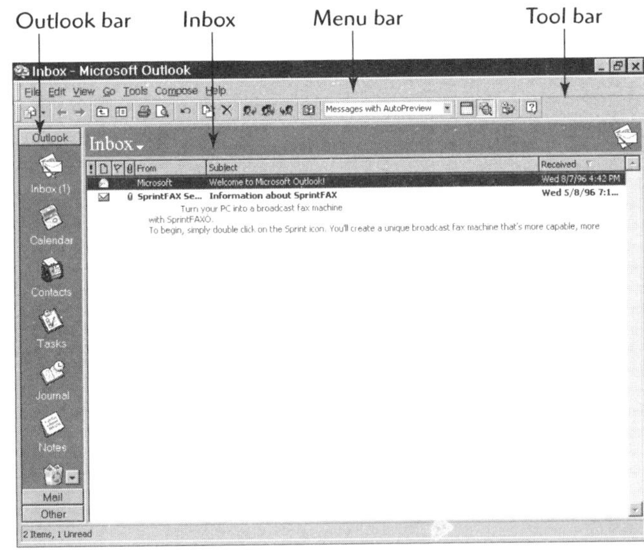

Outlook is different from the other Office programs in one important respect: You don't have to manually save Outlook files. Think of your daily planner notebook: You keep one such planner, and every time you add something to it, whether it's a piece of paper you clip to the inside cover or an appointment you write on a page, you update it. Outlook is your central electronic planner, and every time you make a change it is automatically saved. Although you can manually save e-mail messages you receive through Outlook, and even create and save new Outlook forms, you normally don't have to name and save your Outlook files as you do with Word or Excel files.

You can export information from Outlook to other programs, and save the files there. You can also import information from other Office products into Outlook, and that imported information is automatically saved in Outlook.

This lesson focuses on the scheduling capabilities of Outlook. But first, you get a glimpse at the total Outlook environment and the basics of moving among its different areas.

Using the Outlook bar

Outlook offers several different functions, and you move among them using the Outlook bar.

1. Select Start from the Windows taskbar.
2. Click the Programs submenu.
3. Click Microsoft Outlook.

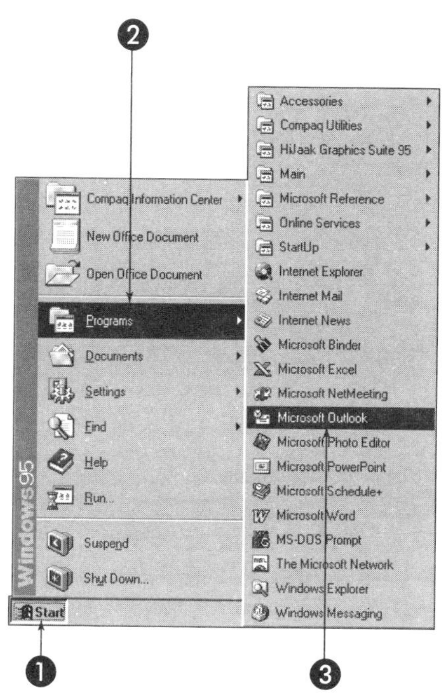

NOTE

If you haven't changed your Windows desktop since you installed Office, you'll find an icon for Microsoft Outlook that provides a shortcut. Double-click it to open the program.

Microsoft Outlook takes a moment to load. When it's done, the Inbox appears. You probably have a message or two from Microsoft, welcoming you to Outlook or alerting you to certain features. Along the left side of the Outlook screen is the Outlook bar. This is used to move among the different features of Outlook.

4. Click the Contacts icon on the Outlook bar.

The Contacts view appears; yours is probably blank, but the illustration to the right shows you this view with some contacts entered. The letter tabs down the right side of this window enable you to easily locate the contact name you wish to look up.

5. Click the Journal icon on the Outlook bar. The Journal appears.

It is likely that you have some journal entries. The journal automatically keeps track of Office documents you create. It's a way of keeping a central record of your Office activity.

6. Click the button with the + sign next to Entry Type: Microsoft Word. Documents you've saved in Word are listed here.
7. Click the arrow near the bottom right of the Outlook bar.

Notice that the last icon in this area, Deleted Items, moves up and the first icon, Inbox, has moved up out of view. Deleted

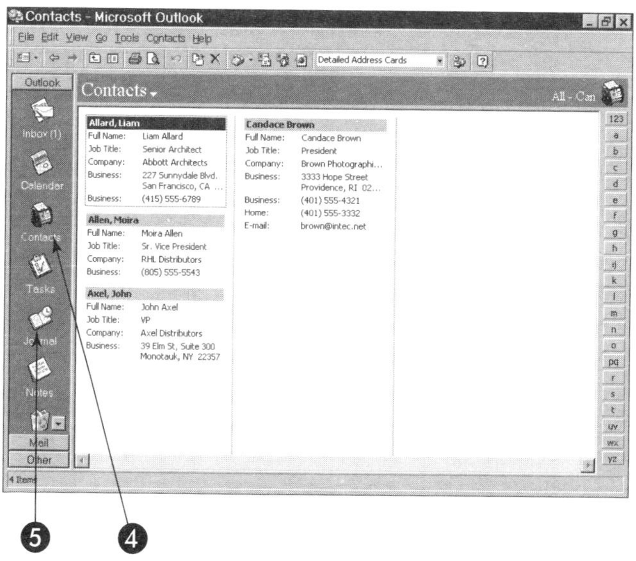

Items is like an Outlook trash bin you use in the same way you use the Recycle Bin on the Windows desktop. You can use the arrows that appear on the Outlook bar to move up or down and see more items. It's even possible to add items to this bar, making this scrolling feature even more useful.

8. Click the Notes icon on the Outlook bar.

   The Notes area of Outlook will probably have the placeholder note, *Where was I going to go today?* The illustration to the right shows a few more notes, as well as a note being composed. This area works like Post-it Notes: little scraps of paper you jot a note on and stick to this note board.

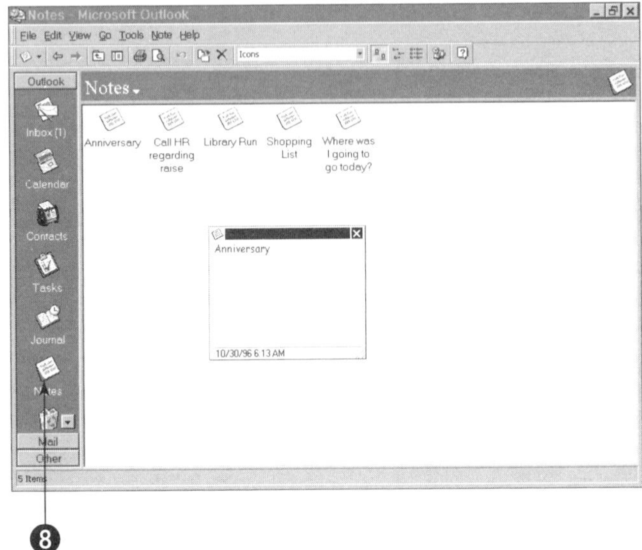

Exploring the toolbar

The toolbar along the top of the Outlook screen changes depending on the feature you display. However, certain tools are common to all features. The following illustration shows the Notes toolbar, with the tools that are common to all Outlook features identified. The first item, New Note, changes its name (New Task, New Appointment, New Contact, and so on), but its function — adding a new element — is identical among the views.

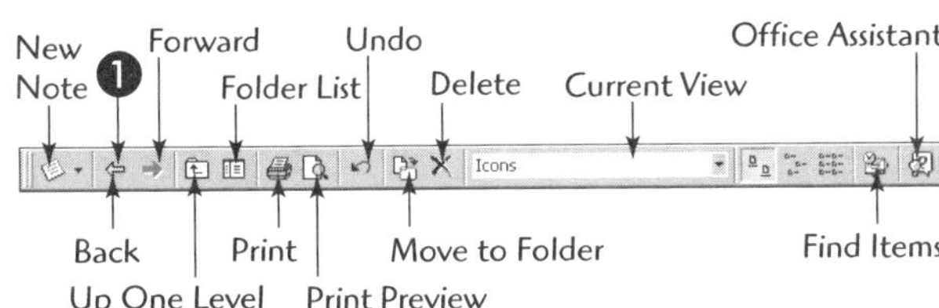

1. Click the Back tool. You return to the last place you were in Outlook, which is the Journal feature.

2. Click the Up One Level tool, which takes you to the Personal Folders folder.

3. Click the arrow next to the Personal Folders heading. This displays the list of folders in Outlook.

4. Select Notes from this list by clicking it.

5. Click the Folder List tool. This displays the Personal Folders list to the left of the Notes feature, providing another way to navigate around Outlook.

6. Click the Folder List tool again to remove the Personal Folders list from your screen.

7. Click the arrow to the right of the *Current View* drop-down list on the toolbar.

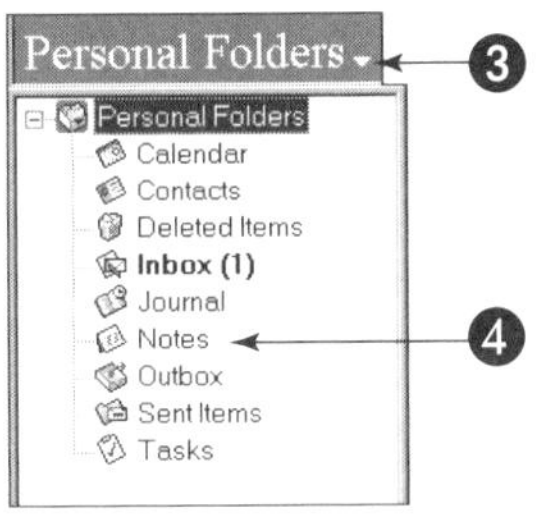

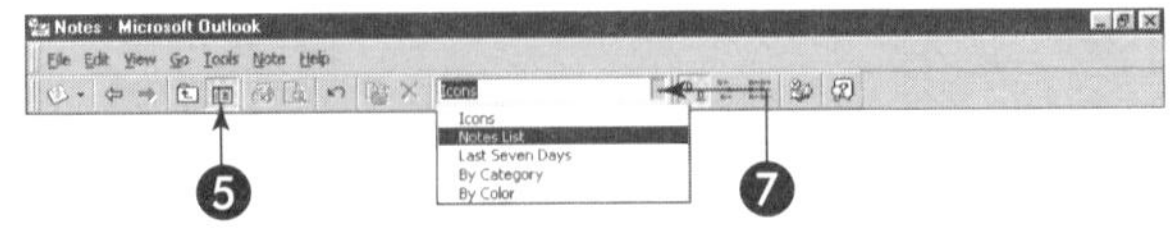

Every area of Outlook has several views, offering you different perspectives on your information. You change views by selecting a new one from this drop-down list.

8. Select the Notes List view from the drop-down list. A different style of listing appears.

9. Select the Find Items tool. The Find dialog box appears.

   You use the Find feature to locate any type of document or entry by keywords or criteria, such as the date of the item or whether it had attachments.

10. Close the Find dialog box.

    You had a quick run-through of most of the different looks and features of Outlook, and you know a little about navigating your way around. It's time to get into the first major function — scheduling. You begin by taking your first look at the Calendar feature.

11. Using the Outlook bar, move to the Calendar feature.

    The bottom illustration shows the Calendar view with a few appointments filled in.

USING THE CALENDAR

There are three categories of items which can be added to the calendar: events, meetings, and appointments.

- *Event* refers to an occurrence that lasts more than one day, such as a convention or vacation. An event isn't placed in a specific time slot on your calendar; instead it appears in a banner on your calendar screen.
- *Meetings* refers to an appointment that you ask other people to attend. You can use an Outlook feature called Meeting Planner to send out meeting requests and schedule resources.
- *Appointment* has a specified time in your calendar. An appointment can be designated as private, and can have a reminder attached to it to alert you when the appointment time is nearing.

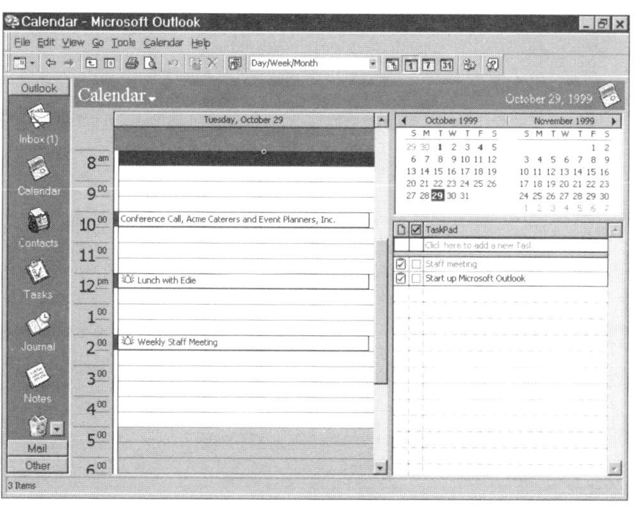

Adding appointments

You can use the different calendar views to focus on certain events. You're currently in the Day/Week/Month view. This shows a daily calendar for the current date on the left, and a scrollable monthly calendar on the right. Beneath the daily calendar is your TaskPad. This is a kind of to-do list, showing the items entered within the Task area of Outlook.

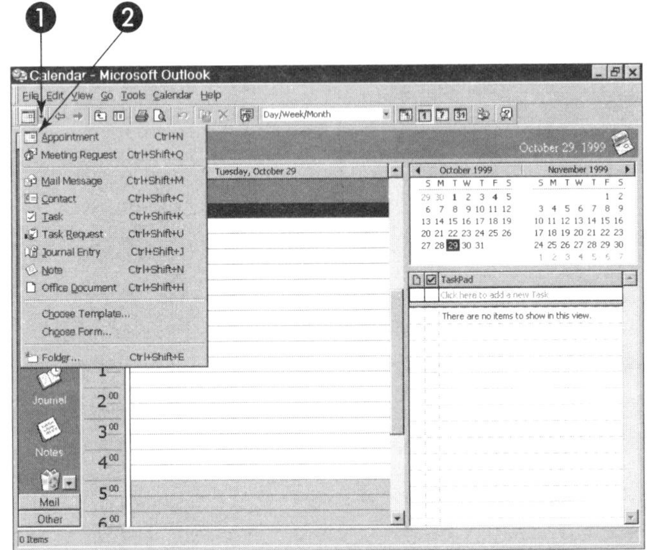

Adding appointments

What would you do without appointments? You know, those meetings, conference calls (more meetings), interviews, and seminars that you have to juggle in your workaday world? Outlook helps with a variety of features.

1. Click the arrow on the right of the New Appointment tool.

Notice that you can create any of Outlook's items here, such as Notes, Contacts, or even e-mail. Also notice the keyboard shortcuts for these frequently performed tasks next to each menu command. You can quickly create a new appointment by clicking the New Appointment button itself, rather than the arrow at the side of the button.

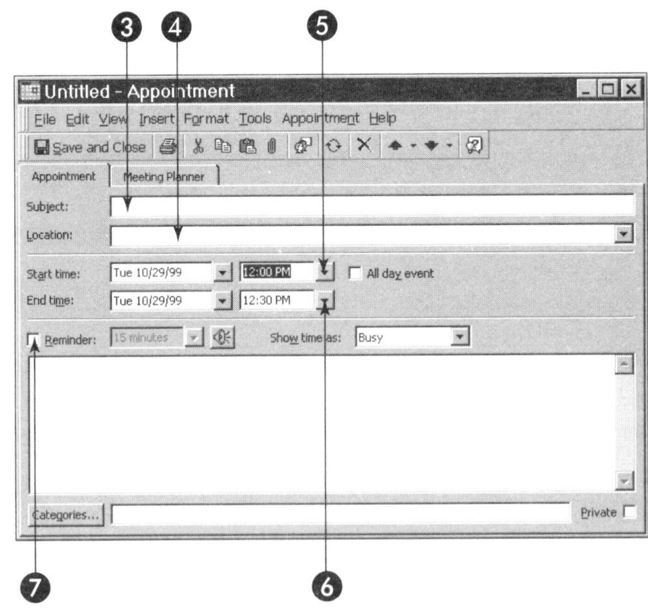

2. Select Appointment from the menu. The Appointment form appears.
3. In the *Subject* box, type **Conference call with West Coast office.**
4. Type **Conference Room 4B** in the *Location* field.
5. In the *Start time* box, select 3:30 PM. The end time is automatically entered as a half-hour later.
6. Open the drop-down list for time in the *End time* box, and select 4:30 PM.
7. Request that Outlook remind you of the appointment by clicking in the *Reminder* check box.

8 Open the *Reminder* drop-down list and select 30 minutes. You'll receive a reminder 30 minutes before the appointment time.

9 Open the *Show time as* drop-down list and select Tentative.

The choices here are especially useful if someone else, maybe your assistant, accesses your calendar. Appointments appear as *Busy* by default, and are therefore blocked out on your calendar so no one else can schedule an event at that time. You may use the color coding of other time categories, such as *Out of Office* (purple) to indicate to someone that you aren't available for any calls or interruptions during an appointment, and *Tentative* (light blue) to indicate that the appointment could be rescheduled if necessary.

10 In the comments field at the bottom of this form type **Bring Durbin folder.**

11 Click the Categories button to open the Categories dialog box.

12 Use the scroll bar to locate the Phone Calls check box and then click that box.

13 Choose OK to close the Categories dialog box.

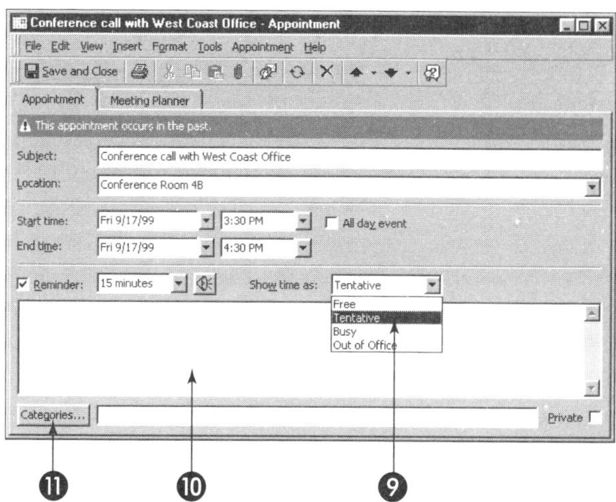

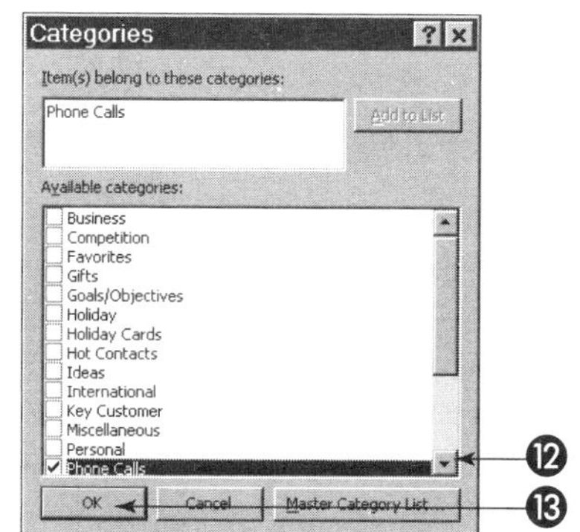

To attach a file to this form, click the Insert File tool. This places a copy of the file you select in the comments box represented by an icon; you can open the document and the application it was created in by double-clicking the icon.

14 To make this appointment a regular, recurring event, select Appointment ➢ Recurrence. The illustration to the right shows the Appointment Recurrence dialog box that appears.

15 Click in the *Monthly* option button to indicate that this appointment will happen every month. You can also control this pattern by setting either the date of the month or the day (every third Wednesday, for example).

16 Choose OK.

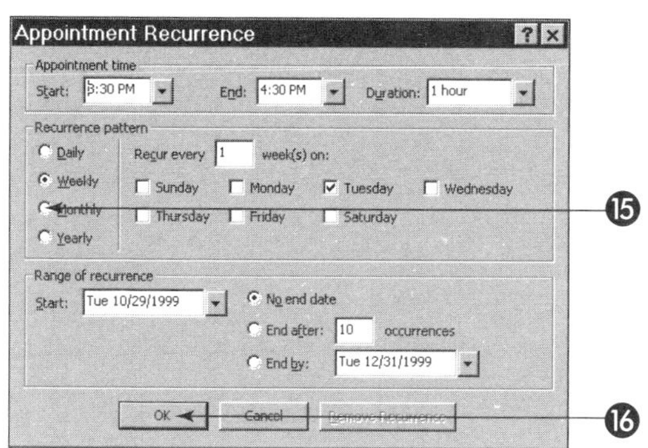

⑰ Click the Save and Close button on the toolbar to save the appointment and return to the Calendar. The appointment is now noted on your daily calendar.

TRY OUT THE INTERACTIVE TUTORIALS ON YOUR CD!

Adding events

Events are added in a similar way to appointments. The main difference is they run more than 24 hours.

1. Click the New Appointment button. The Appointment form appears.
2. In the *Subject* box, type **Off-site conference**.
3. In the *Location* box, type **Maui** (we can dream, can't we?).
4. Click in the check box for *All day event*. Notice the title of the form changes from Appointment to Event and the boxes to set start and end times disappear.
5. In the *Start time* box, select a date two business days from the current date.
6. In the *End time* box, select a date three business days after the first. You may need to use the scroll bar to move to the next month.
7. Change the *Show time as* setting to Out of Office.
8. Click the Categories button.
9. Check the Competition category and choose OK.
10. Click the Save and Close button to save the event.
11. Click one of the dates you scheduled for your conference event in the monthly calendar section of the screen. A banner appears at the top of your daily calendar saying Off-site conference (Maui).

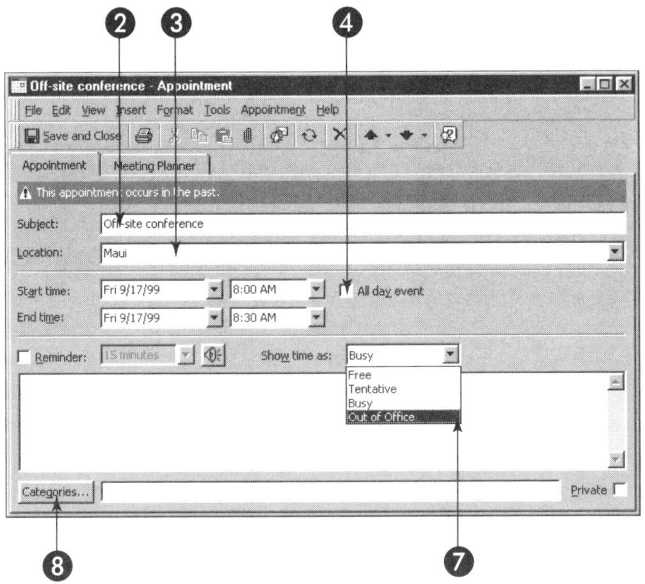

Requesting a meeting

Outlook even helps you get others to appointments, with indispensable meeting scheduling tools.

1. Click the arrow next to the New Appointment tool.
2. Select Meeting Request from the drop-down menu. The Meeting form shown in the illustration to the right appears.

   This form is similar to the Appointment and Event forms, but it has an address line so you can e-mail this request to meeting attendees.
3. Click the To button.

   The *Select Attendees and Resources* dialog box appears. The names of people from your Outlook contact list for whom you've included an e-mail address will appear.
4. Click the New button. A New Entry dialog box appears.
5. Select In This Message Only.
6. Select Other Address.
7. Click OK.
8. In the New Other Address Properties dialog box that appears, enter your name in the *Display name* box.
9. Enter your e-mail address in the *E-mail address* box.
10. Enter the type of online service you have in the *E-mail type* (for example, Internet, America Online, and so on).
11. Click the Required button at the bottom of the form.
12. Click OK to return to the Meeting form, with your name filled in as an addressee. You can repeat the above procedure to add more addresses to this invitation.

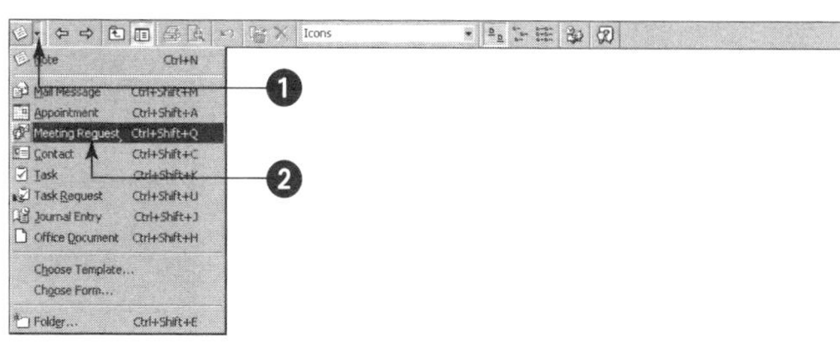

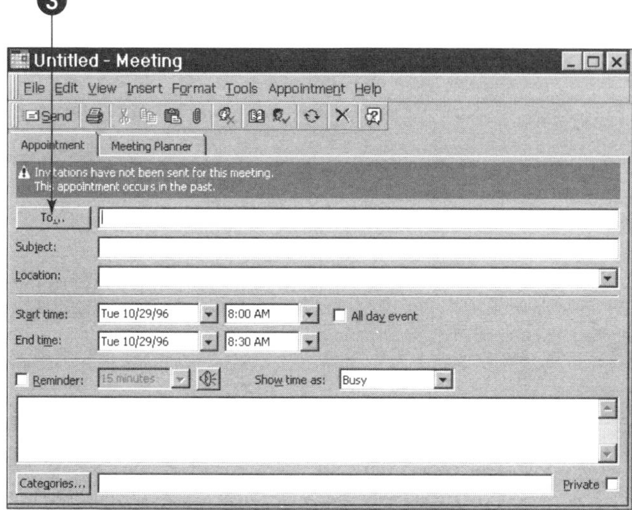

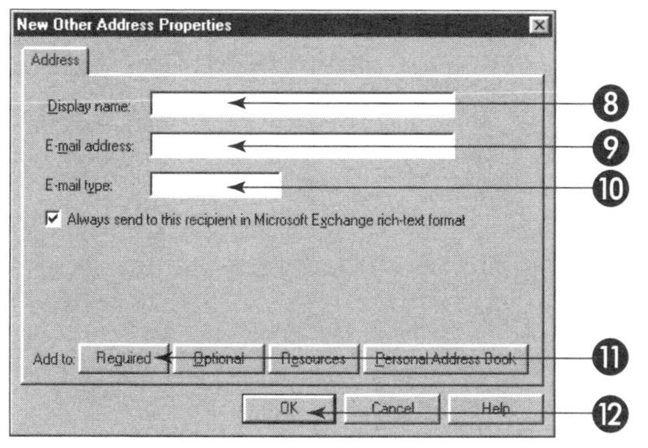

18

Managing Your Schedule

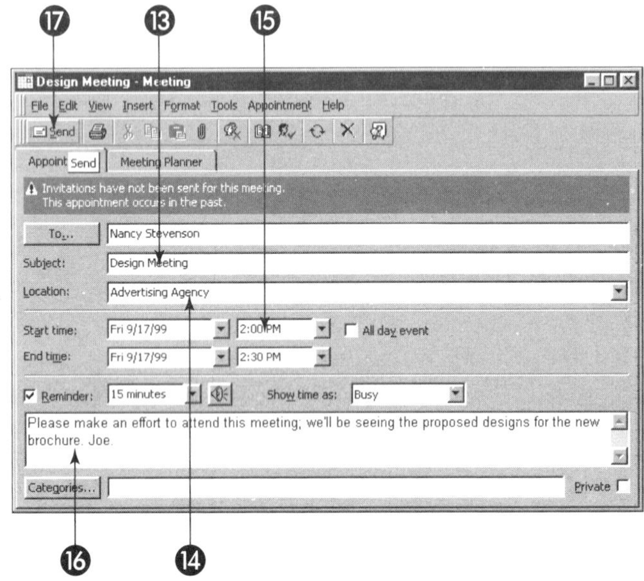

You cannot create new contact entries from here; you can only request the attendance of people already entered as contacts.

13. In the *Subject* box, type **Design Meeting**.
14. In the *Location* box, type **Advertising Agency**.
15. Set the *Start time* for 2:00 PM the next business day.
16. In the *comments* box, type this message: **Please make an effort to attend this meeting; we'll be seeing the proposed designs for the new brochure. Joe.**
17. Click the Send button.

    If you're connected to e-mail, the message will be sent. If not, the message will be sent the next time you do connect, along with any other outgoing mail. Responses to your invitation appear in your Inbox. Outlook has also created a meeting event at 2:00 PM the next business day. If you click that item, a message appears in the Meeting form asking whether any responses to requests have been received.

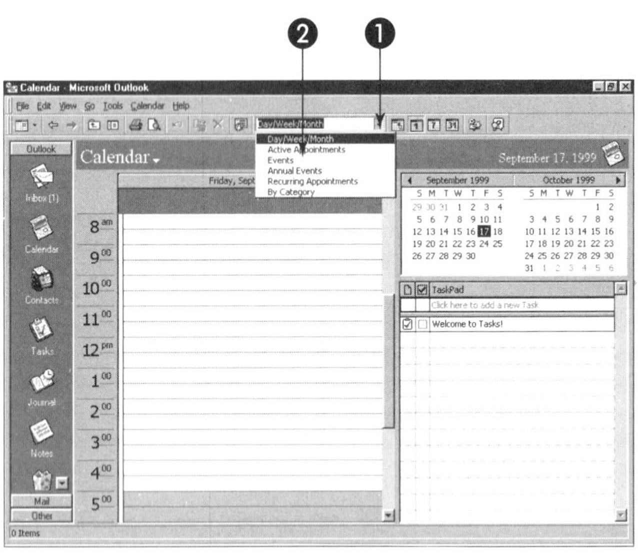

Don't worry about accessing your e-mail with Outlook at the moment. You learn all about that in Lesson 20. When you do, the invitation you just created will get sent.

Changing Calendar views

Now that you've entered some information in Outlook, you can explore some of the different views it offers to see your schedule. You're currently in the Day/Week/Month view.

1. Open the Current View drop-down list on the toolbar.
2. Select the Active Appointments view. The listing shown in the illustration shown at the top of the next page appears.

Changing Calendar views

All the items you've created are listed here. The icon to the left of each indicates its nature: Events and appointments show a small calendar, and meetings display images of two little people. The items are also divided by those with no recurrence, and those that recur on a regular basis.

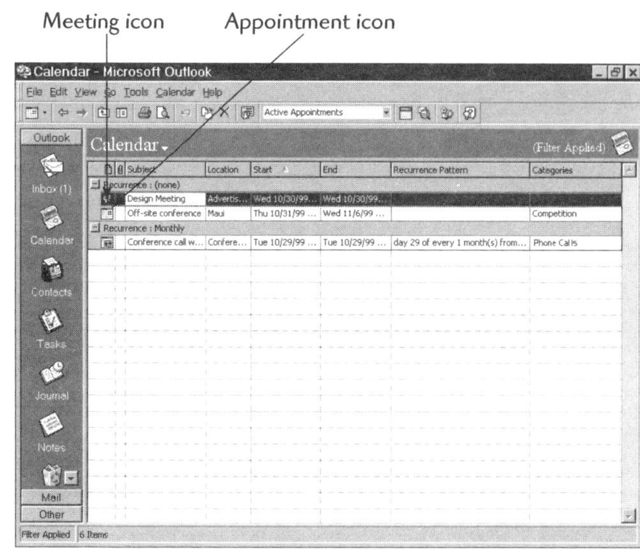

3. Select the By Category view from the Current View drop-down list.

4. Click the + symbol to the left of the item Categories: Competition. The display shown in the illustration to the right appears.

   You can use the plus and minus symbols to open and close the listings by category. Using the views you've just explored and a few others you can see information in your schedule from different perspectives. Any changes made in one view are reflected in corresponding entries in all the other views. Now you learn how four tools available in the Calendar View (just to the right of the Current View drop-down list on the toolbar) help you see different periods of time.

5. Return to the Day/Week/Month view by selecting it from the Current View drop-down list.

6. Click the Week button on the toolbar. This displays a block for each day of the current week.

7. Click the Month button on the toolbar. A full month of calendar is displayed.

8. Click the Day button. You are returned to the single day format.

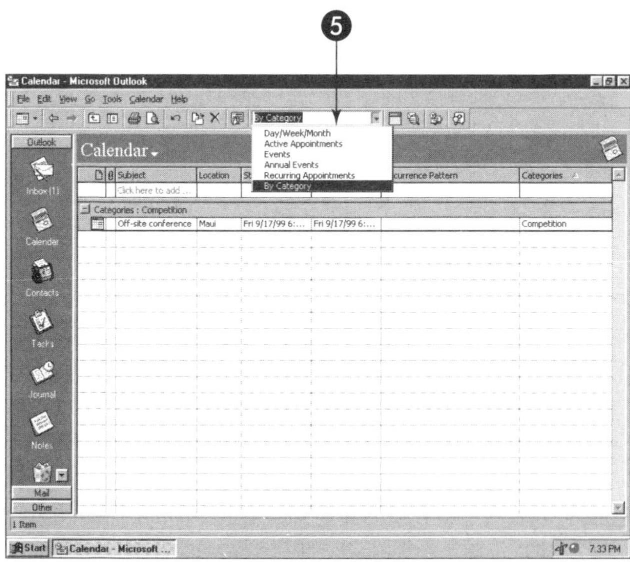

USING THE TASK PAD

The Task Pad is like a to-do list that shows in both the Calendar and the Tasks area of Outlook. You can add new tasks from either place. Tasks differ from appointments, meetings, and events in that you don't associate specific start and end times with the task. The task is left on the task pad until you delete it. To keep track of completed tasks, you can also simply mark it done, and it is left on your pad, but with a line drawn through it to indicate its status.

Adding tasks

Adding tasks

Tasks, by nature, don't have a start and end time (that would be an appointment). Tasks are things like picking up your cleaning, or writing a memo; they need to be done . . . sometime. Outlook enables you to create a due date for tasks, and alerts you when you miss that date, but otherwise they just sit there on that list, taunting you into a guilty frenzy. Try creating a task now.

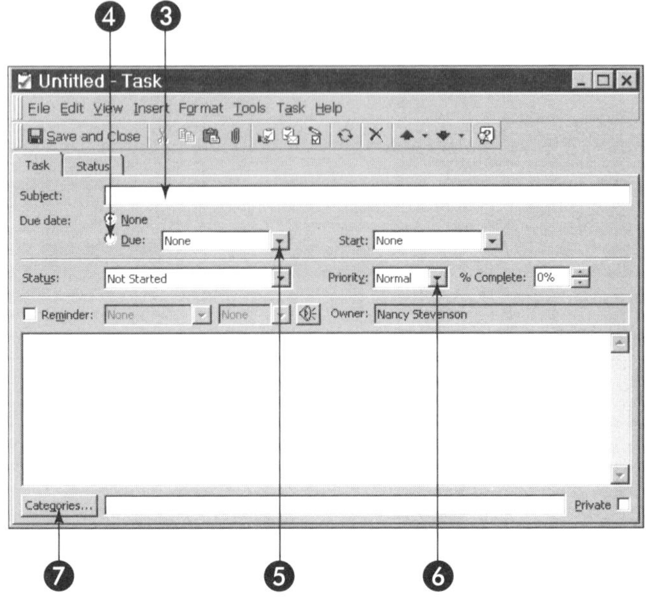

1. Select Tasks from the Outlook bar.
2. Double-click on the space that says *Click here to add to begin to build a new Task* (don't single click: that opens that field for editing).

   The Task form appears, as in the following illustration.
3. Type **Complete Office 97 One Step at a Time** in the *Subject* field.
4. Check the Due option button in the *Due date* section.
5. Select a date a week from the current date from the drop-down calendar.
6. Change the Priority to High by selecting that choice from the drop-down list.
7. Click the Categories button and select Goals/Objectives from the available categories list.
8. Click OK to return to the Task form, and then Save and Close to save the task.
9. Change to the Calendar using the Outlook bar. The new task appears in the Task Pad here as well.
10. Click in the check mark column next to the task. A line is drawn through it, indicating it is complete. *(No, don't close this book: we're just supposing you've finished all the lessons!)*
11. Click the space labeled Click here to add new task. If you simply want to enter a task name, you can enter it right here, without opening the task form.

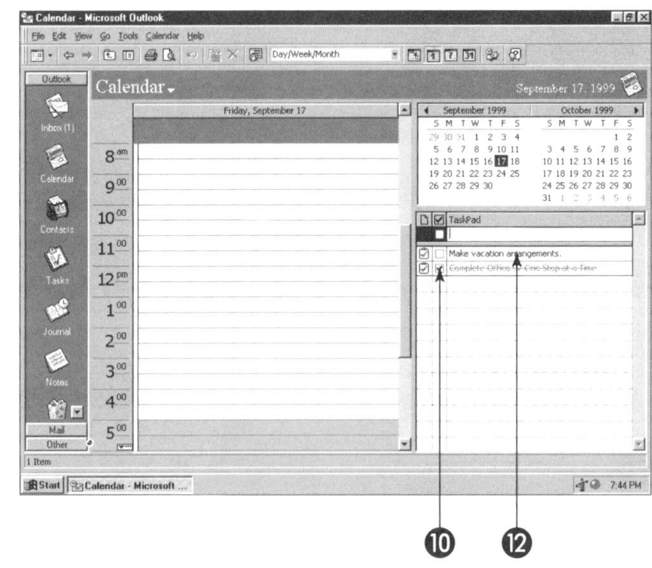

⓬ Type **Make vacation arrangements**.

⓭ Press Enter. The new task appears here and in the Tasks area of Outlook.

Changing Task Pad views

Just as the Calendar had different views, so Task Pad offers different perspectives on your to-do list.

1. Select Tasks from the Outlook bar.
2. Select Completed Tasks from the Current View drop-down list.

   Now only the completed tasks are displayed, plus a few more columns of information. The column headed with an exclamation mark displays the priority you assigned to the task. You can click this column and change or assign a priority from the drop-down list that appears. The column titled Date Completed provides a record of the date when you marked the task complete. The category you assigned the task is also displayed.

You can sort your tasks in different ways by clicking the gray column headings. For example, clicking Due Date sorts task by due date, and clicking the Subject column heading sorts tasks alphabetically in ascending order.

3. Select Active Tasks from the Current View drop-down list. Now only the task not yet marked as complete appears.
4. Double-click this task. The Task form opens.
5. Click the Due option button and select yesterday's date from the *Due date* drop-down list.
6. Click the Save and Close button on the toolbar. The task now appears in red, which indicates an overdue task.
7. Change to the Overdue Tasks view.
8. Click in the % Complete column for the task and type **100**.

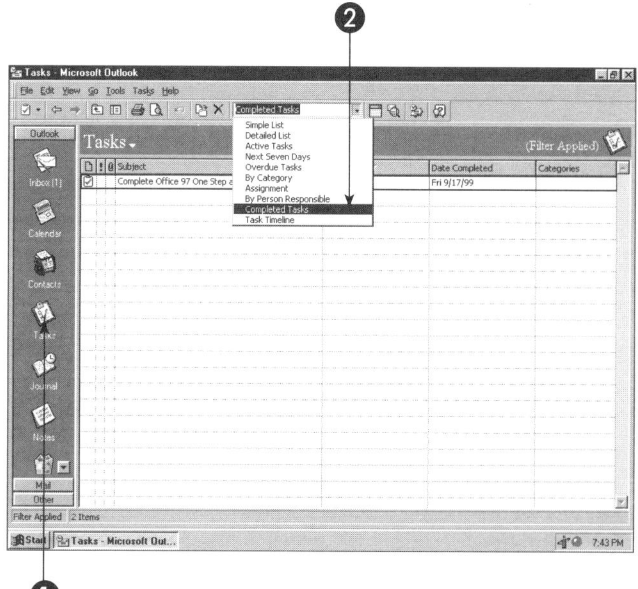

9. Press Enter.

   The now completed task disappears from the Overdue Tasks view.

TRY OUT THE INTERACTIVE TUTORIALS ON YOUR CD!

SKILLS CHALLENGE: UPDATING OUTLOOK

You saw many different features of Outlook. Now it's time to practice getting around and filling up your schedule.

1. Display the Calendar.
2. Enter a dental appointment at 2:30 PM next Monday. Set a reminder for one hour before the appointment.
3. Change the Calendar display to show a week.
4. Indicate that the Complete Office 97 One Step at a Time task is not complete.

From which two places in Outlook can you indicate an incomplete task?

5. In the Tasks area, display the Detailed List view.
6. Change the priority of the task to Normal.
7. Set the Category of the Vacation arrangements task to Holiday.
8. Create an event for the week between Christmas and New Years called Management Retreat.

What is the difference between an appointment, an event, and a task?

9. Make the location of this event Denver, and mark the event as Private.
10. Display the month of December in your Calendar.
11. Request the attendance of two people — a coworker or family member whose e-mail address you know, for example — to a meeting at your house on the first Friday of next month. (Remember, when we connect with e-mail in Lesson 22, the invitations will actually be sent unless you delete them at the end of this lesson!)

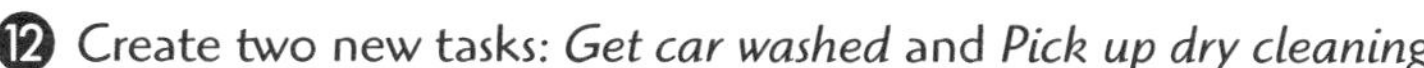

⓬ Create two new tasks: *Get car washed* and *Pick up dry cleaning.*

Name three ways to enter a new task.

⓭ Remove the reminder from the Conference call with the West Coast.

⓮ Change the Show time as choice for this appointment from Tentative to Busy.

⓯ Mark the Office 97 One Step at a Time task as 80 percent complete . . . because it is!

TROUBLESHOOTING

As you explore the possibilities of using Outlook to keep your schedule and remind you of appointments and events, you may run into some questions. The following table attempts to answer some of them.

Problem	Solution
I get a message in the Appointment form saying *This appointment occurs in the past.*	When you open this form, it has a start time of 8:00 AM of the current day by default. If it's later than 8:00 AM, it gives this message. Don't worry: Just choose a time later than the present and the message goes away.
While changing views, I get a message about saving view settings.	If you've changed something in a view, like sorting it or displaying the Personal Folder column, you get this message. Unless you want to change the view defaults, select Discard the current view settings from the message dialog box.
How do I make a recurring task stop being recurring?	If the event is past, just delete it. If one iteration of the event is still going to happen in the future, open the event and select Appointment ➢ Recurrence and click Remove Recurrence.

Wrap up

WRAP UP

You've done a great job getting to know Outlook. You already move around like a pro, having learned the skills to do the following:

- Display various views and move among the different areas of Outlook
- Create tasks, appointments, events, and meetings
- Set priorities for tasks and mark them as complete

For more practice with Outlook scheduling, plan an actual event, such as an office party. Set up an appointment with the caterers, schedule a call to the florist, block a whole day out to decorate the office, and invite ten customers to attend the party. (Again, if you don't want to actually send those invitations, delete them when you're done practicing.)

In Lesson 19 you learn how to use Outlook to manage contacts, and begin to build your contact list.

Managing Contacts

GOALS

Outlook offers several features for managing the many contacts you have in your personal and business life. It's much more than an electronic Rolodex; with Outlook, you can place phone calls, send letters and e-mail, and plan meetings with your contacts, all from one convenient location. In this lesson you learn the following:

- Creating Contacts
- Editing Contacts
- Planning a meeting
- Sending a letter to a contact
- Calling contacts using Phone Dialer

Get ready

GET READY

In this lesson, you use the Contacts area of Outlook. The instructions assume that you haven't yet entered any contacts in Outlook. To complete one of the exercises, you need a modem connected to your computer.

In the following exercises, you build a contact list like the one in the accompanying illustration.

TRY OUT THE
INTERACTIVE TUTORIALS
ON YOUR CD!

BUILDING YOUR CONTACT LIST

What are contacts? Contacts include your dentist, your manager, your best customer, and the phone company. *Contacts* are people you need to be in touch with on a regular basis and for whom it's useful to keep an ongoing record, such as a salesman who might keep one about a customer's account activity. Contacts are organizations you need to call or write to frequently, like your mortgage company or the PTA.

Contact management is a system of organizing and maintaining records about those contacts. Outlook's contact management features act like your own personal secretary — one who efficiently keeps records, places phone calls, and even plans meetings for you.

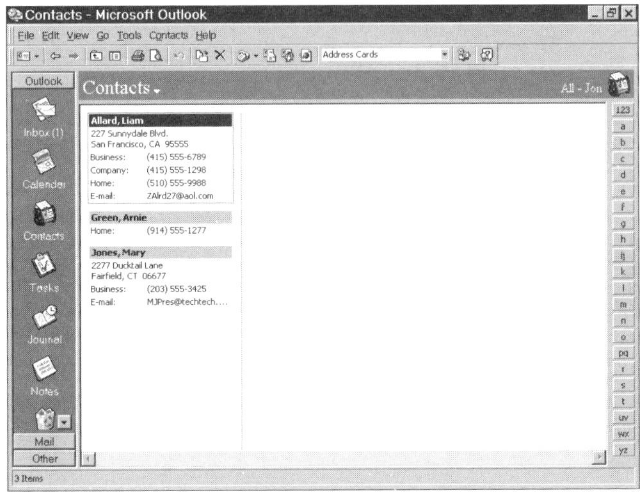

Creating contacts

Before you can manage contacts you have to place contact information in Outlook. Here's how.

1. Open Outlook.
2. Select Contacts from the Outlook bar.
3. Click the New Contact button on the toolbar. The Contact form appears.

   There are four tabs in this dialog box: General, Details, Journal, and All Fields. The General tab is where you enter the most common information for contacts such as name, address, phone, and e-mail address. The Details tab enables you to enter background information about the person, such as his or her department, profession, birthday, or nickname. The Journal tab is where a record of all activity relating to this contact is kept. The Journal tab acts as a kind of log of e-mail, faxes, letters, meetings, and phone calls. Finally, the All Fields tab enables you to display fields of information for this contact by categories such as All Document fields and All E-mail fields. If, for example, you want to see all the possible fields for personal information such as children's names, gender, anniversary, and hobbies, you can display the Personal fields on this tab.

4. In the *Full Name* box type **Liam Allard**.
5. Press Enter. The name is automatically placed in the *File as* box with the last name first, and your cursor moves to the *Job title* box.

If you want to enter a more detailed name, for example one with a title, middle name, and suffix such as Jr. or III, click the Full Name button and use the Check Full Name *dialog box. There is even a check box here if you want this dialog box to appear whenever you type the name incorrectly or incompletely.*

6. Type **Senior Architect** in the *Job title* box.
7. Press Enter. You move to the *Company* box.
8. Type **Abbott Architects** and press Enter. This moves you to the *File as* box in case you want to make changes to Outlook's automatic entry.
9. Press Tab to move to the *Address* box without making any change to the *File as* box.
10. Click the Address button and type this address in the form: **227 Sunnydale Blvd., San Francisco, CA 95555**.
11. Click the Address button. The Check Address form appears.
12. Make sure you check the *Show this again when address is incomplete or unclear* check box.
13. Choose OK.

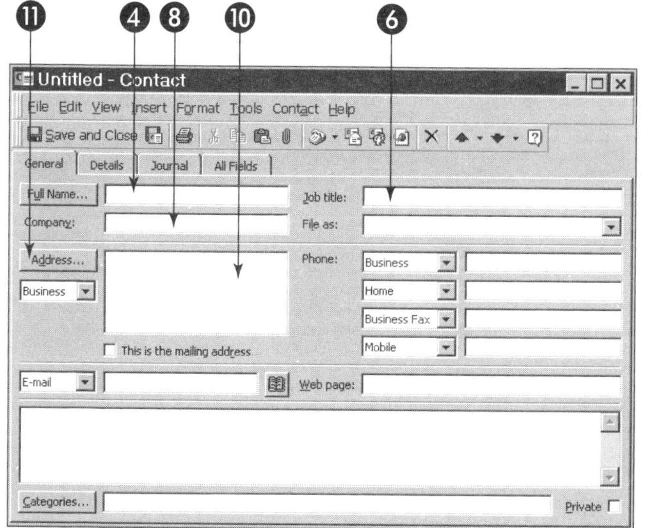

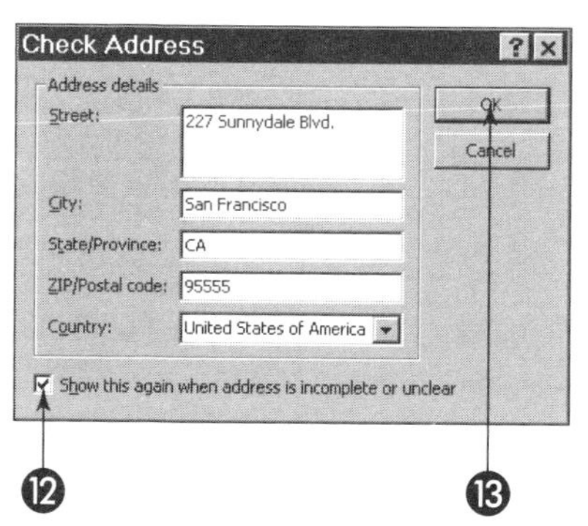

Creating contacts

14. Press Tab to move to the address location drop-down list.

15. Click the arrow on this list to display the choices Business, Home, and Other. Using these settings, you can enter two or more addresses for a contact on this one form.

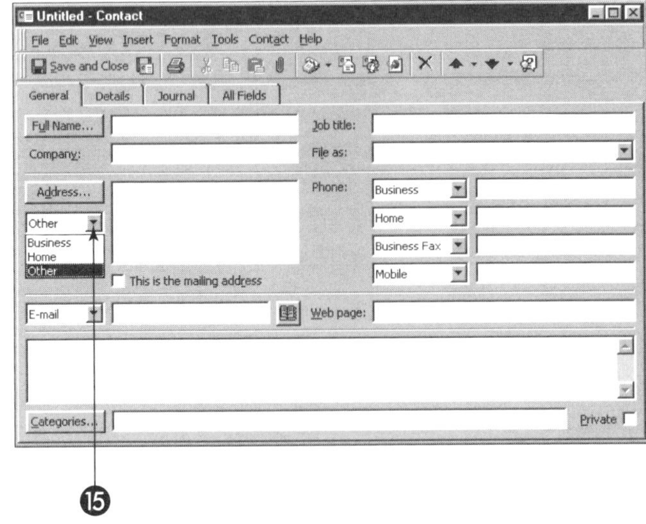

16. Make sure Business is selected and Press Tab to move to the check box for mailing address. If you did create several records for the same contact, you might prefer that all mail go to one address; checking here makes this the default address for any letters you create to this contact.

17. Press Tab to accept the default mailing address designation and move to the Phone section of the form.

18. Click the arrow next to open the first Phone Number drop-down list.

    These four phone drop-down lists enable you to customize the phone designations with items such as ISDN, Car, Pager, Telex, and so on. You can change these any way you like by selecting a different label from each list.

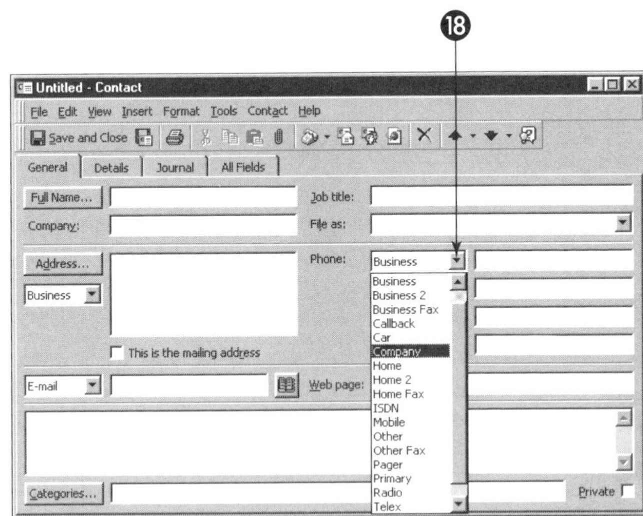

19. Select Company from the list, and then type this number in the phone number field: **(415) 555-1298**.

20. Click in the *Home* phone number box and type: **(510) 555-9988**.

21. Press Tab six times to move to the *E-mail* address entry box. Type **ZALrd27@aol.com**.

The little book icon next to this field opens up a Select Name dialog box. If the contact's e-mail address is recorded elsewhere, you can select it from here rather than typing it in. You can also use this feature as a shortcut if somebody with a similar address is on record. For example, a company such as Acme Tools might have e-mail addresses for all employees that end in @acmetools.com. Place Smith@acmetools.com *here using the Select Name dialog box and just change* Smith *to* Jones*.*

22. Click the Categories button and select Hot Contacts from the list of categories.

23 Choose OK to close the Categories dialog box.

24 Click the Save and Close button to save the new contact. The contact information is displayed onscreen, as in the following illustration.

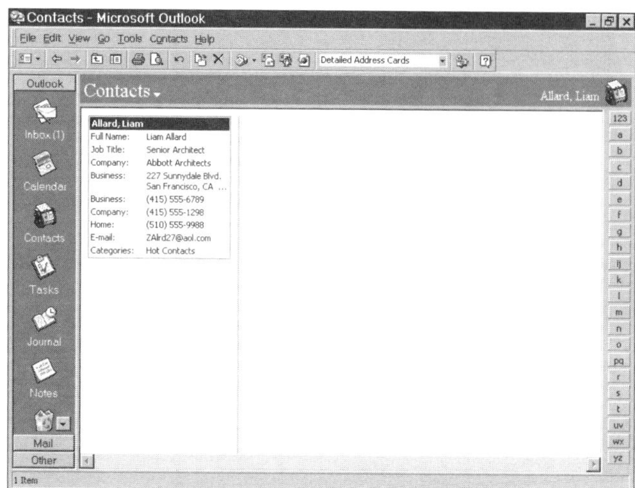

25 Repeat the preceding steps to create two more records with the following information:

- Mary Jones, President, Wright Associates; Business address: 2277 Ducktail Lane, Fairfield, CT 06677; Business phone (203) 555-3425; E-mail address MJPres@techtech.org; Category: Favorites.
- Arnie Green; Home address: 33 Lisle Road, New Paltz, NY 22566; Home phone (914) 555-1277; Category: Hot Contacts.

A great shortcut when you're entering contacts from the same company or living at the same address is to use the Contacts ➢ Create Contact from Same Company command. This opens a new contact form with the company and address already filled out and the area code of the company phone field entered.

Editing contact information

Just as you can add a new phone number to a Rolodex card or scribble a new address in your address book, Outlook enables you to easily make changes to contact information you store there.

1 Open the Current View drop-down list on the toolbar.

2 Select the By Category view.

3 If a message appears about changing the current view, accept the default option of discarding changes by clicking OK.

4 Click the two Category + buttons to display their contents.

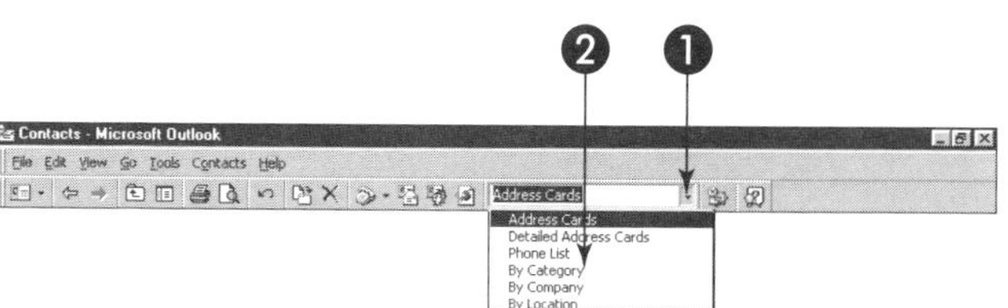

5. Click in the Categories column for Liam Allard.
6. Select the current text and type **Favorites**.
7. Press Enter. The new category information is saved and the record moves to the Favorites category.
8. Double-click the icon on the far left of the line containing the record for Mary Jones. The Contact form opens.
9. Click the Details tab, shown in the following illustration.
10. In the *Profession* box, type **Anthropologist**.
11. Click the Save and Close button on the toolbar.

   You can edit and add information for any contact easily using columns shown in the various views for contacts, or by opening the contact form.

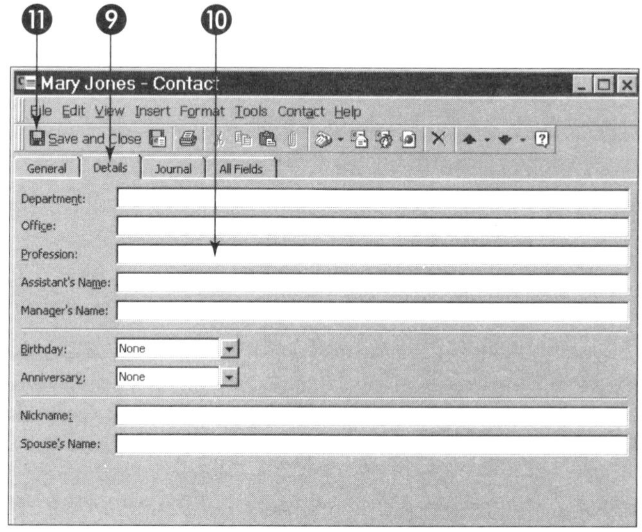

WORKING WITH CONTACTS

Once you've built your contact list using the above procedures, you can save yourself time and effort in communicating with those contacts using several features of Outlook. You can use the contact list to streamline inviting attendees to a meeting, send a letter to a contact letting Outlook enter the address information, and even let Outlook dial the phone number for you.

Planning a meeting

Once you have contacts in Outlook, you can use that information to plan meetings with them. You do this by creating a meeting appointment.

1. Select Calendar in the Outlook bar.
2. Click the New Appointment button. The Appointment form opens.
3. Select the Meeting Planner tab.
4. Click the Invite Others button.

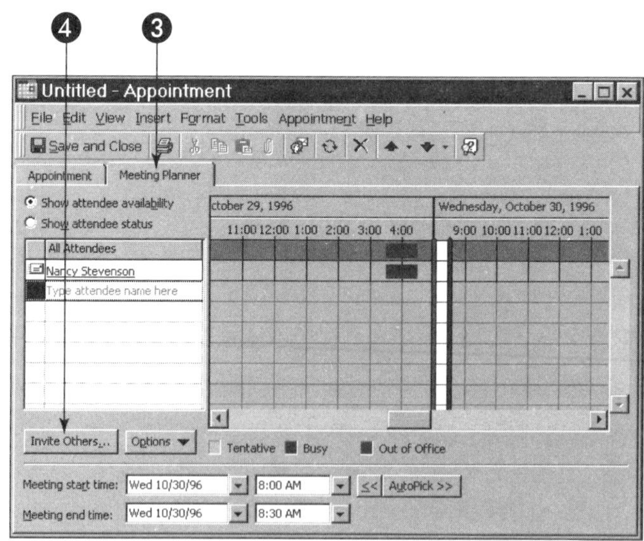

The Select Attendees and Resources dialog box appears with the two contacts for whom you entered e-mail addresses. With Contacts selected in the drop-down list at the top of this dialog box, any contacts you created with an e-mail address will display here. You can also type other invitees in here if you wish, but having the names already in the Contacts area saves you time and possible mistakes made when entering new address information.

5. Select Liam Allard.
6. Click Required to place his name in the corresponding field, indicating that his presence at the meeting is mandatory.
7. Select Mary Jones.
8. Click Optional; her name appears in the Optional field.
9. Click OK. The updated Meeting Planner tab appears with all invitees listed.
10. Set the meeting start time for 4:00 p.m. and leave the default end time of 4:30 p.m.

    My display, shown in the illustration to the right, contains an appointment at 2:00 p.m. on the 29th and says that I'm out of the office all day the next day, because I completed those entries in the previous lesson. Depending on when you went through the previous lesson, you may or may not have other obligations noted on the Meeting Planner tab for the current day. The meeting selection bar with a red and green line on either side in the date display area represents the timing of the meeting.

11. Place your cursor on the right side of the meeting selection bar (on the red line) until your cursor turns into a two-way arrow.
12. Click and drag the column one space to the left. This has changed the length of the meeting, and that is reflected in the new Meeting end time of 5:00 p.m.
13. If you wish to send invitations to the meeting, click Send at this point. For now, close the Meeting form without saving your entries.

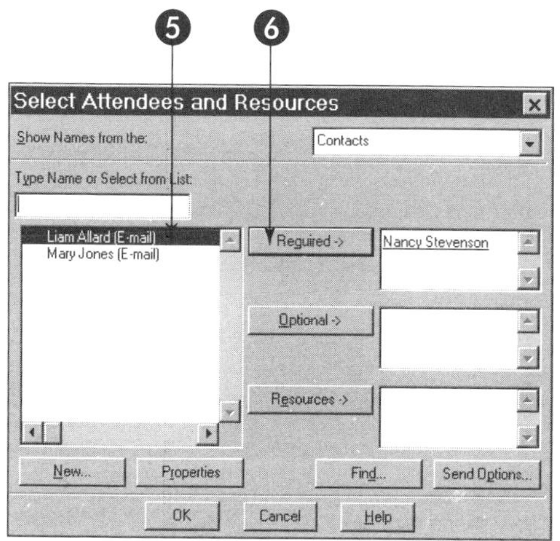

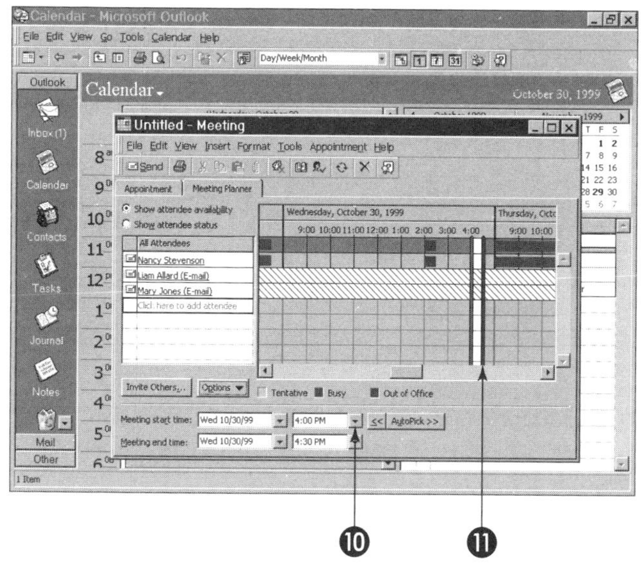

If Outlook has access to the other people's schedules, for example, through your company network, you can use the Autopick button to let Outlook find the next block of open time for all attendees and suggest a meeting time.

Sending a letter to a contact

Meetings don't always suffice: Sometimes you want things in print. When you need to create a letter to one of your contacts, let Outlook work with Word to do it for you.

1. Select Contacts in the Outlook bar.
2. Select Mary Jones' record by clicking on it.
3. Select Contact ➢ New Letter to Contact. Microsoft Word opens in a window within Outlook, and the Letter Wizard appears.
4. Click the *Date line* check box to automatically include a date formatted like the date in the drop-down list to the right of the check box.
5. In the *Choose a page design* drop-down list, select Contemporary Letter. A preview of the letter style appears.
6. Click Next to proceed to the second step of Letter Wizard. Mary Jones' contact information has already been entered for you.
7. Click the *Informal* radio button in the Salutation area of this dialog box.
8. Click next.
9. When the third dialog box of the Letter Wizard appears, offering some variations on cc: addresses and references, click Next to proceed without making any changes.
10. In the fourth dialog box of the Letter Wizard, type your name in the *Sender's name* box.

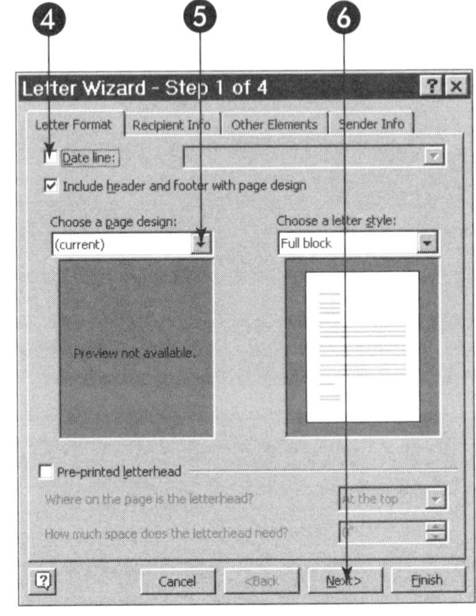

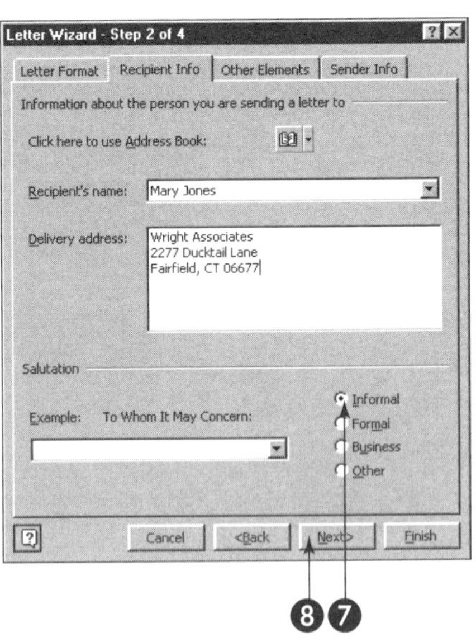

⓫ Enter your address in the *Return address* box.

⓬ From the *Complimentary closing* drop-down list, select Best regards.

⓭ Click the Finish button to create your letter.

The Office Assistant appears, asking if you'd like to rerun the wizard or proceed with entering text for the letter. A placeholder for text is highlighted in your letter. At this point you could continue to enter text for a letter, and save or print it. For now, close the letter without saving it.

⓮ Close the Office Assistant, and then close Word without saving any changes.

Using Phone Dialer

Remember the old days, when people actually dialed the phone themselves? This has become a seriously old fashioned thing to do, especially when Outlook not only dials the number for you, but also helps you record what takes place during the call.

❶ Select Arnie Green's record.

❷ Click the Auto Dialer button on the toolbar. The New Call dialog box appears, with Arnie's name and phone number already entered.

❸ Click the *Create new Journal Entry when starting new call* check box.

❹ Click the Dialing Properties button. The Dialing Properties dialog box appears.

❺ Verify that all the entries for your phone access are correct, and then click OK.

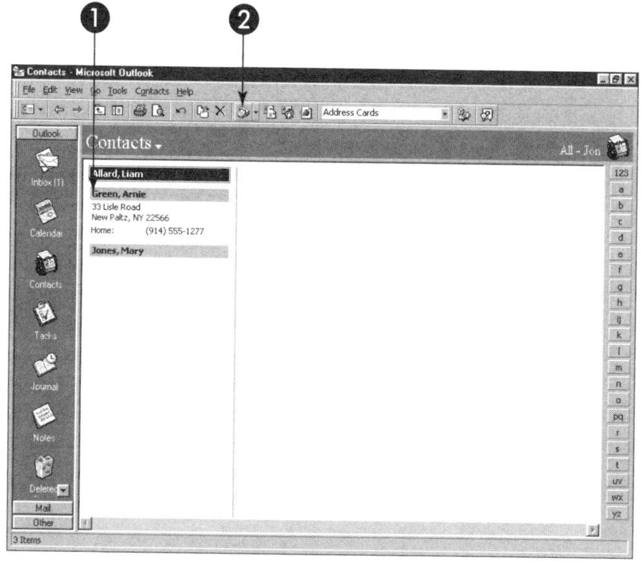

Your default location listed here is your computer's location and the phone line it's connected to. If you need to connect a phone to your computer, check your computer's documentation for instructions.

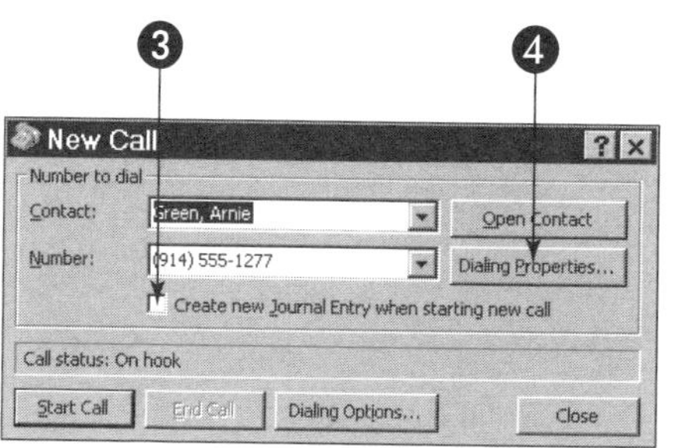

6. In the New Call dialog box, click the Dialing Options button.

   The Dialing Options dialog box in the illustration to the right appears. You can enter information here for speed dialing.

7. Choose OK to return to the New Call dialog box.

8. Click Start Call to place the call.

9. As soon as the call begins to connect, click End Call.

   If the call connects, a Journal Entry dialog box appears at this point.

10. Close the New Call dialog box. The Phone Call Journal Entry form appears now, as shown in the illustration to the right.

    You use this form to enter details of the conversation, or run a timer to record the length of the call. This is especially handy for those who bill by the hour, such as lawyers.

11. Click Save and Close.

12. Select Journal in the Outlook bar.

13. Click the + icon next to the Phone call entry type. Your call to Arnie has been noted.

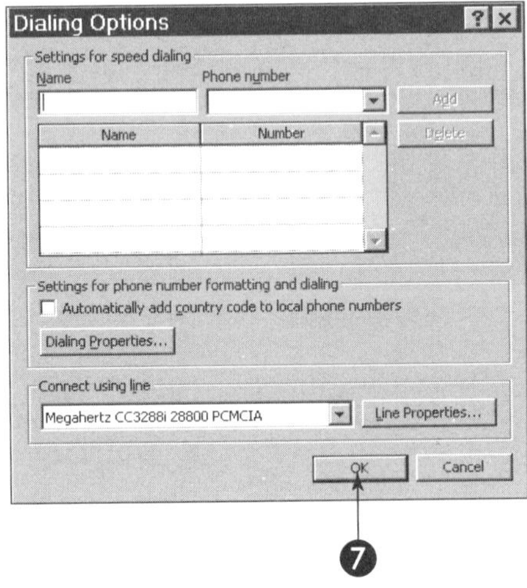

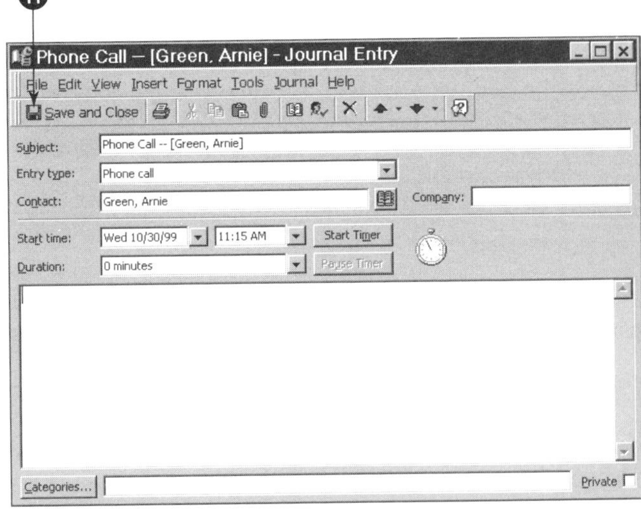

SKILLS CHALLENGE: ADDING TO OUTLOOK

To get more practice with Outlook's contact features, work through this exercise to add and use more contact information.

1. Add yourself, your doctor, and your best friend to the Contacts.

2. From the By Category view, assign all these records to the Personal Category.

3. E-mail an invitation to yourself to attend a two-hour meeting next Wednesday at 3:00 p.m. (If you have any problem with e-mail, don't worry; you cover it in more detail in Lesson 22; for now, just move on to the next step).

Name two ways to set the length of a meeting in Meeting Planner.

4. Place a phone call to your best friend using the AutoDialer.
5. Time your phone call, and write a comment about what was discussed in the Journal Entry.
6. Look up the Journal Entry for your phone call.

Name two ways to go to the Journal area of Outlook.

7. Add birthday and anniversary details to contact records about yourself and your best friend.
8. Write a letter to your doctor using the Contacts ➢ New Letter to Contact command.
9. Create a contact record for your doctor's receptionist using the same address information.

What's the shortcut for performing the preceding step?

TRY OUT THE

INTERACTIVE TUTORIALS

ON YOUR CD!

TROUBLESHOOTING

You've mastered the second major function of Outlook — contact management. However, as you use these features, you may run into some questions. Table 19-1 offers some helpful advice.

Wrap up

Problem	Solution
I've entered several dozen contacts and I can't easily find the one for Dr. Smith.	Click the letter *S* on the tabs that run along the right side of the Contacts Address Card view, or use your scroll bars to display more contacts.
How can I locate someone whose company I remember but whose name I forgot?	You can display the By Company view, or use the Find Item feature.
I want to keep my insurance agent's record by her profession rather than her last name.	In the *File as* box, change the default Last Name, First Name option to the words *Insurance Agent*.

WRAP UP

In this lesson, you covered many of the features Outlook offers to organize and work with contact information. You learned the following:

- Creating records for contacts and making changes to those contacts both in various views and in the Contact form
- Reviewing Journal Entries for contact-related activity
- Using contact information to send letters, make phone calls, and plan a meeting.

In Lesson 20, you explore the third major area of Outlook functionality — e-mail.

LESSON 20

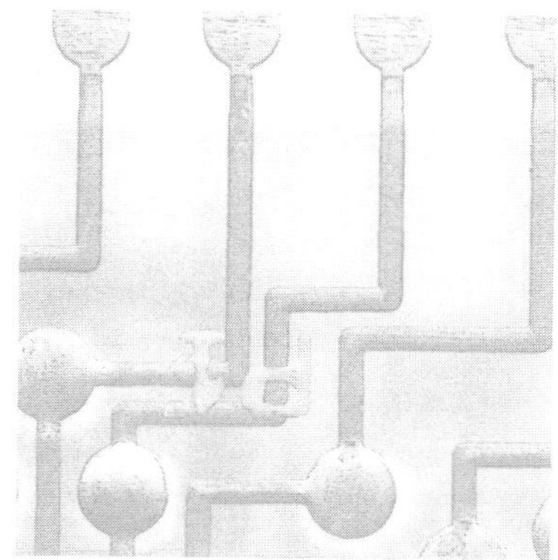

Managing E-mail

GOALS

In this lesson, you learn to connect to the world! Outlook provides features that connect you to your e-mail program so you can send, receive, and manage mail. You'll learn about the following:

- Adding a service
- Connecting to your service
- Composing a message
- Receiving mail
- Replying to mail

Adding a service

GET READY

For this lesson, you must have an e-mail account set up properly on your computer. You also need the following information about your online account: dial-up access number, mail server, mail account name, and password.

MAKING THE E-MAIL CONNECTION

Why should you connect with your e-mail through Outlook instead of through the software provided by your online service? Yes, Outlook has a friendly interface and useful mail management tools, but the main reason to use it is its integration with Office. To truly take advantage of the way Office products connect by using features such as the Outlook journal or applets, you need to work in the Office environment most of your day. Being able to do *everything* there, including making your online connections, offers the convenience of a one-stop shopping trip. If you have more than one online service, the ability to access them both from Outlook makes life even easier.

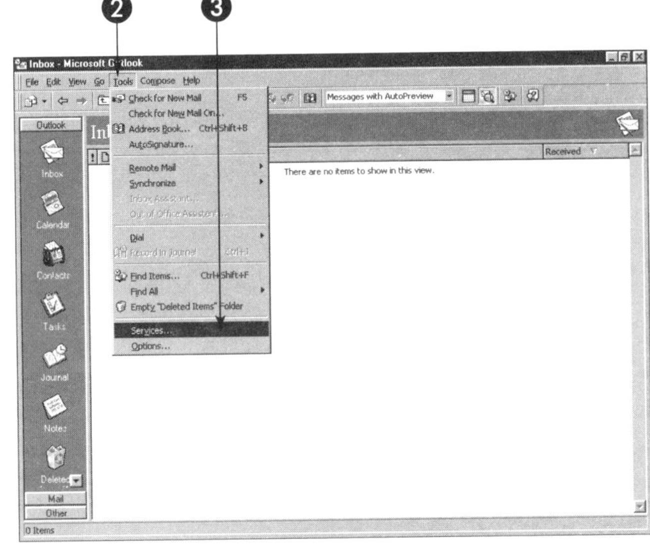

Adding a service

The first step toward sending and receiving mail is to set up your e-mail service in Outlook, whether you use Microsoft's MSN, or an Internet service provider.

1. Open Outlook.
2. Click the Tools menu.
3. Select Services.

   The Services dialog box appears. Make sure the Services tab is active. The Services tab has features that enable you to add or remove online services from Outlook, or to see the properties of services already added.
4. Click Add. The Add Service to Profile dialog box appears.
5. Double-click Internet Mail. The Internet Mail dialog box opens.

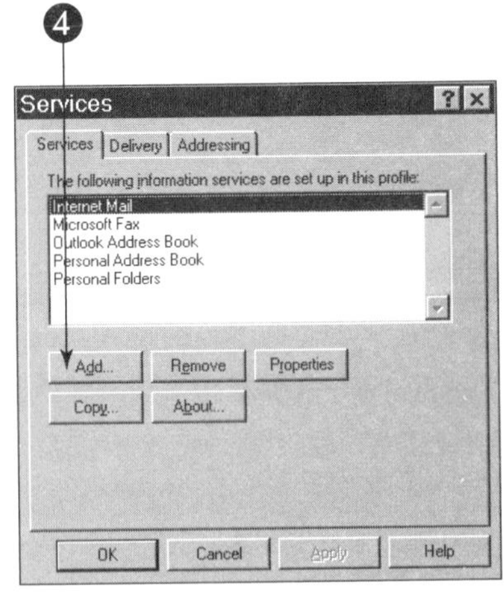

6. Enter your name, e-mail address, mail server, account name, and password. You can get this information from your service provider.
7. Select the Connection tab of the Internet Mail dialog box.
8. Select either the first or second option button, depending on whether you connect with the Internet through your company network or a local modem in your computer.
9. If your connection isn't listed in the drop-down list beneath these option buttons, click Add Entry. (If it is listed, select it and move to Step 14.)
10. In the Make New Connection dialog box, type a name for your provider connection.
11. Click Next to proceed to the next dialog box.
12. Type the dial-up access phone number, given to you by your provider, and verify the area code.
13. Click Next to proceed. The next dialog box verifies the successful creation of a new connection.
14. Click Finish. You return to the Internet Mail dialog box.
15. Choose OK. Two messages appear telling you that the changes won't take effect until the next time you try to log on to Internet Mail, and that you need to exit Outlook.
16. Choose OK for each of the messages above, and then choose OK to exit the Services dialog box.
17. Select File ➢ Exit and Log Off.
18. Restart Outlook.
19. Outlook opens, and connects to the new Internet Mail service that you set up.
20. When you're sure the connection has been made successfully, select Tools ➢ Remote ➢ Mail Disconnect.

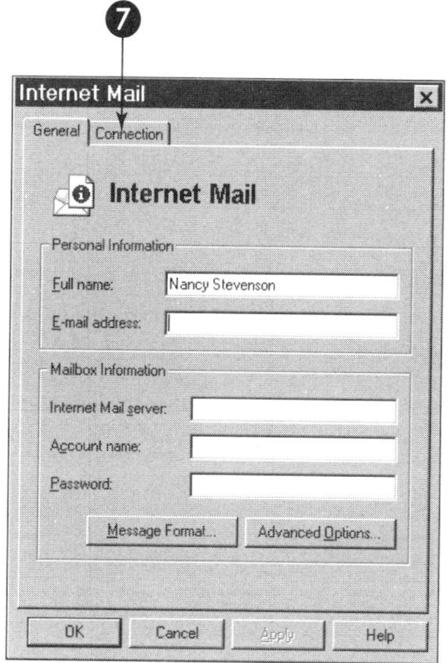

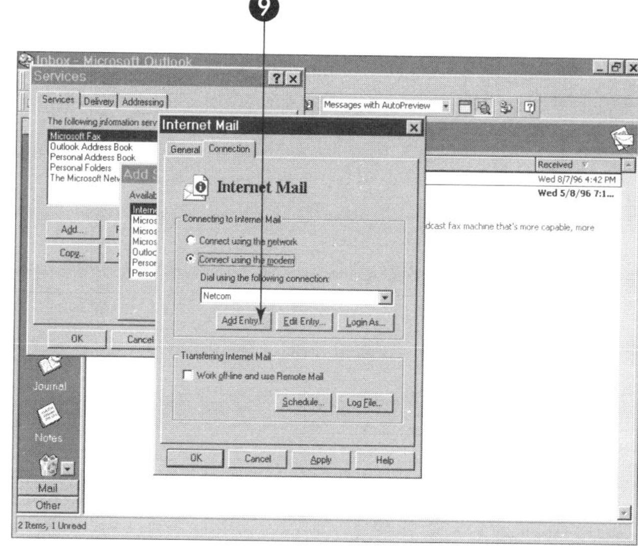

Connecting to your service

If you don't have an online service but would like to connect to one, you can use the Microsoft Network service, which is already installed and listed in the services dialog box. You have to open an account to use the service. To do so, double-click the Microsoft Network icon on your desktop and follow the directions provided.

Connecting to your service

You can set up your e-mail connection using the Tools menu.

1. Select Tools.
2. Choose Remote Mail.
3. Choose Connect.
4. In the Remote Connection Wizard dialog box, place a check in the Internet Mail check box and deselect any services you don't want to check for e-mail, such as the Microsoft Network, if that is not your provider.
5. Choose Next. The second Remote Connection Wizard dialog box appears, as shown in the following illustration.

   You have two choices here: to have Outlook automatically retrieve and send all new mail on connection, or to retrieve only headers of new mail. Because you created a few new messages in the previous lessons that you don't want to send, select to retrieve only messages until the Outbox is cleaned out.
6. Check the option button *Do only the following.*
7. Click the check box for *Retrieve new message headers.*
8. Choose Finish.

   Outlook connects to your service and retrieves any new mail. This may take a minute or two. While it's connecting, you see a message showing the status of the connection.

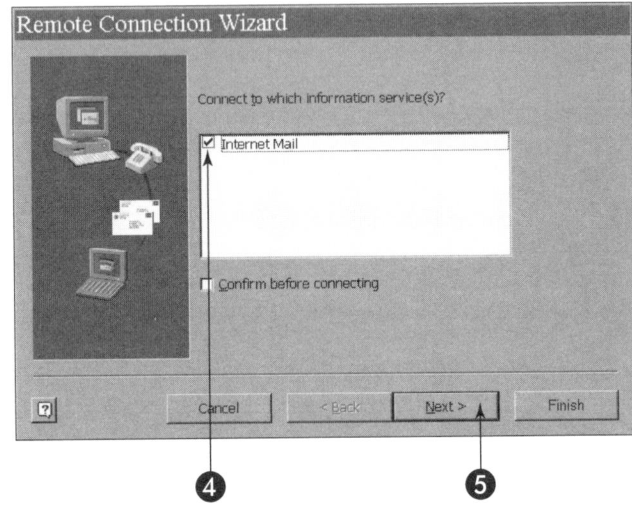

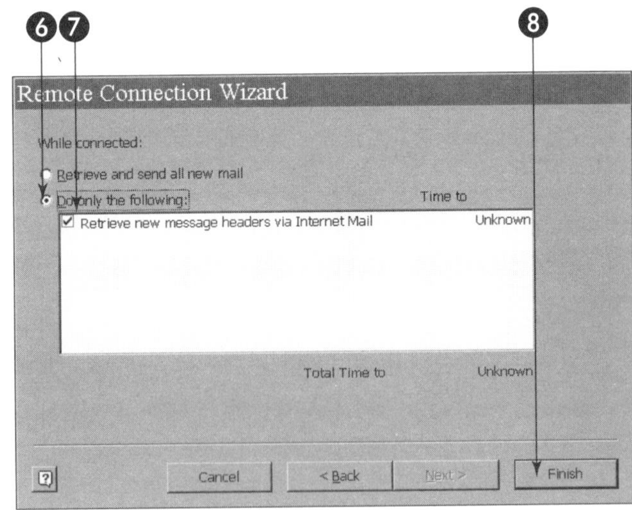

New messages appear in your Inbox, and a note in the lower left-hand corner of the screen indicates how many messages you have and whether any are unread.

Now when you enter Outlook, it automatically connects with your mail account and retrieves any new mail. There are also ways to connect when sending mail, which are discussed in the next section. To try those out, you first have to disconnect from your service. Depending on your service, Outlook may display a connection message with a disconnect button on it. However, you can also use the Tool menu to disconnect.

9 Click Tools.

10 Choose Remote Mail.

11 Select Disconnect.

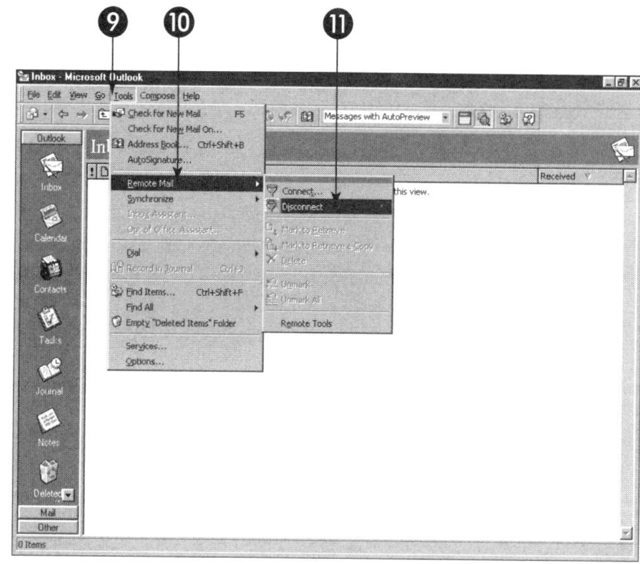

SENDING MAIL

Outlook provides easy-to-use tools for creating mail and sending it via your online account. Outlook also enables you to attach files to your messages. You can manage the delivery of your mail with features that enable you to set delivery for no earlier than a certain date, or track mail with a receipt.

Composing a message

You can easily create a message by filling out Outlook's Message Form and using various options to control how it's sent.

1 Select Compose ➢ New Mail Message. A Message form like the one in the illustration to the right appears (with no addressee or subject filled in at this point).

2 Click the To button. The Select Names dialog box appears, listing the contacts you entered with their e-mail addresses.

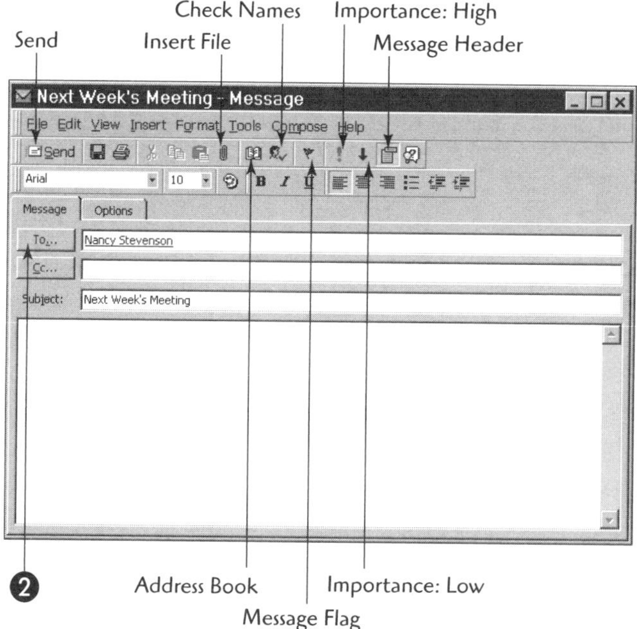

Composing a message

3. Select Mary Jones's name.
4. Click the To button. Mary Jones's name appears under Message Recipients.

   You can use the To, Cc, and Bcc (blind carbon copy) buttons to add addresses for your message. If you have not entered an addressee's name in your Outlook Contacts, you can address this message to the person by clicking the New button in the Select Names dialog box and entering the name and e-mail address.
5. Choose OK to save the addressee and return to the message form.
6. Press Tab twice to move to the *Subject* line.
7. Type **Next Week's Meeting**.
8. Press Enter.
9. Type this message: **Next week's meeting will be held at the Ritz at 3:00 p.m. Thursday.**

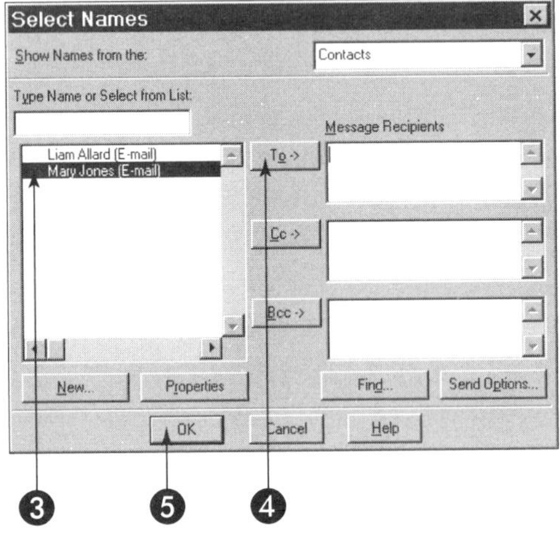

You can use any of the text formatting tools available in this window to change the font and font size, or apply effects such as bold or italic to your message.

10. To set the message's importance, click the Importance: High button on the toolbar.
11. Click the Insert File button. The Insert File dialog box, appears.
12. Select the file Ex2-1 from the accompanying CD-ROM.
13. Choose OK.
14. An icon for the file attachment appears in your mail message window.
15. Click the Message Flag button in the mail message window. The bottom illustration shows the Flag Message dialog box that appears.
16. Click the *Flag* drop-down list and select Call.

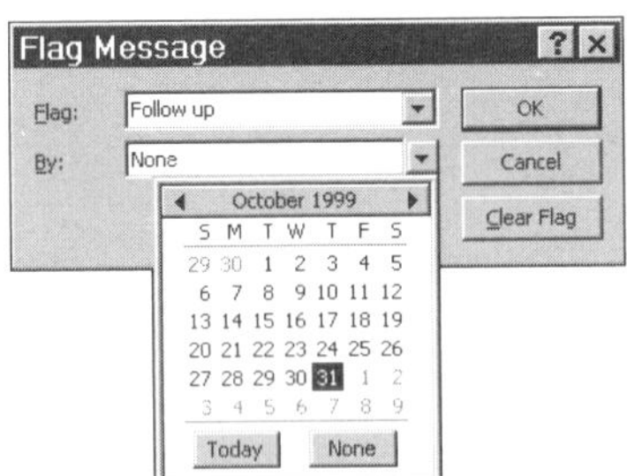

17 Click the *By* drop-down list and select next Wednesday from the calendar.

18 Choose OK.

The message flag feature places a flag symbol in the Flag Status column of the recipient's message list, along with the type of flag, letting the reader know what response or action is appropriate for this message.

TRY OUT THE
INTERACTIVE TUTORIALS
ON YOUR CD!

Managing mail delivery

Just as you can send regular mail certified, first class, or next day delivery, there are several ways to control the delivery of your electronic mail.

1 Select the Options tab of the Message dialog box.

You can use the choices in this dialog box to manage how e-mail is delivered and replied to. The choices include the following:

- *Importance.* Use this drop-down list to set Low, Normal, or High importance to alert your message recipient to the priority of the message.
- *Sensitivity.* This drop-down list enables you to mark the message as Personal, Private, or Confidential.
- *Use voting buttons* places a quick reply button on your message so the recipient can easily respond with an Approve/Reject or Yes/No/Maybe.
- *Have replies sent to* will set up your message replies to go to someone else; for example to your assistant or spouse.
- *Save sent message to* is where you designate a folder to save copies of all your messages; the default is Sent Items.

2 Under Delivery Options, click the *Do not deliver before* check box.

3 Use the drop-down list next to this check box to select tomorrow's date. This is handy if you want to compose mail but send it at a later time.

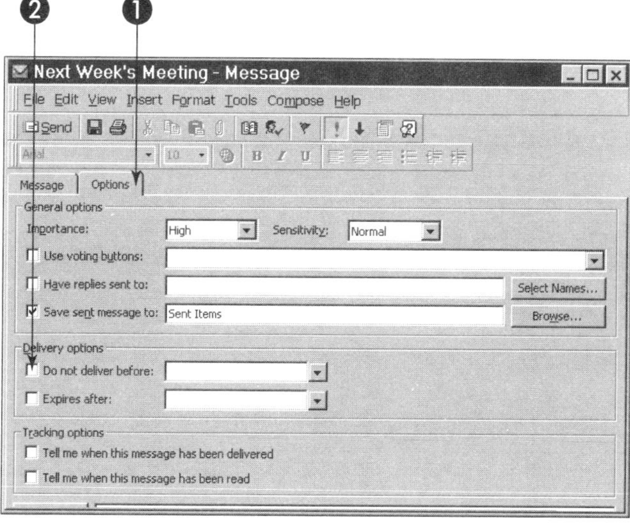

4 Click the check box for *Expires after*, and then select next Thursday's date from the corresponding drop-down list. Once the meeting is over, there's no point in delivering e-mails alerting people to its location.

5 Under Tracking Options, click the second check box to be notified when the message has been read.

NOTE

It can take time from when a mail server accepts a message for delivery and when it is actually received or read. Remember that a delivery receipt is no guarantee that your message has been read.

6 Click the Send button to deliver the message. Outlook places the message in your Outbox.

7 Select Go ➢ Outbox. Your message is listed there, as shown in the bottom illustration.

Notice the various symbols on the message header, including the exclamation point for high importance, the red flag indicating the appropriate response and the paper clip which symbolizes the attached file. The next time you connect with your online service all the messages in the Outbox will automatically be sent.

8 Select Tools ➢ Check for New Mail. Your new message will be sent and any new messages will be delivered to your Inbox.

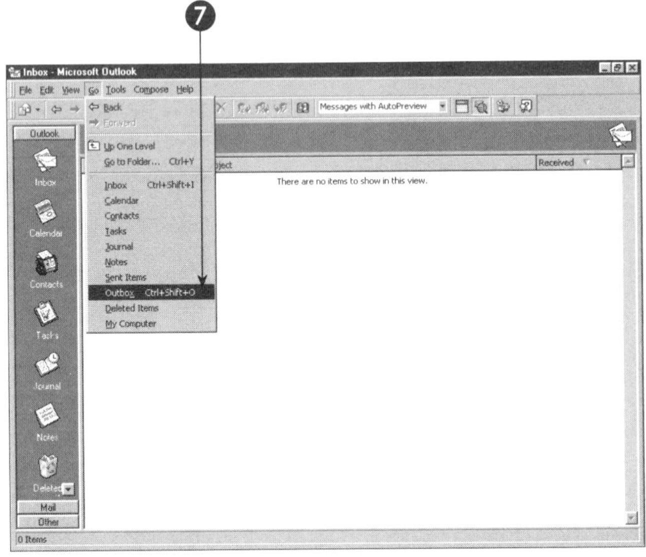

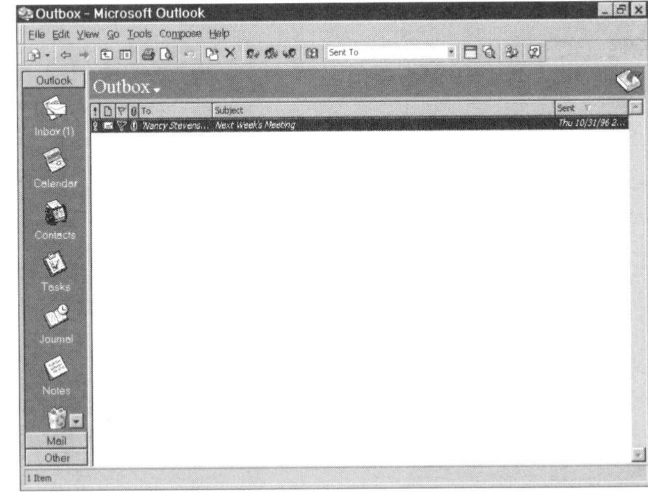

RECEIVING MAIL

Receiving your mail and replying to your correspondents is simple with Outlook. When you first start Outlook, your Inbox is displayed. Outlook connects and retrieves any unread mail. To look for new mail at some later point in your Outlook session, you can select Tools ➢ Check for New Mail. You may have to wait several minutes or even a few hours for the message you just sent yourself to be delivered to you.

Reading messages

You won't just send mail from Outlook, you'll get very popular online and receive a lot of mail, as well. Here's how to read electronic junk (and other) mail.

1. Wait for your message to be delivered, and then select Tools ➢ Check for New Mail.

   Outlook takes a moment to connect and retrieve new mail. When it finishes, it displays new mail headers in your Inbox, as in the following illustration.

   The symbol to the left of messages that looks like an envelope tells you if a message has been read (in which case the envelope flap is open) or is still unread (in which case the envelope is closed). The date the message was received is noted next to the subject line. By default, the most recent messages will be at the top of the list. You can sort messages by clicking the various heading buttons; for example, click From to sort by sender or Received to sort by receipt date.

2. Open your message by double-clicking it. The full message appears.

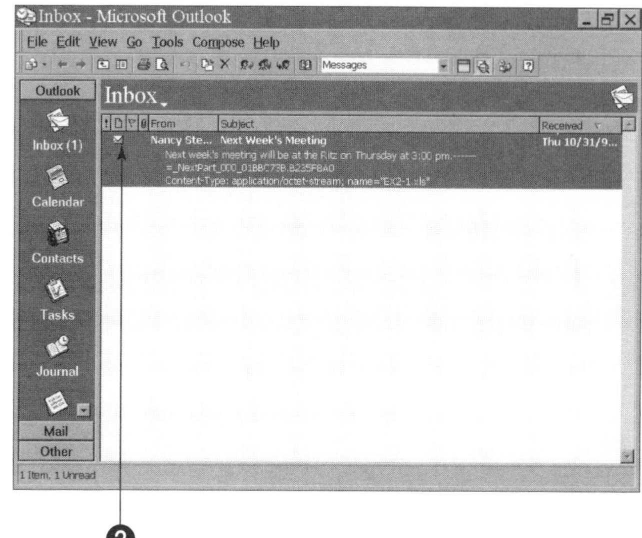

If illegible "garbage" text comes through with a message, you probably have received a file attachment that wasn't properly decoded. To get at this kind of attachment, you have to save it by selecting File ➢ Save Attachment, and then select a destination for the saved file in the Save Attachment dialog box that appears. You can use a program such as WinCode or Xfer Pro to decode the file. These programs are simple to use (you usually just select a Decode command from a menu, and then name the file to decode) and many are available as shareware that you can download from the Internet.

Replying to e-mail

You can use the scroll bar next to the message window to read more of a message. The Previous Item and Next item tools are useful if you have several mail messages to read. These buttons allow you to move among several messages without having to close the message window between each one.

Replying to e-mail

The three buttons on the left of the toolbar in the message window enable you to take action on your messages. You can use them to reply to the sender, reply to all the addressees of the message and the sender, or forward the message to someone else.

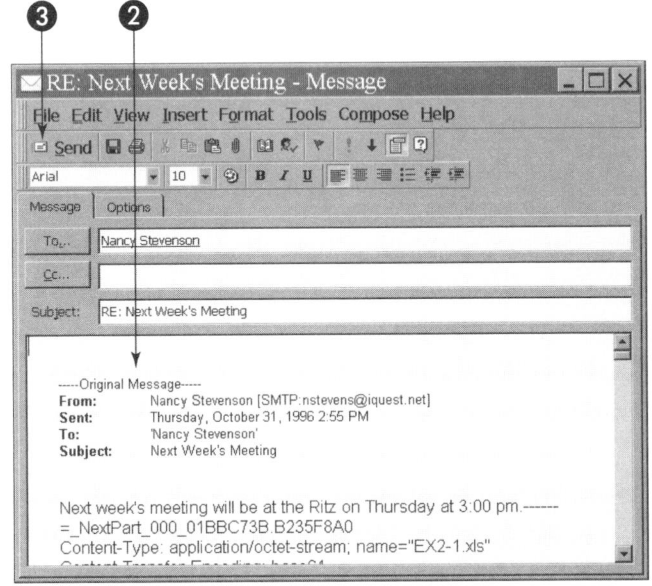

1. Click the Reply tool. The Reply message form appears with the sender's address filled in and the text of the original message beneath your cursor.

2. Type Thanks for the reminder. See you there.

   Once again, you can use the many formatting tools, as well as the flag and importance buttons on the toolbars, to format and set delivery options for the reply.

3. Click Send to send the reply to the message.

   The *Reply to all* option works the same as Reply, except it sends your reply to everyone who received the message. If you prefer to copy just some of the other recipients, or others who never received the original message, in your reply, choose the Reply button and use the To button on the reply message form to select additional addressees.

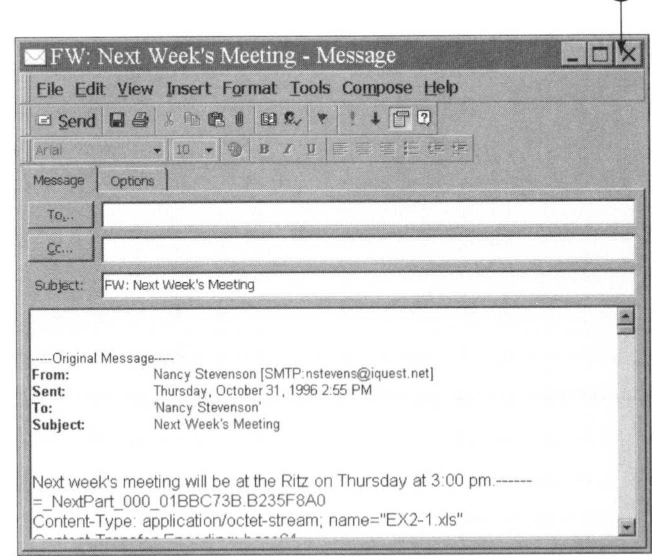

4. Click the Forward button. The Forward Message dialog box appears.

   The Forward message form is similar to the Reply and Reply to all forms, except that no recipients have been filled in for you. You must use the To button to add addressees.

5. Close the message form.

   At this point, you could save the message or its attachment to any folder on your hard drive, or a floppy disk. You simply select

File ➢ Save or File ➢ Save Attachment. You can also move the message to a folder in Outlook.

6 Click the Move to Folder button on the toolbar of the original message window.

7 Select Move to Folder. The Move Item to dialog box, shown in the illustration to the right, appears.

8 Click New to create your own folder for the file.

9 Type the folder name **My correspondence** in the Create New Folder dialog box that appears.

10 Choose OK, and then OK again to close the dialog box.

If you ever want to retrieve the message, you find it by clicking the Folder List button on the toolbar and selecting it from the appropriate folder.

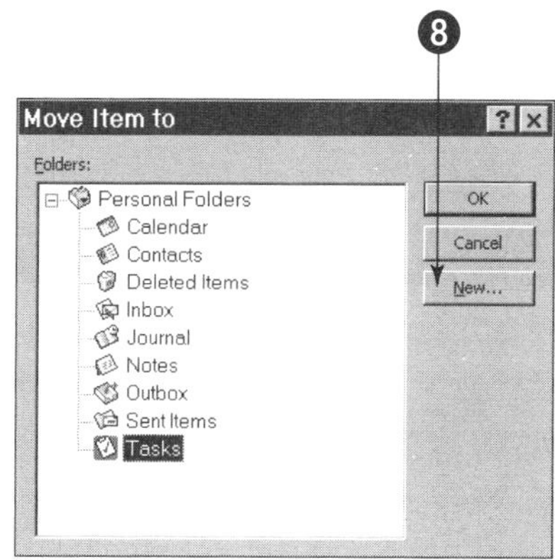

SKILLS CHALLENGE: BECOMING AN E-MAIL EXPERT

It takes practice to become an e-mail expert. Get some practice by working through the following steps.

1 Create a mail message to three of your friends or co-workers whose e-mail addresses you know.

How do you place names and e-mail addresses in your system so they're available to you in the Select Names dialog box?

2 Make one person the recipient, one the Cc:, and one the Bcc:.

3 Set the message to be delivered no earlier than next Monday.

4 Set the Tracking Options to send you a notice when the message has been delivered.

5 Make the importance of the message low.

Name two ways to determine the importance of the message.

Skills challenge

6. Send the message.
7. From Outlook, retrieve any e-mail you may have. If you have none, send yourself a few messages to practice with.
8. View your e-mail by the date received.
9. Move one e-mail to a folder, creating a new folder for it in your Inbox.
10. Reply to a message using High importance for its priority.

Where do you set a message to be confidential?

11. Perform a Find Item search for messages with the words Next week in the subject field. (You should find the first one you sent to yourself with the subject *Next Week's Meeting*).
12. Display the Personal Folders list and locate the e-mail you saved to the My Correspondence folder.
13. Delete the e-mail.
14. Send a message to two other friends asking them to vote on an issue and send their replies to a third friend (Of course, you should let the third friend in on this one!).

TROUBLESHOOTING

The Outlook e-mail feature can be a wonderful way to manage your communications with the world, but it can also bring up questions. Table 20-1 lists a few of the problems you might encounter, with suggested solutions.

Problem	Solution
I just got back from a trip and have 30 messages; how do I find the ones where people flagged me to call them easily?	Change the view of your Inbox using your Current View drop-down list on the toolbar to By Message Flag. Messages will be grouped by the type of flag attached.
My company requires that I sign all e-mail with my name, company, e-mail address, fax number, phone number, and company slogan. Is there a way to save me time entering all that?	Try the AutoSignature feature. Select Tools ➢ AutoSignature. Enter all that stuff once, and select Add this signature to the end of new messages, and then choose OK. Each time you send a message this ending will be added.
How do I get rid of messages without reading them (I get a lot of junk e-mail).	Just select the message in the list in your Inbox and click the Delete tool. It's gone!

WRAP UP

You mastered the basics of surfing the world of online e-mail using Outlook, including the following skills:

- Setting up Outlook to access your account
- Composing and adding attachments, and setting delivery options for your messages
- Retrieving, replying to or forwarding, and filing new message

In Lesson 21, you begin learning about Access and how it helps you manage large amounts of information with ease.

PART VI

Access for Windows

This part introduces you to Access for Windows, Office 97's database program. It includes the following lessons:

- Lesson 21: Exploring the Access Environment
- Lesson 22: Looking at Tables and Forms
- Lesson 23: Getting Information Out of Your Database

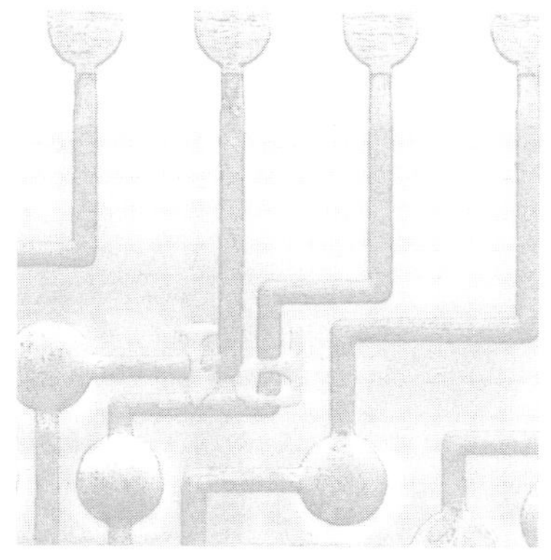

Exploring the Access Environment

GOALS

This lesson introduces you to Access for Windows, Microsoft Office 97's database program. Access helps you to manage data by enabling you to enter, sort, organize, and retrieve that data in a variety of ways. In this lesson, you learn about the following:

- Using the Database Wizard
- Looking at forms
- Displaying a table
- Changing views
- Adding a record
- Moving between records

Get ready

GET READY

For this lesson, you need the file NORTHWIND, which you copied to you hard drive from the accompanying CD-ROM.

TRY OUT THE
INTERACTIVE TUTORIALS
ON YOUR CD!

HOW DATABASES WORK

A database is a program for storing and manipulating data. Data can be names and addresses; it can be dates, dollars, or design specs. In fact, data can be any kind of information. The idea behind a database is that you can organize a set of data in some way and get at that information easily.

Think of the yellow pages — the data set consists of business name, category of business, address, and phone number. The records in that data set are organized first by a category, such as Restaurant, and then alphabetically by the business name. However, you often also find a section of the white pages that takes that same data and organizes it alphabetically by business name so you can look up a company when you're not sure exactly how to categorize its business.

Databases require that you enter all the data once in what is called a *table*. Once the data is in a table, you can organize the same information in different ways so you can find what you need or emphasize one type of information over another. The same table of data can be the basis for a customer order form, merchant sales record, and billing form. The customer, salesperson, item ordered, number of items ordered, and cost may all be included in this data set, but the customer form shows a record of one customer's purchasing history, the sales record provides a total of all sales by quarter or year for that salesperson, and the billing form enables accounting to generate customer invoices every month — all from the same set of data!

You can produce a variety of reports from the table of data or print individual data forms. You can do this because Access enables you to sort data, search data by different criteria, and design reports that show the information you need in the format you want.

VISUAL BONUS: TABLES, FORMS, AND REPORTS

The following Visual Bonus gives you an idea of how the different pieces of Access come together.

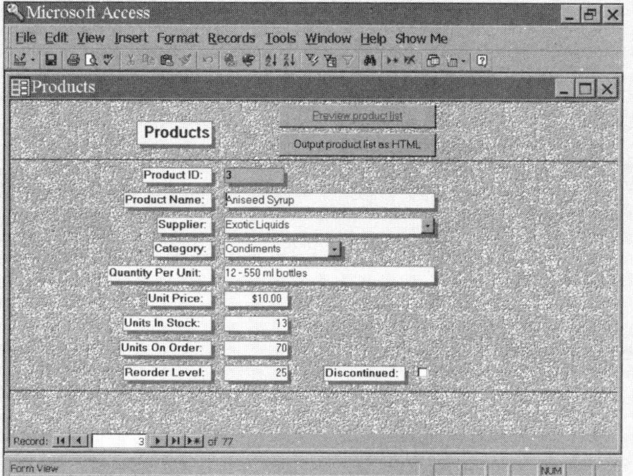

Forms are designed to enable easy data entry.

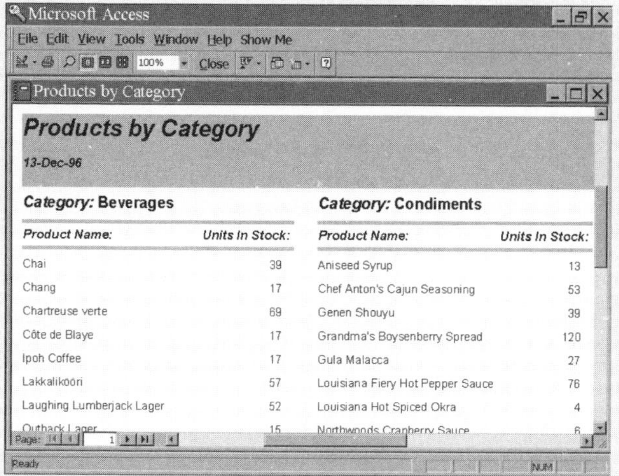

A report can be generated using what is called a query to focus on different aspects of the data.

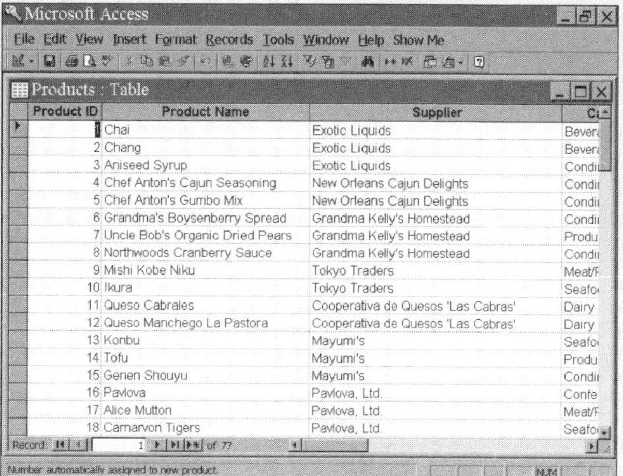

The table is the basis of all the database functions.

Opening a file

YOUR FIRST LOOK AT ACCESS

In truth, Access is a remarkably robust software that can be customized and programmed by computer whiz kids to do very complex things. However, coexisting with this highly technical capability is a database program that is relatively simple to use. In this and the following two lessons, you explore the most user-friendly features of Access: tables, forms, and reports.

Opening a file

You can open an Access file in several ways.

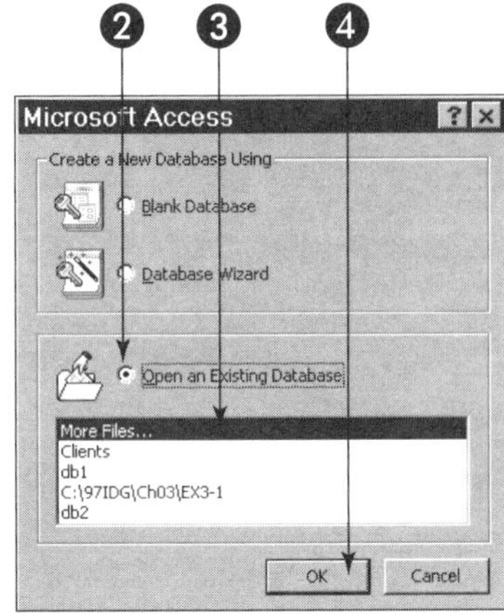

1. Open Access from the Windows Taskbar. The Microsoft Access dialog box appears, as shown in the illustration to the right.

   At this point you have three choices: to open a blank database, to use the Database Wizard, or to open an existing database. Choosing the Database Wizard enables you to open a file based on a database template, which appears with tables and forms already created for you. To create a database that has no predefined contents, you create a blank database.

   In the lower portion of the dialog box is a list of the last files used. If you want to open an existing database and the file you need is listed here, you can select it from that list at this point. If it isn't, you can select More Files to locate the file.

2. Click the *Open an Existing Database* option button.
3. Select More Files.
4. Choose OK.
5. From the Open dialog box that appears, locate the file NORTHWIND from the accompanying CD-ROM and choose OK to open it.

   The window that appears looks like the one in the illustration at the top of the next page. Under the tabs in this window are the various elements that make up an Access database. Several of these elements are already created here for you to explore.

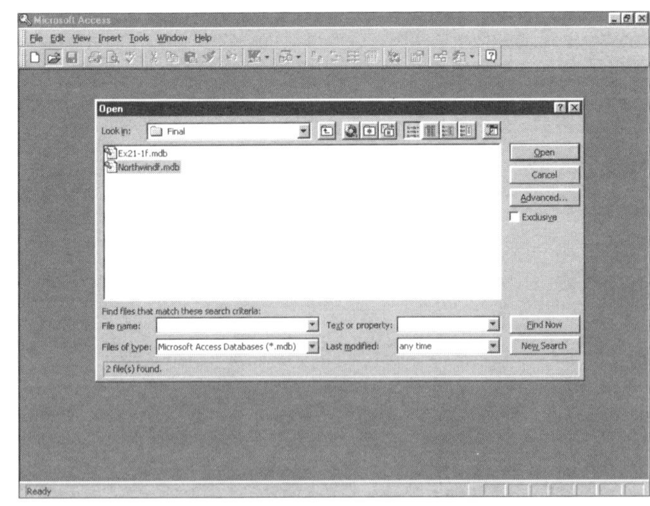

The Show Me menu you see on the Access menu bar is unique to this sample database created by Microsoft — you won't see it in the regular Access screen. You can use it to run demos of various Access features to help you get up to speed.

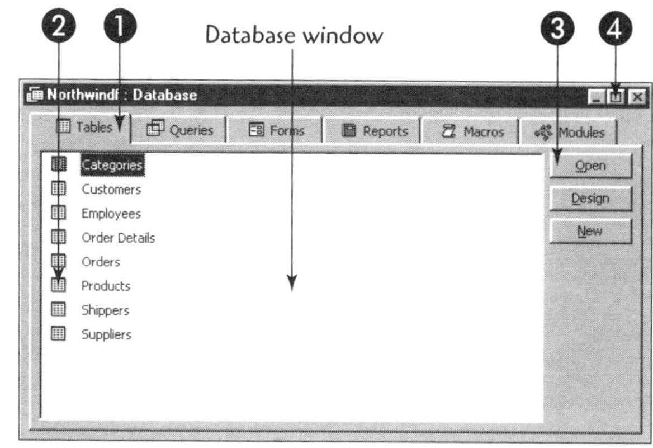

Displaying a table

A table is the basis of an Access file. A table is where the actual data resides; forms and reports displaying different subsets of that data pull the information from the fields in a table.

1. Select the Tables tab if it's not already selected.
2. Select Products from the list of tables.
3. Choose Open to open the table.
4. Click the Maximize button to open the table to full screen view. The window should look like the one in the illustration to the right, which has callouts for some of the tools you'll be using in the Table view.

   A table is a lot like a spreadsheet, with rows and columns of data. At the top of the table are column headings. You can move across the columns using the scroll bar at the bottom of the screen, and down the rows using the vertical scroll bar to the right of the screen.

   A record is contained in each row of this table. A record is one set of data; in this case, one company product and the details about that product. Notice the Record navigation buttons in the lower left-hand corner. These enable you to move from record to record. Try this now.

5. Click the Next Record button. Your cursor moves to the second row of the table.
6. Click the Last Record button. Your cursor moves to the last record, number 77.

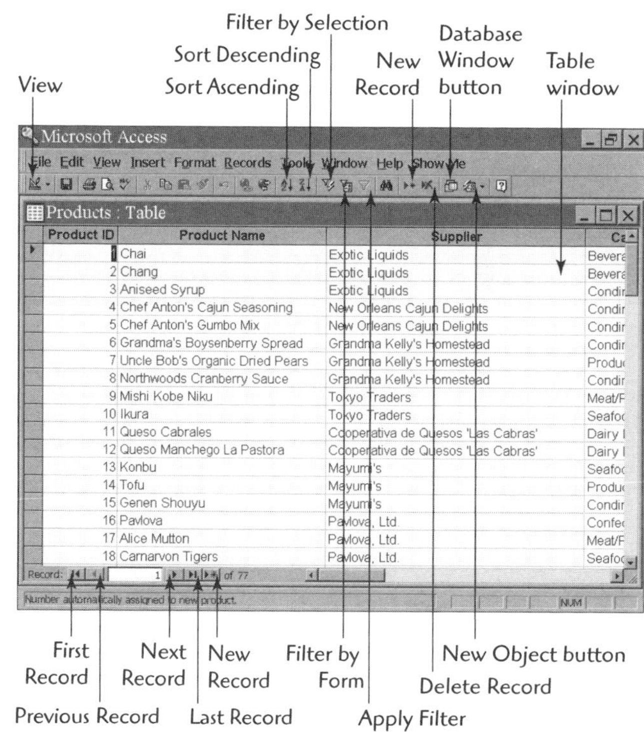

Displaying a table

7. Click the First Record button. Your cursor moves up to the first row, containing the first record of the database.

8. Click the arrow on the right side of the View button and select Design view. You use the form shown in the middle illustration to design the table.

   You learn about designing tables in Lesson 22; for now, notice that the column headings you saw in the table are listed here as field names. A field contains one piece of data. For example, in a database of addresses, the city, state, and ZIP code are fields. Each record in a database contains a separate field for each piece of data.

   The Data Type column shows you the format of each field: in this case, Number, Text, Currency, Yes/No, and AutoNumber. By formatting fields according to the type of data in them, you are able to perform certain operations. For example, an AutoNumber field will automatically place the next number in sequence in this field each time you create a new record. A Yes/No format will force the entry of either Yes or No in that field. A number field can have calculations performed on it; for example, you can program a number field to take the value in a field containing unit price, multiply it times the value in a field containing quantity, and return a value in the number field.

9. Click the Database Window button on the toolbar. The Database window appears.

   While you're looking at this table, take a look at how the table relates to various other tables in this database. In Access, you can create relationships between different tables using matching fields. You can use these matching fields to pull records from more than one table for a report or query. Let's say, for example, you have a customer contact information table and a customer billing table. By relating the two tables (matching a field called CustomerID, for example) you can run a report including the customer name and address from one table and the last billing amount from the second table. Access can match

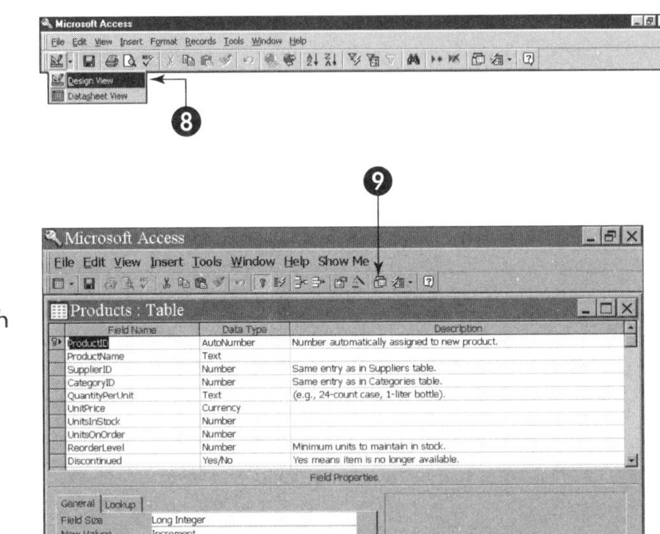

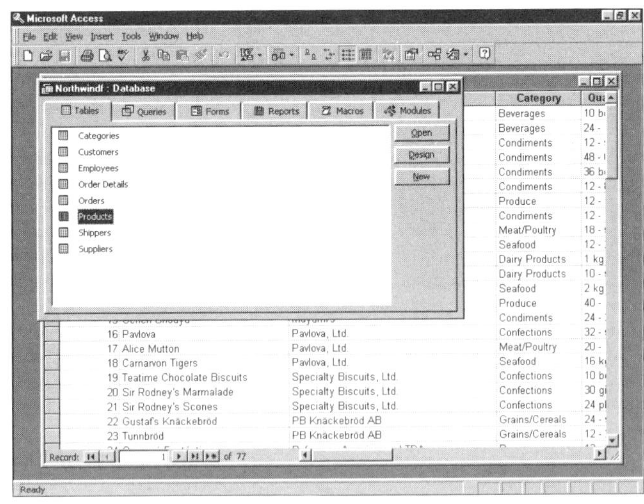

the records from these tables by referring to the CustomerID field in each.

⑩ Click the Tools menu.

⑪ Select Relationships. A window appears showing how many tables have relationships to this table.

⑫ Click the Close button on the Relationships window.

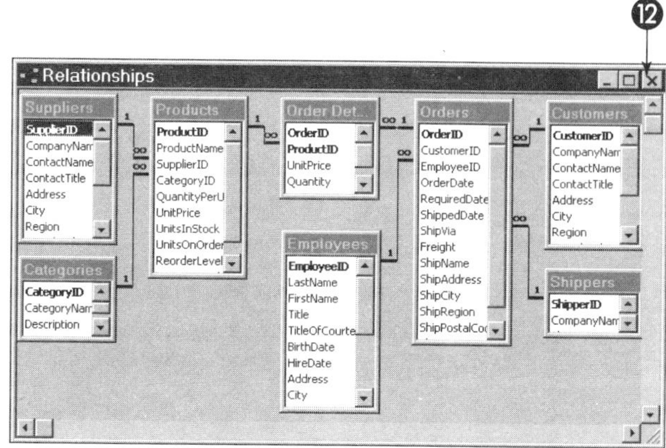

Looking at forms

The second important item in Access to look at is forms. You create a form and associate it with a table of data; and then Access places the information for each record in the table into a separate form.

❶ Select the Forms tab in the Database window.

❷ Select the form called Products, and choose Open. The Products form appears.

The information in this form was taken from one row of the Product table; that is, one record of information. Not all the fields represented by the table column heads are necessarily in all forms based on that table. Once you create a table and a corresponding form, you can either use view to enter or edit the data in each record, or to add new records.

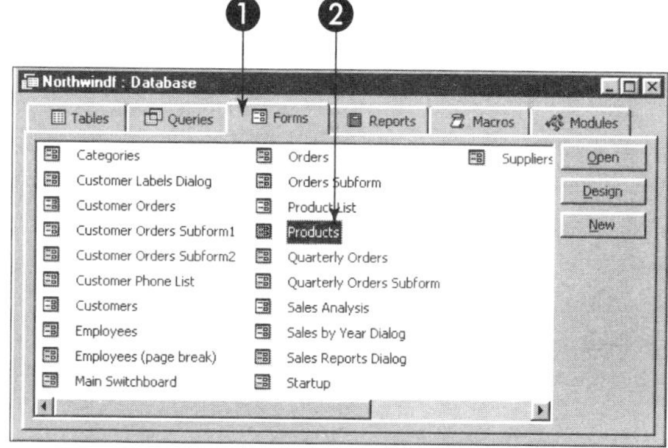

❸ Click the Last Record button at the bottom of the Products form window. The last record appears.

❹ Click the First Record button to return to the first record.

❺ Click the arrow on the right side of the View button on the toolbar.

❻ Select Design View. The Products: Form window appears.

The Form Design view window contains a form header, which is typically the name of the form, and a detail section. The detail section contains field labels on the left and text boxes on the right. The text boxes are where your data will appear.

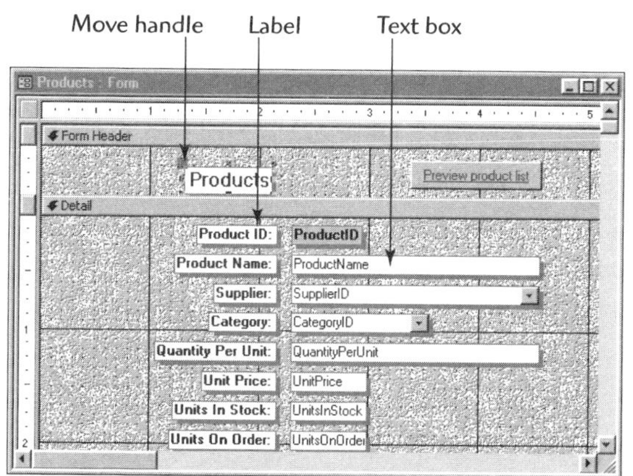

Adding a record

7. Click the arrow on the right side of the View button and select Datasheet View. The accompanying illustration shows the Datasheet view.

   This view resembles the table you saw earlier, minus the lines to separate columns and rows.

8. Click the Close button to close the Datasheet view window.

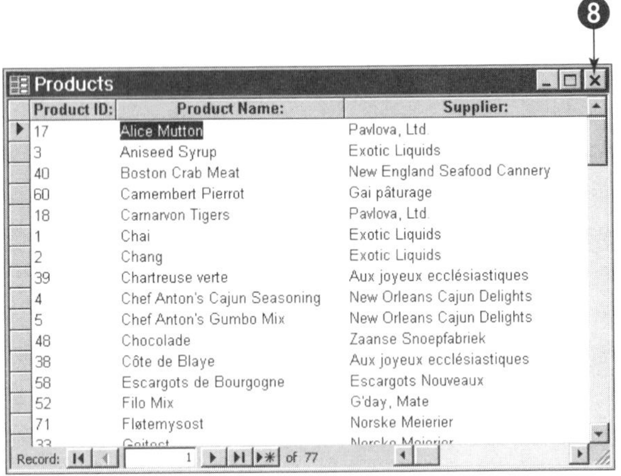

Product ID:	Product Name:	Supplier:
17	Alice Mutton	Pavlova, Ltd
3	Aniseed Syrup	Exotic Liquids
40	Boston Crab Meat	New England Seafood Cannery
60	Camembert Pierrot	Gai pâturage
18	Carnarvon Tigers	Pavlova, Ltd
1	Chai	Exotic Liquids
2	Chang	Exotic Liquids
39	Chartreuse verte	Aux joyeux ecclésiastiques
4	Chef Anton's Cajun Seasoning	New Orleans Cajun Delights
5	Chef Anton's Gumbo Mix	New Orleans Cajun Delights
48	Chocolade	Zaanse Snoepfabriek
38	Côte de Blaye	Aux joyeux ecclésiastiques
58	Escargots de Bourgogne	Escargots Nouveaux
52	Filo Mix	G'day, Mate
71	Fløtemysost	Norske Meierier

WORKING WITH RECORDS

The database you have open has many records already entered, and many forms that have been created to organize that data in different ways. The next two exercises give you practice moving between records and adding new ones.

Adding a record

You build forms based on specific tables. Therefore, you need to build at least the first record in a table before you design a form. After that, records can be added and edited in both tables and forms.

1. Select the Table tab.
2. Double-click the table called Employees. The Employees table appears.
3. Click in the Last Name column, in the first blank cell under the last record.
4. Type **Smith**. Because the Employee ID column is an AutoNumber field, it automatically fills in the next number in sequence for the new record.
5. Press Tab to move to the next column.
6. Type this information in the remaining columns, pressing Tab to move between the columns: **Jane, President, Ms., 10-Feb-54, 09-Oct-79, 22 Willow Way, London**.
7. Close the table window by clicking the Close button.

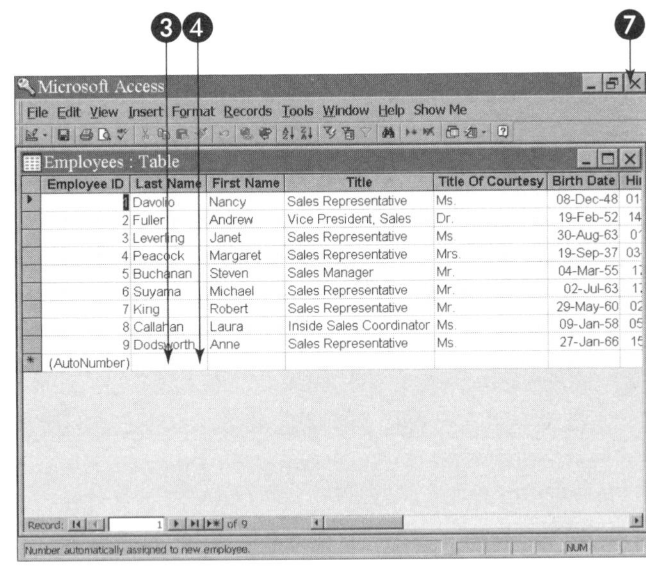

Employee ID	Last Name	First Name	Title	Title Of Courtesy	Birth Date
1	Davolio	Nancy	Sales Representative	Ms.	08-Dec-48
2	Fuller	Andrew	Vice President, Sales	Dr.	19-Feb-52
3	Leverling	Janet	Sales Representative	Ms.	30-Aug-63
4	Peacock	Margaret	Sales Representative	Mrs.	19-Sep-37
5	Buchanan	Steven	Sales Manager	Mr.	04-Mar-55
6	Suyama	Michael	Sales Representative	Mr.	02-Jul-63
7	King	Robert	Sales Representative	Mr.	29-May-60
8	Callahan	Laura	Inside Sales Coordinator	Ms.	09-Jan-58
9	Dodsworth	Anne	Sales Representative	Ms.	27-Jan-66
(AutoNumber)					

8. Select the Forms tab.
9. Select the Employees form and choose Open.
10. Click the Last Record arrow at the bottom of the form. The record you entered in the Employees table has generated this new form.
11. Type **3345** in the Extension field. Your form now looks like the accompanying illustration.
12. Click the New Record button (it's on the far right of the record navigation buttons).
13. Type this information: **John Martin, Marketing Manager**.
14. From the *Reports to* drop-down list, select *Steve Buchanan.*
15. Click the Close button and close the form window.
16. Select the Tables tab and open the Employees table. Notice the new record for John Martin is reflected in the table, as well as the form on which it's based.
17. Use the horizontal scroll bar to move to the last column in the table, Extension. The extension you typed in the Employee form for Jane Smith has also been entered in the table, as well.

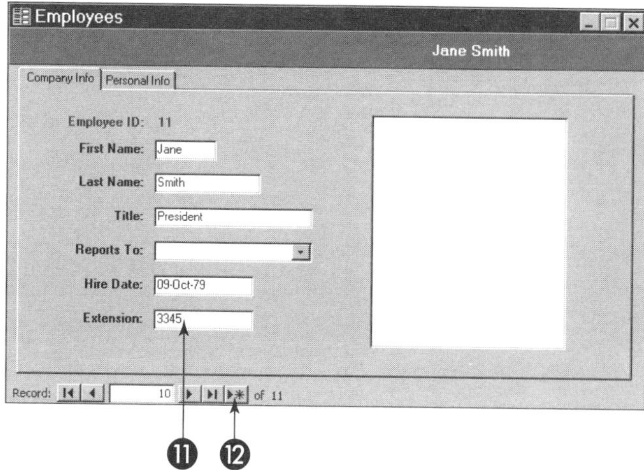

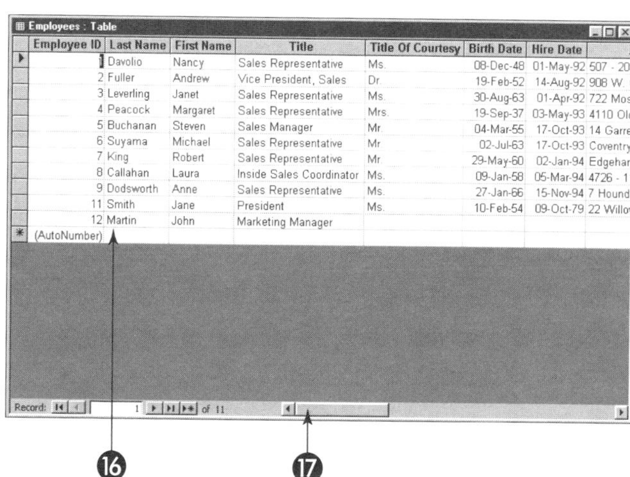

Employee ID	Last Name	First Name	Title	Title Of Courtesy	Birth Date	Hire Date	
1	Davolio	Nancy	Sales Representative	Ms.	08-Dec-48	01-May-92	507 - 20
2	Fuller	Andrew	Vice President, Sales	Dr.	19-Feb-52	14-Aug-92	908 W.
3	Leverling	Janet	Sales Representative	Ms.	30-Aug-63	01-Apr-92	722 Mos
4	Peacock	Margaret	Sales Representative	Mrs.	19-Sep-37	03-May-93	4110 Ol
5	Buchanan	Steven	Sales Manager	Mr.	04-Mar-55	17-Oct-93	14 Garre
6	Suyama	Michael	Sales Representative	Mr.	02-Jul-63	17-Oct-93	Coventry
7	King	Robert	Sales Representative	Mr.	29-May-60	02-Jan-94	Edgehar
8	Callahan	Laura	Inside Sales Coordinator	Ms.	09-Jan-58	05-Mar-94	4726 - 1
9	Dodsworth	Anne	Sales Representative	Ms.	27-Jan-66	15-Nov-94	7 Hound
11	Smith	Jane	President	Ms.	10-Feb-54	09-Oct-79	22 Willo
12	Martin	John	Marketing Manager				
(AutoNumber)							

SKILLS CHALLENGE: WORKING WITH TABLES AND FORMS

Time to practice what you learned in this lesson.

1. Open the table called Orders.
2. Enter a new record with the following information:

   Customer: **Alfreds Futterkiste**
   Employee: **Peacock, Margaret**
   Order date: **July 13, 1999**
   Required date: **August 1, 1999**
   Ship via: **Speedy Express**
   Freight: **$10.00**

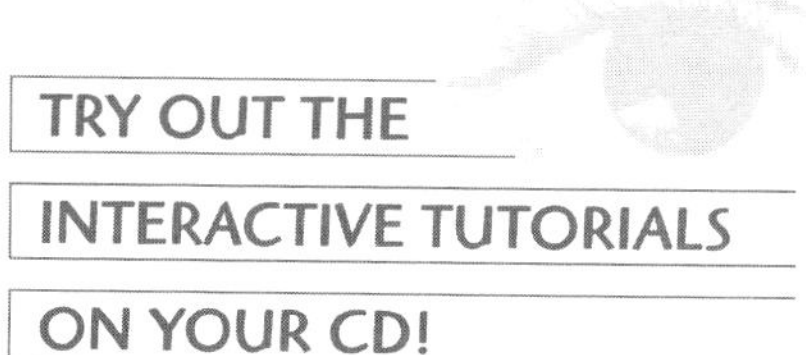

Ship Name: **Alfreds Futterkiste**
Ship Address: **Renstrasse 33**
Ship City: **Berlin**
Ship Country: **Germany**

From which two areas of Access can you enter and edit records?

3. By displaying the design view of this table, identify how many text fields there are (there should be seven).

What does an AutoNumber field do?

4. Display the Forms tab of the database.
5. Open the Orders form.
6. Move to Record 7. This is the record you entered in the Orders table (Order ID 11079).

How can you move quickly to the last record?

7. From the drop-down list, select the *Product Carnarvon Tigers.*
8. Close the Orders form.
9. In the Customer Orders form, go to the first record and locate Order ID 11079 and verify the product ordered was Carnarvon Tigers.
10. Close the file.

TROUBLESHOOTING

This lesson demonstrated a quick overview of the structure and capabilities of Access. This table offers some tips for finding your way around tables and records.

Problem	Solution
I try to create a form, but I get a message that I can't.	You have to have a table of data created before you create forms so you can base the fields of that form on the fields in the table.
I want to save the file, but the Save command isn't available.	Changes you make to a database are automatically saved when you make them. There's no need to save the file.

WRAP UP

In this lesson, you got a brief overview of the tables and forms features of Access, and learned something about the relationship between them. You learned about the following:

- Opening an existing database and moving between its forms and tables
- Entering and editing records in both forms and tables
- Navigating through the records in a particular form
- Displaying design views of forms and tables

In Lesson 22, you use Access wizards to build your own databases.

Looking at Tables and Forms

GOALS

In this lesson, you begin building a simple database. In the process, you learn the following:

- Using Table Wizard
- Naming fields
- Setting data types
- Editing tables
- Establishing a relationship
- Using Form Wizard
- Designing forms
- Looking at form properties

Using Table Wizard

GET READY

You create your own files in this lesson, so you won't need any files from the accompanying CD-ROM.

At the end of these exercises, you'll have a form that looks like the one in the illustration on the facing page.

CREATING A TABLE

You saw in Lesson 19 that tables are the basis of an Access database. Tables are where you store the many pieces of data that make up the database, organized into fields and records. Forms are based on tables, and tables, in turn, enable you to run searches (called *queries*) to produce reports about your data.

Using Table Wizard

For a beginning Access user, the best thing is to use the wizards that Microsoft has built into the product. Using a wizard ensures not only a more polished look to your database elements, but also that all relationships and elements needed to make a database function are dealt with. Start by using the Table Wizard.

1. Open Access.
2. Click the Blank Database radio button.
3. Choose OK to proceed.
4. In the File New Database dialog box, enter the file name **MyMusic**.
5. Choose Create to create the new database. The blank database in the following illustration appears. There are no table forms or anything else here at the moment.
6. On the Table panel, choose New. The New Table dialog box appears.

   The New Table dialog box gives you the option of starting a new table from different perspectives of the design or datasheet views. You can also import data for a table from another source:

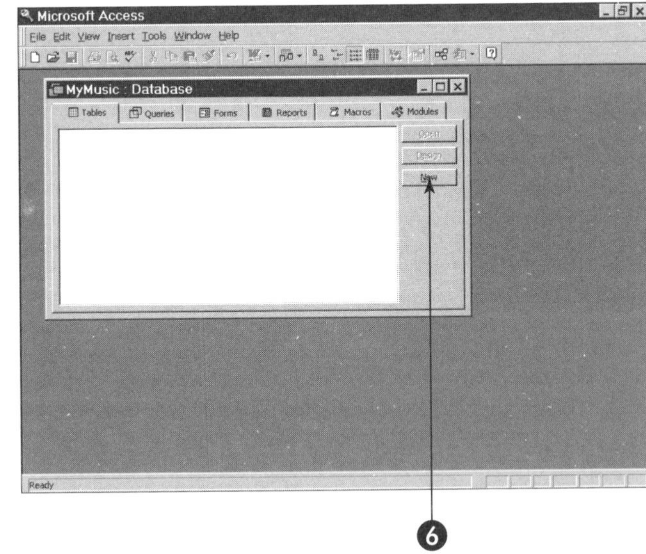

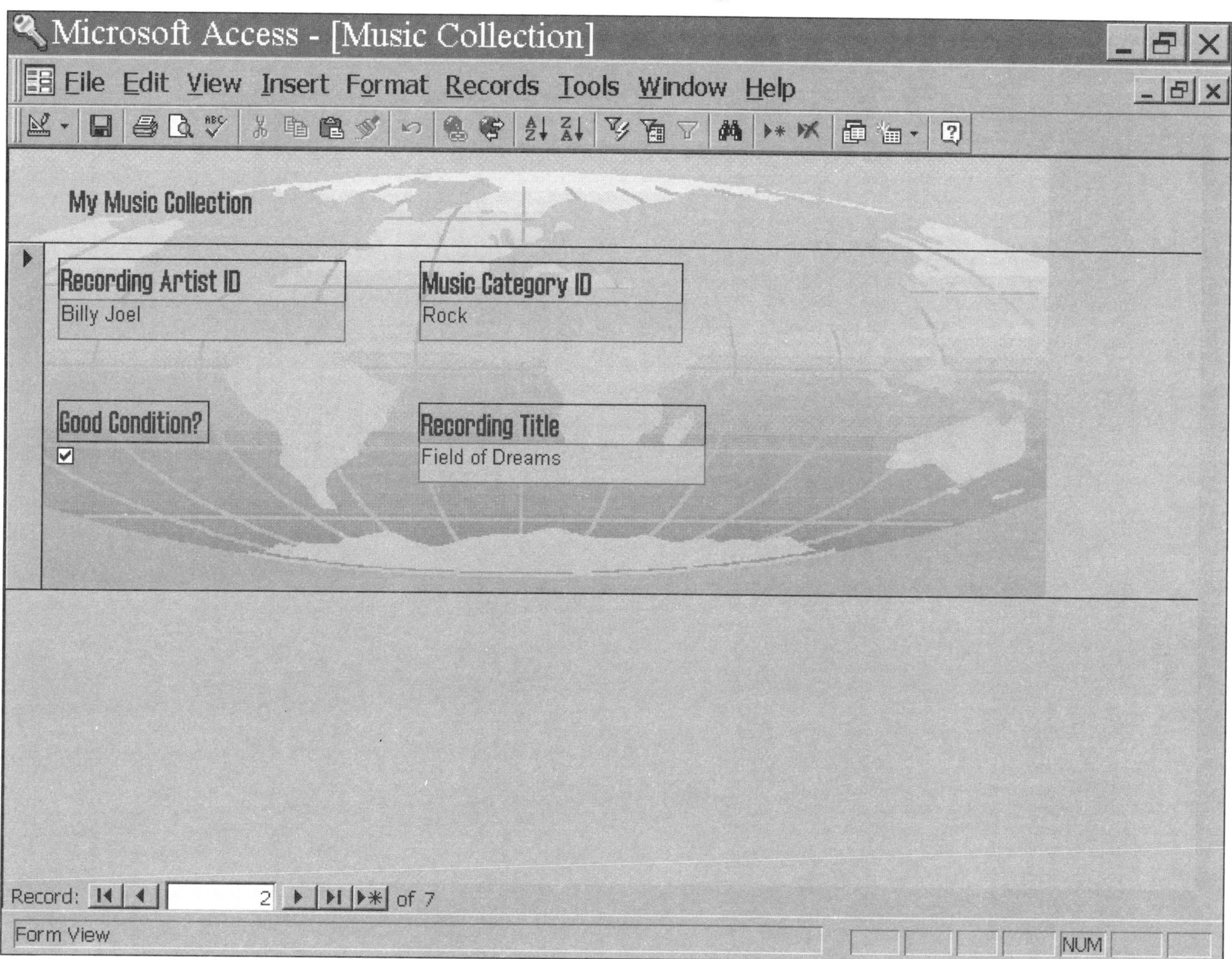
Microsoft Access - [Music Collection]
File Edit View Insert Format Records Tools Window Help
My Music Collection
Recording Artist ID
Billy Joel
Music Category ID
Rock
Good Condition?
Recording Title
Field of Dreams
Record: 2 of 7
Form View
NUM

Using Table Wizard

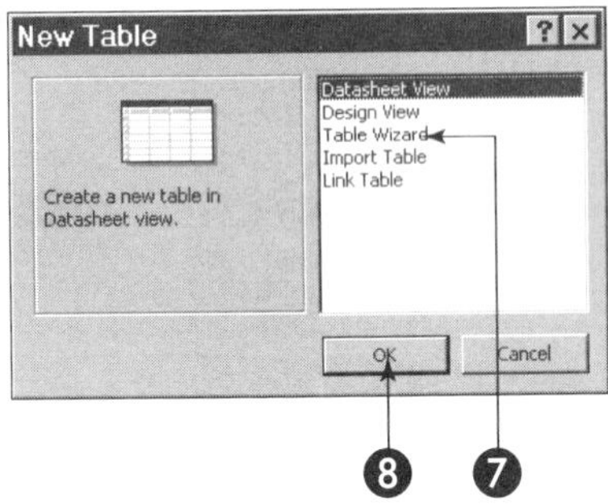

a Word table or Excel worksheet, for example. The easiest way to create a table is by using the Table Wizard.

7. Select Table Wizard.
8. Choose OK to proceed. The Table Wizard dialog box appears.

NOTE

If Access gives you a message that wizards aren't installed, you may have to do a special installation. Open your CD-ROM drive window and locate the folder ValuPack. Within the ValuPack folder is another folder named Dataacc. In the Dataacc folder, double-click the file Dataacc, which runs an installation program for the Microsoft Data Access Pack. When the installation is done, your wizards are available.

TRY OUT THE INTERACTIVE TUTORIALS ON YOUR CD!

9. Click the Personal option button. A different set of sample tables appears.
10. Using the scroll bar in the *Sample Tables* list, select Recordings.
11. Select the *Sample Field* named RecordingTitle.
12. Click the Add button (which looks like a single, right-pointing arrow) to add RecordingTitle to your table.
13. Repeat this step with the fields RecordingArtistID, MusicCategoryID, and Format.

    At this point, you can rename any of the fields by selecting the Rename Field button. You can also rename fields later from the Table view.

14. Choose Next to proceed to the Table Wizard dialog box, shown in the following illustration.
15. Type the name **MyMusic** in the field at the top of this form.

    The rest of this dialog box has to do with setting a primary key. A primary key is like an index of records in a table. Assigning a primary key uniquely identifies each record, making searches for data and other activities in Access possible. You can set any field

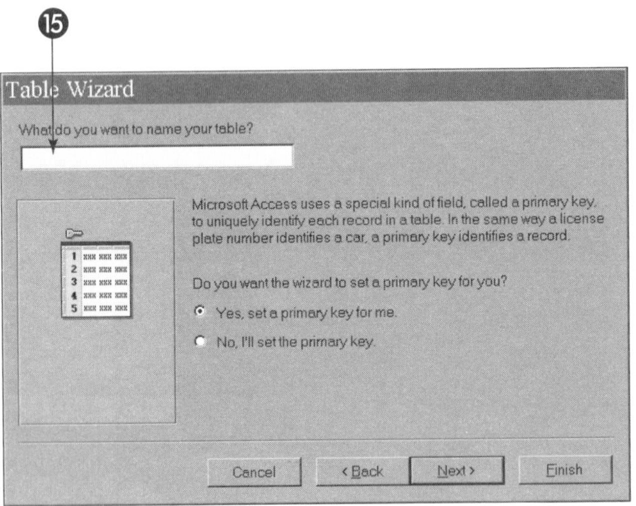

as the primary key, such as the last name field in a customer database. However, using the last name as the primary key when there may be several people named Smith is not as efficient as creating a separate primary key field. When you let Access create such a field for you, it creates a unique primary field key, which is usually the best option.

16 Leave the default choice to allow Access to set the primary key for you, and choose Next to proceed to the next dialog box.

17 Choose Finish to proceed to the table where you can begin to enter data.

The new table appears. The fields you selected while in the Table Wizard are represented as headings of columns. A first record is open, ready for you to enter information.

Notice that the term AutoNumber is in parentheses in the first column. This means the wizard has formatted this field as an AutoNumber field; each time you enter a new record, a new number automatically appears here in sequence. There are times when the wizard's choice of field format does not match how you intend to use that field. However, that's simple to change.

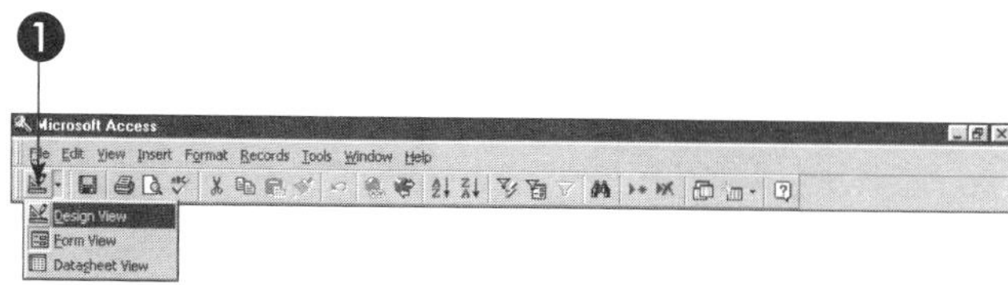

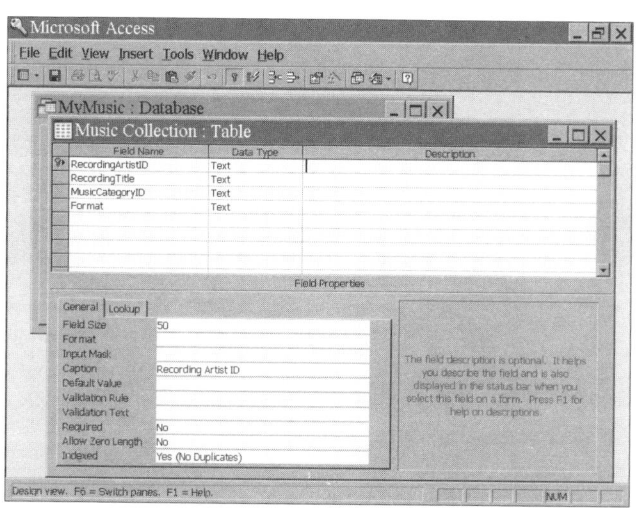

Setting data types

Fields are assigned data types so that Access can perform certain actions on them. For example, to be able to perform a mathematical calculation on a field, it must be formatted as a number field. You can set the data type for each field in your table from the design view.

1 Click the arrow at the right of the View button on the toolbar and select Design View. The window in the middle illustration appears.

2 Click the Data Type field next to the field RecordingArtistID.

3 From the drop-down list there, select Text, because you'll be entering the names of recording artists here.

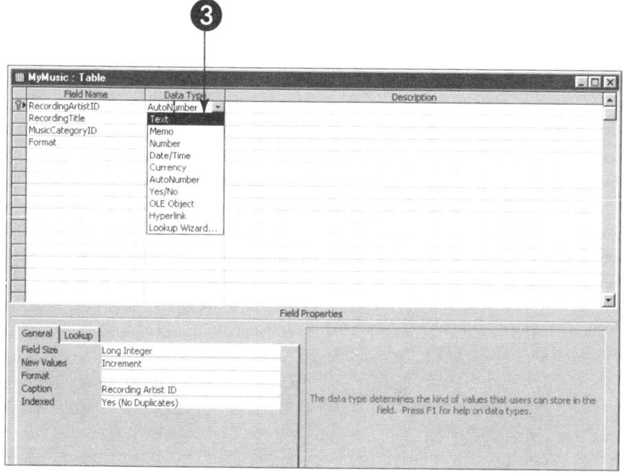

4. Change the MusicCategoryID field to the Text data type.

   The Format field is currently formatted as text so you can enter a recording format, such as CD or tape, so leave it as it is.

5. Using the drop-down list from the View button, return to the datasheet view.

6. When you're prompted to save the design, do so.

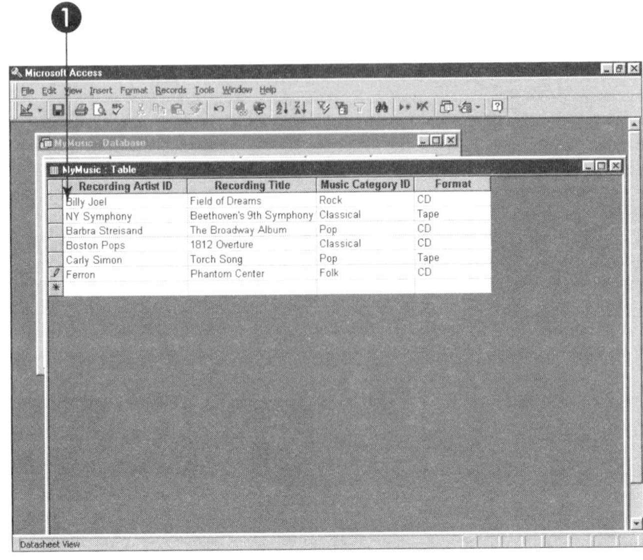

Editing a table

The next step in creating our table is entering some records into it, now that each field is formatted with the correct data type.

1. Place your cursor in the first record in the column Recording Artist ID.

2. Type **Billy Joel** and press Tab to move to the next column.

3. Using the text in the following illustration, complete this record and enter five more.

   Now it's time to learn to edit your table; you'll add an additional field column to your table and resize the columns so the field names can be read more clearly.

4. Select the field column named Recording Title.

5. Select Insert ➢ Column. The new column appears to the left of the selected column with the name Field1.

6. Double-click the cell containing the term Field1.

7. Type the new name **Good Condition?** and press Enter.

8. Place your mouse pointer between the first and second column headings until your pointer becomes a two-way pointing arrow.

9. Click and drag the edge of the column until you can read the entire first heading.

10. Repeat Step 9 to modify any column widths so you can read field headings.

11. Select File ➢ Save to save these changes to the table.

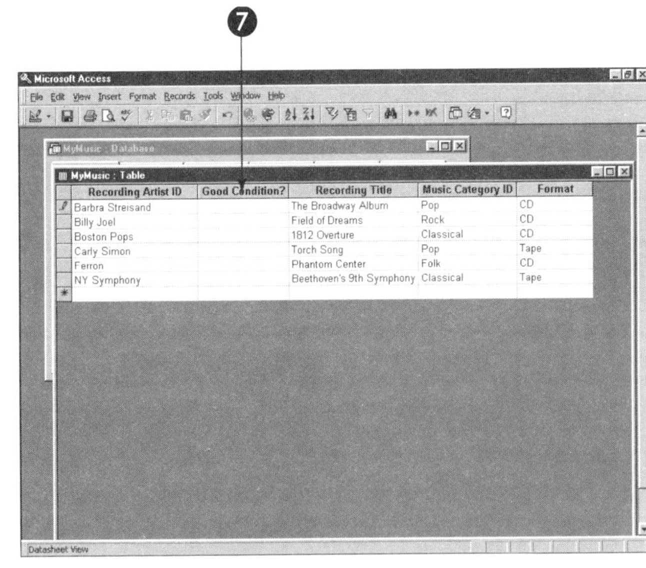

Setting properties for a field

You can program fields to have certain characteristics, called properties. Properties can help make entering data into a field easier. Here you work with the properties of the new field, Good Condition?, to make it automatically enter a default value.

1. Using the View button, change to the Design View.

2. Change the data type of the Good Condition? field to Yes/No. Now there are only two values possible in this field: a check in the field for Yes, and no check for No.

   The selected field's properties are listed at the bottom of this view. You can use these to set a limit for how many characters can be entered in a field, to set a default value for every new record, or to limit text entries to certain choices. For example, if you have a database of part-time employee records and you want to limit entries in a particular address field to one of two states, you can do that here. This can save you data entry mistakes in the table down the road.

3. Type **Yes** in the Default Value field.

   This means that all new records are automatically filled in with a check mark, indicating a recording is in good condition. Someone entering a record would only have to click in this field to deselect it if the recording was not in good condition, saving any change in most cases.

4. Return to the Datasheet view. The new column now contains check boxes.

5. Check the box in the second, third, and sixth records, so your table looks like the one in the illustration to the right.

   Notice the next new record, the blank one at the bottom of the table, is checked automatically. All new records have the Yes value entered by default.

6. Select File ➢ Save to save changes to the table.

7. Click the Close button to close the table.

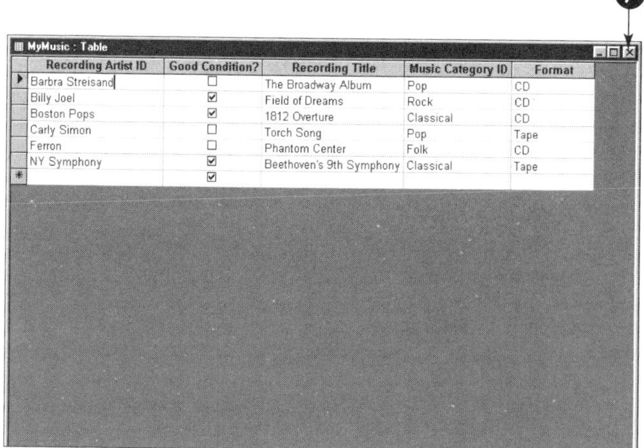

Recording Artist ID	Good Condition?	Recording Title	Music Category ID	Format
Barbra Streisand	☐	The Broadway Album	Pop	CD
Billy Joel	☑	Field of Dreams	Rock	CD
Boston Pops	☑	1812 Overture	Classical	CD
Carly Simon	☐	Torch Song	Pop	Tape
Ferron	☐	Phantom Center	Folk	CD
NY Symphony	☑	Beethoven's 9th Symphony	Classical	Tape
	☑			

DESIGNING FORMS

While tables contain long lists of records, organized by fields in columns, forms enable you to focus on each record individually. The way you lay out information for ease of entry and reading is essential to the successful use of your database. You get a head start on good form design by using Access's Form Wizard.

Using Form Wizard

Form Wizard saves you a lot of time in creating attractive layouts for your forms.

1. Select the Forms tab.
2. Choose New to open the New Form dialog box.

   Use the options here to create quick, simple forms with a feature called AutoForm, or to build a new form from within the Design View. The Form Wizard option helps you design a slightly more polished form with very little effort.
3. Select the Form Wizard and choose OK to proceed. The first Form Wizard dialog box appears.
4. In the *Tables/Queries* drop-down list, the Music Collection table you just created should appear by default; if it doesn't, select it from the drop-down list. The fields in that table are now listed in the *Available Fields* area.
5. Select RecordingArtistID.
6. Click the Add button to the right of it. This field is added to your form.
7. Repeat this procedure to add the fields *Good Condition?*, *RecordingTitle*, and *MusicCategoryID* to your form.

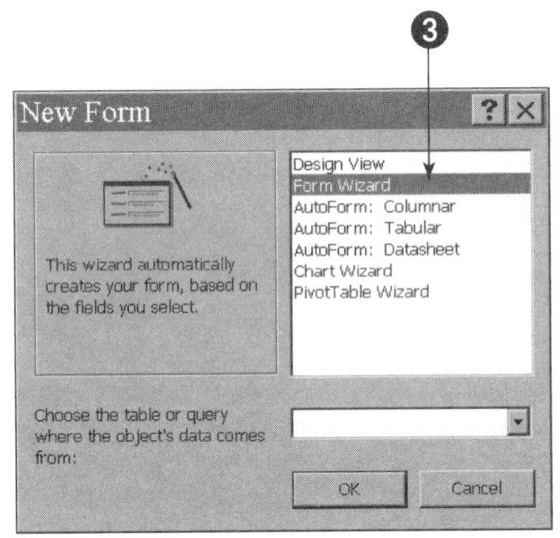

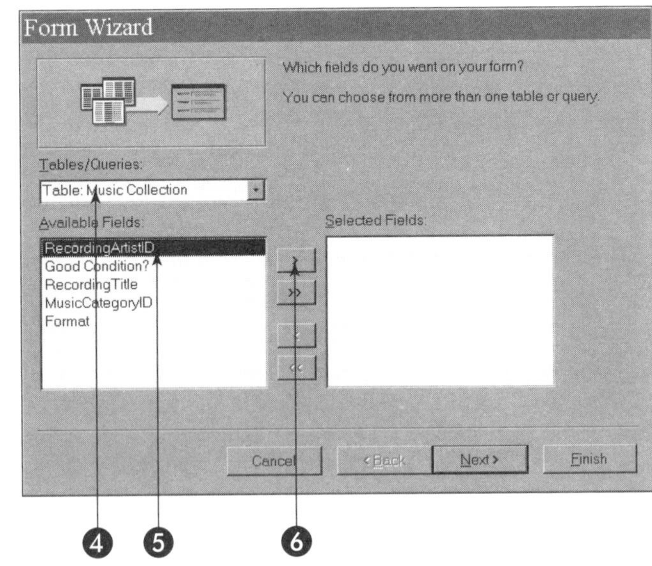

You can use fields from a table in any order you like in a form. You don't have to use all the fields. You can even select another table from the Tables/Queries *drop-down list and add fields from several different*

tables in one form. The form pulls the appropriate data for each record from the tables you've designated.

8. Choose Next to proceed. The second Form Wizard dialog box appears. The choices here concern your preference for a layout style.

9. Click the radio button for Justified, and then choose Next to proceed.

   The next dialog box you see offers several built-in design styles for your form. These styles determine a background pattern, a color scheme, and type formatting settings.

10. Select the International style.

11. Choose Next. The final Form Wizard dialog box appears.

    You can change the name of your form, which is currently taken from the table name. Because any number of forms can be created by taking contents from a table, forms often have more descriptive names; a table may be called Music Collection, while the forms that utilize that table are called CD's Bought in 1996, Classical Collections, and CD Purchase Order.

    The other setting on this form has to do with what you want to do when you finish the wizard. You can go right to Design View to make changes to the design, or right to the form to see what it looks like and enter records.

12. Leave the name of the form as Music Collection, and accept the default choice to open the form by choosing Finish. The form in the illustration to the right appears with the first record from the table displayed.

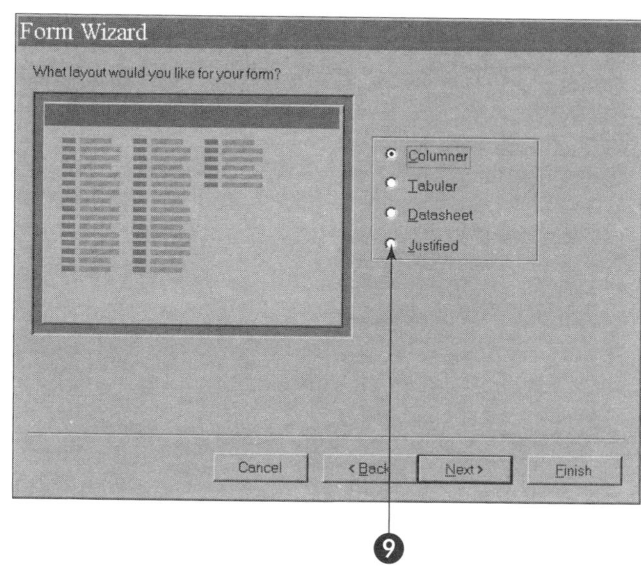

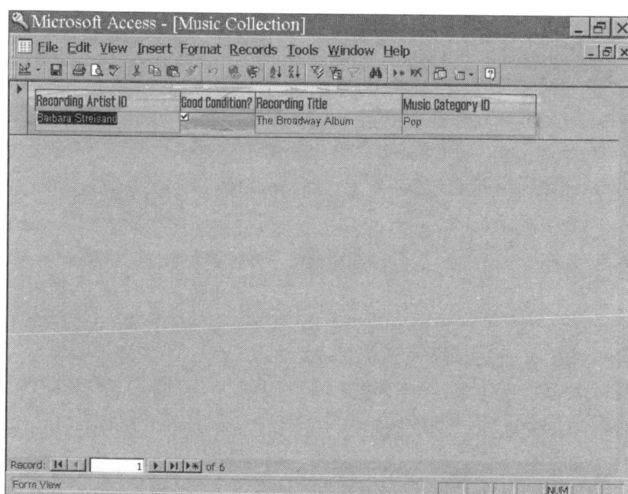

Adding a header to a form

The form designed by the Form Wizard has an attractive, graphic background, a professional looking typeface, and all the records filled in from the table data. However, there are some things you might want to do to redesign forms to make them even more attractive or to suit your purposes.

22

Looking at Tables and Forms

Moving labels and text boxes

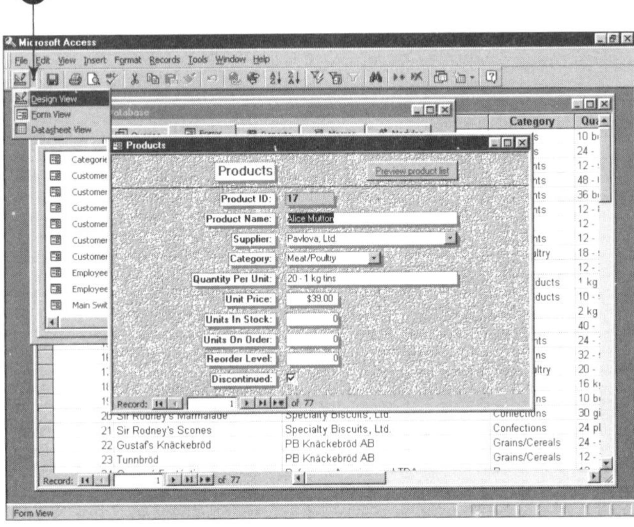

1. Click the arrow to the right of the View button and select Design View.
2. Double-click the bar titled Form Header. The illustration to the right shows the view that's displayed.

   The Design view enables you to move around fields and text boxes, or add graphics, a header, or even buttons, check boxes, and drop-down lists to your form. The property sheets for the Detail and Header section can be used to control how an element on your form functions. For example, you can choose to only display a field when another field is marked Yes. You can stipulate that a field can or can't expand as text is entered.

If you want a different background for your form, access the Form Wizard style choices again. Select Format ➢ AutoFormat and choose a new style from the dialog box that appears.

3. In the property sheet for the header, change the Height to 0.5". The header area expands to half an inch.
4. Click the Label tool on the Design toolbar.
5. Click in the expanded Header section and drag to draw a rectangular text box in the header area.
6. Type **My Music Collection** in the new text box.

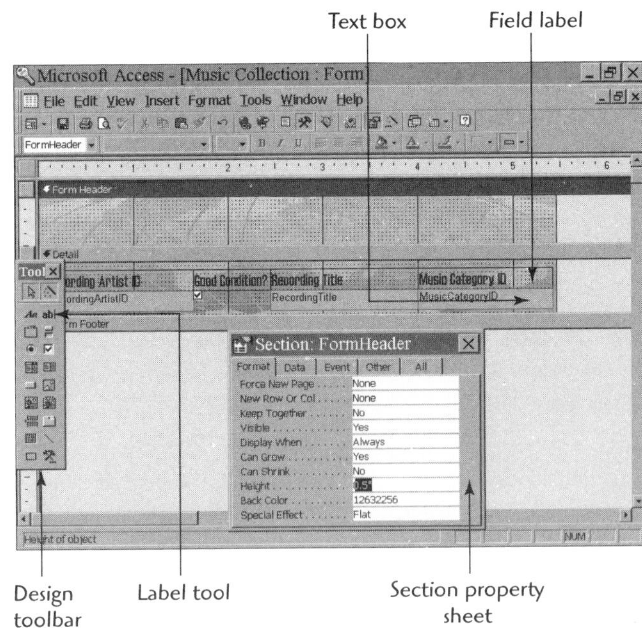

Moving labels and text boxes

Although you had the opportunity to choose from different layouts when you ran the Form Wizard, you may want to move individual elements around your form or resize them. You can do this using the moving and resizing handles.

1. Click the Good Condition field label. A set of handles appears around it; one of these, a large block in the upper left corner, is the move handle.

2. Click the move handle and drag the Good Condition? field label down below the Recording Artist ID text box (about a half an inch below it). As you drag, the Detail area expands to offer more space.
3. Select the check box that belongs under the Good Condition? label and move it down below the label.
4. Using the following illustration as a guide, continue to move labels and text boxes until they are placed in this new arrangement.
5. Using the View button, return to the Form View.
6. Click the New Record button on the toolbar.
7. Type this new record:

   Recording Artist ID: **Indigo Girls**
   Music Category ID: **Rock**
   Good Condition? **Yes**
   Recording Title: ***Rites of Passage***

   The new record, entered in your modified form, looks like the following illustration.
8. Select File ➢ Save to save the changes to the form.
9. Select File ➢ Close. The saved version of this file is available on the accompanying CD-ROM, named Ex22-1F.

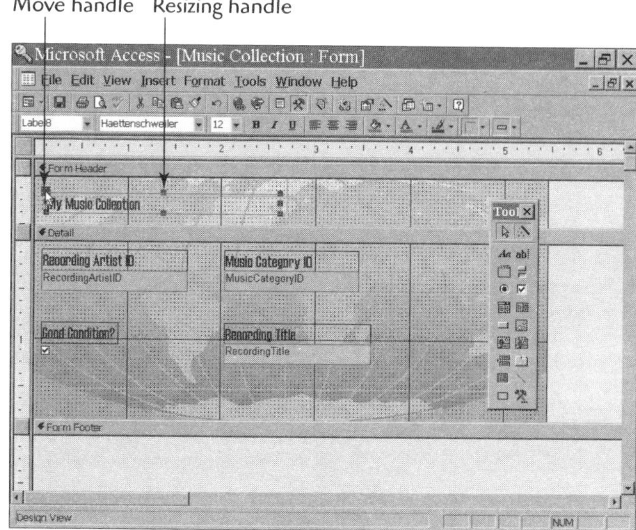

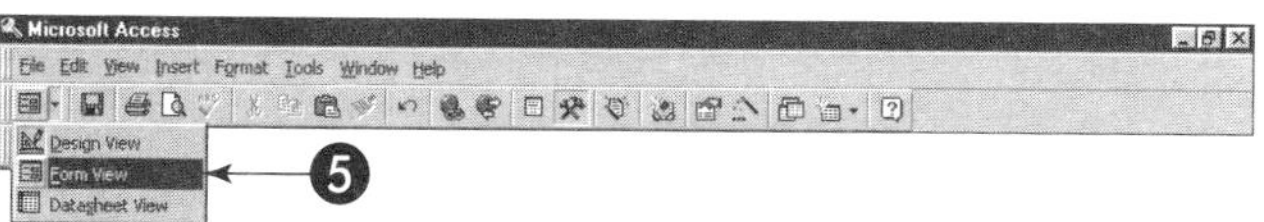

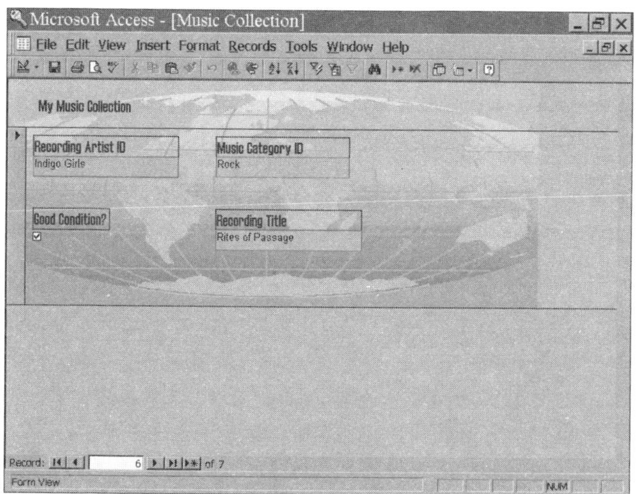

SKILLS CHALLENGE: BUILDING A BOOK DATABASE

Now that you've built a database for your music collection, it's time to take a literary turn. Build a book database in the following steps and get more experience with Access forms and tables.

1. Open a blank new database, and name it **MyBooks**.
2. Create a table using the Table Wizard; make choices that will create a table based on the Books sample table, and include the fields named Title, PublisherName, and PurchasePrice (and any other fields you'd like to include).

Skills challenge

3. Make sure the Title and PublisherName fields are text data types, and the PurchasePrice field is the currency data type.

Can you perform calculations on text fields?

4. Make **IDG Books Worldwide** the default value for the PublisherName field.
5. Insert a column in the table and name it **Author**.

What are two ways to rename fields?

6. Resize the columns of your table so all labels are visible.
7. Enter two records from the table: one for this book, and one for your favorite novel.
8. Using the Form Wizard, create a form based on the Books table. Use the Author, PublisherName, Title, and PurchasePrice labels, the Columnar layout, and the Dusk design style.

How do you change the design style after you've completed the Form Wizard?

9. Add a header to your form with the label field **My Library**.
10. Change the property sheet for the Details section so that it expands if you enter more content than it can accommodate (hint: use the Grow property).
11. Move the Author field in the form to be the last field (if it's already last, make it first).
12. Create a second form; this time take a couple of fields from the Books table and a couple from the Music Collection table to create the form with Form Wizard.
13. Upon completing the form, make some new entries in each of the tables; and then look at how the new entries appear in your new form.
14. Close the file.

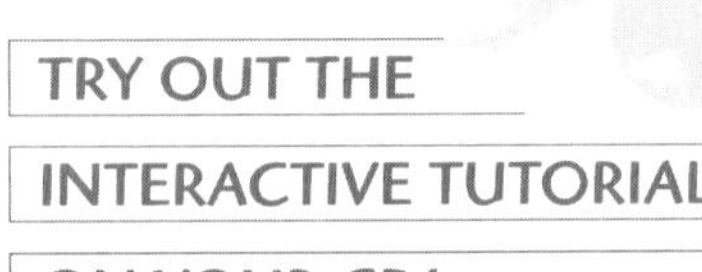

TRY OUT THE

INTERACTIVE TUTORIALS

ON YOUR CD!

TROUBLESHOOTING

You learned the basics of table and form design using Access, so you can now build your own simple databases. The suggestions in the following table might help you handle any unexpected surprises.

Problem	Solution
I want to see the records in my table alphabetically.	Select the column you'd like to alphabetize and click the Sort Ascending button on the toolbar. If you want to sort by last name, be sure to either make separate columns for Last Name/First Name, or enter the records as Last Name, First Name.
What happens if I select the Database Wizard when I start up Access?	This wizard is similar to the Table and Form Wizards, but it covers both functions at once, creating an entire database for you. It's great for standard types of databases, but gives you less control over your choices.
How do I print a form?	From the Form View or Form Design View, select File ➢ Print. If you do this from Datasheet View, a datasheet prints.

WRAP UP

You learned how to work with the basics of two of the four cornerstones of any database, forms and tables. In this lesson you learned the following:

- Using wizards to produce polished tables and forms
- Using design views to modify the properties of elements in tables and forms
- Adding columns to tables and resize them
- Adding headers and text boxes to forms

Wrap up

If you want more practice with these features, try running through the Database Wizard to create a file, and then modifying the design of the forms and tables that wizard creates.

In Lesson 23, you look at two more key parts of Microsoft Access: queries and reports. These are the features that enable you to search and generate reports based on your data.

LESSON 23

Getting Information Out of Your Database

GOALS

In Lessons 21 and 22, you learned about the structure of an Access database, and built some tables and forms to hold data. Now comes the real payoff: you get to search and generate reports from that data, the real strength of database software. In this lesson you learn the following:

- Using Report Wizard
- Modifying reports
- Running queries
- Sorting and filtering records
- Using Print Preview and Page Setup
- Printing output

Using Report Wizard

GET READY

For this lesson, you need the files Ex23-1 and Ex23-2, which you copied to your hard drive from the accompanying CD-ROM. You should also have a printer connected to your computer and set up as your default printer.

In the exercises of this lesson, you produce a report like the one on the facing page.

RUNNING A REPORT

Reports are the logical extension of all that data you enter in your tables and forms. Just as you meticulously write out Rolodex cards and place them in alphabetical order in a plastic base so you can find phone numbers more easily in the future, you enter data in a database so you can generate reports that look at that data in different ways: alphabetically, chronologically, and so forth.

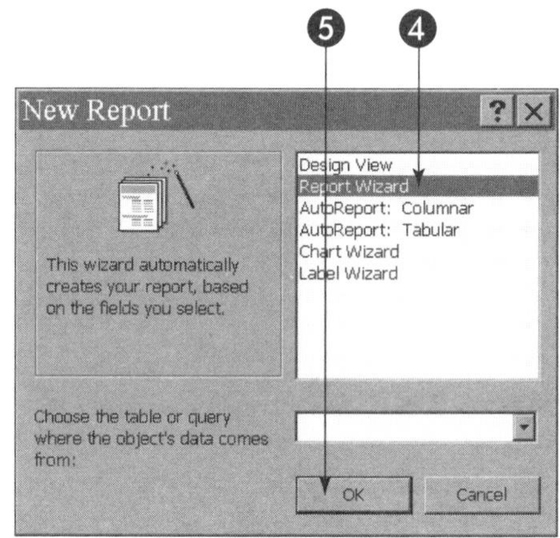

Using Report Wizard

The quickest way to generate a report is using Report Wizard.

1. Open the file Ex23-1. This is the Music Collection file you created in the Lesson 22, with a few added records.
2. Select the Report tab of the database window.
3. Choose New. The New Report dialog box appears.
4. Select Report Wizard.
5. Choose OK.

   The first Report Wizard screen appears, as shown in the following illustration. You can use the AutoReport features here to quickly generate simple columnar or tabular reports, or create a report yourself in Design view.

6. Make sure the Music Collection table is selected from the *Tables/Queries* drop-down list. The fields contained in the table appear in the *Available Fields* list.

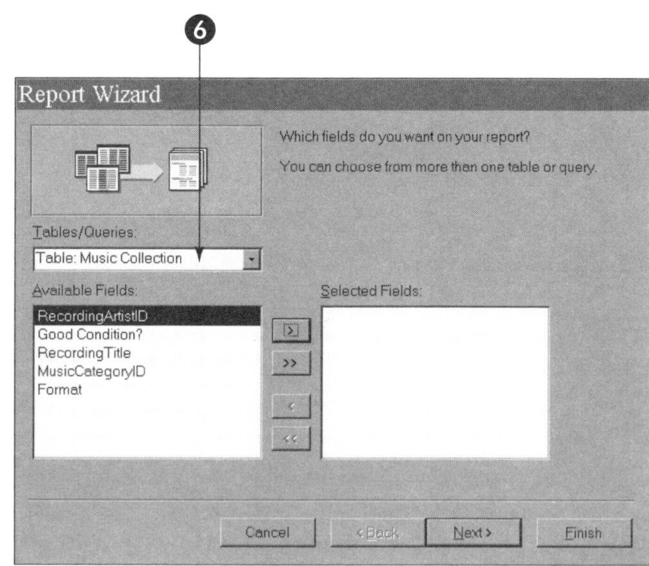

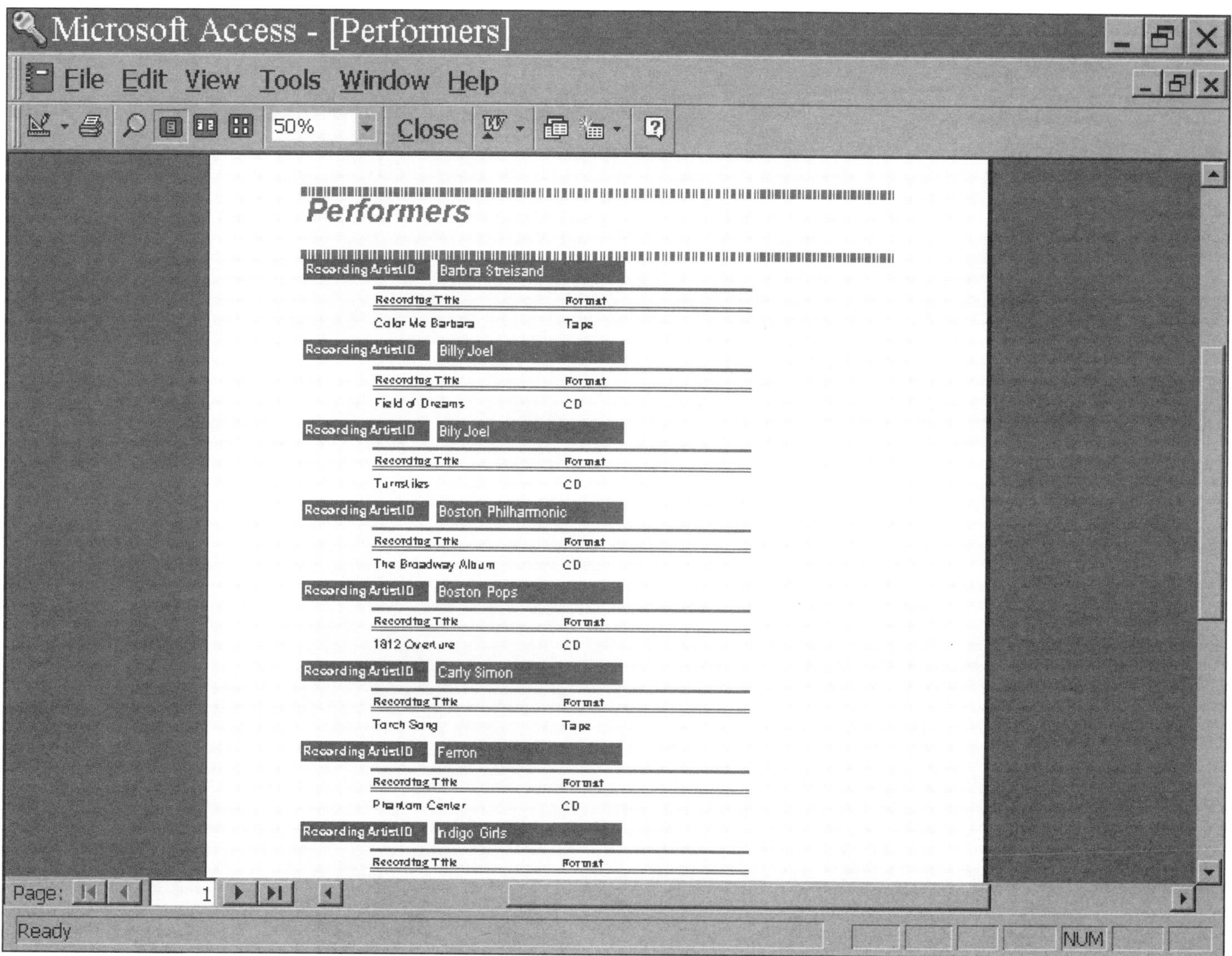
Microsoft Access - [Performers]
File Edit View Tools Window Help
50%
Close
Performers
Recording ArtistID
Barbra Streisand
Recording Title
Format
Color Me Barbara
Tape
Billy Joel
Field of Dreams
CD
Bily Joel
Turnstiles
Boston Philharmonic
The Broadway Album
Boston Pops
1812 Overture
Carly Simon
Torch Song
Ferron
Phantom Center
Indigo Girls
Page: 1
Ready
NUM

Using Report Wizard

7. Select the RecordingArtistID field.
8. Click the Add button to the right of the *Available Fields* list to add it to the *Selected Fields* list.
9. Repeat the previous step to add Recording Title and Format to the Selected Fields.
10. Choose Next to proceed.
11. In the next Report Wizard dialog box, select RecordingArtistID in the list of fields on the top of this form.
12. Click the button with a right-facing arrow to add the field to the grouping list.

    This places this field in a first level, and places the other two fields beneath the first field. This is a way to group levels of information. Think of your television program guide. The first level of a program entry is the title of the program or movie, and beneath the title is its running time and description. The title has been placed at the first level of these records. You see how this effects your actual report in a little while.

13. Choose Next to proceed.

    You can use sorting on up to four fields in your database. Table 23-1 gives you an example of how Access uses sort levels. The records here are sorted first by State, so all the records from the same state are grouped together. The records are then sorted by City, so all the records within a certain city in a state are sorted next. Finally, after records have been organized by State and City, names have been sorted alphabetically within each city .

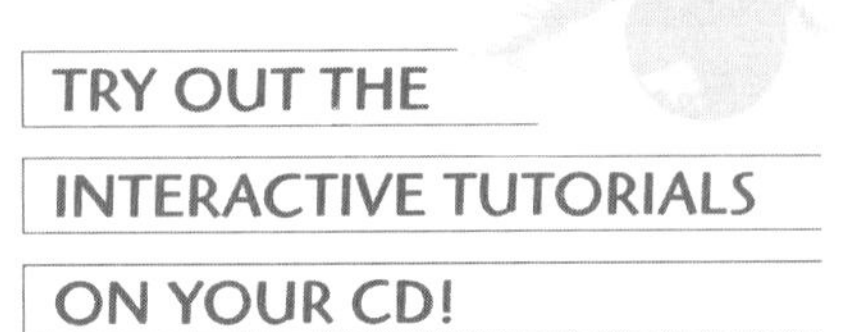

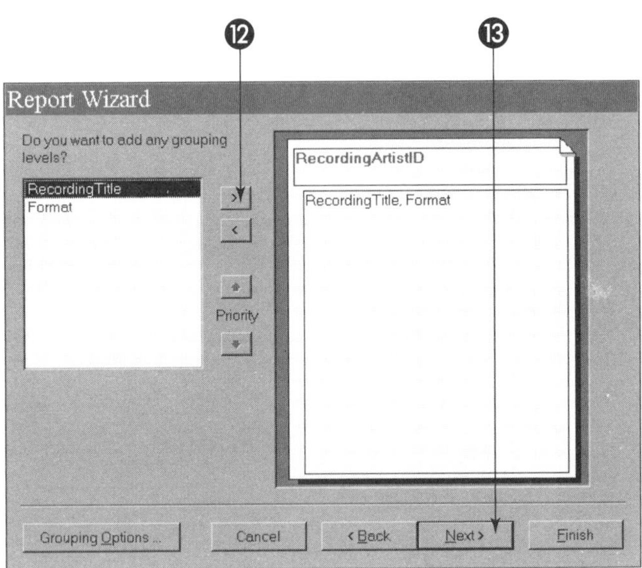

TABLE 23-1 MULTIPLE SORT CRITERIA

State	City	Name
Alaska	Fairbanks	Allen
	Fairbanks	Barnes
	Fairbanks	Smith
	Juno	Adams

continued

TABLE 23-1 MULTIPLE SORT CRITERIA *(continued)*

State	City	Name
Juno	Arkin	
	Juno	Baker
	Juno	Kearns
	Juno	Marshall
California	Bakersfield	Rogers
	Bakersfield	Stanton
	Monterey	Chandler
	Monterey	Quinn

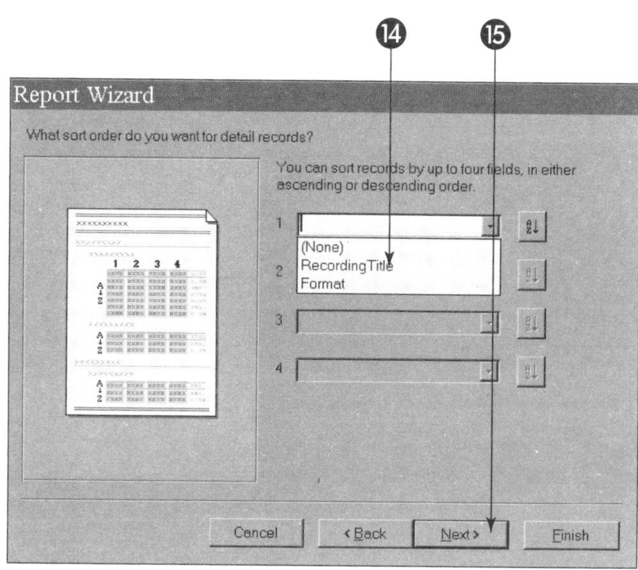

⓮ Select Recording Title in the first sort field.

⓯ Choose Next to proceed.

⓰ Select the Align Left 1 layout for the report and leave the Portrait orientation selected.

⓱ Choose Next to display the dialog box used to set the style for a report, as shown in the bottom right illustration.

⓲ Select one or two styles to see how they differ, and then, with the Casual style selected, choose Next.

NOTE

Sometimes it's hard to tell what a report style will really look like until you finish the Report Wizards. Don't worry; you can always change the style you assign to a report at a later time by selecting Format ➢ AutoFormat in the report design view.

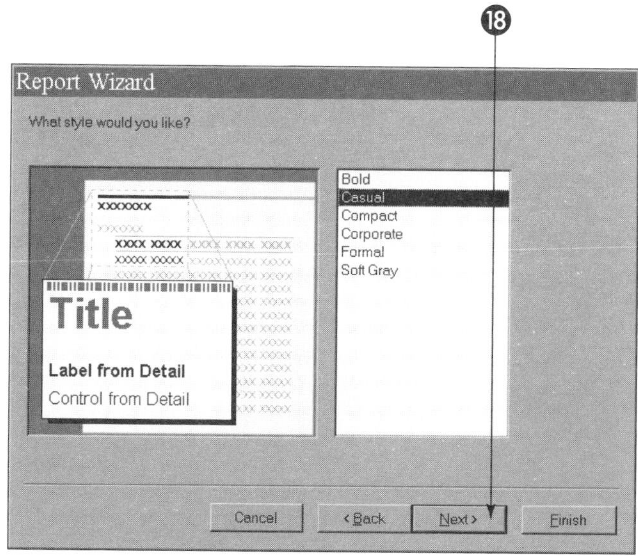

⓳ On the final Report Wizard dialog box shown in the following illustration, type **Performers** for the title of the report.

⓴ Make sure the Preview the report option button is selected.

㉑ Choose Finish.

Modifying reports

A Print Preview view of your report appears, as in the illustration to the right. Notice that the RecordingArtistID field stands above the other fields in the report. This is because you grouped the field to its own level. Because you sorted by the Recording Title field, the two Billy Joel titles, *Field of Dreams* and *Turnstiles,* are listed in alphabetical order.

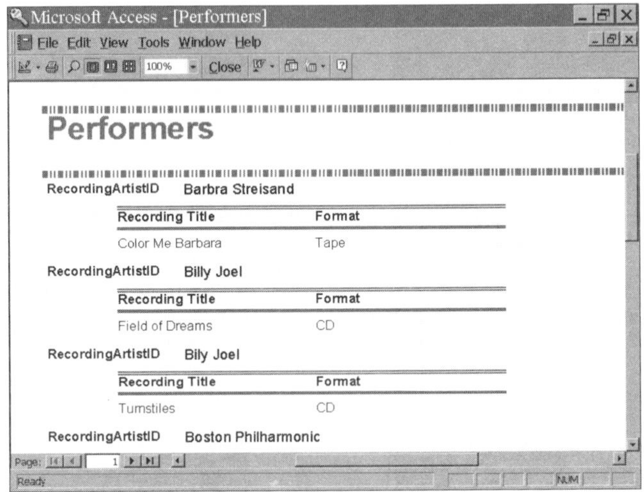

Modifying reports

Once you create a report you can easily make changes to it in the Design View.

1. Click the arrow on the side of the View button and select Design View.

   The Design view for the report appears, containing placeholders for a report header, the two levels of fields and text boxes, and a footer containing date and page information. Notice that there are two blocks that say RecordingArtistID, and two blocks that say Format and RecordingTitle. One of each of these is a field label placeholder, and one is a text box placeholder, where the actual entries for that field will appear.

2. Click the Performers header; handles appear around its edges.
3. Click the Italic button on the toolbar to make this text italic.
4. Select the Recording Title field in the RecordingArtistID Header section.
5. Using the *Font* drop-down list on the toolbar, change the font to Times New Roman.
6. Repeat the preceding two steps to change the font of the Format field in the same header to Times New Roman.
7. Select the RecordingArtistID field (it's the placeholder with that name to the left of the screen) and click your right mouse button.
8. Select Fill/Back Color; the submenu appears.
9. Click a dark blue block in this palette to change the background of the border surrounding this field name.

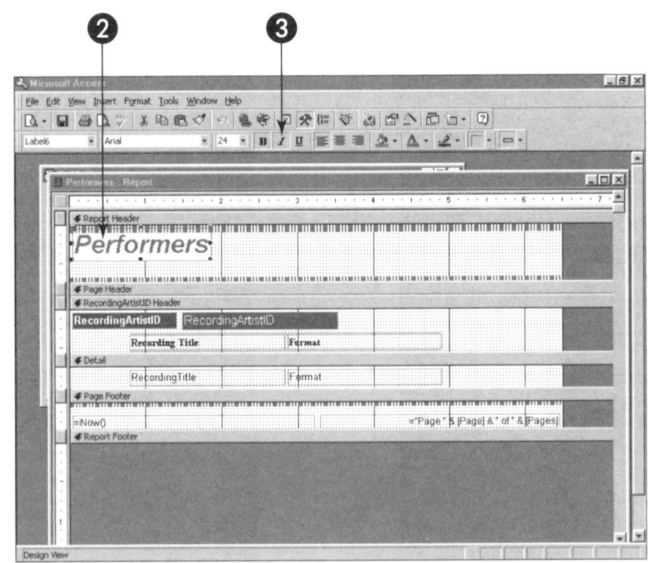

⑩ With RecordingArtistID field still selected, click your right mouse again.

⑪ Select Font/Fore Color, and choose the white block from the submenu. The background of this block is now blue, and the letters in it are white.

⑫ Select the RecordingArtistID text box (the second block with that text from the left).

⑬ Right-click your mouse and select Fill/Back Color, and then choose a dark purple color block.

⑭ Right-click again and select Font/Fore Color, and then choose the white block from the submenu.

⑮ Select Layout View from the View button's drop-down list. The report is displayed again, with your formatting changes applied.

⑯ Select File ➢ Save to save your report and close the Report window.

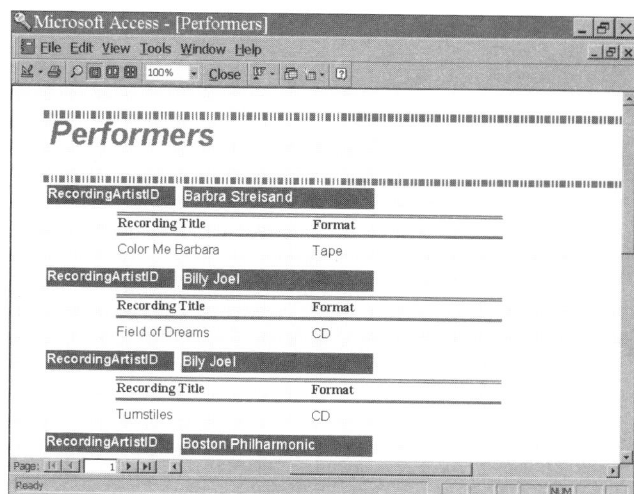

FINDING INFORMATION

Reports are useful for extracting data from your database in an attractive format; once you create a report, you can save it and print it as often as you like. However, there are other ways to look at your data. For example, you can sort or filter information in a table to alphabetize the records by last name or display only records for people living in a certain state. You can also create and save queries. Queries contain a set of criteria that records must meet.

Running queries

Records that match query criteria are displayed on your screen. The ability to save queries means you can run your query at any time, getting the most current results based on any new data you might have entered.

❶ Select the Queries tab of your database.

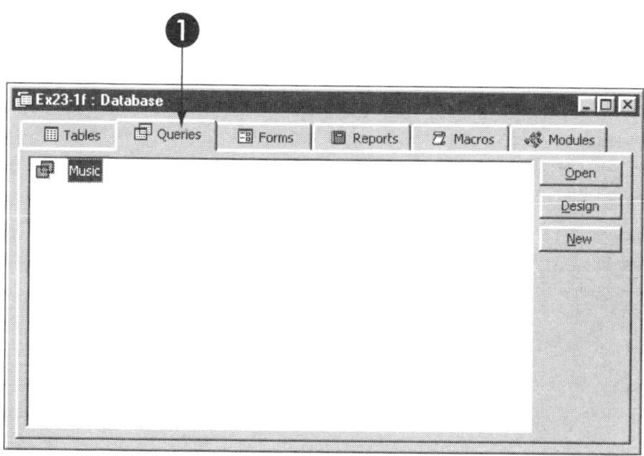

2. Choose New.
3. From the New Query dialog box, select Design View and click OK to proceed. A query form appears.
4. From the Show Table dialog box displayed on the query form, select the Music Collection table and choose Add.

You can actually select several tables to add to your query, and then pick and choose fields from those tables to include in your query.

5. From the Music Collection Table list displayed at the top of the query form, double-click MusicCategoryID. It appears in the first column of the query form on the lower half of the screen.
6. Double-click the fields RecordingArtistID, RecordingTitle, and Format in sequence until the first four columns of the query are filled in.
7. In the fourth column, on the row titled Criteria, type **CD**. Your form now looks like the one in the illustration to the right.

   You can use the Criteria row as well as the Or row to set the parameters of a basic query. For example, by entering **CD** under format, your query will display only records that contain CD in their format field. If you don't type the quotation marks around the entry and press Enter, Access will enter the quotations for you to designate actual text entered in the field.

   You can use these fields in combination. To only see recordings by Billy Joel on CD, you would enter **Billy Joel** in the RecordingArtistID Criteria and **CD** in the Format Criteria. You can enter a second criterion in the row titled Or to ask for records that match two or more criteria. For example, entering **Classical** in the MusicCategoryID Criteria and Rock in the Or row for the same column displays records that fit the Rock and Classical category. If you had a numeric field in your table, you could use equations like ">10" or "Between 10/9/96 and 10/21/96" to see only records with a certain amount or date in a field.

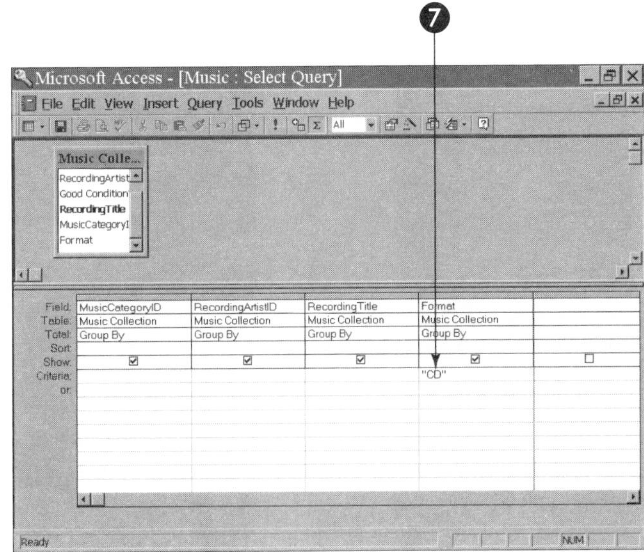

❽ Select Query ➢ Run to run the query. The records that match the criterion of containing CD in the Format field are displayed, as in the figure to the right.

❾ Use the View button to go back to the design view for the query.

❿ Delete CD from the Criteria for the Format column.

What results do you get? You can see in the next figure that records of all formats appear (because you deleted the criteria for format).

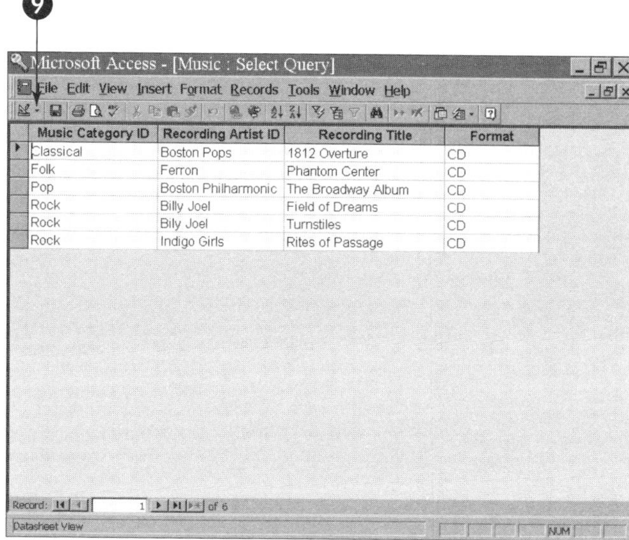

Music Category ID	Recording Artist ID	Recording Title	Format
Classical	Boston Pops	1812 Overture	CD
Folk	Ferron	Phantom Center	CD
Pop	Boston Philharmonic	The Broadway Album	CD
Rock	Billy Joel	Field of Dreams	CD
Rock	Bily Joel	Turnstiles	CD
Rock	Indigo Girls	Rites of Passage	CD

Queries can be as simple as the preceding examples, or extremely complex. You can use a feature called Expression Builder to create queries that have several criteria; for example, in an employee records database, you could look for any records to be displayed when the amount in the salary field and the amount in the bonus field add up to more than $78,000, but only for employees hired after October 1995 who live in the state of Illinois. Look in the Access helpfile for examples of the many variables you can use for building more complex formulas. If you're interested in using these more advanced Access features extensively in your work, you might also want to pick up IDG Book's Worldwide's Access 97 Bible.

⓫ Select File ➢ Save to save the query, and then close the query window.

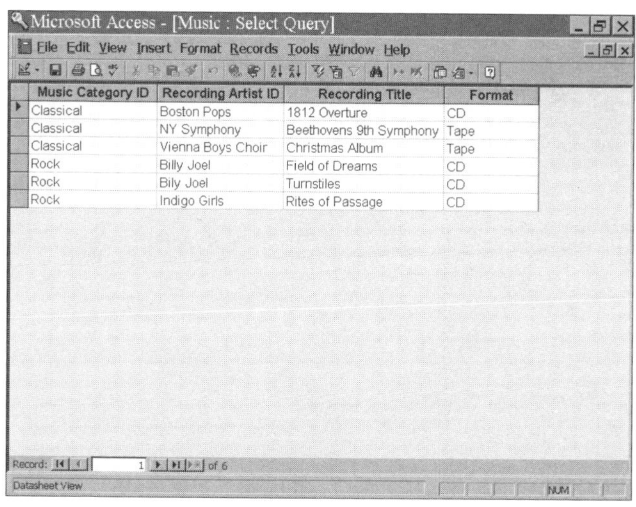

Music Category ID	Recording Artist ID	Recording Title	Format
Classical	Boston Pops	1812 Overture	CD
Classical	NY Symphony	Beethovens 9th Symphony	Tape
Classical	Vienna Boys Choir	Christmas Album	Tape
Rock	Billy Joel	Field of Dreams	CD
Rock	Bily Joel	Turnstiles	CD
Rock	Indigo Girls	Rites of Passage	CD

Sorting and filtering records

There's an even simpler way to control how information is displayed on your screen. You can sort the records in ascending or descending order, and you can apply filters so that only records that meet certain criteria are displayed on screen. Tackle sorting first.

❶ Select the Table tab and open the Music Collection table.

❷ Select the column titled Recording Title.

3. Click the Sort Ascending button on the toolbar; your data sorts alphabetically.

4. To see information sorted by category, select the MusicCategoryID column.

5. Click the Sort Descending button. The selections appear with the Rock recordings first and the Classical last, sorted in reverse alphabetical order by the selected field, as in the illustration.

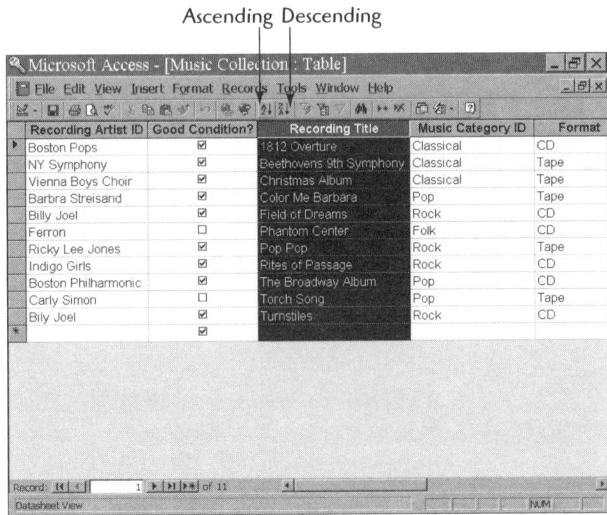

If you want to sort based on two fields, you have to move the fields next to each other, with the first sort field on the left. Select both, and click one of the Sort buttons. The records are sorted first by the field on the left, and second by the field on the right.

6. Click the Filter by Form button on the toolbar to display the Filter by Form view.

7. Click the check box in the *Good Condition?* field. This filters out any forms from your screen display which do not have a check mark in this field.

8. If you want to set filter criteria in any other field, select an option from the drop-down list, such as Music Category ID.

9. Click the Apply Filter button on the toolbar. A table is displayed on your screen, showing only those records for recordings in good condition.

   Filters are a quick way to show only certain records from your database. Also, if you print a table with a filter applied, only the filtered records will print.

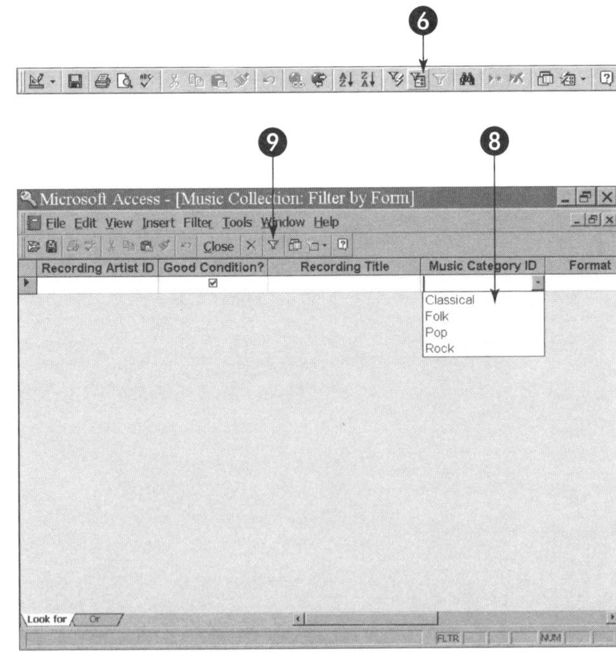

PRINTING FROM ACCESS

Although there are many elements to an Access database — tables, reports, forms, and queries, for example — printing is pretty straightforward. There is only one Print dialog box with one set of choices. You determine what prints by what is selected or displayed, rather than by making that choice in a dialog box as you do in PowerPoint.

The first step in printing is making sure that what you're about to print looks right by using Print Preview, and making any necessary adjustments to things such as margins and page orientation using Page Setup.

Using Print Preview

Print Preview in Access is similar to the Print Preview function in all the other Office products. You use it in this exercise to see how different types of output will look. You should still be in the table view.

1. Click the Apply Filter button to remove the filter that's been applied.

2. Select File ➢ Print Preview (you can also use the Print Preview button).

3. Click the page display to enlarge the table preview, as in the illustration to the right.

   If you want to publish this table as a Word document, use the Office Links button on the toolbar and select Publish with Word. This opens the Word window within Access, so you can use its formatting and publishing tools. To see the preview page display at different percentages of magnification, select different settings from the *Zoom* drop-down list. To create a new element in the database, use the New Object button.

4. Close the Table window.

5. Select the Reports tab.

6. With the Performers report selected, click the Print Preview button on the toolbar.

7. When the report appears, click the Two Pages button on the Print Preview toolbar.

   Two pages at a time show in your preview. Use the page navigation buttons at the bottom of the screen to move between

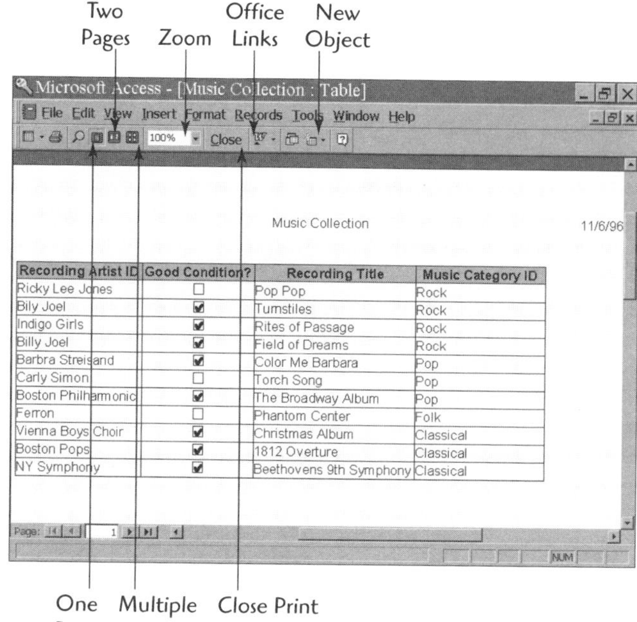

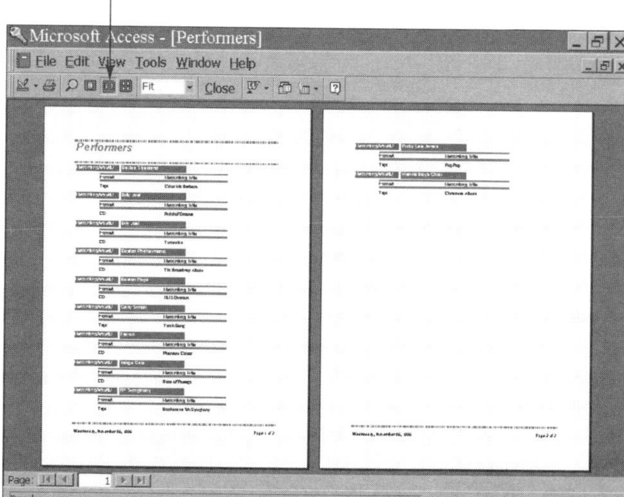

reports consisting of several pages. Now take a look at how forms display in Print Preview.

8. Close the Report preview window.
9. Select the Forms tab.
10. With the Music Collection form selected, click the Print Preview button.

    You can zoom in by clicking the page, and then use the scroll bars to move around the preview.

    Notice that the records don't have any dividing mark between them. You might consider, at this point, redesigning the form to place a page break or line between each record.

11. Click the Multiple Pages button and drag to highlight three page icons.

    When you release your mouse button, the display changes to three pages across.

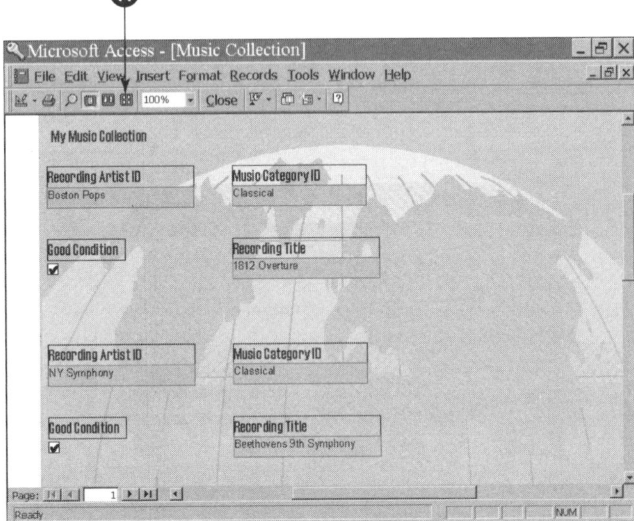

Printing

Once you preview your document, you may want to modify how it's going to print by changing its margins or page orientation. You do that in Page Setup.

1. Select File ➢ Page Setup. The Page Setup dialog box appears.
2. Change the top margin to 1.5 inches. The change is reflected in the sample preview.

If you want to print only data and no graphics, check the Print Data Only *check box on the Margins tab in the Page Setup dialog box.*

3. Click the Page tab.
4. Change the orientation to Landscape.

    Changes in margin and orientation impact how many records you can get on a page and how the space on the page is filled.

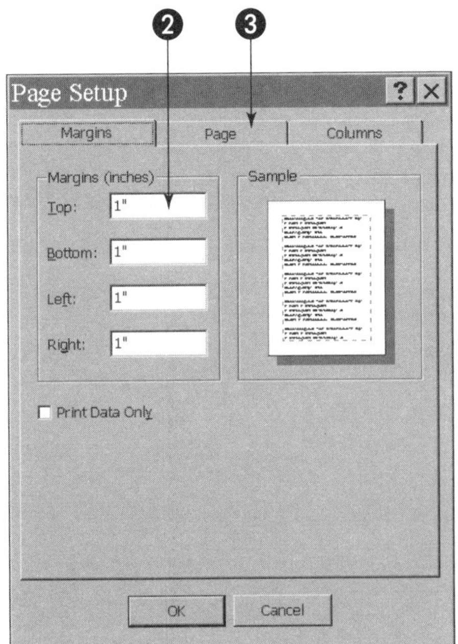

5. Choose OK to save the Page Setup.
6. Select File ➢ Print. The Print dialog box appears.
7. In the Print Range area, click the radio button for *Pages*.
8. Type **1** in the *From* box and **2** in the *To* box. You can select specific records before opening the Print dialog box, and use the Selected Records option to print just those records.
9. Change the number of copies to 2.
10. Choose OK to print the first two of three pages of forms in your database.

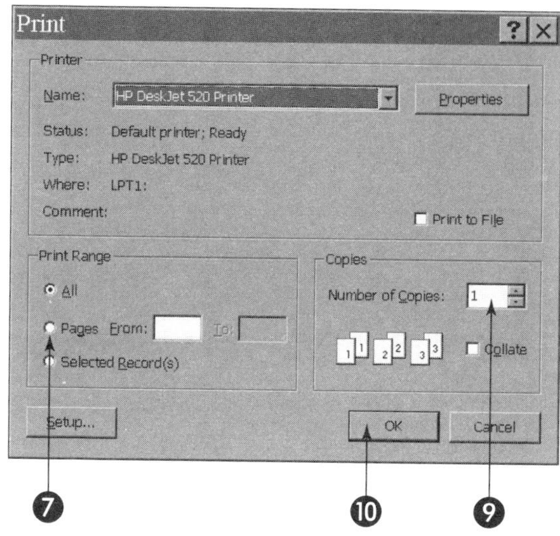

SKILLS CHALLENGE: RUNNING A REPORT AND QUERY

Reports and queries are the big payoff in Access, and the more you use them, the better you get at producing just the information you need.

1. Open the file Ex23-2, which you copied from the accompanying CD-ROM.
2. Create a report with Report Wizard based on the Product table. Use the ProductID, ProductName, Supplier, and Category fields; sort by Supplier, use the Corporate style, and name it Products by Supplier.

How would you change the name of this report from its default name?

3. In the report Design View, change the font for all the text to Times New Roman.
4. Make the background fill color of the report title red and the font/foreground white.
5. Save the report.
6. Create a query based on the Customers table.
7. Set as your criteria to display all records with either British Columbia (BC) or Washington State as their region and run the query.

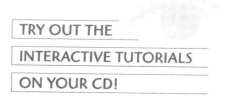

TRY OUT THE INTERACTIVE TUTORIALS ON YOUR CD!

8. Change the query to display any customer record with the title of Sales Manager or Sales Representative in the Contact Title field.
9. Sort the Customer table in ascending order by Country.

How do you sort by more than one field in a table?

10. Use the Filter Form to filter out any forms in the Customer table that do not have the title Marketing Manager.
11. Remove the filter and print only the first six records.

How is a filter different from a query?

12. Preview the Products by Supplier report, displaying six pages in the preview.
13. Print the first page of this report only with landscape orientation.

TROUBLESHOOTING

You finished the book (almost). However, as you continue to use the Office products, and Access in particular, questions will come up. Table 23-1 has the last few troubleshooting tips for using Access.

Problem	Solution
I want to print only those records for people living in Detroit.	You can either select the records you want to print before printing and use the Selected Records option button in the Print Dialog box, or apply a filter before printing to show only those records for Detroit.
Some reports I try to run ask me to fill in a Parameter Value before they'll run.	Somebody created a parameter query; this enables you to set query criteria, such as a date range, each time you run the report. You're being asked to enter a date range, minimum amount of currency, or some other limiting factor for the report.

WRAP UP

You picked up the basics of getting information out of Access using queries, reports, and filters, including the following:

- Creating reports using Reports Wizard and modifying their design in Design View
- Designing a simple query and filter
- Sorting records
- Previewing and printing output

For more practice, try creating a database containing information about your favorite recipes, and create reports and queries to look at information by ingredients, cooking time, or country of origin.

Don't forget to look at Appendix B, Practice Projects. This helps you continue to practice the skills you learned in this book, and master new ones in the weeks to come so that you retain all that hard-earned Office expertise. Now you're on your own: After all, even a tutor has to go home sometime. Good luck!

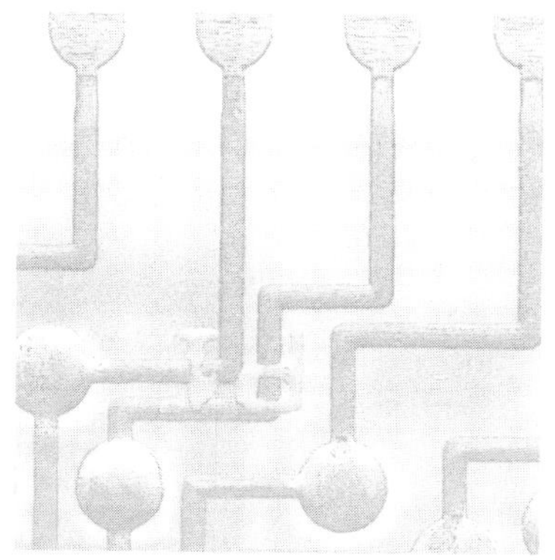

Installing Microsoft Office 97

Installing Microsoft Office 97 on your computer is a relatively simple and straightforward process. However, Office 97 takes up a great deal of hard drive space, so you are forced to make some decisions as the installation proceeds. Appendix A helps you anticipate some of those decisions so you'll know which choices you should make.

Installing Microsoft Office 97

GET READY

These instructions assume that you are loading Office 97 from a CD-ROM, that your CD-ROM drive is labeled (D:), and that you have sufficient space to support a typical installation (about 121 MB). It is also assumes that you are running Windows 95.

You do not have to install all Office programs if you don't need them (or don't have space for them). However, to work through all the exercises in this book, you need to perform a typical installation, and load all the Office programs on your computer.

INSTALLING OFFICE 97

Follow these steps to install Office 97 on your computer's hard drive.

1. Turn on your computer and load Windows.
2. Place the accompanying CD-ROM in your computer CD-ROM drive (typically the (D:) drive).
3. Click the Windows Start menu and select Settings ➢ Control Panel.
4. When the Control Panel window appears, double-click the icon labeled Add/Remove Programs.
5. From the Install/Uninstall tab, choose Install. The *Install Program from Floppy or CD-ROM* dialog box appears.

Office is equipped with an AutoRun feature. Under certain circumstances (such as, you have the CD-ROM in your CD-ROM drive when you boot up your computer), the dialog box mentioned in the previous step appears on your screen automatically, without you having to go through the preceding steps with the Control Panel. If it does, proceed with the steps that follow.

6. Choose Next to proceed. The Run Installation Program dialog box appears, confirming the location of the Office setup file (D:\Setup.exe).

7. Choose Finish to begin the installation. After a moment, the Microsoft Office 97 Setup screen appears, as shown in the illustration to the right.

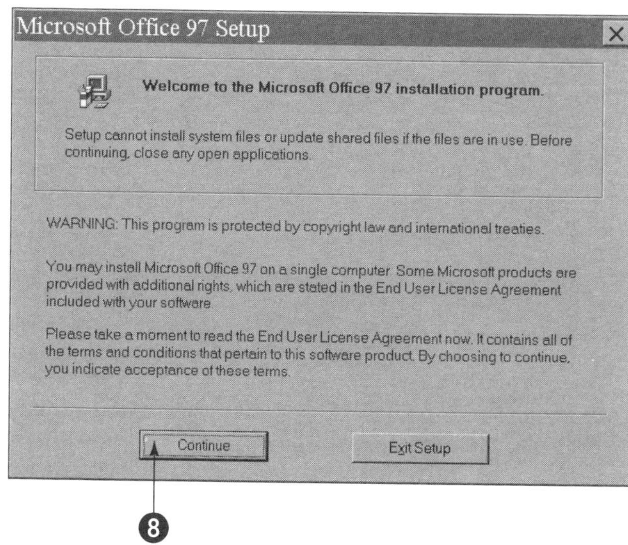

8. Choose Continue. The Name and Organization Information dialog box displays, as in the following illustration.

9. Type your name and, if appropriate, your organization.

10. Choose OK.

    A window appears listing your Product ID number. Make a note of this number; you need to provide it if you call Microsoft technical support.

11. Choose OK to proceed. The dialog box in the bottom right illustration appears.

    This dialog box gives you the option of changing the folder where Microsoft Office is installed. Unless you have a previous version of some of these programs that you want to keep, you should accept the default folder name. If you do wish to have the programs installed to a different folder, you choose Change Folder and enter a new folder name.

12. Choose OK to accept the default folder name. Another dialog box appears offering you a choice of three types of installation.

    - *Typical* installation installs all Office programs, as well as the most commonly used applets and templates. This is the best choice for a less experienced user.
    - *Custom* installation gives you the opportunity to pick and choose what you want to install. This is an option if you don't have enough memory to install all the programs or components, or if you don't need one of the programs at all. If you make this choice, you see a Custom dialog box. You can deselect anything you don't want to install.
    - *Run from CD-ROM* enables you to run most of Office from your CD-ROM drive. However, this makes running the software slow and much less efficient.

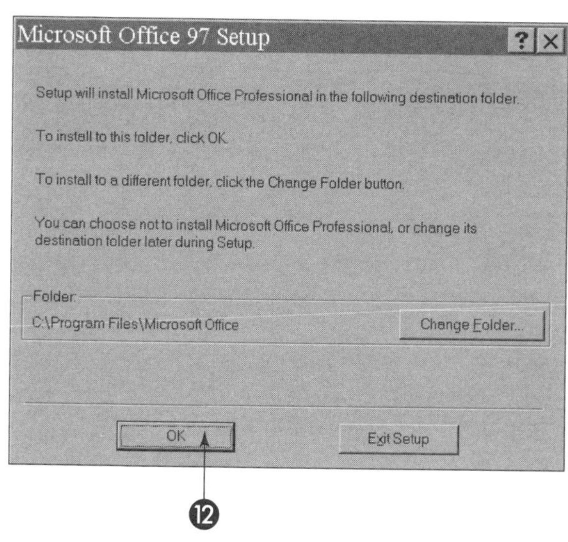

13. Click Typical. The Typical dialog box appears.

    Check the Space required and Space available information at the bottom of the dialog box and be sure you have enough room on your hard drive to install Office. The components that are not selected in the list of Options in this dialog box can always be installed later by running this installation program again. For now, it's best to accept the default typical installation options.

14. Choose Continue.

If you have a previous version of Office installed on your computer, you may see an Upgrade message at this point. This gives you the option of overwriting old versions or keeping them on your computer. Be aware that double versions of Office are likely to use tremendous amounts of space on your hard drive, and choosing to retain older versions may make it impossible to install the new Office. If you don't think you need the older versions, it's best to remove old components when the Upgrade Wizard appears.

A screen appears, tracking the installation with a percentage complete bar. (If you install Office from disks instead of a CD-ROM, you are asked to insert the disks in sequence during this procedure.) It may take several minutes for the installation to complete; it varies, depending on the speed and configuration of your computer.

Some information on the features of Office displays at the top of this screen, which you may want to read to begin to familiarize yourself with the new features of Office 97. When the installation is complete, you see the following screen. If you have a modem installed and wish to register your software online, you can select Online Registration at this time.

15. Choose Restart Windows to complete the installation.

    When Windows reappears, some new elements are added to your desktop: Microsoft Outlook and Setup for Microsoft Office. You can use the latter to install different options at a later time, if you wish.

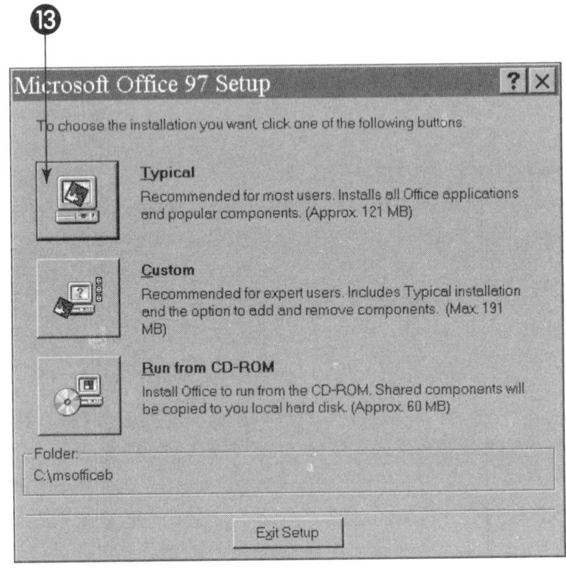

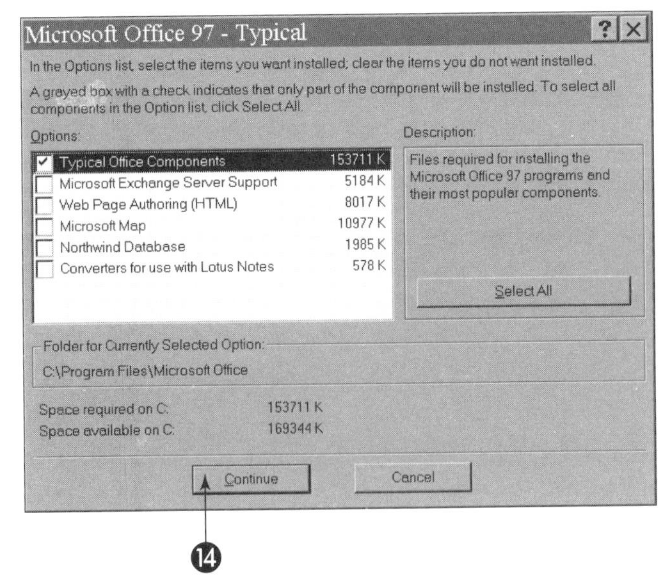

WHAT IF I DON'T HAVE ENOUGH SPACE FOR OFFICE?

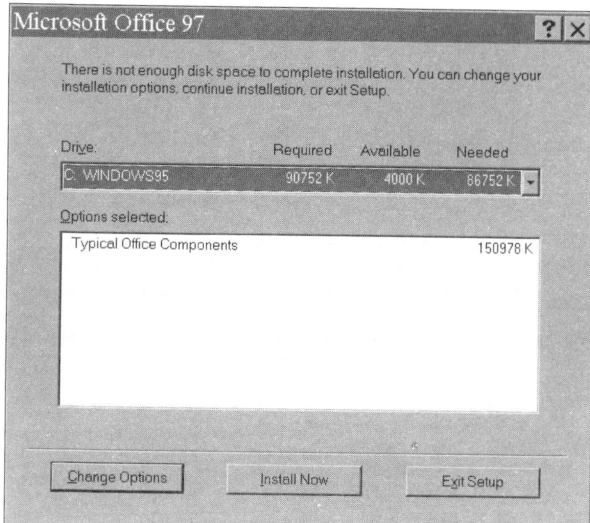

If at some point in the installation process a dialog box appears and tells you that there isn't enough space on your hard drive for Office, you have three options.

You can click Exit Setup to exit the setup program and clean up your hard drive by removing programs you don't need, emptying your Recycle Bin, or running a utility to clean up fragmented files on your hard drive. (You can also consider using a compression program to maximize space on your hard drive.)

You can click Install Now and continue with the installation, knowing that not all components will load and some programs may not run properly.

You can click Change Options. This would take you back to the dialog box where you have a choice of a Typical, Custom, or Run from CD-ROM installation. You could select Custom and choose not to install all programs or components, or run from your CD-ROM, which will be less efficient, but usable.

Only you can determine the best way to make space available for Office on your computer. Remember that the information in this book is based on a typical installation of Microsoft Office.

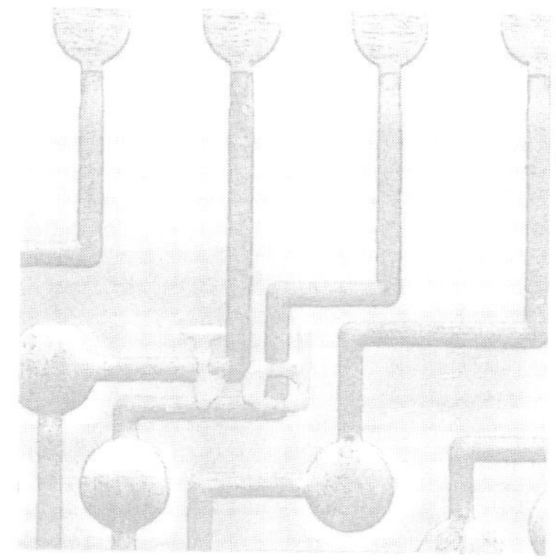

Answers to Bonus Questions

Answers to Bonus Questions

■ Bonus Question 1.1

What are the two ways to close a program?

You can close a program using the Close button or by selecting File ➢ Exit.

■ Bonus Question 1.2

Describe how you would get to this file by opening various folders.

This is an exercise file, located in the folder you created earlier in this lesson. The path is My Computer ➢ (C:) ➢ Personal Trainer Exercises.

■ Bonus Question 1.3

Besides using the scroll bar, how could you see more of the contents of the (C:) drive window?

Click the Restore button to maximize the window, enabling you to see more of the files and folders in it.

■ Bonus Question 2.1

Name four ways to open an Office program.

You can select Start ➢ Programs, and the program name; select Start ➢ New Office Document, and the appropriate type of blank document; locate a file created in that application on your hard drive or a floppy disk and double-click it to open the file and application; or select Start ➢ Document and select a document to open from the sub-menu.

■ Bonus Question 2.2

Name two ways to switch between open programs.

Press Alt + Tab or click the program button on the Windows taskbar.

■ Bonus Question 2.3

Name three ways to close a program.

Click the Close button or select File ➢ Exit; if the program is minimized, click its name on the Windows taskbar with your right mouse button and select Close from the shortcut menu.

■ Bonus Question 3.1

How would you perform the same procedure using a menu command?

Select Format ➢ Font (or, in Excel, Format ➢ Cell). In Excel, select the Font tab; all other programs display the Font dialog box. Select or type a new font size in the Font Size box.

■ Bonus Question 3.2

There are six different ways to move down in a document. Can you name them all?

You can move toward the end of a document using the PAGE DOWN or HOME keys; the down arrow key on your keyboard; by clicking the down arrow at the bottom of the scroll bar; clicking just beneath the scroll box; or dragging the scroll box down.

■ Bonus Question 3.3

What keyword or words could you use to search the Contents and Index feature of Help to get the same information?

Try the keywords *delete*, *cut*, *workbook*, or *worksheet* to get help with deleting a worksheet.

■ Bonus Question 3.4

Name three ways to delete something.

Select Edit ➢ Delete, or press the Backspace key or the Delete key on your keyboard.

Answers to Bonus Questions

Bonus Question 4.1

Do you remember how to see templates listed by file details rather than large icons in the New dialog box?

Choose the Details button to see file details, such as filename and date last modified, in the New dialog box.

Bonus Question 4.2

Can you identify in which view this document appeared?

You are placed in Page Layout view when you base a document on this template.

Bonus Question 4.3

How can you see how your printed document will look without actually printing it?

You can select File ➢ Print Preview to see a representation of the actual printed document.

Bonus Question 4.4

If you want to save this as a WordPerfect file, what change do you make in the Save As dialog box?

In the Save As dialog box, click to open the Save As Type drop-down list. Use the scroll bar in the list to locate the appropriate WordPerfect file format and click it. Proceed to save the file by choosing the Save button.

Bonus Question 5.1

Aside from using the Center button on the toolbar, what is the other way to change text alignment?

Select the text, and then select Format ➢ Paragraph. In the Paragraph dialog box, select Center from the Alignment drop-down list.

■ Bonus Question 5.2

How do you quickly select all text in a document without using your mouse?

To quickly select all text in a document, use the Select All command in the Edit menu.

■ Bonus Question 5.3

If you Cut text, is it deleted?

When you use Cut (or Copy), whatever you cut is placed on the Windows clipboard and remains there until you use Cut (or Copy) again.

■ Bonus Question 5.4

Identify the three fonts used in this document. How was each applied?

Book Antiqua, Times New Roman, and Arial. You applied the Book Antiqua in the Font dialog box, Times New Roman was the font used by the Normal template on which you based your document, and Arial was part of the Heading 3 style you applied.

■ Bonus Question 6.1

What is another way to open WordArt?

You can open WordArt using the WordArt button on the Drawing toolbar.

■ Bonus Question 6.2

How can you add new clip art to the Clip Gallery?

Select Insert ➢ Picture ➢ Clip Art. In the dialog box that follows, select the category where you want to add the file, and then use the Import Clips button to locate a file and open it.

Answers to Bonus Questions

■ Bonus Question 6.3

What other fill effects can be added to objects?

The fill effects available to you are Gradient, Texture, Pattern, and Picture.

■ Bonus Question 7.1

Name two ways to create a table.

You can create a table using the Insert Table button or selecting Table ➢ Draw Table and using the Draw Table tool on the Table and Borders toolbar.

■ Bonus Question 7.2

Name two ways to change column or row size.

You can click the lines of a table, use the Column or Row Division markers on the rulers, or select Table ➢ Cell Height and Width and enter exact measurements in the Cell Height and Width dialog box.

■ Bonus Question 7.3

How would you move the entire table to the right so it lines up with the left edge of the text in the memo?

To answer this one, you have to pay attention to the elements of a table. A table has its own margin marker on the horizontal ruler. With the table selected, drag the table's left margin marker to the right to line up with the left margin of the text.

■ Bonus Question 8.1

Where are the margins indicated in Print Preview?

The gray area on the horizontal and vertical rulers indicate the margins of the page.

Bonus Question 8.2

If you want to see several pages of a document in Print Preview, how do you display them?

Choose the Multiple Pages button on the Print Preview toolbar, and then drag your cursor over the page icons in the drop-down list to select as many pages as you'd like to display.

Bonus Question 8.3

If you want to put your name in the header, what is the quickest way to do that?

Choose the Insert AutoText button on the Header and Footer toolbar and select Created by (assuming you created the document).

Bonus Question 8.4

If you want multiple copies to print in complete sets, what setting do you choose?

Choose the Collate check box in the Print dialog box.

Bonus Question 9.1

If you want a blank line to appear for any records with no data in the Company field, where do you check that setting?

From the Mail Merge Helper, choose Merge. In the Merge dialog box, check the Print blank lines when data fields are empty option button.

Bonus Question 9.2

How do you quickly move to the last record?

Use the Last Record button on the Mail Merge toolbar. (This can be a real lifesaver with a data source containing hundreds of records!)

Answers to Bonus Questions

Bonus Question 9.3

To sort records so that all the records from a particular PostalCode appear in a group, and the higher zip codes print first, what settings would you make in the Query Options dialog box?

Select the Sort Records tab. Sort by PostalCode and check Descending to have the higher ZIP codes print first.

Bonus Question 10.1

What is the formula displayed in the formula bar calculating?

This formula is calculating the average of the numbers in cells B3, C3, D3, and E3.

Bonus Question 10.2

What are the two ways to rename a worksheet?

Double-click the sheet tab itself, or right-click on the tab and select Rename from the shortcut menu.

Bonus Question 10.3

How can you set up Excel to provide five worksheets in each new workbook by default?

Select Tools ➢ Options. On the General tab of the Options dialog box, click the up arrow in the Sheets in new workbook field twice.

Bonus Question 11.1

What tool can you use to quickly change font color?

The Font Color tool on the Formatting toolbar.

Bonus Question 11.2

Name two methods of changing column or row size.

You can use the two-headed arrow cursor to drag the edge of a row or column or select the column or row and select Format ➢ Column or Format ➢ Row, respectively.

Bonus Question 11.3

If you select a column and insert a new column, does the new column appear to the left or right of the selected column?

A new column appears to the left of the selected column.

Bonus Question 12.1

How do you use your mouse to complete a formula?

Enter **=SUM(**, and then drag your mouse over the cells you want to include in the cell range; press ENTER.

Bonus Question 12.2

What operator do you use to designate a range of cells?

The colon (:) is the operator to indicate a range of cells, as in D1:D10.

Bonus Question 12.3

What is the fastest way to place this formula in all three cells?

Select the cell and click the Copy button. Drag your mouse across all the cells you want to copy the formula to, and then click the Paste button.

Bonus Question 12.4

What is the total of costs for this budget?

If you've applied the formula correctly, the total of all costs in the marketing department budget should be $155,500.

Bonus Question 13.1

What are two ways of designating source data?

Select the data from a worksheet using your mouse or type in a range of data in the Chart Wizard dialog box.

Answers to Bonus Questions

■ Bonus Question 13.2

How do you determine that a chart will have a 3-D effect applied?

Choose a 3-D chart type when you first create the chart.

■ Bonus Question 13.3

How do you preview how a chart type will look with your chart?

Use the Press and hold to view sample bar in the Chart Type dialog box.

■ Bonus Question 14.1

Name four ways you can adjust sizing of output.

You can change the margins, adjust the percentage of normal size in the Page tab of the Page Setup dialog box, set the scaling to fit to a set number of pages on the same tab, or modify the width of columns or rows in your worksheet to be smaller or larger.

■ Bonus Question 14.2

Name two methods of changing margins.

Use the settings in the Margins tab of the Page Setup dialog box, or drag margin lines displayed in Print Preview to new settings.

■ Bonus Question 14.3

What percentage does Excel have to use to print this worksheet on a single page?

Your percentage should now read 77 percent.

■ Bonus Question 14.4

Why could hiding these rows confuse the readers of your spreadsheet?

This one's a little tricky, but think about it; if you hide columns whose values are part of the formula in the Total Sales row, the numbers that print in the columns won't add up to the Total Sales value, which could be confusing to someone reading the worksheet. Keep this in mind when using the Hide feature with columns or rows.

■ Bonus Question 15.1

When you first open PowerPoint, how do you start the AutoContent Wizard?

AutoContent Wizard is one of the four choices offered to you on the opening screen of PowerPoint. You can select that option to begin to run the wizard.

■ Bonus Question 15.2

Name three elements or settings for your PowerPoint slides that can be contained in a template.

A template can contain a background color, background pattern, graphic elements, and text formatting including font, font size, and special effects such as bold, italic, or shadow.

■ Bonus Question 15.3

What is the other method of displaying the Slide Sorter view?

Click the Slide Sorter button on the bottom left-hand corner of the screen (just above the Drawing toolbar).

■ Bonus Question 15.4

In the previous step, there are two ways to achieve these text formatting changes. What are they?

You can use the Bold and Shadow buttons on the toolbar or select Format ➢ Font, and make both changes at once from the Font dialog box.

Answers to Bonus Questions

Bonus Question 16.1

What are the different ways to change the order of slides in a presentation?

You can click and drag slides to new locations in the presentation sequence in either Slide Sorter view or Outline view.

Bonus Question 16.2

If you use a layout with two placeholders but you only enter text in one, what appears in the empty placeholder when you print the slide?

Placeholders with no text entered don't print at all.

Bonus Question 16.3

How do you control where on your slide a clip art image appears?

You can't control where clip art will appear on a slide; you'll have to move it after it's been inserted.

Bonus Question 16.4

How do you ungroup grouped objects?

Select the grouped object, and then select Draw ➢ Ungroup.

Bonus Question 16.5

What two PowerPoint features can you display to help you position objects on screen?

You can use the View menu to display Rulers or Guides to help with positioning objects on a slide.

Bonus Question 17.1

How do you apply an animation effect using a menu command?

Select Slide Show ➢ Preset Animation and select an effect from the side menu that appears.

Bonus Question 17.2

What are two ways to apply timing to your show?

Select Slide Show ➢ Rehearse Timing, or save the timings created when you record a narration.

Bonus Question 18.1

From which two places in Outlook can you indicate an incomplete task?

You can do this in the Calendar and Tasks areas of Outlook.

Bonus Question 18.2

What is the difference between an appointment, an event, and a task?

An appointment has a specific start and end time, but is less than 24 hours long. An event has a specific start and end date, but is more than 24 hours long. A task may have a date by which you'd like to complete it, but no start and end time. Note that an appointment can also have a reminder attached to it and can be marked as private.

Bonus Question 18.3

Name three ways to enter a new task.

From the Calendar or Tasks areas of Outlook, you can click once in the Click here to add a new Task field and type the task name; you can double-click in the same field and enter the task in the Task form; you can select New Task from the New Tool drop-down list and enter the task in the Task form.

Bonus Question 19.1

Name two ways to set the length of a meeting in Meeting Planner.

Drag one side of the meeting selection bar until it spans the desired time frame, or enter a specific start and end time for the meeting.

Answers to Bonus Questions

Bonus Question 19.2

Name two ways to go to the Journal area of Outlook.

Select the Journal item from the Outlook bar, or click the Folder List tool and select Journal from the Folder List that appears.

Bonus Question 19.3

What's the shortcut for performing the preceding step?

Select Contact ➢ New Contact from Same Company.

Bonus Question 20.1

How do you place names and e-mail addresses in your system so they're available to you in the Select Names dialog box?

Add names to the Outlook Contacts, making sure to include their e-mail addresses, before composing a new message.

Bonus Question 20.2

Name two ways to determine the importance of the message.

You can use the Importance: High or Importance: Low buttons on the message form toolbar (if you don't choose one or the other, the importance is Normal by default). You can also choose the importance from a drop-down list on the Options tab of the new message dialog box.

Bonus Question 20.3

Where do you set a message to be confidential?

You can choose Private, Personal, or Confidential from the Sensitivity drop-down list on the Options tab of a new message dialog box.

Bonus Question 21.1

From which two areas of Access can you enter and edit records?

You can enter and edit records in tables or forms.

■ Bonus Question 21.2

What does an AutoNumber field do?

An AutoNumber field automatically generates the next number in a sequence when you create a new record.

■ Bonus Question 21.3

How can you move quickly to the last record?

Click the Last Record button near the bottom of the form window to move to the last record.

■ Bonus Question 22.1

Can you perform calculations on text fields?

You can't perform calculations on text fields; you have to use number or currency fields for calculations.

■ Bonus Question 22.2

What are two ways to rename fields?

You can choose the Rename Fields button when you're running the wizard and selecting the fields to include, or you can double-click the field name in the table view and type in a new name.

■ Bonus Question 22.3

How do you change the design style after you've completed the Form Wizard?

Select Format ➢ AutoFormat to select a new design style for your form.

Answers to Bonus Questions

■ Bonus Question 23.1

How would you change the name of this report from its default name?

You can assign a different name for a report on the last Report Wizard dialog box, or right-click the report name and select Rename from the shortcut menu that appears.

■ Bonus Question 23.2

How do you sort by more than one field in a table?

To sort by more than one field, place the two fields next to each other, with the first sort to the left. Select both fields, and then use the Sort Ascending or Sort Descending buttons on the toolbar to sort them.

■ Bonus Question 23.3

How is a filter different from a query?

A filter enables you to take data from your table and specify that records with that data are the only ones that should be displayed in the table view. A query is a more complex operation run from the query window (not from the table window) that can add a variety of parameters to the criteria and can be saved and run as many times as you like.

What's on the CD-ROM

The CD-ROM in the back of the book includes the exclusive *One Step at a Time On-Demand* software. This interactive software coaches you through the exercises in the book's lessons while you work on a computer at your own pace.

USING THE ONE STEP AT A TIME ON-DEMAND INTERACTIVE SOFTWARE

One Step at a Time On-Demand interactive software includes the exercises in the book so that you can search for information about how to perform a function or complete a task. You can run the software alone or in combination with the book. The software consists of three modes: Demo, Teacher, and Concurrent. In addition, the Concept option provides an overview of each exercise.

- **Demo** mode provides a movie-style demonstration of the same steps that are presented in the book's exercises, and works with the sample exercise files that are included on the CD-ROM in the Exercise Files folder.

Using the One Step Software

- **Teacher** mode simulates the software environment and permits you to interactively follow the exercises in the book's lessons.
- **Concurrent** mode enables you to use the *One Step at a Time-On Demand* features while you work within the actual Office 97 environment. This unique interactive mode provides audio instructions, and directs you to take the correct actions as you work through the exercises. (Concurrent mode may not be available to all exercises.)

Installing the software

The *One Step at a Time On-Demand* software can be installed on Windows 95 and Windows NT 4.0. To install the interactive software on your computer, follow these steps:

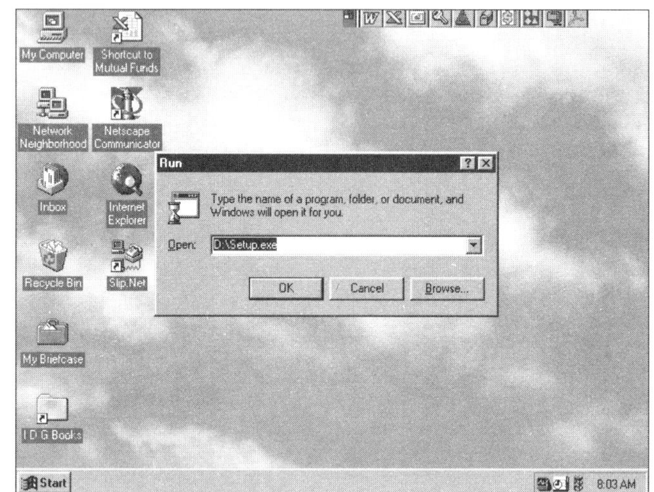

1. Place the *Office 97 One Step at a Time* CD-ROM in your CD-ROM drive.
2. Launch Windows (if you haven't already).
3. Click the Start menu.
4. Select Run. The Run dialog box appears.
5. Type **D:\Setup.exe** (where D is your CD-ROM drive) in the Run dialog box.
6. Click OK to run the setup procedure. The On-Demand Installation dialog box appears.
7. Click Continue. The On-Demand Installation Options dialog box appears.
8. Click the Full/Network radio button (if this option is not already selected).

Full/Network installation requires approximately 150MB of hard disk space. If you don't have enough hard disk space, click the Standard radio button to choose Standard installation. If you choose standard installation, you should always insert the CD-ROM when you start the software to hear sound.

9. Click Next. The Determine Installation Drive and Directory dialog box appears.
10. Choose the default drive and directory that appears, or click Change to choose a different drive and directory.
11. Click Next. The Product Selection dialog box appears, which enables you to verify the software you want to install.
12. Click Finish to complete the installation. The On-Demand Installation dialog box displays the progress of the installation. After the installation, the Multiuser Pack Registration dialog box appears.
13. Enter information in the Multiuser Pack Registration dialog box.
14. Click OK. The On-Demand Installation dialog box appears.
15. Click OK to confirm the installation has been successfully completed.

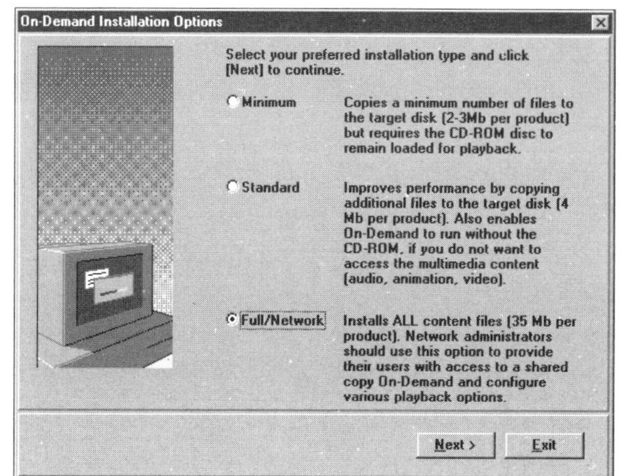

■ Running the software

If you run the One Step at a Time On-Demand software in Windows 98, we recommend you don't work in Teacher or Concurrent mode unless you first turn off the Active Desktop feature. However, Teacher mode and Concurrent mode may not work properly at all in Windows 98. At the time of this writing, the final release of Windows 98 was not available and all topics could not be tested in Teacher and Concurrent modes.

Once you've installed the software, you can view the text of the book and follow interactively the steps in each exercise. To run Demo, Teacher, or Concurrent mode, follow these steps:

1. From the Windows desktop, click the Start menu.
2. Select Programs ➢ IDG Books Worldwide ➢ Office 97 One Step. A small On Demand toolbar appears in the upper-right corner of your screen.

3. The On-Demand Reminder dialog box appears, telling you that the On-Demand software is active. If you don't want to display the dialog box, deselect the Show Reminder check box. Then, click OK.
4. Click the icon of the professor. The Interactive Training — Lesson Selection dialog box appears.
5. Select the Contents tab, if it isn't selected already. A list of the lessons appears, divided into six parts.
6. Click the plus icon next to the part you want to explore, or click the Lessons radio button. A list of the lessons appears.
7. Click the plus icon next to the lesson you want to explore. Topics appear. If you wish to work in Concurrent mode, begin with the first topic of any lesson because the software may direct you to open specific files you use to complete the steps in the lesson.
8. Double-click a topic of your choice. A menu appears.
9. Select Demo, Teacher, or Concurrent.
10. Follow the onscreen prompts to use the interactive software and work through the steps.

In Demo mode, you only need to perform actions that appear in red. Otherwise, the software automatically demonstrates the actions for you. All you need to do is read the information that appears on screen. (Holding down the Shift key pauses the program; releasing the Shift key activates the program.) In Teacher mode, you need to follow the directions and perform the actions that appear on screen.

Getting the Most Out of the One Step at a Time Software

It is strongly recommended that you read the topics in the book as you are using the software (especially while working in Concurrent mode). In those instances where the onscreen instructions don't match the book's instructions exactly, or the software appears to stop before completing a task, the book will provide the instructions necessary for you to continue.

■ Stopping the program

To stop running the program at any time, press Esc to return to the Interactive Training – Lesson Selection dialog box. (To re-start the software, double-click a topic of your choice and select a mode.)

■ Exiting the program

Press Esc when the Interactive Training – Lesson Selection dialog box appears to exit the program. The On-Demand toolbar appears in the upper right corner of your screen. Click the icon that displays the lightning bolt image. A menu appears. Choose Exit. The On-Demand – Exit dialog box appears. Click Yes to exit On-Demand.

■ Copying exercise files to your hard drive

Generally, your computer works more efficiently with files located on the hard drive, rather than a floppy disk or CD-ROM. To make your work in this book easier, copy the exercise files into a folder on your hard drive. You can then open and work with the files from that location when instructed to do so.

1. Double-click the My Computer icon on your desktop.
2. Double-click the hard drive (C:).
3. Select File ➢ New, and then choose Folder from the submenu that appears.

   A new folder appears, with the name New Folder.
4. Type **One Step** to name the folder.
5. Press Enter.
6. Close the My Computer window.
7. Place the *Office 97 One Step at a Time* CD-ROM into the disc drive.
8. Double-click the My Computer icon again and, in the My Computer window, double-click the CD-ROM icon to open the drive where you inserted the disc.
9. Click the folder named Exercise.

10. Copy the selected folder by pressing Ctrl + C.
11. Close the CD-ROM window.
12. Double-click the My Computer icon on your desktop.
13. In the My Computer window, double-click the hard drive (C:).
14. Double-click the One Step folder.
15. Paste the Exercise folder into the One Step folder by pressing Ctrl + V. All of the exercise files are now located within this folder on your hard drive.

Using the Exercise Files

You need to make sure you have removed the Read-only attribute from any files you copy to the hard drive before you start using them. Otherwise, you will not be able to save changes to the files. To remove the Read-only attribute, open the Exercise folder on your hard drive and press Ctrl + A to select all the files in the folder. From the File menu, select Properties. The Properties dialog box appears. Click the Read-only attribute to remove the check from the checkbox.

FINDING OUT MORE ABOUT ON-DEMAND INTERACTIVE LEARNING

You may install additional modules of On-Demand Interactive Learning and find out more about PTS Learning Systems, the company behind the software, by using a file on the CD-ROM included with this book. Follow these steps:

1. Start your browser.
2. Select File from the menu.
3. Select Open.
4. Type **D:\info\welcome.htm**, where D is your CD-ROM drive.
5. Click OK to view the contents.

This glossary contains simple definitions of some of the common computer terms you'll encounter in this book and as you use the Office products. Although this section provides basic definitions of many terms, it's not exhaustive; don't forget that you can also use the Contents and Index choice in each Office product's help feature to search for information on terminology that you may not understand.

A

align To arrange text or an object relative to the document margins, or to another object. Alignment choices are left, right, center, and justify.

annotate In PowerPoint, annotating is the ability to add comments to slides as you present them. In Excel, annotating a cell means to attach a note to a cell.

applet A small application that performs a useful function; specifically an application built into Office that is available to and can be opened from all of the Office products. WordArt and Microsoft Organization Chart are examples of applets.

application A term for a piece of computer software; also called program.

attachment Any file send with an e-mail message is called an attachment.

attribute A characteristic of something, such as a font or object. Examples of attributes would be color or size. An example of a file attribute would be its size.

audience handout In PowerPoint, one type of output which prints the contents of two, three, or six presentation slides on a page to help viewers of a presentation to follow along.

B

bullet A symbol used to precede a list of items in no particular order. Bullet symbols can be virtually any shape, but the most common is a solid circle.

C

cell In Excel, the point where a row and column meet in a worksheet.

clip art Ready-made line drawings that are stored in Microsoft Clip Gallery and available to all Office products. Clip art collections can also be purchased or downloaded from online sources.

collate To print more than one copy of a document so that the pages of each copy print in order.

D

data type The category of information that data falls within, such as numbers, currency, date, and so on.

default Settings in a computer program that will be in effect unless you change them. For example, you can set a default printer, and you will always print to that printer unless you change the setting.

delegate In Outlook, somebody to whom you assign the responsibility for a task.

dialog box A box that appears on your computer screen during certain procedures that allows you to make settings by typing, selecting items from a list or checking boxes or buttons.

download To retrieve a copy of a file from an online source, such as the Internet, and place it on your computer's hard drive, a network or a floppy disk.

drag and drop A function that enables you to drag a selected object from one place to another either within a document or from one document to another. Drag and drop works between documents created in different Office products.

E

e-mail Electronic mail consists of typed messages that can be sent over a computer network with e-mail software installed, or through an online service such as America Online.

embed To place a copy of an object in a document using a technology called Object Linking and Embedding (OLE).

extension A three letter designation at the end of a file name that indicates what program the file was created in or what software format it was saved to. *See* file format.

F

field In a database or form letter, a placeholder for a certain type of information, such as first or last name. Corresponding specific data is then placed in that field through a table lookup or mail merge.

file format The arrangement of and computer standards used for storing computer information. A format may relate to the type of software used to create a file, or the way the information was saved. *See* extension.

file type When opening or saving a file, a file type field enables you to choose the kind of file to use, such as a word-processed document, graphics file, or Excel worksheet.

fill effects For drawing objects and clip art, fill effects can be applied to add color, patterns, or textures to the inside of the object.

filter In Access, a filter can be used to display or print only data records that match certain criteria, thereby filtering out the records that don't match the criteria.

folder A file management device provided by Windows, a folder can be named and used to store individual computer files in groups.

font Also called typeface, a font is a design family of letters, symbols, and numerals with a common look.

footer Information placed at the bottom of each page of a document or section of a document, but entered only once in a Footer dialog box.

formula In Excel, any set of symbols and numbers that define a calculation to be performed on values in a worksheet.

function In Excel, a saved procedure that produces a value. A Date & Time function, for example, when placed in a document, returns the value of the current date and time.

G

GIF Graphics Interchange Format. A file format for graphics files. *See* File formats.

grid In PowerPoint, a display of intersecting lines used to line up objects on a slide. In Access, grids are dots at regular intervals that are used to position objects precisely when designing forms.

grouping To connect two or more objects so that they become a single, larger object.

H

handle Eight small squares that appear when you select objects. These handles are used to resize the object.

header Information placed at the top of every page in a document or section of a document, but entered only once in a Header dialog box.

HTML Hyper Text Markup Language. The language used to create pages on the World Wide Web. It enables online users to open Web pages by clicking on text or graphics.

hyperlink Using Hyper Text Markup Language (HTML), hyperlinks allow a computer user to click on an object and be taken directly to a file in another location. This location can be a file on the Internet or an internal company intranet.

I

import To place a file created in one program into a second program.

Internet A worldwide network of computers with no central operating organization that enables computer users to share information and send e-mail. Originally established for government research, it holds a wealth of resources for information on a variety of topics from universities, museums, commercial data providers, and individuals.

intranet An intranet, on its simplest level, is a network of computers internal to an organization that has hyperlink capabilities.

K

keyword In Access, a term that defines the topic of a data search.

L

Landscape Orientation of a printed page that places the top of a document along the longer side of the paper. *See* orientation.

layout In PowerPoint, a predefined set of text or graphic objects on a slide, such as a title and bullet list.

link To establish a connection between an embedded object and the software program it was created in. The data is actually stored outside the file which contains the link. When a link is in effect, any update to the object in the original software will be reflected in the linked and embedded copy of it.

M

macro A set of recorded keystrokes or actions that can be replayed.

mail merge The process of creating a form document, adding fields for data, and combining the form with specific data to produce personalized documents.

Master In PowerPoint, a feature that allows you to place items you want to appear on every slide, such as a company logo, on a master slide.

menu A set of named commands that can be selected to invoke a procedure or open a dialog box. Menus appear on a menu bar, and sometimes contain sub or cascading menus.

multimedia The use of several methods of communication, such as sound, animation, movies, and text.

O

OLE Object Linking and Embedding. This Microsoft-created technology allows you to place a copy of an object created in one program in another and, with linking applied, the original data for the object is actually maintained outside of the file containing the link and any update to the original object will be applied to the copy.

Office Assistant A help feature new to Office 97 that allows you to enter a question to get help with a topic.

online A connection to another computer through a network or online service such as the Internet or CompuServe that enables you to receive and send information or files.

orientation The angle of the material on a page relative to either the long or short side of a piece of paper. *See* Landscape and Portrait.

P

paste To place an object on the Windows clipboard in a document.

placeholder In PowerPoint, an editable object that indicates the placement of an item, such as a slide title, in the selected page layout.

pop-up menu A menu of choices that appears only when you click on a pop-up menu arrow on a toolbar or in a dialog box.

Portrait Orientation of a printed page that places the top of a document along the shorter side of the paper. (See Orientation.)

program A set of instructions in a specific computer programming language that a computer can perform. Also called software.

Q

query A request for information that matches specific criteria. In Access, a query can result in a report or display of matching information that is located in tables and forms.

R

range In Excel, a description of a set of cells used in formulas to perform calculations. A1:G5 identifies a range of cells, for example.

record A set of data. In Access, a single record might consist of contact information for a single customer.

S

scroll bar A mouse-operated device located on the far right (vertical) or bottom (horizontal) of a program screen used to navigate from screen to screen, page to page or slide to slide.

select To designate an object or text for action. A selected object is often selected with a mouse click, and usually appears to have a highlighted affect.

sound clip A sound file.

Speaker's Notes In PowerPoint, a type of output that places a single slide and speaker's comments on each printed page.

styles Named and saved sets of text attributes.

symbol A typed character other than a letter or number. A dollar sign, bullet, or ampersand are examples of symbols. In Access and Excel, symbols can be used in formulas or expressions to perform queries or invoke calculations.

T

template A named and saved group of settings which can include color, margin and indent settings, font, page orientation, and even text placeholders. Templates act like patterns on which documents can be based. They are used in Word, Excel, and PowerPoint.

tool An on-screen button that provides a shortcut to a menu command function.

Tracking In Outlook, to follow and record activity relative to a specific task. In Word, Tracking relates to creating a record of revisions in a document.

transition In PowerPoint, a multimedia effect invoked when you move from one slide to the next. A transition might be an animation effect or sound clip.

U

Undo A feature of all Office programs that enables you to reverse an action or group of actions in order.

V

View Views are used in Office programs to provide an environment for different types of activity in a program. For example, in PowerPoint, an Outline View enables you to work with the organization of your slide contents, while a Slide View is the best place to add drawn objects and format text.

W

WYSIWYG What You See Is What You Get. This acronym represents a technology that enables you to preview exactly how the printed output of a document would appear on your screen before printing.

window A movable and resizable frame that contains a list of the contents of a directory or drive, help information or a computer program.

Windows A program from Microsoft that provides a graphical interface for computer functions.

Windows clipboard A holding place for text or objects that have been cut or copied from a document. The clipboard is only capable of holding one item at a time.

wizard An interactive routine that creates new documents based on your answers to a set of questions and choices you have made in dialog boxes.

workbook In Excel, a set of worksheets that make up a single file.

worksheet Individual pages of an Excel workbook that contain columns and rows for inputting data.

WWW World Wide Web. A system on the Internet that uses hyperlinks to navigate among the various pages on it.

Z

zoom To view a document at a reduced or enlarged percentage.

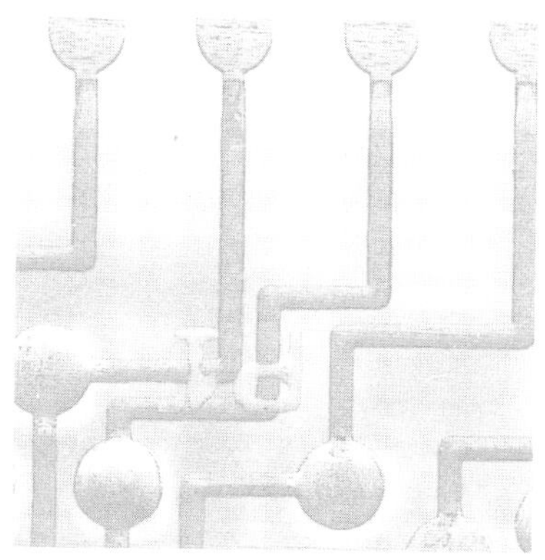

A–D

E

E–I

M–P

Q

R

S

T

continued

IDG BOOKS WORLDWIDE, INC.
END-USER LICENSE AGREEMENT

Read This. You should carefully read these terms and conditions before opening the software packet(s) included with this book ("Book"). This is a license agreement ("Agreement") between you and IDG Books Worldwide, Inc. ("IDGB"). By opening the accompanying software packet(s), you acknowledge that you have read and accept the following terms and conditions. If you do not agree and do not want to be bound by such terms and conditions, promptly return the Book and the unopened software packet(s) to the place you obtained them for a full refund.

1. **License Grant.** IDGB grants to you (either an individual or entity) a nonexclusive license to use one copy of the enclosed software program(s) (collectively, the "Software") solely for your own personal or business purposes on a single computer (whether a standard computer or a workstation component of a multiuser network). The Software is in use on a computer when it is loaded into temporary memory (i.e., RAM) or installed into permanent memory (e.g., hard disk, CD-ROM, or other storage device). IDGB reserves all rights not expressly granted herein.

2. **Ownership.** IDGB is the owner of all right, title, and interest, including copyright, in and to the compilation of the Software recorded on the disk(s)/CD-ROM. Copyright to the individual programs on the disk(s)/CD-ROM is owned by the author or other authorized copyright owner of each program. Ownership of the Software and all proprietary rights relating thereto remain with IDGB and its licensors.

3. **Restrictions on Use and Transfer.**

   (a) You may only (i) make one copy of the Software for backup or archival purposes, or (ii) transfer the Software to a single hard disk, provided that you keep the original for backup or archival purposes. You may not (i) rent or lease the Software, (ii) copy or reproduce the Software through a LAN or other network system or through any computer subscriber system or bulletin-board system, or (iii) modify, adapt, or create derivative works based on the Software.

   (b) You may not reverse engineer, decompile, or disassemble the Software. You may transfer the Software and user documentation on a permanent basis, provided that the transferee agrees to accept the terms and conditions of this Agreement and you retain no copies. If the Software is an update or has been updated, any transfer must include the most recent update and all prior versions.

4. **Restrictions on Use of Individual Programs.** You must follow the individual requirements and restrictions detailed for each individual program in Appendix C "What's on the CD-ROM." These limitations are contained in the individual license agreements recorded on the disk(s)/CD-ROM. These restrictions may include a requirement that after using the program for the period of time specified in its text, the user must pay a registration fee or discontinue use. By opening the Software packet(s), you will be agreeing to abide by the licenses and restrictions for these individual programs. None of the material on this disk(s) or listed in this Book may ever be distributed, in original or modified form, for commercial purposes.

5. Limited Warranty.

(a) IDGB warrants that the Software and disk(s)/CD-ROM are free from defects in materials and workmanship under normal use for a period of sixty (60) days from the date of purchase of this Book. If IDGB receives notification within the warranty period of defects in materials or workmanship, IDGB will replace the defective disk(s)/CD-ROM.

(b) **IDGB AND THE AUTHOR OF THE BOOK DISCLAIM ALL OTHER WARRANTIES, EXPRESS OR IMPLIED, INCLUDING, WITHOUT LIMITATION, IMPLIED WARRANTIES OF MERCHANTABILITY AND FITNESS FOR A PARTICULAR PURPOSE, WITH RESPECT TO THE SOFTWARE, THE PROGRAMS, THE SOURCE CODE CONTAINED THEREIN, AND/OR THE TECHNIQUES DESCRIBED IN THIS BOOK. IDGB DOES NOT WARRANT THAT THE FUNCTIONS CONTAINED IN THE SOFTWARE WILL MEET YOUR REQUIREMENTS OR THAT THE OPERATION OF THE SOFTWARE WILL BE ERROR FREE.**

(c) This limited warranty gives you specific legal rights, and you may have other rights which vary from jurisdiction to jurisdiction.

6. Remedies.

(a) IDGB's entire liability and your exclusive remedy for defects in materials and workmanship shall be limited to replacement of the Software, which may be returned to IDGB with a copy of your receipt at the following address: Disk Fulfillment Department, Attn: Office 97 One Step at a Time, IDG Books Worldwide, Inc., 7260 Shadeland Station, Ste. 100, Indianapolis, IN 46256, or call 1-800-762-2974. Please allow 3-4 weeks for delivery. This Limited Warranty is void if failure of the Software has resulted from accident, abuse, or misapplication. Any replacement Software will be warranted for the remainder of the original warranty period or thirty (30) days, whichever is longer.

(b) In no event shall IDGB or the author be liable for any damages whatsoever (including without limitation damages for loss of business profits, business interruption, loss of business information, or any other pecuniary loss) arising from the use of or inability to use the Book or the Software, even if IDGB has been advised of the possibility of such damages.

(c) Because some jurisdictions do not allow the exclusion or limitation of liability for consequential or incidental damages, the above limitation or exclusion may not apply to you.

7. U.S. Government Restricted Rights. Use, duplication, or disclosure of the Software by the U.S. Government is subject to restrictions stated in paragraph (c) (1) (ii) of the Rights in Technical Data and Computer Software clause of DFARS 252.227-7013, and in subparagraphs (a) through (d) of the Commercial Computer—Restricted Rights clause at FAR 52.227-19, and in similar clauses in the NASA FAR supplement, when applicable.

8. General. This Agreement constitutes the entire understanding of the parties and revokes and supersedes all prior agreements, oral or written, between them and may not be modified or amended except in a writing signed by both parties hereto which specifically refers to this Agreement. This Agreement shall take precedence over any other documents that may be in conflict herewith. If any one or more provisions contained in this Agreement are held by any court or tribunal to be invalid, illegal, or otherwise unenforceable, each and every other provision shall remain in full force and effect.

CD-ROM Installation Instructions

The CD-ROM includes the interactive *One Step at a Time On-Demand* software. This software coaches you through the exercises in the book while you work on a computer at your own pace.

INSTALLING THE ONE STEP AT A TIME ON-DEMAND INTERACTIVE SOFTWARE

The *One Step at a Time On-Demand* software can be installed on Windows 95 and Windows NT 4.0. To install the interactive software on your computer, follow these steps:

1. Place the *Office 97 One Step at a Time* CD-ROM in your CD-ROM drive.
2. Launch Windows (if you haven't already).
3. Click the Start menu.
4. Select Run. The Run dialog box appears.
5. Type **D:\Setup.exe** (where D is your CD-ROM drive) in the Run dialog box.

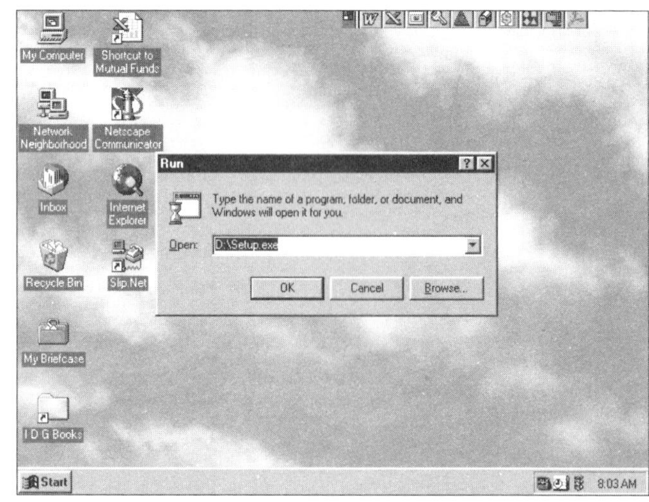

6. Click OK to run the setup procedure. The On-Demand Installation dialog box appears.
7. Click Continue. The On-Demand Installation Options dialog box appears.
8. Click the Full/Network radio button (if this option is not already selected).

   Note: Full/Network installation requires approximately 150MB of hard disk space. If you don't have enough hard disk space, click the Standard radio button to choose Standard installation. If you choose standard installation, you should always insert the CD-ROM when you start the software to hear sound.

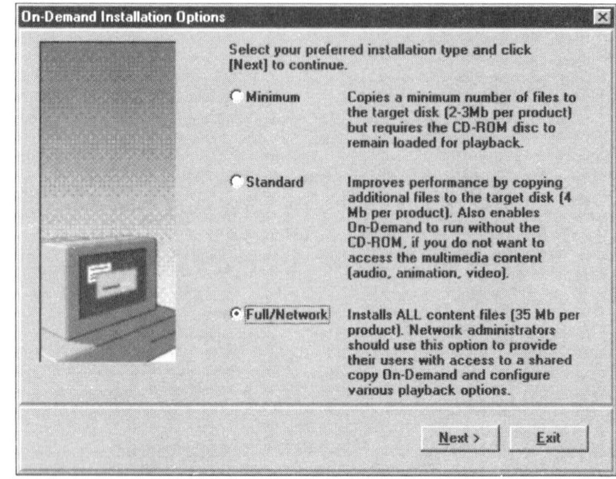

9. Click Next. The Determine Installation Drive and Directory dialog box appears.
10. Choose the default drive and directory that appears, or click Change to choose a different drive and directory.
11. Click Next. The Product Selection dialog box appears, which enables you to verify the software you want to install.
12. Click Finish to complete the installation. The On-Demand Installation dialog box displays the progress of the installation. After the installation, the Multiuser Pack Registration dialog box appears.

13. Enter information in the Multiuser Pack Registration dialog box.
14. Click OK. The On-Demand Installation dialog box appears.
15. Click OK to confirm the installation has been successfully completed.

Please see Appendix C, "What's on the CD-ROM," for information about running the *One Step at a Time On-Demand* interactive software.

■ Copying exercise files to your hard drive

Generally, your computer works more efficiently with files located on the hard drive, rather than a floppy disk or CD-ROM. To make your work in this book easier, copy the exercise files into a folder on your hard drive. You can then open and work with the files from that location when instructed to do so.

1. Double-click the My Computer icon on your desktop.
2. Double-click the hard drive (C:).
3. Select File ➢ New, and then choose Folder from the submenu that appears.

   A new folder appears, with the name New Folder.
4. Type **One Step** to name the folder.
5. Press Enter.
6. Close the My Computer window.
7. Place the *Office 97 One Step at a Time* CD-ROM into the disc drive.
8. Double-click the My Computer icon again and, in the My Computer window, double-click the CD-ROM icon to open the drive where you inserted the disc.
9. Click the folder named Exercise.
10. Copy the selected folder by pressing Ctrl + C.
11. Close the CD-ROM window.

12. Double-click the My Computer icon on your desktop.
13. In the My Computer window, double-click the hard drive (C:).
14. Double-click the One Step folder.
15. Paste the Exercise folder into the One Step folder by pressing Ctrl + V. All of the exercise files are now located within this folder on your hard drive.

Using the Exercise Files

You need to make sure you have removed the Read-only attribute from any files you copy to the hard drive before you start using them. Otherwise, you will not be able to save changes to the files. To remove the Read-only attribute, open the Exercise folder on your hard drive and press Ctrl + A to select all the files in the folder. From the File menu, select Properties. The Properties dialog box appears. Click the Read-only attribute to remove the check from the checkbox.